PUBLICATIONS

OF THE

NAVY RECORDS SOCIETY

VOL. 133

SAMUEL PEPYS AND THE
SECOND DUTCH WAR

Pepys's Navy White Book
and Brooke House Papers

The Navy Records Society was established in 1893 for the purpose of printing unpublished manuscripts and rare works of naval interest. The Society is open to all who are interested in naval history, and any person wishing to become a member should apply to the Hon. Secretary, Deputy Chief Credit Officer, Barclays De Zoete Wedd Ltd, First Floor, St Mary's Court, Lower Thames Street, London EC3R 6JN. The annual subscription is £30, which entitles the member to receive one free copy of each work issued by the Society in that year, and to buy earlier issues at much reduced prices.

Subscriptions and orders for back volumes should be sent to the Membership Secretary, 5 Goodwood Close, Midhurst, Sussex GU29 9JG.

The Council of the Navy Records Society wish it to be clearly understood that they are not answerable for any opinions and observations which may appear in the Society's publications. For these the editors of the several works are entirely responsible.

SAMUEL PEPYS AND THE SECOND DUTCH WAR

Pepys's Navy White Book and Brooke House Papers

transcribed by
WILLIAM MATTHEWS and by
CHARLES KNIGHTON

edited by
ROBERT LATHAM

PUBLISHED BY SCOLAR PRESS
FOR THE NAVY RECORDS SOCIETY
1995

© The Navy Records Society, 1995

All rights reserved. No part of this publication may be reproduced, stored in a retrieval system, or transmitted in any form or by any means, electronic, mechanical, photocopying, recording, or otherwise, without the prior permission of the publisher.

Published by
SCOLAR PRESS
Gower House
Croft Road
Aldershot
Hants GU11 3HR
England

Ashgate Publishing Company
Old Post Road
Brookfield
Vermont 05036
USA

British Library Cataloguing-in-Publication Data

Pepys, Samuel
   Samuel Pepys and the Second Dutch War:
   Pepys's Navy White Book and Brooke House Papers. – (Navy Records Society)
   I. Title II. Latham, Robert III. Series
   942.066–092

ISBN 1 85928 136 2

Library of Congress Cataloging-in-Publication Data

Pepys, Samuel, 1633–1703.
   Samuel Pepys and the Second Dutch War : Pepys's Navy White Book and Brooke House Papers / transcribed by William Matthews and by Charles Knighton : edited by Robert Latham.
   p. cm. — (Publications of the Navy Records Society : vol. 133)
   Includes index.
   ISBN 1-85928-136-2
   1. Anglo-Dutch War, 1664–1667—Sources. 2. Great Britain—History, Naval—Stuarts, 1603–1714—Sources. 3. Pepys, Samuel, 1633–1703—Manuscripts. I. Latham, Robert, 1912–1995. II. Navy Records Society (Great Britain) III. Title. IV. Series. DA70.A1 vol. 133
[DJ180]
949.2′04—dc20   95–1779
                CIP

Printed on acid-free paper

Phototypeset by Intype, London. Printed and bound in Great Britain at the University Press, Cambridge.

THE COUNCIL
OF THE
NAVY RECORDS SOCIETY
1995

PATRON
H.R.H. THE PRINCE PHILIP, DUKE OF EDINBURGH,
K.G., O.M., F.R.S.

PRESIDENT
THE RT. HON. THE LORD CARRINGTON,
K.G., C.H., G.C.M.G., M.C., P.C.

VICE-PRESIDENTS
H. U. A. LAMBERT, M.A.
M. DUFFY, M.A., D.Phil., F.R.Hist.S.
Captain C. H. H. OWEN, R.N.
Professor D. M. LOADES, M.A., Ph.D., Litt.D., F.S.A., F.R.Hist.S

COUNCILLORS
Miss P. K. CRIMMIN, B.A., B.Phil., F.R.Hist.S.
Professor G. TILL, M.A., Ph.D.
A. D. LAMBERT, M.A., Ph.D.
Professor B. McL. RANFT, M.A., D.Phil., F.R.Hist.S.
J. D. DAVIES, M.A., D.Phil.
K. J. JEFFERY, M.A., Ph.D., F.R.Hist.S.
R. GWILLIAM, Esq.
R. W. A. SUDDABY, M.A.
R. J. B. KNIGHT, M.A., Ph.D., F.R.Hist.S.
M. BLACKWELL, Esq.
Admiral SIR BRIAN BROWN, K.C.B., C.B.E.
Rear Admiral J. B. HERVEY, C.B., O.B.E., F.B.I.M.
Rear Admiral J. A. L. MYRES
Rear Admiral J. R. HILL
A. W. H. PEARSALL, I.S.O., M.A.
Captain A. B. SAINSBURY, V.R.D., M.A., R.N.R.
A. N. RYAN, M.A., F.R.Hist.S.
Professor J. B. HATTENDORF, D. Phil.

S. P. ROSE, M.A., Ph.D.
Professor G. E. AYLMER, M.A., D.Phil., F.B.A., F.R.Hist.S.
Lt. Commander L. PHILLIPS, R.D., R.N.R.
E. J. GROVE, M.A.

Hon Secretary:
A. J. MCMILLAN, B.A., A.C.I.B.

Hon. General Editor:
M. A. SIMPSON, M.A., M.Litt., F.R.Hist.S.

Hon. Treasurer
J. V. TYLER, F.C.C.A.

CONTENTS

	PAGE
Preface	x
Acknowledgements	xii
Editorial Methods	xiii
Bibliographical Abbreviations	xv
Introduction	xvii
Part I: The Navy White Book	1
Part II: The Brooke House Papers	269
(i) Pepys's Defence of the Conduct of the Navy	271
– Letter from the Brooke House Commissioners to the Navy Board	271
– Pepys's General Defence	271
– Pepys's Particular Defence	325
– Pepys's Address to the King	330
– Pepys's Address to the Duke of York	332
(ii) Pepys's Brooke House Journal	334
List of Principal Persons	436
Glossary	437
Index	443
Appendix to Index	482

Publisher's Note

Although Robert Latham died before this volume went to press he was able to check the page proofs and supervise the compilation of the index.

PREFACE

These documents, printed for the first time from manuscripts preserved by Pepys in his library, are among the most important surviving records relating to the Second Dutch War. They illustrate the activities of the Navy Board in general and the work of Pepys, its clerk, in particular. It was in these years that by virtue of his talent for administration Pepys established his dominance over his colleagues, despite his comparative youthfulness and his lack of naval experience. The last of the documents – his Brooke House Journal – shows that the King had no doubt about who was his best spokesman on affairs of the Navy.

The first and most considerable of the documents is Pepys's Navy White Book (pp. 1–267), a memorandum book he kept between 1664 and 1672, i.e. during the war itself (1665–7) and the years immediately before and after. These were years when war conditions made the Navy Board particularly busy, and the book's rich detail and comprehensive coverage, together with Pepys's frank comments on incompetent colleagues and dishonest contractors, provide a unique insight into the workings of the administrative machine.

The documents which follow at pp. 269–435 are concerned with the work of the Brooke House Commission, the statutory body appointed in December 1667 to scrutinize the Navy Board's management of the war finances. They have a special value in that the official records of the Commission are scattered and incomplete.

At pp. 271–333 is Pepys's defence of the Navy Board and himself against the criticisms of the Commission in their report (25 Oct. 1669). The eighteen 'Observations' of the Commission are in turn summarised and answered.

Finally, at pp. 334–435 is Pepys's Brooke House Journal (December 1670–21 Feb. 1671) in which he recorded day-by-day his part in the debates held before the Privy Council between the Brooke House Commissioners and the Navy Board on the subject of the Commission's report. No other record of the proceedings is known to survive. Pepys composed it in shorthand, which he continued to use occasionally, although after May 1669 out of concern for his eyesight he no longer kept the shorthand personal diary for which he is best known to the reading public.

ACKNOWLEDGEMENTS

I am grateful to the Master and Fellows of Magdalene College, Cambridge, for permission to reproduce these documents from the Pepys Library, and to the beneficiaries of the estate of Lois Emery Matthews for permission to make use of her late husband's transcription of the shorthand section of the Navy White Book. My thanks are due also to the Trustees of the Leverhulme Foundation for their award of an Emeritus Fellowship which enabled me to carry out the work.

    I owe a large debt of gratitude to Dr Knighton who has played a major part in transcribing and indexing the text as well as in correcting the proofs; to Professor Henry Roseveare of King's College, London, who brought his knowledge of commerce and finance to bear on conundrums I was unable to solve; to Frances McDonald and Dr Eric Sams for help with the shorthand; to Dr J. D. Davies who lent me the typescript of his *Gentlemen and Tarpaulins: the Officers and Men of the Restoration Navy* before its publication, in 1991; to Professor Charles Boxer, Professor J. R. Brujn, Dr Richard Luckett and Dr Richard Saville for information on particular points; to my late wife Linnet and to Richard Ollard for reading drafts of parts of the book; and to Mary Coleman and Aude Fitzsimons of the Pepys Library whose ready assistance in a variety of ways has facilitated my work.

EDITORIAL METHODS

Spelling etc. Spelling, with certain exceptions, has been modernised: 'fadom', e.g. is printed as 'fathom'; 'alway' as 'always'. The exceptions are: names of persons, places, and ships, and words whose spelling represents contemporary grammatical forms, e.g. 'give' for 'gave', 'run' for 'ran'. Capitalisation follows modern practice; superscripts have been lowered, many abbreviations silently expanded, e.g. 'Greench', 'Taylr', and ampersands spelt out except in statistical tables. Punctuation (which hardly exists in the shorthand section of the Navy White Book) is editorial throughout. Paragraphing follows as far as possible the model of the manuscripts.

Dates. A second year-date has been added, if missing from the original, in the cases of dates between 1 January and 24 March inclusive when both Old and New Calendars were in use. Otherwise dates are given exactly as they appear in the manuscripts. Their format, although sometimes unfamiliar to the modern reader, is not obscure, e.g. '(64)' or '*64*' for 1664, '9ber' for November and so on, and '21th' (one-and-twentieth) for 21st and '31th' for 31st.

Abbreviations. In the manuscript of the Navy White Book Pepys often abbreviates recurrent names: Sir William Batten, for example, appears as 'Sir W.B.' or 'Sir Wm B.' or 'W.B.' Many of these shortened forms are retained in order to preserve the character of the document as a notebook. To retain them all, however, would be to make the text occasionally obscure, especially to the reader who is consulting only a part of it. Abbreviations of surnames are therefore extended whenever this is likely to be helpful. Initials listed at the foot of a letter or order are always left unextended since this is the form in which names of signatories were invariably given in contemporary copies. The signatories can if necessary be identified from the List of Principal Persons.

Printing conventions. Italics are used to denote headings and marginal rubrics.

Commentary. These documents were often composed hurriedly and disjointedly, not infrequently for Pepys's eyes alone, and occasionally in a sort of officialese. Some clarification is therefore called for on the page, in footnotes. For the rest, technical and obsolete language is explained in the Glossary, and also in footnotes where that seems to be helpful. Where there appears to be an important error, a suggested correction is given in the text and the error in a footnote. Slips of the pen and accidental repetitions are corrected silently. Persons are in some cases identified in footnotes; an attempt to identify them all is made in the Index and its Appendix. The present whereabouts of the official papers which Pepys quotes or refers to are given wherever they have been found: a number, however, remain untraced.

Cross-references. Pepys's own cross-references in the Navy White Book are here substituted by the relevant page numbers of this edition. His references to other papers are left as they appear in the MS.

BIBLIOGRAPHICAL ABBREVIATIONS

(Works are published in London unless otherwise stated)

Allin, *Journals*	*The Journals of Sir Thomas Allin, 1660–1678*, ed. R. C. Anderson (NRS 1939, 1940)
Anderson	*Lists of Men-of-War, 1650–1700*, pt i, *English Ships, 1649–1702*, comp. R. C. Anderson (The Society for Nautical Research Occasional Publications, no. 5: Cambridge 1935)
Aylmer, *State's Servants*	G. E. Aylmer, *The State's Servants, 1649–60* (1973)
BL	British Library
Bodl. Lib., Rawl.	Bodleian Library, Oxford, Rawlinson MSS
CJ	*Journals of the House of Commons*
CSPD	*Calendar of State Papers, Domestic Series*
CTB	*Calendar of Treasury Books*
Diary	*The Diary of Samuel Pepys*, ed. R. Latham and W. Matthews (1970–83)
Ehrman, *Navy*	J. P. W. Ehrman, *The Navy in the War of William III, 1689–1697* (Cambridge 1953)
Evelyn, *Diary*	*The Diary of John Evelyn*, ed. E. S. de Beer (Oxford 1955)
Firth and Rait, *Acts and Ordinances*	*Acts and Ordinances of the Interregnum*, eds C. H. Firth and R. S. Rait (1911)
Further Corr.	*Further Correspondence of Samuel Pepys 1662–1679*, ed. J. R. Tanner (1929)
HLRO	House of Lords Record Office
HMC	Historical Manuscripts Commission
HMC, *Lindsey (Supp.)*	*Supplementary report on the manuscripts of the late Montagu Bertie, twelfth Earl of Lindsey, formerly preserved at Uffington House, Stamford, Lincolnshire, A.D.*

	1660–1702, eds C. G. O. Bridgeman and J. C. Walker (1942)
LJ	Journals of the House of Lords
Milward, Parl. Diary	The Diary of John Milward, Esq., Member of Parliament for Derbyshire (September, 1666 to May, 1668), ed. C. Robbins (Cambridge 1938)
Naval Minutes	Samuel Pepys's Naval Minutes, ed. J. R. Tanner (NRS 1926)
NMM	National Maritime Museum
Oeconomy	The Oeconomy of his Majesty's Navy Office (1717)
OED	Oxford English Dictionary
G. Penn, Memorials	G. Penn, Memorials . . . of Sir William Penn, Knt (1833)
Pepys, Memoires	Samuel Pepys, Memoires of the Royal Navy 1679–1688 (1690)
PL	Pepys Library, Magdalene College, Cambridge
PRO	Public Record Office
Shorthand Letters	Shorthand Letters of Samuel Pepys, ed. E. Chappell (Cambridge 1933)
Tanner, Catalogue	A Descriptive Catalogue of the Naval Manuscripts in the Pepysian Library at Magdalene College, Cambridge, ed. J. R. Tanner (NRS 1903–23)
VCH	Victoria History of the Counties of England
Duke of York, Memoirs	James, Duke of York, Memoirs of the English affairs, chiefly naval . . . 1660 to 1673 (1729)

INTRODUCTION

I   The Navy White Book (pp. xvii–xxii)
II The Brooke House Papers
    (i)   The Brooke House Commission (pp. xxiii–xxxiv)
    (ii) Pepys's Defence of the Conduct of the Navy (pp. xxxiv–xxxv)
    (iii) The Brooke House Journal (pp. xxxv–xxxix)

I THE NAVY WHITE BOOK[1]

In his Diary for 7 Apr. 1664, immediately after observing that war against the Dutch seemed imminent, Pepys wrote: 'Vexed to see how Sir W. Batten ordered things this afternoon (*vide* my office-book; for about this time I have begun, my notions and informations increasing now greatly every day, to enter all occurrences extraordinary in a book by themselfs).' There was already in existence an office memorandum book (now in the Public Record Office), begun by Pepys and his clerks in July 1660 on his appointment as Clerk of the Acts which registered selected decisions of the Navy Board and other items of general interest to its members.[2] The new book, on the other hand, was to be Pepys's personal record of the Board's debates and transactions and of how, in fact, each member of the Board had discharged his responsibilities. It was designed to be a means of defence against criticism. It also came to be, in Pepys's words, a record of 'matters to be reformed or improved'.[3] The book was a handsome folio bound in white vellum, with the royal arms stamped on both covers in a style identical to that of the larger and more important books of the Office. Its contents consist of memoranda in the hands of Pepys and his clerks dated between 1664 and

---

[1] PL 2581.
[2] 'Conclusions and Memorandums Occasional': PRO, ADM 106/3520.
[3] This is the description he gives in the catalogue of his library: PL, 'Supellex Literaria', vol. ii, 'Additamenta', p. 15. He makes the same point in a letter of 28 July 1667 to Coventry: *Further Corr.*, p. 180.

1672, but principally between 1664 and 1669, followed by a brief Index written and presumably composed by Pepys, not printed here.

The entries before July 1665 (pp. 3–126)[1] were written by Pepys almost entirely in shorthand.[2] They were arranged, with dates and headings, in loose chronological order, and with references to the numbered bundles of official papers on which many are based. Soon after the outbreak of the war Pepys ceased to use the book and made brief notes on loose sheets,[3] which were later copied into the book, almost entirely by his chief clerk, Richard Gibson,[4] whose clear and flowing hand is unmistakable. Shortly after January 1667 the memoranda were once again entered in the book in the same format as in the pre-war section, but in longhand and by his clerks – again principally by Gibson.[5] The number of times that Pepys refers to Gibson's preparing his copy in his presence suggests that he wrote at Pepys's dictation. But clearly the present text is a fair copy.

These post-war entries are longer than those of the pre-war period, being concerned with complicated problems such as the accounts of contractors. But despite the deterioration of his eyesight which forced Pepys to abandon his Diary in May 1669, he continued to dictate voluminous entries in the Navy White Book. In 1669 they occupy over 100 manuscript pages, more than for any other year. Thereafter they dwindle – to 3 in 1670, none in 1671 and 10 in 1672. They end in December 1672, six months after the Third Dutch War had begun, but have little bearing on it.

In the first pages of the book are notes of the preparations made for war from the autumn of 1663 onwards. Pepys already had some knowledge of timber and the timber trade and the measuring of great masts – it was now particularly important for him to understand the making of sails and cordage, which were

---

[1] The page references here and elsewhere in the Introduction, where they refer to the text, are to the pages of this edition, not to pages of the manuscript.

[2] As in the Diary, he used a system invented by Thomas Shelton. For an account, see *Diary*, vol. i, pp. xlviii–lxi.

[3] They do not appear to have survived.

[4] He had been a purser under the Commonwealth and a victualling officer at Great Yarmouth in the war, after which he became Pepys's chief clerk. In 1670 he was made chief purser to the Mediterranean fleet, and returned to Pepys's service during the last months of his tenure of the Clerkship of the Acts. For his career, see *Diary*, x. 155–6.

[5] Judging by the handwriting, Hewer wrote entries at pp. 232, 236–7, 251–3, and Hayter those at pp. 256–60.

more liable to loss by damage and wastage in wartime than any other stores. It is no accident that these two materials are the subject of the longest of the memoranda in the early pages of the book (pp. 27–31, 39–42). About sailmaking it may be that he had learned something indirectly from his upbringing as a tailor's son – certainly he appears to be entirely at his ease in the discussions he records about seams and selvedges, and is able to defend the use of wide canvases in sails against the experienced sailors among his colleagues who favoured narrow ones. He made frequent visits to the ropeyards, learning how to test hemp by trials of its tensile strength, how to spin it and lay it in tar. In these notes Pepys returns to the subject of cordage time and time again, and his long account of the prices of Scandinavian tar and pitch is evidence of his care to familiarise himself with the international price mechanisms which the trade involved (pp. 32–5).

In supervising the supply of stores he had to pit his wits against those of the contractors. The book opens with a note of the hidden profits made by Backwell the financier, and as it proceeds Pepys makes a point of recording cases of price rigging which became more frequent with the approach of war, the most notable being William Cutler's attempt to raise the price of tar by spreading a rumour that the tar house at Stockholm had been destroyed by fire (pp. 97–100), 'Merchants will be merchants', as Pepys observed in another connection (p. 75). But royal servants were often not much better. According to Pepys's observation in these notes, not many dockyard officers could be relied on to put the King's interest before their own. He reports a sad number of cases of embezzlement and corruption, as well as of sheer inefficiency.

In his efforts at reform, in the dockyards and elsewhere, Pepys complains that he received little help from his immediate colleagues. Sir William Batten (Surveyor 1660–7), Col. Thomas Middleton (Surveyor 1667–72) and Sir William Penn (Commissioner 1660–9) were all indifferent administrators; and only Sir William Coventry (Secretary to the Lord High Admiral 1660–7 and Commissioner 1662–7) was constant in his support.

War intensified the problems that had plagued the Board in times of peace: the familiar issues of lack of money, careless supervision by officers of the yards, defective materials, and corruption and embezzlement. In addition war brought new problems – principally those of the recruitment and victualling of seamen. The Admiralty, lacking money for wages, was forced to recruit by means of the press gang, whose tyrannous conduct Pepys more than once criticised in the Diary. In the White Book his comments are rather on its effects on the efficiency of the fighting force. It led to chaos in the allocation of men to ships (pp. 233–4), to undermanning of victuallers' ships so serious that they were unable to carry supplies to the fleet (p. 128), and, most disturbing of all perhaps, to the alienation of the seamen from the King's service, sometimes to the point of mutiny (p. 160).

As for victualling, Pepys had gained close experience as Surveyor-General (a post invented at his suggestion in January 1665), and in April 1666 he attempted some reforms in the office of purser, which was the part of the organisation most easily susceptible to improvement by administrative regulation. But pursers could still evade the Board's scrutiny (p. 129), and the scrutiny, when it occurred, was far from thorough (p. 177).

The Admiralty, he found, was not well-supported in the crucial business of directing the movement of ships. Pilots were too few in number and were often put to work in unfamiliar waters (pp. 129, 134). There were too many delays in despatching pressed men to their ships and in clearing wrecks from the River. Both tasks would be better performed, he thought, if made the responsibility of a single member of the Board (pp. 129, 140). He was probably thinking of the improvements in administration which had followed from his own appointment as Surveyor-General of Victualling in 1665.

The first duty of the Navy Board in the immediate post-war period was to repair the wastage caused by the hostilities. The bulk of the work therefore fell on Middleton, Batten's successor as Surveyor of the Navy, who repeatedly complained of the difficulties caused by Batten's failure to keep adequate records. Middleton himself did not greatly relish desk-work, but he applied himself with vigour to the supervision of the yards. He impressed Pepys by the good sense of his view that whenever a great ship was building, a smaller vessel should be built alongside her, 'there being always so much leavings to be found' (p. 156). Shortage of money in the post-war period was, as ever, the main difficulty. Many contractors now insisted on payment in advance, or on some form of security that was not dependent on the credit of the government (pp. 189–91). Debts outstanding from the war, or before it, demanded attention. Sir William Warren's bills alone for masts, timber and freightage kept the Office busy for months. Pepys, despite his close and profitable alliance with Warren, resisted all proposals from other members of the Board to pay him before he had produced copper-bottomed evidence to support his claims. Among the other principal creditors of the Navy were, of course, the unpaid seamen. They had to be content with vouchers ('tickets') never before used on such a scale. At pp. 164–5 Pepys records a summary of the speech he made on 17 July 1668 to the Privy Council (in answer to criticism in Parliament) justifying the use of tickets on practical grounds even though it meant paying the money to ticket-mongers who bought them from seamen at a figure well below their value. Elsewhere he records other abuses of the ticket system: Adm. Sir William Jennens's attempt to acquire the proceeds of tickets for 800 or so imaginary supernumeraries (pp. 176–82) and Capt. O'Brien's attempt to have a ticket issued for the mistress he kept on board disguised as a man (p. 248).

In November 1668 the Navy Treasury had been put into the hands of political enemies of the Duke of York, Sir Thomas Osborne and Sir Thomas Littleton, who held the office jointly. They did not cooperate smoothly either with the Duke or the Navy Board. They issued new rules without consultation (p. 159); paid tickets for 1666 before those for 1665 (p. 158), and occasionally refused to meet a bill that antedated their own appointment (pp. 189–91).

The combined effects of the war and of political pressure had forced the King in August 1668 to institute an inquiry into the constitution of the Navy Board. The result was a recommendation (made largely at Pepys's suggestion) that no structural changes were needed. All would be well if only the Principal Officers without exception were to perform the duties laid down for them in the Admiral's Instructions. No member of the Board, for instance, should rely on deputies or clerks to do his work for him. Admittedly Mennes had assistants (Brouncker and Penn) to help him with his accounts, but they had been formally appointed, and had been allotted specific duties (p. 176). Again, clerks should not be treated as personal servants who might as a favour be allotted extra duties in order to earn extra pay. Middleton, for instance, had transferred one of his clerks to Brouncker's service without consulting the Board. Pepys was outraged. He set out his views on the affair and on the whole question of the qualifications to be required of Principal Officers and their clerks in a minute which is among the most powerful he ever wrote (pp. 194–9).

Old abuses continued to trouble him: excessive prices paid for petty emptions (p. 145), embezzlement (p. 124) and blatant cases of private trading by commanders (pp. 200–1). The use of impressment in peacetime led him to protest to the Admiral (pp. 203–10). He tells of Sir Edward Spragg boasting that he could man his fleet simply by sending his press gang into the London brothels – a story which John Evelyn heard 'with great affliction' (p. 217). Pepys for his part found it a sad contemplation that seamen took service in East Indiamen simply to escape the press (p. 205).

A little later there is a long report (pp. 221–7) of a conversation on 10 June 1669 with Coventry, whom Pepys admired more than any other public servant. Coventry, after recalling his original opposition to the war, turns to the debate about the employment of gentlemen captains in the Navy. It was a debate which had political overtones: had not the success of Cromwell's navy against the Dutch owed something to the fact that the greater part of his naval commanders were chosen for their skill in war or their experience in navigation – or both – rather than for their gentility? Coventry's argument here was not political but pragmatic, and was based on the simple consideration that ships could not safely be entrusted to landsmen. He had often stated it before. He now develops it rhetorically – at one and the same time making his case and answering objections to it. Pepys's reporting, which gives the impression of missing none of the twists and turns of the argument, is in its way as impressive as the subtlety of the speaker himself. It is also, perhaps, significant of something more. It suggests that Pepys reported Coventry's views so thoroughly because he so thoroughly agreed with them. His own first article of faith was a belief in the importance of professionalism in the King's service at all levels, from anchor-smiths to admirals, and in himself not least. Every page of the Navy White Book testifies to that belief.

II THE BROOKE HOUSE PAPERS[1]

(i) The Brooke House Commission

After the inglorious end of the Second Dutch War in 1667, culminating in the raid on the Medway in June and the conclusion of an unsatisfactory peace in August, two extensive inquiries into its conduct were held, and for a time ran concurrently: a Committee on Miscarriages appointed by the Commons in October 1667 and what became known from its place of meeting as the Brooke House Commission appointed by statute in the following December. Inquiries so wide-ranging into the conduct of royal servants during a war were unprecedented, but the circumstances themselves were without precedent. Only recently, under the Republic, had war on such a scale been undertaken.

The Committee on Miscarriages concerned itself with the conduct of the campaigns and only incidentally with Navy Board matters. The Board was criticised for alleged mismanagement of victualling, which according to Rupert and Albemarle had fatally constricted the movements of their fleets in 1666. It was blamed rather more convincingly for the weak defences of the Medway, but managed to shift the blame on to the Commissioner at Chatham, Peter Pett. The payment of seamen by tickets was the readiest charge against it, since specific sums had been reserved for the seamen in parliamentary grants[2] – but Parliament did not understand that the complexities of naval finance made it impossible to reserve funds for a specific purpose. Nor did it understand that there was no avoiding payment by tickets since *inter alia* it enabled the Navy Treasury when calculating pay to take into account the fact that most seamen would have served in more than one ship. Appearing before the Commons on 5 March 1668 Pepys explained it all in a long speech which encroached on to the members' dinner hour.[3]

The Committee on Miscarriages was poorly designed for its purpose. It was too large, and the 56 MPs who composed it were unable to give it their undivided attention. Moreover, it lacked

---

[1] Pepys never had these papers gathered together or gave them a general title. That given here is editorial.
[2] £30,000 had been reserved for the seamen's pay in the Eleven Months Assessment (1667): *CJ*, viii. 683; 18 & 19 Car. II c. 13, sect. x.
[3] Summary in John Milward, *Parl. Diary 1666–8* (ed. Robbins, Camb. 1938), pp. 207–9. Cf. *Diary*, ix. 102–4.

both the power to compel witnesses to attend and the power to administer oaths. Beyond having an accused person voted guilty of a miscarriage, the Committee could do nothing except attempt to have him impeached – a weapon which it found was apt to break in its hands. (Articles of impeachment were voted against Pett, but he was saved from trial by the prorogation of Parliament.) The Committee's proceedings caused a public stir, but in the end posed no real threat to the Principal Officers of the Navy apart from Pett.

The Brooke House Commission, appointed in December 1667, presented a more formidable challenge. It was set up to inquire not into undefined miscarriages, but into the specific problem of what use had been made of the money granted by Parliament for the war – a matter which directly and principally affected the Navy Board as the main spending department. Since the King's own revenue, which by convention served as the national war chest, was inadequate of itself to provide money and credit for a war on the scale of a naval war against the Dutch, Parliament had granted some £5m. towards the cost.[1] It now claimed the right to inquire into its disbursement.

The origins of the Commission went back to September 1666 when the Commons, in determining the amount which should be appropriated to war expenses, chose a committee to inspect the accounts of the Navy, Ordnance and Army.[2] Accounts were produced by the responsible officials, but the King refused to allow the officials – being servants of the Crown – to be examined on their contents. An attempt was then made in the Commons to remit the inquiry to a joint committee of the two Houses which (they claimed) would have the same power to impose oaths on witnesses as was enjoyed by the House of Lords itself. This move also came to nothing. The Commons therefore in December tried threats. They tacked on to the Poll Bill then before them a proviso designed to empower a committee of nine members of their own House to investigate accounts and swear witnesses. No investigation, no supply. The King refused to have his hand forced, and threatened to veto the bill. Then followed an attempt by the government's critics to enact their proviso in the form of a separate bill, but this foundered in a series of disputes between the two Houses which was only brought to an end by the King's

[1] C. D. Chandaman, *Eng. Public Revenue 1660–88* (Oxf. 1975), pp. 177, 189.
[2] *CJ*, viii. 625.

proroguing Parliament on 14 Jan. 1667. When Parliament reassembled in May, the King made an attempt to resolve the main constitutional difficulty by issuing letters patent appointing a commission composed of judges and members of both Houses, which was empowered to examine the accounts. This fell through with the refusal of some of the MPs to accept nomination.

All difficulties were resolved, however, in the summer of 1667 by the Dutch raid on the Medway and the humiliating peace which followed. The King was in no position to hold out when Parliament met on 10 October after the recess. The Lord Keeper then announced to the two Houses:

> His Majesty formerly promised you that you should have an account of the moneys given towards the war, which His Majesty hath commanded his officers to make ready; and since that way of commission (wherein he had put the examination of them) hath been ineffectual, he is willing you should follow your own method, examine them in what way and as strictly as you please. He doth assure you, he will leave everyone concerned to stand or fall, according to his own innocence or guilt.[1]

By December a bill had been drawn up and passed which established a small body of salaried Commissioners to scrutinize the expenditure on the war.[2] They were to be nine in number, with a quorum of five, and by a resolution of the Commons, none was to be a member of the Lower House.[3] They were to examine not only the expenditure of parliamentary grants made for that purpose in 1664–7,[4] but also the expenditure from customs and prize money – two sources of revenue that were normally under the King's exclusive control. The Commission was to work full time, with the assistance of a staff of clerks.[5] It had authority to enforce the production of accounts, to compel attendance and

---

[1] *LJ*, xii. 116.
[2] 19 & 20 Car. II c. 1.
[3] *CJ*, ix. 28.
[4] For example, the Royal Aid (1664), the Additional Aid (1665), the Poll Tax (1667), the Three Months Assessment (1667) and the Eleven Months Assessment (1667).
[5] William Jessop was appointed secretary, with William Symons and Edmund Portman as clerks. All three had served as government clerks in the Interregnum, and the first two were old acquaintances of Pepys when, in 1655–60, he served as a clerk in the Exchequer.

to impose oaths. It was to expose all 'frauds, exactions, negligences, and defaults or abuses', and was directed to take proceedings in the Court of Exchequer to recover any debts due to the King, employing informers if necessary, and to recompense the seamen for any losses they had incurred through the abuse of their pay tickets. Its powers were to run for three years after the close of the current session, unlike those of a parliamentary committee of inquiry which, unless renewed, lasted only for the session in which it was appointed. It was to report to Parliament from time to time 'to the end that your Majesty and this whole kingdom may be satisfied and truly informed'. Pepys was nervous of the outcome. '[The Commissioners]', he wrote on 30 December, 'are the greatest people that ever were in the nation as to power', and for days after the act was published he could not bring himself to read it.[1]

The nine Commissioners, chosen by the Commons from a list of twenty nominated by a committee, included no front-rank politicians, apart from Coventry's nephew, Sir George Savile, later the Marquess of Halifax. The chairman, Lord Brereton,[2] was an accomplished mathematician, better known perhaps in the Royal Society than in political circles, but admired on all sides for his ability and integrity.[3] He had sat in the Commons in two parliaments in 1659 and 1660 as a supporter of the Presbyterian interest – the party of moderate critics of the monarchy who had been displaced by the republicans at the end of the second Civil War and who had later helped to bring about the Restoration. Since 1660 this group had lost its place in the limelight but was now, after the fall of Clarendon, enjoying something of a revival. Two

---

[1] *Diary*, viii. 601.
[2] 3rd Baron Brereton of Laughlin in the Irish peerage; succeeded 1664, a founding Fellow of the Royal Society. He came of a family of Cheshire landowners and was a grandson of Sir William Brereton the parliamentary general. He was never well-off, and after the Commission's work was done retired to his estate, protected from his creditors by appointment to Court office as a Gentleman of the Privy Chamber. For biographical details see B. D. Henning (ed.), *Hist. Parl. The Commons 1660–90* (1983), i. 715–16.
[3] Cf. Evelyn, *Diary*, iii. 232; Aubrey, *Brief Lives* (ed. Powell, 1940), p. 132; Burnet, *Hist. own Time* (ed. O. Airy, Oxf. 1897–1900), i. 483. On first meeting him Pepys found him 'a very sober and serious, able man' (*Diary*, ix. 10), and like Brouncker he welcomed his appointment (ibid., viii. 577; *CSPD Add. 1660–85*, p. 228). Though impatient with his manner in the debates before the Privy Council, he admired his management of the Commission's inquiries: *Diary*, ix. 10, 68.

of Brereton's colleagues were chosen from the same party – William Pierrepont, one of the most respected men in politics,[1] and Sir John Langham, a prominent London Presbyterian, MP for Northampton in 1661 and 1662.[2] Col. George Thomson was from a different mould.[3] An ardent Puritan, he was a self-made merchant who had given good service in the Commissions of Admiralty and Navy during the Commonwealth, and never tired of extolling the virtues of the Republic (pp. 360, 368). He was far and away the most knowledgeable of the Commissioners in naval matters, and proved industrious to a fault in exposing the shortcomings of the newly re-established Navy Board.[4] With Lord Brereton he was the most active of the Commissioners in the debates before the Privy Council which followed the presentation of their Report. Of the other members of the Commission, Giles Dunster and Sir William Turner (Lord Mayor 1668–9)[5] were experienced London merchants brought in as experts on finance and business affairs. The more obscure John Gregory seems to have been a man of business attached to the service of Sir Joseph Williamson, Under-Secretary of State and Keeper of State Papers.[6] The appointment of Col. Henry Osborne, son of Sir Peter Osborne, of Chicksands, Bedfordshire, is a little difficult to explain. He had been a royalist but had

---

[1] In 1660 he had been both a Councillor of State and an Admiralty Commissioner, but had not sat in Parliament since 1661. He did not sign the Commission's report. For biographical details, see Henning, op. cit., pp. 243–4.

[2] His election to the Cavalier Parliament was declared void in 1662. His nomination to the Commission was the only one to be contested in the Commons: *CJ*, ix. 36. For biographical details, see Henning, op. cit., p. 709.

[3] For his career see Firth and Rait, *Acts and Ordinances*, i. 1010; ii. 1277, 1407; B. Worden, *Rump Parliament* (Camb. 1974), pp. 314–25; Aylmer, *State's Servants*, pp. 204, 399.

[4] See, e.g. *Diary*, ix. 394.

[5] Dunster was appointed Surveyor of Customs in 1671 for his services: *CSPD 1671*, p. 510. Turner was a prosperous dealer in drapery with international business connections. (See his papers in the Guildhall Library, London.) As Lord Mayor he showed great acumen in his management of the rebuilding after the Fire, and in religious matters he was popular with the Dissenters for his lenity. His brother William, a distinguished lawyer, had married Pepys's cousin Jane Pepys.

[6] Pepys thought him 'an understanding gentleman' (*Diary*, viii. 534). When he first knew him he was an Exchequer man, but at the Restoration he moved to the office of Secretary Nicholas: ibid, ii. 232; vii. 116. For his association with Secretary Williamson, see *Diary*, vii. 116; *CSPD 1667–8*, pp. 471, 472, 483; *CTB 1667–8*, p. liv.

never held high public office or been a member of Parliament.[1] He may have been one of those obscure men whose very obscurity, according to Coventry,[2] qualified them for election.

In January 1668 the Commissioners settled into their headquarters at Brooke House in Durham Yard, Holborn,[3] and opened an office near Bishopsgate for the receipt of complaints about seamen's tickets.[4] They organised themselves into 'divisions' corresponding with the subjects of their inquiry,[5] and began to call for papers and information. Their first letter to the Navy Office (21 January) asked for an account of stores, contracts and ship hire – in Pepys's words 'more than we shall ever be able to answer while we live.'[6] Pepys drafted a reply which Coventry advised him to alter as being 'a little too submissive' and as granting 'a little too much and too soon our bad managements, though we lay [them] on want of money'.[7] On the 31st he went to Brooke House accompanied by the Navy Office doorkeeper, who carried a pile of contract books, and 'was received with great respect and kindness and did give them great satisfaction, making it my endeavour to inform them what it was they were to expect from me and what was the duty of other people'. 'I do observe', he concluded, 'they do go about their business like men resolved to go through with it, and in a very good method like men of understanding' – working through the day and 'eat[ing] only a bit of bread at noon and a glass of wine'.[8] In early February the Navy Board sent them *inter alia* 164 sea books, 3 contract books, 3 order books, and 12 bill books.[9] Before the month was up they had ventured on Warren's Hamburg business, seamen's pay, and

---

[1]VCH, *Beds.*, ii. 271. After the Commission's work was over he was made an equerry (his brother John was a Gentleman of the Privy Chamber), and given a post in the Navy as Treasurer for Sick and Wounded: *CTB 1667–8*, p. 11. His sister was Dorothy, later famous as the author of the charming letters addressed to Sir William Temple.
[2]*Diary*, viii. 572.
[3]Once the residence of Sir Fulke Greville, 1st Baron Brooke, the Elizabethan poet and courtier. Since his death in 1628 it had occasionally been used for public purposes. See H. B. Wheatley and P. Cunningham, *London Past and Present* (1891), s.n.
[4]*Diary*, ix. 43.
[5]There is mention of the 'Navy division' in 'Mr Pepys's Defence': PL 2554, p. 160.
[6]Bodl. Lib., Rawl. MSS A 185, p. 314; *Diary*, ix. 34.
[7]*Diary*, ix. 42.
[8]Ibid., ix. 43–4, 56.
[9]PRO, ADM 106/2886, pt I, p. 26.

INTRODUCTION   xxix

the affair of Sandwich's prize goods.[1] This last Pepys might have been involved in had he not sold out his share of the proceeds;[2] as it was, his old colleague in Sandwich's service, Capt. Ferrer, was sharply dealt with by Lord Brereton when he appeared before the Commissioners later in the year and failed to satisfy them that he had provided all the evidence they needed.[3]

On 14 March the Commission submitted a progress report to the Commons which was well received. The occasion is described in the parliamentary diary kept by John Milward, one of the members for Derbyshire:

> Sir Thomas Meers informed the House that some of the Commissioners of Accounts were at the door and desired to give the House an account how far they had proceeded; whereupon it was ordered to call them in, but before they were called in we had a great debate whether they should have chairs set [for] them or not, but in regard Lord Viscount Halifax was not there it was said no Peer was there, for Lord Brereton was not a Peer of England, and therefore they had no chairs, but seats only at the Bar was prepared for them; the Bar was not let down, and Lord Brereton and five more of the commissioners came in. Sir William Turner (who is pricked for next Lord Mayor) was speaker for all the rest; he presented to the Speaker a book of seven sheets of paper written close on both sides. There was a debate whether it should be read or not; it was ordered to be read, and it was a very exact form and method of their proceedings. It did inform that some persons did abscond and would not be brought in to make their accounts to what they were able to charge upon them; they also informed of the great abuse of buying tickets at 7s. per pound and some at 5s. the pound, and also of the irregular paying of such tickets; but they gave us no account as yet of the disposing of any moneys. When the book was read the commissioners were called in and the House gave them their hearty thanks for their excellent method and great care in their proceedings, and prayed them to continue the same, and

---

[1] Ibid., pp. 29, 35, 36, 45, 90.
[2] *Diary*, vi. 314 & n. 1.
[3] See Ferrer's delightful letter quoted in F. R. Harris, *Life of 1st Earl of Sandwich* (1912), ii. 197.

that this House will at all times and upon all occasions be ready to assist them.[1]

Another short report was made in April.[2]

Pepys had the Office keep a register of all transactions with the Commission[3] and did what he could to satisfy their queries. When Brooke House complained that they had been kept waiting for a copy of the survey of the Navy of February 1663 and would report the delay to Parliament if kept waiting any longer, Pepys replied (15 April):

1. That for anything concerning his place the Commissioners had not stayed two days.

2. That he cannot do the whole work of the Navy, and is ashamed it is not done.

3. That he may say, as a matter of complaint rather than excuse, that his fellow Officers did not do their parts to enable him to do his, in the making up and piecing things together.

4. That he hath not heard a word from the Comptroller, Treasurer, the executors of the last Surveyor or the present Surveyor to enable him to write a word for digesting the matter.[4]

The Commissioners' investigations occupied the whole of 1668 and most of 1669. They had to examine the accounts of the Exchequer officials receiving the money and the accounts of the numerous financial officers of the armed forces responsible for spending it. They had to call for papers, receive depositions, interview witnesses, invite comments from officials and in some cases reply to them. It was the autumn of 1669 before they were in a position to present their main conclusions. These took the form of 10 Observations concerning the accounts of Carteret, Navy Treasurer during the war, and 18 Observations concerning the Navy Board[5] which constituted the principal part of the Report presented to the King and to the two Houses of Parlia-

---

[1]Milward, *Parl. Diary*, pp. 225–6.
[2]*CJ*, ix. 79.
[3]PRO, ADM 106/2886, pt I. He also had his clerk Gibson keep a record of the Board's answers to the Commission's inquiries from 21 Jan. 1668 to 23 July 1670. It survives in Bodl. Lib., Rawl. MSS A 185, pp. 313–14.
[4]PRO, ADM 106/2886, pt I, p. 218.
[5]In the Commons debates that followed, the meaning of the word 'Observation' was called into question. The Commissioners denied that it implied legal judgement; it was merely a statement of fact: A. Grey, *Debates* (1763), i. 168, 234. This was a common meaning of the word at the time.

ment on 25 and 26 October. In addition they sent a series of accounts and a mass of letters and other *pièces justificatives*.[1] Included amongst them, attached to an abstract of Carteret's accounts, was a statement that was later to cause a great stir, to the effect that £514,518 8s. 8½d. had been spent 'for other uses than the war'.[2] In early November the two Houses appointed committees to examine the Report, and began with the charges concerning Carteret. He chose not to answer them personally, and was allowed legal representation in both Houses – one of his lawyers being Robert Sawyer, Pepys's old chamber-fellow at Magdalene.

The Lords' Committee, rather oddly, included Halifax, himself one of the Commissioners, and Sandwich, who was involved in the prize-goods affair, one of the items under investigation.[3] It held a series of meetings in November, two of which Pepys attended to give evidence,[4] and ended by exonerating Carteret completely, although it was clear that his accounts were in serious disorder. The Commons, on the other hand, were severe and after discussing each of the 10 Observations concerning Carteret voted him guilty of misdemeanours in regard to all except one, a minor one about payment for slops. On 10 December he was suspended from the House, and on the 11th the Commons were debating a motion to exclude him from office[5] when the King intervened and prorogued Parliament until 14 February.

By this time there had been no discussion in Parliament of the 18 Observations concerning the Navy Board. These had been sent to the Board on 29 September with a request for a reply by 19 October when Parliament was due to reassemble. But Pepys was at that time abroad on leave, and Brouncker and Mennes, the only other survivors of the wartime Board still in post, explained that they must put off their reply until his return.[6] He came back on 20 October, but within days was overwhelmed by

---

[1] The report and its appended papers are in HLRO, Main Papers 26 Oct. 1669, 213 A and 213 B; summary in HMC, *8th Report*, App., pt i. 128–33. There is a summary of the debates on it in the Commons in *CTB 1667–8*, Introduction, pp. lxx, lxxx-lxxxiv.

[2] HLRO, Main Papers 26 Oct. 1669, 213 A, f. 8r; HMC, op. cit., p. 128. The Commissioners later stated that by 'other uses' they had in mind other naval uses: below, pp. 372–3.

[3] *LJ*, xii. 261.

[4] Below, pp. 334–5.

[5] He resigned his post as Vice-Treasurer of Ireland in January 1670, but was in office again after 1673 when he was made a Commissioner of the Admiralty.

[6] Below, p. 334.

a personal tragedy – the death, on 10 November, of his wife.[1] He gathered what papers he could (some were inaccessible at Brooke House) and composed by 27 November an 18-fold answer to the 18 Observations. It is printed below (pp. 271–325). Pepys took it in person to Brooke House on the 29th, and attested it on 14 December.[2]

Soon after the prorogation on 11 December, the King changed the whole situation by transferring the debate on the charges made against the members of the Navy Board from Parliament to the Privy Council. There the accused were invited to defend themselves in the presence of the King, the Lord High Admiral (the Duke of York), and the Council. The move was made to avoid having royal servants exposed to such severe treatment as Carteret had suffered at the hands of the House of Commons.

The proceedings in Council began in late December[3] and were first concerned with matters that had arisen from the examination of Carteret's case. On 3 Jan. 1670 Pepys was called in, with Exchequer officials, to counter the charge that over £500,000 had been spent on 'other uses than the war'[4] – a charge which had aroused agreeable expectations in the public mind that the officials would be found guilty of providing for the King's mistresses out of money meant for the war.[5]

It was a week later, on 10 January, that the Council undertook consideration of the criticisms made of other members of the Navy Board. On that day, before the Council met with members of the Board and of the Commission in the Council Chamber, Pepys, with the King and the Duke of York, withdrew into the King's Closet, and presented the King with a copy of his answer to the 18 Observations, and also a copy of a letter which he had just sent to the Commission on 6 January in defence of his own conduct.[6]

The debates which followed at intervals between 12 January

[1] Ibid.
[2] PL 2554, p. 111.
[3] The precise date is unknown. Pepys (below, p. 335) says no more than that they started in December. According to Starkey, the newsletter writer, they began shortly before 1 January (BL, Add. MSS 36916, f. 157r). The Privy Council Register is almost entirely silent about them. There is a little information in the draft minutes (BL, Stowe MSS 489, ff. 249–66) but what follows here is largely based on Pepys's Journal.
[4] Below, p. 336.
[5] Below, pp. 337–8.
[6] Below, pp. 341–2.

and 21 February, centred on the 18 Observations and were recorded by Pepys in his 'Brooke House Journal' (below, pp. 334–435). A remarkable feature of the proceedings was that the public were admitted, presumably to give maximum publicity to the official case. On the afternoon of Friday 28 January, when the allegation about the King's misuse of the parliamentary grant was at issue, the Council Chamber, according to Pepys, was full to capacity.[1] Starkey, the newsletter writer, who was present, reported that 'hundreds' were there.[2] The government's case was that, far from misusing public money, the King had spent £800,000 from his own revenues on the war; and moreover that the £500,000-odd which the Commissioners claimed had been spent on 'other uses' was a miscalculation due to their failure to take into account the cost of preparing for the war as well as the cost of waging it.[3] The Commissioners immediately, on the same day as the debate, issued a supplementary report stating that they had revised that part of their original report: 'If any person has drawn wrong conclusion from our enquiries, we in all humility hope it may be looked upon as our unhappiness, and not our fault.'[4]

On 14 February, when the Houses re-assembled, they were assured by the King and the Lord Keeper that His Majesty had looked into all these matters himself.[5] The Court party was now completely in control of Parliament and was determined to render the Commission harmless. On 18 February they secured a decisive vote in the Commons which gave supply precedence over inquiries into the war,[6] and went on to grant an unusually generous subsidy. Paradoxically, the Commission was drawn into the business of arranging for the supply. At the same time their correspondence with Pepys continued – about Warren's accounts with the Navy Treasury and on 20 March they appeared at the Bar of the House to present papers on one of the charges in which

---

[1] Below, p. 372.
[2] BL. Add. MSS 33916, f. 162r. The public did not always preserve a respectful silence (below, p. 433).
[3] Below, p. 374.
[4] BL, Egerton MSS 2543, ff. 217–19 (copy); printed in J. Ralph, *Hist. Engl.* (1744), i. 178–9n.
[5] *LJ*, xii. 287; *CJ*, ix. 121.
[6] *CJ*, ix. 124. At this point some 80 of the country ('opposition') MPs seceded. According to Burnet, the votes were secured by bribery (*Hist. own Time*, ed. Airy, Oxf. 1897–1900, i. 486), but this view is discounted by Dr Witcombe (D. T. Witcombe, *Charles II and the Cavalier House of Commons 1663–74*, Manchester 1966, p. 99).

some MPs for maritime constituencies had an interest – that concerning prize ships and prize goods.[1] But the finances of the war were no longer a political issue, and under the terms of the statute establishing the Commission, its duties terminated in May 1671.

(ii) Pepys's Defence of the Conduct of the Navy

On 27 Nov. 1669 Pepys sent to the Brooke House Commissioners a 'General Defence' of the Navy Board against the charges they had brought in their 18 Observations of 29 September, adding that it was to be understood that he wrote without prejudice to his colleagues' freedom to write in their own defence (pp. 271–325). Mennes, Brouncker and Penn submitted their individual answers, and Pepys followed suit with his own 'Particular Defence' on 6 Jan. 1670 (pp. 325–30). On 8 January he submitted copies of his General and his Particular Defence to the King and the Duke of York (pp. 330–3).

His answers to the charges are for the most part convincing. The Commissioners were ill-informed at some points about procedures in the Navy Office, and misled about certain facts, e.g. about the prize ships (pp. 318–23). They were inclined to exaggerate and were unwilling to make allowance for war conditions. But in his counter-attack on the record of the naval administrators of the Commonwealth Pepys is less convincing. They created and maintained a battle fleet of unprecedented size and power, and until the closing years of the Republic kept it well-paid and supplied.

In his defence of his own conduct the most interesting feature is his claim to 'integrity'. There is no denying that like most of his colleagues in the Navy Office, except the lowliest, he accepted gifts in money and in kind from naval contractors, in compensation for the low rate of his salary. No doubt the considerable sums he regularly received from Warren the timber merchant and Gauden the Victualler might have caused him embarrassment if they had become known. But the gifts did not prevent him from criticising his benefactors when necessary.[2] He never became the paid servant of anyone but the King, and there was probably

---

[1]Several members for ports had been employed by the Prize Office in the war. *CJ*, ix. 128, 136; Grey, op. cit., pp. 233–4; A. Marvell, *Poems and Letters* (ed. Margoliouth, Oxf. 1952), i. 100, 101; BL, Add. MSS 36916, ff. 176*r*, 178*r*.
[2]See below, pp. 300, 311 n.2.

substance in his claim that in these private transactions the public interest was always protected.[1]

(iii) The Brooke House Journal

The climax of Pepys's relations with Brooke House came when the Commissioners and Navy Board debated the 18 Observations and the Board's answers before the King and Privy Council in a series of meetings held between 3 January and 21 February 1670. The Council records are almost completely silent about the debates,[2] and if the Brooke House Commission kept a record of them, it does not appear to have survived. It was Pepys's habit, however, when attacked, not only to defend himself but to keep a careful record of his defence.[3] In this case he preserved a report of the debates in journal form, with a preface summarising his part in the events which immediately preceded them. The original manuscript has disappeared and the journal is printed here (pp. 334–435) from a unique copy in the Pepys Library (PL 2874, pp. 385–504). There it is to be found in his 'Miscellany of Matters Political, and Naval' – a collection in twelve folio volumes of copies of manuscripts from public and private sources, made by clerks after Pepys had retired from office in February 1689. Volume VI of this 'Miscellany', in which it occurs, consists of copies of papers in Pepys's own possession. The journal is flanked by two other items of Brooke House material – 'Notes Preparative' (PL 2874, pp. 361–83)[4] and copies of his General and Particular Defences (ibid., pp. 509–81), all in the same unidentified hand. They were compiled by two clerks, one writing at the other's dictation. That the notes were dictated is evident from the occurrence of scribal errors which are clearly the result of mis-hearings

---

[1] See the discussion in *Diary*, vol. i, pp. cxxx, cxxxiii–cxxxiv.
[2] The Privy Council Register has a note at 7 January of an order to the Principal Officers to attend on the 10th at 9 a.m., but no further record of the meeting: PRO, PC 2/62, f. 52r. There are brief notices of some of the debates in the draft minutes of the Council's proceedings made by the Clerk, Sir Edward Walker (BL, Stowe MSS 489, ff. 249–66).
[3] The most remarkable is his 'Book of Mornamont' (PL 2881–2) – the two large volumes of copies of papers which he gathered in self-defence when accused of treason during the Popish Plot.
[4] These appear to have been made when he was composing his General Defence of the Office. They have not been printed in this volume.

rather than of misreadings: 'late' for 'great' (p. 348), 'his' for 'it is' (p. 359), 'in' for 'ill' (p. 361), etc.[1]

Before the debates began the Council devoted four meetings between 3 and 7 January to the discussion of Carteret's accounts, to which Pepys was summoned without his colleagues (pp. 336–41). There followed two meetings at which procedure for the debates was settled (pp. 341–5), after which the debates opened on 17 January. They were continued in nine subsequent meetings and ended on 21 February. Pepys attended all of them, though once arriving late, having stopped on his way in an attempt to see Claude Duval the highwayman carried to his execution (p. 366).

The debates, to which the public (in a remarkable departure from precedent) were admitted,[2] were presided over by the King with the Duke of York at his side, and followed the order of the 18 Observations. Each Observation was read by one of the Commissioners, who then submitted 'a paper of instances'; whereupon Pepys replied by presenting his written answer and elaborating on it. Other members of the Board might follow with their comments, after which the debate would be thrown open, Privy Councillors occasionally joining in. In the virtual absence of other official or unofficial records, Pepys's report cannot be checked. But it is unlikely to have contained serious mistakes of fact – Pepys's personal Diary can hardly be faulted at all on that ground, and the Brooke House Journal, like the Diary, was composed immediately or very soon after the event.[3] But we have no means of knowing if Pepys suppressed or distorted some part of the Commissioners' case. He certainly devotes much less space to their speeches than to his own.

His reports are fluent and copious, and only rarely given in note form.[4] Like the lengthy reports of conversations that are a feature of the Diary, they are evidence of Pepys's powers of memory. Many of his own speeches are in his best official style and are reported in dense detail. They read like memoranda, though here and there they come alive when he addresses reminders to himself – of what he ought to have said (pp. 352,

---

[1] Other examples include 'sure' for 'score' (p. 383), 'done' for 'down' (p. 391), 'lost' for 'passed' (p. 392), 'will' for 'which' (p. 421), and 'and' for 'at' (p. 423).
[2] See above, p. xxxiii & n. 2.
[3] This is clear from the reminders he addresses to himself.
[4] He occasionally includes notes made in preparation for a speech, e.g. the elaborate notes on payment by tickets at pp. 411–16.

383, 391) or of what he means to say later (pp. 354, 360, 406, 410). Of the speakers few are described with the same attention to visual detail that they would have received in the Diary. They are voices only. On a few rare occasions they become persons too – as in the angry scene when Pepys met head-on Brereton's accusation that he had embezzled a seaman's ticket worth £7 odd, and the King 'with a smile and shake of his head' gently scorned the suggestion that his Clerk of the Acts could have stooped so low (pp. 429–32). Throughout the debates the King presided with firmness and good humour, but without any pretence of impartiality. He never lost sight of the fact that he had arranged these proceedings as a means of defending his servants. He exhibited a confidence that came not only from his regality but also from his close knowledge of naval business: the terms of a contract (p. 347), the state of stocks of pipestaves (p. 392) or the global sums spent on the war by the two chief combatants (pp. 400–1).

Early in the proceedings he established a rapport with Pepys, choosing him to help to prepare Carteret's case which was discussed before the charges against the Navy Board were broached. He ruled that the debates concerning the Navy Board should centre on Pepys's answers to the Observations, and that his colleagues should present points concerning their own conduct as they arose in the course of the general discussion. The understanding between Charles and Pepys developed as the discussions proceeded. Like Pepys, the King welcomed any chance of mocking the Commissioners' admiration of the republican régime – ' "those pure angelical times" (saith the King), to which I added "those times concerning which people discourse in matters of the Navy as historians do of the primitive times in reference to the church" ' (p. 371). On the last day of the debates, Pepys protested that the Commissioners were raising charges without giving notice:

> Which method of theirs I showed would ... perpetuate the dispute without any end to be foreseen of it; while answers being given to satisfaction to this day's objection, that satisfaction shall never be owned but in lieu thereof a new race of objections shall be started, so as I plainly told his Majesty, my work must be to get a son and bring him up only to understand this controversy between Brooke House and us, and that his Majesty too should provide for successors to be instructed on his part in the state of this case, which otherwise would never

likely be understood, either as to what thereof had already been adjusted or what remained further to be looked after in it (pp. 432–3).

At the beginning of the proceedings Pepys was asked by the King to be responsible for replying to the charge that Charles most resented – that he had spent money granted for the war on 'other uses'. Arlington followed this by suggesting that Pepys should publish a refutation:

> as he did believe that Mr Pepys was the best informed of any man to do his Majesty this service, so (he added) that though Mr Pepys was by, yet he should not refrain to say that his style was excellent and the fittest to perform this work; though he would have it recommended to him to study the laying it down with all possible plainness, and with the least show of rhetoric if he could (p. 340).

Nothing came of the proposal – perhaps it was thought more effective to counter coffee-house gossip of this sort in the speeches of the King and the Lord Keeper at the opening of the next session of Parliament[1]. Meantime Pepys in these debates forced Brooke House to make an apology (p. 432).

On the subject of storekeepers' accounts (pp. 398–401) and seamen's tickets (pp. 403–10), he stunned his critics by firing off a barrage of detail. In both cases his speeches, for all their length and complexity, lacked nothing in lucidity. The forcefulness of his argument appears in the journal's summary of his speech answering the criticism that the Board had signed the Treasurer's ledgers without first ascertaining the dates of the items of expenditure. He showed

> that the crime here charged upon us was our not doing what was never enjoined us, what in no age was ever practised, what we could not have attempted to have done without unfaithfulness, what in itself is impossible to be done, and lastly what as soon as we were enjoined it and enabled thereto has as far as it is possible been punctually executed (pp. 367–8).

As a debater, Pepys could be hard-hitting. In his examination of Gregory's evidence about prize ships (pp. 432–4) he drove his critic into a corner, challenging him several times to repeat

[1] See above, p. xxxiii & n. 5.

his words. Occasionally, also, he took the contest into enemy territory. He questioned the validity of the Commissioner's inquisitorial methods of inquiry, which presumed guilt in the accused (pp. 365–6, 369). He denied their assumption that deviations from the Admiral's Instructions were always an offence, pointing out, in one of his best speeches (pp. 388–9), that the Instructions were meant to be interpreted with due regard to the circumstances of war. He maintained, like the King, that the only valid ground on which criticism of the Board's conduct could be based would be that their faults had demonstrably impeded the war effort. The Commissioners, he submitted, had not proved, and could not prove, any such charge.

The closing words of the Journal breathe an air of triumph typical of Pepys at his most complacent: 'And so ... the whole business of these Observations ended, with a profession of all satisfaction on his Majesty's part.'

I THE NAVY WHITE BOOK

January 5. 1663[4]. Ald. Backwell about pieces-of-eight. Ald. Backewell was this day sent for to the table about furnishing us with 5000*l*. in pieces-of-eight.[1] His demand was 4*s*. 7*d*. I told the Board, he being withdrawn, that I had informed myself and that I can have them at 4*s*. 6½*d*. and with the same security that he is to have. And my merchant (Mr Bland, whom I did not name)[2] would be contented with less interest per 1 per cent of the King for the forbearance of his money. The proposal was mightily liked, and Ald. Backewell called in to know what interest he expected. He told us he demanded of us but 6 per cent,[3] but that he would not conclude anything therein with us, but did leave it to the King's pleasure and my Lord Treasurer's – with whom he told us by the by in vainglory, that he had had the honour to trust the King since his coming with 500,000*l*. in money, for which to this day he never did receive a farthing interest; and Sir G. Carteret said that at this day he had advanced for the Navy 150,000*l*. But I do well know that he hath not less than 9, 10, 11 and 12 per cent sometimes for his forbearance, though he dare not own it.

But this is it I observe – that we could not make use of this good proposal because we could not bring him to say what interest he would be contented with, and further that it is but vain to beat him down in the price since at this rate he may well (though he does not) offer his money cheaper than any man else since, when he seem to save the King in the price, he can make good to himself above what others can do in the interest which the King pays him and all unknown to us that contract with him.

Jan. 7. Unknown interest the King pays for money. I told the Board again that my merchant (Mr Bland) will let us have them at 4*s*. 6½*d*. and will be content with 6 per cent interest (and herein he tells me that he does act by advice with Viner the goldsmith).[4] Sir G. Carteret could not tell what to say to it more than that he will tell my Lord Treasurer of it and Ald. Backewell,

---

[1]This was in preparation for an expedition against Algiers now about to sail under Adm. Sir John Lawson. Edward Backwell was the government's principal banker.
[2]Pepys, as a member of the Tangier Committee, was dealing with John Bland at this time for supplies. Bland was later Mayor of Tangier.
[3]The legal maximum, but normally 4% was added as 'gratuity'.
[4]Pepys and Bland, according to the Diary, had a meeting with Vyner on the 13th.

and see what he says of it, but cannot undertake that this offer shall be made use of for the King. Nor was it at last, but Backewell did furnish what he[1] had in the town. Sir J. Lawson at last undertaking to deliver them at Cales[2] and supply the occasions of the fleet at 4*s*. 6*d*., to be delivered full weight to the mean. But to be paid his money dead in a fortnight. But here is presently seen how we are bound to Backewell to the King's great and obscure wrong.

June 4.(64). Low credit of tallies. Upon like occasion at the Committee for Tanger we were fain to give Ald. Backewell what price he pleased above it. I particularly knew and did offer to serve them out, ready money, here. For there is nobody in town would deal with us for our tallies but him, so that he may take what gain he would upon us. And by this means he was emboldened to make us an offer and a desire indeed that we would try anywhere else to get them cheaper, but if we could not then rather than we should want he would supply us. But he did afterwards tell Creede (as Creede tells me) that he knew if he had gone away we must have entreated him to serve us and that if he would demand 4*s*. 11*d*. he could make us give it him. This is the unhappy posture of the King's credit. And the effect of making use but of one or two men.

May 20. 1664. An instance of the ill service of the King's own officers discovering to the merchant our wants. Mr [*blank*], son to Mr Ingram,[3] having been several times with me about getting me to help him off with a parcel of port-hinges and other trades left by his father Mr Ingram – which I put off till I knew whether they were good or no and that we wanted them. He came to me today to tell me that we do want them. And as he hath told me several times that Mr Shish tells him that we want, so today he tells me by name that Mr Chr. Pett of Woolwich did also lately tell him that we have now occasion for them for the new

---
[1] MS. 'we'.
[2] Cadiz.
[3] Robert Ingram, a London ironmonger, whose son and executor Richard had inherited his business: *CSPD 1661–2*, p. 625.

ship,[1] and that if we do not buy his we shall be at a present loss for the new ship.

May 26. 1664. Sir W. Warren's contract for dry deals. An instance of our officers receiving goods not answering contracts. Memorandum: that upon a difference today between Sir W. Batten and Sir W. Warren this day at the Board about a late contract of 28 Apr. last for some dry deals – I am to remember that the contract in terms is so good that I did this day forbear to give the money for a thousand more of them to answer the contract.[2] And, more, that though they are not so good as we would have, yet if they answer the contract, he willingly will take them away and the fault is to remain upon them that received them not so good as contract.[3] And we ordered the taking away as many of them as are not spent. But, above all, not only I but Mr Coventry do remember and did this day tell the Board that it was against Sir W. W.'s will that we had these, he himself dissuading from it and would have had us buy better.

May 28. 1664. Fallacy of the storekeepers' manner of keeping their books etc. Discoursing this day with Mr Deane,[4] he did tell me, among other things, that Mr Ackworth the storekeeper doth observe himself and is angry with his servant if he neglects at any time to enter his issues with a great distance one line from another, that so if upon comparing of books with Deane he sees that he can by any advantage set down anything more in his issue than he really did, he may have room to do it with the same hand that writes his book, and by that means gains so much upon his issues.[5] He confirms me in what I have found lately upon my inquiry into the embezzlement of the *Beare*'s cable (*vide* the

---

[1] Shish and Pett were building the *Royal Katherine*, a 2nd-rate, launched at Woolwich on 26 October: *The Newes*, s.d.

[2] The contract was for 1000 deals at £4 per hundred (i.e. 120 by the normal reckoning): *CSPD 1664–5*, p. 133. Batten had presumably objected to their not answering contract, but Pepys was against buying another thousand to replace them.

[3] That is, the dockyard officers who had wrongly certified them as answering contract.

[4] Anthony Deane, assistant shipwright, Woolwich.

[5] Pepys refers to Ackworth's cheating in the Diary at about this time: v. 130 & n. 2, 156. In 1658 he had been temporarily suspended for embezzlement: Aylmer, *State's Servants*, p. 160.

embezzlement, no. 2).[1] Then again he doth never complete his book or any account of goods that he issues or receives presently, but keeps it unentered a good while, by that means getting some advantage by it of having the thing forgotten – as in the business of the old cordage sold to Wood, in part of which the shot of cable of the *Beare*'s was issued. Where, instead of 20 ton or thereabouts, at which it was by computation sold, Deane believes that by letting the quantity slip till it was forgot, he hath at several times issued above 80 tons.

October 6. 1663. The great contest at the table between Sir J. Mennes, Sir W. Batten and myself about Sir W. Warren's contract for knees and Winter's contract for timber (said by them to be as good in its terms as the other, which I denied). *Vide* my Journal of this day.[2]

King's timber measurer trusted by the merchant. Question: what may be drawn from the King's timber measurer (Mr Fletcher) at Deptford being trusted by the merchant Capt. Cocke in measuring his East-Country plank, which I see him do, and so did Sir W. Pen, whom by chance I met there in the yard the last summer while he lay there for his health. *Vide:* page [111], Tinker and Eastwood.

Decembr 15. 1663. It is fit for me to remember against a time of inquiry what I have to say as to the profit which I have made of Capt. Taylor's bills for his ship hired by us to Tanger,[3] which is this. He at first had received 92*l*. 18*s*. 04*d*. by way of imprest upon his freight. The services being done there was the

---

[1] This and similar references are to the numbered bundles of papers on which many of these memoranda are based.

[2] *Diary,* iv. 326: 'Mr Chr. Pett and Deane were summoned to give an account of some Knees which Pett reported bad, that were to be served in by Sir W. Warren, we having contracted that none should be served but such as were to be approved of by our officers – so that if they were bad, they were to be blamed for receiving them ... Sir J. Mennes told me angrily that Winters Timber, bought for 33*s* per loade was as good ... ; I told him that it was not so, but that he and Sir W. Batten were both abused, and I would prove it was as dear a bargain as had been made this half year – which occasioned high words between them and me, but I am able to prove it and will.' Warren's timber had been approved of by Deane. In criticising Winter's timber (from Hornchurch in Epping Forest) Pepys was relying on reports from the purveyor and from Deane: PRO, SP 46/136, no. 94. Cf. below, pp. 57–8.

[3] The *William and Mary.* There is a brief account in the Diary: iv. 414, 423 & nn.

other two thirds due to him, which together is 278*l*. 15*s*. 00*d*. Then for demurrage, so many days according to the rate that we did use to count others, and cutting off half of it,[1] it came to 73*l*. 17*s*. 00*d*., which together is 352*l*. 12*s*. 00*d*., which is the whole of the bill now made out to him. But I thinking that this was too much for him to go away with, beyond whatever he expected for demurrage, I did cast about how to get something of it; and so having told him upon the Change that I had got him 43*l*. 17*s*., he was mighty thankful to me for it. Only, I told him that he must abate 8*l*. 9*s*. for short deliveries of goods, which I did do against a day of inquiry, and this 8*l*. 9*s*. I cast it as it is in the margin:

Butter, 116 lbs at 9*s*. per lb.	1*l*. 9*s*. 0*d*.
Bread, 1000 at 12*s*. per cwt	6*l*. 0*s*. 0*d*.
40 deals	1*l*. 0*s*. 0*d*.
Total	8*l*. 9*s*. 0*d*.

And he was most ready to agree to it, giving me many thanks. Seeing this go fair, well I delayed for three or four days, telling him that I would endeavour to get this granted and confirmed for him by the Commissioners of Tanger, and that I had no way to satisfy myself but by getting something the more added, either to his bill or to somebody's else under another head, and therefore if he would consent to it and keep it secret, he would do me a courtesy. He told me with all his heart, he would, and that he would secure me against all inquiry from his partners hereafter (and by name I did inquire whether Mr Wood was one of them: he told me no, but that Sir W. Warren was, of which I was glad). So we parted, and a while after I came and told him that I had got his bill signed as I told him, with an addition for myself under the name of demurrage, of 30*l*., to which he did fully consent. That is to say, that out of the 352*l*. 12*s*. I should have 30*l*. upon that score and 8*l*. 9*s*. abatement for short provisions. Then he begun to treat with me about my buying of his bill – to pay him at my own time between this and Candlemas. He would give me 5*l*. I would not buy his bill, but if he would give me out of the 221*l*. 4*s*. 8*d*. the 6*l*. odd money, and leave himself 215*l*. clear, upon condition I got him the money paid before Christmas, I would endeavour what I could. He consents. So the next day I got the Treasurer to sign it and this day, being

---

[1] The other half being credited to his partners, presumably. Pepys was reserving half for himself.

the 16th day of December 1663, he did go himself to the Treasury Office, without anything with me along with him (only last night, by other business I did go thither and spoke to Mr Fen) and received his money, that is, the whole bill of 352*l*. 12*s*., only abating his former imprest of 92*l*. 18*s*. 0*d*. – and 3*l*. and the odd money of the sum remaining for their poundage.[1] And so there remained to him 256*l*. out of which he did come to me and brought me 43*l*. 13*s*. 00*d*. – that is to say, 30*l*. for my part of the demurrage and 8*l*. 9*s*. for the abatement for short provisions, which I must take care to reckon myself debtor to the Committee of Tanger in and lay by the money to that purpose, and 5*l*. 4*s*. more for my pains in getting the money thus paid him.

Upon the whole, I am principally to remember these points –

1. That the bill is all writ with my own hand, and was done at the importunity of the man in the absence of Mr Hater, who was then at Portsmouth at the pay of Sir J. Lawson's fleet there, and nobody else here could do it. But however, I did keep it till they did come home and got the Comptroller's hand to it, and would have had Sir W. Batten's too but that Sir J. Mennes had set his hand so near the other that he hath not left room for Sir W. Batten to set his hand between his and W. Coventry.

2. That Capt. Taylor hath not been observed to pay me any money, he bringing it in a handkercher to my office, which nobody observed, and left it with me so. And that he had not any word from me under my hand, or anything whereby he can evidence the payment of any money to me.

3. That if hereafter he should play the knave (for I have not herein done the King the least wrong, nor the man, for he is well satisfied with having the 43*l*. for his demurrage and the whole 73*l*. is not a farthing more than we have all along paid others in proportion), I may, I say, hereafter either put him to prove his payment or say that it is true I did receive money of him, but it was 8*l*. 9*s*. for the Committee of Tanger.

4. That if I be demanded why I did not mention it in the bill of 8*l*. 9*s*. – I had [no] reason so to do, it being so much delivered short to the wrong of my Lord Peterborough,[2] who hath offered to me (by Mr Povy) the gathering of what is due to him upon

---

[1]That is, dues paid to the officers of the Navy Treasury.
[2]Governor of Tangier.

short deliveries; and what I account for the rest, I do purpose to [do] it for this.

5. That none of the Treasurer's people can have the least doubt of my being concerned herein, he himself going for the money, and receiving it all and giving his hand for it. Nor did I take anything under his hand for what was coming to me when I did give him up the bill.

6. I must remember that he had, besides all this, given me a while since a silver plate, to gain my help in this business, so that I have got of him herein a piece of plate of about 4*l*. and 35*l*. 4*s*. clear, besides 8*l*. 9*s*. upon account for Tanger against I am called to give it. However, I will keep myself ready to expect it.

7. He cannot say that he did pay me any particular sum, for he did not tell it. But only, in the morning he brought me 40*l*. in his handkercher and I took it without telling it, laying it by me; and at night he came and paid me the rest (3*l*. 13*s*.) wrapped up in a paper, without telling it at all.

8. That he did take of me the particulars of the provisions: how the 8*l*. 9*s*. did arise, as I have set it in the margin of the other side; but that he left it behind him, and so hath nothing to show of particulars, only in a bit of paper he did take the sum of 8*l*. 9*s*. as the sum that was abated out of the whole upon the account. But now I think of it, I am not very certain of this last head, for I think he did take the particulars of the provisions in two several papers at several times.

December 15. (63). Dispute at the table about Sir W. Warren's great contract of masts.[1] There happened this day at the office, present my Lord Berkely, Sir J. Mennes, Sir W. Batten, W. Coventry, Sir W. Penn, and myself, a great dispute about the signing of Sir W. W.'s bill for his masts delivered lately at Chatham and certified to answer in all points the terms of the contract, and also what to do with other goods which came along with them. He was most shamefully used by Sir W. Batten, and Sir W. Warren's

---

[1]This was for £3000-worth of Norwegian masts: see draft in PRO, SP 29/80, no. 47 (incomplete summary in *CSPD 1663–4*, p. 270). It had been concluded on 10 Sept. 1663 at a meeting from which Batten had been absent. Pepys had negotiated it single-handed and his colleagues had signed it after only one reading and without asking any questions: *Diary*, iv. 303–4 & n. For the disputes which followed, see below, esp. pp. 79–81; and the summary in B. Pool, *Navy Board Contracts 1660–1832* (1966), pp. 26–7.

condescensions were so great that my Lord Berkely did say he never heard so many reasonable answers and agreements in any man in his life, and all the Board, Sir W. Batten and J. Mennes excepted, most fully satisfied with W. Warren. And all things at last, with some loss to him, agreed on.

Sometimes W. Batten said that there was a great many of them boltsprits, whereas there was only, besides 74 good masts, 9 that were shorter than their due lengths, some of them a good deal. But however, after he had endeavoured to have them served in as timber, we did carry it to have them bought as masts, but of less hands; we took them down because of their want of lengths.

Sometimes he said that some of them were a year or two old, and one of them worm-eaten, whereas Sir W. Warren[1] did say that indeed there was one did seem old, but was as good a tree as any in the world, and it was bought.

But most of all, he did repeat the badness of the contract, and would needs have it confessed that it was a bad contract; but since it was made, we must make the best of it; at which I was moved and desired him to say wherein it was so bad a one. He said, and that at last he declared was his only objection, that we was by it clogged with more small masts than we should use in some years, and that we had no need of them. I answered, as is in my letter to Sir G. Carteret, that it is not so many as he[2] had consented to have bought of Wood.[3] He had no other way but to deny that he had agreed to have had them all of Mr Wood. This I did wonder at, it being so false, and argued that he did not only consent, and never in the least did object anything against them, but moreover, that he did well remember, and so did Mr Coventry, that Wood did declare he would not deal for any unless we had all, and upon that score did plainly tell us that he would not sell those two or three masts that we had occasion for but at those great rates; and that if we would have his whole parcel, we should have them as we had the rest. But above all, I bid them remember how, after we had gone through with W. Warren, a while after, Mr Wood did offer his at Warren's rates, and both Sir J. Mennes and he did say that it was reasonable, but I did oppose it. This they denied. But to the truth of it –

[1] MS. 'Batten'.
[2] Batten
[3] William Wood, Warren's greatest rival in the trade, and Batten's friend.

1. I am ready to be opposed,[1] as truly I may, for I most perfectly remember it.
2. My letter that day to Mr Coventry[2] says it.
3. I appeal to their own consciences whether they did not. However, they did persist to deny it, and I resolve to try a trick how to prove it.

That which vexed me as much as anything was that Sir W. Penn, who had often spoke to me in commendation of the bargain, and at my coming to town did send for me on purpose to tell me how he had stood up in my absence to defend this contract, did this day say at table that for his part he was sick we knew all the while, and that he doth remember he was here at the signing of the contract but not at the making of it up, nor knew upon what terms and arguments it was done. But only since, he doth remember he had informed himself, and he found it, so and so, better than the other bargain offered by Wood. But this is not the first time wherein he hath dealt deceitfully, and I hope I shall never forget how to deal with him hereafter. Sir J. Mennes also did say after him, that he also was here at the day of signing the contract, and when I told him I do then believe he was then convinced that it was the better, he told me plainly that he will look better hereafter to contracts, and that I now take the minutes and then draw the contract as I please – which did vex me to the guts, to hear that impertinent fool talk so, when God knows I did it with all the care and faith in the world, and to good advantage I am sure.

December 16. (63). This day at the Change I went on purpose to find and speak with Mr Wood, and did so, first calling Capt. David Lambert and giving him in his ear direction to stand close by and hear what passed between Mr Wood and I.[3] So I begin, after other things, to ask him that when at such a time he came to offer his masts at the price we had bought Sir W. Warren's, and that Sir W. Batten and Sir J. Mennes did consent to it, who it was that hindered it: he told me it was me. I did ask him

---

[1] MS. 'proposed' (i.e. examined).
[2] In this letter (14 Nov. 1663: *Further Corr.*, pp. 6–10) Pepys set out calculations showing that Warren had offered twice as many of the largest masts as Wood, five times as many of the middling size and about half as many of the smallest.
[3] The Diary has only a brief note of this encounter and does not mention the ruse plotted with Lambert.

what it was that I argued then for my so doing: he told me that I did argue their being old; from thence I did seem to offer him an opportunity of tendering them now, and so beat off the discourse from my point; and so parted, and afterwards told Capt. Lambert the whole story of yesterday's proceeding between W. Batten and me and the reason of this question of mine to Wood, and bid him remember; which he said he will, that Wood did confess to me before him that Sir J. Mennes and Sir W. Batten did consent that he should sell us his masts at the price we did give Warren, and that it was I that did oppose it, and by that argument – which is an excellent proof.

But it is a pretty consideration, that hence Wood will go to W. Batten and tell him how I seem willing to buy his masts, and what Sir W. Batten will do therein – for either he must now contradict himself by offering to buy these, when he says we have too many already, or else he must, sore against his will, be contented to have Wood's lie still upon his hands.

June 4th 1664. It is to be remembered that notwithstanding all this great store of small Norway masts which Sir W. B. hath urged against this good contract, we are this day forced to buy at dearer rates of Mr Wood old – last year's – masts, to be sent from hence by the *Augustin* for Portsmouth and some of Mr Blackborough also, old masts (but not so dear) for Deptford, there being not sufficient of 12 hands and under in either place to set forth the few ships now ordered forth for present service from both places. I may also turn to the state of the masts in all the yards the last survey, which I have abstracted by me, where the number of small is not very great in any of the yards – especially if we compare it with the number required to mast the fleet round, which I also have by me.

June 7. 1664. Corruption of a purveyor, Mr Meres. Nay, it is further observable that upon the Change this day, inquiring of Sir W. Warren whether he had any small masts, he tells me yes, he hath above 100 or thereabouts, small masts fresh come in this year, which he is willing to serve in upon his last contract at the same price, and that they have lain at his yards ever since they were brought in, which is three weeks or a month ago. And yet the other day (June 4), I did again and again demand of Mr Meres the purveyor whether he had look all over the River: he told us yes, and that there was not any men in the River had any, no masts of this year's, but Mr Dering a very few – by which means we lose the fresh ones at the old price and give more for the last year's masts.

I charging of Meres (June 18) this day at the table with it, he denies that they did lie then at Sir W. Waren's wharf – which I will take to know more particularly.

Upon June the 23rd Sir W. Batten did take occasion at the Board to tell me that he had informed himself, and that for all what I said the other day, Sir W. Warren hath not nor hath had any new small masts come this year. I asked him whether he was sure of it: he told me before the whole table, yes. I then produced a letter Sir W. Warren sent me yesterday in answer to mine, where he tells me particularly the time and place where and when they came, and do still and have lain ever since they came. At which, not only he was justly shamed, but Meres reprehended by Sir G. Carteret, Mr Coventry and the Board. And such is the disgraces the King hath in everything else.

May 1664. A copy of Mr Harbing's account of the charge of a hundred bales of Noyles canvas; asserting it to be the real charge it stands him in.[1]

100 bales at 172*l*. per bale	£ 17200.00
Commission	£ 00344.00
	£ 17544.00
5848 at 57*d*. per ton is	£ 1388.18
Custom	£ 0080.00
Freight	£ 0050.00
Porterage, wharfage &c.	£ 0008.10
Delivering into his Majesty's stores	£ 0008.02
	£ 1535.10
100 bales reduced according to his Majesty's measure 296 yards per bale makes 94⅔ bales at 16*l*. 15*s*. per bale	1581.00.00

[1]This calculation presumably relates to a recent dispute over John Harbin's bill: *CSPD 1663–4*, p. 560.

A trial of the advantage or loss in our converting of sheathing board; made in the King's yard at Deptford May 3d 1664 by Mr Shish at my direction.[1]

	l. s. d.
4 loads and 43 ft (in 3 pieces) of Dram timber costing (at 39*s.* per load) 9*l.* 9*s.* 0*d.* with the additional charge of 4*l.* 16*s.* 4*d.* for sawyer's work; in all	14. 05. 04
Yielded according to measure by the middle-board,[2] 3218 ft which at 10*s.* per V^{xx}ft[3] (Sir W. Warren's price) comes to	16. 01. 09
And according to true board measure (board by board) 2774 ft which at the same price comes to	13. 17. 00

May 24. 1664. Sir W. Batten taking money of the Victualler for the signing of his accounts. Sir J. Minnes did tell me, discoursing of the victualling business and the passing of his accounts, that Sir W. Batten did demand and hath received of Mr Gauden, 20*l.* a time for the passing of his accounts. And that Mr Gauden hath sometimes said to him that he was in his[4] debt also, but he is resolved never to take it, though he says he thinks it may be found to have been the old practice that the Comptroller and the Surveyor should have 20*l.* apiece at an account, and by name, that my Lady Palmer[5] did always demand it for pin-money. And that Sir Guilfd Slingsby[6] did receive it. And that Sir W. Batten hath often said to him that he ought to have it, and why

---

[1]See Shish to Pepys, 3 May: PRO, SP 29/98, no. 12 (*CSPD 1663–4*, p. 578). Pepys appends to the letter the notes which are given here.
[2]This would be the board at the mid-point between the shortest and the longest, which would give the mean measurement. The average measurement could be distorted by a large number of short or of long boards.
[3]Five score.
[4]Mennes's.
[5]Barbara Palmer, Countess of Castlemaine, the King's mistress.
[6]Comptroller of the Navy, 1611–18 and 1628–32.

did he not demand it; but he will not demand it, but quite contrary, gives 20*l*. a year out of his purse to have it done. But he desired me not to speak of it, for he will know that it comes from him.

March 21. 166³/₄. Effects of survey being ill taken and not publicly examined. By this means it comes to pass that we have more nails and other ironwork than we are able to spend by the Surveyor's own confession these seven years – as appeared by the last survey.[1]

By this means it is that we are in the like case for lignum vitae, by his own confession, at Woolwich.

By this means it is that it costs us so much in a year for transportation from yard to yard.

By this means it is that we have so many treenails lie in Woolwich yard and have long done for many years at Chatham in corners, out of mind, more than will be spent while good.

By this means it is that so many oars have lain unspent, and yet served from other places to Portsmouth (as those of Mr Harrington's).

By this means it is that we ordered so much small timber to Woolwich that we are forced to carry 80 or 100 loads of it to Deptford, which at the same charge might have been delivered there first when it was brought out of Epping Forest.

March 29th. This day, being at the passing of Sir G. Carteret's accounts at his house, Sir W. Batten did say himself to me and Sir J. Mennes before Mr Wayth,[2] that he believed there was 100 tons of hardwood in stores, and most of it lignum vitae, more than would be used these seven years – and much, he said, served in without order.

April 1. (64). Hence it is that at Deptford, last survey, there was found so great a quantity of spars of all sorts, that for certain will never be spent while good. And by discourse with Sir W. Warren this day I find that so great a number of spars and balks was desired of him by Sir W. Batten in his last great contract made with us this last year,[3] only to put him out of a capacity of

---

[1] General surveys, conducted under the supervision of the Surveyor, were in theory held annually.
[2] Robert Waith, cashier to the Navy Treasurer, Carteret.
[3] See above, p. 9 & n.1.

contracting with us – believing that neither he nor any man but Wood (who, out of a presumption of contracting with us, hath got them together) was able to serve us with them – they[1] never selling half so many anywhere else in a great while. But it happened that Sir W. W. did serve them in. One thing more he tells me, that that which are most spent of us, there [are] demanded least, and so put them upon a necessity of using the great ones, for want of worse.

By this means it is that in March last Sir W. Batten with his own hand (the paper may be turned to) drew up a note for some things to be brought from Portsmouth by the *Augustin*: he sends for 25 masts of the small masts of Sir W. Rider's, and accordingly we writ for them – when Tippets presently answers us that they had but 33 in stores and dared not spare them.

June 2. By this means it is that Edgehill the block-maker, being with us today, he tells us that there are more at present in Deptford stores than will be spent of small blocks in a year's while and while good. And yet Sir W. Batten did but two or three days since contract for many dozens, which we may see by our books.

By this means we are forced this day to buy small anchors, there being by Sir W. Batten's confession at the Board not any so much as to set out these three first ships are going out with this fleet from Deptford.

By this means in general, I may observe, it is very true that our many demands at this day made from every yard for the dispatch of twelve ships now going forth with all imaginable dispatch, in expectation of a Dutch war,[2] there is not sufficient stores of all sorts in any one of his Majesty's yards to set forth one ship – without borrowing of some other ship that possibly may be in the River or of the rigging that lies by belonging to another ship, and those are but few too, God knows.

And it is observable that whereas he did the other day deliver under his own hand (which I have) an account of the stores in

---

[1] That is, Wood (Batten's friend) and Castle (Wood's partner and Batten's son-in-law).

[2] They had been ordered out hurriedly by the Duke of York on 18 May on receipt of the news that the Dutch had left harbour: PRO, ADM 106/8, f. 463r. The Dutch, after making a show of force in the Channel, were back in harbour by December: *Diary*, v. 152 & n. 1, 155, 168. War was not declared until the following February.

every yard, and that of Portsmouth, there was but [one] per estimate, and also thereupon did under his hand also make a demand of a year's supply to be made of the principal provisions – it is to be thought after what manner he could do this with any judgement, when we at the Board the last week desiring, at my motion, to have a day appointed for the considering of the stores, he did desire to have a week's time to cast up his survey-book, that he might say what there was in store of each at the last survey; and so we did give him to tomorrow. And it will be fit to consider his report when he doth make it, how it agrees with his late abstract of the stores and his year's demand. *Look a little lower.*

June 3. (64). We meet, as I said above to receive his report, and there was not one thing done; nor could he give us an account of any one particular, great or small, for he did not abstract the goods and reduce them to a head. And so we were forced to show him the way ourselves, Mr Coventry and I beginning with anchors, which held us most of the morning. And whereas he makes no demand in his great demand which I mention above, we do find of many sorts a great many wanting, as appears by our calcule, which I keep by me[1] – besides those small ones which we the other day contracted for.

June 18. (64). Sir W. Pen reports the state of the ships at Portsmouth. This day Sir W. Pen coming to the Board (being come from Portsmouth last night) did, among other things, acquaint us that every ship there, upon his personal survey of them, doth look other-gates repaired in every respect than the Surveyor's book doth speak them to do – whereby much more labour is created in fitting them forth than was expected.

June 23. (64). Having often called for Sir W. Batten's account of stores, which instead of being ready to give, he would say to what end was it, or else that it was already done well enough in the survey-book – which God knows is the most confused thing in the world. At last, by agreement with Mr Coventry, we did

---

[1] 'The Generall State of the Naval-Stores upon a Survey taken March 1663/4' (in Pepys's hand): Bodl. Lib., Rawl. MSS A174, ff. 19–20.

call for his abstract, which he hath so long promised, of the masts only, thinking to settle that, and the rather because Sir W. Warren doth offer us a parcel of large masts. And the time of year for having them spends;[1] and more, I know the plot of making us have Wood's old ones. So we called for it, and Mr Coventry took it and it proved so confused still, and impossible from thence to understand the state of our stores, and much less how to compare it with what we should have to mast the fleet round (which I was forced to collect what number was necessary to mast and yard the fleet round) that I was forced at the open table to take it to my part to abstract his book of masts and to teach them[2] what it is to state a thing methodically. So I did do it, and this day (June 25th) sent it to Mr Coventry. And shall think it labour well bestowed if it may but teach the Surveyor how to do it hereafter, that and other stores.

Jan. 27. 1663[4]. Mr Hempson. Mr Hempson, clerk of the survey at Chatham, did spend a great deal of the morning with me, telling me how desirous he hath been to wait on me, but durst not, for giving offence to I know whom – and by and by plainly saying Sir W. Batten.

That he hath a design to buy Cowly's place, clerk of the cheque at Deptford, who asks five years' purchase; and would have me advise in it and how to gain Mr Coventry's consent.[3]

Myself. In everything he flatters me, and told me how many at Chatham did formerly speak mighty hardly of me, and above all Capt. Pett;[4] but that now all is over, and that he hath defended me always, and I know not what. That I have done great good by making the Commissioner[5] do that of visiting the yards, and I know not what, that he never did in his life before.

Comr Pett. That Comr Pett is as very a knave as lives upon

---

[1] Mast ships usually avoided sailing after the summer.
[2] The dockyard clerks of the survey and their assistants.
[3] Nothing came of this proposal. Cowley was still clerk of the cheque in 1667, two years before he died: *CSPD 1666–7*, p. 509; A. H. Nethercot, *Abraham Cowley* (1931), p. 298.
[4] Phineas Pett, master shipwright at Chatham.
[5] Peter Pett, Navy Commissioner at Chatham, 1648–60 and 1660–7.

earth;[1] and told me many of his tricks, poor sordid ones indeed. And among others, his making a banquet for the King at his first coming into England and making the State pay for it; and yet would not pay a woman for some of the wine that they had, but put her to the Commissioners of the Navy, and then to the Commissioners of Parliament,[2] till at last she said she would complain to us, and by name to Sir W. Batten; whereupon he presently ordered her payment.

That he is noted by all the gentry of the county for a false-hearted fellow, whom none of them can endure, and that it is a scandal to be known to have to do with him.

That for all his pretence of a fire extraordinary, he doth seldom keep any at all.[3] That he makes sometimes four, five, or six labourers work to the removing of his dung and other such works.

Feb. 2. (63[4]). About Sir W. Batten. He told me how Sir W. B., with whom he hath been today (upon a letter he received from him, and which he showed me, reproaching him with neglect of business, and his coming to others of the Office when he is in town and not to him, which indeed was to me (as above), which he had notice of; and Hempson tells me that that is it he means from what James Norman[4] had told him, and in the letter he is discharged of his place, to be gone in such a time (in March next), that he cannot get him to recede from his resolution of turning of him off; and indeed, Sir W. B. did tell us at the Board that he had done it. He tells me that he will make a sound stir before he parts with his place. And that he offered him today a 100*l.* in money and a piece of plate and a hogshead of wine, 23*l.* more. And also near 40*l.* to Tom Newburne, and that Newb. hath told him that Sir W. B. did swear by God, that if he thought that

---

[1] The Pett family and their kindred, of whom the Commissioner was the chief, held a quasi-monopoly of the dockyard offices at Woolwich and Chatham which laid them open to charges of corruption and every manner of malpractice. See Aylmer, *State's Servants*, pp. 157–8.
[2] The Commissioners appointed at the Restoration to pay off the armed forces.
[3] Dockyard officers had allowances of firewood made up from offcuts of timber. Pett was probably claiming the cost of the labour. For abuses of the practice, see R. D. Merriman (ed.), *Sergison Papers* (NRS 1950), pp. 132, 135.
[4] Batten's clerk.

had Hempson not[1] given him 50 pieces (that is, T. Newb.) he should never have had his place.

Sir W. Penn. He told me, speaking of Sir W. P. (who, it seems, he is told should say[2] that he wondered Sir W. Batten had kept him[3] so long), that he heard Sir W. P. say heretofore, that if there were any of the true children of God in this world, they were the Anabaptists, and that he would live and die with them.

And that when he was a flag-officer in the Dutch war, I think he said Vice-Admiral, at the Kentish Knock, he was articled against by a Major for cowardice, for not coming into the fight, and that he was very melancholy a great while upon it, and doubted of ever being employed again; but Sir H. Vane, being of his own religion, kept him in.[4]

May 3d 1664. About Sir W. Batten. That Sir W. B. (as he is able to prove) did take 10 pieces in gold of Capt. Cox to set his hand to his certificate at the King's coming in.[5] And did ordinarily take of others in like manner. And that T. Newborne did take 3*l.* of one poor man to get him entered in the King's yard, and hath often done so. And that Sir W. B. hath often said, "By God, Tom, we must share; thou must have some, and I must [have] some of it". *Vide my Journal this day.*[6]

March 28. (64). Sir J. Mennes's discourse about the falseness of Comr Pett. Speaking with Sir J. M. concerning Comr Pett, that it would be best for the King's service to have him employed in some other yard, where he may not be so well known as he is here, by which means he will be free to find faults and command,

---

[1]MS. 'that Hempson had not' – sc. Batten would not have appointed him in the first place had he not understood that Hempson had given Newburne 50 pieces.
[2]Sc. had said.
[3]Newburne.
[4]Penn was Vice-Admiral under Blake at the Battle of the Kentish Knock (28 Sept. 1652). In the Diary (iv. 375–6 & nn.) Pepys tells these stories from another source. The story of Penn's cowardice – he is alleged to have hidden in a coil of cable – was current for some time: cf. Marvell's *Second Advice to a Painter* (1666), ll. 87–8. The "Major" was presumably Nehemiah Bourne, Rear-Admiral of Blake's fleet.
[5]At the Restoration commissioned officers and office holders had to obtain certificates of their loyalty during the Interregnum to retain their commissions and offices.
[6]*Diary*, v. 141, where Batten's words are reported slightly differently.

which he cannot do here – he told me, among other things, one instance of his hypocrisy and false dealing. Which was, that he complained to Sir J. Mennes and Sir W. Batten the other day of Mr Barrow, how unquiet a man he is,[1] and said: "Why, you may see how while you are here, he is orderly and doth things as he should do; but no sooner will you be gone, but he will be as bad and raise troubles as he uses to do." "And yet," says Sir J. M., "the other day when he was at the table, he would not lay any fault to Mr Barrow, but was wholly silent and cleared him of the business of Mr Gregory's complaint. And yet a day after, when Mr Barrow was not at the table, he did confess a little that he was somewhat unquiet – but in no such manner as he had done when he was at Chatham."

March 11. 166¾. Mr Lewes's discourse upon pursers' accounts.[2] He tells me that it is a most ordinary thing for a purser to bring his certificates one by one – and as he sees occasion from the examination of one, to order or correct his others – and having those returned to them which we do not like, a good while after either bring the same again, when it is out of our minds and we busy and in haste, or another made in a better manner, which we then pass. And that it is even alehouse talk among the pursers – and their sport – that if they can get but Sir J. Mennes to pass anything at one time, they are contented, for at some other time, as they find [him] in an humour, he will be sure to pass the rest – not from his satisfaction that he hath in them now more than before, but only that his humour is different. This I know to be true in other things, and some of this sort too.

The uncertainty of what Sir J. Mennes doth therein. And a most usual thing it is with Sir J. M. to sign a thing, which when he hears questioned, all he says is, that he doubts whether it be his hand or no, or asks how his hand came there, and presently scratches it out. And in a week or two after will sign it again. Nay, and sometimes upon the same paper. As for instance, a bill

---

[1]Barrow (storekeeper at Chatham) had long caused trouble, particularly by quarrelling with Gregory, the clerk of the cheque: *Diary*, iii. 155; iv. 149; *CSPD Add. 1660–85*, p. 136. He resigned, and a successor was appointed in March 1666: *CSPD 1665–6*, p. 308; PRO, ADM 20/9, p. 2.

[2]Thomas Lewis was a clerk in the Victualling Office.

to G. Buckridge, March 28. 1664, for 10*l*. odd money due to him as purser to the *Assurance* for his disbursements.[1]

And more than all that, notwithstanding he had at open table denied that ever he did give order for the purser of the *Breda*, Mr Stephenton, to victual some women that went over for Tanger[2] – yet upon the 26 March 1664 he did acknowledge that he did give such order for it and owned the truth of the captain's certificate to the truth thereof, which he had at open table again and again denied, and ordered the purser to bear the charge thereof himself. Yet I say did this day sign for the purser's being allowed it. The paper is in Mr Lewes's hand, and may be turned to, signed by him and me.

February 22. 1663[4]. Upon Mr Wood's parcel of New England masts and boltsprits.[3] Meeting this day Mr Wood upon the Change (I having followed him very hard at the Board in his business of his New England masts), he told me very hotly that I was resolved to ruin him. And that he could not see but that I am the man; at least, he would not for the present, though he knows others.

And nothing would pass me but what comes through Sir W. Warren's hands, and then white deals should be sold as red.[4] That we could stand to the report of the officers of the yard in anything of Warren's, but not in his. That if we would not refer the business in difference between us about his New England masts to some indifferent man, as he desired, he would petition the King, for he would have me know that he would serve the King as well as any of us. That he could tell (and I think spoke more with respect to me than upon the rest of the Board) and would gather up how the King hath been served by our contracts with Warren. And that what we did was not to serve the King, but to ruin him.

Febr. 11 (63[4]). After long debate this day at the Board

---

[1]Mennes's initials, with those of his colleagues, occur on the office copy of the bill (23 July 1664, for victuals): PRO, ADM 106/3520, f. 20*v*.

[2]Both garrison and town came to have their quota of womenfolk (of all sorts). Pepys found 'very few ... of any quality or beauty' when he went there in 1683: E. Chappell (ed.), *The Tangier Papers of S. Pepys* (NRS 1935), pp. 17, 74, 89, etc.

[3]Contracted for in November 1662 and delivered at Portsmouth at the end of 1663: *Diary*, iii. 268; below, p. 54.

[4]White deals (spruce) were inferior to and cheaper than red (pine).

concerning Mr Wood's New England masts and boltsprits, in both of which I alone did object against their want of length, it was agreed among other things, at the motion of Sir W. Batten, that for the boltsprits, if they do answer the length of the boltsprits now standing in the King's ships of those diameters, we would not stand for any abatement, because nowadays it seems our ships do not require so long boltsprits as formerly.

I wrote down to Comr Pett (*vide my letter in the public book*)[1] to give us any account herein; and he did particularly, and the length of Mr Wood's do fall short of them now up. When I came to show this report to the table, Sir W. Batten would have excepted against the report of Comr Pett [and] would say that he himself had measured them at this time on purpose, because otherwise the report might be made out of some old book of rates of ancient measures. In a day or two, the Commissioner coming to town did say that they were measured on purpose. Then Sir W. B. said that it might be that they did pick out some of the longest on purpose; and therefore, being himself to go down soon to the measure, he would measure them himself.

Feb. 24. (63[4]). An alteration in the dimensions of boltsprits proposed unseasonably. He did so, and reported to us how he found several of the boltsprits now up. And not finding them as he would, he under his hand, and gets Comr Pett to sign to it (as among my papers of masts appears), that they were too long, and some of them they had ordered to be made shorter. Which is an excellent piece of knavery, or at least but an ill-timed alteration of an old rule, to do it just at this time to favour his friend, and cost the King money, without any necessity, we having an old known practice, and their one reference thereto (as above) to back us.

May 4. 1664. Look among many things that have passed us lately about this business of Mr Wood's masts and boltsprits. I think it will be necessary for me to observe hereafter whether this shortening of these masts ordered by Sir W. Batten be effected, and whether any new rule be from henceforward continued to be proposed by Sir W. B. for the practice of the Navy hereafter – which I believe will not be, but laid aside as a thing only started at this time in behalf of Mr Wood.

[1] NMM, LBK/8, p. 95 (11 February).

Decembr 18. 1663. About the flags and flagmakers. Being this day at Deptford, I did among other things call to see the bewpers brought in by Mr Whistler upon the late contract, which he was permit[ted] to make with us for some.[1] And neither the storekeeper nor master attendants being in the way, nor the pattern to be found, I did take two or three pieces home with me, and the next day did examine them; and by chance there being also Mr Michell at the office, I did speak to him about them, and upon the whole I do find that by their being pressed, they do look pretty well and are really better than they used to serve, but not so good as the others, nor altogether the width of the contract. But I did bring also a couple of jacks, which the storekeeper's clerk did tell me were served in the other day from Mr Young of Michell's stuff; by the same token, when I asked him whether they were of Michell's or of the old store of Young's and Whistler's, he told me they were of Michell's, for within this little while since October last, they were utterly without any, either of the one or the others. But the stuff of one being very bad, made me doubt something; and upon conference with Michell, he doth think, and I am really of that mind, that this was never of his stuff; or if it was, the master attendant hath played the knave in certifying it to be so good as the pattern. But looking on another which I brought, which I believe is of Michel's stuff, I do find a demonstration that they do play the knave with his stuff, for it is evident that there is a piece of the jack which is not of Michell's, but wholly different from the rest of the jack; and which is more, is judged of the same hard and naked and open thread which the two pieces are that I brought up of Whistler's stuff – which Michell says he doth think do come from Norwich, but yet are far worse methinks than his pattern.

Asking Michell why he doth not press his stuffs to make them look slick and smooth, he tells me that at first he did, but Mr Davis would not receive them; and yet he doth these of Mr Whistler's.[2]

---

[1] Cf. his tender (24 October) : *CSPD 1663–4*, p. 318.
[2] John Davis was the storekeeper at Deptford. Pepys had for some time suspected that he was in Whistler's pay: *Diary*, iv. 73 & n. 3.

Jan. 22. 1663[4]. Observations on the glaziery.

Being this day at Woolwich, among other things I went into the glazier's shop and there observed –
1. That all the new work done for the King, at least as much as can be wrought there, is wrought there. *Question*: whether it ought not to be done at home, and only the old repaired there.
2. The officers all do say that they apprehend that it is the glazier's contract to have day's works as well for the new work done there as for the old;[1] and so did Mr Chr. Pett, whom I met afterward at Greenwich tell me.
3. Much of the new work, before it went out of the shop, I observed to have plain holes through it, which I caused there to be mended while I was there. *Question*: whether they ought not to be tied to such a substance of glass, or some other terms fit to secure the strength of the glass to the King.
4. That there is no account kept by any officer, either storekeeper, master shipwright, clerk of the cheque or timber measurer, of good panes [that] are needful to be mended in the old work, but what they please to mend they may, and are paid for what appears new.
5. That there is no account taken, for what I see, of what plate or glass is spent on the old work, nor that it is delivered into stores at all. So that the King is at the mercy of the glazier to pay for what he demands.
6. That be the work more or less, there is always work found for his men, two or more. I think there was three or four this day there.
7. Measuring of lanterns ill regarded. Asking the storekeeper's man this day at Deptford how lanterns were measured, whether from the bottom of the neck or no, and who measured them – he told me he knew nothing to the first question, for that Mr Flecher, the timber-measurer doth always measure them. I then went to Fletcher, and he tells me plainly, that he never measured one in his life – nor knew how they are to be measured. So that by this means we may see how the King is served in this particular.

---

[1] Sc. to be paid by the day, which was difficult to check if the work were not done in the yard.

June 1. 64. Measuring of blocks not agreed on. Being at Deptford today, among other things, to inform myself in the business of blocks, of which [we] are now to buy a great quantity to send to Portsmouth for the ships now going forth – I inquired of Mr Shish how they were measured, for we buy them at so much for all so many inches diameter, and so much for all above that diameter. He told me that he measures them always the breadth way. By and by, when Edgehill the blockmaker comes and I asked him the like, he told me that we measure them and take them from him always the length-ways and never otherwise anywhere.[1] Now herein is a great deal of difference, for of some blocks the length is little more than the breadth, but in some above twice as long, and therefore the price is greatly increased. But strange it is, that a thing of so great charge and daily expense as this, should be no better agreed in by the master shipwright, who is the proper judge thereof. And that things are very little heeded what is delivered or how anything is measured into stores.

Jan. 22. (63[4]). Method of rating carver's works. Bad effect of precedents. Calling at Greenwich today to see in what manner Mr Pett and his assistants proceed upon the valuing of the carved works of the *Henrietta Yacht*, I found them standing upon the shore looking upon the vessel, which lay upon the shore also, and in my view did set their prices upon everything distinct. I coming, demanded by what rule they valued any piece; they answered (he and Mr Shish, the other[s] not being there): by the prices formerly given for the work done upon the other boats. And this I found was their only rule – which shows the great consequence of bad precedents.

But by and by, I suppose upon hearing that I was there, came out of a tavern to me Mr Leadman the carver, Capt. Pett, Mr Cowly, and several other officers, all very fine in their best clothes; and upon a little inquiry, I found that Leadman makes a dinner for them today; and at dinner, there the rates are concluded upon – which answers with what I have formerly been told of the same nature at Chatham.

---

[1]Reporting this incident to Commissioner Pett in a letter of 16 July, Pepys wrote: 'which way is the true one I know not, but see that to be sure the King payeth by that that is dearest': *Further Corr.*, pp. 26–7.

Jan. 27. 1663[4]. Sir Wm Petty's vessel.[1] Comr Pett's discourse with me about this vessel was that notwithstanding that she is good for anything, yet he did largely set out the dangerous consequence of bringing in the use of such ships, as I have largely set down in my Journal this day.[2] And I believe will endeavour to stop all encouragement to be given to her. And herein I must needs observe the little certainty he can make in judging of her now, before she is tried, by his seeing her, that he hath these fears about him, notwithstanding that he will not own that there is any true line or part in her according to art.

Feb. 2. (63[4]).[3] At Whitehall I stood by and heard the King and the Duke and all the Court laugh at Sir W. Petty to his face in a most contemptible manner for his vessel, but without the least assignment of any fault in her or other reason – which he took most ingenuously, and I am apt to think she will yet do something extraordinary, though at her first trial she hath not shown much.[4]

March 31. 1664. Comparing the breadths of Hollands duck and West Country canvas and their different pennyworths. Sailmakers profit by the narrowness of canvas. Being at Deptford today to inform myself against the afternoon (Col. Reames being to treat with us about altering the width of our West Country canvas at the desire of Sir W. Batten), I did measure Hollands duck which is the best of all canvases, and find that it holds generally neither more nor less than 31 inches, and for it we pay 22d. per yard. The West Country cloth I found to hold 27 inch wide, and for it we give 18½d. per yard. Now my rule[5] shows –
As 22d. to 31 inches – so is 18½d. to 26 inches, so that the

---

[1] The famous double-keeled ship of which Petty designed four prototypes and for which he made great claims. This was the second, *Experiment II*. See Marquess of Lansdowne (ed.), *The Double-Bottom or Twin-keeled Ship of Sir W. Petty* (Roxburghe Club, Oxf. 1931), passim; *Diary*, iv. 256, 257; v. 28, 33, 47, 353 & nn.
[2] *Diary*, v. 28. Pett argued that because of her speed she would be a danger to merchantmen if captured by Barbary pirates.
[3] In the Diary Pepys reports the encounter which follows under 1 February.
[4] In the previous summer she had in fact beaten the Dublin pacquet boat in a race across the Irish Sea. Pepys, although he continued for some years to be interested in the design (see e.g. *Naval Minutes*, p. 23) came eventually to be sceptical. In 1684, together with Sir Anthony Deane, he laid bets with Petty against his claims for the fourth prototype, the *St Michael*, and won – she never cleared Dublin harbour.
[5] Slide rule.

West Country in proportion gains an inch in width. But then we are to consider that duck works without a seam in the middle, and the other doth not, which takes up above an inch of cloth; so that the advantage is already lost. And then it costs us not only ³/₄d. per yard the more for working with a seam in the middle, but also doth call for more widths of canvas; that is to say, in every 27 widths, one, because it loses an inch in every width, and besides, by that means gives the sailmaker an increase of 4¹/₄d. for every yard of cloth so added. His price being for Noyalls and West Country, 4¹/₄d. per yard for all wrought with a seam in the middle, and 3¹/₂d. for all wrought without a seam in the middle.

Col. Reames's argument that canvas of 22, 24, or more inches is as strong as that of 15 or 10. So many threads in the length of a piece as will make 20 inch, 22, or 24, broad is sufficient to hold the strength of the workman and his brass shutter; and if so many threads as will make 20 inch etc. in breadth be but sufficient, it follows that so many threads as will make but 15 or 10 inch broad must need be too few and weak, and either the workman must slack his hand and weave with less force, or else break all; and so by consequence that Poldavis will be no thicker at 15 than it is at 22 etc.

But to this, then Sir W. Batten and Sir W. Penn did argue that it is not in expectation of having the cloth better, but by being narrower that there will be the more seams, and so the sail will be the stronger. To this, I answer in the first place, that experience tells us that all sails returned from sea are found to be broke at the seams before the cloth wears. And to this, Sir J. Mennes did affirm that in the *Harry*,[1] his sails rent from top to bottom all along the seams, not that the seam itself, that is the twine, gives way, but it tears along the seam in the whole cloth along the holes which are cut by the needle.

Multitude of seams no strength to the sail. I did also affirm and offer wager that sew some cloths together and stitch them, you shall find that they shall six times in seven tear in the seam.

Next, it must be much worse to have a seam in the middle, for that is the weakest place of every cloth, the selvedge being always the closest and strongest.

---

[1] Mennes flew his flag in the *Henry* when he was Vice-Admiral and C-in-C of the Narrow Seas, 1661. On 18 December he had reported damage to his squadron from foul weather: *CSPD 1661–2*, p. 183.

It is to be observed that the Hollanders, the best husbands in the world, do make their best canvas, that is, their duck, broader than any we have, for theirs is 31 inch broad, which they would not do if the width did spoil the sail.

It is true that seams supports it up and down, but Mr Lewen the sailmaker tells me that the bolt-ropes is sufficient for that with the little help of the seams of the cloth at the width it is made now.

He tells me too, that the merchants that are good husbands are forced when their sails begin to wear to lay a list three or four inch broad up and down to cover and strengthen the seam, knowing that there it begins to split first.

May 24. 1664. Col. Reames, Sir J. Mennes and myself being together, Mr Harris the King's sailmaker did tell us that our Englishmen could never make so good canvas as the Holland duck, not only from their different skill in the spinning and weaving of it, but from the nature of their stuff, which he says is much better than ours, and he thinks is all flax. But then by and by in discourse he told us that West Country cloth will yield to the needle in the sewing better than the duck, it being a softer thread, and next, that it will not be so soon galled with the ropes as that which is so hard and apt to fret itself, and not so woolly as ours is.

Quality of different canvases. Hollands duck is an even thread, whereas the West Country is here and there gouty and in another place small. And then again the warp of the first lies pretty close one thread to another, whereas the latter lies further asunder, which doth make the woof seam the bigger; but then it is so little covered with the warp that it must needs be sooner worn; and then again, if a thread of the warp breaks, it must needs make a greater hole by much than the duck, which hath its woof hid almost with the warp.

May 27. (64). Suffolk cloth is generally said to be apt to mildew, which Mr Wayth confesses that it doth so for want of the washing which the other cloths have, which by that means also look whiter. But that they can make theirs as white and as free from mildewing as any of the other if encouraged; and to that purpose, took me to a sailmaker's, one Lewen's, and there showed me some Suffolk cloth in my eye little inferior to either duck or West Country. And yet he will make a sample of better.

May 28. 14d. offered by Sir W. Batten for 18 inch which (in proportion to $18\frac{1}{2}d.$ for 27) would be but $12\frac{1}{8}d.$ I stopped at a full Board, Col. Reames being there, Sir W. B.'s project of bespeaking the West Country cloth to be of 15 inch wide – or 18, which the Board seemed inclined to have. And very high Sir W. B. was with me how he should not understand a sail better than I. And he offered 14*d*. a yard for 18 inch would come in proportion to 18½*d*. for 27 inch, it should come but to 12¼*d*. and a little more. Besides, the loss of cloth in the increase of seams – increase of labour to the sailmaker, and spoiling of the sail – which I will at leisure draw up something upon.

June 22. (64). Mr Harris's discourse about the different selvedges of all French canvases, and their degree of goodnesses. Discoursing with Mr Harris, he tells me that to have a sample lie, sealed in each yard, of a middling sort of Noyalls, and also of the best of the seconds, will be a good security to the King therein. And [that] that is worse than the best of those to be sold for seconds or carried away again.

He tells me that all French canvas, Noyalls and Vittry (and those only, for neither Holland duck nor any English is so) have a different goodness in the selvedges, the one taut, which is the stronger and that by which it ought to be measured by; the other slack, which is bad and not only that which gives the occasion of some sails (as Sir J. Mennes reported) splitting all along by the seam (for it is worst there, and so by degrees grow better and better till you come to the other selvedge); but in measuring, you shall lose commonly a quarter of a yard in every 10 yards and in the best cloths five or six inch in 10 yards (and sometimes five or six yards in 100).

He knows not, he says, the issue of it, but so it is always.

He says that for width, there was never any other that he knew full 27 inch broad but lacks generally three quarters of an inch, although the constant term of the contracts of this Office have been 27 inch. Nor hath any defalcation been ever known by him to be made for want of breadth. But the reason of our breadths said in our contracts he cannot tell me. He says that there is not any known difference between the first and second sorts of canvas, so as all do agree that this is one and that the other. And therefore it is necessary to have samples of both agreed on. And he doth confess to me that of the first sorts taken in (as I did observe) there is 30 or 40*s*. in a bale difference between them sometimes. The same course he would have in

Vittrys also, of which there are from 10*d*. to 17*d*. per yard, till they come to be as fine as to serve for sheeting. Also, of West Country too, of [which] he observes that Capt. Plea never served but one parcel anywhere but at Portsmouth, which was at Deptford, and there he did offer some, which he said would not have been refused at Portsmouth, of which Harris did reject five bolts – which Plea did offer him after we would not receive them at 2*d*. in a yard cheaper than our price. And he doubts he makes such to pass at Portsmouth.

July 22. 1664. Mr Harris the merchant. Matter of Holland's duck. Having sent into Holland, at my request, purposely to inform himself of what the Hollands duck is made of, he tells me that there is of three sorts – the first, which is all of hemp; the second which is of hemp and flax; and the third, which is all flax – and that which is made all of hemp, the sail dearer by 2*s*. in a piece or more than others that are not.

March 23. 166¾. Discourse about tar and pitch. Stockholme tar (says Mr Staply) is the best for all uses, but Bergen as good or better for cordage than it, especially being wrought in hot weather – that of Stockholme, through its thinness, being apt to run out.

The barrels of Stockholm (says he and Stacy) commonly weigh about 3 cwt and more, sometimes 3½ cwt, but then the tare of the cask being great comes to ½ and sometimes ¾ cwt itself. And the vessels generally hold from 30 to 36 gallons.

Russia is (they both confess) very good, but the cask little. Stacy says that such is the difference in their contents, that he demanding 9*l*. 15*s*. per last for his Stockholm, he tells me (upon my request of his opinion freely in the matter of Russia, which Mr Hebden is now tendering from Archangell) that what we give about 9*l*. for Russia we give too much.[1] He says it holds from about 28 to 30 gallons. The tare of the barrels is not so great, being thinner. Yet Mr Hebden doth not offer to contract that a barrel (cask and all) shall weigh above 2½ cwt.

---

[1] Hebdon's price was £10 per last: *CSPD 1663–4*, p. 344.

March 26. 1664. A trial of the different measure & weight between Stockholm & Russia tar.[1]

	Cwt	Q.	L.
One full barrel of Stockholm tar poized[2]	3.	00.	07
The content of tar (being emptied) 22 gallons & the tare of the cask was	0.	03.	08
But the general weight of a Stockholm barrel of tar is commonly (as the workmen say)	2.	03.	14
We weighed the tare of two other barrels, which were	{0. {0.	02. 02.	16 08
We took also the tare of two Russia casks, & were	{0. {0.	01. 01.	10 15

We measured moreover (with water) the content of two Stockholme casks and two Russian & found the first {24 / 25}

The second two to be {17 / 20}

Bergen tar, its weight & tare.

	Cwt	Q.	L.
One barrel of Bergen tar poized	2.	2.	9
Tare of its cask	0.	1.	20
Net tar	2.	0.	17

The cask (upon measuring) contained 23 gallons beer-measure. Upon inquiry I find that the difference between this measure and the contents which commonly are reckoned to the several sorts of tar (as to Swedes 32 and 34 gallons) is reconciled by this, *viz*: that merchants by gallons of tar mean so many 8 pounds (and selling in retail always 8 pounds to him that demands a gallon) and so 24 gallons if liquid measure may yield 32 times 8 pounds, or thereabouts (as appears in the instances above).

---

[1] Pepys was assisted in these enquiries by John Falconer, clerk of the ropeyard at Woolwich. For Falconer's report, see PRO, SP 29/95, no. 48 (*CSPD 1663–4*, p. 530).
[2] Weighed.

An account of the cost of one cask [of] pitch and another of tar served us in upon account by Sir W. Rider and Mr Cutler and Capt. Cocke,[1] *according to computation upon Edmond Yorke's loading from Gottenb., viz:*[2]

Tar 1663	
One last (great band)[3] cost	rd. 27. -
Custom & charges of shipping aboard	rd. 6. 42
Commission & postage of letters	rd. 0. 40
	rd. 34. 34 of Gottenb.
Rd. 34. 34st. deduct for legio of 6 per cent[4] rd.	2. 3 is Hamb.
Rd. 32. 31. which at 8*s*. per rd. is Vla[5]	*l*.13. 1. 2
Brokerage & postage of letters Vla	0. 1. 0
Commission for ordering at 1 per cent	*l*.0. 2. 7 Sterl.
At 34*s*. 6*d*. the exchange Vla	*l*.13. 4. 9 makes *l*.7. 13. 08
Assurance & charges of 2½ per cent	*l*.0. 3. 10
Custom & charges of ship hire	*l*.1. 13. 00
Postage of letters 4*d*. &	*l*.0. 07. 10
provision[6] of 4 per cent	7*s*. 6*d*. *l*.9. 18. 04

---

[1]A contract was concluded with this partnership on 24 March 1663: *CSPD 1663–4*, p. 84.
[2]The calculation here is in Swedish copper dollars (*riksdalern*) and stivers (1/48 dollar). Here and elsewhere in the notes to these tables I am indebted for information to Prof. H. G. Roseveare.
[3]A 'last' was a measure; 'great band' a (superior) variety.
[4]This was the commission commanded by Hamburg bank money. 'Legio' appears to be a mistake for or variant of 'agio' (commission).
[5]The Hamburg rixdollars were now converted into Flemish (*Vlamische*) £ s. d.
[6]Commission.

Pitch

One last cost	rd. 41. 24
Carrying aboard 6 st. postage	
of letters 6 st.	rd. 0. 12
Provision of 2 per cent	rd. 0. 40
	rd. 42. 28 of Gottenb.
Rd. 42. 28 deduct rd. 2.1 for legio of 5 per cent	
is Hamb. rd. 40.27 which at	
8 s. Vla per rd. is	Vla £ 16. 4. 6
Brokerage & postage of letters	Vla £ – 1. 2
Provision & ordering at 1 per	£ – 3. 3
cent	
at 34*s*. 5*d*. per *l*. sterl.	Vla £16. 8. 11 make sterl.
	£ 9. 11. 1
Assurance at 2½ per cent	£ 0. 4. 11
Custom & charges of freight	£ 1. 13. 0
Postage of letters & provision	£ 0. 9. 6 £ 2. 7. 5
at 4 per cent	£11. 18. 6

Calculation of one last of pitch from Stockholme served us in as on the other side, 1663.[1]

One last cost	Copper dollars	200. –
Custom		rd. 11. 1.
Provision of buying 2 per cent		
if drawing ½ per cent and		
brokerage ½ per cent		rd. 5. 3. 4
		rd.217. 0. 4

At Hamborough

Rd. 217. 0. 4 at 19 marks makes rd. 45.34 st.	
which at 8*s*. is	Vla £18. 5. 0
For difference of specie & bank 1⅝ per mark[2]	Vla £ 0. 0. 7
Post of letters 4*d*., brokerage 1 per mark 4*d*.	Vla £ 0. 0. 8
Provision ½ per cent on 18.06.11	Vla £ 0. 1. 10
	flem. £18. 8. 9

---

[1]This calculation is in Swedish copper dollars (*riksdalern*), marks and őre.
[2]By specie is meant current money used for foreign exchange dealings; bank money carried a variable premium.

At London

Vla £18.08.09 at 34s. 9d. is sterling	£10. 12. 04
Freight 48s. caplaken[1] & premio[2] 2s.	£ 2. 10. 0
Lighter money & waterbaily[3] 1s. pro custom & entry at Chatham 3s. 4d.	£ 0. 4. 11
Charges at delivery 3s. 6d., assurance at 2½ per cent 5s. 8d.	£ 0. 09. 2
Provision of 4 per cent on 13. 16s. is	£ 0. 11. 1
	£14. 07. 06

Vide other computations of this nature in my Pocket-book.[4]

Dec. 22. 1663. About Mr Wood's contract for New England masts. Mr Wood came this day with a bill for his masts from Portsmouth, wherein the master shipwright alone certifies only that they are fit for the King's service. I stayed without saying anything, till all was silent, and especially Sir W. Batten who said nothing good or bad. And seeing that the bill was likely to pass, only Mr Coventry did ask me whether they did answer contract or no. Whereupon, I told them what a poor certificate we had, short of the certificate we had the other day in Warren's, and is his duty to give. Besides, here is a bill also made for some deals that he brings, besides his masts, though nothing of it in the contract; yet these are received without order, though Sir W. Batten did, when he was at Portsmouth the other day, command the deals that came with Sir W. Warren's masts not to be received (as appears by his letter to us thence) though by contract he had a power to bring them (though perhaps he will say that then he did not know of any such condition in Warren's contract). But that which is most in my eye is that I do not find that these masts do answer in their length to the length which they ought to have. And I the rather think so because of a letter which I had this day from Deane at Woolwich [which] tells me that those at that place prove most of them too short – for which Sir W. W. was

---

[1]Gratuities, usually given to the ship's master, and originally put into his cap.
[2]Premium.
[3]Water baillage: dues levied by the City of London on foreign imports.
[4]A notebook, now untraced, which Pepys carried when gathering information about prices of supplies. A similar pocket book of abstracts of contracts (also untraced) is mentioned in the Diary (viii. 540).

forced to make a sound allowance,[1] as appears by the particular papers thereof.

Jan. 7. 1663[4]. I having lately sent for and got certificates from all the master shipwrights and others of the true rule granted among all for the measuring of masts – I did this day, upon Mr Wood's coming produce all; and at first he denied those rules to be true, saying that in a mast of 24 inch diameter that gives but 24 yards length, when it ought to be more, and his are more. I showed him Comr Pett's hand, particularly in the very example for me and for the rule which is given to be the true rule – and showed him that his masts of that diameter was not so long.[2]

He fell to cry out of his bad usage, and that he would furnish us with his Gottenb. masts 5 per cent cheaper than Sir W. Warren's; which the Board liked of, and bid him bring his tender. I expect here to see Sir W. Batten how he will be taken either owning what I said, that he did once agree to the taking in all his after Sir W. W.'s were bought (which he says he never did, and lay the fault of Sir W. W.'s contract upon our buying too many of these little masts), or else he must oppose the buying of them, which I am sure will trouble him mightily.

Mr Wood insisted mightily upon having the whole referred to indifferent men. We consented to refer the point concerning the true rule of measuring masts, and nothing else. And so broke off for that time.

Apr. 6. 1664. Sir W. Warren tells me that he was told by Capt. Taylor's foreman in his yard that his master's masts for all the other's bragging are better than Mr Wood's, for he says Wood's were plugged some of them in the River – which it seems is to hide a rottenness discovered at the butt, and that the plugs continue in them at Woolwich still.

March 10. 166¾. Mr Wayth's discourse of ironwork. Meeting Mr Wayth at noon upon the Change, we went to the coffee-house together, and there in discourse upon the business of ironwork he did tell me that from the buying of the old iron at the last

---

[1] See above, p. 10.
[2] Cf. Pepys to Coventry (7 March 1664): 'every mast (be its length what you will) is so many yards long and six more as it is hands (or 4 inches) in compass [diameter].' The rule did not apply to New England masts because of the 'irregularity of their bodies'. See *Further Corr.*, pp. 21–5. Pepys's calculations are set out in detail in a memorandum of June 1664: Bodl. Lib., Rawl. MSS A 174, ff. 19–20.

sale at Chatham Sir W. Batten was offended at it and had been told by somebody that others might have it. And that notwithstanding all the house[1] did laugh at him for what he did, saying that he had burned his fingers in giving so much for it and, more than that, Sir W. B. did say so himself to me I well remember, and did say that he had caused before the sale a great deal of the best to be culled out by the master shipwright that had been first laid by for sale. Yet Mr Wayth says that the master shipwright did stand by him at the very sale and did tell him that there was a great deal as good as the best new iron that was served into stores, and that upon his encouragement he bought it. And since Sir W. B.'s last going down the other day, he at his survey did view it again and writ us word that there was as good stuff for bolts for the new 2nd-rate ship building at Woolwich[2] as any could be made – which is very strange.

Nay, Wayth tells me more, that there is hardly a sale but as at this, so everywhere else, there is good iron that was never used for the use it was made for, but being unfit perhaps was flung among the old iron that is sold afterward for old iron. He minds me that if there had been any good survey kept heretofore, how comes it to pass that we are so clogged with nails, that will not be spent in ordinary spending these seven years.

He tells me, moreover, that he believes that some of the King's smiths cannot tell us the name of their ironmonger that they buy half the iron that they sell off into the King's stores – it being bought by them of seamen and workmen, that is stole by them out of the King's ships and yards.

That it will be much for the King's profit to have extra and ordinary ironworks made at the same rate, for now it is in the power of the storekeeper's instrument to make what he will (that is, report to us what quantity he will) or ordinary, and what otherwise. So that then he will have but one way of deceit left, which is by overweight.

That the Surveyor's open design of keeping the book of the surveys from the Board or anybody is to have it in his power not only to bring in anybody to sell, upon pretence of want, or to keep out anybody, by pretence of plenty, but also to be able to gratify any man of the King's officers in the yard with what

---

[1]That is, the coffee-house.
[2]The *Royal Katherine*.

expense they please upon their houses, or if he be corrupt, with the embezzling of what they will.

March 22. 1663/4. Mr Weston the iron merchant about that commodity. He says that Spanish iron comes generally, if not only, from Bilbo, and is for all uses the best in the world – especially for ships, it being able to bear the blows of the greatest sledges, which Swedes or other will not do without breaking or bowing when they are wrought into bolts. And this yields now about 15*l.* or 16*l.* per ton, which in the Dutch war[1] was at 22 and 24*l.*

That the best sort of Swedes is very good. And our English forest iron (except that of Sherwood) [is] as good as the world hath, but it is not nor can be brought so cheap as the other is brought in at, and so our works are undone and will every day decay more and more – foreign iron being brought in almost without any imposition upon it, and ours cannot be exported without great duties[2] – a folly continued to us from our forefathers, who did make that law with reason enough when we had none imported and not so much of our own to spend as now.

Great was our consumption of our English iron in the Dutch war, for the making of shot, and it seems it was made most into bars, and the whole world is said never to have known such good shot as we shot against the Dutch, as they themselves will confess. And Blake used to brag of it – for it is also reported, that being once at the Admiralty chamber when the shot-maker's bills were examined, he would not suffer any abatement to be made in it, because of the good shot he made, which it seems could not be found at any time to be bowed or buckled at anything it met with.

The ordinary iron of England is turned to pots and other such ordinary uses, of which, though there is great store brought from Holland, yet theirs being much heavier than ours, and not being so white, ours are in much better esteem than theirs. And more, he says that great guns with good preparation might be made of English iron as good and almost as light as them of brass.

---

[1] The First Dutch War.
[2] The duty on the export of iron amounted to £16 per ton (i.e. 1*s.* in the £ on the value in the Book of Rates), compared with £7 per ton on the import of foreign iron: 12 Car. II c. 4.

Dec. 23. 1663. Discourse of hemp and tar and cordage. This day upon the Change I met with Mr Stapely the rope merchant and advised with him about our working of the great quantity of Russia hemp which we have at present, whether to work it with Riga or alone. He tells me that they generally do work them together; but inquiring of him the reason of it, he told me that it was not to better the Riga or to make it take tar as it was urged, for that takes tar enough of itself, and hemp may take too much tar till it burns the cordage, as oftentimes it doth.[1] But for these two reasons – first, because the Russia is too bad generally of itself to work into cables that are put to any stress, and therefore is mixed with Riga to give it strength. The second and main, and so he confessed indeed the true, reason, is that masters of ships will not go to the price of all Riga, and therefore when they do bespeak any they will, according as they will lay out their money, contract to have it half or threequarters or a quarter Riga.[2] And herein he says the ropemaker that will be a knave makes his advantage, for it is impossible after it is tarred and laid ever to distinguish whether it be Riga more or less, but the word of the ropemaker must be taken.

He therefore doth advise by all means to work the Russia by itself if it be of any goodness in running rigging, wherein if it fail the matter is not great.

He tells me too (upon my inquiry about Russia tar) that they do generally prefer Swedes tar above all for cordage, and that they do generally mix that and Bergen together for their daily use – and seldom use Russia.

He told me also that mooring cables of Russia hemp, where they are not liable to much stress of tide or weather, is as good in a fresh water as the other – for it seems, he says, the fresh water doth rot a cable presently, and therefore if they can help it, they do never let a new cable be used first in the River. And that for all that they make to be used in the River, they do always lay them steeping in pickle (salt and water) 24 or 48 hours.

Dec. 30. 1663. I met this day again with Mr Stapely, having two days since given him Sliter's letter about the reason he thinks of the failing of these cable strands. Which Stapely says he thinks are foolish, for it is true there is a steam rises always, and

---

[1] Selling by weight, the merchant was tempted to use too much tar.
[2] According to Hollond it was generally agreed that a half-and-half mixture was best; *Two Discourses*, ed. Tanner (NRS 1896) p. 189.

which (it is as true) doth always make wet the upper halls,[1] and therefore they do use to lay mats upon them; but this doth only wet, not spoil, the yarn, and therefore he concludes that it was the ill laying of them, by the knavery of the workmen, to spite the foreman (which is usual), or neglect, by laying too great press upon these strands, more than they ought to have.

Jun. 26. 64. Concerning the wages, measures, and day's works of Ald. Wood's ropeground, *vide* Bundle no. 1.

June 23. (64). Discovery of the fallacy in ropemakers undertaking to serve us with Riga and Quinsborough cordage. This day comes one Burchet, and after him another, by Sir W. Batten's order, to the Board, to proffer cordage, which, say they, is made all of Riga and Quinsborough hemp. And Sir W. B. did at the first word offer them what we have been forced for want to give to others; but the want, thanks be to God, is at present over. I came in and demanded whether the yarn was already tarred or no. They said, yes. And upon my further demand did grant that we must trust to them to know what hemp it is made of. But they do affirm that it is all Riga and Quinsborough. I told Sir W. B. that I am sure there is ne'er a ropemaker in town that, unless it be bespoke, doth make one cable of all Riga and Quinsborough hemp. He said the contrary. I appealed to any of the workmen in town, and did ask these men, affirming that what they offer is not all Riga and Quinsborough hemp, or if it be, it is not Rine hemp. They did then confess that a third of it (and I believe a great deal more) is pass hemp – which is as bad as any Russia. By this means we escaped buying of it, Mr Coventry coming in and joining with me therein. And I hope have stopped the current of Sir W. B.'s design if we should have gone on in buying of cordage.

Aug. 3. 1664. Our cordage worse than that bought from Holland. Comr Pett in his letter of the 3d of August (64) tells us that our cordage we now make (and that is all of Riga or Quinsborough hemp) doth upon trial prove worse and weaker than that bought lately and brought from Yarmouth, bought from Holland.

August 16. 1664. Discoursing with Stapely about working some of our hemp into yarn for us, because at this time we cannot work it so fast as we shall need it – and he tells me clearly that their gain is in the making it into cordage, and so will work it

---

[1] Of the ropehouse.

for 5*l.* 10*s.* per ton, delivering back in cordage weight for weight for hemp. And will have 6*l.* for delivering it back weight for weight in white[1] yarn.

We work nothing so cheap (for labour) as the merchant. Talking with him further, whether it would be profit for us [to] have it done either of these ways, or hire a field ourselves and so do it – that it will be best to put it out for that we cannot do things in any part of the Navy, nor particularly in this, so cheap, by almost one third, as the merchant doth. He says, for instance, that for the loading or weighing a bundle of hemp, we use 16 or 20 men; they use never above five or six. In the laying of a great cable, we use 20 men more than they do, and so in all other things accordingly.

Aug. 29. 1664. Spinning bettered during double day's works. Comr Pett (by his letter of the 20th of Aug. 64) tells us that he hath with much ado convinced the ropemakers of their ill spinning and laying. And that it is now done beyond any exception. And moreover (which is a strange mystery to think), that since, through haste, he hath put the men of his own accord, and indeed against the advice of the Board, to double-day's works, by which they do two days' work in one day, he never saw them spin better threads.

Sept. 15. 1664. Sizes of threads in spinning for cordage. In order to the contracting for the spinning of some hemp into yarn we sent to Mr Bodham, clerk of the ropeyard at Woolwich – and there consulting with the master ropemaker, these were returned to be the proper sizes –

Size in inches	Threads
3/4	6
1	9
1½	12
2	18
2½	30
3	45
3½	57
4	78
4½	96
5	114

[1] Untarred.

Computation of the charge of working hemp into cordage per contract for the King. *Vide paper [blank] number [blank].*

Octobr 3. 1664. Our cordage upon a trial found stronger than the Hollands. This day, Mr Coventry and myself being at Deptford, we made a trial of strength between our cordage and that of Holland, by cutting off two fathom of each sort of two inch beginning (within a tenth of an inch): the first that was tried was the Hollands, and that bore 17¼ cwt before it broke. Then the English of our making, and that bore 24¾ cwt before it broke – both, as near as we could, hanging the same time to stretch, and stretching alike. Then we tried with the same length of another Hollands cable of the same beginning and that bore 20½ cwt before it broke. So, contrary to report from the other yards, ours doth prove the strongest, though Mr Coventry came with some expectations (and in some degree wishes that the other might prove very good, because of his being instrumental in the buying of it) to find it otherwise.

Decembr 24. 1663. Manning the Guiny ships at low wages.
I sent down on purpose to Eriffe to muster the *Sophia* and *Wellcome,* lent by the King to the African Company and manned by them. I afterwards went to the *Leopard,* an expedition now manned by us and going forth and lying there also.[1] And I find the other ships better manned than ours, take man for man, and their wages (to which purpose I went) – not any the best men they have above 18*s.*, and those but very few. The rest 17 and 16*s.* And several I met with that were able young men of 22 and 23 years old, that have served their seven years as seamen, that had but 14 and 15*s.* – and their officers but 21 and 22, or at most 23*s.* per mensem.[2] I also found that after they had entered their men and paid most of them a month's advance, it falling out that we had a fleet to set out for Argier, several of these men did run away and listed themselves (as is believed) in the

---

[1] The *Leopard* was an East Indiaman hired to convoy merchantmen to the Mediterranean and the Levant: *Diary,* iv. 241, n. 1; Duke of York, *Memoirs,* pp. 87–9.

[2] In the Royal Navy the monthly pay of captains varied from £7 to £21 according to the rate of the ship, and under-officers earned at lowest 24*s.*: M. Oppenheim, *Hist. Administration of R. Navy* (1896), p. 360.

King's ships, after they themselves had desired, and were in no respect forced to serve the Company at these wages.

March 24. 166¾. An eminent instance (in some joinery) how the King's work is performed by the day. There having been spent (as Sir W. Batten upon examination of the clerk of the cheque's books did inform us) about 49*l.* upon the planing of deals and preparing of boards for the joiners' work for the new ship now build[ing] at Woolwich,[1] it was afterwards thought fit to have it done by the great;[2] and coming to agree upon the price for doing thereof with Mr Dowson, the King's joiner there – he confessed that he believed that work already bestowed on the boards did cost the King about 47*l.* or 48*l.*, but yet (though he be master workman for the very purpose, to see the other people do their work) he offers to allow us but 26*l.* for all the work which so cost us 49*l.*; and at last we were forced to give him it for 28*l.* (for so it is valued in the 130*l.* we give him for the whole work of the joinery upon the ship), which is a plain demonstration how the King is served. *Vide Dowson's letter,* March 22. 166¾.

December 30. 1663. About sails and sailmakers. This day there followed me from the Change to the office, and we walked together a great while in the Court, Mr Harris the sailmaker, who tells me of one Robt Gyles who mends the sails at Portsmouth, whose visible profits are not more than 30*l.* per annum, and yet he spends after the rate of 100*l.* – and is worth money besides; and moreover (upon an offer of bringing in somebody to work with him), he will rather let work stand still than have anybody brought in to work there besides himself and his own servant. Mr Harris doth not allege anything further against the man as any known cheat of his, but from hence concludes that he is not honest; and upon my demanding how he could cheat the King and no notice be taken of it by the storekeeper under whose keeping all the sails are, he told me after much unwillingness, that there were several ways he might do it. I urging him to tell me, he told me that some of them were, that what warrants come to the storekeeper for the issuing of old canvas for the

[1] The *Royal Katherine.*
[2] At an agreed price for the whole.

making of sails for boats or for other uses to the boatswain or carpenter, he may give them what quantity he pleases, for he cuts it out and delivers it without any check upon him. And then again, the warrants for issuing to a boatswain such and such a sail or sails coming to him, he may give it of what bigness he pleases, or what goodness, for nobody else looks after it. Besides that, he only hath the spending of the twine there, and nobody else observes what he demands or spends.

And therefore, he would have another man, that he knows to be honest, to be put in to work with him, that he is sure, he says, will not agree with him; and by this none of the work will be left undone, and the other will not so securely cheat. Or to avoid the charge of keeping another employed, he offers that the servant of this Gyles may be discharged, and this man entered in his room. Only, when there is work for more, then the other's servant may come in and be set at work.

May 28. 1664. Corruption of officers in the business of Mr Wayth's and Potter's Ipswich canvas. We this day contracted with Mr Wayth for some Ipswich canvas, notwithstanding Sir W. Batten did argue mightily against buying any, as a thing not [necessary] for the service, because he found by discourse that Potter would not serve us cheaper than he had formerly done. But I made it appear how much was computed by Mr Harris necessary for to serve the fleet round with that sort of cloth forasmuch as we could expect but small supply in proportion of West Country to serve single in the room of double. We did, I say, contract with him for 150 bolts. But when he came to serve it into stores, great scrutiny there was (the master attendant and clerk of the survey declaring themselves unable to judge of it without the sailmaker, and how fit a man he is to judge on the King's behalf will be worth consideration hereafter); and afterwards I heard that they were likely to reject it, Sir W. B. beginning to talk at the table of it – though Wayth doth assure me that he buys it of the very same man, and that it is made by the very same hands, that that Potter uses to serve in. And never any fault found with his.

June 2. (64). This day, Sir W. B. orders Potter to come, and urged at the table why he should not serve rather than another man if he would come to Wayth's price, which before he had refused. And by the way, this I must observe as a very bad encouragement to any man to sell cheap. But, however, we did buy 50 bolts. And being served in, Mr Wayth tells me that there was a present damp upon all their high discourse before the yard, and the other received and no discourse afterwards of it, but bills made out for both – though he tells me his was rather, if any difference, the better of the two.

March 26. 1664. Observable in the complaint the master shipwright (Mr Shish) made this day of the shipwrights. This day comes to the Board in a great heat with a very sad complaint, Mr Shish, that contrary to the Duke's late order for the carpenters and others to come at half an hour past 5 to work, they do come (it is true), but will not fall to work till the clock strikes 6. And that all of them, as well the shipwrights in ordinary as others, do all refuse it.[1] And when they do work, they work so lazily that they value not his speaking, but whereas he hath heretofore sheathed a ship of 400 tons in a day, now they have been eight days sheathing a vessel of 120 tons, and knows not yet when he shall have done it. And that now the power of the master shipwrights is quite lost.

I bid him give me the names of some of the warrant officers, shipwrights. He would not do it, but told me two others. I again desired him; he said he could not. I bid him again; he told me he would step aside and do it. I would not be contented with that, but bid him think of the names and I would set them down; he told me he could not think of them presently, he was so disturbed. So W. Hewer reached a call-book and there read the names of them all to him. Then he begin to say that some of them were very willing to work, but that others would not let them. And yet by and by that they all hung together. This made me mad, and thereupon I told him that he did counterfeit this complaint if he did not tell us the names of some that did really deserve complaint, or else he had so carried himself that he durst not complain by name. At last I forced him to tell me, man by man, one after another and of the whole number of the ordinary; he would say but six of them were faulty, and by name; the rest he said were all willing and diligent – and that the others would only forbear till it was 6 o-clock. So that when I asked

---

[1]This was at Deptford. The Duke's order (16 February) was to apply to the summer months (mid-March to mid-September) and brought practice in the royal yards into line with that in private yards, where the hours were laid down in the charter of the Shipwrights' Company: PRO, ADM 2/1725, f. 136r. Several of the King's shipwrights – Shish included – had private yards.

him whether the refractoriness of these could alter the degree of dispatch of the work as he had said – he answered me that he had not now the power of rewarding men as he could before, to give them double-day's wages or a night and a tide – by which men were willing to work better.[1] So that there I see is the bottom of it; he hath a mind to have that power again – or else, as I thought before and do still, he hath carried himself so that he dares not complain of them, and so they crow over him.

And after he had first accused all the ordinary, and then picked out only six of them, he would have excused them too, and told me of two other extra men that were the negligent persons that stopped and hindered all. And when I exam[ine] I find that one of them is a friend of Mr Wayth's and his clerks, and kept in by him. Now, between Wayth and him there hath been an old grudge, and that is the reason. And thus I find that the King is served among them – either officers never complain, or when it is, it is out of some design to vex some other rather than do good to the service.

March 31. (64). Mr Shish came to the Board himself with all the carpenters of whom by name the other day he complained, and there did, before their faces, desire they might be re-entered, saying that they did no more than all the rest. That they were good and very able workmen, such as he could give 4*s.* a day to in his own yard.

However, reading his letter (which we keep by us) to Mr Coventry concerning them,[2] and remembering the manner of his coming to us the other day, we did continue their suspension.

April 4. (64). He wrote to Mr Coventry (I have the letter by me) that the men are sorry for their fault and do promise never to be so again.[3] And therefore desired their being permitted to work again. So this day we did under their petition to the Board re-admit them upon their promise. But now to see how Mr Shish hath concerned himself in the getting of them employed again (which I will never believe could proceed from any good cause) is very strange.

March 31. (64). Mr Chr. Pett about Capt. Cocke's East-

---

[1] As an incentive they could be paid double or for extra hours – 'by the night' (five hours extra) or 'by the tide' (one and a half hours extra): J. Ehrman, *The Navy in the War of William III, 1689–1697* (Camb. 1953), p. 93 & n. 2.
[2] *CSPD 1664–5*, p. 530 (26 March).
[3] Ibid., p. 544 (4 April). He also pleaded that it was their first offence.

Country plank. Mr Chr. Pett being at the Board this day, speaking of the East-Country plank, which Sir W. Batten would now again have him use for the deck of the new ship he is building, he told him he would, if he was ordered to it, but not otherwise, for he durst not.[1] "Why," says Sir W. B. (which he hath often told the Board and me before), "Mr Tippets doth not only use much of it (all he had) under water, which is the most dangerous service it can be put to, but did give Sir J. Mennes and me thanks for so good supply," which Sir J. Mennes did also witness. "Then," says Mr Pett, "Mr Tippets is in two tales, for he did say when he was last in town, with his own mouth, that he had not nor durst use a jot of it under water" – which Sir J. Mennes and W. Batten replied they knew was false – for they saw some of it used, I think they said.

Apr. 2. Mr Pett told me at Woolwich that he would lose his head if there was one bit of that plank use[d] by Mr Tippets upon the new ships.

And the Heneretta's anchors. And that whereas Sir W. Batten did the other day reproach Bowyer, the smith at Woolwich, for his dearness in his work, and that whereas he would not take under 40s. for working the anchors of the *Heneretta Yacht* (which was made last), another, by name [*blank*], did do it at 32s. per cwt. "I could," says he, "have told him that what was done was not worth 22s. per cwt, and if the bill had come to me, I had branded it – for Capt. Pett was fain to borrow the *Kitchin*'s anchor, for he durst not use hers, and said that he would strike off the palms of hers with a hammer."[2]

---

[1] For the new ship, see above, p. 5 n. 1. The use of East Country plank, made from Bohemian oak, was becoming increasingly necessary as supplies of English oak were exhausted, but in the face of prejudice among some shipwrights of the royal yards who would use it only for decks. It was however widely used in the construction of English merchantmen and of foreign warships. In 1686 a committee of shipwrights and Navy Board officials approved its use for men-of-war: Pepys, *Memoires*, pp. 35–47.

[2] Anchors were often made not of solid iron but of iron bars welded together and covered with sheet iron. Methods of manufacture and of testing were alike unsatisfactory. See below, p. 94; R. B. Merriman (ed.), *Sergison Papers* (NRS 1950), pp. 146, 159, 160, 161, 162.

March 31. (64). About colours. Being at Deptford today, I did measure two ensigns and found –

| one of 14 breadths | 6¼ yards long | 4½ yards broad |
| one of 12 " | 5¾ " " | 4 yards broad, 3 inches short |

Octobr 4. 1664. Mr Young at a pinch refuseth to serve without serving all. This day, the Duke having ordered two days since the setting out of a new fleet (the Guiny fleet being dispatched), we foreseeing a want of bewpers and so sent to the office for Mr Young (present Sir G. Carteret, Sir J. Mennes, Sir W. Batten, Mr Coventry and myself), and there, after many disputes, Mr Young did declare that if we would come to a contract with him to serve all for a year, he would do it, but he would have no competitor. Only, he did forbear to be obliged to take all that Michell makes for six months. And this he would do at his present rate of sixpence,[1] which otherwise he would expect to have increased. When I told him how we at this day do give Michell 5*d.* and that if his were not found as good as theirs I would give my consent he should never serve yard more to the Navy – he answered that if we would agree with him to serve us for 20 years together, he would do it at that price, but otherwise not. And would not hear of anybody to be employed as a competitor. We brought it to the issue at last, whether he would serve the King so many yards per month, let him name his own quantity, great or small; he answered, no, unless he might do all, and so we broke off in that manner.

Sir G. C. and Sir J. M. and all but Sir W. B. did agree in confessing now, how apparently he endeavours to set the price upon us at this pinch – and crying shame of it, as well as his inhumanity to this poor man. But at last, he being gone, I proposed Sir J. M.'s way of making them of calico,[2] which Sir J. M. says he hath known the experience of; and Sir W. B. only opposes it. But however, it was voted that we could make a trial of it.

Young will not endure a competitor, for that makes him hold up to his goodness[3] – which, should he get all to his own hand, he would never keep to.

[1] Per yard.
[2] They were normally of wool.
[3] That is, maintain the quality.

Octobr 5. This day Mr Young met me upon the Change and there mightily argued for our letting of him work all our flags, and that he would, not only for six months but as long as he wrought them, that Michell should work for him at the same price he doth, and have his money paid upon the table down to him as he brings home the goods, and work when he can. When I told him what the apparent reason was of his demanding that Michell might not serve to the King, but to him, which was to keep his good cloths from coming in to disgrace their bad ones – he said no, but it was that two men might not go to the market, for that makes one another pay dearer than they would do. I told him, how could that be, when he makes himself all he served; he says no, but he doth not; and though he doth, he buys the stuff he works where they do. So that now it is plain, they confess, he buys and works the same stuffs, whereas heretofore they confess he buys at the same market with them.

Octobr 6. Mr Young and Whistler came both to the Board and did offer that since they could not be admitted otherwise, they would serve us what quantity we pleased for a certain time. But when we came to the price, they would have 6*d.* per yard. I acquainted the Board that not only Michell doth now serve to this day at 5*d.*, without demanding more, but also that I do find that calicoes may be made at 5¼*d.* to us clear. And therefore, it would be unfit for us to give more than we give to Michell. But they refusing to take that, I did advise the Board to offer them a farthing more, which they refused. And then said that they have great quantity lying upon their hands; when Mr Young did the other day say that he had but 3000 yards. Now they say now they have, by order of Sir J. Mennes, provided 20,000 yards, which they demand to serve in at 6*d.* This appeared most incredible. But to stop clamour, we did vote they should be suffered to serve in 4000 yards apiece and no more, for which they should have 6*d.* – and an order is to be given accordingly for their receipt. They did own to the Board that Michell did go to their market for stuffs and yarn and did cause the price to be raised.

April 2. 1664. Chr. Pett's second report of Sir W. Warren's knees after his former blemishing them.[1] Being at Woolwich, Chr.

[1] Above, p. 6 n. 2.

Pett did tell me that the knees which Sir W. W. hath lately and is still serving in (though he himself did formerly blemish them) are as good as ever he saw, and serve the occasion of the new ship[1] fully, and that himself, if he had occasion of them, would not think much to give 4*l*. a load for them.

Apr. 2. (64). Saturday. Manner of valuing Mr Wood's New England deals. This day Mr Wood took the opportunity when none was to be there but Sir J. Mennes and I and Sir W. Batten, who forebore going to the House[2] on purpose today) of this day to demand his bill to be signed for his New England deals – demanding what Mr Tippets had said they were worth – which was 7*s.* per piece. But I would not give way to allow more than for their wood in proportion with what we did give Mr Harrington, which came to 6*s.* 9*d.* per deal; only, they forced me herein to make no abatement for the difference in wood between this and those of Sprucia.

Apr. 7. 1664. Mr Ackworth about the service[3] intended as a perquisite to the master attendant. He tells me, discoursing of the business of the old service which Sir W. Batten did at our first coming in in Nov. 1660 direct under his own hand the storekeeper, Mr Ackeworth, to deliver to Capt. Boddily as a perquisite – which Ackeworth denied to do, and hath ever since got his ill word for it – and Sir Rob. Slingsby[4] under his hand comman[ded] him to stop the delivery of it also – and it would have cost the King as Ackeworth says, 500*l*.[5] – he tells me that afterwards at a sale, Sir W. Batten, to make it appear a small matter, did set it up at the candle at 6*d.* per piece and Ackeworth being licensed to bid, did raise it up to 4*s.* 6*d.* per piece, and so it was sold. And whereas Sir W. B. did the other day rail against Ackeworth for it, saying that they raised it only for his reproach, but that it was never fetched away, he says that it was presently sent for away, and the money paid for it. And that the parcel which Sir W. B. speaks of was bought afterward by Phin. Pett of Limehouse, and

[1] The *Royal Katherine*.
[2] He was MP for Rochester.
[3] Presumably a dinner service of silver plate.
[4] Comptroller, 1660–1.
[5] MS. '500*l.* per annum'.

that he will fetch it away also speedily. But that this was not of the first parcel of which this dispute was.

Apr. 7. 1664. An eminent instance of Sir W. Batten's severity to Sir W. Warren in a bill for goods long ago delivered. An eminent instance this afternoon how Sir W. B. did force the table against all reason, because he said he remembered very well that the timber was white woods and small which was above three year ago delivered in. It is true it was delivered without contract, but at the desire of the King's officers; and the King's service lacking it, it being good, and employed as the bill mentions in sheathing board – and certified to be worth 12*d.* per foot or very near it a foot, which is 50*s.* per load. Sir W. Batten hath all along opposed the having a bill made out for it; but only Sir W. Warren did request it of the Board when he was out of the way, that at Mr Davis's going out[1] he might then (or never) have it out.

Sir W. B. did, contrary to this certificate – after three years – stay for his money; and though goods at that time were all sold dear, and he himself did direct the giving 12*d.* a foot for the same sort of Dram balks at Chatham to Sir W. Warren a month or two ago, and that he himself did say that he should have as much as ever any had had for Dram timber, which when I told him was 46*s.* per load, he fell from again – and would not yield to the giving him more than 38*s.*

Apr. 7. 1664. Sir W. Batten's ill way of evading a contract with Mr Deering. Mr Deering comes to the table with a tender of 100 bales of Noyalls canvas at price certain – and 400 bales more at the then present price, to be delivered all by Christmas next. Sir W. B. did give him a very short answer, that we would not buy a pig in a poke, for that it was not yet come over. When I told him that we had done the like with Harbing, who I knew was without, expecting to come and contract, he told me it was true, but he would never do so again (though he hath, both with Harbing and several others, as appears by our contract books). So I bid Deering withdraw and called in Harbing, who tendered 100 bales which is ready here, his price 17*l.* 10*s.* – and the lowest 17*l.* I desired Sir W. B. to consult so as that the King's merchants

---

[1]John Davis ceased to be storekeeper at Deptford in 1663.

might have no just reason to complain for our giving to another that asks more the offer of our money before the King's merchant that offers at less. However, without asking where they were, or directing anybody to go and see the goods, as he pretended in Deering's case, he at first word offers him 16*l.* 5*s.*, the price Deering demands, and I am confident would have taken less. Which [after] a great deal of do, Harving, little thinking that in truth we were offered so, was at last forced to take.[1] And that being done, I was forced to urge Sir W. B. to take some of Deering's, and was forced also to give him the price he asked.

Apr. 7. (64). Discouragement to Michell the bewpers-maker. This afternoon, as one vexation more to poor Michell about the flags, Mr Uthwayte (who by the Surveyor his master is brought to sign to all bills, and God knows what the consequence of it will be) caused him to bring a great provision of bewpers back, which he had carried to Deptford but would not be received, saying they were not so good as the contract. When they came, they were many of them opened, and not one worse than the pattern, not in Uthwayt's confession – and at last said, indeed, that he did except but against one white piece; but though the man offered to take his oath that he had brought all that they looked upon at Deptford, he could not find that or any other that he could except against. It is true they do object against the colours, though compared with what the other people served in heretofore or the merchants now use, they are as good. Besides, Mitchell did since bring his dyer to me, who tells me that he did, and doth still, dye all Mr Young's while he served the Navy, and that he hath as much as this poor man, and that he doth it with the same care that he doth any man's that he dyes for.

August 31. 1664. The daily clamours and controversy now ended about Michell's bewpers. It is wonderful to consider that to this day, ever since our order for Young and Whistler to serve in some colours ready made at 6*d.* per yard, though upon my being there I did take up one off the ground indifferently, in the sight of the storekeeper, one of theirs and another of Michell's, and brought it to the office, where they are, and the difference of

---

[1]Warrants were issued on 9 April to the officers at Deptford and Woolwich yards to receive 100 bales from each contractor at £16 5*s.*: *CSPD 1664–5*, p. 133.

goodness is to the advantage of Michell's side, and he is to have but 5*d*. per yard delivered in made. Yet since that day to this, there hath neither been any demand made nor want complained of, nor much less any fault found with Michell's stuffs, though to be sure no better than before, and the best that ever he sent never passed above three times or four without some contest or other.

April 7. (64). Sir W. Batten's not signing the most excellent contract with the platerers.[1] When the contract that I had been so long making of for the platerers, and approved of as it deserves by the whole Board, and commended to the Duke, and indeed is generally 40 per cent, I think, below the former practice of Hardwin – Sir W. B. refused to sign it, there being none but Sir J. Mennes and I there besides, toward the evening, because he said he had not read it, and that it would not be fit for him to sign it. I cannot for my head guess what the meaning of this should be, when he is a man that values not in his heart what he signs to, but unluckily refuses to sign to that now, which is the best thing he hath had to sign a good while, or likely will have again.

April 30. 1664. Instances of the unfaithful certificates of the King's officers in the masts served in by Capt. Taylor and Mr Wood lately from New England. Upon ending that business and my papers about my management of the business of valuing and filing the bills for Mr Wood and Capt. Taylor's masts, about which we have made so great and so long dispute of late,[2] and my pains therein being visible in the bundle of papers which I have laid up touching that business – it occurred to me that it was not unfit to set down what I observed in the bills made out for these masts:

1. Comes that from Portsmouth, wherein with great cunning [it] is expressly said that they are of due bigness at the rounds and all other points mentioned; only, is silent in saying that they are of length fit for their bigness, and instead thereof sets down

---

[1] Concluded this day with Thomas Stanes for lanterns, plates and glass: *CSPD 1664–5*, p. 132.
[2] See above, pp. 22–3.

their lengths and bigness, leaving us to do that, believing (as may easily be thought) that we would never look after them. And especially after so fair a character of theirs and the master shipwright's saying, without any brand upon them, that they are fit for the King's service.

This was done upon Castle and Wood's son going down thither and causing them to be so certified to the best advantage, and I know not how to blame the poor men for doing so, since they are so much awed by Sir W. Batten and this his son-in-law.[1] But I being forewarned herein by Deane of Woolwich, did examine it, and so stopped the passing of the bill, and wrote down a letter to Mr Tippets from the Board (dated Dec. 22. 1663) reprehending him for his bad and commending a more particular certificate.[2] He thereupon makes out a new bill and certifies (as by a copy in my bundle of papers touching this business appears) largely, that some were too long and some too short, and that, one with another, the long ones make good the short ones – only, two of the masts and three boltsprits, which he says ought to be shortened in the value (and their shortening alone, without any of the rest, comes to 75*l*., which is something to be saved by his own second letter, which he omitted and might have supplied us in the overseeing by his first bill). Being not well satisfied in the whole business of masts, I had a mind to inquire thoroughly into it, and among others, wrote to Mr Tippets for the rule by which he measures all masts, as well Gottenburg as New England, to which he answers me very particularly, and upon examination, the best of any man I wrote to. But there he tells us (besides that it is a folly for him or any man to think that a yard of length of any mast can make good the real shortness of another by a yard or two – for the latter is much more costly to mend than the profit of the other can make up) what the true length to every diameter is, and there it is clear that the very masts, where he says that long ones make good the shortness of the others, by his own rule doth not come nearer it than 1276*l*. is to 1073*l*. – for so much by my computation (to be seen in my bundle of papers) the difference between the price, according to contract to which his first bill would have led us, and the price his own rule afterwards sinks it to. And yet himself in his letter to me says that respect is to be had in their value to the shortness of

---

[1] Castle.
[2] Cf. Tippetts to Navy Board, 21 and 26 December: *CSPD 1663–4*, pp. 384, 390.

masts, none of which respect appears to have been had by him in his first bill, and but very little in his second.

2. From Woolwich comes a bill with a little more caution (as coming later) and for that I had on purpose a week before wrote to Mr Chr. Pett to give me an account of the rule of measuring of masts. Where he tells me: first, the Gottenburg rule (wherein all agree),[1] and then that for New England there is no other than to bring them into hands, and so observe the other rule[2] (only he adds, which was his cheat, that from thence the greatest come commonly a yard or two short of the rule; but all that doth bring no exception to the rule, which he himself sets up and is the true one, but only justifies the reason why we should give so great a difference in price, because of the difficulty of bringing them of their due dimensions).

Hereupon in his bill, he prepares and wisely draws it up that they are generally sound and of length such as commonly comes from that place – only, excepts three, of which he makes a small abatement. I being displeased at this blind certificate, writ myself (Jan. 6. (63[4])) about it. And received his answer (in my bundle), where he says they are of lengths only, they must be lengthened, and excepts two more than he did before, with a small abatement. Yet it was more than at first he said was necessary – and yet no nearer the truth than 1451*l.* is to 1233*l.* for the price is the price by contract, and the latter the price according to the rule which he himself says is the only rule he knows. Besides, both in this and the other parcel, we abate for the boltsprits in this 14*l.* difference, and in the other, 20*l.*

3. From Chatham, a bill comes for Capt. Taylor's masts, without the least want in the world, either in bill or certificate. Only, one may see in the certificate that upon having notice of the scruples we made, he hath added to what he had wrote, and concluded, by a line drawn to it, that he excepts three of them, which are only fit for boltsprits, whereas we find reason in his bill to abate 140*l.*; and according to the true rule of measuring, it would have been, I think, 70*l.* or 80*l.* more abated.

Thus I have set down how these bills would have supplied us. How far we did remedy the King, though not to the true height which we should have done, my papers will fully show, which I keep by me.

---

[1] See above, p. 36.
[2] The "Gothenburg rule".

Aug. [blank]. 1662. Instance of the ill use of receiving bad goods from the merchant upon pretence of his fetching them away again; and of delaying the making out of bills. Being at Deptford, among other things to inquire into the business of our flags, I looked over what we had in store and found them mighty bad; and that I might compare them the better with our pattern in the office (the pattern not being to be found there, Mr Davis being out of the way), I brought one or two home, not of the worst of them neither – and found them much beneath the pattern, by 3*d*. in a yard as to the price we pay them.

The next day, Mr Davis sends me word that I should not blame him for the badness of these flags, for he had not received them into stores nor given out a bill for them, but was fully resolved to send them back to the flagmakers; and since he tells me that he did send them, and it may be so.

But this I am to observe, that they were up in the price, as those are that are the King's, and as good as some of them which afterwards I found at Woolwich to have been received by Davis and sent down thither. And lastly, I do not upon inquiry find that ever Davis did find fault or reject or send back any goods that ever came to him before from those flagmakers.[1]

June 9th 1664. Considerations upon Sir W. Batten's neglecting ancient practice where it opposes his design – though he relies upon it so much at other times. Upon discourse of tarpaulins today at table, for which there is great want of old canvas through our indiscreet selling so close at our last sale – and Sir W. B. (who did in my presence command Capt. Bodily to cast some (when he told him there was none) for he would have some cast), finding that he cannot cast enough, though he hath I fear done more than was fit to do thereupon and never before argue against the making of tarpaulins and coats for masts of old canvas, for he says we use them double, and it takes up too much tar and doth no service, and that merchantmen do not, but make them of new stuff. But it is to be considered that our canvas is not worn so low as merchants wear theirs, and therefore may do good service. It is true, rather than buy old canvas that is not

---

[1] Whistler and Young: for their suspected collusion with Davis, see above, p. 24 & n. 2.

half so good as what [we] may cast ourselves at $6\frac{1}{2}d$. per yard, I am apt to believe that it is better to use new Ipswich.

But this makes me recollect the practice of Sir W. B., who rather than not have his mind and have any pass that should reflect on him, values not the denying of any old practice, though in another point, where ancient practice is for him, he makes it weigh down all other arguments.

Thus lately it was in the business of canvas, when he found that Mr Wayth was resolved to undersell Potter:[1] he cried down Ipswich cloth as a thing not to be used in the Navy, so base and unserviceable, when in all my life I never heard him speak one word against it while Potter served. And yet again, when Potter saw that Wayth did sell, he did come down to his price, and there (if I turn to it) I may see what is observable in the delivery thereof.

Another considerable instance there is in sheathing board with Dering or anybody else that he had a mind to could sell it at 14*s*. a hundred weight. All was well when[2] at last I brought in Sir W. Warren to sell from time to time at 10*s*. and that nobody of his parts[3] would be contented to serve it so, though many endeavours made to raise the price again. Then, without any consideration on his part, he reports it to be bad husbandry for us to buy sheathing board, and that it was plainly best to make[4] it ourselves. It is true, what the issue of it is I have observed (page [14]), but if it be right, we may thank Sir W. Warren's selling us so cheap, not through any understanding or care of his,[5] which might as well have told us sooner of it – and so corrected the ancient practice of buying it, which hath, as I find in my books, for the most part been in the Navy, excepting when we had any old masts which were fit for nothing else.

June 19. (64). Sir W. Batten's discouraging of all men when he finds they do anything like honest men against his designs. It is worth considering too, that no man did cry up Mr Deane, assistant at Woolwich, as he did; and particularly, he and Sir W. Penn did observe and report him mighty active in the business

---

[1] See above, p. 44.
[2] That is, until.
[3] Intelligence.
[4] MS. 'sell'.
[5] Batten's.

of the *Assurance* being sunk.[1] But so soon as he saw me to favour him, and that he did inform me of the truth in the business of Hornechurch timber,[2] he could never endure him, but presently he and Sir J. Mennes cried out that he was a useless officer, that there was no need of such an office, and what do we do with him, and I know not what.

The like for the boatswain of the Woolwich yard, he did use to speak well of him, especially after we have seemed to obey him in his design of getting the old stuff for the master attendant (in which Mr Ackworth opposed him),[3] but at the sale he cannot endure him, and says just as he doth about Dean, that he is an unnecessary officer, and so said to Mr Coventry – as Mr Coventry himself told me.

The like for Mr Ackworth, whom he could never endure since the time that he opposed his will about the old stuff, the particular story whereof I have in this book[4] – though before that, friends good enough. But since, to this day, cannot endure him.

His man Hempson, as I have set down at large in this book,[5] he put away of [a] sudden, only from his hearing that he came to me to the office – though at that time he was as good friends as ever he was with him, notwithstanding the many complaints of his neglect of business.

Jan. 1664/5. How when the same man that he hath discommended becomes useful to him, he will cry up that man to the highest. Yet it is observable in the business of Deane, that Sir W. B. having been down at Harwich (where Deane is now master shipwright) to settle his business of the lights there,[6] in which it seems he hath made some use of Deane – he did not only there, as Deane writes me word, but at his coming up, did both privately and publicly at the table, of his own accord, and did tell me that he could tell the Duke the same, and Mr Coventry also – that we had been all this while kept in ignorance touching the worth of Deane, whom he finds a very able man, and hath been kept in a cloud all the while he was at Woolwich, and that he hath seen

---

[1]She sank off Woolwich in a December storm: *Diary*, i. 313 & n. 2, 315.
[2]See above, p. 6 & n. 2.
[3]See above, pp. 5–6. The boatswain was Richard Smyth: PRO, ADM 20/5, p. 25.
[4]See above, ibid.
[5]See above, p. 19.
[6]On 24 Dec. 1664 Batten had been granted a licence to erect two lighthouses there: *CSPD 1664–5*, p. 129.

his draft and is able to build the ship himself that is to be built there[1] – and a man that deserves as much encouragement as any man in the Navy.

July 14. 64. An instance of tradesmen's imposing on us; Mr Howell[2] *in a parcel of lignum vitae.* Meeting Mr Hempson this day upon the Change, he told me how to his knowledge, this is true and he will make it appear: that one Scott, formerly a clerk of this Office, living at Portsmouth, had a parcel of lignum vitae to sell, and offered it to Mr Tippets, who valued it at 7*l.* 10*s.* per ton. But before he received it, Mr Howell heard of it and stopped his receiving it, saying that it was his right only to serve in that sort of goods by his warrant. So Scott was forced to sell it to Howell for 5*l.* And then Howell served it in, and Mr Tippets, not thinking anything, upon the bill certified it to be 7*l.* 10*s.* At which Howell was very angry, and did say here in London how Tippets had wronged him, for if he had let the bill come without any such certificate, he was sure to have 10*l.* for it here at this office.

June 19. 64. Merchants not to be believed. Mr Harbing in his contract for Noyalls canvas. It is fit to consider how little faith is to be given to the words of merchants, and none to them that we have the greatest confidence in. As in Mr Harbing the French merchant – who (as appears in the third leaf before this)[3] did with a great deal of judgment before the beginning of the discourse of a Dutch war come to Deering's price of selling us Noyalls canvas at 16*l.* 15*s.* – a while after the report of a Dutch war beginning, and we had a mind to make sure of some more. We sent for him. He cries out of his last bargain, protesting that he should lose by the last bargain, and Mr Deering a great deal more. By his violent protestations, we were led to believe him, and offered him 16*l.* 10*s.*; he would not take it, but two or three days after we got him to take 16*l.* 12*s.* 06*d.* For 200 bales, I think. Presently after comes Col. Reames, and when the discourse of a war was at the highest (and Harbing pleaded the buying up of all the commodity in France) he contracts with us for 100 bales at 16*l.* 5*s.* So did Mr Stanly after him of Southampton, his being

---
[1] The *Rupert*, a 3rd-rate completed in 1666 and greatly admired by the King and the Duke of York: *Diary*, vii. 127.
[2] Richard Howell, turner to the Navy.
[3] Above, pp. 51–2.

to be fetched from France too. So did a son of Sir Rd Ford's for a quantity he had. And which is more, Col. Reames, almost a stranger to the trade, and whom we doubted we had misled into a sudden bargain to his loss, performs his contract presently at Portsmouth with stuffs Sir W. Penn both writ and approved also himself yesterday to the table to be as good or rather the best of any had been there delivered by any man. And likes the price so well that he came again June 2nd and contracts with us (notwithstanding the great quantity we have bought and bespoke and the high discourse of a war) for 300 bales more to be served by Michaelmas at the same price.

July 1. 64. Moreover, I am to observe that Reames's, upon my particular inquiry and report under Sir W. Penn's own hand (and mouth, when he was in town lately) is as good as any hath been delivered. And by letters from the sailmaker and storekeeper there is but two bales of a great parcel of Harbing's found to be of the first sort – and the other second[s] and thirds.[1] So that they refuse to open any more or receive any but them two.

June 16. (64). Another instance in Morisco the tar merchant[2]. Being in some want of tar, we endeavoured by Sir W. Rider and Mr Cutler (who [are] under contract with us for some from Stockholm but are doubtful how late it may come) to engage Morisco, to whom all the tar comes, to give us the refusal of what comes next – which they did tell us he upon motion promised them – though I did tell Mr Coventry that I feared Morisco dares not displease by disappointing his constant customers to supply us. This was about a month ago. This day Sir W. Rider and Cutler came to the office to tell us that there was some now come on ships' loading, and that Mr Morisco was forced to part with some to his customers but hath reserved 40 or 50 lasts for us to have if we please – at 11*l.* per last. I wondered at the price, and stopped the Board from giving any present answer till I had inquired; and then at the Change met Mr Hill, who though a dear man, yet did offer to sell us 50 lasts at present and 200 lasts within these six weeks (though neither this nor what he expects is other than what he hath of Morisco) at 10*l.* per last. I offered him 9*l.* 15*s.* And he desired a day to consider of it – and returned

[1] Cf. the storekeeper's letter (25 June) in *CSPD 1663–4*, p. 626.
[2] Charles Marescoe: q.v. H. G. Roseveare (ed.), *Markets and Merchants of the late 17th cent. The Marescoe-David letters 1660–80* (Oxf. 1987).

answer he would take no less than 10*l*. But we expecting some of our own to come soon, we would not give it him. However (June 28) we did contract at 10*l*. with him – and the 30th with Stacy for 100 lasts of the very same tar out of the same ships, never landed.

June 17. 1664. An instance of the delay in making out bills. Birkhead the coppersmith. Mr Davis, late storekeeper at Deptford, delays the making out of any bill to Birkhead the coppersmith from Dec. 60 to Jan. 63 just upon his going out of his office, and then makes him out a bill for 65 cwt of copper, amounting to 500 and odd pounds. I stopped the signing of the bill; and this day inquired first of the clerk of the cheque, whose hand is to the bill, who tells me that he took no notice of any receipts of stores till Aug. 62, when the instructions came to him. And since that time I searched his book to January last, the term of this bill, and find in several parcels as much as comes to about 8 cwt – which was in a year and half. And in the former part of the bill, which is but another year and half, he must then have served in 57 cwt – which is a thing hard to be believed. *Consideration*: how many ships were brought in when the King came in, and laid up and their kettles taken on shore and, as there was occasion, used.

Thence I went to Fownes, who was Mr Davis's clerk (and now Harper's), who tells me he never knew that there was any bill made out to Birkehead – nor ever entered it, but it was done by Mr Davis himself, which is another ill circumstance – and not likely for nothing, for a man to delay the calling in his money, so great a sum and when for a year and half he served in so little ware.

June 22. I sent for Mr Davis, and he did bring me a particular of copper kettles that Birkehead hath, as he says, delivered at several times according to the bill; but God knows how we shall disprove it – though it is very unlikely that he should be willing to stay so long without his money without any cause for his delay. And also no likelihood appears that we have spent so many kettles, there being so many ships abroad at the King's coming in, whose kettles might certainly have served those that have been set out since, without buying of many new ones.

Observations I made in passing the Treasurer's account ending Dec. 1. 1663

1. I observe bills signed by the clerk of the cheque of every yard and summed up without words at length, but only in figures, and never cast or examined in their casting by us – which may lead us to great errors.

2. A bill of Maxwell's was altered (though it is true made right) from 59*l*. to 68*l*., without being corrected in the Comptroller's book at all – but altered after it was passed him and his clerk's entries.

3. The workmanship of the twice-laid stuff is now borne in the ropeyard's book, without any notice taken thereof as to the casting or value of it or the quantity of it in any record – besides that the waste in the binding of it is allowed for at the discretion of the clerk of the ropeyard alone.

4. A bill may be signed by us and altered afterwards, that is falsely altered by the Comptroller's clerks, who may make his ledger agree therewith, and by that means do the King what wrong he will, unless my clerks or some others cast over every bill also. Therefore, fit my clerks' letters-to-be to them;[1] nor will that do unless they cast them over after they are entered in the Comptroller's ledger. (Thomas Lucy for netting-rope, 1663.)

5. Clerks' allowances for the making up of books too great, without being empowered thereto more than we are.

6. A bill made out in lieu of another formerly made out and said to be lost. This second bill is paid and brought to us upon passing the Treasurer's account and passed. I demand how the King is secured that the first bill hereafter (which hath no brand or anything to put us in mind of a second made out) be not paid, or if paid be not passed by us in a future account of the Treasurer's? And for anything I can at present think, I cannot see how it is to be done but by help of the Comptroller's book being brought and examined all along with the Treasurer's at our passing his accounts, and to have the second bill entered, or noted only, by the side of the first, that so we may be warned of a double payment.

7. We allow at this day the old conduct money (as in time of

---

[1] Sc. make sure that in future the clerks' letters correspond with the bills entered in the Comptroller's ledger.

pressing) for the carrying down of the surgeons and their chests to their ships. And also for transcribing their bills at 6*d.* each.

8. The title of disbursements breaks all that method which appears in the Treasurer's accounts, for under that head comes more or less of everything which we expect should be reduced[1] under their several heads.

9. The Comptroller's book not brought till with much arguing and denying to proceed without it, I caused it to be sent for; and when it came, the bill not standing there in the method of the Treasurer's, we could make no use of it – it costing us half an hour almost to examine four or five bills.

10. Capt. Lambert's bills (of the yacht)[2] for pilotage are now many, and we may pay two or three times for aught we know for the same work. It were better to have them quarterly.

11. A bill of Mr Young's for flags served in before our time for 56*l.* 16*s.* 10*d.* was brought to us, examined by Mr Pew, and had been paid. But I observed and stop its allowance.

12. A bill of 40*l.* for oil bought by Sir J. Mennes and Sir W. Batten at Portsmouth of Arth. Smith and paid there by their order to Mr Wayth,[3] without the least notice taken of it by any clerk upon the body of the bill or entered in the Comptroller's book.

I find also several bills in like manner signed abroad, without any notice taken in our books thereof. And some signed here in the office and carried away without any entry thereof by either of our clerks. To be prevented no better than by desiring the Treasurer that none may be paid without both our clerks' letters to every bill.

13. We lose the use of the ledger by having the bills entered in them in short, so that we cannot turn to precedents, nor oftentimes understand our prices and proceedings as we should do.

14. Great charge I find the transportation of goods from Chatham to the Hope or the Downs comes to. And upon inquiry, they tell me that it is one of the knaveries of the boatswains, not to take all their stores on board at first, but leave something to carry down after the ship, by which they have the opportunity of

---

[1] Arranged.
[2] Capt. James Lambert commanded the Duke's yacht, *Anne: Diary*, iii. 63.
[3] Cashier to the Treasurer.

stealth.[1] The like they tell me is done every day at Deptford and Woolwich.

15. It is necessary to revise the variety of tonnage[2] of several provisions – for they differ much, and if not well proportioned must in so great a service turn greatly to the King's wrong. And one thing I am told, that generally the rate is more for small things than for great in proportion.

16. I find it very inconvenient to send out of our hands[3] the accounts of purveyors, messengers or others that have the laying out of money for us, or are employed in many and upon ordinary services – for though it is fit a copy should go along with the bill, to keep us from too great a security in paying away the King's money without submitting the particulars of every allowance to the view of the Auditors,[4] yet we may, by not having copies of them by us, be also led to pay the same over and over again.

June 16. (64). Practices of the clerks of the cheque. Mr Ackworth came to me this afternoon to the office, and discoursing of many things in the yard,[5] he tells me that we are liable to mighty abuses in the petty warrants made by the clerk of the cheque while ships lie there fitting to go to sea – and would have them all to be signed by one or more of the Commissioners before they go to the Victualler. But I must confess, till I have more time, I do not apprehend the depth of it, but will take a time to understand it of him. This I remember he told me: that the last time the *Wellcome* lay there but a fortnight, the dead purser ([he] did say, I think at least) did get 20*l.* by the petty warrants; and further, he says that when he goes about any business to the clerk of the cheque,[6] if there be ever a purser with him they are of a sudden very hushed and silent while he is there about anything – and what they discourse is mighty private.[7]

[1]Boatswains were notorious for stealing. Cf. J. R. Tanner (ed.), Hollond's *Two Discourses* (NRS 1896), p. 101.
[2]The cost per ton.
[3]Sc. to the Exchequer.
[4]The Auditors of the Exchequer.
[5]Woolwich, where he was storekeeper.
[6]William Sheldon.
[7]About a year earlier Ackworth had reported to Pepys similar malpractices by Sheldon, who in collusion with several pursers was falsifying the books of the ships in harbour so as to collect wages and victuals for absentees: *Diary*, iv. 241. The present occasion is also reported in the Diary (v. 181): 'Mr. Ackworth came to me (though he knows himself and I know him to be a very knave) ... to discover the knavery of other people, like the most honest man in the world.'

He tells me moreover, that in the yard's book, the clerk of the cheque will sometimes set down a man short as to his time, and by that means give him cause to complain to him; and then tells him that the next [time] he will give him so much the more time to make it good; and so by this means hath a pretence to get money extraordinary allowed to this man privately on his books the next pay, and receiving it himself (pretending the man to be out of the way) will pay the man what he expects and keep the rest (which he by this advantage had in his power to make what he would) to himself. Nay, sometimes he will say to a man, "There is so much due to another man; I will give you so much time upon your head[1] too much," and by that means be able to pay him. So the man when he receives it, will bring what was above his own pay to the clerk of the cheque and he keeps it.

June 28. (64). Mr Lever's account. This day, after more than two years' time and many offers and denials, comes Mr Lever's account to be signed as Purser-General for the fleet that went with my Lord to the Straits.[2] Sir J. Mennes hath signed it and led Sir W. B. to sign it also. This has been done before it came to the table. Mr Coventry being here, he did raise some questions, which the Comptroller did give some answer in general to: that he had looked over the great oath taken in Spayne[3] and the several certificates besides. So not knowing where to fix any certain objection, he signed it. Then it came to me, and before signing it I did declare that what I did was upon the confidence of Sir J. Minnes's examining it thoroughly – for I had not time to do it myself. He thereupon did tell me that he would not upon that condition have me to sign it, for he would be security for no man and that I was as much concerned to examine it as he. And would have put out his name out of the bill; whereupon Mr Coventry did bid him, if he put out his, to put out the rest. I desired him not to do it of a sudden from anything I said, for I did confess I could not place any certain objection to argue

---

[1] Sc. on your score.
[2] In 1661–2 a fleet under Pepys's patron the 1st Earl of Sandwich had sailed to take possession of Tangier and to bring Charles II's bride, Catherine of Braganza, from Lisbon to London. Thomas Lever had provisioned it mainly from Malaga and Cadiz: R. C. Anderson (ed.), Sandwich's *Journal* (NRS 1929), pp. 17, 113, 114.
[3] Lever's oath which comprehensively certified the accuracy of his accounts.

against it. But in general, I did fear there might be something extraordinary in the case – for first, when he first came over he was hard to be put to come to any account, and did get letters from my Lord to excuse his not bringing of certificates for all, and that it was impossible to have them in a time of hurry, as that was. And thus it hung for above a year and half, he always complaining that he could not be demanded certificates for all his issues in any reason. Now all of a sudden he is said to bring sufficient vouchers for everything, and all clear, and he creditor to the King above 500*l*.

Further, I considered that Mr Lewes[1] was the man that both publicly and in private to me have often said that he was not able ever to make an account, and that he was an idle fellow. Whereas now he defends the account and says that all is clear. And moreover, Sir J.M. did often publicly at the table complain of him, and did argue much the unfitness of the office and this man for that office, and how far he is from bringing any account; and now all of a sudden he is satisfied in it.

Now for this man that was so loath and so far from mentioning himself to be creditor, besides that we believed him (and so I believe he was) not worth a groat, now to be come of a sudden a creditor to the King 5 or 600*l*. – and yet at the table he says this day that he is a loser by his employment above 300*l*. – is very strange.

Upon these considerations I thought fit to excite Sir J.M. by my orders to look the better to the account, as I have often done to him in private. And when at one time he did say at the table that he had examined all his vouchers and found them clear, I did desire to see them. He then, nor any of his clerks, could find them. Mr Lewes was sent for; he had them not. And it appeared that at that time Sir J. Mennes had never looked upon them, nor any of his people had them in their hands.

It ended thus: that I caused the bill[s] to be entered in my office with Sir J.M., Sir W.B. and Mr Coventry's hands to them, and so let go to Mr Turner, out of my hands, for him to deliver to the Comptroller to do what he please with the bill. (*Turn over.*)

Mr Lewes a knave. This night at Mr Rawlinson's I met with Mr Pierce the purser, and speaking with him about this, he

---

[1]Thomas Lewis, clerk in the Victualling Office.

tells me that Lever hath been and is a very idle loose fellow, and never had been able to have passed any account but for Mr Lewes, who of a sudden is become his friend from the greatest foe that could be, and that Mr Lewes is the man that doth all this; and more, that he is the most corrupt villain that ever was employed or can be. That there is not a purser can have any account pass without giving him 5 or 10, 15 or 20*l*. And that for want of this he hath undone many a poor man and his family. And for this he will make any man's account passable and bring a man debtor or creditor, as he pleases. He told some instances – of what was given him – and where he hath certified for men to be creditors upon their accounts, where upon examination or he being offended, they have been found to be 1000*l*. in debt, and 400*l*. another in debt upon accounts before the King's coming in.

That Sir J. Minnes is the public discourse among all pursers, how he will let anything go out one time and cross any the most just thing another, as he would have done to this thing today of Lever's.

And pretty it was to observe, how when I said that what I now said in words, the others did intend; that is, that they signed not upon any examination but only reliance upon his care – and applied myself to Sir W.B. – Sir W.B. answered me that he had examined it by his clerks. When I endeavoured further to know who, I find that it is T. Willson, who indeed is his clerk, but is hired by Sir J.M. to look after the business of the victualling, and so they mean the same person.

June 30. (64). Mr Wood's old masts. Going down by water with Mr Wayth to Deptford this afternoon (in the morning Mr Wood having made us a tender of his old parcel of masts) I called at the several places they lie at in the River – when every parcel almost, but what was brought in this and the last year, are overgrown with weeds as high as my thigh. It is true, contrary to my expectation, when I came to pluck the weeds, I found they were only mud generally hanging about the trees which bred the weeds. But however, to be sure, where there is any hole or shake there it grew fastest – and hard to pull out. However, we may thence infer that they have lain there.

And it is to be considered that of themselves they at the best must be the worst of the parcel, for he being a mastmaker, he would be sure to pick out and make the most money of what would yield him most. As appears further by some of them having been tried, and part of their bodies wrought and left off working, upon the finding some fault I suppose in them.

I must not forget that out of all these he could not find us two to serve us for the two yachts formerly,[1] when he made us pay 25*l.* per mast for them.

And thus, should we buy these when we may have fresh brought hither, and they may lie at his charge here (for to be sure, we may have them when we please) better than at ours – for we buy not for present use but for stores.

Going down to Woolwich, I discoursed with Mr Chr. Pett; and discoursing with him in general of old masts, without telling him whose I mean, he doth assure me that it is no husbandry at all to tell how far the water hath eat into them. He says too, that though the natural sap of a tree doth do good and preserves it while it remains sound, and therefore he advises to have a little left about a tree – yet when this is eaten out by wet and dry lying and becomes rotten, and the wind and water gets in further, that this doth spoil (and shorten, as he calls it) the grain of the wood, and makes it become frow. And that though the merchant do cut away all that is unsound, till it comes to the sound wood, yet that then it will not be so strong nor serviceable as a fresh tree of that diameter by a very great matter.

June 30. 1664. My journeys and disbursements expressed in a bill. This day I offered to the Board a bill of my disbursements for some things – among others, for five journeys to Woolwich and Deptford, 1. 15. 00. Sir J. Mennes would by all means have had me taken more – "for," says he, "why will you have less than the clerks? And it is too little." But I would have it go as it was, saying it was as much as it cost me.

When it came to Sir W. Batten's hand, I observed he pointed to the bill to Sir J.M. What he meant I know not, for there is nothing I need fear examining. Only, the copies of the clerk of the cheque's books printed, which did not cost me so much the printing barely to Moxon.[2] But at the worst, it will be made out that the paper and all might well come to the money, which I think was 5*l.* 7*s.* 0*d.*

[1]The *Charles* and the *Jemmy*, royal yachts built in 1662: Anderson, nos 298, 299.
[2]Joseph Moxon; he supplied printed stationery to the Navy Office.

June 30. (64). Mr Wayth about chips. This day, going down to Deptford, he told me, among other things, of one man that used to have his breakfast brought to him two or three times in a morning, for his wife thereby to carry out chips every time. And he says that he himself hath bought of that man 40*s.* or 3*l.* worth of chips of one month's gathering. He knew them to be but of one month's collection, because that at the end of the former month he had bought of him 4 or 5*l.* worth before. This man was a sawyer, and it seems the slabs of every piece of timber they used to carry away as chips, which was good for many uses besides firing.

Mr Falconer about tar barrels. He and his wife dining with me this day with Mr Wayth, we were talking at table of tar. And she begin to ask me whether that which I told them we had contracted for this day be the tar with thick barrels. "For," says she, "my husband gives me them for my fees, all that is left that the fire doth not spend. And those that are thin yielded me little; but for the thick ones I have 6*d.* apiece" – selling them to people that use them for vessels to keep wash for hogs in and such like uses. If this be so (and the truth is, for fire, [as] Mr Wayth well observed – they have more wood than three faggots in them) then we have contracted this day for 100 lasts; which at 6*d.* per barrel comes to 30*l.* – besides 25 last we bought the other day, and a great deal more in of our own from Stockholm. That at that rate her vails are very good.

Mr Wayth about men going out to breakfasts. Alehouses: too many near the yard. The men at Deptford are mighty desirous at this time, and have petitioned to us, to have the leave of going out to breakfast again.[1] Mr Wayth tells me that the keeping them within the yard at breakfast doth save not only much time as to their call[2] and to the carrying of chips out – but many embezzlements might also be prevented if good use were made of it; but the porter doth nothing of his duty therein, but suffers the masters to go out of the yard as they please, leaving only their servants

---

[1] This had been disallowed since the recent disturbances there: *CSPD 1664–5*, p. 189; above, p. 45 & n. 1.
[2] Roll call.

in the yard. And then there are so many alehouses, that whenever they can carry out, be it a packet of nails, a deal or anything, there are places presently to make money or drink of them. That it were to be wished there were not so many alehouses. And more, he says that it were worth trying to have the gate toward the town shut for a while, and make all people go in and out the other way; he says we should soon hear an angry cry among the alewives, and find less carrying out of goods out of the yard.

July 22. 1664. About timber measure. Mr Shish a master shipwright his inability therein. Being this day at Deptford at the burial of Mr Falconer, and coming a little too soon, I walked up and down the yard; and among other things got Mr Shish to measure a piece or two of timber, but very rawly and uncertainly. At last, to try him, I took him to a piece of timber that was flitched and brought into the yard die-square, 6 inch deep one way and 20½ inch the other and 32 ft long. He measures it, and makes it 37 ft of timber in it. I observed how he did it, and seeing him bring it so false out, I asked him plainly again and again whether he found that a true way of measuring of this piece, to take the half of the two depths for the square of the piece; he without any doubting replied again and again that it was, and he would maintain it to be right – when, as I told him, that it was but 27 ft in content.[1] And Mr Fletcher coming by, I bid him do it, and he by his line of numbers and a pair of compasses did it right, but a great while he was in doing it over me by my ruler.[2] And ashamed he was of Mr Shish, though he durst not appear so to him. Now this piece could not cost the King less than a 5*l*. per load, which is 20*s*. less to him in a piece of timber of 27 foot content.[3]

---

[1] Strictly 27⅓ cu. ft.
[2] Richard Fletcher's 'line of numbers' was a carpenter's ruler inscribed with a scale of logarithms; Pepys's 'ruler' was presumably his recently acquired slide-rule with the logarithms inscribed on a spiral line: see *Diary*, iv. 85; v. 17 & nn.
[3] In his account in the Diary (v. 217) Pepys has a slightly different calculation. He there calculates the loss to the King on a piece of timber 28 cu. ft in volume at 12*s*.–13*s*.

July 29. 1664. Measuring of blocks and grindstones not agreed on. It is strange to consider (as I have formerly observed, page [26]) how things are received into the stores time after time from judgement to judgement, without any certain rule known therein. Not only in the great things of New England masts, sorts, breadths and degrees of goodness of canvases – but in usual things of daily receipt, as blocks and grindstones, in both which by several letters within these two or three months, but particularly by one of July 12th, and another of July 29th 1664, Comr Pett himself desired to be informed in the manner of measuring, as doubting that there may be a fallacy therein, but yet never thought of till now.[1]

August 17. 1664. Lightness of the King's weights in store. Mr Bodham becoming clerk of the ropeyard at Woolwich in the room of Mr Falconer, who is dead, he begun his office with the trying of the King's weights there, which hath not been in four years before; that is, since the King came first in; and in this time he finds (as by his letter of this date)[2] that in 19 cwt they want 33 lb. and ½ oz. Which answers to above 35 lb. to 20 cwt or a ton. Which at 43*l.* medium (and more than that we have lost us, one sort with another, since the King's coming in) it hath lost us 15*s.* upon every ton of hemp. Besides the loss of weight in the spinner's day's work, which he[3] computes together in these four years time hath lost the King about 500*l.*, but I believe much more.

And the like I fear in the other yards.

Aug. 22. 1664. Plating of bread-rooms when advised against[4]. I never remember to have heard anybody discourse against the plating of bread-rooms till after Stanes came in to Chatham to serve the plating there, not with the good opinion of the Commissioner, though with most considerable profit to the King.

---

[1]Pett's letter of 29 July about his method of measuring grindstones is in PRO, SP 29/100, no. 127. As for the measuring of blocks, Pepys had inquired of Pett on the 16th if they were to be measured by diameter, or, as Shish did (according to Pepys), by length: see above, p. 26 & n. 1.
[2]*CSPD 1663–4*, p. 668.
[3]Peter Pett.
[4]Bread rooms, where the ship's biscuit was stored in canvas bags, were usually lined with lead or tin. Cf. R. C. Anderson (ed.), *Journals of the Third Dutch War* (NRS 1946), pp. 66, 76; Sir W. Beveridge, et al., *Hist. prices and wages in Engl.* (1965), i. 657.

And then the Commissioner did at his coming to town first discourse against the plating of them, and that he would line them with slit deal. Which it seems he hath hitherto done, and this night I was told of it by Stanes's brother, who came to complain of it, that a great part of the little profit Stanes hath is by this taken away by design of the Commissioner.

Aug. 23. 1664. About shortness of breadth in canvas not observed. Master attendant's ignorance and negligence therein. It is strange to think that notwithstanding all our contracts for Noyalls canvas (of which we spend so much) are and have ever been, time out of mind, expressed to be of 27 inch broad – yet that a little while ago, the master attendant himself, Capt. Boddily, should tell me that he never minded the breadth of canvas, and that he thought these were as broad as they ought to be, and never made any abatement for want of breadth (as I always supposed by their not taking notice of any shortness of breadth that they had done) and as I think they do in Ipswich's. So that this day comes the first bill wherein that defect was ever certified to the table, and this is a bill of Mr Harbing's daughter's, August 5. (64), and what we have lost, God knows, thereby – it being, I perceive, generally an inch and ¾ inch. Nay, [I] remember he would face me down, notwithstanding there was pieces there to be judged by; yet so little was his skill, as well as memory, that he would face me down that time out of mind the practice hath been to put the best piece of canvas in the middle of the bale, which we know that it is always the worst. Which is a sad thing, that this man, which is the King's only security in this commodity, should know no better.

Breadth of Noyalls canvas made good. Memorandum: that out of a bill bearing date the 5th of Aug. 1664 made from Deptford to Mr Harbing for Noyalls canvas, by him delivered therein, I did cause the narrowness of the breadths to be abated out of the bill for so much cloth as they wanted. The abatement came to 6*l.* odd money, but the precedent will do us a great deal of good. And this is the first that ever was made of it yet in any man's memory, as Mr Turner[1] says. But yet the letter of their contract, that it shall be 27 inch broad, will bear us out in it.

August 31. 1664. Bills ill made out. It comes in my head to set down the effect of our late urging the storekeepers by letter to express goods upon their bills to be as good and answer contract, and not in general fit for the King's service.[2] For presently after comes a bill from Portsmouth for canvas of Col. Reames – and certified on the back side thereof, so much answering contract, and so much fit for the King's service, but not answering contract.

August 31. (64). King gets most by others' differences. Mr Wood (as Sir W. Warren the other day told me) did go down to see and sent one also to measure Sir W. Warren's masts that came in last – which to be sure was not done out of goodwill to the King.

Mr Wood's great mast chargeable in its lengthening. Mr Deane tells me that the lengthening of one of Mr Wood's last New England masts (about which we have so much ado) to make a main mast for the new ship building at Woolwich[3] will, as the mastmaker himself confesses, cost above 50*l.* I have bid him give me the particulars, which I will demand of him.

Aug. 31. 1664. Sir W. Pen about getting his daughter an annuity of 80l. per annum of Mr Falconer and his ill using of his widow when dead.[4] It is worthy remembering Sir W.P.'s receiving of a gold watch of Mr Falconer at his getting him his place; and more than that, got a present of him to put his daughter Pegg into an estate for her life of 80*l.* per annum. And yet his usage most base to his widow after his death. But I think God Almighty hath punished him by taking away Mr Falconer before he could

---

[1] Thomas Turner, clerk-general of the Navy Office under the Commonwealth; now clerk to the Comptroller.
[2] See above, p. 62.
[3] The *Royal Katherine*. For the 'ado', see above, p. 36.
[4] John Falconer, clerk of the ropeyard at Woolwich had died on 19 July: *CSPD 1663–4*, p. 646.

get her[1] life put in in the room of his former wife, for this woman[2] finds by his writings that the thing is not yet done. *Vide* my Journal of Aug. 1664 from Mr Falconer's death to this day.[3]

Aug. 31. 1664. Sir W. Batten orders rails and posts to be made him from Deptford. A week or two ago Mr Wayth did show me a note which he says he took up from the ground at Deptford, which was a note wrote and signed by Sir W.B. (he showed it to me) to Uthwayt and Shish for their causing some posts and rails to be made and sent to Bow for the making him an arbour.[4] The lengths of the rails and posts are therein set down – and directs them to send them to one Chockely for him at Bow.

Aug. 26. 1664. Sir W. Rider's bargain with Clothier at Woolwich for cordage for the King and how it proves. This day I went down to Woolwich and took Pumfield the ropemaker with me to look upon some cordage yet unsent by Clothier, with whom Sir W. Rider (among other parcels and persons that he by our entreaty hath contracted with all for some cordage for us privately) had contracted for some cordage of Millan hemp at 40*s*. per cwt, when he himself contracted with others for Riga stuff[5] at the same very price. Pumfield finds the goods well enough made, but of most cruel coarse stuff, that the shivers[6] stood in it as thick as could be, or at least the hemp unshackled.[7] And told me that he would not condemn the cordage otherwise than by saying that he would help me to some as well as others, and of the same hemp for 34*s*. per cwt. So I directed Capt. Teate, who was to take it in for Portsmouth, among other things he is carrying thither, not to take this cordage unless Clothier would let it go at 34*s*. per cwt. So away I went, and at Deptford see Pumfield's cordage, which looks and is as good. And agreed with him for it (it was about 2 tons) for 33*s*. And the next day Capt. Teate comes and tells the Board that Clothier is willing to let it go for 34*s*.,

---

[1] Peg Penn's.
[2] Falconer's second wife, now his widow.
[3] *Diary*, v. 248, 249, 253.
[4] Presumably for his country house at Walthamstow.
[5] The best variety.
[6] Loose filaments.
[7] Uncombed.

when he should have had by contract, and will have for what is already sent when the *Augustin* went last, 42*s.* per cwt. So we wrote to the storekeeper from the Board (as our books show) to receive Clothier's at 34*s.* and no more – and to Deptford storekeeper to take Pumfield's at 33*s.*

Here appears that merchants will be merchants, and Sir W. Rider will do as other men when it comes in his way – for he gives this man as much for his Millan as others for Riga goods. And when all done, it proves that this hemp that Clothier works is now or hath been Sir Wm Rider's own, and that he hath some finger in the pie himself – he being a great friend to the supplying and setting up of this Clothier – and had a parcel of Millan a good while since, which we would not buy in the Navy, that hath lain here all this while – as he hath also a parcel of Christiania deals that have lain there these two or three years.

The worst of all is that I did take Russell[1] once thither and he did freely give me not only a good account that it was good and worth the money, but did give it me under his hand that it was very good.

August 31. 1664. Sir R. Ford and Sir Wm Rider's finding passage for some soldiers to Tangier with good cunning and profit. The Committee of Tangier upon the death of my Lord Teviot[2] having occasion to send over some recruits of men – among other ships taken up for the speedy carrying of the men thither, and we being in some haste, Sir R. Ford and Sir. W. Rider did at the table offer it with great kindness that they had a ship going that way, and they would neglect their own matters to spare room for some men; which was taken mighty kindly from the Duke and by all of us – and left to me to agree with them as reasonably as I could – they declaring they would not get by it, but let go some of their own concernments to serve the King herein. So speaking a while after with Sir R. Ford at the India House, he demanded 30 and I did consent to come up with what we had given my Lord Tiviott, which was 25*s.* a head for their transportation, only without victuals. The vessel was the *Loyalty*; Capt. Norwood[3] and his men went in her.

[1] Peter Russell, master of the ropeyard, Woolwich.
[2] Governor, 1663–4.
[3] Col. Henry Norwood, Deputy Governor of Tangier, 1665–8.

A good while after comes complaint that the ship was kept for want of convoy at Plymouth and for want of victuals, and one in the behalf of the master of the ship came to tell me how Sir W. Rider and Sir R. Ford would not consider them for the time they lay there and lost of their intended voyage, by reason of the carrying of these soldiers, but would only give them x*s*. a head, which they had contracted with the master for, though they promised him that the men should be presently put on board and no delay caused to them here or anywhere.

So that here these gentlemen have got thanks of us, and a profit of 15*s*. for every man that was carried, which was 106, and all for nothing.

Sept. 19. 1664. Mr Coventry about his having a salary given him extraordinary in place of fees. Duke's promise in behalf of Navy clerks. This day we, all the officers of us, waiting upon the Duke, as we do every week, Mr Coventry, after all other discourse was done, did tell the Duke and us that according to his own desire, the King had granted him by his R.H.'s favour a set allowance instead of a casual one of his fees – which had given occasion to much discourse – (which it seems is 500*l*. a year)[1] and that from this day or six days backward, he did not only consent but desire that if ever any of us doth hear that he receives any kind of gift or gratuity for any places in the Navy, we should tell the Duke of it, desiring only that he might at the same time know it, that so he might be able to justify himself. Only, he desired that it might not be denied that a clerk of his might take a crown or half-a-piece, and not more, upon the passing of any such grant. And upon a motion of Sir J. Mennes's at the same time, and seconded by all the rest, the Duke did promise that our clerks, as being the fittest men and those that deserve it best, should be advanced into places as places fall.

Sept. 24. 1664. Corruption in the Office of the Ordnance more than in this of the Navy. It is worth considering how Col. Legg, being lately brought into the Tanger Committee by Sir. H.

---

[1] A privy seal for that amount had been issued on 6 September: Longleat, Coventry MSS 98, f. 127*r*. The number of his fees and gratuities had been criticized in the Commons. See V. Vale in *Camb. Hist. Journ.*, xii (1956), pp. 107–25.

Bennet, hath given great attendance, which I always construed to arise from his care of the King's business. But the other day, upon occasion of sending some supplies of stores to the garrison, I did speak of deals, that it would be cheaper to have them go straight thither, which I thought would be done at 6*l*. 10*s*. per centum, whereas it was then made appear to us by Col. Reames and Sir Bernard De Gum that my Lord Tiviott did sell all his at half a piece-of-eight a deal, and by name he told me they were Normer deals.[1]

Upon my saying that I could get them served so, Col. Legg said that he would consult (with him of the Tower that used to supply them) against the next meeting, and bring an estimate of the value of all things now to be sent. So he did, and brought, among other things, deals at 5*l*. 15*s*. per centum, calling them Normer 10-feet deals. Now I know that they are the ordinary and the least sort of ordinary deals. I told them again that they might be furnished, I believed, upon the place for 6*l*. 10*s*. Col. Legg at first seemed very indifferent; and if the King might be served some he was glad of it. But by and by he begun to say that the officers of the Ordnance ought to do this, and did ever do these things. Mr Coventry argued that these were not ammunition, and therefore not properly under their care. But above all, that these were now to be bought out of the fund of the garrison, and then properly to come to us – being not of a distinct privy sale kept to the officers of the Ordnance.

But while they were saying that these were but estimates only, and so no matter how great they were, the King not paying by them but by the prices they paid – to that I said we might guess that there was no great latitude left for that. For I instanced in one particular, iron, which there they demand 18*l*. per ton and he said that their smith did assure them upon his oath that he did pay 17*l*. 10*s*. this last week, or very lately, himself for his iron. So that here was but 10*s*. exceeded in the estimate. And yet I know that at this day the best Swedes iron may be bought every day in the week at 14*l*., if not less.

Col. Legg could have been very angry, as appeared by his words: that he would bring the officers of the Ordnance hither to inform us of their reasons for their demands – and that the D. of York had directed that they should provide them. But being well seconded by Mr Coventry, I did except against the price of

[1] Unidentified.

candles (6s. 6d.,[1] when I bought myself the other day, and may do at this, for 5s. 6d. anywhere) and other things. And rise with a desire to Col. Legg that he would see at what prices his officers would procure these things. But whereas before he had given the Secretary his estimate to keep, as he used to do others – he took it up again and put it in his pocket so that I could not have my will in carrying of it home with me to consider of. But I took the last that he made a month ago, and upon comparing them with the prices we pay for the same goods in the Navy, and those generally the highest we have paid, or at least the highest we at present pay, and upon view and consideration of the goods themselves, I find the difference to be as follows –

	Their demand	Navy price	
	l. s. d.	l. s. d.	
Deals per centum	06. 10. 00	04. 00. 00	
Balks 20 ft long	00. 04. 00 each	00. 02. 04	
Deals slit per centum	08. 00. 00	05. 07. 00	(9 ft in a deal at
Steel spades	00. 03. 06 each	00. 02. 00	3s. per centum
Wire per pound	00. 01. 02	00. 00. 08	sawing comes to
		(*Turn over*)	27s. per centum
Sheet lead per centum	01. 02. 00	00. 19. 06	deals)
Tallow per ton	56. 00. 00	48. 00. 00	
Ash per ton	04. 00. 00	01. 18. 06 ⎫	
		01. 10. 06 ⎭	
Pitch per last	45. 00. 00	16. 00. 00	
Tar per last	13. 04. 00	10. 00. 00	(offered me this day 100 lasts)
Tarred rope per centum	02. 07. 00	02. 00. 00	
Copper kettle			
of 8 gallons	04. 10. 00 ⎫	of 60 gall. sent the other day	
of 6 gallons	03. 00. 00 ⎭	by me to Tanger	
		04. 06. 00	
Spars per centum	06. 00. 00	{ small 01. 03. 00	
		middle 03. 00. 00	
		boom 05. 00. 00	

One thing more I may observe, that though there is reason now to rise rather than fall in the price of deals, yet for those they demanded 6l. 10s. per centum they do demand but 5l. 15s. – which must needs arise from my chance to speak of it the other day before the estimate was brought in.

[1] Per doz. lbs.

From whence we see how the King is served bad at best, and very bad in other places, compared with the present prices we buy at in the Navy.

Sept. 29. 1664. Mr Hill's knavery in abusing us with bad tar among good. Discovered by Sir W. Batten's cheat in tar. After many and great complaints of a parcel of bad tar (sent out of a parcel of Bergen bought of Mr Shorter) delivered at Portsmouth by the *Augustin*, I did yesterday make inquiry, and under the storekeeper's hand of Woolwich (as appears by my papers, no. 5, annexed)[1] report to the Board this day that there was none of Mr Shorter's sent to Portsmouth. After I had said so, Sir W.B., who had so often repeated that it was his,[2] now tells us that he knows from a sure hand that it was none of his, but of Mr Hill's; but desired that he might not be brought upon the stage to prove it, but he knows it was so, for he did send part of his last contract of this bad sort of tar – and said withal that this is the second time that he hath endeavoured to play such open knavery with the King. The thing I believe is true, but wonder to see the time so changed, that Sir W.B. his quondam support and patron should now be the discoverer.

Sept. 29. 1664. Meres the purveyor his neglects in providing of bad screws for Portsmouth. This day a man that made us some screws to send for Portsmouth did this day come to have his bill signed. The Board was for giving him his screws back again from Portsmouth, which, rather than have nothing for them, he would have taken; but I moved that if the King be wronged, he may be righted by the offender. For this man made them to satisfy the King's officer appointed to direct him in the making them and approve of them when made – which was Mr Meres the purveyor. So the man had his bills allowed him, but I fear nothing will now be looked after to right the King of his own instrument.

Octobr 8. 1664. A most disgraceful charge brought by Sir W. Batten against some deals of Sir W. Warren. But most effectually

[1] Untraced.
[2] Shorter's.

removed. This day, after some months having had them received into the yard at Deptford, Sir W. Warren came to the Board to desire that Mr Shish might have an order to call Mr Chr. Pett to his assistance in the valuing some deals and other goods that were along with his last ship of masts. Sir W.B. was mightily against it, that Mr Pett should not go. That it was better to [employ] somebody that is a stranger and that buys deals in the town. Which I told him is not only a new case, but argues the King's officers unfit to be trusted in anything, if not in this. At last he told us the reason, and that is that Mr Pett did value the same deals served in another ship at Woolwich at 5*l*. 5*s*., and they were paid for so by this Board in his absence, which are not worth 3*l*., being all white deals[1] and bad woods. And therefore Pett must for his honour rate these so too. Now, that is a folly, for we pay not absolutely because they value things, but because the quality being sent us, along with their opinion of the price, we think things worth it. And he said that Sir G. Carteret and Sir J. Mennes and he had seen them in the yard, and wondered to see so bad goods received in, and that somebody that understands deals as well as any man in England said they were not worth 3*l*. per centum. Sir W. Warren was called for in, and I told him what was said against his deals. He said that one known very well to this Board had given himself, to sell again, 5*l*. 5*s*. per centum for the very same deals out of the same ship. This was so thundering an answer, that I took it up; and though he would long have concealed his name, yet I did urge him to tell, and it was Mr Wood, and promises to give us the deals if this be not true. Sir W.B. would have gathered some argument from their being the master's[2] deals, and so he could pick out the best. To that, Sir W.W. answered they were indeed the master's deals, but sold with his knowledge and by his direction, and were his own very deals, and no better in any sort, but the very same. This struck all dead, and Sir W.B. quite mad, and Mr Coventry and myself did declare very ill doings and intentions to be meant to Sir W.W., if this be so – as he puts the value of all his goods upon the truth of it.

Octobr 11. 1664. This morning Sir W.B. brought Mr Wood to the office to clear this business, I alone being there with him. And Mr Wood says, as I then took it from his own mouth, that

---
[1]See above, p. 22 & n. 4.
[2]The ship's master's.

he hath not bought a deal these two years. That his son indeed bought some of the master of Sir W.W.'s vessel at 5*l*. per centum, but they are x*s*. better than these the King hath.

Octobr 12. 1664. I this day made inquiry of Sir W. Warren again, telling him what Mr Wood says. To which he answers that his instrument in Sweden sold the master all which the master hath here sold, of the very same without difference, with the rest of the loading. That the master did here sell all he had to Mr Wood, or it may be to his son; but they were landed at Mr Wood's yard and still lie some of them there. That the master did then tell Sir W.W. that he had 5*l*. 5*s*. for them, and that thereupon Sir W.W., to prevent all objection that might be raised (as it now is) that his goods were picked, did stop the delivery of any more to Mr Wood, and did give him 5*l*. 5*s*. for them which remained of what he should have delivered to Mr Wood; which he offers to make oath of, and that he delivered these very deals (as knowing no difference between them and the rest) into the King's yard. And that the master did yesterday assert to him again that the price agreed for with Mr Wood was 5*l*. 5*s*., and that from that time he had nothing for his selling them; he never thought nor reckoned any difference to be between his goods and the rest of the ship's loading. This Sir W.W. desires the master may be discoursed with concerning, and put to his oath. And more – "The master," says he, "cannot be mistaken about the price, for he was paid for them but yesterday, and that after the rate of 5*l*. 5*s*." – only Mr Wood says that he will make the master pay the lighterage, which is 12*d*. per centum. If so (which is not yet decided) he will have but 5*l*. 4*s*.; if not, then Mr Wood gives 5*l*. 6*s*. He says also that old Mr Wood did treat about them, though the young may be said to make the bargain.

Octobr 6. 1664. Calicoes introduced for colours in the King's service. I have already elsewhere set down (page [49]) what passed the Board this day touching the putting off of Young and Whistler. Now I come to set down the manner of bringing in the serving of ourselves with calicoes. Sir J. Minnes had a long time ago bespoke it of his own experience – saying ourselves (Octob. 4, as I have already observed) how Mr Young would have impressed on[1] us, I did revive the vote. The Board then committed

[1] Sc. put pressure on.

it to me to inquire into. I did and reported this day that it might be done for 5¼d. per yard of the present breadths now accounted – which was well received. Sir J.M. again and again urged the use and experience of them. Sir G. Carteret also his own knowledge of the practice of Spain and other places abroad. Sir W. Batten acknowledged that these are stronger and will last better than the bewpers, but opposes them (upon discourse, he says, with Sir W. Rider and others of the East India Company), that they will not fly, being heavy – to which I shall (though I have already weighed them) prepare an answer upon observation. Sir G.C., my Lord Barkely, Sir J.M. and Mr Coventry with great earnestness, and Sir W.B. not opposing it, did desire me to see it done. Besides, Sir J.M. did cause two flags that he had made and dyed at Lisbon[1] to be brought as a proof of his experience – by which I guide myself.

Order and distinction of colours in time of war. Vide Bundle no. 6, which Sir J. Minnes did report upon [at] my desire at the table. But being crossed therein by Sir W. Penn, he did in a hot answer swear what he said was true, and he would give it under his hand; which I in knavery desired he would do, and so very hot he did it and give me it.

Octobr 26. 1664. About my treating with Nellson for blufers. This day it came in my head and I did go to Nellson's house, where Michell had told me Young and Whistler buy all their blufers. Nellson was not at home; the servant shows me some, the same he told me Whistler buys, and showed me the book where one Williamson in Thames Street and others do pay 7s. 6d. per piece. He had only five pieces in the house; I bought and paid for them at 7s. 6d. The servant told me they were to have more tomorrow, and promised me twenty pieces. So I went away well satisfied, promising to take them twenty pieces, and what more I could have.

27th. This night I went thither again[2] and met with the servant again, who told me his master had none come this week, and

---

[1] In 1650 Mennes, commanding the *Swallow*, was, with the rest of Rupert's squadron, blockaded by Blake in the Tagus for several months: E. Warburton, *Mem. Rupert and Cavaliers* (1849), iii. 303.

[2] Recording these visits in the Diary (v. 305–6, 308) Pepys reveals their purpose. It was to bring down the price, or, failing that, to buy direct from Nelson. 'This jobb was greatly to my content.'

seemed very churlish to me, not knowing when his master would have any, when yesterday he told me plainly he had 30 or 40 pieces every week. I asked for the master; he carried me to an alehouse. I with him and with the master came home, and there demanding of the master of a sudden, he did confess he had pieces come yesterday, but told me plainly he had not enough to serve his constant customers, and therefore could not let me have any, and much such language. I would not be put off of my twenty pieces, but took him to the alehouse back again, and there he and I talked calmly and came almost to conclusion, that taking a certain quantity for a year and giving good payment, he would not value Whistler nor Young, but would serve me as good, and the very same that he did them at this day or ever did, and as cheap. That they had endeavoured to get away his workmen in the country to work for them, which they never did attempt before. And therefore he was at liberty. So he took me home and showed me Whistler's name in the book, the 16 of this month, for twenty pieces of narrow bluffers, 7*l.* 10*s.* 00*d.* and two pieces of broad, 3*l.* 00*s.* 00*d.* So, in great hopes to come to an agreement with this man and wholly defeat them, I went home, contented mightily, and now able with demonstration to convince them of their imposing upon us heretofore. He, the man, tells me that he did serve them cheaper and worse stuffs heretofore than now about a year since or two, which is the time that I have made all this ado.

Octobr 31. This night (I suppose, and did afterwards find by their words, that it was upon knowledge of what I had done with Nellson and what I had bought of Bridges for calicoes),[1] Young and Whistler did come to me in a most humble manner,[2] to desire that the trade of flagmaking might not be undone by my bringing in foreigners to work them. That they would not be against Michell's serving us with what and how much and for how long we pleased. Only, that they might have their share. I told them what I had done and what I could do. How all was now in my power. I showed them a great heap of colours of calico brought home, and some of their own blufers, which they know I had bought of Nellson. But they answer they have bought none for

---

[1] On 8 October Pepys had come to terms with Richard Bridges, linen draper of Cornhill, for 100 pieces of calico: *Diary*, v. 292.

[2] Cf. ibid., v. 310: 'There came presently to me Mr. Young and Whistler, who find that I have quite overcome them in their business of flags; and now they come to entreat my favour, but I will be even with them.'

less than 8*s*. and 8*s*. 3*d*. these two or three months – when I did see in Nellson's book that Whistler had bought for 7*s*. 6*d*. the 16 of this month. They owned these I showed them to be the same they do and shall serve, and that better they cannot promise, and leave me to make the price. And do own that Michell's pattern is as good or better than theirs, and that Michell doth now serve in good stuffs but that he did not at first. That they will serve these stuffs made at 5³/₄*d*. per yard. I used all plainness, and told them what my calicoes cost, and showed them Bridges' hand – by that means convincing them of what I did, that I made no gains by it.[1] And upon the whole, made the matter appear very much against their content, I am sure; and so leaving them to make a lower demand, but yet giving them good words, I sent them away.

Nov. 2d 64. Meeting Mr Young at night in the street (I being then going indeed to Nellson's), among other discourses, he told me that he had received a letter this day from Norwich from his mother that makes the stuffs; that he is in fear of pressing, and therefore desires a protection,[2] and that that is the reason that he could send no more stuffs this week, nor so many as he used to. And thence Mr Young would argue that the stuffs will grow dearer, and that he is not able to supply us so soon with the 8000 yards as he intended – nor make four flags extraordinary, all blue, to be used for distinctions as Sir W. Penn desires, I having put out the reds and the whites somewhere else. By this means it appears what little reason he and Whistler had the other day to plead their having so many thousand yards upon their hands.

Nov. 3. 1664. This day (after I had in the garden given Mr Coventry an account of all my proceedings in the calicoes and blufers) I did call in Young and Whistler – and we offered them 5¼*d*. and then 5⅛*d*. I did then, when they had refused it, offer that Michell should serve what he did not make himself with the same stuffs, which I there brought to the table that I bought of Nellson, and which is to be their pattern, at 5¼*d*. promising due payment. So they accepting of my offer, the others were sent away. At last I did give Mr Coventry a private note of Michell's incapacity of doing it if there be any doubt of the payment, as I feared there might; and therefore said I was willing, for fear of any disappointment thereby, that we should give 5½*d*.; which they were called in for and took it, but a great while insisted upon

---

[1] In fact he gained over £50 from the deal with Bridges: *Diary*, vi. 24.
[2] A certificate of exemption from impressment.

their doing all which was denied them by Mr Coventry, but I had made that sure, by making a contract with the other[1] on Tuesday. Mr Coventry was also against the giving these men more than him, and nothing did carry him and me to consent to it, nor had Sir J.M., Sir W.B. and Sir W.P. anything to urge, but only the uncertainty of payment and the abilities of these men to give us credit. And so this great business is ended, they being to serve us with 2 or 3000 yards weekly for a year. But strange it is to see how these men, that cry all their stuffs are better than Michell's, will by no means be persuaded, though we desired it again and again, to serve us as good as his, and that his might be the pattern. But more horrid it is to think that Sir J. Minnes that did give us the first advice to this, commending it in every respect, did yesterday before the Duke (Mr Cov. tells me) and this day clear himself of having to do with calicoes, and that they would be too heavy and would not hold colour. And yet again by and by, when he saw some of these that were brought to the table today, did swear they would hold colour, and that his that he made had been washed in the Tagus and yet have a good colour.

Nov. 4. Being now come to agreement with them, and finding, upon casting up, that we want 40,000 yard of stuff, Young told me that they have not above 5000 in their hands, whereof almost three is to make up their 8000 yards.

Octobr 22. 1664. Cheat in oars. Negligence of timber-measurer. Faults seldom punished. Having lately bought great quantity of oars of a sudden of Mr Lowe – for the obtaining of which he had used my recommendations by friends by letters to us all – and from the willingness of Sir W. Batten to have them of him; and lastly from Comr Pett's late complaint that not one in eight were good, I did this afternoon at Deptford inquire after them. Fletcher the measurer told me they were all good that were received there; that there was none now in the yard, but in a hoy going off to Harwich there was some which I might see. So it being late, and fearing it might be upon presumption that I would not stay that he did offer me the view of them, I did stay, and caused half a dozen to be taken up as he proposed, that being taken impersonally I might judge what the rest were. When I saw them, two of them had great rotten holes, one through the blade

[1] Mitchell.

and the other through the loom. A third had no blade left almost. A fourth hath a great knot in the middle of the loom, and the other two were sorry crooked things. The four first I caused to be laid by to be looked upon by anybody.

I complained of this next sitting day at the Board. And Flecher ordered to come to us the next. Which he did, and some hard words given him but no punishment, nor anything like it. And that which I see doth spoil all, that a man for vainglory, to recommend himself, will be glad sometime to be seen to find fault, but it is not his business he thinks to see it punished, and so lets it go; by which I have yet seen very few men punished for any fault they have committed.

Observable in the ill circumstances of this matter. It is worth considering too how the timber-measurer pleaded he was only to see the lengths true. And yet by the way he told us (when we objected he could not do that without seeing these faults) that he laid a hundred together end by end, and so took the measure of one, and that sufficed for all – which is a bad way of measuring, as being impossible thereby to tell the true length of all; and where we pay different prices for different lengths, a mistake in the length doth not only require a price for more length than we have, but an increase of price upon the whole length of what it really is. He said the master attendant and clerk of the survey was there to see the goodness. But the first it seems was busy elsewhere. The other too said he did not see them measured, nor taken up, at least not all, nor could, having so much business. And yet he, as I observed to him, did certify under his hand the goodness of all these oars – which he confessed he did upon trust in Flecher. And thus the King's work is done.

Nay further, I can observe here that some men's goods can be neglected the surveying wholly, while others, let their business be what it will (as Sir W. Warren or Michell) can be inquired into every particular piece or parcel.

Novembr 4. 1664. Eastland merchants' foul dealing with us for hemp which they promised us at the market rate. The beginning of the year, when it was time to send to market for hemp in the course we had for two years done with good success, by sending our money under the care of Sir W. Rider, Capt. Cocke and Mr Cutler – the Eastland merchants did by private applications to

Sir G. Carteret and others and myself, desire we would not take their trade out of their hands, to which they were bred. That our money coming to market did raise the price to them, and us too, for when a King's ship comes all the world knows she must be loaden, and so they raise the price of their commodity. That they doubt not but to bring the King as good a supply and better cheap than these men can do it. So having good stores, all our houses full almost, we were willing to gratify the Company (the D. of York first giving us his consent) with trusting to them one year, upon their promise that the King should not want hemp, for they would bring in as much, and that they would tender the King it at the market price, without imposing on him, and they doubted not but the price would be cheaper than yet it had come to us – which that year was under 42*l.* per ton.

About August we bought two or three parcels of Riga and Quinsborough hemp of their own seeking, without our request, of Mr Knip and Upton at 42*l.* 10*s.* and 41*l.* 10*s.*

The looks of the Dutch war coming in our view, we thought fit to demand of the Company their supply promised, and so brought to them in September. They came to us and offered what they had, but not at the price we had bought, saying that they that had sold it so[1] they doubted might be breaking men that sold that for want of money and the like, and that they were not bound to their price. So with some angry words we parted and heard nothing of them more.

In October I moved that they might be written once more to – which was done; and being positively demanded their price and quantity, Sir R. Chiverton and Mr Harrington appeared and offered us 120 tons of theirs, saying there was more in the town, and demanded 45*l.* per ton, nor a farthing would abate. We were very high with them, Mr Coventry particularly – alleging their promise to take the market price, which we had and now offered them. They first denied that that was or that there could be any such thing as a market price in nature, every man buying for his own price. And then that for some time past (which was Nov. 1. (64)) they did sell in the market for 44*s.* 6*d.* [per cwt] and 45*s.* now, and less they would not take. So, very angry, we parted, offering them 43*s.* and 44*s.* But to no purpose.

I had however order given me by the Board to contract with them in their absence at their own price if they would not abate.

[1]That is, at that price.

This day, Nov. 4, I met them upon the Change and did tell them our minds, of giving them their price – which Mr Harrington for the rest took. But Lord, with what delays, and he must have this and that ready money, and delivered in this place, and a deal of "We must have this and we must have that" – which went against my stomach, but I was fain to promise all, and so we agreed.

By and by, meeting with Mr Stapely the ropemaker, I talked with him about cordage: he asked me 42*l*. a ton. And among other reasons, "Thus," says he, "Quinsborough hemp is now come to 43*l*." I asked him whether he had paid so: he told me no, he had bought some a month since at 41*l*.; but now he is asked 43*l*. After I had given him hopes of selling us some cordage, I inquired further, and he told me that he was offered on Monday last (four days ago) but 43*l*. and believed that he might have it today – and is sure of it, unless our giving so much to some hath raised it all over to others – which he told me he feared might do it; but if that doth not do it, he is sure to buy some so. So here is the fair usage we have of these merchants, to be lorded over by them at their own price.

Nov. 10. 1664. This day came Ald. Barker and sold us about 100 tons of hemp more, at 45*l*. – obliging himself to let us have all [the] Riga hemp he hath with it – at the same price. Which minds me that Cheverton and Harrington did argue for the justness of their price, saying that how all that should have come to Riga did this year come to Quinsborough and so it is as good [as] and the same with the Riga. And that themselves would afford the Riga as cheap, but that they had none; but whatever they have, they do now offer us a tender of it, and will hereafter. And yet I must observe that Sir W. Batten did tell me that he is informed since that they have Riga, and had then in their hands, and do keep it [in] expectation of getting in a little time 50*l*. for it, and that Mr Gould told him so.

Nov. 8. 1664. About Sir W. Batten's carriage and cunning in the management of his son Castle's bargain of knees. It is observable this day (Mr Coventry being gone out of the office but a quarter of an hour) that Sir W.B. did order his son Castle to come in, my Lord Barkely only and myself being there) and offered his knees (which indeed are well squared, but not in that proportion) and got (by saying himself that they were worth 4*l*.

10*s*.) my Lord B. to offer 4*l*. 12*s*. at the first order; which was too late for me to recall or remedy but by stopping my Lord to offer more, which I did.

Nov. 10. And his abusing of Sir W. Warren's. And yet could not hinder Sir W.B. this day, being alone with me in the office, to offer his son 2*s*. more. But he will not take less than 4*l*. 15*s*. and I know will get it at last – though at this time of dearth of work in the town, there is nobody can buy them of him but us.

Knavery of purveyors in Sir W. Warren's knees. But above all is observable, his cunning to raise an inquiry after some ill-looked knees at this very time of Sir W. W.'s, and in my conscience did get some bad ones to be brought thither on purpose, and now to make complaint of them, that by their being seen they might raise the value of his son's goods – and will have the fault laid upon Sir W.W., though the contract says he is to serve none but what our people mark, and his people will swear that these very knees were marked by the King's own purveyor[1] upon this contract, and all the remedy the purveyor [has] is to say that he never marked these, but that they are brought by Sir W.W. without their choice (which Sir W.W. will bring all his people to answer the contrary) and the timber-measurer, who now says they were not received into the yard, did when I was there lately inquiring and finding fault with them, say that he had measured and received them, but that they were first chosen by Mr Meres, and said that where the timber is very much too rough upon them, he did make abatement for it, which did satisfy me then.

Nov. 10. 1664. Sir W. Batten's knavish course in carrying on a contract that he hath a mind to. And particularly in some goods of Mr Wood's. He will when Sir J. Mennes or I alone are with him at the buying of any provisions that he hath a mind to buy, he will bid and then raise the price by great steps (as this day in some timber bought of on Monday), as by 2 or 3*s*. in a load, without any reason or consideration of ours, or whether we agree, and so impose upon us the denying to consent to what he so openly offers at the Board. And thus he did the other day on Tuesday last with Mr Wood, when I said I would give no more, he would give more and offered it. And when at last I told him that I would not give a farthing more, Wood went away; and

---

[1] Robert Mayers (Meres), timber purveyor, Woolwich.

being gone, he told me that we should lose this bargain, it being of Dram timber – and some deals and pieces of fire timber[1] of 10 ft in a piece (which he would never have heard of of any other man's), and that it being at Harwich it were good to have them: when I told him there was no necessity, for at the very time we had a whole and greater ship's loading of the same goods and better, and masts unlading of Sir W. Warren's there. Yet he told me he would not lose it, and by God would send to him that we would have it – when he knows that his ship was put in, being almost shipwrecked there, and if we had not the goods must have landed them and put them off there, for the ship was rendered highly uncapable of going to sea. This is so, and this he knows.

Novembr 16. 1664. Observed upon the charge in building the Royall Katharine, *begun May 1662 and ended Octob. 1664.*

Whereas the estimate of the carpentry and caulkery of the ship was given in and signed to by us. . . . 2250*l*.

I find by the book, as I have caused it to be kept, and as the clerk of the cheque hath by my desire cast it up and given it me under his hand – as follows –

Shipwrights employed in building her	5094	
Shipwrights employed in laying ways &c. for the launching of her	0300	5520*l.*
Caulkers	0126	

vide no. 7. [*blank*]
vide no. 8. He reports it 1200*l*. less. *Q*. the reason of it?
          Dec. 23. 1664 – having since spoke with him he tells me that the first he made only by estimate and the latter by exact computation from the book.
vide no. 9. An abstract of the provisions expended in the new ship.

---

[1]Timber used for fuel, e.g. in ships' galleys.

Nov. 17. 1664. Computation by Mr Chr. Pett and Mr Shish of the charge per ton of building a 2nd-, 3rd-, 4th-rate ship and a ketch.

Rate	l. s. d.	
2 ...... at	11. 00. 00	
3	8. 10. 00	per ton.
4	7. 00. 00	
ketch ...	5. 00. 00	

Nov. 16. 1664. Considerable[1] in the circumstances of Sir W. Batten's opposing of Sir W. Warren's knees and complaining about bad knees of his in Deptford yard. It is to be remembered that in the beginning, when we were first thinking of contracting with Sir W. W. about his knees, we were mightily opposed by Sir W. B. that the knees of roots were not as good as those of the arms; nay, Mr Chr. Pett was got in word or writing to say the same. But being afterwards informed, we sent down to see them and found them so good as in Aug. 63, I to contract for 50 loads, reserving a power to ourselves, if we needed them, to have 50 more. These we had, and in July 64 contracted for 200 loads more, having a liberty given us to have our instruments to go and mark them, and none else to be brought down. These were all brought to Woolwich and the new 2nd-rate ship[2] almost wholly built with them, and Mr Pett commended them to me many times, saying they were worth 3*l.* 10*s.* per load between man and man,[3] and the better than they proved he never saw any, nor was any fault found with them all the time that Sir W. B. was in the yard during the whole time of their lying there while the ship was building.

Again, in Sept. 64 we contract for 100 loads more to be taken and marked by our own instrument, out of 1000 loads of timber – part of which was brought in at Deptford, being of the same timber with what was formerly, and marked by the same man that heretofore did it, who is no ordinary labourer (as Sir W. B. says) but an able shipwright, as Pett and others tell me, and hath been a master of the yard many years ago, and able to judge of timber as any man in England.

However, Sir W. B. finds bad ones in Deptford yard, and bad

---

[1]Matters worthy of consideration.
[2]The *Royal Katherine*.
[3]That is, on average.

they were indeed. But Sir W. W.'s instruments will swear that they are the very same that was marked by the King's officers. Now Sir W. B. would needs have somebody go thither after the Woolwich man had been there and marked them, and Meres should be the man, but not to go alone, though I urged [it] – which in my conscience[1] he would not suffer, because then he would be the sooner suspected, but I do verily believe that Meres (though Deane did go along with him for colour) did spitefully mark some of these on purpose at this time. For now, because Mr Castle hath a ship loading of Ribadeux knees come, and the better to put a gloss upon his (which indeed are good, or at least well hewed and well looked), these are found out – not before, nor any stir afterwards,[2] that we had contracted for Castle's.

Timber-measurer's knavery. But one thing is most strange – that being down at Deptford yard, I did take notice of them, thinking of nothing, and demanded the measurer what the contents of such a piece was; he told me so much, and that it was one of Sir W. W.'s knees, and showed me that he had measured it and measured it – telling me too (as also Sir J. M. had said a little before, that he had the answer given him by him) that he doth make abatement where the timber is not well hewed away. But now when this pursuit[3] comes, they all answer that they indeed did receive them, but it was upon a Sunday, only to keep them from being carried away in the River, and that they never intended to receive them.

We pay 4*l*. 15*s*. for Castle's knees, which is known cost him 3*l*. 8*s*. Now I am told that upon Comr Pett's seeing them the other day, he caused one of them to be hewed, and the grain of it did show that it was not among knees, but a forked piece which now appears a standard[4] – but with quarter of the strength that must break another this will be broke in the joint, it being not knit as standards are that grow in a natural knee.

Dec. 10. 1664. Corruption in the officers of the Elias *(lately lost) in charging all the clothes on the dead men.* Upon examin-

---

[1] Sc. upon my word.
[2] Sc. nor as the result of the disputes ('stir') caused by Batten's insisting on Castle's being awarded the contract.
[3] Inquiry.
[4] A straight piece.

ation of the account which Capt. Hill, James Coleman, master, and Henry Miller, boatswain, of the *Elias*, lately cast away in her coming home from New England (and they being the only surviving officers of the ship) did give of clothes issued during the voyage before the ship was lost – which account they did give in behalf of the slopseller – the number of men borne in their book being 119, whereof 21 were saved, 12 had been discharged and 86 were drowned. They do charge not one rag of clothes upon any of the saved or discharged men, none of them owning a farthing received of clothes,[1] and these officers confessing they could not disprove them; and yet of the drowned men they could charge clothes upon 56 of the 86 (the rest of them also, God knowing who they were, being cleared of clothes) to a very penny every man, some men twice or thrice as much as another. The whole amounting to 90*l*. 14*s*. 11*d*. And yet they themselves do to me confess that they had no rule either of papers, observation, memory or anything else to go by in this account, but only guess – which is the most ignorant piece of false dealing that ever I saw in all my life. And themselves afterwards did confess it, and desire the paper might be burned, for they confess their ignorance and that it was nothing else, for it could be no profit to them to make it so. But what they might have to do with the slopsellers in this is easy to think.[2]

Jan. 17. 1664[5]. I this day found out that by the confession of the captain, the purser who is drowned had laid out several of the slopseller's goods at New England, as is pretended, for provisions for the ship to the value of about 100*l*. and thereby it arises that they do not only frame an account (as above said) in behalf of the slopsellers, but have, as I hear, with the master and boatswain made out a certificate to the widow of the purser for her to be repaid for the provision, though they owe[3] the slopseller the money. And then again, this day the captain brings a bill signed by the master boatswain for about 80*l*. in provisions, laid out by himself for the ship's company. And so they help one another, these three officers that are alive.

---

[1] Slops were paid for by money docked from the seamen's wages.
[2] Pepys this day composed a three-page memorandum on this matter: PRO, SP 46/136, no. 239 (summary in *CSPD Add. 1660–85*, p. 119).
[3] Sc. it is they who owe.

Decembr 24 (64). Observable in the manner of the King's officers certifying upon bills for provisions. This day a bill of Mr Harbing's was brought to us and signed for [blank] ton of yarn at [blank] per ton – it being French yarn. And certified by Peter Russell, our master workman at Woolwich that it may be good for to serve as mooring cables, but not fit to go to sea.

Jan. 3. 1664[5]. Abuse in anchors. A letter of this day came from Capt. Jere. Smith of the *Mary* in the Rolling Grounds[1] says that her sheet anchor broke in the shank near the stock – it having not one inch of hold, all the rest being broken iron and beaten over to cover it. He keeps what is left to show us. And says that several captains in this fleet have been served in the same manner.

Jan. 15. 1664[5]. Col. Middleton about different pennyworths between ready money and buying on credit. This day I received a letter from Comr Middleton at Portsmouth,[2] wherein he shows the advantage of buying with ready money, and good use may be made of it.

Unthriftiness in cordage. And moreover, doth much complain of the extravagant demands made by commanders upon their coming in for new cordage, when he says he knows that they are not the worse for wearing, and such as he will be contented to ride in the Downs with in a storm of wind at S.S. East. But knows not how to do, but doth it, without taking the miscarriage of any ship for want thereof upon himself, which he desires not to do, but doth complain of the evil of it. We answered him, if I mistake not, the 17th at night – in a letter from the Board, which I may turn to. That the evil is great, but dangerous to remedy:[3] but for his guide, we advised him to make no such supplies without the opinion of the master attendant and clerk of the survey that the old cordage did need it.

---

[1]Off Aldeburgh. For the incident, see Smith to Coventry, 3 January, in *CSPD 1664–5*, p. 161.
[2]Ibid., p. 171.
[3]Accidents might follow if the cordage were in poor condition.

Jan. 18. 1664[5]. Col. Middleton about defect[s] in our shrouds. In a letter this day put up (no. 10)[1] he did give me in a large discourse the great evil we suffer by the bad making of our shrouds, and that that is it that causes so many spendings of masts as we have had of late. And since this letter, two, *New Yorke* and *Mary*, have through the same evil lost theirs, and he says the commanders of ships do much complain of them.

Cutting of cables for swabs and other mean uses. He observes moreover, in a letter to me of the 19th of Jan. 1664[5],[2] that cables which he judges are generally issued at 110 fathom long, are returned above 80 or 85 – the bosuns telling him that they are forced to cut them to make swabs, spun yarn and other necessaries. To this, he tells me that though he cannot discover this, yet were he commander of a ship, he believes he should make the bosun know sorrow that should cut a cable to make swabs of.

April 1664. Augustin *intended to save money by transporting of goods, is employed by Sir W.* Batten *on private scores; as in this case of Mr Wood's masts. Danger the King is in as to the return of goods lent.* Some times in a month the *Augustin* (a ship at great charge made from a great ship – a man-of-war before – into a vessel fit to carry masts and long provisions and kept at no small charge in constant pay)[3] was loaded to Portsmouth and in a great strait we were for the carrying of some hemp thither as much as we could, having not convenience at Woolwich to receive some that we had bought. And finding that the *Augustin* did not take in near the quantity that we expected, I went down to see the reason of it, and there I find four great masts of Mr Wood's, it should seem by a private order under Sir W.B.'s hand all to Capt. Teate (which he showed me) to receive them aboard and carry them to Portsmouth. They had been it seems (I mean the like of them) borrowed heretofore by some merchants, neighbours of ours at this office, and Mr Wood says to make others, and they do send them down. So here I find that not only the Surveyor hath it in his power to take or never take back goods lent, or to take what he will. But here he puts the King to the

---

[1] Dated 16th January: ibid., p. 172.
[2] PRO, SP 29/110, no. 93 (summary in *CSPD 1664–5*, pp. 173–4).
[3] She was a prize taken in the First Dutch War. In 1665 she was sunk for foundations at Harwich: Anderson, no. 193.

charge of hiring vessels afterwards to carry hemp down, while he in the meantime gives his word for filling the King's ships with merchants' goods, and for certain doth it not for nothing, but either the merchants pay him or Wood (which is the same thing) for their transportation.

I spoke to Mr Falconer to send me word what the masts took up stowage of hemp and he writes me word, 40 tons – though afterwards the storekeeper reports it less to me. Both their reports I keep in my Bundle no. 11.

Jan. 1664[5]. It did come in my head about this time to speak to Mr Andrews, the merchant for whom these masts were sent (in lieu of others formerly borrowed by him) and inquire what it was that he paid Mr Wood for the charge of those four masts for him to Portsmouth: he told me that he did give him 5*l*. – which, though it be but very little, yet it is too much for him to get by the use of the King's own ships, when at the same time and before and since we have been continually sending hemp to Portsmouth in hired ships at 20*s*. per ton, which therefore would have saved the King near 30*l*. at least. But no matter to get a private man 5*l*. if the King loses 30.

July 10. 1664. A balance of the expense of ordinary deals at Deptford for 2 years. It may not be unworth consideration what manner of balance it is that Mr Shish hath made and (by our order) sent us this day of the expense of ordinary deals for two years past – *vide* no. 12.

A general state [of] the naval stores March 1663/4, with a general demand for the following year – vide no. 13.

A general state of his Majesty's store of masts and its wants, in June 1664 – vide no. 14.

A state of cordage at Woolwich and our wants at Portsmouth, Nov. 1664 – vide no. 15.

Novembr 1663. An account of the storekeeper's issues to the Hill House[1] *between May 1660 and Octob. 1663 – vide* no. 16.

May 1664. A computation of the quantity and quality of canvas for a suit of sails for two ships of each rank, and for making a double suit of sails for the whole Navy – vide no. 17.

Salary and profits of the clerk of the ropeyard at Woolwich – vide no. 18.

[1] At Chatham.

June 1664. Mr Ackworth's proposal about the present ill method of the ropeyard – vide no. 19.

April 1664. Two instances of craft used in the persuading the Board to raise their prices for goods. Both in tar. Mr Hill and Mr Turner. Being now in view of a war with Holland, or at least of our necessity to provide against a war – among other things, we laid out for tar and bought a good quantity, as well as contracted with Sir W. Rider and Cutler for more in time. But on a sudden there comes Mr Turner of our office with a tender from Mr Hill of 80 or 100 lasts, saying that a private man unknown to him had come to him to buy it and he feared it was for the Hollanders, and that he sold it to his neighbours for 12*l*. – and demands of us 11*l*. for it. We being full of this (though we had given no such price before) did yield to his price – what we had given last (10*l*. 6*s*. 00*d*.) may be seen in my books, and what we bought after for also (it was 10*l*. 10*s*. 0*d*. or 10*l*. – which, I do not remember) – but if we did buy any cheaper afterward it was but little I think, having once raised the price. For this, *vide* no. 20.

Jan. 1664[5]. Mr Cutler's dealing with us about a great parcel of tar at a great price. Mr Cuttler the merchant brings word to Sir J. Mennes first, he coming first in his way, and then to me as a great secret, that he hath late advice that the tarhouse at Stockholme is burnt; and then goes to Sir G. Carteret and tells him the same – declaring upon the truth and the freshness of his relation. [This] doth all of us apart concern to desire him[1] that he will go up and down the town and buy up what tar he can for us, before the town hear of it. He readily seemed to embrace it, and comes the next day and tells us as a secret of great profit (and dexterity of his) that he had made sure for 200 lasts, but less than 12*l*. 10*s*. 00*d*. per last would not be taken. We desired him to get it as cheap as he would, and we would make good what he promised. He told us after another day's trial (as he seemed to take) that lower than 12*l*. 10*s*. 00*d*. he could not take for. The news was broke out, and that the merchant[2] would and did offer him money to release him of his promise, but that he doth hold him to it, vowing to God that he did it as for himself

---
[1] ? Sc. this led each of us in turn to desire him.
[2] The merchant who offered to sell at £12 10*s*.

only as our factor, and would willingly have the tar himself, and that he is sure the merchant would give 100*l.* to be released of the bargain.

Jan. 7. 1664[5]. He comes to me to desire that the contract might be drawn up. I did purposely demand what name he would have it in. He answered in Sir W. Rider's and his, for Mr Morisco, who is the merchant, would not deal with any but with them – not giving me any reason why Sir W. Rider's name should be put in, nor I demanding it, intending to let it go on as far as it would. So away he went, and I presently after drew up the contract.

Jan. 13. This day Sir W. Rider, who never appeared before, nor ever spoke to us or was spoke to by us in this business, comes with Cutler to sign the contract. But did not like my drawing of it, unless I would first, as to the time of payment, directly say that it should be paid so much by such a day, and so much by such a day, and that Sir G. Carteret would, before we had the tar, give them good assignments upon Backewell or Maynell for the money, and that one of them should undertake to the payment of the money at those days. And that the word 'precisely' should be added to the word 'payment'. And that they would be at no cost or charge at the delivery more than to bring it to the wharfside, and there we to fetch away at our charge. And that we should take 40 lasts of Wiburger tar to make up the 200 lasts. And lastly, that they would have it inserted in the contract that they should have each of them 2 per cent for their commission for getting of this done.

In compliance withal, which we were fain to make, the payments in the contract at those precise days, and though the word 'precisely' was not put into the contract, it was because before they did sign the contract, Sir G. Carteret had assured them their payment by Ald. Backwell or Maynell, I know not which. We were fain to promise to receive the tar at the wharf, and to take the 40 lasts of Wiburger, which everybody knows is above *xs.* per last worse than the Stockholme. And though I persuaded them not to stand upon having directly their commission named (it being no office day and I could not promise them anything certain), yet they would not sign unless I would make a memorandum on the contract that for their commission they would refer themselves to the Board, that so, say they, "we may have it remembered that we do expect and deserve some commission for it." And thus we were forced to come to their terms and take the tar as they would sell it us.

But it remains to be considered that the last price we paid for tar before this being not above x*l*. since we paid but [*blank*] and they promised 12*l*. x*s*. before, as Cutler says, it was known by the merchant that the tarhouse was burnt. Next – that he did not go over the town to inquire in many places, but only to Morisco, who it is very unlikely should not have the news of the burning of the house at Stockholme as soon as anybody, being the sole factor for the tar company there. Then – that presently after we had finished our contract for the tar, the news came that there was no such thing as a burning of the tarhouse at Stockholme. Add to this, that at the same time when with all these difficult circumstances, he led us to bid [for] this tar, saying that the merchant would give us 100*l*. to be excused, Mr Hill (who is no cheap man), upon my question on the charge, did offer me what he had (who buys all he hath of Morisco) at the same price when the news of the burning of the tarhouse was at the highest, and deliver at the King's yard without any particular difficulty as to payment, and without any consideration of commission or provision of any kind, but hath taken the price in full for all. And from that day to this (Jan. 27) hath again and again offered me it upon my demanding his price; but, hearing I doubt not of what we have given elsewhere, will not be got now to sell it lower.

Lastly, let me observe that Sir W. Rider and Cutler do expect commission, notwithstanding they say that Morisco (besides that he is unwilling to deal with any of them) will not take any security for his goods but Backwell's and Maynell's, so that these gentlemen demand 2 per cent apiece in a business wherein they are at no disburse of money nor use of their credit, nor any personal labour in seeing the goods weighed or carried down to the King's yard, or anything but barely that one of them may have spoken to Morisco and got him to sell it us much dearer than they would have done that buy it from Morisco to sell again.

Feb. 8. 1664[5]. Mr Stacy this night (to whom I had committed the learning of something out concerning this business) doth assure me that at the same time, so soon as the talk was of the tarhouse at Stockholm being burned, he did go to Mr Morisco, who not only had no news of it, nor did then or ever believe it, but he had letters at the very same time from Stockholme, wherein not one word was said of it. He offers to lay me ten to one that Morisco never said that he believed it, and that he had any news of it.

That he hath inquired about the prices that Cutler should pay for it, and he doth gather that he did pay a good deal above 11*l*. and it may be, he says, 12*l*. But doth not think that they paid 12*l*. 10*s*. – for he says he knows that of the same parcel of which we have part, out of the same ship, the *Sampson*, at the very same time, Morisco did sell some at 11*l*. And doth confess to me, upon my remembering it to him, that he did at the same time offer me upon the Change, and would have been willing and glad thereof, to have served me for 11*l*. 10*s*. per last. And believes with me that therefore it cannot be true that Morisco, who believed and knew this news to be false or very unlikely to be true, should, being paid so highly above the present price he then sold at to others, should offer us 100*l*. to be released of the bargain – he knowing that it was the only folly of Cutler that did give him reason to ask or expect more than 11*l*. He says he doth not hear that Sir W. Rider ever meddled with it or did appear in the business, but only Cutler – and yet Sir W. Rider, without any kind of reason, is brought in to demand commission. *Vide* [106].

Octobr 1664. An instance of our unadvised refusal or acceptance of a bargain tendered. I well remember that Mr Cutler did offer us a parcel of Flanders Rhine hemp at 38*s*. per cwt, which we then refused – which he hath since sworn he was ready to give as much for, and did offer it only as a service to us but had no thanks for his labour. Whereas the very same parcel being about 30 tons, we have agreed for with Capt. Cocke for 41*s*. per cwt and he himself pays but 37*s*. 06*d*. per cwt – which parcel of hemp we bought of Cocke Dec. 24. 1664.

An instance of abuse to King and subject in the levying of taxes as it is usually managed. To show how unequal the King's revenue is collected, I may instance in the business of the assessment upon office.[1] Where in London, by the report of Sir Rd Ford (whom I had had the good fortune to detect in one or two knaveries he was putting upon the Office),[2] who was one of the Commissioners of the City, the three Principal Officers of the

---

[1] By the terms of the Royal Aid (16 & 17 Car. II c. 1) passed in November 1664.

[2] He had supplied defective yarn: *Diary*, iii. 101–2, 102, 130, 136, 283. He had similarly over-assessed Pepys in the tax of 1662 levied for the relief of loyal and indigent officers: ibid., p. 283.

Navy living here in this office were thus rated – the inequality whereof, whether we were rated according to our old or new salaries,[1] will equally appear.

	Old salaries	New salary	Assessment
Comptroller	275*l*.	500*l*.	36*l*.
Surveyor	245*l*.	490*l*.	24*l*.
Clerk of the Acts	182*l*.	350*l*.	42*l*.

Wherein is seen that I am valued by my new salary (at 12 per cent, which was the declared rule)[2] while the others are valued by their old (though Sir R. Ford must needs know in his conscience that I was the meanest, both in estate and office, of the three); and which is more strange, Sir J. Mennes is rated at something above his old salary, and Sir W. Batten something below it – for:

$$12 = 100 \quad\quad 36 = 300$$
$$12 = 100 \quad\quad 24 = 200.$$

January 1664[5]. Merchants' price for masts to the mastmaker. I think it worth noting to see the difference (where shall be occasion of inquiring it) between the King's making or buying of masts and the merchants. For being at this time prising of merchants' ships for men of war, we have taken up the *Loyall Merchant* – which at present wants masts; and the captain of her, upon our demanding when they would be ready, he told us he could not well tell, but he had contracted with Mr Wood for a main[mast]:

              inch
Mainmast ... 26 ⎫
Foremast ... 23½ ⎬ for 150*l*. – only he gives him the old masts,
Boltsprit .... 23 ⎭ valued at 40 or 50*l*.

The ship, he says, measures about 600 tons or upwards.

---

[1] Salaries had been raised at the Restoration.
[2] This would make the assessment £36, which is the figure Pepys in fact gives in a letter of October 1665 to Carteret: *Shorthand Letters*, p. 68. He was assessed at £42 (the figure given in the text) under the 1662 tax: *Diary*, iii. 283.

January 1664[5]. Question touching ballast. It is a thing I believe worthy inquiry whether we are not liable to great abuse in the business of the price or, which is more, of the quantity of ballast we pay for – it being nobody's care for aught I can see to see what we have for our money – unless the lighterman, who gets so much the more by howsomuch he overvalues the quantity in transportation.

Jan. 28. 1664[5]. An instance of the various abuses discovered in a bargain of knees of Mr Castle's. For the better understanding of this business of Mr Castle's knees, I must look back to pages [91-2] and my letter to Mr Shish entered in my particular letter book Dec. 7. 1664.[1]

Jan. 21. Sir W. Batten's practice. Bills signed without consideration. Bills ill-certified. Now I must begin to observe the method used in the making out and getting the bill for these knees. Sir W. Batten, that hath not missed the Parliament one day before since their last coming together,[2] was at the office this Saturday morning (as he hath heretofore in jobs of Mr Wood's) to get signed the bill of his son Castle for his knees – Sir J. Mennes being sick in his chamber, and he sure that nobody could be here but myself and my Lord Bruncker. So the bill was brought and signed by himself and then my Lord Bruncker of course,[3] he being newly come in; and among other bills, it came to me, and minding not of it, I, among other bills, signed it of a sudden. But turning of a bill to see how it was certified, I found it was not said that they were according to contract, but only fit for his Majesty's service. So I put up the bill and this 24 Jan. wrote a letter to Mr Shish and Uthwayt, who signed the certificate (and which letter is in, entered in the same book)[4] that they should do it. And also to send me word the reason of their not taking the whole quantity, which though I knew already yet I would under their own hands have it – believing that I should find a

---

[1]NMM, LBK/8, p. 140 (not printed in *Further Corr.* or *Shorthand Letters*). Castle's contract (17 Nov. 1664) was for 80 loads of knees at £4 15s. per load: *CSPD 1664–5*, p. 136.
[2]The session had begun on 24 Nov. 1664.
[3]That is, as a matter of course.
[4]NMM, LBK/8, p. 149 (not printed in *Further Corr.* or *Shorthand Letters*).

great many more as fit (for the same reason) to be objected as they.

Contract not consulted. I observe the letter by Russell the purveyor, who brings me word this morning (Jan. 23), that he delivered it to Shish this morning, and Shish answered him that he never saw the contract, and thereupon called to Mr Harper and he did give it him to see. By and by comes Mr Castle into the yard, he thinks by chance, but I rather think it was from my having sent him word yesterday that I had returned his bill to be certified as it ought to be.

Castle comes by and by to the office and spoke with me about other business but took no notice in the world of that at all.

Defects in provision ambiguously certified. Anon comes an answer from them, telling me that they had nothing to do to certify the quality of the goods, but only the quantity and something also, to which I returned an answer, and had another from them the next day (both which are in my Bundle no. 21), which is worth reading over again and again to see how, though they do send back the bill with the words added that they agreed to the contract in all but the quantity, yet when they came by being so plainly urged to it to confess the fault of them, they will not say cross-grained, but that the grain runs too near the throat, which is not sense. A more palpable design of abusing us I think never can be expected to be discovered. I wrote the same night in a letter, among other business, to Comr Pett (to whom I had done the same once before, but could not get an answer) taking notice I had heard that he had made some observation upon Mr Castle's knees and of their cross-grainness.

Comr Pett's failure and worse. His ability rendered useless to the King. But now to see the wonder of a false man that hath no other merits to make him worthy employment but only his ability of shipbuilding, of which hitherto since the King's coming there hath been no use – (and which is worse now that we are going to contract for making of ships, he is going to make a ship himself for the King by contract,[1] and so we cannot have his help so much as in ordering of the contract to advantage, because, becoming a party, he is no more to be trusted than a stranger, which was the answer the other day of the whole Board when I proposed the sending to him Mr Castle's contract to be perused and corrected before finished); or if he hath anything else whereby he is

---

[1] No such ship has been traced.

eminently able to serve the King, it is his skill in the goodness and worth of provisions, and herein under his hand to me in answer about Mr Castle's knees, to his shame he says – that as to Mr Castle's knees, he had been too forward already, and therefore must be wiser and hold his peace. This letter is folded up with the other of Mr Shish's and Uthwayt's (no. 21).

Jan. 28. 1664[5]. The merchant's confession. This day, speaking with Mr Wayth about the business, he tells me that he hath lately had a great discourse with Mr Castle about them, begun by Mr Castle himself, and talking plainly of this crossness of grain. Castle answered that it is true they are so, but they do use them so in Spain, and if they were grown as we would have them, he would not have sold them under 15*l.* per load; and Mr Wayth says he thinks really, they would be worth 10*l.* per load, they are all so well hewn. And he says really, that he will, if not with his own force, with a little more, break some of the best of these.

Mystery in knees. And more, it is, he says, observable that whereas other knees, growing very seldom within square[1] naturally, men are forced to cut away part of their throats usually to render them so. These growing the other way are generally more within the square than is needful, and are many of them cut away within the top of each arm to make them less within square.

Memorandum. In my own defence, that though I have let the bill pass me at last, yet I did not do it (though on a sudden I had signed it) before they had wrote that they did answer contract in all but their quantity – which will justify me in the letting it go at last, being not then sufficiently enabled to prove their badness.

He that brought them, his name is Webber of Greenwich, of whom I will endeavour to know the real quantity that he brought, because of the difference between 80 loads Castle computed them at and 47 that are delivered – and whether it be likely that any of them are carried elsewhere.

Partiality in the King's officers. I have wrote a letter (Jan. 28)[2] with all the indifference I can to Mr Tippets to know his opinion of knees cut in that manner, and believe his answer will be taken as a very moderate report. But to see that Shish and Uthwayt, who in business of Sir W. Warren turn and chaw upon every

---

[1] Bent at an angle of less than 90°.
[2] NMM, LBK/8, pp. 150–1.

syllable to answer me in their first letter, as men that have proceeded to certify for the goods as far as the contract led them – had not (as Russell's report is) so much as seen it at that time when my first letter came to them.

I have since received an answer from Mr Tippets (Jan. 31) wherein one may see that he knows not what answer safely to give. Yet says that they are not so strong as knees that grow as they should do, and that indeed he would not use them as knees where others might be had.

But I have since discoursed with Lewsly of Chatham, who hath abundantly shown me in discourse how the practice is frequently in converting of timber, where there is the least compassing in the world, to hew away a very great part of the timber, which turns them to account to make so as to be sold for compass, though it be rendered so by having the grain cut away. And the like for knees also, where he hath seen knees forced out of almost a clump of straight timber, or at least having a little spur only at the root, and with cutting make it more a knee. But he hath this day (Febr. 27) given me a very good answer to this business of Castle's knees, I having given him a copy *mutatis mutandis* of my letter to Tippets – which is very plain and satisfactory.

Jan. 1664[5].
The Victualler's allowance of
extraordinary provisions[1] *to seamen in lieu*
of ordinary, viz.

Brandy	one gallon for 16 gallons } of beer.
Wine } Cider }	one gallon for 4 gallons
Flour	3lbs.
Fruit or Suet	0½lb. { in lieu of 4 lbs of beef or 2lbs of pork and a quart of pease. The like allowance for a sized fish.
Oatmeal	one gallon for a sized fish.
Oil	¾ lb. in lieu of a pound of butter or 2 lbs of cheese.pa
Rice	3 lbs for a sized fish.

[1] For the Mediterranean and Caribbean.

Jan. 1664[5]. Extraordinary rise of the price of masts. It was worth observing a tender come from Portsmouth, sent by Comr Middleton, of a few masts – the difference being so greatly risen above the price we are at present under contract with Sir W. Warren for. And yet lower than these prices will not be taken there. And in approbation thereof, the merchant hath got our purveyor to approve of them, and the approbation is writ by the storekeeper –

Masts	Hands	Demanded l. s. d.	Sir W. Warren's price	
3	14	6. 00. 00	4. 15. 00	
14	12	4. 10. 00	2. 08. 00	per mast.
30	10	2. 15. 00	1. 08. 00	

Jan. 30. 1664[5]. Profitable queries touching the expense of masts. From a letter this day from Mr Pett, builder at Chatham[1] (upon one from us demanding whether there were there any decayed masts to send to Harwich to make a floating stage), wherein he answers that there is none, all being, for want of fire timber, cut out the other day for the erecting the new ropehouse there – it may be fit inquiry whether a very great part of all our masts be not cut out into ordinary uses. And what is the difference between the price of masts and timber. And whether it were not fit to have an account kept of all the masts spent – for what use, for what ship, or what diameter rough and what it made wrought.

About Mr Cutler's dealing with us in a parcel of tar. Vide [97]. Further, I have to say in the business that upon Mr Stacy's information, I have inquired of Mr Prichard and received it under his hand, which I keep by me (no. 22), though he is ready at all times to testify it, that he did about the first of January buy 15 lasts of tar of Mr Morisco out of the ship *Sampson* which was not received of him till the 23d (during all which time we did treat with Cutler and brought to the price we paid), and that he paid 11l. per last, showing me Mr Morisco's servant's hand for the whole sum paid for the same.

[1] Phineas Pett.

Febr. 15, 16, 17. In all these times and two or three days before, Mr Ackeworth were here in town to look after the receipt of the tar, but none would be delivered by Morisco without present money. I sent to Cutler, who told me the same, but that Sir G. Carteret hath promised them payment presently, and then we shall have the tar. *Question*: what I may infer from hence.

But more, I am told the part of the tar we are to receive is very bad tar. But more of this when it is received.

Febr. 24. Ackeworth tells me that they would have had us have more Wibrough tar than the 40 lasts contracted for, and that the Stockeholme casks also, though the tar be good, yet are found to have more water than usual – four or five gallons. And at this day Morisco doth say he will not deliver any more than what he hath till he hath the rest of his money to the full value of his tar, he having I think received about 700*l.* before he parted with the first 100 lasts. So little service doth Cutler do us in it, either in his credit or pains, that he turns our officers to go and contend with Morisco about the goods when we have nothing to do with him but with Rider and Cutler.

Jan. 1664[5]. Price paid by the merchant for new masts made and set. Memorandum: that upon contracting with Capt. Risby for the *Loyall Merchant*, he told us she was ready, all but her masts, which Mr Wood hath undertaken to make for him in such a time, and to furnish him with single or other masts at these prices –

	Inch Diameter		
A mainmast	25½ or 26	at 75*l.*	
A foremast	24	at 54	per mast.
A boltsprit	24	at 32	
A mizenmast	[*blank*]	at 16	
		177	

Towards payment for which he was to receive his old masts (four years old) of the same dimensions at –

The old mainmast	10*l.*
foremast	8
boltsprit	5
	23

Febr. 15. 1664[5]. Of New England tar. This day at the Board, one Capt. Clerke, a New England man, came to treat about his ship lately come from thence, which we have now marked for the King's service. And inquiring of him touching the tar in New England, that there is of two sorts: *viz*.:

Of Plymouth, which is thick and bad. Will burn the rope and is usually boiled up to make stuff of for pitch and is sold for x*s*. the vessel, which holds about 16 or 18 gallons.

Of Kennedicutt,[1] which is thin and good, very clear, and generally used for ropes and sold for xx*s*. a barrel, which holds about half a hogshead.

Febr. 19. 1664[5]. Want of masts. By a letter of this date to me from Sir Wm Pen at Chatham, I find that at this time, before we have stroke one stroke with the Hollanders, they are forced to cut a 14-hand mast to make a foretopsail yard for the *Portland*, which is coming in there to have new masts – having lost hers the other day. The letter I keep, no. [*blank*].

Febr. 24. (64[5]). King's business not taken to heart by anybody as their own. This day I seriously set myself to consider how little the King's business is laid to heart by anybody, and it was occasioned to me from two observations. First, when any loss is of ships or the like. This nobody after a day or two considers it. I can instance in the *Elias*,[2] how sorry an inquiry was made into it, nay though the seamen upon oath did lay her loss to her being ill searched and caulked at Woolwich at her going out. But the very men that swore it before a Master in Chancery – all the ship's company – that that was the chief reason of the loss of the ship, when the very master came to speak before Mr Chr. Pett, nay Capt. Hill himself and the bosun, they did mince the matter very much. Nor were we ourselves at the table concerned in our inquiry at all, but did it as a thing that we cared not what or where the fault lay, and so the business is hushed up. The like I expect, and in part found, in the business of the *Nonesuch* and *Phoenix*, lately lost by negligence in the Straits in not keeping

[1]Connecticut.
[2]See above, pp. 92–3.

their reckoning and mistaking one side of the Straits for the other,[1] as most think.

Comr Middleton's observation upon the manner of the King's business being done. Then again, how often hath Comr Middleton wrote to me, and I wrote and spoke[2] for the getting of two or three galliot prizes full of rotten chestnuts to serve us to take out guns out of the ships coming in to clean. And though the thing is granted, yet it hath been now near two months demanded and hath cost the King three times their value, and of their cargo too, and yet nothing is done in it. Comr Middleton doth further plainly confirm me in his plain letters, telling me how different the husbandry he hath been bred to in his merchant's way is to what he finds practised in the King's service. And that he is cursed every day already for his taking notice of anything.

His advice about cordage, and the rigging of the King's ships. His complaints and advice touching our making and stoving of rigging in several letters from him about this time[3] are worth my looking over at leisure. Among other things, he tells us that nobody minds to employ what is best for this or that service, but that that first comes to hand; and further, that the badness of our cordage is the gains of the boatswain, for it sooner comes to his share, and therefore they will never complain. He instances in the *Yarmo.*, which upon the spending of her masts the other day hath not one bit of rigging saved which he looks upon as the most extravagant thing that ever he knew.

And in one of his late letters says he, 'Where the fault is [I] cannot tell; but this I will say, that I never yet saw any of the King's ships rigged either with running or standing rigging as they ought to be, and this I do give under my hand.' [*verte.*]

Decembr 1664. A further instance of King's business not being taken to heart by anybody. 500l. worth of hemp lost, by being damaged, yet not looked after. As a further instance that the King's

---

[1]They ran aground in the Bay of Gibraltar in heavy seas during the night of 1–2 December. Other ships in the squadron only narrowly escaped disaster. Allin, who commanded the squadron, wrote, 'Of so many ancient masters and officers never was such an oversight': *Journals*, i. 185.
[2]MS. 'spoke above'.
[3]*CSPD 1664–5*, pp. 188, 200, 204.

business is not taken to heart as men do what is their own – I must remember; which is this: a small vessel, the *Tho. & Margt Ketch* of Margett, Danll Jenkins master, was taken up for the carrying of hemp from London to Portsmouth[1] – 25 tons, which then newly cost us 45*l*. per ton was put on board him. In his way, through the leakiness of the vessel, the hemp is spoilt. Delivered at Chatham. Some of it good. Some so far spoiled and the charge so great in the drying it, that comes to 169*l*. And so much quite spoiled as comes to 360*l*., in all 529*l*. I wrote once or twice to Mr Comr Pett before he would give us any particular account of it. And then did by letter Jan. 2 and with it a certificate from the officers of the same day[2] concerning it. So it was his care, though I wrote to him about it, as not to consult what to do or dispose of this bad hemp or seek reparation of the fellow, but suffer him to go away with his vessel, so that at this day, Feb. 25. 1664[5], we cannot hear of him or his vessel to get reparation. And when he comes to town the other day, he was so far from complaining or stirring in it, that when I spoke of it, he endeavoured to excuse the fellow by saying he was poor, and we might undo one man but all he was worth would not pay it, the vessel not being his own.

Besides that, neither he nor the Surveyor neither, nor the Board in general, did ever from that day to this speak or do anything concerning it, but lets it die; only I have caused a protest to be drawn,[3] and do hope to get some reparation though little. But the thing is forgot by them, as much as if it had never been.

Febr. 1664[5]. Royall Charles *like to be lost at Portsmouth through carelessness, but no inquiry made after it.* The *Royall Charles*, going out of Portsmouth harbour (after being cleaned there) was by the confession of Comrs Pett and Middleton cast on shore and there forced to lie till the tide carried her off (and all by the negligence of the officers of the ship, as their letters,[4] among my office letters, show) to the great endangering of the ship. Yet nothing of this look[ed] after nor inquired into, because

---

[1] MS. 'Chatham'.
[2] MS. 'did'.
[3] The protest, made on 19 January before a notary public, stated that the ketch had been forced to discharge her cargo at Chatham because of leaks and that the hemp had been damaged to the value of £500: *CSPD Add. 1660–85*, p. 125.
[4] *CSPD 1664–5*, p. 210.

it happened that the ship received no present visible hurt. Which would have been a sad thing if it had, and the life of him that occasioned it not to be considered with the King's loss at this time. But all is nothing; nothing was said to it.

March 7. 1664[5]. London blown up. The *London*, coming about from Chatham into the Hope, manned with 350 or 400 men, was blown up about the Buoy of the Nore.[1] It is true there is little room left for inquiry after the manner of this miscarriage, but I do not find that (at this time of difficulty neither) any of us are concerned in the loss if it were our own, but as soon as the tale was told were as merry as ever – (Sir W. B., Sir J. M., Sir W. P., P. P.).

Febr. 23. 1664[5]. King's officers chosen by the merchant in cases against the King. Being to receive from the owners of the *Eagle*, a merchant to be hired into the King's service, the names of two[2] persons at Portsmouth (where the ship now is) to join with two on our behalf in the value of the said ship and apparel, in case she should be sunk or taken by an enemy – they chose Capt. Tinker our master attendant and Mr Eastwood our purveyor, the very men which I for my part had in my thoughts to propound to the Board to have appointed in behalf of the King, as the most proper officers the King hath about him. *Question*: what may be intended from hence.[3] *Vide* page [6] about the timber-measurer.

March 6. 1664[5]. Bad method of contracting to take merchants' goods when brought without obliging them to bring them. Question: some inconveniences there are plainly in it. But it is worth considering what more there is in our making contracts with persons at this great time of want by agreeing with persons what their goods shall come to, [or] give them what we did buy for last goods of the same quality. For by this means they are sure to have the best price, and are at liberty whether they bring any or not; or if they do, whether we shall have it or can tell

---

[1] Over 300 men were lost. The news came to the Board on the 8th and is given in the Diary entry for that day, but no mention is made there of any merriment.
[2] MS. 'what two'.
[3] In these cases Pepys smelt collusion between dockyard officers and merchants.

how to demand of them. But we can make no measure of our stores by this. For we can depend upon nothing certain, but are in a liability – if the war should cease – to be overburdened, because we are bound to take them off them when they come and offer them.

Instance in an agreement between Sir G. Carteret and Sir Wm Davidson. This is the case of a private contract between Sir G. Carteret and one Sir Wm Davidson for 500 lasts of tar and 100 lasts of pitch and 500 lasts of Russia hemp.[1]

And it is and hath been the like of other men. A copy of this contract is at hand – no. 24.

March 8. 1664[5]. Bad use made of bills of imprest. It is worth considering the manner of Comr Pett's arguing with me this day for the getting an allowance of his charges in frequent journeys coming up to the King's business and being formerly a while at Greenwich building a yacht (the *Katharine*), that what he demands for it will cost the King nothing – "for I have a sum of money lies out against me as an imprest against me; it will clear me and so take no money out of the King's purse" – as if the forbearing the receiving of what money is due to me be not as much in effect as giving of what I have in my purse. This use, I fear, is too often made of getting money upon imprest.

March 8. 1664[5]. Comr Pett ready to discover the faults of another but not his own. This day, in discourse with Comr Pett (lately come from Chatham), first I find him most ready to discover all that he could collect of any disorder in the yard – thereby to show his ability and care – when I well remember, and he knows I did publicly observe it to be him when Mr Coventry and I were at Chatham, which is the yard under his own eye – that it was impossible for any place to be more full of disorder than that. And even in many or most of those very things which he doth now complain of.

Ill manner of signing the storekeeper's books of issues. Two things more particularly it will be of use to remember – *viz.* that

---

[1]Davison was a Scottish merchant settled in Amsterdam. The contract was private in that it was made by commission.

he finds that it is true the shipwright there doth sign to the storekeeper's book of issues according to his warrants. But it is only at the end of every book that he doth it – all at once – when it is impossible for him to remember anything of what he signs to.

An ill account of the seeming orderliness in Portsmouth yard above others. Next – that it is true that master-shipwright Tippets and all the rest of the officers he will not say but that they are in themselves and in their places good officers (unless the storekeeper Johnson, who he says takes the greatest liberty of neglecting his business of the whole yard); but this he very well observes (and says he had several occasions of finding it so), that they have this principle among them, that none will find fault with his fellow-officer whatever fault he observes him to commit in his own places – "for", says he, "what have I to do with it?" And hence only it is that we hear of no more disorders nor clamours from the yard. And this I fear may be too true.

Boatswains' practices in abuse of cables. One thing more he tells me, that there is not a greater evil in the Navy than the custom boatswains make of cutting of their cables – few that go out 100 or 110 fathom coming home more than 70 or 80. And this arises from their pretence to a perquisite of the clench and splice,[1] by which they defend themselves in whatever they are found taking away. Whereas this ought not therefore to be a perquisite; or if it were, yet if the clerks of the survey did do their duty in calling the boatswains to a good account herein, it were not to be carried away so.

Dec. 15. 1664. Sir W. Batten's dealing in the great contract of timber made by Sir W. Warren and Mr Castle,[2] very remarkable. Vide *papers no. 25.*

March 4. 1664[5]. Sir J. Lawson's having 2000l. given him out of the seamen's groats which should have [been] spent on a

---

[1]The odd lengths left after clinching and splicing. Lengths of up to six fathoms were allowed as perquisites: A. P. McGowan (ed.), *The Jacobean Commissions of Enquiry of 1608 and 1618* (NRS 1971), p. 32.
[2]See above, p. 9 & n. 1.

minister.[1] Methinks it was not only a thing of very repute in general to Sir G. Carteret, Capt. Allen and others that have had the benefit of the groats that are taken from the seamen out of their pays for want of a minister and which therefore they ought to keep, that so they may not be punished both in soul and body by the negligence or wickedness of the captain. And that by this means it shall be the interest of the commanders of fleets or the admirals to neglect and discountenance ministers, because their profit will arise thereby by begging of the groats. But methinks for Sir John Lawson, so lately one of the greatest criers up of religion and zeal, and himself preaching and breeding up others to preach in the fleet, should now be begging of 2000*l*. to be paid out of the poor men's purse and at the charge of their souls, that is very strange – yet it is so.[2] *Vide* paper no. 26.

March 27. 1665. Col. Middleton's opinion of the miscarriages in the King's service. Comr Middleton doth very particularly and happily express the evils which the King's service suffers – saying that he wonders not anything is done amiss but that anything is done otherwise in the Navy. How the officers do their pains herein, and how the profit of some of them is the badness of the provisions served in, for as much as they decay, the sooner and the sooner become perquisites.

He is preparing observations and remedies thereto, and offers to save the King 20,000*l*. in the keeping of 40 ships eight months at sea. *Vide* no. 27.

April 6. 1665. Mr Wood's and Grey's practices offered for the putting off their parcel of old masts. Private contract of theirs about some masts worth observing. It is worth remembering how Mr Wood and Mr Gray after the failure of many of their tricks for two or three year together to get us to buy all their bad old masts, as by catching at opportunities of time when we needed. And then by buying a few new ones to put to them, and when we needed did offer the new ones, but not without buying all the old ones too. Then (sometimes in one of their names and some-

---

[1] Ships' chaplains were paid from a fund provided by deductions of 4*d*. in the pound from seamen's pay.

[2] The payment was authorised by the Board on 7 March: *CSPD Add. 1660–85*, p. 133.

times another, or both) by offering to sell us their old ones with abatement for what our officers should say they are worse than new ones, wherein they knew they could do what they would, for herein Sir J. Mennes and Sir W. Batten did concern and had like to have carried it, but I did by my care prevent it. Then by causing the old ones that were bad indeed to be new wrought over and the sappy rotten part to be cut over, but then they raised their price, so as to make them dearer than before and would have the rest go off with them so never offering to sell any part alone; and this was done in their tender Febr. 23. 1664[5] – which is by me, among my tenders, wherein they do not only ask their great price for the masts they have wrought over as I said before, but a third increase expressly of the price that we did last buy at of Sir W. Warren, and for which we have at this hour some hundreds to come. Their last trick was by Mr Gray, to bargain beforehand with Capt. Taylor, who was to bring some great masts from New England for us for all that he brought under our dimensions. By this means, still continuing as they have done with everybody, to engross all the masts in the River to themselves. And when now Taylor's masts are come, he suffers the little ones to be delivered into Chatham stores with the others, and then tells us they are his; and there being but twelve of them, doth offer them at such a price, provided we would take his other 200 masts, otherwise not. This is his practice,[1] and how I shall prevent the King's being so abused at this time of necessity I do not see, but I will do what I can. The contract between Taylor and him about these masts is worth observing, and a copy I have caused to be taken and is among my papers no. 28.

April 4. 1665. Comr Pett owns himself to seek about his dimensions of a 5th-rate ship. Being in great haste about the contracting for the building of ships – I wrote to Comr Pett for his opinion as to the dimensions of a 4th- and 5th-rate. He keeps it a great while in hand,[2] and returns me my copy of a 4th-rate that I have sent him of an old contract, with his opinion thereon. And afterward, I writing to him about the 5th-rate, he answers me in his letter, Apr. 4 – which is among my papers no. 29, that he is at a very great loss as to the determining the main dimen-

---

[1] Underhand scheme.
[2] He wrote on 26 March promising an answer: *CSPD 1664–5*, p. 274.

sions of a 5th-rate ship – which is very strange. And though he promised me, however, his opinion by the next, he then instead of an answer sends me word that it will be fit to advise with the shipwrights who is to build them, and therefore he will come up to town on purpose. Which methinks is a strange thing, that such as he should at this time of day be to seek in this matter.

Apr. 15. 1665. Chr. Pett's discourse heretofore of the uselessness of an assistant turns to his inconvenience. It is observable that Chr. Pett, who, as Sir J. Mennes and Sir W. Batten doth affirm, now, and hath done it often heretofore, that there was no use of an assistant in Woolwich yard and that he could with his foreman do all himself, and that during the difference between him and Deane and while those two knights had also a spite to him – that Chr. Pett should write me a letter this day,[1] desiring an allowance of his assistant's pay to himself, for extraordinary pains in the little interval between Deane's going to Harwich and Fletcher's coming in, which was between the 15 Octob. and 7th January 1664[5]. Which Sir J. Mennes did, upon my acquainting the Board this day with his request, swear that now he saw that what Chr. Pett had so often said concerning Deane was in spite, and that it was a shame that he should make this demand, and so did Sir W. Batten also in express words.

April 25. 1665. Col. Middleton about an unreasonable demand of cordage for breechings. The *Madras*, a merchant ship hired by us into the service for a man of war, and being at Portsmouth, the Officers of the Ordnance did desire, and we did give leave, to have her supplied with some cordage for breechings etc. out of our stores, they having not sufficient there. Now, by a letter of this date from Col. Middleton, he writes me thus – 'You were pleased to order cordage for the *Madras*. 14 coils were demanded for breechings and tackles. It drives me into a passion. Answer was made me it was no more but what the Officers of the Ordnance allowed. I confess I am not to inquire into the business of the Officers of the Ordnance, but I made four serve instead of fourteen, and breechings of 4 inch serve instead of 5½. Nothing doth trouble me so much as to see these things and cannot

[1]*CSPD 1664–5*, p. 412.

remedy them. The *Eagle* (another merchant ship hired there also) had five coils of 4½ inch rope to make breechings for her guns, but they had them not from hence. Two should have served their turns. Because I have been a gunner. For if the King be not cheated of four of those six, I shall lose my mark.[1] Sure there might be a way found to be honest to the King as well as the merchant.' By Col. Middleton's letter to me of the 30 of April, he tells me that these great issues are command of the Officers of the Ordnance – and that the five coils are actually delivered to the *Eagle*.

In his letter to me of the 2 of May, he tells me more. That he demanded of the officer of the Ordnance at Portsmouth what order he had about cordage. 'He told me he had order for 2½ coils of rope for breechings, which I judge to be (if laid at the full length) 300 fathom of cordage. I begun to reckon with him the length of every gun and to give the allowance fit for every gun. And did make it appear to him that less than one coil by much would serve. For if I mistake not, 88 fathom will do the work. So take 88 from 300, and remains upon account credit to the gunner, 212 fathom. Do but trace this story, as indeed I judge it ought to be, and you will easily find how matters are ordered.' And the truth is, as in this, so in almost all other matters.

[In] his letter May 7th, he tells me that the gunner of the *Happy Edward* demanded and would have been allowed 280 fathom of rope for breechings, and he hath persuaded him to take but 50 fathom, which is not one fifth part of what he was allowed.

May 5. 1665. Reflections upon Mr Castle's building a ship by contract.[2] This day all of us, that is, my Lord Brunkard, Sir W. Batten, Sir J. Mennes, Comr Pett and myself, being down at Deptford, did visit the ship Mr Castle is building there. And my Lord Br. and Comr Pett do find much fault with the timber as to goodness, and then as to scantlings, that are not 8 inches, where by letter of the contract they ought to be 14, this they said to my face. However, by his relation to Sir W. Batten he stands to their teeth, and tells them that the timber is good – and better than some of that that is used in the King's own shipbuilding by

---

[1] Sc. I shall be badly mistaken.
[2] The *Defiance*, a 3rd-rate: *CSPD 1664–5*, pp. 165, 192.

Shish; and that for the bigness, it is big enough, whatever the contract says. Which, though it be true, another man would not be suffered to argue so boldly to us all – nor so shall he.

But to see that Sir W. B., who is Surveyor of the Navy and one so pressing to have the shipwrights consulted with in all our building of ships by the King's own shipwrights, and more than that, is got to be surveyor with Sir W. Rider for the City upon the new ship to be built by Taylor,[1] and intends now, since his own son Castle came in, to have a surveyor appointed to view the work, but let it go on till I thought of it; and yesterday got for the present Chr. Pett and his assistant to be ordered to survey it. But what that will do, whether good or hurt, I know not.

Apr. 29. 1665. Cheat in the weight of cordage made and weighed abroad. Among other abuses in our buying of cordage from abroad, made in other men's yards, one pretty one is this. That ordinary yards not being able to lay so great cables as the King's, we have been contented to have them lay the strands only in other yards, and then serve them in in strands and we lay them. For when we came to weigh the strands in the ropemaker's yard, they have weighed so much, and when these afterward have been laid into a cable, they have been found to lose of the weight – which must be by the ropemaker's cutting off of part of it after it hath been weighed, and our officers gone, or by his false weights, or some other fraud on one side. For instance, Baddicott the ropemaker was to serve us with some strands for 15 and 14½ inch cables –

	Cwt	Q.	L.	
Cable of 15 inch poiz...	50.	3.	5.	at his yard in strands
	47.	1.	14.	at the storehouse
Cable of 14½ inch	45.	1.	2.	at his yard in strands
	27.	2.	21.	at the storehouse

Memorandum: the bands were to be abated out of his weight at home. This was certified to us by Mr Harper, storekeeper at Deptford, under his hand, which is upon my file, no. 30.[2]

---

[1] The *Loyal London*, a 2nd-rate; launched 10 June 1666 at Deptford: Anderson, no. 367.

[2] PRO, SP 29/121, no. 27 (12 May); (summary in *CSPD 1665–6*, p. 362).

May 4. 1665. Proof of English hemp against French. Col. Middleton having bought some Dorsetshire hemp, which by his letter of the [*blank*] of the last month he commended mightily, I did desire him to make a trial of it against the French hemp. Which he hath done, and by a letter this day answers me thus –

'I have made trial of the English and French hemp. The English wasteth[1] 4 per cent, the French 10 per cent. In the labour of dressing, the English 5*d.* per cwt difference, the English less than the French. I caused two coils to be made, one of each; and to tell you the truth, all our weights here are not able to judge which is the better rope. I caused them to be laid without, that we might judge of them as they are without. One mound[2] we shall have tar yarn, then they shall be tarred to see how we may judge of them when tarred; and being tarred, shall send them to you to London that you may give your judgement of them.'

May 9th. He writes me word that he hath tried their taking of tar of two coils. The French weighed without 34 lbs; when tarred, 42 lbs. So it took 8 lbs. The English weighed without 32 lbs; when tarred, 37 lbs; so it took up but 5 lbs of tar.[3]

May 28. 1665. Comr Middleton in his letter to me this day tells me how he hath found out, and it is confessed by all the parties, that the boatswain of the *Eagle* did sell a hawser of 4½ inch for 4*l.* 10*s.*, which cost the King 12 or 15*l.* He sold it to a master of a ship that brought coals hither for Mr Gawden. His name Mark Cooke.

June 4. 1665. Sunday. Discourse with Mr Howell touching abuses in the management of the Treasury of the Navy as now ordered by Mr Fenn. This day, having sent for Mr Howell the turner, upon other business of making some brushes or scrubbers for the use of the fleet, by desire of Mr Coventry; and coming to discourse of the price of them, wherein I endeavoured to get them as cheap as I could, he told me, among other arguments, that it may be he might be forced to sell his bills, as others do every day nowadays, for 18*d.* per centum loss. Thence we fell

---

[1] In the spinning.
[2] Uncertain reading of shorthand.
[3] Earlier, in August 1663 Pepys had come to the conclusion that English hemp was better than any other variety except Riga: *Diary*, iv. 259 & n. 4.

into discourse of our payments of the Navy, and he told me that it will never be well till it comes to pass in the Navy as it is in the Office of the Ordnance since the late Commissioners, my Lord Berkely, Sir Jo. Duncum and Mr Chichly came in.[1] That every week an account of what money, upon every estimate, is received is brought in by the Treasurer and that persons that delivered goods upon that estimate, according to the date of his bill, is paid, whether he be there or no to look after it, for his name is set up and notice sent to him if he doth not come, so that ever since this method came in use, he says he never was at the paymaster's house or ever went to look or ask for his money. So that, though they may owe him upon some estimate or other 1000*l.* at this day, yet it is his satisfaction and others' that they shall be paid in course as soon as money doth come in and that they shall not be postponed at the will of the Treasurer or his clerk as heretofore and so is now in the Navy. Which, though it be not so applicable to the business of the Navy, because we have not such particular estimates for everything we do (and yet that might be ordered a little better than it is), yet we might order that every bill might be numbered, whether upon one estimate or other, and so paid in course – by which means we should not [only] have better cheap but people would be concerned to serve in their goods as fast as they can, which now they take a liberty of serving it in their own time and as their profit or loss over the market leads them, because they know that if they can but do this or that, and make this or that friend, they shall be paid as soon if they bring in the goods six months hence as they shall if they serve it in tomorrow, unless they use the same courses.[2]

From thence we were led to discourse of the profit that the goldsmiths make of the having of all bills paid by them, for when they have any money to pay the Treasurer, they do pay so much of it in bills. "But," he says, "do not think that all this profit can be thought to go to the goldsmith, because it is in the power of

---

[1]They were appointed in October 1664: H. C. Tomlinson, *Guns and Government* (1979), pp. 87, 223.

[2]New rules for the payment of bills in the Navy were issued in June and December 1665. Bills of over £20 were to be paid in course; if a portion of the goods contracted for was delivered, a bill was to be made out within four days: PRO, ADM 106/3520, ff. 26*r*, 27*r*; ADM 2/1733, ff. 230*v*–231*v*.

Jack Fenne[1] to ease him of these bills the next day, if he will; and then it is so much clearly and presently got, and there are many ways of J. Fenne's having of the same thing done elsewhere, to his own great profit, if the goldsmiths did not give him a sufficient satisfaction for this privilege."

Upon this subject, he did give me a very particular instance. Says, "About two year and half since, I was to hire a new house in Tower Street, and by agreement was about such a time to pay 600*l*. in, whereto that I might be sure of my money, I was resolved to make my way sure enough by letting Mr Fenn, the old man, know it, and told him that I was about such a time (which was four months beforehand) to pay 600*l*. and desired that he might have it in his mind that between this [time] and that he might be furnished with the money, for he rested upon it." [The] old man from time to time promised he should not want it. At last the time drew near, and he then went to Mr Fenn the father to put him in mind of it and desire the money. The old man answered, that indeed he had no money, nor could procure him any. At which Howell being much surprised, having let go other ways of providing himself, and the time being very near, pressed him very hard that he would not suffer him to be disappointed and disgraced in this business. Whereupon, says the old man, "All I can do is to tell you that Sir G. Carteret hath lately given Ald. Maynell an assignment upon the customs for 10,000*l*. with a liberty for to pay him the said 10,000*l*. in bills" (that is, Maynell hath a liberty of paying Sir G. C. the 10,000*l*. in bills). "Now," says he, "go to Ald. Maynell and show him your bills; and though," says he, "I do confess 2 per cent is too much, yet," says he, "better give that than lack your money: and that I believe he will take." Upon this, knowing it to be near as cheap as he could have had it of Fenn himself, he was pretty well satisfied, and went to Ald. Maynell, who demanded 15 per cent. And in a word, was fain for his necessity at last to give him after the rate of 10 per cent, paying him 60*l*. for his 600*l*. This he told me he had entered into his books for a memorial of the Navy payments to posterity, and is in every syllable true.

"But," says he, "there is something more than all this in it

---

[1]The paymaster to the Navy Treasurer. The goldsmiths bought contractors' unpaid bills at a discount, and then, when required to advance money to the Navy, passed them on to Fenn at a smaller discount. Fenn was eventually paid the face value of the bills from the Exchequer – hence his profit. Or meantime he would 'ease him[self]' by passing the bills on, again at a discount.

why I may think myself ill used in this business – for I had reason to expect kindness of Mr Fenn – and that upon this score. I and several others", meaning Mr Wood, Mr Harris the sailmaker, Mr Deane, and others, "were led by several invitations to build a ship for Mr Fenn's son, which was built at Portsmouth. Which we did do and paid for, and fitted her for sea. Myself a 16th and Mr Wood three 16ths, and others more or less. Nay, besides that, we put him into a stock to trade with, by raising 800*l*. every share, his 50*l*. and I among the rest, I mine. And after fourteen months' voyage, he came home and brought us, instead of profit, 27 dollars principal for our 800*l*." And he believes that for his voyage, which he hath made since, and is now newly come home, they shall every man of them lose 100*l*. They were led into this adventure by being promised by this young Fenn that they should in all their payments in the Navy have good usage when their bills came to his father's hand, and said that he was directed by his father to promise it them. And Howell tells me that at this time of demanding his 600*l*. he did put the old man in mind of it; but it did but displease him, and hath done since, when very lately he did speak of it; and instead of favour, hath [done] rather an injury to him and them.

I hereupon told him that perhaps heretofore payments might have reason to be worse, but that of late I did hope [neither] he nor others had reason to say any such thing. He told me that every day people are forced to sell their bills, and did give me an instance (and at my request, told me the name of the person, which was one Boke of Chatham, a blockmaker) of a man that lately came to town complaining that he could get no money and that he durst not go out of town without 40*l*. He came to Howell, and he directed [him] to Mr Fenn, and failing there, to Ald. Maynell, where he could not have a farthing under 2*s*. per librum[1] or 10 per cent. "Whereupon," says Howell, "knowing that he was a man that did earn his money with the sweat of his brows, and that honestly, I was resolved to furnish him, if I might do it without danger of suffering by it, and therefore asked him whether he would be contented to give him 18*d*. per pound." The man did thankfully accept of the offer, as that which was a great favour to him, and he did supply him with 40*l*. and did stop 3*l*. in hand for the loan thereof, and hath his bills in his hands, signed by the blockmaker. "This," he says, "is very likely in some

---
[1]MS. 'centum'.

few days." Running on in this disc ourse, I did observe that the paymaster doth require half per cent, which if the year's expense comes but to 1,200,000*l*. (whereas it is likely to be 1,600,000*l*.)[1] his profit will come to 6000*l*. for this year. "But," says he, "it is only the old man that contents himself with half per cent, for he indeed doth not demand or[2] defalk no more – and will be very angry if anybody discourses of more. But then," says he, "where[as] he deals for 1000*l*., he directs people to his son Jack for 50,000*l*., and there there is no taking of half per cent, for he that doth not give him 1 or generally 2 per cent shall never be welcome again, and at that rate this will come at least to 12,000*l*. for the year – besides what greater profit Mr Gawden is forced to give for all that he hath of him for his victualling; who is a man necessitated for [other] men,[3] and yet the most open-handed man in the world."

"And", says he, "to think that Sir George suffers Mr Fenn to go away with all this is against the judgement of all that I meet with, who reckon Sir G. Carteret a wise man, and know well enough that this is a place[4] to be disposed of to one or more of his sons, or may be employed by persons that would give him so much out of it per cent or per annum, that would maintain his family and money to spare, besides his own threepences."[5]

Our discourse ended in his informing me how much all people of state and fashion do condemn the dealing with us in the Navy, because they must come cap in hand to such a proud fellow as Jack Fenn, that will send the best man of them away with a curse, while he is sure no man dare open his mouth against him to Sir G. Carteret, for fear of being the worse dealt with by Fen, at least for the time to come, if not by Sir G. C. himself, whom all tradesmen do believe to be concerned in this practice of his paymaster.

---

[1] The Navy's method of accounting makes it difficult to give an accurate figure for running costs, but the higher figure is, as Pepys suggests, the more likely. See the calculations in Tanner (ed.), *Catalogue*, i. 100–1.
[2] MS. 'but'.
[3] Sc. Gauden is forced to allow young Fenn his 1% or 2% though he himself is under obligations to other creditors (e.g. the merchants who supply or transport his victuals) to whom he is more generous than Fenn is to him.
[4] The post of cashier to the Navy Treasurer.
[5] The Navy Treasurer's poundage (3*d*. in the pound) on all sums paid to him by the Exchequer.

June 2. 1665. Rundall's practice in making of estimates: particularly for a new pair of gates at Deptford. Mr Rundall, our house-carpenter at Deptford, did by order bring in an estimate of a pair of gates to be made at the new wall on the back side of Deptford yard, with a draft of it. And brought it to 55*l*. I sent this estimate to Mr Bodham, who sent it me back with Ellery's offer to do [the] very same thing for 43*l*. Thereupon, a while after inquiring very close upon Rundall whether he would not take less than 55*l*. considering that he is under the King's pay at the very time when he works by the great, as well as at any other time, and being very pressing with him, he told me yes, he would do it for 45*l*. – and lower he would not go.[1] But that was a good fall from 55 to 45. *Vide* no. 31.

June 25. 1665. Mathews the bricklayer and Mr Shish their practice in estimating the brick wall at Deptford. Being at Deptford, I observed the new brick wall in building round the back yard. And have this to remember upon it. That Mathews the bricklayer was directed with Mr Shish to bring in an estimate of the charge of building that wall; which they did under both their [hands] that it could not be done under 4*l*. 4*s*. 11*d*. per rod. Sir W. Batten afterwards meeting with our neighbour Norfolke, and inquiring of him, he did offer to do it at 3*l*. 10*s*. 00*d*. Whereupon we sent for Mathews up, and telling him of it, all he could say was that [he] could not well do it so, but rather than another should do it, he would do it so; and so doth at this day build it at that price.

Apr. 18. 1665. Boatswain of the Beare *abusing a cable. Effect of perquisite.* In a letter of this day to me from Comr Middleton, he writes thus: 'I have to advise you that at the coming in of the *Beare*, the bosun comes for a demand for a supply in the room of what was expended – among other things, a new cable of 15 inches. I ordered him to bring the old one on shore. It could not be come by was his answer. I did imagine what I found. A new cable must be had; the old one I was resolved to have. The bosun pleaded want of plates, mats, swabs, woods, and I know not what more. In fine, I commanded it to be brought on shore. And I am

---

[1]There are similar criticisms of Rundall in the Diary (iv. 284 & n.2).

ashamed to tell you how it came. In fine, eight or ten pieces of as good a cable as we can make, and being measured was 83 fathom. I presume the cable cost the King 120*l*. at least, and had it not been cut, it had not been 10*l*. worse for wearing. I have advised Mr Coventry the same by the same ship. Were no perquisites allowed, the cable had not been cut; but under that notion, you cannot imagine the mischief that is done. Until I see it I could not believe it.'

April 30. (65). Mr Coventry and Sir Wm Pen do in their letter this day[1] complain of our cables being made of different sorts of hemp and their bad wearing: no. 32.

July 25. 1665. Comr Middleton about the charge of all that is done in the King's yard above what the same thing is done for by private men. How little right the King hath from juries, especially where the King's officers are to be witnesses in the case. He says thus: 'But this I observe in these two vessels (namely, the two sloops now newly built there, one by the King at Portsmouth, the other at Emsworth[2] by the great), and I beg of you to mind it (for I have taken special notice of it – that this vessel built at Portsmouth shall cost the King full as much (I am apt to believe very much more) barely in the workmanship than the King payeth for the *Emsworth sloop* being wholly fitted. The *Emsworth* not having above five men at any time to work on her, and sometimes not above two or three, and was built in as little time or less than this hath or will be, and we have had seldom less than 10, 12, to 20 and 30 on this here; and from thence ariseth this, judge you. I am confident we can do as much as other men, but matters must be as they may. A greater experiment in point of labour cannot be, being both of one length and breadth, some difference in the depth, which is not considerable; and may this be amended and, shall it not be, I cannot help it.'

In the same letter: 'We have had at Winchester a gaol-delivery. Three [? prisoners][3] have lain there 18 months. The Grand Jury found the bill Ignoramus, albeit the King's goods found in the house, which was 5 cwt of white[4] yarn, stolen the day after it was

---
[1]They were with the Duke of York on the *Royal Charles* off the Dutch coast.
[2]The *Portsmouth* and the *Emsworth*. The latter was employed as a scout: *CSPD 1667*, p. 377.
[3]Word omitted.
[4]Untarred.

spun. Another was quitted, albeit the ropes found were some new, some of them, and by the master ropemaker affirmed to be laid by him not three months before stolen. But I thank God one was burnt in the hand, another whipped, and that was but for small faults. But the witness against him doth not belong to the King's yard; for the truth is, we that are the King's servants here are of so good nature one to another, that we are loath to hinder any poor man, albeit to cheat or steal, or what else it be, so-all[1] he is a poor man and he hath helped me to steal, and why should I be a witness against him? It will ruin his wife and children, which is an act of cruelty. Besides, he may do as much for me hereafter, or it may be can do it now; and according as I order him, so I may expect the like from him; for in faith, Sir, I believe we are all k[naves]. I pray God make us better, for I protest to God we are ashamed of nothing, of neither theft nor idleness; yet it is to be amended.'[2]

Janry 23. 1666[7]. Memorandum: that at the Board's attendance on his Royal Highness this day I reported to his Highness that the cost of the victuals remaining at Livorne in Mr Clutterbuck's hands[3] amounted to about 6125*l*., and that whereas Mr Clutterbuck had in his letter of the 18 of October 66 to Sir Wm Batten[4] offered but 8208 pieces-of-eight – (as appears by the letter itself resting in the office) – which would amount but to about 1946*l*., I, if it might be accepted, was ready to propose a person of credit who would give 3500*l*. for them in the condition Mr Clutterbuck then writ them to be. The person I forbore to name that so his Highness and the Board might be freer in their judgements, but it was Mr Gawden with whom I had industriously consulted therein, out of my observation of Sir Wm Batten and Sir Wm Penn's readiness to conclude Mr Clutterbuck's offer reasonable, whereas Mr Gawden very readily offered 3500*l*., and so as I concluded would be brought to more. To this proposition they with the whole Board then present had nothing to object but declared it a matter fit for them to entertain, and particularly Sir Wm Batten and Sir Wm Penn were directed by his Royal

---

[1] Nevertheless.
[2] At this point Pepys ceased to enter his memoranda in shorthand. The remainder of the book is entered by clerks in longhand from his dictation.
[3] Richard Clutterbuck was the Navy agent at Leghorn.
[4] PRO, SP 29/175, no. 46, esp. App. II (summary in *CSPD 1666–7*, p. 200).

Highness to consider of it, but especially Sir Wm Batten who then owned to the Duke what he had done at the Board of his inclination to have accepted of Clutterbuck's offer. At the next sitting of the Board I acquainted them with the person that propounded it – namely Mr Gawden – but nothing [was] done then in it.

Objections against Mr Wells' proposal of his having all his Majesty's old cordage above five inches and all bolt-ropes, and in lieu thereof to ease the King of all charge in port-rope, netting-rope, lashing line and black oakum.[1]

1. Many good ropes are made unserviceable by shot and may better fit other purposes to the saving of new, than to be delivered out thus to be wrought out.

2. 'Tis questionable whether he will work out any of the best, or not rather convert that to private use, and serve in only the worst.

3. The old cordage will doubly or trebly suffice making all twice-laid ropes needful, and the charge of working is no more than 3*l*. 10*s*. 0*d*. per ton.

4. This discommodity may ensue his employing of the King's marked cordage to private uses (which he shall think too good to new-lay) – that it will colour embezzlements.

5. The advantages of the present practice of working out ground tows in the King's own yards will be laid by, and this disposed of to less profit, when all the twice-laid ropes shall be supplied by another hand.

6. The King will be constrained to buy part of it again for boatswains and gunners.

7. Boatswains will hereby have a secure way offered them of selling him these twice-laid ropes again, and the King's new cordage suffer for it.

8. Some cables will not serve at sea and yet may be employed for moorings which Mr Wells will crave and possibly

---

[1]This memorandum appears to relate to a meeting held on 10 Jan. 1667 at which William Bodham, clerk of the ropeyard at Woolwich, and John Uthwayt, clerk of the survey at Deptford, criticised proposals made in 1666 by John Wells, who until 1663 was storekeeper at Deptford (*CSPD 1663–4*, p. 322). There is a page-long note on the subject dated 16 January in the office memorandum book: PRO, ADM 106/3520, f. 33*v*. Cf. also BL, Add. MSS 9316, ff. 50–79.

endeavour to debauch the King's officers in getting serviceable ropes cast[1] to augment his quantity.

9. The officers of the yards may save the proposer a considerable expense of twice-laid cordage by sparing his ware, and being profuse in spending the King's new.

10. The present way is safe, the King sure of good work, the charge known and certain.

A collection of loose notes which I had occasionally taken in shorthand (most of them within the time of the late war) containing matters for future reflection.

~Disturbances in having the men of one ship pressed away by others.[2] The trouble raised in the releasing of these, and other inconveniences attending it, amongst which the disappointment of having victuallers[3] stopped in the River for want of men, and of ships lying useless in the River while the fleet wants them. It was the effect of this disorder that cost the King 297*l.* in not taking out the *Society*'s guns in two months after she came in. *Vide* our letter to the Officers of the Ordnance Octob. 11. 66 and their answer of the 15th.[4] *Vide* also Mr Gauden's letter to me Dec. 3. 66 telling me how the Rear-Admiral of the White[5] had taken most and frightened the rest of the men from 13 victuallers then at the Swale:[6] so that there is not men on any victualler to bring their ship to the side of any of the King's ships which are now ready to victual and going out thence.

~The long lying of a merchant ship in freight by the dexterity of the owners on their part and the negligence of the King's officers on theirs upon pretence of a little beer or other provisions or stores left in her.

~Soldiers paid and not seamen.

~Fireships, victuallers, ammunition-ships lie idling at every place in the River for want of a constant officer and vessel to take account of them.

~*Aug. 23. 66.* Of all our 24 water ships and victuallers not one

---
[1]Included in the count.
[2]That is, to other ships.
[3]Victualling ships.
[4]The Ordnance Commissioners explained that they had lost workmen to the press gang: *CSPD 1666–7*, pp. 200–1.
[5]Kempthorne. For the letter, see ibid., p. 315.
[6]The channel between the Isle of Sheppey and the Kent shore.

(or not more if one) have been in the River this many weeks lying all loaden and we forced to take up colliers, and who we can get to carry victuals, who we cannot expect should make haste, but take their own time. Or else our victuallers keep out of the way, nobody being appointed to check them nor able to dispute whatsoever pretence they make for their stay. Would it not be best for all these hired ships, ketches and smacks to be taken up with condition for his Majesty to have the choice of their masters?

~Delays in pressing of men. This Office troubled with it and their business interrupted thereby; whether it were not fit for [it] to be put to the care of some one of this Board to keep a constant understanding of the dispatch made in the pressing of men and the determining in all cases, and writing of all applications touching that matter?

~*Septemb. 1666.* Comr Midleton in his letters at this time[1] largely inveigh[s] against commanders' ignorance and indifference in making and signing to boatswains' and other men's demands, and about their suffering sails to be put up now with holes as big as a man's head in them; that he could give great instances of their ignorance but thinks it unsafe.

~We never know what victuallers are doing.

~Pursers because not to be disturbed in the midst of their employments have their faults generally passed by till the occasion be over of correcting them. And the like of other officers.

~*Novemb. 10. 1666. Vide* a letter this day to Comr Pett about our being forced to press men for the manning 15 frigates newly come in, while there is I believe above 2300 men in pay and no ships abroad or going out presently but them, and particularly all the great ships newly come in and landing at Chatham, all the men in pay.

~*Novemb. 15. 1666. Vide* our letter of this day upon the failure of Trinity House about pilots for the Gottenburg fleet which is at last gone without one pilot recommended by them, having (as I think) if any at all not above two or three, and those strangers recommended by Sir William Warren.[2]

~Cask. The King gives Mr Gauden 26*s*. per ton – though it be

---

[1] See his letters of 16, 18 and 23 September summarised in *CSPD 1666–7*, pp. 131, 136, 159.

[2] There was a continuing shortage of pilots at this time: cf. *Naval Minutes*, pp. 23, 38.

old for ought we know when it goes out. It carries water down to the Nore perhaps and is there employed and brought back, and the King allowed by Mr Gauden but 14s. per ton for the same returned; then is the same, it may be, refitted in a week's time and the King have it and gives another 26s. *Quere*: whether this be not the case. Heretofore a storekeeper was appointed in each [yard][1] to receive all returned cask and provisions to sort, keep and dispose of them. Now D. Gauden alone receives, surveys, appraises them, and allows the King what he pleases, for so much of them as D. G. pleaseth to own his receipt of.

~Most of the victuallers employed this year have through the whole year's service been employed no further than the Nore, Ipswich, or Portsmouth to carry victuals to and again. *Quere*: whether D. G. should not do all this. Whereas he does not bring any account of anything he does of that kind in any ship of his own.

~As an instance of the imperfect passing of tickets, there were two soldiers (John Medcalf and Cuthbert Allin) petitioned, that having delivered into the Office their tickets and the same being lost they might have new ones made out. Mr Carkess[2] certifies with the petition (xb. 10. 1666) that no tickets for any such men had passed that Office. Upon the 15 the tickets formerly made out were found in our Office examined several weeks agone by Mr Whitfield and signed by me having been mislaid here for want of persons to call for them. Mr Hayter had put them up against they were inquired for. Upon this being observed, we called for Mr Carkesse who did this 15 day affirm again, that he had examined and could not find any entry of any such tickets passed their Office.

~Upon ships to be repaired in merchants' docks. The ships are brought into their docks and then surveyed by our master shipwrights or their assistants, without surveyors or anybody else overlooking them. At the same time and in the same manner the works to be done are appraised, which I observe ever more to come very near the merchant shipwrights' demand, nor anything in either done by the surveyors, nor anything towards the seeing either the full or well performing of their contract at last coming to agree with Castle and Johnson upon the report of Ch. Pett and Shish. Very few words were used but all instantly agreed.

---

[1] Blank in MS.
[2] James Carkesse, clerk in the Ticket Office.

But when afterwards Sir W. Batten who managed the whole business comes to treat with Boyce many faults are found and no agreements to be made without great abatement of his demand. It is true Sir W. B. does say that Boyce's demand doth more exceed Pett's and Shish's than the other. But who knows (since that is the only declared measure and the only visible one I could discover to be by him taken) how far the estimates of the two former were made by favour, beyond that of the third ?

~Selling of prize goods by the Prize Officers, while we have neither credit nor money to buy them for the King's own use, and this done notwithstanding our letters Janry 15. 1666[7], and another before to Sir G. Carteret and W. Coventry,[1] and the King's own command sent by me from Whitehall on the 16 to my Lord Ashley; who was mighty angry at it. And my Lord Ashly's note of my writing by his direction at the House of Lords to the Commissioners of Prizes at London, which I went and delivered at their Office to Capt. Kingdom for stopping the sale of the hemp, tar, timber, deals, spar[s] and knees. Sir W. Batten went by my desire on the 18 in the morning to my Lord Ashley, and was (as he told me afterwards) soundly schooled for his pains and the things sold.[2]

~Unruliness of captains in demanding whatever they please to be done to their ships as to supplies of stores or anything else, and without any reason or knowledge sometimes, as Comr Midleton has often complained to me (by his discourse when here in town as well as by letters), particularly of Capt. Obryan, about his anchors and cables which he would have changed, and I think something of like nature from Capt. Hubbard. And Mr Deane in his letter of the 25 of October 1666 says he had like to have been knocked in the head by a quarrel arising upon his refusal to do something on a ship which he judged unfit.

~Commanders and masters taking money to excuse men they press. *Vide* the case of Nathaniel Scave master of the *Sophia* put out of his place for so doing by the Duke of York's letter Janry 22d 1666[7].

~Much complaints of ships leaky at sea, and out of repair, even on ships newly sent out of the King's yards. This occasioned a letter of the Duke of York Janry 28. 1666[7] for us to inquire

[1]The letter to Coventry (on the 10th) asked him to stop the sale: NMM, LBK/8, p. 441.
[2]Cf. *Diary*, viii. 15–16, 20.

into it. Mr Shish says that it is an ordinary thing for captains to come in upon pretence of wants when they need it not. Sir Wm Batten, Sir Wm Penn and Shish (being at the table) do lay much fault upon the carpenters of ships that they do nothing for the keeping their ships so much as dry, which rots all and spoils the ships in little time. They observed too that the over-gunning of ships makes ships old too soon. *Vide* Comr Midleton's letter of the 5 of February 66[7] touching this point, and the other which the Duke of York in the same letter takes notice of: *viz.* the frequent wrongs done the King's ships by running on board one another. Which they do in vanity because one or t'other will not bear up: an evil the King suffers much hurt by. See Comr Midleton['s] answers were fully to both these. *Vide* also a letter from Comr Taylor on the same subject Feby 5 1666[7], lodged among my letters and papers of my White Book.

~Purveyors frequently lie long in town upon or under pretence of want of money. *Quere*: whether or not sometimes upon design – they being paid by the day (work or not) and upon less charge lying here than when abroad.

~*Janry 31. 1666[7]*. After long delays and letters and answers Comr Pett was this day at the Board and discoursed the matters in difference about Castle's and Johnson's ships, the *Warrspight* and *Defiance*,[1] and said that there was not a verier rag[2] in the Navy than that of Mr Castle's the *Defiance* for badness of timber, badness of scantlings, showing him where they fell short of contract. It was plain to me from what I observed that the setting of mean men to be surveyors of a ship in building for the King (especially where the builders are friends of the Board's) is to no purpose but a mere betraying the King's service. Comr Pett himself not adventuring to do more than whisper what his thoughts were about the bad performance of this ship, so that the King is on all sides deceived. He says that the *Defiance* has cost the King already above 150*l*. at Chatham in the shifting of her beams and other works on her quarter-deck and elsewhere and almost new making her coach. *Memorandum*: that since this day he did upon our demand by letter send us a particular certificate of several material things done short of contract in

---

[1] Both built by contract.
[2] 'Verier' is the comparative form of 'very'; 'rag' signifies anything badly made: *OED*.

scantlings, unreported by the first surveyor, and not valued by him in his report of the overwork.[1]

~*February 1666[7]*. Ships brought into docks (and particularly merchants' docks) to be repaired, while for want of money and by the ill usage of them we dare not discharge them being out of hopes of their coming into the service again. The men therefore are kept in victuals and wages on board, but having no place to dress their victuals in, nor fire, they tore down the carved works and whatever else they can break, and who knows but the merchant builders encourage them to it to increase their work, where nobody can control him in what he shall think fit to value it at. Besides danger of fire to the King's ships and other great unruliness.

~*Febry 5. 1666[7]*. The captain of the *Swallow* comes to us to tell us that his ship had now all her victuals and stores on board with about 150 men on board but he cannot go to sea for want of glass and brick and plumbers' work for the furnace.[2] And this is the case of several other ships. A little while since the *Convertine* went away without her furnaces neither being able to have it done here, nor from Chatham, as we desired he should when he fell down, but was forced to get it afterwards done at Dover.

~We have been forced to pay our smiths with Swedes' iron for want of money, taking the opportunity of the iron brought by Sir Wm Warren in his Majesty's ships; tell by letter Febry 2d 1666[7].

~Comr Taylor complains that 19 of 20 bolts are broke in the driving into the new ship building by Mr Deane.[3] And everywhere else the like complained of in good reason to suspect it.

~*Febry 19. 1666[7]*. Mr Upton and Doggett offered us 100 tons of Riga and Quinsborough hemp at 50s. on the Poll Bill[4] or 56s. on the first three months of the Eleven Months Tax last given.[5] The next day we laid it before the Duke of York at our public attendance on him, Sir George Carterett being present. The Duke of York did direct us to give the 56s. on the tax rather than 50 on the Poll Bill which is already charged. The merchants came to us the 21 and broke off notwithstanding our offering these

[1] Superstructure.
[2] The captain, Bernard Ludman, was still in the Hope, and still complaining, on the 15th: *CSPD 1666–7*, p. 518.
[3] The *Resolution*, a 3rd-rate.
[4] 18 & 19 Car. II c. 1, passed 18 Jan. 1667.
[5] 18 & 19 Car. II c. 13, passed 8 February ('last given' in the sense of lately given). This was not to come into operation until the following January: hence the higher price charged by the merchants.

terms, because we would not take their pass hemp off their hands together with their Rhine.

~*March 18. 1666[7]*. Capt. Perryman brought us an account (being sent down the River to that end) that several of the West India fleet are ready to sail but no pilot to be got, they complaining that the rewards are too small and not to be got paid when ordered, by which the whole design may be lost, we having present apprehensions that the enemy may get abroad and block up our River.[1]

~Capt. Perryman tells me that among other discouragements to seamen this is a very great one, that instead of able seamen, able to take upon them the charge of a ship upon the miscarriage of a master or mate's, commanders do make their own servants and trumpeters midshipmen, though at the beginning to encourage those able men to go with them they promise to give them the benefit of midshipmen's pay.

~*March 24. 1666[7]*. Sir John Harman in discourse this day with me observed that there is constant fraud amongst the colliers (this discourse was upon the great present difficulty of getting seamen to get out the West India ships out of the River though it be earlier in the year, few ships abroad and few to go out) that they get protections for the master and it may be five men and a boy, but do carry frequently away 16 or 20. Now to save the pressing away of their men in the River they use to put out some of their best men into Albrough, and there take them in again when they come back and thus whereas he was saying he hoped to get a supply of men out of the next coal fleet he recollected himself that he should meet with this defect therein.

~*March 26. 1667*. Comr Midleton: a letter tells us of his being fain to empty tar barrels to make fire to bream the ships with instead of broom, and for want of rosin to grave the ships with to pay them with pitch and for want of pitch for that purpose to boil up some of their tar.

~*April 16. 1667*. Comr Midleton's letter gives extraordinary instances of embezzlements and the dexterity of the thieves that rob us.

~*Febry 1666[7]*. Fit to be considered the liberty taken by commanders of beating their masters, whereof Sir Wm Penn did complain to the Board of Capt. Elliott's beating of his master,

---

[1] The Dutch invaded the Thames and the Medway in the following June.

and promised to give me the particulars thereof in order to a complaint to the Duke.

~*May 5. 1667*. Comr Midleton's letter tells us of ships staying in port there after made clean till they were foul again for want of money to pay men for the inviting[1] them to go abroad again. He tells us also of Silverster the smith his buying a stolen anchor for 12*l*. and serving it into the King's stores where it is now found. *Quere*: what he made the King pay for it.

~*May 7th 1667*. Comr Midleton gives us notice of some nails of the King's marks sold by the carpenter of the *Saphire*. He tells us that much of this arises from the carpenters neglecting their work at sea in confidence of having their ships' work done in harbour and so all the stores he can save is his own. By this means the King is cheated of his stores and put to the charge of more repairs and loss of service by the ships coming into and lying in port.

~*April 21. 1668*. Comr Midleton at the Board largely found fault with the over-ballasting of ships by taking in so much at first as buries her, and all through the vanity[2] or jolliness[3] of the masters for the keeping the ships stiff when they shall be lightened of their provisions, which he says might be remedied by their being enjoined to fill their beer casks with water as soon as emptied.

He complains also and so does Capt. Tincker in a letter from Portsmouth of this date[4] that a third of the hold is taken up in storeroom, by which his Majesty loses the convenience of having so much the more provisions carried to enable ships to continue abroad.

He does very much also enlarge upon the usefulness of Portsmouth harbour beyond any of the rest in the River, saying that he would have all the 3rd-rates and under brought in thither, being a place of much greater dispatch for ships coming in and going out.[5]

~*Memorandum: May 16. 1668*. That the agreement between the Board and Maj. Nicholls about weighing the wrecks in the

---

[1] Inducing.
[2] Foolishness.
[3] Presumption.
[4] PRO, SP 29/238, no. 173 (summary in *CSPD 1667–8*, p. 353).
[5] At this time Portsmouth was mainly a repair base and victualling station. Its development as a large-scale yard began with the French wars of the 1690s.

Medway[1] being signed by the said Nicholls and four of the Board[2] – *viz.* Lord Anglesey, Lord Brouncker, Sir John Mennes and Col. Midleton upon the 14 – but forborne to be signed by me to prevent its being fully passed without Sir Wm Penn's hand, partly from the importance of the contract, and partly from his being forward in the making of it, was this day sent several times from the Board to him to be signed upon pretence of indisposition was refused, till the major's importunity caused the Board to send it once more to him by John Wren,[3] who brought it back to me with this message from Sir Wm – that he would not sign it till I had first done it and thereby testified that it was according to the resolution of the Board, notwithstanding the hands of every one of the Board (saving Mr Tippett's now at Portsmouth and never present at the debate) were to it, and the same sent to Sir Wm Penn by his clerk by the joint directions of all the said members of the Board then sitting. Upon which I signed it (though far from having been forward in the promoting of this agreement as to have been several times reflected on at the public Board[4] by the major for being the only objector to it) and he thereupon did the like.

~*Memorandum*: as a further instance of Sir Wm Penn's industry to avoid signing to anything that notwithstanding his absence from the Board was on his own occasions (I meeting him abroad in the afternoon) yet at night he refused to sign things of ordinary natures though of importance because not present at the Board today, insomuch that I was forced to have some of them go only with Sir John Mennes's hand and my own and keep others till the next meeting that I could get more hands. *Viz.*:

1 – letters to his Royal Highness
2 – letters to Mr Wren
1 – Sir John Shaw
1 – Sir Wm Coventry.

---

[1] These were the wrecks of ships sunk in the Dutch raid of 1667. Nicolls undertook to clear the 14 which impeded navigation for £300 down and a further £100 on completion: P. G. Rogers, *The Dutch in the Medway* (Oxf. 1970), pp. 156–7; *CSPD 1667–8*, p. 401; *1668–9*, p. 406.

[2] That is, one short of a quorum.

[3] Presumably a clerk in the service of Matthew Wren, secretary to the Lord High Admiral. The relationship is unknown: Matthew was a cousin of the architect.

[4] A meeting attended by clerks and members of the public having business with the Board.

Orders

4 – to Sir Denis Gawden
1 – to the officers at Deptford.

~*Memorandum*: that he in like manner totally refused to sign any of them prepared upon the 19th for the same reason of his being absent at the Board.

~*Memorandum: July 25. (68)*. That of eleven letters and orders entered in the book this day and carried to Sir Wm Penn in the evening to sign, he signed but three of them, refusing to sign the rest and giving no reason for such his refusal, so that they went without his hand, notwithstanding that there was not one of them but was ordered expressly by the Board in the morning, himself being present, and two of them – *viz*. the letters to Capt. O'brian and to the officers of Chatham about Norwood's pretence for satisfaction for sand[1] – were of his own propounding.

~*Memorandum: 29 7ber 66*. The Board made very sensible of the inconveniences arising to the service by the same man being storekeeper of the King's yards and storekeeper to the Prize Officers, it being his interest in the latter to delay delivery of those prize goods we are in daily want of, which in his former capacity (without the latter) it would be his duty and interest to find out and press for. The instance given is that of Capt. Taylor at Harwich.

~*Memorandum: November 5. 1668*. The letters prepared this day being sent to Sir Wm Penn this night to sign, he returned them unsigned with this answer – that being not at the Board today he would not sign them, though one of them (*viz*. that to the Duke of Yorke about the state of the King's ships) he had been at several discourses at the Board about it, being a thing of great importance.

~*9ber 7. 1668*. That Sir Wm Penn spending the evening of the 4 inst. at the office assisted by Lord Brouncker, the Surveyor and myself in the examining of the demands of several pursers and allowing or disallowing the same, and among others those of several pursers belonging to Sir John Harman's fleet lately in the West Indies, Mr Hayter, after I was withdrawn, inquired of me whether I was satisfied that the King had right done him as to the present of provisions made by those[2] of New England to his

---

[1]John Norwood was a lighterman and ballast merchant: *CSPD 1666–7*, p. 509.
[2]Sc. the people (cf. below, p. 351 & n. 1).

Majesty for relief of his fleet there, and then in distress. Which hint I taking returned to the Board, asking Sir Wm Penn about it, who answered me that it was the first word that ever he heard of any such present made, and that therefore it could not be expected he should be able to charge any pursers therewith. I told him that I had not only heard the King and Duke speak of it, but that Sir John Harman also had by discourse acquainted the Board heretofore with it, which Lord Brouncker recollected also. But Sir Wm Penn continuing in his total ignorance of it, I propounded that Sir J. Harman might be presently writ to about it, which was done, and this 7 of 9ber Sir Wm Penn brought Sir John Harman to the Board, telling us that Sir J. Harman had delivered in an account six months since of the victuals by him distributed to the several pursers of his fleet in the West Indies. Upon which, I gently reminding Sir Wm Penn of his disowning the other night his having ever heard of these proceedings, he presently answered me with some concernment that the account was delivered to him only as an account of provisions bought by Sir John Harman. To which I replying that I could not believe but that there was some mistake in that, forasmuch as Sir John Harman could not be thought to bring that to account as bought which cost him nothing, Sir Wm Penn hastily answered that the account was delivered to him as of provisions only bought. But Sir John Harman presently stopped him, saying that he did deliver it distinctly in his account what was bought and what presented. Which having awakened Sir Wm Penn in this matter so as to put him upon doing the King right in it, I suffered the discourse to fall, urging it no farther to the unnecessary offence either of Sir Wm Pen or Sir J. Harman. But am thoroughly satisfied that to this hour the King had not been secured by Sir Wm Penn in having any fruits of the present, though I have no suspicion of its being designed to be brought to account as so much bought.

~9ber 7. 1668. It comes in my mind to set down my observing what little security the King hath in the referring of his matters to under-officers. Example: a bill of Sir Wm Warren's being lately to be filled for New England masts whereof some proved considerably shorter than they ought in proportion to their diameters.[1] It was thought fit to refer it to the master shipwright Mr

---

[1] The measuring of New England firs was difficult because of the irregularities of their trunks. Similar complaints were made about other consignments: see above, pp. 22–3, 36 & n. 2.

Shish, and Cadbury the mastmaker at Deptford, for them to report a fit abatement. Which they shortly returned to us by awarding an abatement of 13*l.*, which appearing to the Board a gross undervaluing, and they sending for Mr Shish to give an account of the measures of his abatement, he at the Board excused himself by laying it on the mastmaker, whose judgement he confessed he concurred with without examination, praying excuse and offering to do it better. Which he did against the next sitting, reporting it then at 56*l.*, at which, being much ashamed as well as troubled, I advised the Board to think of doing something that might show their resentment of this miscarriage, but the Board partly in a silent pity of the poor man and partly from their general indifference in all matters of this kind fell from this to other business, acquiescing in the bare correction of the former report and filling the bill accordingly. The bill bears date 9 9ber 1667 for 924*l.* 15. 5.

~*Augst 17th (65)*. Col. Middleton says he will undertake to do the King more work with 200 men than 3 or 400 now do for want of money and thereby food.[1] And in a late letter of the 1st inst.[2] he tells us that a fourth part of all the King's charge at Portsmouth might be saved and the work better done.

~*April 22d (65)*. Mr Lewis tells us the hindrances in sending down the beer – *viz.* the small haste the masters make in fitting their vessels to receive it. The unwillingness of some to hire hands to stow it. The neglect of others to go when loading. But the principal, either want of men to stow it or sail the ships, the watermen being generally unfit or unwilling to work, others doing it by fits only and refusing to lie on board, and then come on board again about 10 and 11 o'clock, others deserting the ship as by a list by him annexed.[3]

~*24 June 66*. Capt. Butler Barnes of the *Royall Charles* merchantman gives the Board an account of a general mutiny among his men in his absence,[4] some already got on shore, the rest resolving to do the like as they could get opportunity, beating the centuries[5]

---

[1]See his letter to Pepys of 17 August: PRO SP 29/129, no. 49 (summary in *CSPD 1664–5*, p. 522); a plea for the provision of board wages for workmen forced by the Plague to work away from home.
[2]Summary in *CSPD 1664–5*, p. 499.
[3]Lewis's letter makes it clear that the main difficulties arose from the workmen's fear of the press: *CSPD 1664–5*, p. 323.
[4]This was in a letter of this date to the Navy Board: *CSPD 1664–5*, p. 455.
[5]Sentries.

and threatening to kill the master. That upon his coming on board he hath reduced all to obedience.

~*Memorandum*: about this time the complaints are infinite of seamen's running away from the service, not only those we would bring into it but those already in it, by leaping overboard, and that though they have much pay due to them, and Maj. Halsey particularly gives me an account of this being done in Holmes's own ship. Daily stories are brought us also of outrages committed upon the persons employed in pressing seamen.

~It is to be wished that captains might be ordered to receive no pay before their officers account.

~The King's houses and ground in yards taken up for private uses.

~It were requisite that upon the death of an officer at sea, captains should be bound to take care to the remains of stores, books, papers, etc.

~Hired ships for transportation of goods lying long in loading and unloading. Of the former an instance Augst 16. 68 in the *James* of Southampton to carry hemp to Portsmouth from Woolwich, where she lay for lack of dispatch, till the demurrage came to above 60*l*., when the freight of what she carried arose but to 38*l*., and we forced at last to compound with him for the whole at above 65*l. Vide* the bill to the master Cotton and the letter of the officers at Woolwich dated 29 Augst (68).[1]

~River's lying long uncleared because not properly the work of any particular officer.

~Most of the Board's time taken up in impertinent talk, confused discourses upon different matters at the same time or petitions, applications, and debates relating to the particular officers of some of the Board which ought to be dispatched elsewhere.

~Repairing and building of ships by contract committed to very mean instruments to inspect without the care of the Board or Surveyor.

~The list of particulars remaining undone (daily provided by the Clerk of the Acts) never to this day 7ber 2d (68) overlooked or called for by the Board, and with difficulty time allowed to him sometimes to mention to them those that are most pressing, and that for the most part without time appointed for the finishing of those matters, or if appointed not kept to.

---

[1] For the letter, see *CSPD 1667–8*, p. 562. The dockyard officers disclaimed responsibility for the delay which had increased the charge for demurrage.

~Demands from the yards neither made the Surveyor's [responsibility] nor no man's else to see examined, judged, answered and dispatched. Instance in supplying Sir Tho. Allen's going to the Straits from Portsmouth Augst 68, which after being demanded by frequent letters for many weeks together and undertaken by the Surveyor to see sent both by sea and land, and asserted by him and his instruments to have been so, were sent neither one way nor other, or if sent never came to him, but was forced to go without them, being supplied with a flag of the *Soveraigne* much too big for the *Monmouth*.[1]

~It is not thought that ever any purser's account was compared with the Victualler's account to see whether the Victualler was not allowed more on this account than really the purser owns to be received in his. And for this account of the purser's we never see our warrants, and so the Victualler may trust him so far as he pleases, and then the purser breaks or never passes his account, and so the King loses it, and we do for the most part, I doubt, content ourselves with a receipt under the purser's hand though we know not the hand. Mr Gibson says that the Victualler has sometimes in kindness to a purser trusted him with the value of a month's or so much more victuals.[2]

The casting of provisions during the voyage prevents the indifferency of officers now used in most cases where they are called to certify to the King's wrong after they are out of his service, and so under no fear of losing their places, while we have time before and at the pay to examine all matters while the company is together.[3]

~*March 16. 1665[6]*. Notes on the Victualler's account now in passing. Comr Pett frequently orders victuals to caulkers etc. on occasions of careening, and the like to men to carry down ships to the Hope. [The] master [of the] *Harwich* hoy (Bond) has two clerk of the cheque's warrants produced by Mr Gawden for 4 men's victuals for 5 days, *viz.* from Septembr 1st to 5th 1664.

---

[1] The *Royal Sovereign* was a 1st-rate and the largest ship in the Navy; the *Monmouth* a 3rd-rate. Allin was forced 'to go to sea with rags': *CSPD 1668–9*, p. 536; cf. ibid., pp. 518, 520, 526. He sailed with four of his ships still short of provisions: *Journals*, ii. 34, 35.

[2] Gibson (himself once a purser) wrote a 12-point memorandum (undated) on the collusions practised between the Victualler and pursers: Bodl. Lib., Rawl. MSS A185, ff. 319–20. 'Victualler'/'victualler' usage explained in Glossary.

[3] Sc. if records were kept of the issue of provisions during the voyage, the pursers and other officers would not be so inaccurate as at present, and could be held to account before they left the service.

Quere: what may be the ill consequences and to whom of our allowing the Victualler victuals upon producing the clerk of the cheque's warrant without the purser's receipts.

~*November 1666. Quere*: how shall we know that a steward shall not be disowned by the purser – we accepting of the steward's hand in Mr Gawden's accounts?

~*Quere*: our warrants to the Victualler are not seen by us at the passing his accounts, but the purser's receipts alone are accepted for the Victualler's discharge.

~What may be the effects of that, he being the passer of the pursers' accounts – may not he for his profit by agreement with them deliver them what victuals he pleases beyond our orders and discharge them thereof again in what manner he thinks fit?

~*Quere*: about Mr Gawden's taking the care of giving us an account how the several victuallers[1] do dispose of their loadings which in his accounts he takes no notice of.

~Let us see whether none of these victuallers be of his own hiring.

~Do not our victuallers carry his victuals where he is obliged himself by contract to deliver them?

~*Quere*: how far is he to carry them?

~Are not the loadings of the victuallers of more worth than their freight, which as Mr Gawden owns is the only security the King has for their right deliveries – then ought they not to give security as pursers do?

~How does the King know that any victualler[2] comes to account and gives a good one?

~How do we know that Mr Gawden does duly charge the several pursers or others with the provisions each victualler brings certificates of the delivery thereof?

~How will the King be secured against this evil – *viz*. Mr Gawden is allowed for all provisions put on board victuallers. He hath also the passing of each victualler's account before the victualler's freight be paid him; this account of the victualler's is made up by his bringing certificates of the pursers to whom he delivers the victuals; these certificates are lodged in Mr Gawden's hands. *Quere*: how is the King secured against Mr Gawden's having allowance of us for those very certificates of the pursers (which he was once allowed for as delivered to the victualler) for he

[1]Victualling ships.
[2]Provision merchant.

may very easily demand the same and have it, being able to show how the purser discharges himself thereof.

~*Augst 31. (68)*. Ships found allowed victuals in D. Gauden's accounts passed, which we now are at a loss what ships they were.

~*Decembr 1st 68. Memorandum*: that the foul play, which I have at large set down in a distinct narrative thereof, lately observed by me in Sir Wm Penn and (by his means as I suppose) the Lord Brouncker's managing of Mr Clutterbuck's accounts lately before the Board[1] for his providing victuals for the King at Livorne, gives me occasion to set down what follows on another matter relating to Clutterbuck, *viz*.:

That Mr Hayter tells me that there was lately offered him by Pointer, Sir John Mennes's clerk, a bill signed by his master Sir Wm Penn for 296*l*. 0*s*. 4*d*., which he desired to have entered in my office. The bill Mr Hayter took from him and, without communicating to me his intent, kept it without entry till it was signed by more of the Board, upon his own doubtfulness that there was some contrivance in the thing, as he since upon my inquiry tells me.

This morning therefore at the Board he tenders it to the Lord Brouncker, who, being not acquainted it seems by Sir Wm Penn with it, asks the question at the Board whether they were satisfied with it. Whereupon he delivering it to me at my demand to see it, I forthwith applied myself to Sir Wm Penn, who presently answered that he was a stranger to it and he signed it only as being led thereto by Sir John Mennes's hand. To which presently turning myself to Sir John Mennes, Sir John says that he had not examined it otherwise than that he was made to believe – he knew not how – that it was a very fair thing, and looked upon Sir Wm Penn, who thereupon seeming to recollect himself said that he believed it was for the clearing him of a bill of imprest of that value which Mr Clutterbuck he was sure had given long ago an account of, they[2] having been only charged upon him for

---

[1] See above, pp. 126–7 & nn. The narrative referred to here has not been traced. According to the Diary, there had been 'a great deal of do' about this matter at the Board on 3 Nov. 1668 and Pepys was convinced that Penn, if not Brouncker, was 'a very knave'.
[2] The victuals.

the clearing of Mr Pett's account,[1] but said for further satisfaction that Mr Clutterbuck was ready at the door to inform us further in it. Who was called in, and Sir W. Pen was very quick in declaring his answer satisfactory and that the bill ought therefore to be presently passed, which I convinced the Board it was not so, and therefore respited it till the bill of imprest was examined and the matter understood, towards which it was most plain not one step had been yet made. Upon this Pointer and Cluterbuck were directed, by a letter to the Commissioners of Accounts their clerk, to take a copy of their imprest out of the Treasurer's Ledgers,[2] which was done and brought to the Board the 3d inst., who thereupon found that it was imprested to him in three several sums, one of which Sir W. Pen had now prepared himself, to show that the King had had right done him by alleging (how true I know not) that, it relating to victuals delivered to the *Bonadventure*, he had charged it on the purser of that ship to the value of 79. 14. 1, for which therefore a perfect bill was presently made to Mr Clutterbuck; though here I am to remember that Mr Gibson at the instant of his writing this tells me (what Sir Wm Penn omitted to take notice of) that the said purser is dead and no account passed, and so the King never the better for charging it on him. There was likewise another bill made and signed for 9*l*. 10. 0. upon account of postage of letters, journeys, etc., which Sir Wm Pen pressed and the Comptroller declared himself satisfied in.[3] For the remainder Sir W. Pen did also much urge that Mr Clutterbuck might not be delayed in the having a bill, though I showed and satisfied the Board that there was no preference for it but that of an account said to be lodged by Sir John Lawson in the hands of Minors, purser of the *Ann*, without the least appearance that ever the account was so much as approved on by Sir John Lawson, much less allowed or seen by this Board, so that till Minors were writ to, there could be no justification for our clearing Mr Clutterbuck of this sum. Which the Board was convinced in and accordingly ordered a stop to the making out of the bill, to the great dissatisfaction of Sir Wm

[1]John Pitt had been secretary and deputy-treasurer of Lawson's fleet in the Mediterranean, 1662–3.

[2]The Commissioners of Accounts (the Brooke House Commission), appointed to examine the Navy Board's expenditure on the late war, had in 1668 taken possession of many of the office papers.

[3]At this point Pepys mistakenly turned over two leaves, adding corrections in the margin on this page and three pages later. Here the pages have been printed in their correct order.

Penn, who (however just the business may in the end prove) is most palpably guilty of endeavouring the surreptitious obtaining of this 296*l*. 0*s*. 4*d*. to be allowed for Mr Clutterbuck without any true account given of the reason thereof, and endeavouring also to dissemble his own practice[1] therein or knowledge of it by fathering[2] it upon Sir John Mennes, whereas he has not only at all times taken a liberty of refusing to sign anything without better satisfaction than that of Sir J. M.'s single hand, but at this particular time professedly avoided to put his hand to the least thing relating to the victualling (because of his present partnership therein)[3] though to the gratifying of Mr Clutterbuck he has thought fit to do it in so studious a manner as hath been said.

Decembr 5th 68. This day discoursing with Mr Hayter (lately made purveyor of petty emptions in the room of Mr Turner advanced to the storekeeper's place at Deptford upon the death of Mr Harper) touching the extravagant prices hitherto paid for provisions and the prices which he informs me they may be had for ready money, which he lately in writing laid before me and I the like to the Board, as also touching the fraud his Majesty is liable to by the looseness of the terms wherein some of the settled contracts for these goods do run and particularly that of Mr Foley's for ironwork, in which for instance under the general word of 'London dovetails' (of which he tells me there are four sorts he is at liberty to serve with what proportion he pleases of the smallest though his price be calculated for all of the best, and we find he does send us in of all the sorts and without any regard had by the King's officers to the proportions of the one or the other). As also that of hinges of several sorts and other goods commonly bought and sold by pairs, which in this contract he is to have so much per dozen without distinguishing per dozen or dozen pair, and upon our examination it appears that [in] the ironmonger's bills they sometimes run with per pair and sometimes without. He tells me, and proved it by some examples which he brought me, that the King is not only abused in the price by from 30 to 100 per cent but that he suffers as much in their quality, his hatchets falling in pieces in three or four blows

[1] Trick.
[2] MS. 'favouring'.
[3] See below, p. 146 n.1.

etc., and that the King is so far from being righted in it by any survey of the goods when taken in, as that the officers did not only declare to him that it was impossible for them to do it, but upon his desiring to see several species of the goods in order to the sealing of patterns according to his letter to me of the 28 9ber 68 and mine to the Board and theirs to the Surveyor of the 1st inst., both young Harper who did the whole business of storekeeper in the life of his father (disabled by constant sickness) and Mr Turner, the present storekeeper, and the other persons under them attending the stores declare themselves ignorant which were the things meant by such and such names in the ironmonger's contract, but showing them the ironwork in general said that they thought that they must be such and such. By which we are led mainly to doubt that not only in the quality and price but even in the quantity also of the goods paid for his Majesty has lain wholly at the mercy of the merchant. Wherein I am confirmed by what Mr Turner the other day, upon his entrance into that employment told me, that upon several people's coming to him for bills for goods delivered in the time of his predecessor, he finds no book of entry kept, but only the merchant's notes, that come down with their goods, filed or lying loose up and down, out of which bills it seems used to be made, which how safe it can be thought to his Majesty, whose security rests upon the merchant's own notes and those liable to be shifted and changed at the pleasure of the storekeeper or his meanest instrument at the temptation of the merchant or his servants, it is high time to consider.

5 Decembr 68. That discoursing with my people today about Sir W. Penn's proceeding in the passing of pursers' accounts,[1] they tell me that he keeps a book of what he has saved his Majesty in this his office, which puts me in mind not only of what I have heard touching his discourses in company of his great savings for the King by his employment of what would otherwise have been lost, but of his giving his Royal Highness an account once in writing in the presence of the Board of what he had to that time saved the King, and his late reply to the Duke's reflec-

---

[1]Since January 1667 Penn had assisted the Comptroller in the victualling business. His failure to check the Comptroller's scrutiny of pursers' accounts was more than once criticized by the Board.

tions wherein he expressly says that he has saved the King above 18,000*l.*,[1] and also that he has frequently let fall that he expects other considerations for his pains than his bare salary; whereas it is most manifest that, as to the casting work, he leaves it wholly to his clerks and the Victualler,[2] and that for the business of allowance[3] there is not one made but what he craftily gets the Board to sign with him in, not only declaring industriously that he makes no allowance but by direction of the Board, but for more sureness prefaces his letter of the 30 of 9ber 68,[4] which design of his I have all along laboured to prevent him in by refusing to sign anything of the victualling till he has signed it, and declaring that I am guided thereto by his hand and the light he gives me, as also by the answer of the Board the 1st inst. to his said letter.

But here I would observe two things. First, his dealing with the Board, whom he would fain make sharers with him in the blame due to all mistakes in his work (as he more largely labours in his said letter), and yet challenges[5] to himself all the thanks and honour that shall be due to what shall happen to be well done. Secondly, his usage of the pursers, not only by an apparent slubbering over[6] and easy allowing of the accounts and giving easy access and dispatch to whom he pleases, and provoking the Board to the cutting off of others, and disown cutting off afterwards the allowances due to them after affidavits made by his own direction; which practice my Lord Brouncker and myself have ever cried out against as a thing unfit to make them swear to the justice of the whole and then arbitrarily to prevent them of the benefit thereof, which nevertheless he has asserted his practice of saying that he gave them enough (which seems to be the less fair, by how much[7] he is not only a judge in this case, but a party too by his pretence to a reward in proportion to the greatest of his savings), but also by his common pretence to the pursers whom he uses worst by telling them – as their friend – that he had with much difficulty prevailed with the Board to allow them this or that, when himself has been the greatest

---

[1] Penn to Duke of York, 11 Sept. 1668: printed in G. Penn, *Memorials* (1833), ii. 514–19 (see esp. pp. 518–19); copy in PL 2242, pp. 82–7.
[2] He admitted as much in his letter of 30 Nov. 1668: see below, n. 4.
[3] The allowance made to the Victualler.
[4] *CSPD 1668–9*, p. 81.
[5] Claims.
[6] Hurriedly dealing with.
[7] In that.

instrument in what they have been cut off. A dealing so suitable to his practice in other things as to be the less doubted in this that is thus reported of him touching pursers.

An account of some proceedings of the Board relating to the adjustment of matters with Sir Wm Warren for the freight of the Great Duke *of* Yorke *sent during the late war for masts for his Majesty from New England.*

December 4th 68. At the Board's meeting this day on this business my despair of ever seeing a good (if any) end of this account, while managed by Sir J. Mennes,[1] was so far confirmed as that I was forced to make it known privately at the Board to my Lord Brouncker by writing: *vide* my entry thereof in my Letter Book, with the grounds thereof and what followed it.[2]

The end of this meeting amounted to the pressing Sir J. Mennes expressly to bring in to the Board in writing a state of the case, what thereof he was satisfied in and what not. Which he did upon the 15 of xber 68, bringing it to the Board under his hand that which he called a state of the case, and delivered as the copy of what he had put into the Commissioners of Accounts and that which was the result of his whole inquiry.[3]

This the Board thought fit by their letter to Sir Wm Warren of the 15 of xber 68 to transmit to Sir Wm Warren, desiring his answer to what was there objected to his demand, signed by Br., J. M., W. P., T. M. and S. P. (*vide* the letter).

---

[1]Negotiations about this account (for the purchase and freight of 29 masts, plus charges for demurrage) had been going on for over a year, and Pepys had now concluded that the only solution was to have Mennes moved from the Comptrollership to a Commissionership at large, where he would be harmless. Brouncker agreed; so did Matthew Wren, the Duke's secretary, and so did the Duke himself, according to Pepys. But the Duke decided that it would be unwise to make the change when his own political enemies (Buckingham and his group) were pressing charges against him in the inquiries conducted by the Brooke House Commission. Warren's New England account was not settled until 1675.
[2]Pepys scribbled a draft and wrote the letter itself during the meeting, with the help of a tube held to his eyes: *Diary,* ix. 384. The letter is printed, with two accompanying memoranda of 4 and 11 December in *Further Corr.,* pp. 199–202, from his letter-book (NMM, LBK/8, pp. 549–52). In the letter he proposed that the Board should appeal to the Duke to take the whole matter out of Mennes's hands.
[3]PRO, SP 29/250, no. 124 (15 December; summary in *CSPD 1663–4,* p. 106), enclosing Warren's letter to the Navy Board (8 December). The latter (misdated 18 December) is in HMC, *Lindsey (Supp),* pp. 147–50.

xber 23d 68. Sir Wm Warren attends the Board with his answer to our letter signed by himself and entered in the book which he had formerly put into Sir J. Mennes's hands, containing a state of the case as he had drawn it up, with copies of the vouchers attending it.[1] I say at the end of this collection he had entered Sir J. M.'s said state, getting Mr Pointer, Sir John's clerk, to attest the truth of it, and in an opposite column set down his reply.

After the Board had observed to Sir Wm Warren that this entry of his answer in his own book, joined with other things of his own, could not be taken for a formal answer to them, and therefore desired that his answer might come to them in a distinct paper (which he promised), they proceeded to the comparing Sir J. M.'s and his notes. Wherein after much time spent in a loose discoursing this matter, some things found granted by Sir J. M. to the King's prejudice (as himself confessed and openly charged that same upon his being misled by his clerk Pointer, who asserted his having writ nothing but with his concurrence), and other difficulties met with, which (it appeared) were never taken notice of by Sir J. M., and lastly I showing the Board that not one original letter or order quoted by Sir W. Warren in the justifying of his demand (either of ours to him or his to us) had been ever examined by Sir J. Mennes, but both himself (and by him the Board) let to allow of the force of Sir W. Warren's allegations out of Sir W. Warren's own pretended copies. The Board began manifestly to discover[2] a universal despair of being ever able rightly to determine this account, till put into some other hand, and so with a seeming loss what to do in it seemed inclined to rise; which I took the opportunity of, for my going to the Exchange, leaving them in the office, and particularly my Lord Brouncker offering at a proposal of coming to a composition with Sir W. Warren, which I stayed so long as to declare my dislike of from the want of that light which should enable us to proceed with any judgement, and so went away.

The same evening going to my Lord Brouncker at his lodgings to discourse of some other matters before the Board, he told me (which I being abroad had not till then heard of) that he and the rest had met this afternoon and concluded upon a composition

---

[1] Bodl. Lib., Tanner MSS 44, ff. 64–5.
[2] Express.

with Sir W. W.[1] Which I being surprised at, and professing my total ignorance of the measures that could lead them to the doing it with any safety, and desiring to know whether it was with the advice of Sir J. Mennes; he told me that it was, and that as he believed it was a better bargain than ever could have been made of it by disputation while managed by Sir J. Mennes (who had granted more in his paper to the King's prejudice than all the benefit arising from his[2] inquiries would amount to), so it was to be put into writing by Sir J. Mennes and should be signed by him before himself should ever sign it, being (as he freely declared himself) very sensible how unsafe any man is even in doing well where so weak a man as Sir J. Mennes is concerned.

To which nothing being left needful to reply, I let fall the discourse, leaving the discharge of my further duty therein till it comes to be signed at the Board.

Janry 2d 68. Saturday. I observed that Sir W. Warren's bill upon this composition was brought to the table by Mr Pointer by whom it was drawn up, and that it was signed by my Lord Brouncker and after him (Sir John Mennes being absent) by Col. Midleton, who among other papers laying it before me I for the reasons above mentioned declined it as a thing I could say nothing to (for or against), and therefore without exception handed it over with others to Sir W. Pen, resolving to take notice of his proceedings therein. Who when he came to it looked upon it, and without making any observation or at least offering anything to the Board thereon in order to the doing the King right therein, he tacitly laid it with other papers then before Mr Tippetts, who without more ado signed it. And so at the end of our meeting it was without any discourse upon it carried to the several offices to be entered.

The meeting being over, I considered many ways how it was fit for me to proceed in this matter, having no more sufficient light whereby to find fault with it than I had to concur in the signing it. Besides that I had (as I thought) abundantly signified to my Lord Brouncker my opinion therein. And after thinking some time to offer my advice yet once more to his Lordship by writing, I was prevented by other business of leisure to do that,

---

[1] The composition was in the sum of £3430 14s. 10d. When the account was declared in the Exchequer in 1675 the Auditors reduced the allowance for demurrage by £1457 19s. 5d.: HMC, *Lindsey (Supp.)*, pp. 121–2.
[2] Brouncker's.

and therefore resolved before the bill was sent out of the office to find a time of making my mind known to my Lord by discourse. Which I did by finding him out at Court on Monday night January 14th, where among other discourses, I introduced the advising his Lordship to remember the caution I gave him lately and which he so readily owned the advisableness of, of having this bill of Sir W. Warren signed first by Sir J. Mennes, which I told him I observed he had forgot by signing it not only before but without Sir J. Mennes. He gave me thanks for my second advice therein and promised he would make use of it the next day, which he did, January 15th, by tendering it to Sir J. Mennes at the Board, who after many difficulties made therein, sometimes saying that he understood it not, sometimes that it was not necessary, sometimes that his queries were not answered, and lastly that if he did sign it (which he would do since it was desired of him) it should be because it was first signed by the Board. Here he beginning to sign it, I thought fit to stop him, telling him that before he signed it I desired him to observe I had not only not signed it, but that (whatever my Lord Brouncker and the rest did who were assisting as I thought at the concluding it) I had not been at all privy to it, so that I did not conceive myself fit to sign it, or if they did expect it of me, it must be only to signify my not being able to make any present objection to it, and that my signing should be in a professed reliance upon my seeing Sir J. Mennes's hand with the rest there before me. Here my Lord Brouncker answered that if I did sign it, he acknowledged it must be by implication only, as not having been consulted with in the doing it. But Sir J. Mennes upon my declaring that my insisting upon the force of his hand, he fell back from his intentions of signing it, and so continued going to other business till about two hours after, when of his own accord I observed him to sign it and lay it towards me. Which seeing, I took it up and as before delivered it to Sir W. Pen, who (as he had before silently refused it, though within two minutes after he found occasion of declaring to the Board his not scrupling to sign bills without examining them where he sees my Lord Brouncker's hand), so he now without any account given of it lays it tacitly by, and so it went away at the end of the meeting without any other hands than those four – *viz.*, Lord Brouncker, Sir J. Mennes, T. Middleton, J. Tippetts,[1] without so much as one original letter

[1] One short of a quorum.

examined on behalf of the King by the Comptroller or any else, though I have often declared the want and neglecting of it, and offered my assisting him with what letters on this subject he should think fit to call for.

January 9th. Mr Hayter came to me at the Board with this bill, telling me (which I had not understood before) that my Lord Brouncker had ordered him not to deliver out the bill [till] it had been signed by Sir W. Pen and myself, and, as Mr Hayter tells me since, it was carried to Sir W. Pen who refused to sign it, saying he would not till I had signed it. Upon the bill being thus put into my hand, I took the opportunity of the office's being at my desire on another occasion voided (*vide* page [170]) to observe to them (*viz.*, Lord Brouncker, Sir J. Mennes, Sir W. Pen, T. Middleton, J. Tippetts, the Treasurers not being then come in) first, that I was not privy to any part of the debate when the bill was concluded on, and therefore that my hand could not be by me judiciously set to it. Which my Lord Brouncker particularly and the Board in general owned, remembering well that only Br., J. M., T. M., J. T. were at the debate, but that it being a thing extraordinary they thought it necessary to desire its being full signed to denote no man's having any objection to make to it. To this I then in the second place showed them that though I could not apply any particular objection to the bill as it is drawn by them, yet I had my old objection to make, *viz.* that there had been no examination either of the accounts of the Board in their letters to Sir Wm Warren on this business or of Sir Wm Warren's to them. So that if they have founded their present composition on no other measures than what I ever yet see before them, *viz.* a state of the case drawn by Sir W. Warren made up of a collection of pretended letters between us and him with his inferences thereon and narrative of his proceedings, I told them that I could not apprehend with what strictness or safety they could proceed therein. To this they answered, that they took for granted Sir J. Mennes's having done that part of his work. Which I having asserted never to have been to my knowledge done, Sir J. Mennes with much earnestness averred and repeated it that he had by himself and instruments a great while since done it by calling for and employing his people at by-times to peruse his books. In which resolute assertion of his the Board acquiesced, and myself thought it becoming me to submit to it, and went on in the third place to observe to them that my Lord Brouncker particularly had the other day declared his signing of the bill upon Sir J. Mennes's being present at the debate and satisfied in the conclusion they came to thereon, and that he relied upon Sir J. Mennes's owning it as his account and an account which Sir J. M. also would look upon as his part to justify on behalf of the Board.

I observed too, that at the same time Sir J. Mennes was unwilling to own it as his account, saying expressly that if he signed it it should be as seeing it signed by three of the Board before him, *viz.* Br., T. M., J. T., and so led thereto by plurality of voices. That therefore I neither did then nor shall now think it fit for me to sign to that where not only the party that expressly stands charged with the seeing right done the King in it, but everybody else declines the owning it and justifying it on behalf either of the King or the Board. To this Br., T. M. and J. T. did declare that Sir J. M. was present and assisting and concurring at the whole debate and conclusion of this business, and that their signing it was in confidence of Sir J. M.'s owning it and justifying it. Which Sir J. M. for a great while showed himself wholly unwilling to acknowledge, but rather urging the contrary. Upon which the rest were mightily disturbed, and particularly my Lord Brouncker, who thought fit solemnly to protest against Sir J. Mennes's dealings with them, declaring his resolution from that time forward never to contribute his assistance to another man in the doing of his particular work, as he had now done in his kindness to Sir J. Mennes, unless Sir J. M. did him right in this case. To which my Lord and the other two reminding Sir J. M. of particular circumstances of his presence and assent in the finishing of this business, Sir J. M. did at last declare his owning it, and his part to justify it on behalf of the Board, and thereupon with the rest desired and insisted upon my signing of the bill. Upon which I, desiring that a memorandum might be entered of this declaration of Sir J. M.'s, and declaring that by my signing I would have no more understood than my not objecting anything to the matter of it, but submission to what the Comptroller and the Board had agreed upon therein, both which was expressly yielded both by Sir J. M. and the rest, I signed the bill, and thereupon with the like declaration touching the limitation of the force of his hand, Sir W. Penn did the like.

Memorandum: that some of my own clerks being within the hearing of this dispute (*vide* page[s 169–70]) are able to justify me in the substance of what is here set down, *viz.* Mr Hayter,

Gibson and Wm Hewers, as upon my asking them they afterwards told me.

The memorandum above mentioned entered in our Memorandum Book under the 9th of Janry 1668[9][1] runs in these words, *viz*.: that at the Board's tendering this day to Sir Wm Penn and Mr Pepys for their signing the bill lately granted to Sir Wm Warren for 3430*l*. 14*s*. 10*d*. for the freight of the ship *Great Duke of Yorke* due to him upon an agreement made for the same between the Board and the said Sir Wm Warren in the absence of the said Sir W. Penn and Mr Pepys, it was declared by Sir J. Mennes that he had according to the duty of his place as Comptroller thoroughly examined all vouchers and circumstances leading him and the Board to the said agreement and that he will at all times be ready to justify the same. Br., J. M., S. P.

Which was signed at the Board by all then present Janry 14; which done at Sir J. Mennes's desire, I delivered Mr Pointer the bill, having declaredly forborne to do it till this memorandum was entered and signed, as it is this day by these; and shall be tendered to the rest for signing as they shall happen to come to the Board.

Accordingly it has been since signed by J. M. and J. T.

Decembr 29th 1668. That the nailer ought not to live near the King's yards. Discoursing this day with Mr Wilson, storekeeper of Chatham, about the quality of ironwork generally served in and the price paid by the King for it, and acquainting him with our intentions of coming to a new contract for those goods, he advised that I would take care for the obtaining a clause in it for prohibiting the ironmonger to make any nails within any moderate distance from any of the King's yards; giving me as his reason that a nailer living near is so ready a way for the workmen's safe embezzling of his Majesty's nails by selling them to him, that they are under none of the difficulty which they would otherwise meet with of disposing of the King's nails, because marked with his mark. And as a proof of it in the practice, he tells me that the nailer belonging to Chatham who works under Folley has from nothing within a few years raised himself to an estate gener-

---

[1]The memorandum is printed in HMC, *Lindsey* (*Supp.*), p. 150. The office memorandum book referred to has not been traced; presumably it was the successor to PRO, ADM 106/3520 which ends in May 1668.

ally reputed at 3000*l*., and added further that the practice of the master shipwright upon all occasions of demanding nails for this or that work is always to demand by even hundreds or thousands, though not one nail ever yet known to be returned.

This and my reflection upon Mr Ackworth's late expedients of purging himself under his being accused of employing the King's nails marked with the King's marks on his private work (which was, by pretending his buying them of Mr Folley's nailer, whom he got to swear that being then unfurnished of nails unmarked he was forced to sell him others that were, and that he was paid for them by Mr Ackworth, though his confessions of another kind to Chayford rendered that oath too very suspicious) makes me think this advice of Mr Wilson's worthy notice and therefore to be made use of in the framing of the next contract.

Decembr 29. 68. About working of ground tows. Upon discourse this day at the Board touching the mistaken husbandry we are under of working ground tows into ropes (occasioned by a motion for the putting to sale several old and useless provisions, among which ground tows was one, at this day pestering the stores) the Surveyor who led us to the observing of this mistake told us that at his late being at Chatham observing the badness of the ropes then bringing in by the party that works them at so much per hundred, he demanded of the party the price he wrought them at, who answering 9*s*. per hundred, the Surveyor demanded of him whether he would take the goods he brought in in payment for his labour, to which he says he was answered that he would not. And further the Surveyor tells us that the goods made of this stuff will when wet swell from half an inch diameter to twice as much more, so as presently to rot and become useless.

Quere: what part of the work it is that is here meant at 9*s*. a hundred, because as I remember some part of the ground tows (wrought into lines as I take it) costs the King a great deal more.

Decembr 29. (68). The King's boatswains not to be masters of lighters. Vide *the Board's letter to the Surveyor 30 xbr, his answer the 4 Feb., and the letters to him the same day.* The Surveyor this day took occasion of showing the Board the very great injury it is to his Majesty to have the boatswains of his yards masters of the lighters, it occasioning very great charge to the King, and abuses which might be avoided by the King's having lighters of his own, to which end he advised that the King should build some in each yard.[1]

Husbandry in building a smaller vessel at the time of building a greater. Which gave occasion of another discourse, *viz.* that there cannot be better husbandry, at a time when the King is building any great ships (which is the present case in every yard), than at the same time to fall a-building of less, there being always so much leavings to be found in the former, as will not only do the latter, but be liable to be worse employed if not employed on the latter, besides many circumstances of other kinds rendering it of advantage to be building both at the same time. In this he was fully seconded by Mr Tippetts, who tells us that the *Nonsuch*, a 5th-rate newly launched at Portsmouth, received not only her dispatch by being furnished with materials for its building out of the leavings of the 2nd-rate ships now on the stocks there, but (comparatively) cost the King little more in her building than the labour. The like was instanced by them in other ships built elsewhere.

Decembr 29. (68). About pickling of sails. Upon discourse at the Board touching the preservation of his Majesty's sails, the Surveyor told us that the want either of judgement, care, or honesty in commanders and boatswains is it that occasions so great a destruction of sails, not only by their failing to take all opportunities of drying their sails but suffering them to lie and heat in their wet and thereby becoming mildewed, but not observing to wet their sails in salt water as himself (and as he says all careful masters of merchantmen) use to do as soon as they come into the Downs, or else pickling them before they go out, which he says upon his experience renders a sail twice as durable as others not so ordered; and therefore offered it as his advice that there might be a large vessel like a brewer's vat provided in each yard, and an allowance made of salt for the pickling of all new sails before delivered forth. He gave us too as his observation,

---

[1] But in his later letter of 4 Feb. 1669 Middleton argued for hiring rather than buying lighters because they were needed only at Deptford: *CSPD 1668–9*, p. 182.

that a mildewed sail when dry appears as fair as any other; but when wet will discover itself by black blotches everywhere the mildew has seized it. The care of putting this in execution the Board committed to the Surveyor.

By his letter to me of the 4th of Febrry, he upon some difficulty urged by the masters attendant on the keeping of sails thoroughly dry, desists from this his proposition though confessedly against his own experience.[1] *Vide* his said letters and the Board's answers of the 5th.

The Surveyor's allowing a boatswain what was denied by the clerk of the survey. The entering of this gave Mr Gibson occasion of taking notice to me of a passage which he was lately advertised of by Mr Homewood, namely, that upon the *Maryner*'s late return to Chatham from the Straits her boatswain bring in his account two topsails blown out of the bolt-ropes. One of which Mr Homewood, as clerk of the survey, says he found reason to allow, but not the other. Soon after which coming to town and meeting Capt. Darcey, the commander of that ship, the captain (as he took it) by way of upbraiding him told him that the topsail which he refused to allow of, the boatswain upon application to the Surveyor himself had got it allowed and a good dinner to boot. *Quere*: the truth and ground of it.

Decembr 29. (68). About cordage lying long in tar. The Surveyor's moving the Board this day, that notwithstanding we had no prospect of any great fleets to go forth this year, yet that it would be expedient to give order to the ropeyards to make up what cordage is wanting upon a supposition of the whole fleet's being set out; I put the Board in mind of what I remembered (as I thought) Sir Wm Batten to have frequently declared – that the long lying of cordage in tar was so far from being advisable, as that the longer it lay the more it burnt the yarn. To this the present Surveyor[2] answered that this was true in cordage carried into hot countries; but where cordage can lie tarred in a cool country his own practice and experience assures him that a tarred rope so kept for two years would outlast that that has lain but

---

[1] PRO, SP 29/255, no. 82. (The summary in *CSPD 1668–9*, p. 182 does not include the point made by the master attendant.)
[2] Middleton.

one, and so three years two, and so on the longer the time is the more it betters it.

An instance of what the King is liable to suffer from the bad keeping of the Surveyor's books and papers; by Col. Midleton's ignorance in what loans were made in all his predecessor's time, and particularly of four score prize masts delivered us at Newcastle during the war and never yet accounted for to us, or by us disposed of. *Vide* the Board's letter to Col. Middleton Feb. 4th 1668[9].

3[1] *Janry 1668[9].* This day being Sunday the Board, *viz.* T.O., T.L., Br., W.P., J.M., S.P. attended the Duke in the afternoon at Whitehall, where among other things Sir T. Osborne in behalf of himself and T. Littleton,[2] after opening the present state of money, did declare to the Duke a rule they had set themselves of paying no money of any kind to any person other than for cutting off growing charge[3] or answering present pressing services (without the least taking notice of the Board either before or now in it), if his Highness approved on it. To which his Highness made an indifferent answer as to a thing which became them of course to consult his Majesty's best advantage in. By and by Sir T. Osborne went on to tell his Highness that upon a late supply of 20,000*l.* from the Lords of the Treasury they had at the motion of my Lord General[4] undertaken forthwith to fall a-paying the tickets of 1666 by 300*l.* a week; which, upon some motion now made for the using of some money, they used as an excuse for their being unable to answer. Here the Duke showing much discontent told them that by my Lord General's favour he had as much reason to stand up for the payment of the tickets of 64 and 65 when himself was in person in the fleet as his Lordship had for those of 1666, or else that his Admiralship signified but little. Which being seconded by Sir Wm Pen and myself, who hinted at such inconveniences as on the sudden occurred to me therefrom, the Duke returned with more vehemence and expressions of displeasure to tell them that as he never had adventured to order any payments partially himself, so he must

[1]MS. '2' (which was Saturday).
[2]Newly appointed (in November 1668) as Joint-Treasurers of the Navy.
[3]Debts at compound interest.
[4]Albemarle; with Rupert he had commanded the battle fleet in 1666.

oppose my Lord General's doing of it now, bidding him tell his Lordship so, and directing them to take care that before they pay those of 66 they should begin with those that are older date, to which with some surprise and trouble they submitted and it ended.

Discoursing of this with Wm Hewers going home, he tells me that the Treasurers have by posting it on their gate and by other ways published for several days together their invitations to all owners of tickets of 1666 to bring them in there to be registered for payment, and have to that end employed one of their instruments day by day to take them in exclusive to all that have been brought them by several persons of elder date.

This I acquainted Mr Wren with on Monday morning the 4th, who thinks the Duke has done enough for the declaring his mind thereon, and that therefore we ought to see how the Treasurers will acquit themselves in it, in obeying the order of the Admiral against the verbal direction (which they acknowledged to be all they had for it) of my Lord General.

The same day at night meeting with Lord Brouncker at Court I told him of it, acquainting him with the inconveniences that may arise from it not only to the discouragement and raising a despair in persons concerned in tickets of before 1666 but to the dissatisfying of those whom their invitation has occasioned the trouble of bringing in theirs of 1666, when they shall find themselves deceived in being first paid. I reflected also to my Lord upon the trouble and censure this Office has gone under in Parliament and even by these very gentlemen, for a supposed partiality in payment of tickets,[1] when of partialities there cannot be either a plainer, or more scandalous and injurious instance thereof than this which themselves have here adventured upon without the least advice or knowledge of his Royal Highness or the Board.

Here my Lord Brouncker began very vehemently to complain of the arbitrariness of the proceedings of the Treasurers without any regard to the asking the orders or advice of the Board, or valuing them when given, so as they would seem to have it in their design to act independently and in defiance both of the Duke and the Board. And went on to instance, in the case of Capt. Narborough whose bill for 100*l*. in reward for his wounds

---

[1] Both Osborne and Littleton were members of the Commons committee which had condemned the alleged misuse of tickets as a 'miscarriage': *CJ*, ix. 4, 55.

they would not accept of till they see the order on which it was grounded, which when they saw they said they wondered that the Duke would give such an order and questioned his power of doing it. Next, he observed that notwithstanding the no reason which we at the Board several times made appear to be for the paying the Chatham pressed shipwrights, which at their own desire had been discharged there by Col. Midleton without promise (as themselves confessed at the Board, the Treasurers themselves present) which we had also a little before for the satisfaction of the Lords of the Treasury wrote to their Lordships upon occasion of their importuning those Lords for their payment; and notwithstanding that the Board did declare the discouragement which the rest of the men of the yard would receive, who would most of them be desirous to be discharged on the same terms; that we would by breaking of their tickets undertake to satisfy their creditors at Chatham for whom they pretended their importunity to be occasioned; that it was manifestly their design to get the money into their own hands, and lastly that this their mutinous manner of soliciting in crowds and with threats and curses to the Surveyor, who happened at their own desire to discharge them, might prove of very ill consequence if encouraged, and that if they were paid by proportions equal with the yard it was not only all that was promised them, but what would by their liberty of working elsewhere be of better support to them than they meet with who are continued to work in the yard without money; yet for their own peace or at least by their own advice contrary to that of the Board and without the notice thereof they paid these men three-quarters pay notwithstanding the many occasions for small sums of money which we at the same time had acquainted them with and which they declare themselves unable to answer. He observed also their questioning very frequently the reason of the Duke's laying up the *Harpe* in Ireland and not bringing her into England, as being a thing never known and that which need not have been, etc., though we know upon how many necessary reasons it was done.[1] He observed too their ready promising of Sir John Chicheley the payment of his

---

[1] An imprest for her repair was cancelled in April 1669. She was then laid up in Kinsale harbour where the cost of maintaining her fell on the Irish Treasury: *CSPD Add. 1660–85*, pp. 290–1; cf. ibid., p. 98. She was a frigate built at Dublin in 1656: Anderson, no. 259.

bills, I think for his pension,[1] as also their constant denial to make the Board any one weekly return of their receipts or payments notwithstanding both a copy of the Duke's order for it[2] given them and the Board's daily pressing for it, they fathering their denial upon Mr Waith's not giving them an account of the tickets formerly paid, which can be no excuse for their not giving us an account of their receipts and net payments. His Lordship also remembered the several difficulties they made of paying a bill of exchange of Sir John Knight's,[3] though recommended to them by the Board's particular letter. These and some others make my Lord very sensible of their imposing upon the Board and the consequences of it, and that it imports us to find some means of giving a stop to it in its infancy, and thereupon upon my moving that we should speak with the Duke this night on some other occasions, he made use of it to the laying this matter also open to him. Which was done by us both with the Duke's good liking, who abundantly expressed his own reflections upon and resentment of the same thing, saying that he would take occasion at our next attending him to direct the Treasurers in all things to act with the privity and advice of the Board, and that he would expect to see it done. And so the discourse ended.

Janry 5th 68[9]. It happened that this day Sir Tho. Litleton only being at the Board Sir Laurence van Hemskirke tendered him his bill for the 100*l.* gratuity lately given him by the King, and which the Duke did largely on Sunday last declare that his Majesty did expressly direct (though the Secretary forgot to express it in his warrant) that it should be paid out of the 200,000*l.*, for the present year's service, and therefore directed

---

[1] He appears to have claimed six months' pay for expenses incurred in fitting out his ship (which never sailed) in the early summer of 1668: see his letter to Pepys, 29 Oct. 1668, in *CSPD 1668–9*, p. 41.

[2] By an order of 8 Dec. 1665 the Duke required the Navy Treasurer to present to the Board statements of receipts and expenditure every Saturday: PRO, ADM 2/1, f. 2*v*. Volumes of these printed certificates survive (e.g. in Bodl. Lib., Rawl. MSS A 215, pp. 1–9.

[3] Navy agent, Bristol; he had pressed for payment incurred in building the *Edgar* and the *Merlin* yacht: *CSPD 1668–9*, pp. 32–3, 75.

that they would pay it him out of that money.¹ Sir T. Littleton demurring first the words of the order 'for service done and to be done', answered that he could not pay it without an order of the King and Council out of this 200,000*l*. Then upon further considering he added that if the King himself would signify his pleasure, it may be he might accept of that in release of the order of Council by which the 200,000*l*. is restrained to the service of the present year. Upon my asking whether that order of Council was directed to Sir T. Osborne and himself, he answered not, but that it was to the Lords of the Treasury, who in pursuance thereof had restrained it in their order to them. Upon my observing to him that in all naval matters the King's pleasure by word of mouth delivered to the Admiral was as authoritatively declared as by the Admiral to all persons as it was in other matters by a Secretary of State,² and thereupon asking him whether, if the Duke should in writing tell us or him that this was the King's pleasure, or that we should rest satisfied therein and so direct it to them, that either of them would satisfy him – he answered that neither would, not anything less than the King's pleasure signified in writing and as he thought in an order of Council. I reminded him of what the Duke said on Sunday touching his desire of easing the party, being a stranger³ of the charge and trouble of getting a new order from the King. Upon which he finally answered that he could say no more in it at present, but would consider of it with Sir T. Osborne against the next meeting, and so Sir Laurence was for the present dismissed, though he declared his design of going down to his ship tomorrow at Portsmouth and that for want hereof he must stay whatever came of the King's business. Thus it now ended, wherein I have been the more particular in regard of the Duke's honour concerned therein.

¹The King told the Duke of York by word of mouth to order the payment of £100 'without account for services performed and to be performed': Duke to Navy Board, 2 Jan. 1669 (PRO, ADM 106/17, f. 289*r*). Payments made 'without account' were normally for secret service. Heemskerck was an agent of Dutch origin whose information had led to Holmes's successful attack on the Dutch coast in 1666. An order had been issued on 9 Dec. 1668 for the immediate payment of the £100 because he was about to leave the country: *CTB 1669–72*, pp. 308, 310, 331.

²Pepys himself when Secretary to the Admiralty in the 1670s often acted on oral orders from the King: see *Naval Minutes*, p. 197.

³Sc. unaware.

Janry 9th 68[9]. A letter came from the Duke declaring it the King's pleasure that Hemskirke's 100*l.* should be paid out of the 200,000*l.* for the present year.[1] Which the Board signified by subscribing the same to his bill and declaring it, showing the Duke's letters by and by to the Treasurers at their coming to them, who read it and silently laid it aside expressing nothing of their intentions touching the paying it, nor the Board offering anything more about it. So I shall observe what they do in it.

Memorandum: that yesterday Janry 8th at the Board's attending the Duke, the whole Board present, the Duke did with great plainness and some decent sharpness advise the Treasurers in this beginning of their office to adventure upon the resolving and doing nothing without his advice or the Board's, showing how easy it is in such cases to fall into errors, as they in particular had done in the late business of 1666, telling them (what I had informed him but concealing my name) that they had posted up invitations to people to bring in those tickets.

Which they denied and further said that though they did not think it necessary to have propounded it to the Duke, yet it was in their intentions before they paid any of these tickets to have acquainted the Board with it. Here thinking it not requisite for me to occasion any growth of difference between the Duke and them, I forbore to interpose by making good the truth of what the Duke said, and the Duke also was contented to pass it over. But after we were parted Will Hewer told me that he is very well assured that two or three persons have for some time been employed in the taking in and registering of these tickets at the Treasurers' office, and that he has heard and does believe that upon inquiry it will be found that it was published upon the gate. But from this the Duke fell earnestly upon pressing them to send in weekly certificates such as their predecessors had done, not giving way to anything urged for their forbearance of it, and ended with enjoining them in all things to proceed by the order and advice of himself or the Board.

To which the Treasurers promised obedience, but seemed not a little disturbed.

[1] PRO, ADM 106/17, f. 307*r.*

Occasions of Supernumeraries

Men to man other ships.
Sick men recovered.
Subjects out of stranger ships.
Saved men out of ships in distress.
Prisoners.
Noble[s] etc. and their retinues.
Reformad[o]s.
Soldiers distributed where ships have had their number, but not fully qualified.
Seamen pressed though the ship have been full manned to better the quality of the complement.
Passengers to other ships entered only for their victuals.

17 July 1668

Heads of discourse prepared to satisfy the Council this day.[1]

1. Whence it is that the number of tickets that shall be made out upon any ship can at no time be ascertained so as to say thus many shall be issued and no less.

2. Whence it arises that every seaman discharged has not his ticket delivered him at the time of his discharge.

That the charge of a ship shall be so much and no more may be ascertained at the day of payment of each ship, saving the inconsiderable difference that may arise by removal of R's.[2]

That it shall be so much and no less [is] at no time ascertainable before the whole book be paid, which can never be thought to happen within any certain time for:

1. A man left behind the ship (instance *Chesnut*) or transferred into another without his ticket (instance Hispaniola ships).[3]
2. Men put out of the King's into a merchantman for a long voyage.

---

[1] Copy in Pepys's hand in BL, Add. MSS 11602, f. 341*r*. On 8 July the Council, in an effort to meet parliamentary criticisms of the use of tickets, had asked the Board to find ways of putting an end to them. These 'Heads' are based on the Board's answer of the 16th: PRO, PC 2/60, ff. 196*v*–197*v* (printed G. Penn, *Memorials*, ii. 517–19). Pepys acted as the Board's spokesman and, according to the Diary (ix. 263), 'did discourse to [the Councillors'] liking'.

[2] Runaways.

[3] Ships engaged in the capture of Hispaniola, 1655.

3. A man taken prisoner.
4. Or a slave.
5. Or may die and his death not in a long time known.
6. The length of the voyage in the King's own ship *viz. Chesnut* cast at the Indies and the men wanting conveniences of coming home. Perhaps got into the Dutch employment.
7. Ships lost, some men afterwards escaping.
8. Dispute of right. A man hath 3 wives – master and servant.

Clerks have it not in their power nor practice to make out tickets without special order.

The frauds of pursers suggested in their making men D.[1] who ought to be R's or not at all, in expectation of their own season of getting them afterwards paid, not practicable without the positive or privative[2] assistance of the commanders and fellow officers.

Discharging of men without tickets arises from:
1. Want of printed tickets aboard.
2. Withholding them to secure the men.
3. Prisoners.
4. Sick.
5. Absence of pursers or the steward's want of books.

No frauds practicable in this whole matter for prevention of which there are not sufficient rules provided if executed.

23 December 1668. Memorandum: that the Board having several times of late taken occasion of complaining to the Surveyor of the want of his survey books or of any person in his absence to give the Board any satisfaction or receive any advice from the Board in matters relating to his office; to which the Surveyor has made answer that he could not prevent it by reason of one of his hands Richd Maddox's being taken from him to assist in making up the Treasurers' books in Broad Street; upon which the Board did openly declare their disowning his being employed there by his command otherwise than with his, the Surveyor's, advice and therefore desired that he would recall him thence. And it falling out that by Mr Ackworth's restitution to his place at Woolwich Theophilus Curtiss was at liberty to attend the work at Broad Street; the Board by their order of yesterday

---

[1] Dead.
[2] Negative.

directed Curtiss accordingly to attend there in the room of Maddox.

Upon which the Surveyor this day at the Board takes occasion to complain that his clerk should be called thence and prayed that he might be restored. To which the Board silently assented, myself only in behalf of the rest telling him what I have already here writ, and that where an officer shall for the advantage of his clerk (as in this present case) insist upon his being employed on matters wherein he is not concerned, he ought not to expect that this his clerk's employment should be accepted in excuse for any omissions in his own work, and that therefore I advised him, the Surveyor, to consider whether the work of his office was not sufficient to employ both his clerks. To which he answering that it was not, I replied that if it were so (which I declared I could not apprehend) and that my Lord Brouncker who stood accountable for that work stood in want of one, I thought his Lordship might very well employ him. To which my Lord Brouncker answered that since the Surveyor desired it he would, and accordingly an order was signed for it by Br., J. M., T. M., which being offered to me I refused, declaring to the Board my opinion that there was need of him for the doing the necessary work of the Surveyor's own office, which I would not so far contribute to the [work] not being done as to give order for the taking away one of his clerks. Which the Lord Brouncker declared to be his sense too, and that his signing to the warrant sprang from the Surveyor's desire and asserting his not needing him at his own office.

Memorandum: that in the evening discoursing with my Lord at his lodgings about several businesses of the office, he took notice of this passage of the Surveyor's, expressing his wonder at his perseverance in it after the freedom I had used about it; adding, that for his own justification in the signing of the warrant, he had taken a memorandum of the grounds on which he did it; telling me too that for the making room for Curtiss he had discharged young Barbour, whom he found not so fit for it.

An account of the proceedings of the Board touching the freight of a ship of Sir Wm Warren's called the Sunn[1] *sent in*

---

[1] In the Navy Board papers usually referred to as the *Golden Sun*.

the year 1666 to fetch masts from Portsmouth. Sir W. Warren having forborn presenting the Board with his demand for the freight of the said ship till as I take it it was from that time till 9ber 1668 depending between us who should be accountable for the loss of time or any other misbehaviour of the master, who was now gone, after being taken tripping in some falsities with the Board (as appears in the minutes thereof kept in the office) and leaving only a copy of his journal behind him; Sir W. Warren disclaiming him for his master and we the like for his being ours. So that I was at last driven to draw up a state of the case, in order to the having it decided by the Council, when Sir W. Warren for saving time as he pretended and all further stops that might arise therefrom, declared to the Board his willingness to take upon him a responsibleness for the truth of the said copy of the journal and an accountableness for whatever we could charge upon the said master. Which being done the Board thought it then ripe to be committed to the care of the Comptroller Sir J. Mennes, who took the journal into his hands and directed Sir W. Warren to attend him with his demand and vouchers in order to their being examined. In which condition it lay till Janry 7th 68[9] when Sir J. Mennes brought it to the table, declaring that he had examined the journal and found it very fair and that he had no objection to make to it. Whereupon Sir W. Warren being by and desiring that a bill might be drawn, Sir J. Mennes answered that he had nothing to say against it, and so Sir W. Warren tendered a bill to the Board which they committed to Pointer, Sir J. Mennes's clerk, to prepare for them, Sir W. Warren adding that for the answering some occasions and some accounts depending of his own between him and one Pemble, pretended part-owner of the ship, he desired that the bill might be made in his[1] name. To which I excepted, that Pemble's name had never been yet used in this matter, but only Warren's; that it might better be in the name of Warren and Pemble; but most properly Warren's alone, who by an assignment of it might answer any end he seemed to design towards Pemble; and lastly that the concealing of Warren's name could not but administer great occasion of jealousy in whoever should observe it in our accounts; besides that it would not appear how Warren was satisfied in case of any future demand from him or his executors. To this Sir W. Warren offers to discharge the Board by a letter under his hand desiring

[1] Pemble's.

that the bill might be made to Pemble on his behalf. With which the Board seemed at present satisfied, and so directed Pointer to go on. But before they rose I took an opportunity not only of reviving this and insisting upon it that Warren's name should be used, but of asking who it was that the Board would rely upon for this business being well examined on behalf of the King. To which they replying Sir J. Mennes, and Sir J. M. declaring that he had examined the journal and had proceeded therein (to use his own terms) as a man jealous[1] of everything that came from Sir W. Warren, and that after all he had no objection to make to it, I was forced to reply that he was so far from expressing any jealousy as in the allowance of this account to take all for granted that Sir W. Warren says, having not examined the truth of one paper either in the King's or merchant's side quoted in the journal, nor inquired whether there were any such papers as are there pretended, nor what more might be found that might be of advantage to his Majesty. To which Sir J. Mennes having not one word to answer but to confess it and that all he had done was to run over the journal, the Board was much dissatisfied, praying that he would not offer to make out the bill till he had performed what I had now discovered to have been undone; which he undertook, and so it rested.

Janry 9th 68[9]. My Lord Brouncker came to my closet before the Board was sat, telling me that Sir Wm Warren was without, and had offered him an argument which made it necessary on the King's behalf that the bill should be made out to Pemble, *viz.* that Pemble (whose name I believe if the truth were known was heretofore made use of by Sir W. Warren in a contract for timber at Portsmouth) had formerly received 1000*l.*[2] by way of imprest never yet cleared. Which Sir W. Warren telling us that the said Pemble is dead makes it necessary for the King that his name should be used in this bill thereby to get this imprest cleared. To which I made no present answer but repaired with his Lordship to the Board, where with J.M., W.P., T.M. and J.T. being sat and this business first offered to debate, I upon inquiry found that several perfect bills of Pemble's have been signed and all paid, without any regard had by the Comptroller to provide for the clearing of the imprest. Which gave me occasion of enlarg-

---
[1] Distrustful.
[2] £2000 according to Warren's papers: HMC, *Lindsey (Supp.)*, p. 154.

ing upon the evil consequences his Majesty has been subjected to of this remissness of the Comptroller, which for ought I know may upon inquiry be discovered in many more cases than this, and did convince and had it declared by the Board and by them urged to Sir J. Mennes that it is his particular province to prevent the payment of any perfect bill before the imprests (where any) be cleared. Which Sir J. Mennes owned, expressing his hopes that the instances of this kind of oversight were not many, and directing his clerk Pointer at the Board for the time to come to take special care in it. Which the Board desiring Sir J. Mennes himself to see observed, they went on to Sir W. Warren's business and concluded that by this occasion it was become requisite for Pemble's name to be used, and accordingly for the present passed over that point, and went to the other point of the signing of the bill, which was brought to the Board by Pointer drawn by him. At the sight whereof and my Lord's going to sign it, I stopped his hand by asking him whether his own satisfaction in it, or satisfaction derived from anybody else, led his Lordship thereto and was to lead the rest of the Board. He readily replied that it was Sir J. Mennes's examination of the business and declaring himself satisfied therein; which, being owned by Sir J. Mennes, he presently signed it and after him Sir J.M., W.P. and T.M. It being then laid before me I forbore to sign it, asking Sir J. Mennes again whether he would have it believed that he had examined this account as it ought to be. To which he replying readily that he would, I did publicly at the open board – many persons standing by and particularly Wm Hewers at my elbow – declare myself in these words: "Then I pray God keep me from having any accounts examined by you, where I shall be concerned as the King is in this." And so Sir J. Mennes making no reply other than by disgust signified in his looks, I forbore to say anything more at present in an open office,[1] but took an opportunity by and by of stepping to my closet, and there making Mr Gibson write a note with my letters to it and deliver it privately to my Lord Brouncker in these words:

> My Lord, I pray I may have opportunity by and by to deliver my mind to the Board in this business of Sir W. Warren's, which Sir J. Mennes will, I fear, otherwise greatly mislead us in.
> 9th Janry 68[9].   S. P.

[1] A meeting attended by clerks and members of the public having business with the Board.

Which my Lord Brouncker readily made use of, causing by and by the office to be voided by strangers and the clerks (myself only having directed Will Hewers to keep himself within the hearing of what I said to the Board in order to its being remembered). Which done, I told them that though I might be thought to have done enough already for my own safety in this matter, by declaring so openly my dislike of the bill and my not signing it with the rest, yet I thought I could not acquit myself of my duty to the King and care of them, if I did not once more declare my mind too in it, and that in terms more plain, *viz.* that whatever Sir J. Mennes has thought fit to take upon him touching his examination of this business, I do affirm that he had not examined the truth of one letter quoted by Sir W. Warren to have been by us writ to him or him to us, but that, whether there were any such letters or no or others of more advantage to the King, he did wholly rest upon the integrity of the merchant; and thereby wholly neglected to satisfy himself in the terms of the agreement for this ship, wherein my memory I told them so far served them as he tell them, 1st, that she was taken up at Dover in such haste as to be limited to the number of days in which she was to be gone, though as I take it she stayed much longer. (This I ground upon a letter which I remember I wrote to him, and which Mr Hayter tells me he lately see in Sir W. Warren's hands, though I find it not entered, wherein I tell him she must be gone in two or three days at the furthest.) 2dly, that Sir W. Warren was told the work she was to go upon, before she went, which was by him accordingly undertaken, though when she came to Portsmouth she was found unfit. So that the disappointment of the service seems too much for the King to bear without paying for her freight. Lastly, that though it is reasonable that she should be paid for her service in carrying of goods from thence to Plymouth, it ought to be inquired into what pretence Sir W. Warren has for our seeing her back again, I believing that there was not originally any such covenant, and am sure that none has been yet made appear to the Board, nor I doubt ever demanded by Sir J. Mennes.

Which last as well as that of the non-examination of the letters being confessed by Sir J. M., and that all he had done was but the reading over of the journal as he said (which Sir W. Penn largely showed to be a matter wherein he and everybody else may without possible prevention be imposed upon) without entering into any examination of the terms of her freighting, the Board expressed much trouble at what they had been led to by Sir J. M., who did the like for his no better examining this matter, promising that he would yet do it before the bill went out of the office.

Which the Board pressing upon him with many expressions of dissatisfaction and shame, the matter ended.

Janry 12. 68[9]. I find by discourse at the Board that the bill had been carried home upon the 9th by Sir W. Warren, and was upon this my discourse to the Board called for back again by Sir J. M., who told us this day that he was upon new examination of it.

Janry 23. 68[9]. Sir J. M. told the Board that he had now examined the business of the *Sunn* and finds no such letter, as Sir W. Warren alleges, in his[1] journal from the Board for her being employed, but on the contrary a letter of mine obliging her to be ready in two days, whereas she went not in a month, and that as I said she was found unfit for the work when she came to Portsmouth etc., as I had hinted to him, and that therefore he had cancelled the bill and would examine it afresh; to which end he the same day wrote to me for some information about the matter, which coming to me the 25 I the same day returned to him an answer to be found in my Letter Book.

Febry 13. (68[9]). Sir W. Warren being at the Board desiring dispatch of his bill for the *Sunn* according as it was now corrected, I find that Sir W. Warren was willing to relinquish his pretence to any freight due to him from the ship's going from Dover to Portsmouth, and seemed to press now only for the remainder. So that so much is clearly saved in the beginning whatever there will be in the end of the voyage; wherein I perceive Sir J. M. yet wholly unprovided how to state this matter.

March 13. (68[9]). Looking over this book occasionally this day I was led to an inquiry what was further done in this business of the *Sun*, and find that a bill hath been passed by the Board not in Sir W. Warren's name but John Pemble's.[2] The time and

---

[1] The captain's.
[2] It was issued on 20 Apr. 1667 and survives among Warren's papers: HMC, *Lindsey (Supp.)*, p. 154.

manner of its doing I do not at all remember, nor believe that my hand is to it, or if it was, I signed it among other bills without any particular animadversions. But I find that her freight is reckoned to commence but at Portsmouth, so as I have occasioned the cutting off all from her being taken up at Dover to that time. How they justify the allowing all the time of her stay at Plymouth and return to the Downs, and the making the bill out in Pemble's name, I know not; but the bill is made for 7 months and 20 days at 7*l*. per ton, the ship reckoned at $322\frac{44}{94}$ tons, amounting to 865*l*. 5*s*. 7*d*., the bill formerly made out having made it 987*l*. 10*s*. 1*d*.

Memorandum: that I find this bill above mentioned for 865. 5. 7. signed by Br., J.M., T.M., J.T. and not my myself as the same is entered in the Comptroller's Book.

Janry 7. 1668[9]. As an instance of the Surveyor's great strictness in his reading over nowadays everything that he signs, since my late overthrowing him in the business of Coleby's contract,[1] it was pretty to observe this day that Sir Wm Penn speaking at the Board something of such importance as to press for the Board's attendance to what he said, and particularly to tell the Surveyor (who was reading over a paper) that he need not lose his time in the reading of that, it being but a thing of course (*viz.* a bill of sale of the *Zeland* sold to Mr Young) the Surveyor with much earnestness answered him: "I must and will read it before I sign it, for it may be a bill of sale of myself for ought I know."

Janry 9th 1668[9]. *Memorandum:* that particularly this night, besides some others of late, word has been brought me upon my sending of letters to sign to the Officers, that as to Sir W. Penn's, though he was in his parlour below, that none of his servants could be got to carry them in to him, declaring that they durst not. And the 2d and 5th inst. they were carried to him, himself and Sir John Robinson being then talking and drinking with him, but he would not sign them but bid the messenger carry them to somebody else, for he would not.

---

[1] On 7 Dec. 1668 Middleton had accused Will Hewer of accepting a bribe from Coleby in return for favours in the grant of a contract for kerseys and cottons. On the 18th was forced to withdraw the charge in the presence of the Board: *Diary*, ix. 388 & n. 2, 394–5.

Janry 28th 68/9]. Byland, shipwright's assistant at Woolwich, writes us that the crop this year of reed got out of Ham Creek will amount to 20*l*.; that the charge in cutting and bringing it in will be 6*l*.[1] To this adding 18*l*. per annum rent for the creek, the charge exceeds by 4*l*. the value of the crop. This I intimated to the Surveyor in writing this night, that he might consider whether the benefits accruing to his Majesty from this creek besides the value of the reed are such as will compensate this loss.

Janry 28. 68[9]. Ill success of our undertaking to fetch masts from Scotland. Memorandum: that the bill for the freight of the *Arthur of Bradley,* one of the three ships lately employed for fetching part of his Majesty's masts from Scotland, came to 764*l*. 11*s*. 6*d*., whereas the Surveyor this day showed the Board that the whole loading (so bad are the masts) is not worth 390*l*. He told us too that the other two ships delivered in Ham River (this being at Chatham) were a worse pennyworth. 'Tis true, the Surveyor's reckoning is calculated I doubt by the present market, while our occasions are small, stores full, time of peace for having more, and no prospect of any occasions of wanting them, all which circumstances were quite otherwise when this project of fetching masts from Scotland was set on foot. But the design will undoubtedly be found very chargeable and Mr Pett in Scotland blameable for encouraging it, as he did upon his first survey, when sent thither to that purpose.[2] Yet this Office not to be condemned, it having sprung from the Court and Council, upon the advice I suppose of my Lord Lauderdale[3] etc. of that country. It was once I understand attempted heretofore in the late times and with no better success. The *Michaell's* freight, John White master, amounted to 738*l*. 19*s*. 0*d*., while her loading is valued

---

[1] Edward Byland to Pepys: *CSPD 1668–9,* p. 171.
[2] Phineas Pett the shipbuilder had visited Scotland in 1666 and 1667 to choose timber. In 1666 Pepys had been concerned with Penn in an abortive plan to employ Pett (unofficially) to buy Scottish timber for house-building in London after the Fire (*Diary,* vii. 298 & n. 3) – a use for which it was better suited than for shipbuilding. Deliveries for shipbuilding arrived in English ports in December 1667 and December 1668. The latter shipment was described by the storekeeper at Chatham as '155 pieces of sorry firewood': *CSPD 1668–9,* p. 118; cf. also ibid., *Add. 1660–85,* pp. 204, 278.
[3] Secretary for Scottish Affairs.

by Mr Shish but at 219*l*. 2*s*. 0*d*. *Vide* Shish's account in my File no. 33.

Janry 29. 68[9]. Lord Brouncker, discoursing of the scandalous mistakes which he finds in the pay books made up at so great a charge by extra clerks, told us among other things of the great loss the King will be found to suffer by clothes, not only by them charged upon runaways, but others doubly allowed, *viz.* upon two books where books have for accommodation of payment been forced to be split. As also another abuse in this matter he took notice of arising from payment made of ships and the pay books made up without examining the muster books, an instance of which he gave us in the frigate *Victory*, where the clothes allowed on the pay book exceed what ought to have been by the muster books by 100*l*. and odd pounds.

Proceedings of the Board touching the passing of Sir W. Warren's Hambrow account.[1]

Memorandum: that after several imperfect endeavours and discourses of Sir J. Mennes to the Board from about two years since about these accounts, with a pretence of employing a merchant in the City for his assistance therein, and his having drawn up several exceptions (as he call them) to the account which he could never obtain answer to from Sir W. Warren, who I remember has several times taken notice of them to the Board as weak and insignificant; which accounts, papers and exceptions Sir J. M., as he informs us, did deliver unto the Commissioners of Accounts many months since, and has received them or copies of them back again in order to their being first stated at the Board. Sir W. W. did upon the 23rd of Janry 1668[9] by a letter (thoughtfully drawn) take notice of the return of the said papers to Sir J. M. and proposing several things relating to the dispatch of his accounts as also about the masts lying at this day at Gottenburg and New England; the latter of which the Board pressed the Surveyor to

---

[1]This concerned five bills for purchases made by Warren under commission from the King and the Duke of York, together with charges for freight and demurrage. When the account was finally submitted to the Exchequer in 1675, the merchants called in to examine it – Sir Richard Ford and Sir John Banks – found that Warren had overcharged by more than £2000: HMC, *Lindsey* (*Supp.*), p. 117.

have in his particular care according to the Admiral's late directions, which the Surveyor readily took upon him. The former the Board directed themselves in to Sir J. M., who also as readily embraced the same, insisting upon his former endeavours therein and exceptions drawn up by him against the account, and that in so doing it remains that Sir W. W. should bring in his answer, upon which he would speedily bring it to an end. Here, remembering the incoherence of Sir J. M.'s discourses heretofore on this matter and his easiness in being over-reached to the King's prejudice in matters of this difficulty and moment, I did take the liberty to tell the Board that I did not believe that one original paper which passed between the Board and Sir W. W. in this business had been examined by Sir J. M., no more than they now found them to be in the business of the *Sunn*,[1] at least that none of those in my custody had been yet called for. And besides that, I found Sir W. W.'s present letter writ in terms so worthy the best care of this Office and particularly of the Comptroller in obviating the force of them, that I durst not but give it as my advice to the Board that some means may be used for getting some able help to Sir J. M. in the managing of this account. In this my Lord Brouncker in words and the rest in their countenances expressed their present concurrence. Only Sir J. M. was dissatisfied with it, saying that he had already had the assistance of as able an accountant as any was in England and that the account should be presently finished, if Sir W. W. would but bring in his answers to his exceptions. Hereupon I replied that what I said was out of goodwill as well to himself as the King, for neither of whom I thought it was safe that accounts of this weight and perplexity should depend upon his single examination and adjustment, whose age and infirmities by frequent sickness, with the muchness of works of other kinds on his hands, rendered him unfit to go through so great a care, and that therefore I might exonerate myself in this matter, being very sensible of the daily prejudice his Majesty receives or is in danger of receiving while no better secured in the adjustment of accounts of so great value as these of Sir W. W. and others. I did desire them to take notice that I did here make it my solemn request and advice to Sir J. M. that he would be pleased to make it his request to his Royal Highness that he might have some effectual help allowed him in

[1] See above, pp. 166–71.

the execution of this part of his Comptrollership also.[1] Forasmuch as till such help was given him or he otherwise eased thereof I could not think either his Majesty or the Board safe in their passing of these accounts, besides Sir W. W. and the clerks, and particularly Mr Hayter and W. Hewers then at my elbow and Mr Waith. There was then at the Board Br., J.M., T.M., J.T. and myself, who all of them remain awhile silent at this my declaration, when Sir J. M. first spake, without excepting against my advice, but running afresh into his old discourse upon his exceptions to the accounts and appointing Sir W. W. to be with him in the afternoon, and so the business went off without any hopes remaining on my part now of seeing anything done to the relieving of the King in this matter, by anything that I can now see resting in my power to do towards it.

An instance of commanders their compliance with his Royal Highness's instructions for the keeping an account of the entries and discharges of their men, and their capacity thereby to prevent supernumeraries, and correct the pursers' books.[2]

Janry 15th 1668[9]. At the Board's attending on his Royal Highness he was pleased to put into their hands a petition of Sir Wm Jenings's for the allowance of about 2000 supernumeraries on his book for the *Saphire*, that thereby the customary suspension of his wages might be removed.[3] This petition we were to examine the grounds of, which we did by giving Sir Wm Jenings several hearings, the result of which I collected and was as follows:

Sir Wm Jenings's case about supernumeraries in the Saphire.
1. That this ship was out under his command from the 20th of April 1667, in which year the Dutch came into the River, to the 7. 9ber.
2. In his petition to his Royal Highness delivered to us by the Duke of York Janry 15. 1668[9] he owns near 2000 supernumeraries and desires allowance of them, expressly charging them upon the Dutch coming into the River of Thames, when he saith he

---

[1] Penn and Brouncker had already been assisting him since January 1667 in the business of victualling and of pay tickets respectively. Brouncker was now appointed to assist him in dealing with Warren's account: see below, p. 193 n. 1.
[2] Dated 1 Jan. 1669: PRO, ADM 2/1, ff. 14–15.
[3] PRO, SP 29/256, no. 79 (summary in *CSPD 1668–9*, p. 216).

thought it not fit for him to reduce his number from 180 to 160 as was ordered but rather to increase his number what he could.
3. That the Dutch came into the River about the 10 of June 1667 and went away about the 23 July.
4. That instead of near 2000 supernumeraries owned by Sir Wm Jennings it is but 1264 that he is charged with.
5. That whereas he charges the whole number of supernumeraries upon the Dutch being in the River, it is certified from Sir Wm Penn's office that all the supernumeraries borne within the month of June 1667 amounts to but 202, so as that excuse is made use of for justifying six times as many supernumeraries as was indeed borne then. By which means also above 1000 supernumeraries of the 1264 are left without any ground given in the petition for their being borne.
6. That at the Board's observing this to him Janry 16th, he answered:
(1) That his petition was grounded upon his being informed by his purser that there was 2000 supernumeraries and that they were occasioned only by the Dutch being in the River.
(2) That we over-reckon the supernumeraries by taking in the times of many run[away]s whose wages the King will never pay, and therefore we ought not to count them here, though in expectation of their returning, he forbore to mark them either with D. or R.[1] And upon my taking notice hereof to the purser by way of reproach, he tells me that he dare not make them D. or R. without the special command of the captain. To which we replied that they standing open, we ought to reckon them as supernumeraries in regard they being open their wages may be demanded at any time by themselves or others. But *Quere:* the ill consequence of this practice and how much the report of what the Commissioners of Account have discovered of this kind touching Sir William Jennings's practice in the *Ruby*[2] may ground our suspecting his integrity here.
(3) That he did keep a book of the entry and discharge of men during the whole voyage, and that by that book he was so far from giving way to any supernumeraries as that at the end of the voyage he did not think there had been one upon the ship during the whole time, nor can believe this day that there was, or could conceive how there could be one.

---

[1] Columns headed 'Dead' or 'Runaways' were provided in the pay books.
[2] See below, p. 180 n. 1.

7. That upon his offering in discontent to leave in the King's hands as much as the victuals of those supernumeraries would amount to, and our answering him thereto that it was not victuals but wages also that the King was wronged in and expected reparation for, he seemed to receive that as a motion of great injustice to him and is therefore on this occasion to be submitted to his Royal Highness to be determined in.

8. The Board finding the supernumeraries thus disowned by Sir Wm Jennings and that grounded upon a book kept by himself, they thought the sight of that book might be useful in detecting the knavery of the purser whose books makes so many, and therefore desiring him to let them have the perusal of it, he promised it, but upon the 23 returns and tells us that he had examined the purser's victualling book by his own and found it right as to entry and discharges, and therefore thought it not necessary to bring us his own. To which being answered that this ought to have been done before when he signed the victualling book, and not to have been left to do now, he replied that he did do it, and had corrected it many places to the King's advantage. Upon which the Board finding it reasonable to insist nevertheless upon seeing that book of his, he on the 26 brought us that which he called his book, which we find to be a bare muster book containing only a list of the men's names written for him by the purser by which he mustered the ship sometimes during only the year 1668, without any account kept of the entry and discharge of any man, so as it plainly appears that by that book he could in no wise enable himself to correct the purser's victualling book when he signed it, nor be able to understand whether he had supernumeraries or no. Which being observed to him he answered, as to the first, he did besides this book keep a particular book with his own hand of the entries and discharges of men, though that book after being frequently demanded doth not yet appear. To the second, that as to the casting of the book to know whether there were any supernumeraries or no, he was not bred a clerk, nor thought it his work, nor believed his Royal Highness expected that his commanders should trouble themselves with that.[1] To which it being answered that it was plain by the Duke's Instructions by which the pursers are forbid to victual supernumeraries without an order in writing under the commander's

---

[1] A new post of captain's clerk was introduced in 1672: J. D. Davies, *Gentlemen and Tarpaulins* (Oxf. 1992), p. 45.

hand specifying both the number and the reason of bearing of them, that his Royal Highness's mind was that every captain should be able to know when his complement was full, it requiring no more than the telling of twenty, and that himself in his petition would have it thought that he knew both that there were supernumeraries, and how many, and from what reason borne. Whereto he returned that he did not know of any supernumeraries, nor thinks it his part to know; but whether he ought or not to know the same he was sure he gave order for none, and therefore if the purser victualled any without his order, by the Duke's own rule the purser is to bear them, and to that issue he brought and so left it.

9. Hereupon the Board, demanding the answer of the purser by what order he victualled the supernumeraries, he by one paper under his hand charges the whole upon the Dutch coming into the River, exclusive to anything in 1668; in another, adds to that of the Dutch in 1667 the sickness of his men, and taking in others to supply them in the year 68, but confesseth that he never cast his books but depended upon his shortness at some times to make up his supernumeraries at another time, and so takes the blame upon himself.

So the sum of it is, the captain disowns the knowledge or giving order for any supernumeraries yet justifies the truth of the purser's book, as to entries and discharges, though at the same time the purser could neither enter nor discharge a man without the order, nor as the captain saith did without his privity.

The purser in the meantime gives some reason for the supernumeraries and yet takes upon himself the blame of bearing them without casting his books whether he had any or no. And though we find him unsteady in the grounds he pretends for these supernumeraries, yet he justifies under the captain's hand the reality of his bearing and victualling them.

I having drawn up this rough state of this matter against our weekly attendance upon his Highness Janry 29. (68[9]), I did by the assent of the Board report the same by discourse to his Highness (present T.O., T.L., Br., J.M., T.M., J.T., and Mr Wren) according to this abstract, verifying the same by showing the papers evidencing every part of it. Upon which Sir Wm Jenings being called in to us (sitting in the Robes Chamber at Whitehall) he received a severe rebuke from his Royal Highness as well for his negligent performance of his duty as his pride in thinking himself too good to do it better, and accordingly we were ordered to detain in his Majesty's hands so much of his wages as would indemnify the King both for the wages and victuals for the whole number of supernumeraries, being 1264.

Accordingly the Board at their next meeting Febry 2d gave order by writing to Mr Hutchingson, the Treasurers' Paymaster, for the payment of Sir W. Jenings's wages detaining in the King's hands 94*l*. 15*s*. 4*d*. on the account aforesaid.

The papers relating to this matter remain in the office.[1]

Memorandum: that the Treasurers and Mr Hutchingson coming into the office after the said order was signed, Sir Tho. Osborne advises us that by letter from Mr Shales to Mr Hutchingson they were informed that Sir W. Jenings had made out and got paid to himself the tickets of some runaways, and it being demanded of him by Mr Shales that the money be repaid to the King, he refused it, saying that by reason of the men's being runaways the money belonged to him and he would keep it. Upon which Sir T. Osborne moved and it was readily agreed to that this money also should be stopped out of Sir W. Jennings's wages. But partly from Sir W. Jenings's denial of the thing (though with much hesitation in his terms), partly from Mr Shales's being then ill, and Mr Hutchingson's not having the letter about him (though he persisted in it that this was the effect of it), we could not come to a final adjustment either of the sum or matter, but left it with direction to Mr Hutchingson to forbear any payment of Sir W. Jennings's wages till the letter should be produced and Mr Shales spoke with.

Memorandum also: that I calling upon Mr Burrows[2] this day at the Board to review his calculation of the supernumeraries, and to ascertain a little better the number thereof borne during the Dutch being in the River (which was not as he had before cast them between the 1st and last of June but between the 10th of June and the 23d of July), he after one or two mistakes brings them from 1202 to 661 for a day, as appears by his certificate[3] annexed to the rest of the papers relating to this matter.

Thursday Febry 11. (68[9]). Sir Wm Jennings brings us a fresh

---

[1] PRO, SP 29/256, nos 74–80 (partly summarised in *CSPD 1668–9*, pp. 215–16). Pepys's conclusion was that 'from the discrepancy of Sir Wm's statements, his delays in producing proper books, his attempt to throw the blame on the purser, and his former practice in the *Ruby*, there is great ground to suspect him of want of integrity'.
[2] Chief clerk to Penn.
[3] PRO, SP 29/256 no. 75, dated 16 Jan. 1669.

reference from the Duke of York upon a new petition of his; the substance of which and the Board's thoughts thereon were delivered to the Duke of York by discourse Friday 19th as follows:
1. He owns his error in charging all his supernumeraries upon the Dutch being in the River, saying that part of them were occasioned in his voyage to the Straits.
2. He owns his error to have arisen from his reliance upon the purser, whom he thought more concerned to keep an account of them as being not to be allowed for them without his order, which he knew he never gave.
3. That he hath always studied the King's advantage, instancing in the giving the whole ship's company four days' fresh victuals at whole allowance at his own charge,[1] and relieving the sick the whole voyage. But this I find by Mr Burrows the King to have no benefit by in the purser's account. He adds further that he and his company redeemed three Christian slaves, and that he advanced to the ship's company their short allowance[2] in money before he received it.
4. That he took some of the King's subjects on board him abroad, which he saith is the only occasion of his supernumeraries for that year.

Upon the whole the matter seemed now ripe for his Highness's determination, how far his supernumeraries should be allowed him, which were of three sorts, *viz.* first, those borne during the Dutch being in the River, and before the 29 of June when the order for the reducement of her number from 180 to 160 took place; second, the same after the said 29 of June to the 23 July when they left the River; thirdly, those that arise from the King's subjects taken into the ships abroad.

Upon which the Duke was pleased to resolve that the first only and the last should be allowed, and accordingly his Royal Highness's order was sent us April the 15. (69) in these words, *viz.*:

'Gentlemen, Sir W. Jennings having made his humble request unto me for allowing several supernumeraries which were borne upon the *Saphire* which he commanded when the Dutch

---

[1] Marginal note: "Mr Gibson since tells me that he understands that this was no more than that he made the purser, at the purser's charge, give the company so many days' victuals extraordinary (without benefit to the King) for their pains in cutting of wood in the island of Furmetera [Formentera] for the use of the purser."

[2] The compensation for short allowance of victuals.

came up the River, of which I think fit to allow 200 men for a day which were borne until 29 of June 1667 at which time his complement of men was ordered to be reduced, as also 4 slaves for the time it appears they were aboard, and all those which were taken out of foreign ships according to the general instructions, and I do desire you will cause allowance to be made of the said supernumeraries accordingly. I am, your affectionate friend, James.'

Febry 6th [1668/9] Credit challenged and allowed to the minutes of a member of the Board. Memorandum: as an instance of the credit sometimes given by the Board to the least minutes of a Principal Officer, that Mr Boyce, the shipwright, this day attending the Board about his bills for work done upon the *Milford* in the year 1666 by agreement between Sir Wm Batten on behalf of the Board and him, which by the death of Sir Wm and non-appearance of this agreement no more than the rest of the books and papers relating to his office, has lain ever since his death to this day unallowed by the Board for want of other proof of the agreement than Mr Shish's acknowledgement of the particular of the works pretended by Boyce to have been done upon her, which the Board was not satisfied but that the said particular might have been framed by them since the death of Sir Wm, and the rather for that the present Surveyor finds her so out of repair as that she cannot reasonably be thought to have had a quarter of the value of his demand bestowed upon her so lately, though Boyce's particular, if it may be admitted as good, answers that objection by showing that the works he did lay in such parts of her as do not at this day need repair, he this morning, and no sooner, observes in justification of this his particular, that it was writ upon the bottom of it with my Lord Brouncker's hand the day and year as follows – 3rd Janry 166⁶/₇, which my Lord, interpreting to be the day of its being tendered to the Board, challenged it in honour and right to his own hand that the paper be admitted as authentic, and his demand made thereupon and sworn to be allowed. Which accordingly was by bill signed the 13 Febry 1668[9] for 560*l*.

Febry 6th 1668[9]. An instance of the bad husbandry of employing the King's own vessels in the fetching goods. The

THE NAVY WHITE BOOK   183

Adam & Eve – omitting the consideration of the time she had lain idle before her going – sets out from Greenwich for Stockwith in the river of Humber[1] the 13 of 9ber (68) as the master's journal declares, and returns to Deptford Febry 5th following, loaden with 36 loads of timber, which at the rates that Capt. Gibbs served us during the war at 20*s*. per load would have cost the King 36*l*., whereas this vessel being thus employed 3 months 0 weeks 1 day (besides the time she lay idle both before and at the end of the voyage) cost the King as follows:[2]

10 men at
{ 28*s*. wages 42. 0. 0
  20 victuals 30. 0. 0
  28 wear & tear 42. 0. 0

His bill of charges brought in for this voyage   5. 10. 8

Total   119.10. 8

Memorandum: the like to be expected in the several other vessels of the King's employed in this work, whereof three which set out with her at the same time not yet come in, though upon their way.

Febry 18. (68[9]). Seamen fittest to command ships. Upon occasion of the Board's treating with some persons this day for some merchant ships to be employed this year as convoys to the Fishery,[3] some of the owners, and particularly Mr Wood, did among other conditions insist upon it, that his ship might be commanded by a seaman; declaring his unwillingness to have her commanded by a man that understands not either himself or to check others in the good or ill husbanding of the ship's stores. Which being by the Board laid before his Royal Highness Febry 19th (68[9]), his Highness allowed of the reason, and said it was what he intended as much as he could both in the King's own

---

[1] *Recte* Trent.
[2] Later, in April 1669, the master asked for repairs to be authorised: *CSPD 1668–9*, p. 280. The vessel was a hoy, taken prize in 1665 and in 1673 sunk for foundations at Sheerness: Anderson, no. 359.
[3] The organisation (since 1664 a commercial corporation) which protected British fishing rights in the North Sea.

ships as well as merchantmen. Wherein he was confirmed by Col. Midleton the Surveyor, who solemnly protested that in his own affairs he would rather choose to let that ship for 80*l*. a month to be commanded by a seaman, than the same ship for 100*l*. to be commanded by one that was not so, and that he was confident there was no less difference than that in the expense of all his Majesty's ship's stores and the use of the ships.

Febry 23d (68[9]). Books and papers of Sir Wm Batten's office as Surveyor either never kept or not found. Memorandum: that the Surveyor this day advertised the Board upon some new occasions of resorting to Sir Wm Batten's books and papers that he has not to this day been possessed of one book or paper that should evidence Sir Wm Batten to have ever been Surveyor of his Majesty's Navy, but one survey book of the year (63).

Febry 23d (68[9]). An instance of what the King suffers in the ill performance of the survey of ships. Memorandum: that this day after many propositions from the Surveyor touching the burning, breaking in pieces, or laying up in Ham Creek the wreck of the *Royall James*, he did this day by writing jointly with Mr Tippetts give us his opinion that she should be made a hulk for Deptford or Woolwich, being wholly unfit to be rebuilt upon for what she was before.

Quere: what would be thought of our having led his Majesty to 3 or 400*l*. charge in the fitting, manning and bringing about this wreck from Chatham into the dock at Woolwich, with the charge of some master shipwright's being sent down to Chatham on purpose to survey her and the *Royall Oake* and *Loyall London*, the second of which had some charge upon her too and at last is broken to pieces.[1]

Sir Wm Batten's neglect inquired after. Quere: what can be said in defence of the Surveyor then in being who might have done the same then at Chatham as the present Surveyor has done here and prevented the loss of so much money, she being after all by the Board's letter to the Duke of York propounded to be

---

[1] These ships had been burnt in the Dutch raid on the Medway. The *Royal James* was converted into a hulk at a cost of £1635, and the *Loyal London* rebuilt at a cost of £10,000: *Further Corr.*, pp. 196, 227.

turned to a hulk, and accordingly ordered so by the Duke of York March 10. 1668[9]. *Vide* page [247].

Febry 23. 1668[9]. Sir John Mennes's weakness instanced in his management of the account and suit between the King and Mr Cutler. Memorandum: that after more than two years and more than 30*l.* expense to his Majesty, as Sir J.M. himself confesses, in the sueing of Mr Cutler about the business of Lyell sent to Lieth during the war for buying up for the Navy here such prize goods as should happen to come up there,[1] the Board did upon some late desires of theirs and solicitations of Mr Cutler's receive from Sir J.M. what account he could give of the true state of the controversy between the King and Cutler, and of the three only points which he propounded as matters of difference, I did, to my own great trouble to see how weakly all matters in this Office are managed, satisfy the Board (Mr Wren also present) upon my first hearing them that the first two were not only injuriously denied to Mr Cutler, so as if we had persisted in the suit the King must certainly have been overthrown in all the costs and damages attending the same (and these points were Lyell's buying of clapboard, and supplying of Strachan[2] with 30*l.* for the victualling of the vessel that brought the goods hither), but that though Cutler had in his very first account demanded allowance two years ago of this 30*l.* by charging it on Strachan even before Strachan's coming away from Scotland, yet Sir J.M. is found to have suffered Strachan to bring the goods, pass his account for victuals and receive both his own and company's wages, and (after several months' stay here in doing thereof) depart back to Scotland wholly discharged of the King's service without so much as ever charging him with this 30*l.*, or so much as seem at this day ever to have taken any notice of it; so as the sum must be given up as wholly lost, the Board being fully satisfied that Cutler had done his part. The third point related only to casting, which ought to have been done long ago, and may now in half an hour's time, and was accordingly committed to Mr Pointer presently to dispatch. Thus has the King been at double loss and might have been at more; the merchant also put to charge and his reputation

---

[1]This was in 1666. Lyell was acting on behalf of the contractor, Thomas Cutler: *CSPD Add. 1660–85*, p. 166; *1665–6*, pp. 548, 555. The suit was in the Prize Court.
[2]Capt. John Strachan, Navy agent at Leith.

prejudiced without any the least ground appearing from anything that Sir J.M. has discovered; and yet when all is done I do verily believe from the broken memory which I have of this matter that Cutler has really played the knave with the King therein, and doubt not of being able to recover how, if I can get time to recollect myself about it, which I shall endeavour. But in the meantime lie under the trouble of seeing both him and the King made to suffer where there is no ground, and the latter left unrighted in the points wherein he has been truly abused.

An instance of the imperfection of our estimates. In answer to a demand from the Board, grounded upon an order from the Committee of the Council for the Navy, an estimate was provided by Mr Christopher Pett, master shipwright at Woolwich, of the charge of building two 2nd-rate ships to answer the *Royall Katherine*,[1] and sent to the Board, wherein he estimates each of them at 9176*l*. 1*s*. 0*d*., so as both of them amounted to 18,352. 2. 0. Upon which, without any examination of the grounds of his calculation, the Surveyor approves on it and recommends it to the Board for their approbation; which was given and a regular estimate provided, signed by J.M., W.B. and S.P. 9ber 5. 1664, and sent to the said Committee.[2] By whose approval returned to us, the Board soon after directed their order signed by the same hands for the putting in building, the one at Chatham, the other at Woolwich, two ships of that quality, burden and dimensions.

These ships, being shortly after put in hand, lay slowly advanced upon until Febry 166⁵⁄₆, when upon joint advice of Col. Midleton, the Surveyor and Comr Tippetts, the Board was put upon representing to the Duke of York the injury his Majesty would receive if we were not by money to buy materials and pay workmen able[3] to finish them this year, which the Surveyor urged might be expressed (and a letter was accordingly drawn up, though afterwards by the rest of the Board thought fit to be spoke in softer terms) by saying that it were better to have what is done upon them burnt than proceed upon them with fresh upper works after the bottoms shall have lain wet and dry in dock one year more.

[1] A 2nd-rate; much admired (*Diary*, v. 306 & n.3).
[2] *CSPD 1664–5*, p. 55.
[3] MS. 'enable'.

When this representation came to be finished I advised it as a circumstance to be added, that we should tell the Duke what positive sum would be requisite for the enabling us to finish these ships, which they approved of, and by the Surveyor's advice they resolved upon putting down the sum which the Surveyor had in his late book presented by the Board to the Duke valued the same at, abating only about 2000*l.* in a ship for what further work and materials may have been spent upon them since that time, which was in [*blank*] last. I also at the same time propounded it to them whether it might not be convenient to take notice to the Duke of York of the value of the King's loss if these ships should not be seasonably finished, and to do it by giving him an estimate of what the works and materials already spent upon them [cost]. Which at the Board's desire, the Surveyor and Mr Tippetts did then at the Board compute and agreed that it could not come to less than 16,000*l.* (says Mr Tippetts), 20,000*l.* (says the Surveyor). But it was thought unnecessary by the Board to give the Duke any present account thereof.

Hereupon I proceeded to the preparing a new draft of the letter to the Duke, but in doing it found that what was here valued at the lowest at 16,000*l.* for what was done already to them, and 27,000*l.* for what is yet to do (the Surveyor in his said book having valued the finishing that at Woolwich at 13,000*l.*, and that at Chatham at 18,000*l.*, together 31,000*l.*) both amounting to 43,000*l.* was in the Board's before-mentioned estimate valued but at 18,352*l.* 2*s.* 0*d.*, which is 3*l.* less than half the real cost.

This I acquainted the Board with Febry 27. (6⁸⁄₉), who were with good reason astonished at it and in their considerations how the same (if observed) could be answered in extenuation of the Board's remissness in their making the estimates, nothing else could be pitched upon them than that the builders have greatly exceeded their dimensions and scantlings, and consequently greatened the charge both of labour and materials – a liberty which I took the occasion of observing to them the many ill consequences of, especially at a season when both money and materials (and the more by how much they are the greater) are so hard to be procured, and the Board censured in other things (though without reason) for the greatness of the naval expense.

This nevertheless was held an excuse which might in some measure serve the Board if the present matter should happen to be inquired into, it being thought less safe to ask a less sum than would really do the business, especially having so lately under our hands demanded a certain sum 31,000*l*. However, it was thought fit to make use as far as they could of the just pretence of having some work done to them since that demand, and therefore concluded of lessening it now to 25,000*l*., according to which the letter was prepared and signed by the Board March 2d 1668[9] by Br., J.M., T.M., S.P., J.T. So that at their lowest computation these ships will cost the King 41,000*l*., which the Board had under their hands estimated (in order to the providing money for the same) but at 18,352*l*. 2*s*. 0*d*., which is yet less by 2000*l*. than half of the true cost.[1]

Another instance of the imperfection of our estimates. Vide the case of the R. James wreck. Vide page [185]. *Memorandum:* that the order for turning the *R. James* into a hulk was grounded upon a joint survey, report and estimates of Col. Midleton and Comr Tippetts, who by letter under their hands value it at 750,[2] according to which the Board reported to the Duke and he to the King and Council, who allow of its being done and we upon the Duke's order on that behalf send down our warrant to Woolwich for putting the same in hand, enjoining the master shipwright to keep within the estimate. Who answers us by a letter signed by Mr Shish and Byland that this work could not be done for less than 1635*l*.,[3] at which the Board being amazed, and the Surveyor at a loss how to defend the former valuation otherwise than by alleging Mr Tippetts's concurrency therein, we sent down to Portsmouth Shish's and Byland's particular, by which they so much exceed the former estimate, praying Mr Tippetts's opinion thereon, who in his next letter returns us his allowance of Shish's valuation as far as to 1350*l*. and sends up his reasons of exception against the rest. Which reasons being sent to Shish and Byland, they answered by a letter of the 2d of April that they cannot depart from their former estimate of 1635*l*., and pray that we would take the opinion of any other shipwrights in the River for our satisfaction. Accordingly we by letter desired Mr Castle and Mr Graves, merchant shipwrights, to view and give us their opinion herein, who by letter of the 8 of May report the

---

[1]The ships, both 1st-rates, were finished in 1670 – the *Prince* being built at Chatham and the *St Andrew* at Woolwich: Anderson, nos 448, 450.
[2]*CSPD 1668–9*, p. 205 (22 February).
[3]Ibid., p. 260 (2 April).

particulars insisted on by Shish and Byland not only to be necessary, but that the work will cost 1982*l*.[1]

March 9th 1668[9]. The Treasurers' proceeding at the Board in relation to contracts and payments. Memorandum: that the contract book being this day tendered to the Board for their signing of what contracts had been drawn up and entered by agreement made at the Board within a meeting or two before, I observed that the Treasurers refused to join in the signing to what did not appear that themselves were not present at the making; and that so far as reciprocally to decline the signing what one of them was absent at, though the other was present and did sign to it.

In the next place I observed that the Board being in very great want of Sprucia deals and upon being informed that the merchant, one Mr Boddy, who offered us a parcel, as the Surveyor reported them, of excellent goods and a good pennyworth,[2] refused to deliver his goods without the money were first secured for his payment in a third hand imprested by bill of the 2nd inst. [of] 600*l*. to Mr Mayors the purveyor,[3] that so the merchant's scruple might be removed, and we secured in our promise of payment, the goods being also as the Surveyor told us much solicited for by Mr Johnson and Castle, shipwrights in the River. The Treasurers did this day utterly refuse to pay the bill, alleging the consequence of that practice, *viz.* that nobody would trust us without the money were first in the like manner secured, which they said they foresee they should not suddenly be able to do. Upon which the Board urged not only the consonancy of the practice to the Duke's Instructions and a constant use and design of purveyors, but as we durst not any more undertake for payment, so neither will others accept of our undertaking, especially such as, like the present merchant, did at this day lie under the inconvenience of the credit they had formerly given us. Besides, that if ever we intended to buy at the market price we must be furnished so as to be able to buy of strangers, which had no knowledge of us more than by the ill report of our payments. All which they made no other answer to than that they believed there was something

---

[1] *CSPD 1668–9*, p. 317.
[2] On 17 February Body offered his deals at 15*s*. per 'piece': ibid., p. 635.
[3] Mayers had reported favourably on Body's deals: ibid., p. 216.

extraordinary in this, that their payment should be rendered so doubtful, who, as they challenged any man to complain of the want of payment upon any contract to which they concurred in the signing, so they declared they would take care never to be found failing in the payment of such contracts, and thereupon desired that this merchant might be presently sent for, which he was (from the Exchange), who after a long denial did, upon the earnest protestations of the Treasurers touching his payment and the joint importunities of the Board, was prevailed with to trust us upon assurance of payment the very next day after his bill shall be signed.

I also at the same time was informed by W. Hewers that the Treasurers had this morning at the Treasury Office made great difficulty of yielding to the payment of the bill for 300*l.* dated [*blank*] imprested to Mr Hayter, purveyor for petty emptions, for providing of some goods of like necessity which could not be had (at least at the market price) but with ready money; though they it seems did afterwards agree to it.

The consideration of all which made me take occasion March the 11th to observe to the Board the danger wherein the whole credit of the Office now was, the Treasurers having (according to many instances I then gave them, as in Mason's late contract, etc.) expressly disowned their being under any obligation to satisfy bills upon contracts made before their time, and declared their singular care to those contracts wherein they are concerned, so as for my own part, as I had for some time forborne to sign to any contracts till the Treasurers had signed them, so I held it now unnecessary to sign where their names are, the assurance the merchant had for payment being now professedly placed not upon the credit of the Board but of the Treasurers singly, which by the late changes in the hands of the Treasurers may be doubted will not be sufficient to answer the occasions of this Office while people are so sensible that more changes may be expected. I told them, however, that if as they seem to desire I did sign any of those contracts, I declared that I would not have it construed to my charging myself with any undertaking for or owning any assurance which the Board could have of being enabled to make good the payment, but to the signifying my concurrence with them in the terms or my attestation (according to the intent of the customs of my predecessors heretofore, as I lately more largely told them in my letter upon the Surveyor's late dispute about the

THE NAVY WHITE BOOK 191

Board's proceeding in a contract with Coleby for kerseys,[1] and myself in the signing of all contracts before the signing of the Board) that the said contracts are drawn according to the direction, sense and order of the Board.

To which they yielding, and then discoursing awhile in general of the truth and consequence of what I had then said touching the Treasurers' proceedings, the matter rested.

2 April 1669. Substance of my discourse alone to his Royal Highness about the general administration of the Navy. Memorandum: that having four days since desired his Royal Highness's allowing me half an hour to attend him alone about some particular matters of the Navy, I by his appointment waited upon him this afternoon in his closet at Whitehall, where (among other things) I gave him by discourse a relation of the management of this Office, with all the changes that has therein been from the farthest backward that (in my late searches) I can meet with any record of, and offered him my humble advice touching the method wherein it might be most convenient for the Board to represent the same in writing in pursuance of his late order in that behalf. Which advice he was pleased to approve of, and commanded me to see followed.[2]

My advice that Comr Tippetts and Capt. Cox should begin their attendance as Commissioners, the first at Chatham, the latter at Portsmouth. He was likewise pleased to approve of the reasons I gave him for Mr Tippetts's taking his first turn at Chatham and Capt. Cox his at Portsmouth. It being hard to expect from either of them the same vigour in regulating matters as Commissioners in a place where but the other day they were but equal with

[1] See above, p. 172 & n. 1.
[2] On 13 February the Duke of York had at the King's request ordered the Board to draw up a report comparing the existing administration of the Navy Office with that of 'the late times': BL, Add. MSS 36782, f. 81*r*. Pepys, having searched the records from 1618, composed a memorandum (17 April) defending the existing constitution and concluding that the Commonwealth was 'not more husbandly than we' (*Diary*, ix. 484). The original is in the Duke of Leeds MSS, Yorks. Arch. Soc. DD5/12/10 (inf. from Mrs S. Thomas); copies listed in *Diary*, ix. 525 n. 1.

those they are now to command, as in place where they lay under no such restraint by old acquaintance, familiarity, relation, or interest.[1]

My advice to the Duke about Sir John Mennes's present inability to manage the office of Comptroller. I in the next place showed his Royal Highness a letter of Sir Wm Warren's to the Board of the 1st of April (69) complaining severely of those delays which he had not long since by petition[2] done the like about to his Royal Highness, and concerning which, upon his Highness's reference on that petition, the Board had by their letter of the [blank] to his Highness and I by another to Mr Wren dated the 3d of Janry last and by discourse both to Mr Wren and his Highness Janry 4th (*vide* my Letter Book Janry 3d 166⁸⁄₉)[3] abundantly as I though informed his Highness not only that the delays in this matter lay on Sir J.M.'s hands, but that the whole business of the Comptrollership lay on the like delay and non-performance through the general incapacity of Sir J.M. to execute it. That it was true that his Royal Highness had on this my advice resolved to lay it before his Majesty, but that I doubted whether what his Royal Highness may have done by discourse to his Majesty may always be remembered, when the ill effects of continuing so weak an Officer in so weighty an office shall be observed, as soon or late they undoubtedly must, to the occasioning great blame. To which his Royal Highness answered me that he had so often spoke of it to the King and sometimes prayed his Majesty to remember that he had done so, that he cannot doubt his Majesty's remembering it whenever there shall be occasion. To which I returned that though I hoped this might be enough to justify his Highness as to that particular, yet I thought that more might be done than yet was done for his Majesty's security and the subject's ease until his Majesty shall think fit to remove Sir J.M., and that was by authorising one of the two members of this Office (already acting as his assistants

---

[1]Tippetts had been master shipwright at Portsmouth, and Cox master attendant at Chatham. Neither in fact was moved on his promotion.
[2]PRO, ADM 106/17, f. 265r (20 Dec. 1668).
[3]NMM, LBK/8, pp. 555–6 (printed *Further Corr.*, pp. 204–6).

in some particular parts of his work)[1] to take the care of easing him in the adjustment of several accounts of moment which have long lain unevened and are likely to continue still so, with extraordinary prejudice to his Majesty, reproach to his service and grievance of many private men, unless some other hand than Sir J.M.'s be charged with the management and dispatch thereof. Here his Royal Highness answered me that he had already a good while since upon my discourses heretofore to him on this subject spoken to my Lord Brouncker to give Sir J.M. his assistance on the particular accounts of Sir Wm Warren. I replied that I well remembered it, and that my Lord Brouncker hath indeed intermeddled with those accounts since that time, but that I do perceive that he does not interest himself therein with that vigour, strictness and attention as such matters ought to be handled with, and as I doubt not his Lordship would do, were he authorised and enjoined to it by some written order from his Highness. To which he answered that he would direct Mr Wren forthwith to prepare such an order to the Lord Brouncker and send it him; and accordingly, when at the determination of our discourse and going forth of the closet his Highness met Mr Wren, he directed him to draw up an order for my Lord Brouncker's assisting Sir J.M. as I should advise him, and particularly in the settling the accounts of Sir W. Warren.

Mr Wrenn's unwillingness to take off more work from Sir John Mennes than is just necessary. Hereupon the Duke's going away Mr Wren demanded my advice about the order, which I gave him, observing to him that there are many other accounts to be adjusted and those of very great moment to his Majesty as well as to private persons, wherein Sir J.M. doth equally want help with those of Sir W. Warren's. Whereto Mr Wren made me the same answer as formerly, that it is a pity to offer more seeming discouragement upon a gentleman that has served the King so long as Sir J. M. has than is necessary, and that therefore, no complaint having yet come of delay from any other person than Sir W. Warren, and that his Highness having only mentioned Warren's case, he was unwilling to offer at intrenching upon the poor gentleman any farther than what related to that particular.

[1] Brouncker and Penn had been appointed to assist him with the Treasurer's and Victualler's accounts respectively by a Privy Council order of 16 Jan. 1667. The Navy Board then set out their respective responsibilities in detail: PRO, ADM 106/3520, ff. 34v–35v (n.d.).

I told him here, that though no other private person besides Warren had complained to the Duke, yet that very many others had made their complaints to us, and that almost daily; besides, that my importunity in this business respects not so much the satisfaction of private men but that it is much more grounded upon the sense I have both of the reproach this whole Office suffers, and the unspeakable damages his Majesty's service and treasure are exposed to by the weakness of his one Officer. To this he replied that the present order should be drawn up with respect only to Warren's case, leaving the rest to his Royal Highness's further consideration of this matter, and declaration of his pleasure therein. And so this matter ended.

3 April 1669. Upon occasion of the Surveyor's tendering to the Board this day some loose accounts of boatswains and carpenters, not examined and allowed by himself (but only by the clerks of the survey of the yards), much less drawn up into a declaration according to the 5th article of his duty for the ready perusal of the Board,[1] and yet would have it thought that he had therein fully complied with his duty; and again upon considering the answer he gave to my Lord Brouncker and myself when we urged it as his duty not only that the said accounts should be fairly and abstractedly stated to the Board, but that the same should be all of them signed by himself in testimony of his having examined and allowed them, which answer of his was that he would not for a thousand pound a year no more for any reward in the world be obliged to examine all boatwains' and carpenters' accounts with his own hand, although I did then tell him and do heartily believe that all the accounts then showed us as the growth of the first year of his Surveyorship might be examined with the assistance of one of his clerks in less than a month's time, spending but an hour or an hour and a half in a day, I was led to the reflecting on what I believe will be found very true, that no greater error can almost be committed in the choice of a Principal Officer of the Navy or any other of like trust, than the choosing of such whose age, infirmities, ignorance or aught else renders them unable or whose slothfulness makes them unwilling or condition in the world renders them too great, too good, or under no necessity to attend the execution of the office with their own

[1] *Oeconomy*, p. 65.

hands. The truth of which is easily verified by Sir G. Carterett, Sir Wm Batten, Sir J. Mennes, Sir Wm Penn, and by this present Surveyor, all of whom from one or other of the precedent causes were led (though in different degrees) to the sparing their own hands and heads and delivering up the work they were entrusted with to be managed by their clerks or not at all, and accordingly their work hath sped to the ruin of the service and Office. Whereas in such as Sir Wm Coventry, Sir Robt Slingsby and my Lord Brouncker, who applied their own heads and hands to the management of their works, the effects of their pains have in their particular places been very laudable and really advantageous to his Majesty, though the failures of the greater number have involved their endeavours of the rest in the same blame and ill success with those that most deserve it and to whom the ill success of the whole ought to be imputed. Upon the same occasion further matter for meditation was administered to me by his reply to what I moved touching his calling home to his own proper work that clerk of his, Maddox, which contrary to the public advice of the Board (as appears by what I have in another place heretofore taken a memorandum of)[1] he hath kept in continual employment at the Treasury Office in making up books at 7s. per diem extraordinary. His answer to which was that if he were not there another must be there, and therefore he might as well be continued there where he is, and the Board allow him to take another clerk extraordinary to do this work. To which I answered, first, that the doing the work of the Treasury Office was not under his care or any of the Board's but my Lord Brouncker particularly, who has been so far from desiring or needing Maddox's help as to have put out Maddox and appointed another in his room, until upon his (Col. Midleton's) dissatisfaction thereat, and declaring that the work of his own office could spare one of his clerks, he was set at work again there, thereby only to entitle him to 7s. a day extraordinary wages. Next I observe to him, and was therein seconded by my Lord Brouncker, that while he continued him there as his clerk the King paid him not only the 7s. a day but 30l. a year, whereas if he took him home to his own work 30l. a year would pay him, and the 7s. per diem provide another to do the work at the Treasury Office. To which he then replied that this clerk Maddox is not qualified to serve him in the business of his Surveyorship. Whereto he was readily

---

[1] Above, pp. 165–6.

answered that the King put him under no necessity of entertaining or keeping a clerk that was not fit for his service, and so with some dissatisfaction to the Surveyor this discourse ended. But not without leaving me an occasion of reflecting upon another great evil in the Navy in reference to clerks, which upon recollection I find to have been very rarely chosen by their fitness, and having been bred to anything that might fit them for the Navy in general, much less for the particular service of the Officer he is to serve, but either for money, such as Sir Wm Batten's clerks, not only those of the survey of the yards but (as is reported) even Gilsthrop that attended him at the office, whose education had been the being a clerk to a justice of the peace. Others, as Pugh to Sir John Mennes, John Davis and Aldridge to Lord Berkely, Seddon, Gibbons, Waterson and Clapham successively to Sir Tho. Hervey, Jo. Lake to Sir Wm Batten, John Sheeres at present to Mr Tippetts, Hanbury and Maddox to the present Surveyor, all which have been manifestly chosen for the sake of acquaintance, kindred, or some other ground in which their present qualifications bore no part. The consequences of which method of choosing clerks are these. First, that being brought in either for the profit of the master, or the particular advantages of the clerk, all ways must be found of employing those clerks so as their employments may be beneficial to them. Thus before they are entered upon any other work whereby to initiate them into the knowledge of the Navy, they must be sent to the Ticket Office, or to the making up of pay books at the Treasury Office, or to the attending the paying off of ships and yards; to the end that by these means they may be entitled to travelling charges, or extraordinary allowances of 7s. a day for the making up of books, or the profits which they have opportunities of making (how just I will not say) by making out of tickets and getting them paid. All of them being works calling not only for great integrity and industry (whereof they have not yet had time to give any proofs), but as much ability and experience in the methods of the Navy and the evils they are to obviate, as any other pieces of clerkship belonging to the Office. Secondly, by this means the proper work of the Officers of the Navy is neglected, the clerks allowed them thereto by the King being for their private benefit sent to other employments than what their masters' duties call them to. Thus Sir Wm Batten employing his clerks on works foreign to his own office but such as their particular advantage led them to, not one part of the work of his own office was ever performed, the books of survey never kept, no account of loans, no accounts of boatswains ever examined. So that since his death his successor Col. Midleton has frequently declared to the Board that at his entrance into his place he found not one book or piece of paper by which he should understand that there had ever been such a man as Sir Wm Batten Surveyor of the Navy, but only one old survey book for the year 1663 or 64.[1] Nor after several letters on that behalf from the Board to my Lady Batten, or any to be found elsewhere. By which means, among many other ill consequences, we are left wholly ignorant of all loans, and what goods of his Majesty's lie out of his yards; so as it is only by accident that we have sometime since his death been informed of goods of a considerable value lying out of the King's hands; as there are no doubt many more which for want of survey books we cannot inform ourselves of, and so the King likely to lose them. Hence it is that not only in the Surveyor's business but the Comptroller's we are so unable either to secure the King, satisfy the Commissioners of Accounts, or justify ourselves in anything almost belonging to those two offices.

Sir John Mennes (like Sir Wm Batten) taking care that Pugh shall be ever attending one or other extraordinary work of private profit; so as nothing is done relating to the standing work of his office, but what one hand (Pointer) can do, which is the reason that so little is either done well or done at all. Thirdly, by this means, clerks being employed upon works foreign to their masters, their masters have no check or eye over them, but they left to do as much or as little, as carefully or as negligently, as they please. Thus it comes to pass that the clerks employed in the making up the books without any command over them, the work is not only for their interest lengthened to double or treble the time it needed and the King's charge thereby greatened (as may appear by the bills which have been granted to them, amounting to many degrees more than their bare salary of 30*l.* a year), but the work so done (partly from their negligence aforesaid, and partly from their ignorance) as that my Lord Brouncker lately informed the Board that he had in reviewing some of their books found so many faults as that he doubted all that had been for two or three years at so much charge been done must be done over again. And no wonder, it being a business wherein our clerks had not their own negligence and ignorance only to betray

[1] Cf. above, p. 184.

them, but the interest and subtlety of the paymaster to connive at their errors, if not to lead them into them. Fourthly, lastly, by this means the Principal Officers and Commissioners themselves (which is indeed one of the pests of the Navy) being either too great, too good, or by age, inexperience, or other infirmities or negligences unqualified for doing their work themselves; whilst in the meantime care is not taken to breed up clerks, but strange faces introduced with every new Officer and those shifted for convenience and still for new ones and only for the private advantage of those thus brought in, and this to the discouragement of those few that have been bred to the Navy, who by being fit for it are therefore necessarily kept to do the drudgery of the office; it happens that there are very few clerks able to do any thorough services; or that have any more acquaintance with the business of the office than just to some one particular to which for their private advantage they have applied themselves. Hence it is that Sir John Mennes, being unable to do anything himself, has not one clerk able to manage his business, but that gross mistakes are found in all that passes that office, as appears by my daily returning them for correction even after Sir J.M. has been led to sign them. Hence it is that upon the Board's late insisting with the Surveyor upon his personal overlooking the boatswains' and carpenters' accounts, which he would have excused by want of a clerk to assist him, I took the freedom to advise that he would call to him that clerk of his, Maddox, which he had ever since his coming into the Navy employed in the making up of books at the Treasury Office, contrary to the desire of my Lord Brouncker and the Board. He thought fit to answer the Board that since one must be employed at the Treasury, this clerk of his might as well be there as another, and the King allow him to entertain a third, who might be fit to serve him in the work now propounded, which he declared Maddox not to be.

From whence it is observable, first, that here is a clerk entertained and employed not where the master needs them, but [where] the man may be most profited. Secondly, that the proper work of the master has been suffered to lie wholly neglected for want of hands well chosen, though at the same time the King is put to the same charge for a person unfit. Thirdly, that the private convenience of the master or clerk is so much considered before the advancement of the work they are properly concerned in and the charge the King is at for the doing of it, that rather than a clerk shall be removed from an employment of profit though he has nothing to do in it, the King shall be made to bear not only the standing wages of 30*l.* a year and an allowance of 7*s.* a day, but entertain a new clerk at a new charge, rather than the old one shall be removed from his trade of profit to attend the work that belongs to him, when in the meantime, were he put to do the work he ought to do for the salary he receives as the Surveyor's clerk, enough able clerks might be found to attend at the Treasury Office for less than the 7*s.* a day he receives over and above.

Which I told the Surveyor plainly at the Board and was seconded therein by my Lord Brouncker, besides what we said to him on this subject in writing dated [*blank*] April (69). Fourthly, lastly, what the consequences are likely to be of the Surveyor's late proposition of having the whole care of all stores and provisions lodged in the commanders, and that to that end boatswains, gunners, pursers and carpenters should be at the sole choice of the commanders, when in the Surveyor's own choice of the instruments allowed him by the King such an instance is given of the manner wherein the King's work is done without having hands either qualified for it or duly applied to it.

April 6th (69). Upon discourse this day to the Board with the Surveyor, touching the extravagant expense and demands of boatswains, and the ignorance or knavery of commanders in vouching them, Mr Homewood the clerk of the survey at Chatham being then present, did give me an instance of two where boatswains have brought their captains' allowances of expense of stores more than ever the boatswains stood charged with.

April 9th 1669. Memorandum: that after the Board's waiting upon his Royal Highness this day to confer with Sir Thomas Allen (who came to town yesterday from Portsmouth, being newly arrived there with his fleet from the Straits) about getting forth of another fleet with which he is to return to the Straits, I in my discourse in several places find the coming back of Sir Thomas Allen extremely censured as having left the greatest wealth of our English merchants now in the Straits to the mercy of the Algerins, that have been there a great while, Sir Tho. Allen having patched up a disadvantageous peace,[1] and the same having been violated by the Turks since his making that peace, and before his leaving of the Straits, as among others by taking out the gold out of one of our Company's ships, Godolphin master, going to the East Indies.[2] And that which I most observe is people discoursing universally of Sir Tho. Allen's and the rest of his fleet's having practised more the trade of merchantmen, not only in bringing home goods but carrying of goods from port to port in the Straits, than doing the work of men-of-war. And thence I find they agree in the imputing the coming home of the fleet to the commanders' concernment of profit to bring home the goods they have taken in. How true this is I cannot tell. It being as much denied by Sir Tho. Allen as asserted by the merchants, and Capt. Perryman particularly, who since his coming home as a merchantman has given me many particular instances of the truth thereof which himself see when lately in the Straits. But this use I would make of it, *viz.* to consider whether it might not be of use before the pay of every ship to have the commander's and master's journal delivered to the Comptroller, which (as in other respects in reference to the checking of boatswains' demands for loss of anchors, cables and sails when possibly in port, etc.), so it may be useful to discover especially in voyages to the Straits or elsewhere where action and keeping the sea is required, to discover how the King's ships spend their time abroad.[3] Besides that I find it suggested that this way of commanders turning merchantmen with the King's ships is it that does many times occasion the commanders complaining of the ill condition of their ships, want of stores and provisions, etc., thereby only to bring about their being called home to the bereaving the King of the service which their ships might otherwise do him by continuing abroad.

Memorandum: that I am confirmed in my last suggestion by what I understand this day (May the 4th 69) from Mr Gibson, who tells me that he is very well informed that upon Sir Thomas

---

[1]The peace, concluded on 2/12 February, allowed the Algerians to take as prize any ships in which slaves were found: Allin, *Journals*, vol. ii, pp. xl, 227.

[2]The ship was the *Morning Star*, freighted by the E. India Company, taken off Cadiz: *CSPD 1668–9*, p. 234.

[3]Commanders of fleets were already obliged to deposit a copy of their journals with the Admiralty, and the present suggestion does not appear to have been put into effect. On 23 Apr. 1669 an Order in Council was issued forbidding the carriage of all goods, except gold and silver, in royal ships. Allin was reminded of this order when he set out for the Straits in the following July: *Journals*, ii. 233.

Allen's hearing at Tanger (by letters overland) that a stop was likely to be put to his coming home, he, to prevent his receipt of any such orders, sails that very night towards Cadiz, where staying very few days, no more than was just necessary for taking in provisions, he dispatches away thence so far off to sea as might bring him out of the road of meeting with any intelligence from England, and by the greatness of the compass he took did not only prevent his meeting with any orders for his stay and so came home, to the astonishment of the Exchange, who publicly declared that he came home only to bring home the goods that the King's ships had taken in, but made his voyage to the King's cost much longer than otherwise it might have been, being near six weeks, and the wind so as several of their fleet were astonished (as is said) at his tacking to and again for several days, and so getting further into the sea when he might have been coming directly home.

May 4. (69). I can never enough wonder at the improvidence of some men, who rather than not seem in some measure concerned in behalf of the King, will be found frequently falling foul upon the enormities of such as themselves are in particular charged with the preventing of. Such as the Surveyor this day fell (as he frequently does) upon the knavery of boatswains, occasioned by a demand of Spanish tables for the ships now going out, saying that they were rogues and should not be supplied for that they never returned any.[1] Upon which I asked him whether they did not indent for them, and if so, why they were discharged of them in their accounts. Whereto he answered that they generally brought them in in their accounts either as stole or taken away by their captains. Whereto I replied that if this account of them be good, why should the boatswains be now blamed? If bad, how comes the boatswain to be discharged by the clerk of the survey certifying that he hath made a fair account, and the captain not to be charged therewith if delivered to or taken away by him? To which he made no return, but as heretofore on like occasions suffered the matter to rest, yet will undoubtedly in a day or two fall to the like complaint again.

---

[1] Spanish tables were a variety of trestle tables commonly used on board ship. On 13 May Middleton wrote to the Board suggesting that they should be made of deal: *CSPD 1668–9*, p. 325; see below, pp. 214–15 & n.

The same day I had fresh occasion of taking notice of and considering the consequence of the practice of the present Treasurers (every day used by them) of inviting merchants to trust us by appealing to them whether they have heard of any failure in payment for any goods bought within their time – which implies the reducing the credit of the Office in general to the credit of the Treasurer in particular, who by death, disfavour or otherwise, being many ways removable (as we have already had instances),[1] how many will think themselves unsafe in trusting where they find a Treasurer solicitous of paying none but what's contracted for in his time, leaving that of his predecessors unregarded. The case wherein this argument was used was that of Mr Stacie's about tar, pitch and oil, who upon this very score and consideration as himself declared at the Board, denied to sign to his contract entered the 17 of April (69), wherein he is promised payment within fourteen days after delivery, until this day that he obtained a clause for having 200*l.* advanced to him beforehand, refusing otherwise to deal with us upon any promise of payment after delivery.

A third particular fit for reflection occurring to me this day was the Treasurers' moving with great vehemence as an expedient they had found out for the effectual prevention of the cheats the King is liable to from the pursers imposing clothes in great sums upon the King in the cases of men dead and run, which expedient was that in all the books they deliver in from time to time to the muster-masters, clerks of the cheque, or to this Office, during the voyage, they should set upon those books what clothes each man had to that day received from him. Which was no sooner propounded by the Treasurers but embraced as an extraordinary motion by Br., J.M., T.M. and J.C., and particularly by J.M. as a thing which he had often wished for and spoken of, and accordingly it was concluded and referred to me that something should be digested in order to the putting this in execution, when I showed them that the thing has long since been done and expressly enjoined, and books provided at the King's charge ruled on purpose with a column for clothes, and showed them muster books from the muster-master in the Downs whereto the same thing is actually done. Which when they see they silently signified their well liking of it, but expressed their doubts that it was but seldom executed. Which I told them was in the hand only of the

---

[1]Carteret had resigned in 1667 and Anglesey had been removed in 1668.

Comptroller of the Navy, before whom all those books and that whole matter lay, to see these good rules observed in this particular, and cause the neglect thereof to be punished. And so this matter ended, but the use I would make of this occurrence is to consider in what a case the King's service is, when not only rules made and left us by our ancestors and grounded upon their experience, but those which were made by ourselves not three years since, shall be so little practised or regarded as to be wholly forgot, and then the service must go to wreck as if there were no rule in being. Which shows also (among many other useful inferences) how little safe the King is in the committing a trust promiscuously on many, when of many he only that perhaps suggested and formed the rule (as myself in this particular) shall remember it, while not only the multitude but even he whose particular province it is to see the King have the benefit of that rule, as in the present case Sir John Mennes and of late my Lord Brouncker, shall have forgot it, as if no such rule had ever been.

Notes for my discourse to his Royal Highness tomorrow May 14th 1669 about the practice of impressing men as it is now managed.

Impressing of men and its management considerable,[1] first, as it is a charge to the King, secondly, as it reflects on the reputation of his service abroad,[2] and as it is attended with interruption of trade and a necessity of raising wages in the merchantmen at home,[3] as well as the price of goods.

Little pressing all the first Dutch war, at least with very little confusion or noise or oppression complained of, to be imputed not only to the rise of seamen's wages in the State's service from 19*s.* to 24,[4] and its good payment, and a larger supply of soldiers and those better chosen, exercised, led by their commanders, more obedient and willing to assist the seamen in their sea labour, better set out as to clothes and shifts, than now they were, and yet not preferred in payment to the seamen as now they were, but to the temper, fair usage, and care of commanders.

[1]To be considered.
[2]Its public reputation.
[3]Seamen deserted the merchant service and took jobs on land for fear of impressment: see below, p. 205.
[4]This was the rise in the monthly rate for able seamen effective from January 1653.

None [pressed] (or at most very few, as I shall by and by mention) after the King's coming in, though a much greater number employed at once, namely at my Lord Sandwich's Algier voyage,[1] than are now called for; and this notwithstanding the great arrear of wages then cut off by the Parliament.[2] And that this is so appears by complaints then made to this Office against commanders for their unwillingness to entertain men, though able seamen, without a covenant for part of their wages, and this found practised in some ships to great numbers. And as a further instance R. Gibson tells me of his knowledge that at that time Capt. Poole in the *Advice* as having his full complement turned away above 20 able seamen tendering him their service that voyage, and one of them John Smith, who R. Gibson had known to have served several years as coxswain and quartermaster in the *Saphire*, and then sent with a special recommendation in writing by Sir Thomas Allen to be entertained by Poole as an able seaman, but refused by Poole though since that and at this day employed by Sir Tho. Allen as a quartermaster, coxswain or midshipman. And the same was done to his knowledge by Capt. Smith in the *Newcastle* and others.

That when the last war came they fell to pressing, and with such disorder and charges as was never before heard of, nor can now be in any wise justified but by the war, though that not sufficient when compared with the little noise it was done with in the first war.

That now the war is over not any of the captains undertake to man their ships without press warrants, though the whole of the ships now fitting forth call but for 2946 men, towards which the ships lately and in present discharge might supply them with 1925 men. So as (officers considered) the whole number wanted, and those in several places, *viz.* London, Chatham and Portsmouth, come not to 1000 men. Besides that, not less than 200 sail of ships, great and small, are said to have come in from the West and Southward since these ships have been in fitting, so as five men out of a ship would without any disturbance have supplied all we want.

But instead of this, the whole town rings of our pressing of men, and complains of the trouble offered thereto to trade, as

[1] In 1661–2.
[2] The Act of January 1661 (12 Car. II c. 27) provided funds for arrears of pay from 14 March 1659 only.

much as we ought to expect for ten times the number. And the force of it appears plainly in the particular of coals, which before the late fleet of colliers came in were at 16s. 6d. per chaldron in the Pool, and are notwithstanding the fleet's being come in, at 19s. 6d., and myself this day paid 23s. brought to my house, who bought upon advice that they were still likely to rise, and all imputed to our pressing of their men, to the general dissatisfaction of the people and (as some employ[1] it) to the reproach of the government.

What wages merchantmen give at this instant I cannot presently say, though I hear that the press has by making seamen disappear raised the merchants' wages; but sending this day by W. Hewer to Mr Blackborne[2] to know what wages the East India Company (whose service is always reputed harder than the Straits voyages and all other but Guinney) at this day gives, he answers me that the medium of the wages given by the Comptroller to the *George* and *Returne*, the ships last and lately by them set forth, amounted to 23s. per mensem. Which is to be reputed much inferior to the King's pay when besides that it is but equal in money to what the King's seamen actually receives, the merchants' service is accompanied with much more labour, more waste of clothes, more hazard, less satisfaction in diet, and a liableness to defalcation out of the mariners' wages for all goods damaged, and a loss of all if the ship be lost, and one month less in the year than the King allows, which is thirteen, and lastly no allowance of wages for the time the ship lies in delivery after she is come home and at anchor at Blackwall, and but at half pay till her passing Gravesend outward bound, whereas in the King's service they have their full pay from their first entry.

What makes this so burdensome to the people is the method used by captains in pressing by committing the execution of their warrants to a lieutenant or meaner officer, who without distinction presses men of all sorts, whether on board merchant ships or on shore, and then, as is generally reported, for a piece of money discharging them again; by this means, where 40 is wanting, it may be 80 are pressed, and as an instance of the further disorder with which this is done I may show the Duke how some of the commanders, *viz.* Sir Edward Spragg and Capt. Herbert have even at this day demanded a supply of printed passes from

---
[1] Imply.
[2] Robert Blackborne, Hewer's uncle, secretary to the E. India Company.

the Office, provided during the war when many press warrants were abroad at the same time for preventing the re-pressing of men already pressed, while for a few days they remained on shore for providing themselves for sea. The exercising which practice now must imply either that there is at this day the same disorder used as there was in the heat of the war in the pressing of one another's men, or that it is designed by the officers entrusted in the pressing to enable them to press who they will and discharge them again, with a protection from being pressed by any else.[1] Neither of which need to be, did they press now as they sometimes indeed did heretofore in peace since the King's coming in (though but rarely) – which was to press only at sea out of ships homeward bound and near home.

And here it may not be amiss to observe what I hear confessed by commanders universally, that they do not make any matter of pressing men at sea without giving them any press money, which I doubt is a ceremony essential in law to the impressing of any man, and consequently necessary to the obliging him to continue in the King's service as that without which he cannot be punished as a runaway, if he deserts it. And this seems the more considerable, if, as I have been informed, [they do not make any matter] of hurrying men away from the shore into the press-masters' boats without their press money.

It may not also be amiss to mention our present practice (as Sir John Mennes this day acknowledged to me) of paying the seamen their whole wages at the pay table without defalcation of their press money, which is confessed to be contrary both to all ancient practice and the practice of the late times, and consequently to the King's loss in so such money. To which, it is true, Mr Haytor answered me that should the press money be stopped, it is most probable that the seamen would then insist upon having the other part of the ancient practice made good, which is for every pressed man to have conduct money given him to carry him to the place from whence he was pressed, which would be treble the charge, considering the great numbers pressed out of the West Countries and the North as far as Scotland. Which nevertheless does not satisfy me, it being to be feared that this may be reckoned among the hardships imposed upon the seamen which, though silently by them borne, contributes to their making

---

[1] For which the seaman paid.

them shun the King's service to the greater prejudice of his Majesty.

But, by the way, I doubt the captains' unreadiness at the pay table to declare distinctly which were and which were not pressed men might contribute to this practice, it being to be feared that their late bringing in their accounts for their press money springs from some convenience they receive from the delay; it being probable that fewer seamen would be found at the pay table to own the receipt of their press money than the captains afterwards do charge the King therewith.

But now to consider whence it is that seamen are thus backward to serve the King, I cannot find it ascribable to any other reasons than two:

First, the severe and disobliging deportment at this day of most commanders to their seamen, expressed either in beating them, in the multitude of servants, friends, and retinues, to the rendering the labours the heavier to the few that are seamen, the dividing the pay of midshipmen and under-officers to their barbers, fiddlers and other creatures of their own, or lastly the denying them an allowable liberty of going on shore, when it may be done without prejudice to the King's service. Here we may instance in the little difficulty which some commanders are found at any time to meet with in the manning of their ships, such as Sir John Lawson, Mings and Wager, the two last of which would not only indulge their company by turns with going on shore, but joining in their sports on board, and yet none more beloved, more followed, better obeyed, or having the King's work better performed. The like may be said at this day of Sir John Harman, Capt. Hayward, Lloyd, and others who are put to press very few men. Whilst on the contrary some others, seamen do openly declare their abhorrency of, whose names may be spared.

The second is the illness of their pay as to their certainty thereof. It is true, it may be said, that some proof has been given for the last year or two of the bettering of their payment, but first, this is only for their present earnings, their arrears being as they think desperate;[1] next, that even this has been with much uncertainty, my Lord Anglesey having paid them from Janry 66[7] forward by money, from thence backward to the first of Augst 66

---

[1] Marginal note: 'But the arrears of '59 may be objected. But then they hoped by the King's coming in that they would be paid, or at least that no such thing could be any more. Which they now find reason to dread the contrary of.'

by tickets, and from that time further backward not at all. The present Treasurers they endeavour and have hitherto made shift to pay the whole wages due upon any ship paid off since their time all with ready money, but yet with much uncertainty whether they shall be able to go on to do so, the 67 money being all spent, that of 68 almost the same, and 69 already overcharged and a liableness (as they think) to the like difficulties hereafter, either by changes of hands,[1] or men's minds, or new limitations in the applicableness of moneys; tending to the rendering the King's pay very hazardous to all that are to serve for it.

I might here mention what the seamen generally complain of touching their being wholly defrauded of the benefit of the proceed of the prize goods taken between decks, whereto by Act of Parliament they are entitled,[2] and of which valued at 100, some say 200,000*l.*, the seamen hath never yet received one farthing dividend, though gathered in the several ports by persons appointed by the Flag Officers and by them disposed of (as was pretended) for the seamen's use. This complaint is universal, but how far just, I have not yet had opportunity of making any particular examination.

Another thing that hath been thought very burdensome by the seamen has been their being tossed from ship to ship, sometimes with and sometimes without tickets, to serve under commanders whom they have less liked, and at last forced to hunt after their wages from several ships and wait to receive it at several times.

But these two latter I may reserve for future use, after better examining them, and in the meantime close with advice to his Highness, as the only means left of regaining the love of the seamen and removing the present reproach of the King's service both at home and abroad, that he will effectually mediate for the payment of the arrears of wages due to seamen, and consider what may be done towards the bringing up among commanders a desire and study of obliging and encouraging them, and as a way of proving what commanders do practise this most, as also to remove the world's dissatisfaction for the present pressing of men, to call in the press warrants, by which it will be seen which commanders are soonest manned and therein can best serve the King, and which of them by being unable to do it ought to be

---

[1]That is, by the appointment of new Treasurers.
[2]By the Navy Discipline Act of 1661 (13 Car. II c. 9) they were allowed all goods on or above the gun-deck.

made to give way to those who can, as many such there are undoubtedly to be had, both wanting and desiring as well deserving employment.

Memorandum: that this business was discoursed of at the time expected, but (through want of time) prevented in its being thoroughly heard. And thereupon deferred to another hearing this day May 21th (69), when I had liberty to go through the whole, and opportunity of offering further the following considerations, *viz.*:

That the inability of some commanders to get men without pressing brings a necessity of pressing on others who would not otherwise need it, as Sir John Harman at this day owns, that consequently not only good commanders are hereby prevented in doing the King the service and preserving the honour which otherwise by their interest in seamen they might do, but his Majesty and Royal Highness [are] prevented in knowing and rightly distinguishing touching the true value of commanders in this particular. That as pressing in men for the King raises the wages of seamen in merchant ships, as from 21*s.* their late common wages to 30 and 35, and from 40 and 45 the voyage to Newcastle in colliers to 50 and 55*s.* and to be clear from the shovel,[1] and consequently the price of coals from 16 and 17*s.* to 22*s.* the chaldron; so reciprocally the high wages in merchantmen prevents the King's ships being manned at the King's wages. That much of the seamen's good or bad disposition to the King's service depends upon the temper and virtue of the commander, as appears by Capt. Hayward, now in the *Foresight*, who told me yesterday that he was manned with volunteers till he was forced to discharge some as supernumeraries, and all good men, and that he hath within a day or two refused above 20 more. Here the Duke of York added the like of Capt. Darcy. That among the other discouragements which seamen meet withal in the King's service, a great one is their being turned over from ship to ship, not only as it brings difficulties upon them in the procurement of their payment (as has already been mentioned), but as it occasions their continuance in the service from voyage to voyage, to the robbing them of the satisfaction which most of them expect from many reasons in being at liberty at the end of the voyage to dispose of themselves as they see fit; the truth and force whereof is illustrated to me by R. Gibson in the Hollands' East

---

[1] Sc. not required to load or unload.

India Company, who found it very hard to get men till they gave over their first practice in obliging men to a continuance there beyond the time promised, and falling to a strict making good of their word for their not keeping them longer than four years, which is said to be their practice at this day, and whether true or no in fact carry much reason in it.[1] But touching the true occasions of the loss of the seamen's affections and the variety of them, as also what was necessary for recovering them, I told the Duke of York that it was a work worthy its being carefully prepared for his Majesty and Royal Highness's seasonable debate, if there be any prospect of his Majesty's needing them again, and that as to my particular, I was endeavouring to furnish myself with all that is to be gathered on that subject, which I hoped will enable me in some time to give his Highness some competent light therein; and for the present I moved that his Highness would put a present stop to the press warrants that were abroad here, which the Duke of York and the Board yielded to with full satisfaction, as far as concerned their being executed on this side Gravesend,[2] and accordingly his Royal Highness directed Mr Wren to publish his order on that behalf.

Memorandum: another discouragement of seamen is the commanders' partiality in choice of men to send first on board and man prizes, which ought to be and was heretofore done by lot. *Vide* further on this subject page [215].

May 7th 1669. Memorandum: that his Royal Highness's telling me this afternoon that his Majesty had this day declared his satisfaction in the account lately given him of the constitution of the Office, there having yet been no objection brought to him against the same after so long expectations of it, and our late letter and book containing the said constitution left at my Lord Arlington's office for view to those of the Lords or others that were desirous of it;[3] and therefore that he would not longer forbear the appointing somebody to succeed Sir Wm Penn, and

---

[1]They contracted to stay in Asia for five years exclusive of the voyages: J. R. Bruijn et al., *Dutch-Asiatic shipping in the 17th and 18th centuries* (The Hague 1979–87), i. 147. I owe this reference to Prof. C. R. Boxer.
[2]Above Gravesend seamen on board outward bound merchantmen were on half pay. Below it they were in service and were paid at the full rate.
[3]See above, p. 191 & n. 2.

therefore named Sir Jeremy Smith, whom it is true the Duke of York had a good while since propounded, but his Majesty, my Lord of Buckingham, and those that seemed dissatisfied with the Office had for a good while spoken of Mr Child; yet now his Majesty of his own accord named Sir Jeremy Smith.

Which choice, as being a seaman, no merchant, and one for whom his Royal Highness is concerned as well as his Majesty now pleased to propound, I think it unfit for me to offer any objection to. But being doubtful that this gentleman is but very moderately qualified for this particular work, I thought it so far my duty to prevent as much as might be the ill effects of an ill choice, as to draw up a clause wherein is described the work and trust of this Officer in order to the putting the same into his patent, and this being drawn, to show it both to his Royal Highness, thereby to inform him in the weightiness of it, and Sir Jere. Smith that he might not be ignorant of the task he was undertaking. And this I did – Mr Wren present – in his Highness's chamber at St James's Thursday morning May the 13th (69),[1] when not only his Highness perused, considered and approved of the requisiteness of having a clause inserted in the commission, but Sir Jeremy Smith did the like, and took upon him the care of seeing it put in. To which end by his Highness's direction the old warrant delivered some days since to the Attorney-General was recalled and a new one drawn and sent him wherein the said clause was inserted, in the words following, *viz*.:

> And in a more especial manner, to take upon him the trust and care of performing all that part of the duties of the Comptroller of his Majesty's Navy which was or ought to have been performed by Sir Wm Penn, Knight, late one of the Commissioners thereof, in the examining, comptrolling and balancing the accounts of the victuallers, pursers, and all other persons concerned in the victualling of his Majesty's ships; thereby as well to see right done between his Majesty and the said accountants, and all covenants on his Majesty's behalf contained in the present contract between his Majesty and the victuallers of his Navy rightly executed as to be able at all times to inform the Lord High Admiral and the rest of the Principal Officers and Commissioners of the Navy in every

---

[1] According to the Diary Pepys spent the whole of this morning in the office and did not go to St James's until the morning of the 14th. But the Diary entries, because of his eye trouble, have several mistakes at this time.

matter relating to the expense, debt and management of that branch of his Majesty's naval action.[1]

24 April 69. As an instance of the negligence with which his Majesty's business of the greatest moment is performed, let me remember, that upon some late occasion given us by the Commissioners of Accounts, I observed that a true list of his Majesty's ships was not to be made up out of any or all of the lists given me from the several offices of the Treasurers, Lord Brouncker, Sir J. Mennes and Sir W. Pen, and that thereupon the consideration came into my head, in whose hands it must be *ex officio* to have a constant knowledge of the number and names of all his Majesty's ships and vessels, and thereupon concluded that though by accident others may, and by my particular curiosity I am certain I have by me a perfect list of all the ships that his Majesty hath at any time had since anno 1660 and hath at this day,[2] yet that the keeping a clear and constant account thereof is lodged nowhere *ex officio* but with the Surveyor.

Upon which, being willing to make the experiment whether this was to be found in his office, so as upon any occasion his Majesty might readily know the greatness and condition of his naval force, I did several times at the Board move from one occasion or other that the Board might have a list from the Surveyor's office of all the ships great and small which after so many changes remain at this day belonging to his Majesty, which accordingly the Surveyor undertook, and directed his clerk to prepare it for them. Which after several callings for was brought to the Board by his clerk – himself present – and there lodged.

Which upon perusal I finding short of the true number, I called his clerk to me, to whom observing the same, he answered that this was all his master had notice of, or at least that appeared in any of the books in his office, as being all whereof he had had notice by any surveys taken since his master's being Surveyor, which was in Jan. 1667[8] to this day, though most of those missing are or have been at home in a way of being surveyed within that time. Besides that, the books of his predecessor (if

---

[1]These duties (not included in Penn's original patent of August 1660) had been transferred from Mennes to Penn in January 1667: see above, p. 176 & n. 1.
[2]Several such lists survive. There is one dated 4 May 1669 in BL, Add. MSS 32094, f. 212. His final cumulative register covering 1660–88 is in PL 2940 (printed Tanner, *Catalogue*, i. 253–306).

any had been kept) ought to have been sufficient to have informed him in this particular, and this want of a constant provision for a ready knowledge of the state of his Majesty's ships of how much scandal it is to this Office and of what prejudice it may be to the state as well as reproach to the general management to its affairs is worthy considering. And how great this want at this time was appears by the number of ships underwritten, which being unticked were not taken notice of in this the Surveyor's list, *viz.*:

1st-rate

Charles the
2d √
Soveraigne √

2nd-rate

St George √
Henry √
James √
Royall
Katherine √
Rainebow √
Tryumph √
Victory √
Unicorne √

3rd-rate

Ann √
Cambridge √
Dreadnought √
Dunkirke √
Edgar √
Fairfax √
Gloucester √
Henrietta √
Lyon √
Mary √

Monck √
Monmouth √
Mountague
Plymouth √
Resolution √
Revenge √
Ruby √
Rupert √
Warrspight √
Yorke √

4th-rate

Adventure √
Advice √
Anthelope √
Assistance √
Assurance √
Bonadventure √
Bristoll √
Centurion √
Crowne √
St David √
Diamond √
Dover √
Draggon √
Faulcon √
Foresight √
Greenwich √
Hampshire √
Happy
Returne √

Jersey √
Kent √
Leopard √
Mary Rose √
Newcastle √
Nonsuch √
Portland √
Portsmouth √
Princess √
Reserve √
Ruby √
Saphire √
Stathouse van
  Harlem
Swallow √
Sweeptakes √
Tyger
Warwick
Constant √
Yarmouth √

5th-rate

Dartmouth √
Eagle √
Forrester √
Fountaine √
Guarland √
Guernsey √
Mermaid √

Milford √
Nightingale √
Norwich √
Orange
Oxford
Pearle √
Richmond √
Speedwell √
Success √
Victory Litle
Victory
  Prize

6th-rate

Deptford
  Ketch
Drake √
Emsworth
  Sloope
Fanfan √
Francis
Harpe
Portsmouth
  Ketch
Portsmouth
  Sloope √
Roebuck
Roe Ketch
Spie √

Truelove	Small	*Tower Smack*
Wevenho Ketch	vessels	*Lighter Hoy*
	employed	*Chatham*
	for	*Smacke*
Yachts	transport	
Ann	*Adam & Eve*	
Besan	*Black Dogg*	
Henrietta	*Friezland*	
James	*Hope Galliot*	
Katherine	*Marygold Hoy*	
Mary	*Musterboate*	
Merlin	*Smack*	
Monmouth	*Harwich Hoy*	
Roe Kitchin	*Seaventure*	

May 13. 1669. Memorandum: for an instance of the fruits of advice given to a fellow Officer in the performance of his duty, *memorandum*, that the Board by their letter of the 11 inst. to the Surveyor then at Chatham, upon occasion of some fresh demands from thence of Spanish tables,[1] having pressed him to the remembrance of the 5th article of the Surveyor's duty and his Highness's late reflections thereon,[2] and our letter of the 10th of April last on the same subject, touching his personal examination of the proceeding of the clerk of the survey in the passing of boatswains' and carpenters' accounts (*vide* his letter of the 11 inst.), he answers them in one of the 13 as follows:

> As for that which I presume you lay to my charge, I must take the boldness to give you this answer, that I have not at any time been negligent in my duty so far as I have understood it, and I think I may say without any presumption that I do understand as much of the King's naval affairs as any that shall undertake to teach me; but if new work be cut out daily, there

[1]Cf. above, p. 201 & n. 1.
[2]For the article, see *Oeconomy*, pp. 64–5; for the Duke's particular 'reflection' (in a letter of 26 August 1668), see e.g. BL, Add. MSS 36782, f. 75; cf. *Diary*, ix. 289.

is no one man in England shall ever be able to know an end of his work, neither how to do it.[1]

Wherein, besides what might be observed touching the general style of this answer, it is worth taking notice that the pretence of being a new work is made use of in excuse for the not doing of that which has in all ages been reckoned and so prescribed as one of the essential parts of the duty of Surveyor.

Memorandum. May 24. (69). That discoursing with Mr Gibson afresh upon the present business of pressing of men (*vide* page [204]), he tells me that the steward of the *Foresight*, Capt. Hayward commander, which lies at this day near Halfway Tree[2] a little distant from Capt. Beach of the *Jersey*, both designed for the present expedition against Algier, the steward told him in discourse that they had not on board his ship one pressed man, but contrarily that he does believe his captain has refused a hundred that have voluntarily proffered themselves, and further, that upon his telling his captain that a couple dozen of his men had discovered some troublesomeness in finding fault with their victuals, his captain found himself so far from needing to comply with them as to direct their being presently turned ashore, and did the like to about fourteen more whom the master had without the captain's direction pressed, and brought on board. While at the same time Capt. Beach lies pressing so as all the River rings of it, and yet is unmanned; those he has endeavouring to run away from him and adventuring to swim ashore, in which two or three have been drowned, whilst in the meantime he keeps sentinels night and day in his ship with their cutlasses drawn to prevent them. Moreover, he further says that Beach's men have openly wished that they could come to serve on board Hayward, and that if Hayward's boat were brought to the buoy of their ship, they would strip themselves and swim to them, rather than serve under Beach.

Memorandum further: that the Board took notice to Beach by a letter of the [*blank*] instant of the several complaints brought against him, we having had three petitions upon his pressing of men out of ships outward bound, which we ordered to be released

---

[1]PRO, SP 29/260, no. 49, in slightly different words (summary in *CSPD 1668–9*, pp. 325–6).
[2]Half-way mark between Deptford and Rotherhithe.

by subscribing one of the petitions and writing letters in case of the other two. In answer to which subscription of ours on the petition, without taking notice of the letters, he by letter of the 22d May 69 tells us plainly that pressing of men has raised merchants' wages, and that so without pressing it is not to be expected that either his ship can be manned or any other, saving one (by which I presume he mean Capt. Hayward), and that he has got some of his men from him, saying that he had 130 volunteers at his coming from Deptford which have since deserted him, and that therefore he had discharged one of the two men and kept the other till further order, saying that without leave to press he should be able to carry but few able men to sea, and consequently [not] likely to do good service. A full instance of the different influence of commanders upon seamen.

Since this it was publicly reported that one of his company was by his sentinel shot in endeavouring to leave the ship, but it proved not so as to the killing the man, but that one was shot at.

June 11. (69). At the Board's waiting on the Lords of the Treasury, Col. Birch mentioned with great severity the dishonour his Majesty receives by the present press, as well as the merchants dissatisfied by their ships being molested.[1]

By and by, attending the Duke, and mention made of the great injury done few days since to the *Guarland* in the beating of her head and knee by a merchant ship falling foul of her, Col. Midleton told the Duke that the master had been with him and in his defence complained that so many of his men were taken out of him and so few that were left so fearful of appearing for fear of being pressed away as the rest were, that he was not able to govern his ship. Which being proved, the Duke was at a loss how to expect any reparation for the damage done the King's ship. Which damage nevertheless, though considerable, is not to be compared with what the King will suffer from the loss of time, service, wages and victuals while the ship must lie in full pay and manned, till her provisions can be taken out and the ship lighted.

But most scandalous it is methinks to the King's service that it should be publicly told to the Duke before the whole Board the 4th of June (69) by Mr Wren that Sir Edward Spragg had told him that he was the day before at Damaris Page's, the most

[1] Col. John Birch, MP, was a member of the Commission for Trade.

famous bawd in town,[1] and there had made so much of her that she had already furnished him with about forty seamen to man his ship the *Revenge*, and that she would do more. In the truth of which I was confirmed by Sir Edward Spragg himself who, sitting by me at dinner at Trinity House June the 7th[2], I industriously asked him the success of his late visit, and was answered by him publicly that as long as Damaris Page lived he was sure he should not lack men. This among others Mr Euelin heard and took notice of it to me with great affliction. *Vide* more page [230].

Memorandum, May 24. (69). Upon discourse with Mr Gibson about masters, he observed to me that in passing of pilots' bills he finds no regard had to the certificate of the Trinity House by which the master is recommended as fit to take charge to the Westward, Northward, Southward, etc., by which it falls out that the King pays pilotage there where he is supposed most conversant as much as anywhere else.

On which subject it is further considerable how secure the King is under those partial certificates, in case of a miscarriage in any place not contained in the certificate; and how seldom it is that any man is employed to that part without being called to some other coast. Nay, how rare it is for us to choose any master by the quality of the certificate or with any regard to it, at least after the first voyage, which upon strict examination may in case of miscarriage be found very hard to be defended by the Office.

Again, it is to be considered with what blind and unsteady arbitrariness pilot bills are filled which might be reduced in a great measure to a certainty, thereby righting the King, and the reputation of the Office, as well as remove the discontent to private men by seeing others at one time have twice as much for the same service as themselves have at another. Cases of which kind do easily occur in our bill books, but this not to be mended without an able Comptroller.

An eminent instance of a boatswain's bringing discharge of stores spent beyond what they ever received, showing either great remissness in the clerks of the survey and honesty in the boatswains in charging themselves with what they receive better than

---
[1] 'The great bawd of the seamen': *Diary*, ix. 132.
[2] The Trinity Monday feast, celebrating the annual election of officers.

those with whom they are to indent, or great craft and knavery in the boatswains, with as much ignorance, negligence, or unfaithfulness in commanders.[1]

And in the third place this particular instance discovers grounds of believing the knaveries of boatswains to be practised with so much security and elbowroom with their commanders, that they are under no difficulty how to make their demands and accounts meet, but only take care to demand enough, it being improbable otherwise that the boatswain in this case would either have got vouchers for so much more than he had in some things, or omitted to get them for the full of what he had in others, while in this case to [o] his exceedings (which profit him nothing) is by many times more than those wherein he fall short, which must be a real loss to him by being made to pay for them.

The instance is the case of the boatswain of the *Lyon*, brought to the Board this day by the Surveyor (the first that ever he did so) May the 25th (69), signed by Mr Homewood, clerk of the survey at Chatham, as follows:

Lyon *44 months and odd.*
(*Supposing all his expense under the several commanders' hand allowable*).

Expense exceeds what I can charge him with:	Coils of 3½ inches............One
	3......................368 fa.
Boats' Grapnels......................2	2½......................528
Marlin Spikes........................11	2............................209
Long Boat..............................1	1½......................380
Other Boats 2	1............................238
Boat Oars.............................31	Lashing line.........................10
82 fathom of cable in parcels	Netting-rope..........................5
Two cables for barricades	Junk....................168 fa.
Cable of 10 inches.......120 fa.	Tarred lines.........................28
Cablet of 6½ inches.....328 fa.	Spritsail.............................One
6........................137	Mizen topsail ....One
Hawser of 7 inches..........One	Edw. Homewood
4..................430 fa.	

---

[1] To prevent collusion between commanders and boatswains Pepys had in 1664 proposed that the deputy-treasurer of the fleet should keep a record of boatswains' expenditure abroad: BL, Add. MSS 32094, f. 15*r*.

His expense wants:
Gromets & staples	5 doz. pr.
Bilboes	1 cent.
Can-hooks	2 cent.
Hamacco nails	440
Thimbles	12
Bowls	12
Large staples	24
Brooms	9 doz.
Ipswich Canvas	22 yds
Hamaccoes	153
Winding tackle blocks	4
Handspikes	2 doz.
Boat hook spars	8
Flag of 18 breadths	1
Ensigns	2
Pendants	2
Vanes	3
Cablet of 7½ inches	22 fa.
5	50 fa.
3	1 coil
Hawser of 5½ inches	40 fa.
4½ inches	60 fa.
Old rope	280 fa.
Twine	90*li*.
Cabin lines	8
Mizen	One
Tin trucks	4
Leather	⅞ back
Top lantern	One
Wood axes	3

Edw. Homewood

June 11. (69). This day the Board attending the Duke, I took notice of the great complaints that we meet with at this day of the incapacity of many of the ships going to the Straits to take in their provisions, so as to the King's great prejudice the ships must go away without them and so be shortened in their staying abroad or supplied by letters of credit, which has its great inconveniences, or some vessel hired on purpose to carry the surplusage. I thence descended to the considering in general whence this want of stowage arises, which was either from the taking in too much ballast, ill stowage of the provisions and stores, or their taking up too much of the hold by too large or too many accommodations for the officers and company, arising either by the arbitrary and interested ordering thereof by the shipwright or his assistant at her first building, or the liberty taken of enlarging them at sea. Most of all which must arise from the negligence, corruption, or ignorance of the commander, touching the latter of which Col. Midleton gave a pregnant instance how, after a captain's complaining of want of room for his provisions and stores and declaring his inability to take in a considerable part of both, he himself then at Portsmouth went on board, rummaged the hold and made room, though he found the ship full crammed not only for the whole quantity both of stores and provisions but for fifty ton more. But here it is to be reflected on of how much importance this must be to the King, and yet how impossible it is to be otherwise where the commander is not a seaman, and consequently knows not either the manner of well stowing of provisions, nor what room the hold can afford or the goods require, nor how large the cabins and storerooms to be allowed to this and that officer ought reasonably to be. Capt. Cox observed how the *Henry*, after having ever taken in 300 ton of ballast and been ever found to draw 21 foot [of] water, he when at Chatham fitting her forth for Sir John Mennes[1] would not put in more than 200 ton, by which besides the gaining so much stowage she was ever since found to sail better than heretofore, and draw when fully set forth not above 19 foot. To this the Duke himself added his own observation the other day of the great deal of do made by Capt. Hart for want of room to carry his provisions, he being to transport home the Spanish Ambassador,[2] insomuch as his Highness had once commanded us to hire a vessel on purpose to carry about 50 tons of the Ambassador's goods, and afterwards order was sent him[3] for the putting out 20 or 25 tons of his beer into the *Victory Prize*, going the same way, for the enabling the *Portland* to carry the Ambassador's goods with him.[4] Whereas at last the Duke himself observed that without any noise or difficulty at all, upon some considerations doubtless from the Ambassador, the *Portland* not only takes in all her own provisions but takes in the Ambassador's, too. Upon all which my motion was that the Duke would commit it to the Surveyor, Mr Tippetts and Capt. Cox to consider and propound in writing what may be established for the rectifying of this evil for the time to come, both in the present ships and what may be hereafter built. Which the Duke approved of and directed, and I took care to confirm by a letter to that purpose from the Board directed to those three gentlemen and dated the 12 June (69).

---

[1]Mennes was commissioned captain to the *Henry* in 1661: Tanner, *Catalogue*, i. 383.
[2]The Conde de Molina, who sailed in the *Portland* from Plymouth c. 22 June: *CSPD 1668–9*, pp. 374, 377; cf. *Diary*, ix. 544.
[3]Capt. Hart.
[4]Marginal note: '*Vide* order from the Board to the captain of the *Victory* and purser of the *Portland* dated 15 May (69)'.

10th June 69. Memorandum: that discoursing this day with Sir Wm Coventry about business of the Navy and some passages relating thereto during the late war, he was pleased to show me a copy of a letter of his wrote in 9ber (64) to my Lord Falmouth,[1] wherein upon occasion of my Lord's desiring his opinion in the point, he most ingeniously and with demonstration showed that whatever was then hoped for at Court to be saved to the King out of the 2,500,000*l*. voted by the Parliament for carrying on the war,[2] it was not to be expected, supposing the war to last two year. He also laboured to remove the expectation of great profits to the King then (as it seems) mightily depended upon from the prizes that should be taken.

He showed me also a copy of another paper by him wrote at that time upon a design then very hot on foot of having the King's ships commanded by lords and other persons of great quality, the Duke of Buckingham, my Lord Berkeley, and others offering themselves on this score.[3] Upon which occasion he most amply showed how unadvisable the thing was and ineffectual it would prove. That the great argument of courage could not be held of much force, courage having showed itself to the utmost degree in commanders ordinarily born, and that were the greatness of quality only attended with courage,[4] and with courage only without skill how to know the true way of improving that courage by the taking all advantages in the conducting of the ship to the annoying of the enemy, but must be led wholly by the master or meaner officers, whose skill he must submit to, and consequently to the dictates of their cowardice (in case they must not be admitted to be valiant), the King's service would be found very unsafe under such a conduct, and possibly worse by how much such commanders will not probably content themselves to

---

[1] Keeper of the Privy Purse; a favourite of the King. The letter is probably that surviving among Coventry's papers as an undated copy-draft, endorsed 'A paper about the Dutch warrs showed once to my Ld Falmouth and to none else': BL, Add. MSS 32094, ff. 50*r*–52*v*.

[2] This was the Royal Aid granted in November 1664, much the largest grant ever made to a Stuart government. Pepys thought it would cover two-and-a-half years' war expenses: *Shorthand Letters*, p. 20.

[3] Coventry's undated copy-draft of this letter survives in BL, Add. MS 32094, ff. 43–5, endorsed 'Reasons against sending commanders to sea who have not used the sea'. His views (and the similar views of Sandwich) may well have confirmed Pepys in his distrust of gentlemen captains: see J. D. Davies, *Gentlemen and Tarpaulins*, ch. 3.

[4] Here follows a series of subsidiary clauses, the main clause being resumed at 'the King's service would be found very unsafe'.

be led by the master and other the officers the most capable of advising well, but by some other who by an appearance of more confidence and valour though of less judgement and ability to direct, shall be thought the fitter man to be advised by, though to the ruin of the service.

But it seems the project was, where any of these gallants went, they should be assisted by another captain who should be a seaman. To which W. Coventry answered: first, that (as before) if this seaman have not courage as well as a nobleman, he will be easily able to impose upon the other a thousand things upon him that shall make the other's courage signify nothing by pretence of dangers, disadvantages or advantages tending to the bringing the ship out of harm's way. If he have courage, then to what purpose is this increase of charge to the King by the introduction of a gentleman commander that signifies nothing? Besides, how can it be thought that a seaman thus qualified can with any stomach serve the King and hazard himself when the reputation of good success shall redound all to the valour of a gentleman, and the blame of the bad be imputed to the envy, ignorance, negligence, or cowardice of the seaman.

But further, it's well known that courage is a thing very uncertain and of different sorts,[1] and very rarely found in difficulties whereto the encounterer is so great a stranger as a land gentleman must necessarily be thought to be to that of sea service, where tempest, fire, springing of leaks, are terrors so surprising to a person unacquainted therewith. And I remember he takes notice of what has been generally said touching Cromwell's soldiers which were employed in the fleet in the first Dutch war, that though men used to fight and of tried courage at land, yet they were not suddenly brought to bear and contend with great guns, such as the sea service most depends upon.

He adds the considering what little love a landman can expect among seamen, or awe over them, who shall find neither themselves nor their trade understood by them, and as an instance mentions a story, which the King himself (as he says) sometimes tells, how among other ships that in the late times went away to the King, there was one into which the gentlemen of Kent had put a land gentleman of their acquaintance to command her, called Capt. Bargrave. Which ship, when she was come to the

---

[1] Cf. Coventry's disquisition on courage reported in the Diary (v. 169–71). That report makes no mention of landsmen at sea.

King, and the boat coming off with the commander, who the King believed was coming to kiss his hand and present him this ship, it proved that the seamen came to make that compliment, and declared that they had brought their captain with them that his Majesty might be pleased to dispose of him as he saw fit, and find them another that could understand the word 'abaft'.[1]

He concludes, as I remember, with that great argument which I have sometimes had urged to me by Mr Wren, who is a great asserter of the great requisiteness that the Crown should bring all the military power both at land and sea into the hands of the nobility and gentry,[2] and that is, the practice of former times, in which it is said that of twenty commanders of ships in the time of Queen Elizabeth nineteen were men of family, and that the like in great proportion is found in the time of King James.[3] To which he answers upon a supposition (though not granted) that this is true in fact, that Queen Elizabeth had no enemy considerable at sea but the Spaniard, who, taking the same course of commanding their ships by noblemen and gentlemen, might be contended with by the same kind of conduct; though they paid dear then in the success[4] of their fleets for that kind of conduct, and their continuance of it may be reckoned among those other circumstances that have rendered the Spaniards to this day so behindhand with the rest of the world in seamanship. Besides that, even in those times all that were considerable in that quality were seamen bred, such as Drake, Hawkins, and others. And though the same practice might in a great measure be continued under King James and the late King, yet first, that was principally in times of peace when ships went abroad under my Lords of Buckingham and Northumberland for pomp only, and next, that when active times came we find that the Parliament judged it necessary to employ seamen and found success of it, though as might be further urged, if they could not find gentlemen to serve

---

[1] This incident occurred during the royalist rising in Kent in May 1648 at the beginning of the Second Civil War, when the seamen of several parliamentary ships in the Downs mutinied. Bargrave (either Richard or Robert, of Bridge) was one of a number of royalist gentlemen who went on board the ships to carry them to join the royalist squadron which lay off the Dutch coast: Clarendon, *Hist. Rebellion* (ed. W. D. Macray, Oxf. 1888), iv. 336–7.

[2] A not uncommon view at the time, especially among the nobility and gentry after their experience of civil war and revolution.

[3] The medieval tradition that the upper classes were the natural leaders in warfare was still alive. Cf. Pepys's observation about the commanders of the English ships in the Armada campaign: *Naval Minutes*, p. 119.

[4] Ill success.

them, yet they could not want of their own relations and interest landmen enough that might have been gratified with this employment. But that which seems above all to silence this way of arguing is that the enemy we have at this day to deal with is not like those formerly, but made up of seamen bred, from the common man up to the Admiral, that knows the whole trade and cannot be offered a greater advantage than that of our meeting them with landmen in the head of our fleets. Which is a consideration of that force and so plain as not to need the least enlargement upon.

I remember he takes notice in one place of the preposterousness which every man would blame his proposition for who in the choice of leaders for a land army should offer sea-commanders for that service who had never been conversant with anything but the sea; and yet it may very reasonably be urged that the labour, mystery, accidents and requisites appurtaining to the trade of a sea-commander do both in bulk, variety and difficulty, very far exceed that of a commander at land.

He doth also hint at what in discourse I took occasion to enlarge further upon, touching the discouragement which it would be to the whole race of seamen to find themselves reserved only for the toil and hazard of the trade, while they shall observe themselves excluded from the best rewards of [it] – *viz.* wealth and honour. For as it cannot be denied, where so many instances thereof can be produced, that an Englishman of any capacity at sea is every whit as sensible and ambitious of honour as at land; so no man can think that a seaman can ever hope to lay up anything considerable for the support of his family till his service shall recommend him to a command, and that seconded by sharing with others in voyages of advantage, which are now and are ever likely to be, while the same reason remains, not only generally bestowed upon gentlemen but even made on purpose for them, as is manifest in the King's being put to the charge of sending a ship of his own, the *Leopard*, with Sir Daniel Harvey to Constantinople the last year only avowedly to make a fortune for Capt. Obrian.[1]

And here I took occasion to desire Sir Wm Coventry's opinion of the real force of that argument generally given for the bringing

---

[1]Charles O'Brien was a court favourite in command of the *Leopard* which took Harvey as ambassador to Turkey. His instructions from the Duke (19 July 1669) left him free to call at will at any port on the return voyage: Duke of York, *Memoirs*, pp. 151–2.

the government of the naval force into the hands of the gentry, namely, the interest of the Crown. To which he answered, that there is much force in it, that the gentry by one means or other, *viz.* by their alliances, education, higher conversation,[1] and an elevation of their minds thereby contracted, by their own and their families' honour and some principles of gratitude for the favours and estates obtained from the Crown, are under much more formidable obligations of adhering to the Crown, than those of meaner birth and spirits, and who by the lowness of their fortune and distance from the eye and favour of the Prince are under no such visible obligations as the other are, but on the contrary look upon themselves as creatures neglected, and therefore under an easy temptation of being led away by any faction[2] which may put them into a possibility of making themselves better, while they know themselves not liable by any success[3] to make themselves much worse. And this, as he observed, is the sum of that argument, and is not without some force. But then, says he, this is calculated only in prevention of a civil war,[4] touching which the Crown is at this time more concerned by all possible means to prevent it, than provide for it in one particular only of so remote a consideration as this, where that provision against the inconvenience that may happen in the time of a civil war shall be of so constant and important evil consequence to the Crown till that shall happen.[5] Besides, says he, should (which God forbid) a civil war arise, that which must save the Crown in every other particular will do it also in this, namely, the securing to itself the City of London, the being master of that and of this River being it that probably shall ever govern the interest of all places else, and particularly the fleet, which cannot reasonably be supported by any power of this nation that hath not London, where not only lie the magazines of provisions and stores, but which is the general home to the seaman and his relations. And in proof of this he very well observed that the losing of London

[1]Manner of life.
[2]The reference here is probably to the faction of Buckingham, principal enemy of the Duke of York.
[3]Eventuality.
[4]Coventry is here sceptical of the view that after the Medway disgrace a recurrence of civil war and the overthrow of the monarchy was likely. For the prevalence of the view, see *Diary*, viii. 377–8, 390, 556; ix. 373.
[5]Sc. it would be unwise for the King to weaken his navy by the appointment of gentlemen commanders in order to protect himself against the purely imaginary danger of civil war.

did not discover itself of prejudice to the late King in anything more than in his fleet, which as at the best what he saved thereof was inconsiderable, so that which he had was never able to do him service, but on the contrary was ever more a charge to him, serving at the best but as pirates, and its gettings turning to the profit only of the persons employed in them.

Besides (he adds), if the Crown shall think it necessary to forecast so far in this particular, there seems a more natural method of doing it than by a continual imposing of land commanders upon seamen, who as they can never do the King's work as seamen, so shall they never have the affection of them they command; the effects thereof are (as I showed him) to be learned from that example of the ships' revolting to the late King. Where the captains were beloved they were obeyed; where no, their ships were disposed of at the pleasure of their companies (the particulars of which story I shall endeavour to get a more satisfactory account, it being a very proper use and very instructive in the present case).[1]

But the method here mentioned is either the King's bringing it about for the nobility and gentry to send their children (designed for the sea) young to their trades, and in a quality not too great to submit themselves to the learning and practising all the duties of a seaman, or the King's obliging of the natural seamen by his favour and eye, by his bounty and honours as he has hitherto done the landmen; all families having had their beginnings to a title, and their being nobody among the stiffest assertors of the power of gentility in the establishing of loyalty who (as he conceives) will doubt that Sir Robt Holmes, whose descent is [not] known,[2] is as sure a friend to the Crown, and expect that others should think so of him, as any other that can pretend to an honour of longer date?[3] And whether the same may not be as reasonably thought of Lawson, Tiddeman, Mings and others, the sons of the sea, whom the King has been pleased to give honour to, is submitted to consideration, having given the

---

[1] These events took place in May 1648 during the Second Civil War, when ships of the parliamentary navy sailed from the Downs to join the King's forces in Holland. The ship of the C-in-C (Rainsborough) was taken over by her crew. Pepys never apparently composed the account he refers to.

[2] MS. 'Known will think himself.'

[3] Holmes's knighthood dated only from the 1666 campaign. He was the third son of an obscure Irishman, Henry Holmes of Mallow, Co. Cork: R. Ollard, *Man of War* (1969), p. 17.

best proof thereof in the sacrificing their lives to the King and his service. And thus ended this discourse on this subject between Sir W. Coventry and myself.

But here at my setting down these passages there occurred to me to be added, first, the influence that the honouring of seamen shall have upon the generality of that sort of men, in the encouraging them to serve the King; evidences in the great numbers of men which the sea-commanders that are bred seamen do commonly come attended with into the King's service,[1] such as those above mentioned, Smith, Wetwang, Saunders, Wager, Sansum and others from Newcastle, Scarborough, Hull, Yarmouth and other places, where a landman can never hope as such ever to do anything of that kind.

Next, that it is worth considering, and for form's sake to discourse with Sir Edward Walker or other persons conversant in the vain doctrine of the rules of honour, what it is in the trade of a land soldier that shall so universally obtain in the reputation of a gentleman, or what stops there are in any other kind of worth by which that title is acquired and to which it is avowedly granted, and whether the same be not in every part and degree to be matched in the trade, duty and service of a seaman.[2]

Next, Mr Gibson gives me occasion of inquiry what was the reason of the mutinies at Portsmouth among the seamen of the King's ships at their going out to the service to the Isle of Rhe, as well the ill success of the service there; whether the ships being commanded by gentlemen were not an ingredient if not a principal cause in it.[3] Another thing is to inform myself in some particular instance of the daring courage of seamen, not only at sea but on shore, as among others those at this day and ever since the English had the island of Jamaica in their attempts upon the Spaniard both by sea and land, and those at the siege

---

[1] On the importance of 'followings', see N. A. M. Rodger, *The Wooden World* (1986), esp. pp. 119–23.

[2] This, and similar questions about the status of seamen, are a recurrent theme of Pepys's *Naval Minutes*, written ten years and more later: e.g. (at p. 62) 'Have any of our Heralds allowed in express words the seamen for a gentleman?'

[3] Two abortive expeditions were sent in 1627 and 1628 to relieve the siege of the Protestants in La Rochelle. There were riots among the seamen gathered for the first expedition in London and Plymouth, and at Portsmouth before and after the second. The principal grievance seems to have been shortage or lack of pay: S. R. Gardiner, *Hist. Engl. 1603–42* (1884), vi. 168–9, 291, 348.

of Dunkirke.[1] As also during the late civil wars, in their services in defending of Lyme, Plymouth, Hull, etc.

Having done with this subject about the difference about land and sea commanders, we fell to discourse in general touching the late war, touching which I shall only observe that he[2] showed me a paper writ, all (as the other two) with his own hand, as being the original foul draughts wherein he excellently laid down his judgement against the war, wrote, as he told, about 9ber (64);[3] wherein by the way he discourses touching the true value of what we so generally and deeply concern ourselves for, namely, a pretence to the dominion of the sea, showing the present inconsiderableness thereof in truth to the Crown, and the little question that has been made of it by our neighbour princes otherwise by the pens of a few scholars,[4] and that therefore it ought not to be thought a matter either in itself (or if ever yet not yet) worthy the charge and dangers that attend a war. He showed, too (though I cannot remember enough to do it right in expressing it) that though it be the part of a prince to support his subjects, and particularly of our King to support his, and especially in their trade, yet that it ought to be considered whether this ought to be done to the prejudice of the Crown, such as the making a war in defence of it may prove to ours, either by the ill success of it, or the necessities the Crown may be brought under, and particularly that of being at the pleasure of a Parliament, in case after being involved in a war the Crown shall be brought under a want of money to carry it on.

He then shows from one foreign trade to another how few of them the Crown is so far profited by as to deserve its running any hazard for the protecting them.

He shows how many contingencies of winds, sands, sea and fire not to be foreseen or provided against, a naval war is subject to; how incapable of being concluded at pleasure when once entered upon, and how necessary when entered never to conclude it but upon terms of conquest, or a peace so honourable as should show the King's care of his people, the wisdom of his conduct,

---

[1]Jamaica was taken in 1655. The references here are to Blake's attack on the Spanish treasure fleet at Santa Cruz, Tenerife, in 1657, and to the capture of the Fort of Dunkirk by an Anglo-French force in 1658.
[2]Coventry.
[3]See above, p. 221 & n. 1.
[4]E.g. by Grotius in his *Mare Liberum* (1609), making claims for the Dutch of freedom of the sea which were controverted by Selden in his *Mare Clausum* (1636) on behalf of Great Britain.

and give them satisfaction in the fruits of the money it has cost them. This he did very expressly, as well as it has proved prophetically. And tells me that he gave it only to my Lord Falmouth, who showed it the King, but without success; though he seems to believe that if my Lord Falmouth had lived, we should have had a peace, he being become very sensible of what was to be looked for from the war.[1] And he is fully satisfied that the end of the year 1665, when the King was at Oxford, the Dutch would have given almost any terms of accommodation,[2] at least so far as to the delivering up Polyroon,[3] the granting us to hold whatever we had then taken from them and a round sum of money to satisfy all the demands of the merchants injured – Buatt,[4] who was afterwards beheaded by them, having particularly declared that having cast out some words to Beningham[5] that the States would do well in time to offer terms of peace, and that it was not impossible but the King of England might listen to an accommodation, Benningham replied (after great professions of service to the King and complaining of his misfortune in being represented to the King as one opposite to his interest) that did he think his Majesty would listen to peace, he would go *a la naige en Angleterre* (or swim to England) to receive his demands. But so remiss were we at that time in minding the affair, so unthoughtful of the consequences, or at least so little questioning our success as not to be ready at any time to say what we would have, till we were forced to take what they would give.

As an instance of the manner wherein the King is to expect to be served by gentlemen commanders, let us consider the case of Capt. Obrian, whose quality and gift of dancing recommending him to the Duke of Monmouth and Duchess, Lady Castlemaine and other ladies, the *Leopard* must be sent to Constantianople with Sir Daniel Harvey contrary to the mind of the Council, even to the bringing them to a resolution and vote that it should not be brought in precedent for the King to be at the charge of sending any ambassador thither but that the Company should

---

[1] Falmouth was killed in the first battle of the war.
[2] This view is not supported by later authorities. See, e.g. K. Feiling, *British Foreign Policy 1660–72* (1930), pp. 196–200.
[3] Pulo Run, a spice island in the East Indies, disputed between the Dutch and the English since the 1620s.
[4] Henry Fleury de Culan, Heer van Buat, a leader of the Orangist opposition, executed in October 1666.
[5] Coenraad van Beuningen, Dutch ambassador in London.

bear it,[1] and all this professedly to make a gainful voyage to Obrian, over the head of a great many old and better deserving commanders. And see the fruits on't, in his keeping out the King's ship [for] his own pleasure, calling from port to port and staying there his own time; to so great a charge to the King, as all the Exchange takes notice of it, and, upon my observing it to his Royal Highness two days since, he told me he did intend to make a very strict inquiry after it; as it well deserves, and its issue recorded.

Vide page [217]. *June 22d (69).* Discoursing this morning with Mr Wren touching the long delay of the fleet going out to the Straits under Sir T. Allen, and asking him the reason of it, he told me that the backwardness of the Victualler gave some occasion to it, but that if that were over there would be yet another hindrance, namely, the want of 3 or 400 men, which, says he, cannot be supplied while we make a scruple of pressing, and therefore his Highness must give one general liberty to press without restriction when the fleet is in all other points ready; by which means we shall at once do our business and away.

Which being sorry to find his Majesty's service still reduced to, I did by and by take an opportunity in my return home to discourse with Mr Tippetts, asking his opinion touching this necessity of pressing and the reason of it. Who told me, as to the former, that he doubts men are not to be had without pressing, forasmuch as very many of the men from home he lately by order at the discharge of their ships stopped 5, 6 or 7*l.* a man to secure them to the service on other ships of this fleet going out, which money was to be paid them before their going out at the Spithead, very many of these men (he tells me) rather choose to make their escape, though with the forfeiture of this money, than preserve it by staying in the service. As to the ground of it, he professed himself at a great loss what to think it to be, considering the many apparent advantages which the King's service affords them above the merchants', of which he enumerated several mentioned already in those by me set down in my former notes on

---

[1]This was the normal arrangement. For the *Leopard*'s voyage, see above, p. 224 & n. 1. O'Brien carried with him a retinue of 26, including the Earl of Castlemaine, husband of the King's mistress: *CSPD 1667–8*, p. 535; ibid., *1668–9*, p. 455.

this subject,[1] but told me that all he could judge it to arise from must be either from the want of the good usage and encouragement which they use to have from commanders, or their aversion to the being constrained to any service against their wills, and much more to the being forced to serve under this or that captain, telling me of several that if they must serve declared against serving under such and such commanders, and complaining of it as a grievance that they might not choose under whom to serve, or lastly a general distaste to the King's service contracted by the late ill payment of their wages, and other ill treatments, which he believes (though an amendment in these things may hasten it) yet nothing but time can thoroughly remove the memory and impressions of.

June 24th 69. Meeting this day with Capt. Poole, I propounded to him the same question, who was telling me that, do what he can, seamen do desert the service, and that after he hath given several men that have come to him as volunteers notes to the clerk of the cheque to enter them, the men have never appeared but as is to be supposed made use of these as they do of printed passes to preserve them from being pressed into other ships. And to my question he answered that he cannot satisfy himself in any measure what the reason should be of this aversion of seamen to the King's service, while the advantages of his service do evidently exceed those of merchantmen's. But tells me that which he meets most with amongst seamen as the reason given by them for it, is their being kept too long in the King's service when they are once in it before they can get their pay for the relief of their families, or be at liberty to follow their other occasions, or please themselves in the change of their service, which either on the account of the voyage, ships, commander, or many other circumstances they may frequently find reason to desire, and do therefore reckon their being debarred from as a mark of slavery, the varying of voyages being matter of general delight to seamen, who also think it but their due that while they are willing to serve they may have the liberty of serving where themselves upon some of the considerations foregoing shall think best. Which argument of theirs hath certainly much force in it.

But here, mentioning of Capt. Poole, R. Gibson took occasion to tell me that he did not wonder that Capt. Poole particularly

[1] Above, p. 227.

should meet with difficulties in the keeping of his men, who was observed to keep so little command over his under-officers as to suffer his lieutenant Salkield[1] to beat and abuse his under-officers and men, though to his own knowledge and confession unjustly, and that so apparently as upon occasion of his own, going from on board, to be forced to give leave to some of his under-officers to go from on board also to prevent their being abused in his absence by the lieutenant, who it seems is a gentleman and consequently one whom the captain durst not exercise that command over that he ought and would undoubtedly have done over a seaman. The same consequence of introducing of persons of too great quality into the King's ships which R. Gibson gives me another instance of in the late Capt. Seamour, who when but a reformado in the *Yarmouth*, under Capt. Wager, had more observance paid him, and the officers and company more fearful of disobliging him, than of any officer in the ship.[2]

But as to our former subject, Mr Gibson does tell me of another discouragement to seamen which never yet occurred to me but seems very considerable – *viz.* that whereas in all merchants' service if a seaman deserts the ship at the beginning or during the voyage he indeed forfeits his wages, but if it be at the end after the ship is come into port, he forfeits no more than the master's charge in hiring another to do his work in the delivery of the ship. Our practice in the King's service is such, that if after a ship is come into port, lying there without anything to do but in expectation of being paid off, and this after being abroad a year; if, I say, at this time a seaman either for health, business, visiting of his family, or, it may be, pleasure, shall not attend on board, though there be nothing for him to do, nay and the King be profited by his absence in the saving of his victuals and might also save his wages during his absence, yet this will not suffice, but that the seaman shall forfeit all his wages past. Which (for instance) is the present case of one Thomas Haggon now petitioning the Board, who coming as a volunteer to serve Capt. Scott and served him as a midshipman fourteen months in

---

[1] Ralph Salkeld came from a North Country landed family. He was possibly the son of the 'Ralph Salkfield', commissioner for the assessment of 1643 for Berwick-on-Tweed: Firth and Rait, *Acts and Ordinances*, i. 93.

[2] Hugh Seymour, third son of Sir Edward, the 3rd Baronet, and brother of Edward, later 4th Baronet and Speaker of the House of Commons, was a member of the prominent West Country family of that name. He had many friends at court, including the Duke of York himself: H. St Maur, *Annals of the Seymours* (1902), p. 291; C. H. Hartmann, *The King's Friend* (1951), p. 121.

the *Victory Prise* and therein continued a week after her coming in to be laid up, then with his captain's leave went on shore to visit his friends and happening to marry in the interval, which was five weeks before the ship's being paid, and in that time being missed at his musters, he was denied his whole pay for the voyage and is still so now the ship has been paid off above ten months, and Capt. Scott himself not only certifying the truth of the premises but at this day soliciting for him as for a very able and deserving seaman, and who by his coming in as a volunteer and serving as a midshipman cannot be reasonably judged a runaway. Which practice of the Navy seems very well worth considering; and the rather for that at the same time I do remember that the absences of seamen have been punished by defalcation of wages only for the time they have been absent, though absent for six weeks, without forfeiting any more. Which latter practice condemns the former, and while both are continued bewrays unsettledness in our methods. *Vide* what was done at the King's coming in to the 65 ships then lying long in expectation of being paid off,[1] when, as I remember, leave was published to the men to visit their friends with the forfeiture only of their victuals.

June 26th (69). Speaking on this subject this day with Sir Jeremy Smith, he tells me that he cannot think anything contributes more to the present aversion of seamen to the King's service [than] the ill usage they receive under their commanders by beating and otherwise and by their seeing a rout of rascally landmen brought on board to the filling up of all cabins and taking away all the encouragements and conveniences which seamen (as they deserved) used to enjoy, with commanders making them wait, nay and give money to some one or other of his gang that he entrusts with the keeping and delivering of their tickets, and in short that they do find themselves wholly neglected and commanded by men who neither mean nor understand how to oblige them.

July 3d (69). This day Mr Hosier desired the Board's direction how he should answer several seamen who, having been pressed out of merchantmen into Sir Edwrd Spragg's ship the *Revenge* now going to the Straits, and many being pressed above

---
[1]Cf. below, pp. 258–9 & n.

the complement of the ship in order to the picking out a complement out of the best, these are discharged and come to Hosier as clerk of the cheque at Gravesend for tickets for the time they have served, which they being supernumeraries he would not grant them without our direction, who in right to the poor men did direct him to give them tickets, but by this means his Majesty is not only already run into a charge of supernumeraries, but the poor men oppressed by being turned out of one ship into another with great trouble to get their wages, in the meantime the merchant suffering by our stripping them of men, and all through the negligence, ignorance or oppressive proceedings of our people in the use of their press warrants. And this puts me in mind of the old complaint of seamen during the late war and in the time of the Plague of turning them on shore without their tickets, by which they were bereft of anything whereby to challenge their wages. Besides the real and general discouragement given seamen by their being forced so much to take their satisfaction in tickets, the trouble, attendance and other difficulties in the getting them made, delivered, signed and paid, and relief in case of tickets lost, imperfectly made out or signed by the officers, and sometimes made out and paid to wrong persons without their privity, etc., being such as the condition of a poor seaman, his wife or widow is not able to undergo. *Vide* page [243].

June 26. (69). This afternoon going to my Lord Brouncker in his lodgings at the office, I found him in company with Sir Tho. Allen, Sir Jer. Smith, Sir Edwrd Spragg and Capt. Langston, where discoursing loosely of several things, Sir E. Spragg fell to tell us that he had lately been before the Commissioners of Accounts[1] on this occasion – *viz.* that one of his company being drowned at sea, he did in kindness to the friends[2] of the party (to prevent their being at the charge of taking out letters of administration) give order that he should not be made dead upon his book, but discharged, and that at the end of the voyage among others whose moneys in kindness to the parties or their friends he took care to get paid, he received this. That upon his coming to the Commissioners of Accounts they asked him whether that he had ever received such a man's money. He answered yes. They

[1]The Brooke House Commissioners.
[2]Relatives.

replied, "Whence is it that you keep it from the person that hath right to it?" He answered because to this day it was never demanded of him, and that he was now ready to pay it, which they ordered him to do and the party[1] to attend him for it. That accordingly the party came to him, and whether he received his money or no he did not say, but he told us that his arm being ill he durst not at that time venture to strike him as he was resolved to do, but ordered him to come to him the next day, against which he swore he had provided a parcel of good cudgels with which he was resolved to drub the rogue as long as he could stand. But the fellow as he believes suspecting his design and so escaped a drubbing. To which when I asked him, as Sir Tho. Allen also did, how he could justify to the Commissioners or anywhere else his making out tickets in this manner and receiving and keeping the money when perhaps the ticket might never have been called for, and so the money would have been saved to the King. To which he answered with an oath, that he looked upon those windfalls (so he called them) to be his own, at least that he would take them, for that he thought it reasonable that the commander should have them rather than anybody else, and somebody or other he was sure would prevent the King's having the benefit of them. Which as it was a most bold confession on his part, and what the company seemed silently to take deep notice of, though the place thought unfit to say what otherwise ought to have been said upon it; so it naturally leads me to reflect upon the wonderful injury his Majesty and poor seamen are liable to by this practice, the easiness and temptation of which does from this acknowledgement of his make me fear its being too common, and leads me also to look upon the charge of keeping the ships' books after they are brought into the Ticket Office (as well as before) as a matter of greater trust than I had hitherto thought it.

July 3d (69). Telling this passage of Sir E. Spragg this day to W. Hewer, he observed another evil therein not here mentioned, which is that the party being dead yet appearing but as discharged upon the book, his friends supposing him yet alive, and not knowing but that he may have had his ticket, or at least having no ground themselves of demanding one, the money may probably lay for ever unasked for, unless by accident the books in the

---

[1] Presumably a seaman impersonating the dead man.

Ticket Office should happen to be searched and there a ticket found to have been made out. In which case nevertheless the ticket being paid and (as it is ordinary with us to find) no name expressed to whom it was paid, the party remains as far as ever from relief.

W. Hewer at the same time told me that he hath been well informed that this practice hath not only been proved at Brooke House against Sir Wm Jennings but avowed by him there, and that not only in the case of dead but of runaways, nay and that there was one poor man's case found, where by the captain's beating him and other ill usage he was forced for his own preservation to run away, and being gone Sir W. Jenings was afterwards found to have made out a ticket for this runaway and got it paid to himself; and being afterwards discovered therein, he pretended that he did it to make himself amends for the wrong the fellow had done him. And from this fund it undoubtedly is that commanders are able to live and spend after the rate they do, beyond what their known wages and allowances can maintain them in.

June (69). *Vide* a paper on my file of this date from Mr Wilson at Chatham containing a discourse upon the present practice of mooring ships by swivels, and upon his conference (by my advice) with Boatswain Moore, his opinion that it is less safe and more chargeable than the old way of hawsers. And instances in the late loss of the *R. James*, *Loyall London* and *R. Oake* at Chatham.

July 6th (69). *Memorandum*: waiting at St James's I in the outward room heard Capt. Digby,[1] lately come home from the Straits, discourse with another about the merchants' beginning to talk of Capt. Obrian's coming home loaden with merchants' goods in the *Leopard* from Constantianople and other ports in the Straits[2] (where, by the way, I heard Mr Wren this day speak very largely touching the length of time he was taken in his coming home, calling and staying from port to port) in which discourse Capt. Digby took occasion to enlarge on this subject,

[1]Francis Digby, 2nd son of the Earl of Bristol, a gentleman captain in command of the *Montagu* in Allin's voyage to the Mediterranean 1668–9: Allin, *Journals*, i. 30.

[2]See above, pp. 224, 229–30 & nn.

saying that he did not doubt but the world would be as ready to find fault with Obrian though without cause, as they had done with him, who with others lay lately under censure for his private trade, whereas he swore that he would give the King his pay and 400*l*. more to clear him of all his expenses this last voyage and leave him but a saver. And that he believed not any of the fleet were the richer by the voyage but Sir Tho. Allen, to which the other replying that he did believe that two or three other might get 100*l*. apiece or so, he answered that he believed not, or if they did he was confident Sir Tho. Allen['s] share was fifty out of every one of their hundreds. Where I taking notice of their discourse put in and said: "Are you used then at sea to compound with one another?" He replied that though it had never been his lot to do it or have occasion of doing it, yet others did, and seemed to insinuate very hard things of Sir Tho. Allen particularly. Then being asked whether he was for the sea then or no, he replied not he, till the King would make his service fit for a gentleman, which it was not now as not being sufficient to support a gentleman according to his quality, and that therefore since tarpaulins must be thought the only men that can do anything (though he knew how much they were mistaken that thought so), the King's service should continue for him in their hands as being fittest for them, who know not how to make any difference between the honour of a merchantman and a King's ship, and this in time of peace when the honour of the King seems to be the sole end of the charge of setting out ships.

Here discoursing on this subject with R. Gibson at my entering this note, he gave me as an instance of the value the late Parliament put upon this pretence of honour to the nation, that Capt. Grimsdich, then lieutenant under Pen in the *Fairfax* and left at Iueca in the Straits in charge of the *Great Alexander Prize* then lately taken, where he remained with her till the return of Pen from the bottom of the Straits,[1] he during that time run himself out by his high expenses above 400*l*., and, finding himself prevented by Penn in reimbursing himself out of the prize goods, attempted at his coming home by his interest in Desborough and others to get allowance, from them then in power, of his charge

---

[1]This was in 1651 when Penn was hunting down Rupert's squadron in the Mediterranean. The *Great Alexander* was a French prize left in the harbour at Ibiza ("Iueca", later in this entry "Iversy") until she was taken to England in May: G. Penn, *Memorials*, i. 311, 332, 336. (Ibiza was spelt in various ways at this time. In this passage the variants were multiplied by the fact that it was dictated).

pretended in the treating of the Governor and Friars[1], etc., at Iversy for the honour of his country, to which Haslerig and the rest that he appealed to gave him no other answer than that instead of reward he deserved to be turned out of the service, having done more dishonour than honour to his country by his prodigality in entertaining of a Governor whose duty to his master the King of Spaine, then in alliance with us, ought to be held sufficient obligation to him to behave himself well to us without being invited to it by the prodigality of such a fellow as he.[2]

Talking further on this kind of matter, R. Gibson gave me a pleasant instance how seamen are corrupted by being tempted to imitate gentlemen while they observe gentlemen to be most regarded. The instance is Capt. Robinson's vanity when he lay commander of a squadron of ships at Gottenburgh during the late war, where inviting company on board his own ship and being merry he must needs pretend to dance, and having so done till he was weary, he concluded, saying that he danced as he fought. Whereto Digby[3] was heard to reply that he knew not how he fought, but he was sure he danced like a fool. And being interpreter for Capt. Robinson to the company that were strangers, while Robinson thought that he was doing him honour to the company, Capt. Digby thought it necessary to desire the strangers that they would not judge of the behaviour of the English gentlemen by this of Capt. Robinson, who was but so and so, and better could not be expected from him. This Robinson is he that to recommend himself the more by getting himself the name of the Lieutenant of the Tower[4] (who ever since has called him cousin) took upon him the name of Robinson, though both himself and his father before him (a schoolmaster at Great Yarmouth) had ever writ themselves Roberts.

R. Gibson did give me at the same time an instance of how a commander that is a landman may be imposed upon by his underofficers even to the hazarding the reputation of his valour, for which alone landmen do particularly value themselves, and it is of DuTell, whom his Royal Highness to this day honours as a man of great courage, though turned out afterwards of his com-

---

[1]The clergy of the cathedral.
[2]Penn himself gave a present to the Governor for his help: Penn, op. cit., i. 360.
[3]See above, p. 236 n. 1.
[4]Sir John Robinson, Bt.

mand by the Duke of Albemarle for a coward.[1] Whose present case was this, that in chasing some ships in sight of the Flag and himself particularly being the headmost of our ships besides the windermost by at least a league, his Royal Highness saw among the ships [that] was chased a square-sterned ship which he took (as well as the rest of the fleet) to be a man-of-war because she sailed something better than the rest of her fleet (though indeed she afterwards proved to be but a merchant ship come from Guinny) and put his whole hopes in DuTell taking her, which he might have done more easily than any other man-of-war in the fleet, but by one Dry, his master, was persuaded it could not be and that they might, by seeking to get her, lose some others they might make sure on, did give over his chase and man two or three other sorry flyboats, which was imputed to his cowardice in taking that occasion to eschew encountering the man-of-war (as it was thought to be). This passage and of his Highness's meeting Dutel at the entering port and being ready to strike him, R. Gibson was an eye witness of, though afterwards by his Highness's present opinion of him it seems that his Highness was satisfied in this matter; though in 1666 he was finally turned out by the Duke of Albemarle for a coward, though the Duke of York never mentions it but with dissatisfaction for his so doing.

June 29. 1669. As an instance of the condition pursers are in in reference to their accounting with their captains, and obtaining right of them in the certifying the allowances due to the purser, *vide* the following case of Danll Sindry, purser of the *Jersey* under Capt. Holmes to Guinny, as the same was presented this day to the Board and sworn to by the said Sindry as follows:

That in the years 1663 and 64 the said ship was upon the coast of Guinny, where falling short of provision the said Sindry was required by Sir Robt Holmes, then his commander, to give a bill under his hand of 42*l.* for provisions short for his cabin, which accordingly he did.

That by order of the said Sir Robt the said Sindry upon the

---

[1] Jean-Baptiste Du Teil, a French favourite of the Duke of York, was temporarily under a cloud after the Four Days Fight, when his guns had done more damage to his own side than to the enemy. But he was later given a post in the Duke's Household and knighted: J. R. Powell and E. K. Timings (eds), *Rupert and Monck's Letter Book, 1666* (NRS 1969), p. 71; *Diary*, vii. 163; viii. 147.

ship's arrival gave all his prepared certificates, vouchers and papers into the hands of one Wm Roach to be firmed by the said Sir Robert, and when they were redemanded they were denied to be returned unless the said Sindry would pay him 30*l*. for getting Sir Robt's hand.

That the said Sir Robt Holmes arresting the said Sindry for non-payment of his bill, he forthwith deposited 42*l*. in the hands of Mr Phineas Pett to satisfy that debt, in whose hands it remained two months and was denied by Roach to be received without 3*l*. more to pay the bailiffs for the arrest.

That prosecuting the law, the said Sindry is confined to the King's Bench upon execution.

That although the said Sindry offers Sir Robt responsible security to pay out of the balance of his account the 42*l*. bill and the 30*l*. demanded, Sir Robert refuses to accept thereof and detains the papers.

That Sindry is content for Sir Robt's better satisfaction to continue a prisoner till the account be passed and balance received.

All which the said Sindry humbly offers to your Honours' consideration, humbly begging that his said papers may be delivered, and proceedings against his security stopped whiles the account is passing, he paying the charges at law.

And as bound, etc.,
Danll Sindrey.

Sworn by the said Danll Sindry all the contents hereof to be true before me this 29 day of June 1669.
Samll Starling.

Upon which the Board thought fit to write to Sir Robt Holmes the following letter, forbearing at present to take notice of any more than what was necessary towards obtaining a capacity for the purser to pass his account, leaving the rest relating to the price the purser was to give for his certificates to a particular enquiry, after the first shall be got.

The letter from the Board to Sir Robt Holmes follows:

Sir,

Among the many pursers against whom this Office is at this day proceeding by course of law for their not passing their accounts, Daniel Sindry happens to be one, who was purser of the *Jersey* under your command in your voyage to Guinny 1663, and does now pretend to excuse his not having passed that account from the want of those necessary certificates which (as he says) were long since signed by yourself on his behalf, but have been to this day detained from him by reason of his non-payment of a debt of 42*l*. which he acknowledges to be due to you from him and which he tells us he is most willing to pay you out of the balance of his account, and in the meantime to secure you therein either by bonds to your satsifaction, or by continuing your prisoner (as it seems he now is) until the same be actually performed.

What we have to say upon this matter is, that we are obliged by many considerations on his Majesty's behalf to press this man to the passing his account, which being impossible for him to do without the vouchers necessary thereto, we desire to be informed from you how far those his pretences are true, and that rather than his Majesty shall be prevented in having this account cleared we will take upon ourselves the seeing you satisfied by him the aforesaid debt before he receives any part of what shall be found due to him upon the balance of this account. Whereto entreating a word or two in answer. We remain,
      Your very humble servants,
      Br., J.M., J.S., S.P.
Sir Rob. Holmes,
29 June 1669.

Memorandum: upon Saturday night July 10. (69) Sir Robt Holmes meeting me at Court, he told me that the letter above written from the Board found him upon the road, where he could not answer it, and that he now desired me to tell the Board that he had many years since assigned over to another man (Roach) what was due to him from the purser and had delivered to that man all the certificates relating to the said purser's accounts, and which he had at that time signed; so as he neither had anything to expect from the purser nor could say anything to him, as to his demand of certificates, the purser being to apply himself to that person only, who where he at present is, he told me he knew not. To which I answering that by this means the purser being disabled from ever passing his accounts, not only the purser will be ruined by the want of what will be coming to him upon the balance thereof from the King if creditor, and Roach be by that means for ever prevented in the payment of the sum due to him; but the King also prevented in what the said purser upon his accounts should happen to be found debtor in. Whereto he made me no other reply, than that he could not help it, and so we parted.

Thursday July 1st (69). Sir Thomas Allen this day taking leave of the Board, and having 7000*l.* imprested to him for answering the contingencies of the fleet,[1] he was very earnest with the Board that it might be declared in writing before his going, that if he should die in the voyage Sir Edwrd Spragg's order for the disposal of what part of the money should be then remaining in his hands might be a sufficient discharge to his executors for the same. To which the Board answering that the thing was wholly new, and without precedent, and that they had no cognizance that Sir Edwrd Spragg was designed to succeed him in the command of the fleet in case of death, nor had the authority of making any such order if they did know it, he insisted with so much earnestness upon the thing, that I began to suspect his having some extraordinary ground for it, and therefore asked him privately what was the true reason of his being so much concerned in this particular. He answered me by putting his head between Sir Jeremy Smith and me, so as Sir Jeremy heard and took notice of it as well as myself, that if he should die it might be very dangerous to his family if he did not first secure them against Sir Edwrd Spragg's disposal of the money, who he was sure would lay hold of it, and what he would do with it be would be loath to answer;[2] which hearing, I thought he had but too much reason to do what he now did, and gave the Board a little intimation thereof, who nevertheless did not find they could do more in it than advise him to ask his Royal Highness's direction therein. And so it ended.

Saturday July 10th (69). One told me that Sir Edwrd Spragg has heard of this discourse of Sir Tho. Allen's, and inveighs against him most bitterly, swearing that he need not be so jealous of what will become of the money that he leaves behind unless he were more honest himself in the laying of it out, swearing again that he is sure Sir Tho. Allen would poison the fleet or let

---

[1] He sailed for the Mediterranean on 17 July 1669 and returned on 6 Nov. 1670.
[2] Spragg had a reputation for avarice, according to Evelyn (*Diary*, ed. de Beer, iii. 606), and he and Holmes were old enemies.

them starve rather than lose the advantage of laying out the money to his own profit. Upon what grounds he says this may be fit for inquiry. But I remember that, three days since, discoursing with [blank] in Lincoln's Inn Fields touching the condition of the Navy and persons in command therein, he told me that when first Sir Edwrd Spragg was nominated to command a ship of the King's, he did hear my Lord Falmouth make a question openly whether it could be thought safe to put one of the King's ships into his hands, lest he should run away with her, his condition being so necessitous, and his former dealings of no better reputation.

Sunday July 11th (69). Capt. Eliott and Lieut. Ward dining with me, and discoursing of the temper of seamen, and in particular under commanders or masters whom they do not love, Ward gave me an instance of a merchantman wherein he then was, which being chased by a Spaniard, the master commanded them to make ready to fight, which the men one and all refused as being a man that had disobliged them, and therefore chose to run her aground, which they did; and having turned the master ashore and then of their own accord fitted their ship, met the Spaniard and fought him three hours in the sight of the master, till they were forced to deliver the ship, upon terms of being all with their clothes and private trade set safe on shore.

Vide page [234]. As a thorough demonstration of seamen's present aversion to the King's service we may consider what Sir Tho. Litleton acquainted the Board with this day, that of the money stopped in his agent Ridge's hand at Portsmouth out of seamen's wages to oblige them to continue in the service for manning of the fleet now newly gone to the Straits under Sir Tho. Allen, which money so stopped was to be paid them at the Spithead before the sailing of the fleet, there is above 700*l.*, now the fleet is gone, left in his hands uncalled for, by men who have chosen rather to forfeit the money stopped, being 4, 5 and 6*l.* a man, than save it by returning to their ships.

July 28. 69. Being at Whitehall this morning I meet with a too pregnant instance of the easiness at which the King's treasure is nowadays to be parted with, the confidence of some men in asking what they do not deserve, and the hardships which the modest painful man lies under who sees this, yet has not assurance enough to ask anything, nor so much as to make his pains known. The instance is Sir Wm Penn, whom I found this morning attending the King and Duke and afterwards understood by him that he had asked of them and obtained their promise of allowing him the same six months' pay which was allowed the last year to several commanders, who having received their commissions, attended the fitting their ships and manning them, furnished themselves for the sea, brought the same on board, and put themselves by all other employment for that year, were, by the sudden stop put to the going forth of that fleet, discharged the service before any pay was grown due to them.[1] Whereas Sir W. Penn was so far from being in their case as:

1. To have no commission ever granted him;

2. Though he was indeed first designed by the Duke to command the fleet, yet such was the exception taken thereat by the Board, and universally by the Parliament,[2] though the thing was but only suggested (the Duke having done nothing publicly to show his intentions herein) that the Duke found it necessary to give out that himself would go, and invite the Prince[3] to go with him as Vice-Admiral, which he accepted of.

3. That Sir Wm Penn was sick of the gout the greatest part of the time of this fleet's preparation, and I remember himself then told me discoursing of this matter, that God Almighty had determined the matter about which the world did so much trouble themselves, that he should not go to sea, meaning by his sickness.

4. I believe he was so far from any preparation for the sea, or being at 5*l.* charge towards it, that not only all discovery of any such thing either by his own or family's discourse was wholly wanting, but if (which I do not remember) he did at all go down

---

[1] A squadron under Allin had briefly patrolled the Channel in the spring of 1668 on receipt of news that the Dutch were out: Duke of York, *Memoirs*, pp. 147–8. On its return the Duke (16 June) had allowed full pay even to those commanders who had remained in harbour – as a reward, he alleged, for their zeal in fitting out their ships: PRO, ADM 106/16, f. 229*r*. Cf. above, p. 16 & n. 2.

[2] He was under threat of impeachment for his part in the prize-goods scandal of 1665 until Parliament rose on 9 May 1668. (As Vice-Admiral under Sandwich he and other commanders, including Sandwich himself, had seized cargo from Dutch E. Indiamen before the goods had been declared prize. See *Diary*, vi. 231 n. 1).

[3] Rupert.

the River or do ought else of that kind towards the dispatch of the fleet, it will undoubtedly be found that he was paid for it by a bill for travelling charges, the work being but his duty as a Commissioner of the Navy.

Besides that, Capt. Cox as I remember received this six months' allowance as commander of the ship *Charles*,[1] in which the Duke was to go, and had the whole care of her.

But (which is more stupendous) Sir W. Penn declared to Mr Wren and me this morning, that he expected to be paid after the rate of 3*l*. a day as assistant to the Admiral, as he was in the *Charles*[2] the first year of the war, which was a thing wholly extraordinary then and would have been held much more so in time of peace, the Duke having so able a commander under him as Capt. Cox.

And lastly, if it shall be thought reasonable that this be done to Sir Wm Penn, how much more reason would the Prince have to expect the like consideration suitable to his quality, and what other charges may attend it also is not presently to be foreseen.

Augst 3d (69). Upon discourse with Mr Gibson touching the proceedings of the last West India fleet under Sir John Harman,[3] he happened to mention a vessel heretofore taken notice of somewhere among my notes, which Sir Wm Penn supplied the King with at Portsmouth by some kind of private dealing between him and Capt. Hubbert;[4] a sorry mean vessel for which as I remember [he] got a much better of the King.[5] This vessel happening to be sent a fireship with Sir John Harman to the West Indies, proved so unserviceable as not only to lose the opportunity offered of doing good service there, but that Capt. Poole (who was left behind Harman to command the remaining squadron there) was (though they had no other fireship left – the *Joseph* being burnt) forced to sell her for 120*l*. or some suchlike sum. It is worth reflecting upon at leisure, the bargain which was imposed upon the King in this ship, taking in the charge of fitting

---

[1] The new *Charles* of 1668: Anderson, no. 443.
[2] The *Royal Charles* taken by the Dutch 1667: Anderson, no. 231.
[3] Harman returned in April 1669 after almost a year on the station.
[4] The *Prosperous*, sold to the King in 1667: see below, p. 246 & n. 1.
[5] The *Flying Greyhound*, a privateer which until then he had shared with Pepys, Batten and Sir Richard Ford: *Diary*, viii. 441 & nn. 1, 3.

her, with the wages and victuals spent in her, and the service finally lost by her unserviceableness.

Memorandum: that the notes above mentioned about this vessel, the *Prosperous*, I have here caused to be inserted.[1]

March 2d 66[67]	Comr Midleton is desired by letter from the Principal Officers to receive the *Prosperous* and fit her for a fireship.
19	Comr Midleton complains of her bad condition.
21	The Principal Officers write to him to tell him they know not upon what terms the King hath her, and therefore know not what to say, only desire an inventory of her.
24	Comr Midleton's letter gives a full account of her.
26	Comr Midleton sends a particular inventory of her furniture.
September 22	Comr Middleton to me in answer to mine lately about it.

July 30th 1669. Being (which is unusual for me) at the Board this day while Br., J.M. and J.S. were under examination of some part of Sir Denis Gawden's accounts, I took notice of their being busy in cancelling of papers, and for my satisfaction demanding what they were, my Lord Brouncker and the rest presently answered me, that Sir Wm Penn in all the accounts of Sir Denis Gawden examined in his time had led the Board to the signing and allowing Sir D.G.'s demands for all allowances by him made to pursers upon their accounts by virtue of the certificates by them produced allowed by this Board, and this Sir W. P. had led the Board to do without seeing one of these certificates cancelled, but, on the contrary, leaving them to lie in Sir D. G.'s hands, at his liberty to be brought again to account if he should at any time think fit to do so. So that the King, to the unanswerable reproach of this Board, might have been easily twice charged with them, had not Sir D.G. himself of his own accord brought

---

[1]These papers have not been traced, apart from Middleton's letter to Pepys of 19 Mar. 1667 reporting the purchase of two fireships, the *Francis* and the *Prosperous*, from Capt. Hubbard: *CSPD 1666–7*, p. 573.

them to the Board to be cancelled, which as my Lord told me had been their work for several meetings. And it is to be doubted whether the King has not been used with the like neglect, in the allowing pursers credit for provisions delivered to other ships without seeing the pursers of those ships duly charged for the same.

Vide something on this subject in the Board's letter to Sir Wm Penn July 31. (69).

Vide pages [184–5] and [188]. *Augst 2d (69)*. This day the Board did receive a certificate dated the 1st inst. and signed by the Surveyor, Comr Cox, Mr Shish and Mr Byland in answer to the survey pursuant to the Duke's late order (upon the Board's late advice) for the sale of the wreck of the *Royall James* now lying in dock at Woolwich. In which certificate they value her (and the Surveyor told me they did it at the highest) but at 200*l*.[1] A thing so scandalous for the Board considering the charge in bringing her from Chatham into this dock, and the filling of the dock so long, which the Surveyor has frequently said was of more worth than 1500*l*. a year, I advised and the Board agreed with me not to proceed to the sale till we had from the Surveyor his opinion of the charge of the King's breaking her up in dock and the value of her material which may be saved. Which [we] would then lay the whole before the Board, and accordingly was demanded of the Surveyor by their letter of this date.

Augst 7th 69. This day Capt. Obrian newly come home with the *Leopard* after his keeping her abroad so many months at his own pleasure[2] came to the Board, to tell us that Sir J. Mennes and Capt. Cox, at the late pay of his ship at Chatham, denied to pay some tickets wherein he was concerned because the party did not appear, and that he was therefore now come to bring one of them to us, whom when we saw we found him a landman who he said had been with him all the voyage but not entered as one of his company, but since his return to Smirna where he had a vacancy to put him in. But that which I would here mention is that he desired we would allow the present payment of one of

---

[1] She had been wrecked by the Dutch in the Medway in 1667. The valuation was based on the assumption that the purchaser would reduce the larboard side to be equal to the starboard before launching her: *CSPD 1668–9*, p. 436.

[2] See above, pp. 224, 229–30 & nn.

his tickets which is of a kinsman of his own name that went with him this voyage and is already gone into Ireland and so cannot be produced. To which the Board answering that they must refer this whole matter till the return to town of Sir J. Mennes and Capt. Cox, he departed; and being gone, my Lord Brouncker acquainted the Board privately that to his knowledge that this person whom he calls his kinsman and declares to be gone to Ireland is a woman that he carried with him in man's apparel (of which the whole Exchange hath long since and doth at this day ring) and is at this day in London. *Quere*: is this a practice under which the King's service can ever be well minded or honoured, or God's blessing ever expected upon it? *Quere*: in what is a commander to be believed after so plain a prevarication as this; and if so, how unsafe is his Majesty while a charge like that of such a ship as the *Leopard* is committed to no better hand? *Quere*: is it likely that the King can be well served when a Commissioner of the Navy of my Lord Brouncker's quality shall find himself under such a restraint as not to think it safe for him publicly to be the discoverer of such a piece of villainy, and is it probable that he would have made the same scruple if Capt. Obrian had been a plain tarpaulin?

I have since asked my Lord Brouncker and Sir J. Mennes about this pretended kinsman, who tell me that they know the woman and that she stood entered all the voyages under the name of Francis Obrian. And the Surveyor tells me of a passage between Capt. Obrian and his master, that being in the Arches among the Islands[1] where the master thought it fit to make the best way he could to prevent his lying among them in the night, the captain commanded him to hand[2] his sails. Wherein being denied by the master and he still commanding it, the master at last told him plainly that himself had the charge of the ship and would therefore execute it, and desired him to let him alone and go down to Mr Francis Obrian. *Vide* page [249].

Memorandum: August 6. (69). Upon the petition of the widow of May,[3] boatswain of the *Breda*, a man reported by Sir

---

[1]'Arches' was the seaman's word for archipelago – in this case the Cyclades in the Aegean.
[2]Haul in.
[3]Marginal note: 'A landman, kinsman to Sir Geo. Carterett and killed at Bergen'.

Jeremy Smith, Capt. Cox and others to have been an extraordinary good officer, I say upon reading her petition before the Duke this day desiring to be discharged of several stores, for the expense of which (and among them a quantity of kerseys), she in the passing her husband's accounts finds herself unable to satisfy the clerk of the survey, an oath is produced wherein one belonging to the commander of the ship, Capt. Seale, swears that he was sent by his commander into the boatswain's storeroom to cut off so much of his kerseys as was necessary for the furnishing his cabin with curtains, carpets, and for his bed, and that, while he was doing the same, the boatswain came in and demanding by what order he did it and being answered by command of the captain, he submitted to it, complaining only and saying that thus went his kerseys away. A fair instance of the condition under-officers lie in in reference to the commanders.

Vide page [248] which is a great instance how the King's ships will or can be commanded by men of quality and pleasure.

Tuesday Augst 10. (69). Sir J. Mennes and Capt. Cox being returned from the pay of the *Leopard* at Chatham gave the Board a short account of what they have discovered by the journals they met with touching Capt. Obrian's calling at almost every port both outward and homeward and staying his own time at each, to the spending as they moderately calculate it full five months upon his own occasions. A thing not to be named without reproach. They purpose to prepare an abstract of the journals and present it to his Royal Highness.

Thursday 12 Augst 69. Being upon the Exchange and a-discoursing with the Hublons, and mention being made of Capt. Obrian of the *Leopard*, they told me, with great sense of the dishonour his Majesty suffers therein, that they had silver brought home in her, the invoice of which runs 'Shipped on board' not 'his Majesty's' but 'Capt. Obrian's frigate the *Leopard*'; and do very much bewail the consequences of introducing gentlemen to commands of the King's ships and laying aside tarpaulins, unless (as they were saying) the gentry would send their children young which they designed for the sea. The contrary (whereof they tell me) they find to be matter of universal discouragement to seamen both ordinary and masters of ships.

Decembr 2d (69). This being the first day of my coming to the Board after the death of my wife,[1] I found the Board very busy in engaging themselves in freighting of ships for the carrying of a supply of provisions to Sir Tho. Allen. Thereof inquiring the reason, and whether they did not remember that the King had by his late contract[2] engaged the Victualler to look after that work, they did not only all of them declare their having it not in their mind, but, applying myself particularly to Sir Jeremy Smith as most concerned therein,[3] he in his excuse voluntarily declared that he had not yet read over the Victualler's contract, adding that his clerk had but newly taken a copy of it. Whereof taking notice to him and the Board as a matter greatly importing the King not only in this small circumstance, but in those of infinitely greater weight relating to the passing of victuallers' and pursers' accounts, and others wherein he daily will be and has for many months been concerned in, he forthwith called for his copy out of his office, and being shown by me the article relating to this particular, the Board forthwith wrote a letter to Sir Denis Gawden requiring him to do it, and Sir Jeremy Smith promised to betake himself forthwith to the reading and informing himself in the whole of the Victualler's contract, in order to his making use of the same in the future discharge of his duty.

December 16. (69). This day the Earl of Anglesey[4] coming with Mr Waith to the Board in order to the dispatching several matters depending touching his account, the Lord Brouncker did among other things acquaint us and him, that however Sir John Mennes and himself and the Board were led to the passing Sir Georg. Carterett's accounts of his payments for widows and orphans, there appearing nothing by which this Board could take cognizance thereof, unless it were that the order of Council by which that business was established directs the payments of these orphans and widows to be made by the Treasurer of the Navy,

---

[1] She had died on 10 November.
[2] Concluded on 18 Mar. 1669 with Gauden and his partners (Penn and Benjamin Gauden, his son): Bodl. Lib., Rawl. MSS A 216, pp. 217–37.
[3] See above, p. 211.
[4] Treasurer of the Navy, 1667–8.

the Board might look upon themselves as the implied judges of that account.[1]

That the Earl of Anglesey could not nevertheless expect the Board's interesting themselves in his accounts for that affair, in regard that the order says 'The Treasurer of the Navy' without the addition of 'for the time being.' At which both the Earl and Mr Waith being wholly at a loss how to discharge themselves in this part, as the Board in general was how to justify themselves for what they had already done in relation to Sir George Carterett, I began to recollect that some order from the King had been passed in that matter, and therein calling Mr Haytor, he looked me out a copy of an order of Council dated the 23d of Augst (67) expressly provided for the very case before us both in reference to what had then and should afterwards be done therein by the Treasurer of the Navy.[2] Which I thought worthy noting, as a wonderful instance of the perfunctoriness wherewith matters are done in this Office, when neither Sir John Mennes nor my Lord Brouncker remembered how to justify themselves and the Board in what they had already been led to do, nor knew after so many months as this account had lain in their hands in what condition they were for passing it, nor Mr Waith who negotiated the passing the like account for Sir George Carterett as he does now for the Lord Anglesey was able to remove this difficulty, though by a memorial entered upon this copy of that order it appears that the original thereof did lodge with him.

December 8th (69). This day the Board attending upon his Royal Highness at Whitehall, his Royal Highness acquainted us that after so long deliberation taken, since our presenting to the King in the beginning of this year with our account of the constitution of the Navy,[3] somebody had now at length presented

---

[1]The order authorizing payment of royal bounty to widows and orphans (21 Feb. 1665: PRO, PC 2/58, ff. 179v–180v) had made no mention of any allowance made to the Treasurer on this score.

[2]This order, issued at the beginning of Anglesey's term of office, provided that tallies or assignments of money payable to Carteret as Treasurer were now to be made payable to Anglesey, Treasurer for the time being, and that Carteret should be discharged of all such sums: PRO, PC 2/59, f. 275.

[3]This had been submitted in April and left in Arlington's office for members of the Cabinet to inspect and comment on. No comments had been made by 7 May. See above, p. 210.

his Majesty with observations thereon, and the defects therein, and that he should have them from the King this night.

Decembr 9th (69). Being very impatient of understanding the effect of these observations, I went early before the Office met to Whitehall, where speaking first with Mr Wrenn, he showed me a paper wrote with Mr Gibson's hand, which he said was the paper the King had delivered the Duke, and was as he believed the same with the late observations sent by the Duke himself to the Board as heads of matter for regulation;[1] and thereupon delivering it to Mr Billop[2] to examine by the original of the Duke's, Mr Billop showed me the original wrote in my Lord Brouncker's own hand, as he presented it first to the Duke. Which being compared with the King's paper proved the very same. At which being much astonished, and most of all for its being writ with Mr Gibson's hand, I went up to the Duke, where he was pleased presently to clear to me the whole mystery, by telling me that the King told him that he found it lying upon a table in his laboratory, where without question it must have been left by Sir Robert Murray,[3] to whom my Lord Brouncker had given this copy. With this I went to the office where by my coming late my Lord Brouncker conjectured where I had been, and asked me what news of the observations the Duke spoke of last night. I told him, very pleasant news, for that they proved no other than a copy of the Duke's own propositions lately sent to the Board. At which I presently observed my Lord to blush, and make no other reply than that it was very pretty, that those propositions should come from two hands, wholly avoiding to be thought in any wise particularly concerned therein. But when at my coming home I understood from Mr Haytor and Mr Gibson the whole method of my Lord's and the Board's proceeding upon this paper, with what neglect of me and my deputy in my absence,[4] with what injunctions of secrecy to Mr Gibson employed in (though

---

[1]This was the letter (largely composed by Pepys) which the Duke had addressed to the Board on 25 Nov. 1668. It called for a few procedural reforms but made it clear that the principal reform necessary was stricter obedience on the part of the Principal Officers to their duties. Summary in Tanner, *Catalogue*, i. 31–2; see also ibid., pp. 28–31; *Diary*, ix. 360, 370, 374 & nn.

[2]Thomas Billop, clerk to Wren.

[3]Moray, Keeper of the King's laboratory; friend and scientific associate of Brouncker.

[4]Hayter had acted as Pepys's deputy during his absence abroad. Pepys had returned on 20 October.

but ill rewarded for, that is to say below what in like cases they had allowed their own clerks), the transcribing copies thereof for them, the great speed made in my absence to finish a report therein; and all this managed personally at the Board by my Lord Brouncker by taking the mind of the Board himself and keeping the papers in his own hand to this day, their total giving over[1] any advance therein since my coming home, and lastly my Lord Brouncker's utter silence to me therein, though at my first coming and since, I had given him several occasions of speaking of it, having understood something thereof in general from the Duke at his first seeing me, as also from my clerks though nothing particular, I say these considerations provoked me to the taking notice of this matter in writing to my Lord Brouncker, giving him hints (inoffensive though quick[2]) of my resentments thereon and desiring him to go on with the answering of the Duke's demands. Which I did by letter of this day entered in my Letter Book,[3] well knowing that the shyness[4] of my Lord's proceedings of this matter arises from what he is conscious of having propounded therein in reference to my particular duty.[5]

Decembr 11. (69). My Lord appears to me at the Board very much disturbed, but wholly silent, otherwise than by reaching to me a paper, saying, "This is the paper you demand", which without reply I received, and put up into my paper-case without any present looking into it.

December 14. (69). I acquainted the Board that my Lord had put into my hand a paper which I thought contained some late propositions of the Duke's, and that I desired they would appoint a time for their being considered. Which they presently concluded should be on Saturday next the 18, and that to that purpose the Treasurers should be writ to to be with us, which was accordingly done. But to see the luck of it – no sooner had I done this, but in comes a letter from the Duke (obtained no doubt by my Lord Brouncker, though to very little purpose) taking notice of his

---

[1]Preventing.
[2]Sharp.
[3]NMM, LBK/8, p. 634 (printed *Further Corr.*, pp. 261–2).
[4]Secretiveness.
[5]The Duke's letter of 25 November had included the proposal that the Clerk of the Acts should keep a register of attendance. This proposal may have originated in a suggestion from Brouncker.

want of answer for so many months to his said propositions, and commanding us to dispatch the same.

December 18. (69). Sir Tho. Littleton only of the two Treasurers coming to the Board this day and that not till past twelve, the Board adjourned this matter till Wednesday next in the afternoon being the 22d.

January 31. (69[70]). To this day the Board has either never been full, or so late, and most of us so much diverted by other matters relating to Brooke House and the examining of their Observations before the King, that the Board has never had opportunity of entering upon this matter since.

Novembr 69. About this time the Board being thoughtful of supplying Portsmouth with tar, and by the high prices demanded there put upon[1] sending it from hence, the Surveyor was desired to inform himself of the cheapest way of sending some, who thereupon afterwards informed them that with some difficulty he had got one to do it at 24*s.* per last, he having much stood upon 30, which accordingly was loaden and sent at that price, while at the very same time Mr Haytor informed me that as much freight and more than we had occasion to use might be had at 16*s.* per last, whereof the Surveyor was acquainted and by Mr Haytor's means a parcel sent at that price by a vessel,[2] one Roberts master, while nevertheless the Surveyor went on with his vessel and sent her away loaden at 24*s.*

Febry 3d (69[70]). Mr Hosier's instance of the obstructions given him in the balancing storekeepers' accounts. And therein of the imperfect performances of the Surveyor's duty. This day a letter of the 2d from Mr Hosier, clerk of the comptrol at Deptford, gives an account of the obstructions he meets with of the balancings of

---

[1]The phrase in this sense of 'decided upon' is not recorded in the revised *OED* (1989).
[2]The *James*, a hoy frequently employed on similar business at this time: *CSPD 1668–9*, pp. 497, 582, 623.

the stores:[1] *viz.* (among other things) the survey's not taking notice of the dimensions of sails, and the clerk of the survey's denying to give it him, with design (as he supposes) to prevent his balancing of stores, and his knowing what becomes of the old canvas in their repairs or alterations. The survey's not distinguishing between double and single portnails, which ought to have been taken distinctly. Some stores in the survey set down without weight. The survey's taking no notice of several of his Majesty's stores and goods remaining in the officers of the yards' houses. His finding many issues of stores to greater quantities, and sometimes where the storekeeper is not charged with any quantity at all thereof in the survey book. The master attendant's frequent receiving stores into the rigging house without giving any account to what ships the same are issued, whereby he is left at liberty to dispose of them how he pleases. The master attendant's and clerk of the survey's not giving a weekly account what sails and their dimensions are made or repaired, and out of what sails or canvas they were made, and what other materials were expended thereon by the sailmaker. His being disabled to charge the storekeeper with the return of boatswains' and carpenters' ledgers into store, for want of the clerk of the survey's certifying to the storekeeper's weekly account of the same. And all this at a time of the greatest leisure.

An example of the perfunctory performance of the Surveyor's duty in the casting of ships. The Surveyor having several times pressed the Board to dispose of several little vessels which as he said was kept at great charge to his Majesty and fills the wet dock at Deptford, and were both unfit at present, and deserved not to be made fit by repair for any future service; and being as often desired by the Board to bring in his report in writing upon examining of his surveys, and conference with the master shipwright of the particular vessels which he would have so disposed of, and being directed by the Duke to see the same done (upon mention thereof at one of our attendances on him), the

---

[1] Francis Hosier to Navy Board, 2 February: *CSPD 1670*, p. 48. In 1668 he had submitted a long memorandum, with tables, (now PL 1788) on the subject of storekeepers' accounts. At Hosier's suggestion five extra clerks were appointed in March 1669 to audit storekeepers' accounts: PRO, PC 2/60, f. 47r; *Diary*, ix. 374, 474 & nn.: *Further Corr.*, pp. 240–1.

Surveyor did upon the 13th of September 1670 deliver to the Board under his hand the following report:

An account of vessels, fit to be propounded to his Royal Highness for sale as being unfit for the charge of repair, and unserviceable in the condition they now are.

Trulove..		
Black Dogg		
Adam & Eve	Galliots	
James		at Deptford.
Hope		
Harwich hoy..................................		
Harwich muster boate...................		

Freizland fly boate .... at Chatham.
Harpe... in Ireland.

Tho. Middleton.

Upon which the same day the Board reported the same under their joint hands with his by letter to the Duke. Which lying with the Duke till our waiting upon him the 21: he was then pleased to inquire after the *Truelove* and *Freizland*, the latter as being reputed an able flyboat, the former as having received large repairs about the end of the war at Harwich, and thereupon asked the grounds of our putting them in this list, and whether the former might not with some slight cost serve as a fireship, and the latter on the occasion she heretofore did, and save the buying of others for those uses when there shall be occasion. To which the Board referring him for satisfaction to the Surveyor, the Surveyor replied without any manner of hesitation that the *Freizland* was indeed a good flyboat, and might be useful again, but that Mr Shish had told him that the bottom of the *Truelove* (though she had been repaired in her upper works) was very weak, and that thereupon he put her into this list. Whereupon the Duke commanded that the *Freizland* should be presently struck out,[1] and the *Truelove* too in case upon our personal view of her very speedily, we did not give him satisfaction to the contrary. Whereupon the Board going down the River on other occasion, upon the 23 they viewed the *Truelove* at Deptford, and upon conference with Mr Shish, the

---

[1] In December 1670 the Board ordered that she should be repaired and converted into a fireship: *CSPD 1670*, p. 586.

Surveyor himself present, concluded her fit to be kept for a fireship, and so to the reproach of the Office, and honour of the Duke, these two vessels are saved from sale.

Visiting the new ship the *Prince* October the 3d 1670 now near finishing at Chatham, I observed from the openness of the seams on her decks and the cracks throughout all her plank a sufficient instance of that sort of evil arising from our inability of making seasonable provision of materials, and our being thereby reduced to the making use of green stuff.

Visiting also at the same time by surprise at night upon the 1st inst. the ships in ordinary, I found not one officer on board any of the ships there, saving the cooks upon the *London* and *Royall Katherine*, and upon most of them could make no person on board to hear me. Being the next day attended at Chatham by many of the officers in ordinary to make their excuses to me, I found most of the blame laid upon the absence of the pursers, and that justified by a pretence of their being at London to pass their accounts. Which though if true it renders not – no more than sickness – the officers' absence excusable, yet it administers to me a new consideration of the inconveniences arising from the delay of passing the accounts of pursers and other standing officers.

Discourse also at this time with some poor workmen about the imperfect service the King receives from them compared with what is done in private yards, gave me fresh occasion of considering whether it is not necessary that the wages and encouragement of men in his Majesty's service be made equal to what they meet with from private men, in reference to wages earned both on ships and in the yards, and whether his Majesty may not reasonably be thought to pay dear for the advantage he may be thought to receive from his prerogative of impressing men into his service at his own pay.

The building also of this ship the *Prince* so as to equalize most of the first-rate in charge, burden and force, whereas she was designed by estimate but for a second, gives a particular sort of instance of the method of our running into debt in the Navy, and the necessity of having estimates deliberately made and strictly kept to.

2d Janry 167$^1/_2$. Memorandum: that this morning being surprised with the news of the King's resolving to bring into the Council a proclamation to be there passed for the postponing of all public payments in the Exchequer,[1] and reflecting immediately upon the ill influence the same might in particular have upon the Navy, I took an opportunity before Council of telling my mind therein to the Duke, and by his direction put the same into his hand in a written memorial, which was by him tendered to the King in Council, but without success,[2] in the following words:

> Offered to be considered by his Majesty in the present debate touching the stopping of payments in the Exchequer, whether a difference were not fit to be made between the case of the banker who originally lends money with express condition of extraordinary profits, and the merchant, who having served his Majesty with naval stores at the market price, has for want of other payments been driven to accept of public securities for their money.

April 29. (72). Discoursing with Mr Gibson upon what Col. Middleton in his letter of the 28vo writes about seamen's (and particularly those of the *Tyger*'s and *Adventure*'s) giving no attendance on board in harbour on ships going out, expecting that the ship should be made ready to their hands, adding that nothing but the hanging of half-a-score of them would remedy it, Mr Gibson observed to me that 'tis nothing but bad pay does it, nor anything necessary but good pay to remedy it, telling me of his own knowledge, and quoting Capt. Wm Poole, now in the *St David*, for instance, that at the King's coming in, on the confidence seamen then entertained of having good pay, confirmed therein by the King's present paying off of the twenty-four ships put into his charge before the Parliament had paid

---

[1] The proclamation was issued this day. The 'Stop of the Exchequer', as it came to be called, postponed payment of interest on bankers' loans, and (for a year) payment of most Treasury orders, in order to meet the cost of preparing a fleet for the coming summer. According to the proclamation the King was unable to raise the money by loans because his revenue was already anticipated.

[2] Similarly a deputation of bankers attended the Council on this day with a petition. The petition was read but the deputation was not admitted: BL, Add. MSS 36196, f. 236r (newsletter).

their sixty-five,[1] men were so ready to prefer the King's service and pay before the merchants', that captains have had their full complements entered in their own muster books before they come to be taken notice of by the clerk of the cheque, and consequently before they entered into the King's pay. Nay (and this circumstance I have some remembrance of myself), seamen have so far stroven to get into the King's service, that they have proffered and given their attendance and labour in rigging their ship gratis, only to secure their being entertained into the King's service when he was fit to receive men.

The loss of which desire after the King's service has arisen by degrees as our pay has been worse rather than from the hazard of a war – witness the backwardness with which seamen were come to resort to it for some time before and ever since the end of the last war, there being little difference between what we met with during the whole interval from the end of that war to the beginning of this now on foot and what was and is under the wars themselves.

Mr Gibson tells me he believes that by the contrary course of good pay and good usage (which latter also goes very far with the former in the rendering the service uneasy to seamen, from the general tyranny exercised by our hectoring commanders) the Dutch, who fit all their ships in their yards, not entering any men into sea service but by beat of drum after the ships are entirely fitted, they for the whole year's service are not at more charge for wages one capital ship with another than for six months, while half the wages of the whole with us is spent in the spaces from our beginning to enter [the men into service] to the ship's being full manned and its being full manned to the time of her being paid off, the seamen in both giving little if any attendance to work.

Besides, whereas from the hopes of plunder seamen are found much more inclining to serve in the lesser ships[2] and therefore endeavour when they must serve so far to get into such ships as to leave the greater ships incapable of being manned in any reasonable time by other means than by forcing them out of a lesser, to the great discouragement of the men, the Dutch avoid

---

[1] 25 (not 24) ships were paid off in September 1660 and shortly afterwards (*LJ*, xi. 171; *Diary*, i. 245 & n. 1); the main body of the fleet was not paid off until the spring of 1661, by which time additional funds had been provided and the ships had come into port.

[2] Because the plunder was shared.

all that trouble, disorder and loss of time by giving some advance of pay to the capital ships by which they are said to be as easily manned as the rest.

Men too, being as they are with us, removed from one ship where they have long served to another without the receiving their pay to that ship, or liberty of refreshing themselves on shore between the voyages, the service is rendered burdensome to seamen. Which liberty of refreshment on shore of how much value it is reckoned by the seamen, may be guessed from their known practice in the times of best payment, that they could never be kept from going on shore as soon as come into port although they were sure to be paid next day.

One thing Mr Gibson tells me by the way touching the indifference seamen are generally come to in all that relates to religion, that when Capt. Heling in the *Mary* (now newly dead) was driven at Port Mahon to make his men do some work necessary on a Sunday and would have invited them thereto by saying that after they had done it, they should go to prayers and then be at liberty all the rest of the day, they answered one and all that if they must go to prayers they had as lief work. Whereupon in punishment Capt. Heling made them work the whole day.

An instance of the different reports after an engagement of the state of the ship, viz. between that of the commanders and that of the officers of the yard.

Harwich, May 29. (72). Capt. Ernle to his father:[1]

I have never a mast nor yard, but a mizen mast and foretopmast that will never be fit for use. Our mainmast, maintopmast and all the rigging belonging to it being shot overboard. Our sails all shot to pieces.

Capt. Taylor in his letter to the Board of the 29th of May 1672 giving advice of the *Dover* and *Success*'s coming in thither from the fleet out of the engagement has these words:

The *Dover* lost twenty men and thirty wounded. The *Success*

---

[1]John Ernle was captain of the *Dover* and his father, Sir John, was a Navy Commissioner. The engagement was the Battle of Sole Bay, the first of the Third Dutch War.

though she lay for long (as they say) by De Ruyter's side, yet lost but one man and six wounded. They lack betwixt them a maintopmast and a foremast and boats. Had I stores here they should be refitted in a day or two.[1]

An observation about chips and the charge of gathering them.

Extract out of Col. Middleton's letter to the Board the 16th of July 72:

We are now raking up all our chips which hath been taken from our masts to burn our plank and to heat our water to wet the plank when burning it. [I] presume it may save the King 40s. and cost him 50 in labour to get them together, yet they are forced to do for want of burning – and a good shift too, otherways the carpenters may stand still for want of burning but we shall have brush faggots come in shortly the store bought, but if it were not for them chips at present I know not what we should do. Here is about 700 old iron hoops which were on board the *Vivenhoe Pincke*. I ordered them up I know not whose they are but are served in the King's stores. I believe they do belong to the *Prince* and to the Company, etc.

A trial concerning carpenters' apprentices in the yard deserving their wages better than their masters, doing the same work and as well, while their wages are less.

An extract out of Col. Middleton's letter the 19 July 72:

I am now to tell you a pleasant story – Mr Pett your builder hath done the King an excellent piece of service, and in good earnest I have thanked him for it.

Finding that Sir Thomas Allen was troubled that so many apprentices were in the yard, to show the apprentices could deserve their wages as well as their masters, he put all the prentices together, half of the one side of the *Lyon* and the other half of the one side of the *Henrietta*, and their masters on the other sides of both ships. Their work was equal. The

---

[1]PRO, SP 29/325, no. 114, p. 250 (summary in *CSPD 1672*, p. 98). The spelling is slightly altered in Pepys's text.

poor apprentices, to show that they would deserve their wages, I confess did work like Tartars, did accordingly to my observation do their work full as well as their masters did, and kept somewhat before them. The masters, I presume and do verily believe, did work as hard as they were able, but I believe did wish their servants hanged, for I assure you, you would have admired[1] to see the work go on so fast. I confess I have sat down and laughed heartily to myself, but not let any man know the reason. I am afraid some of the old men will be crippled, for I assure you they did not use to work so hard. I would sometimes commend the young men and tell them they did well, and I did not believe before that they had been so good workmen. Some of them, as I have been informed, have said they were resolved to work their masters to death if they could, but this believe, that so much work hath not been done in Chatham yard this seven years in so short a time with such a number of men as hath been done within this month. I confess it's to my admiration considering what hath been done formerly.

Which is all at present from your very humble servant,
Thomas Middleton

The Board's answer the 20th to that paragraph in his letter:

We must acknowledge ourselves not at all less pleased than you seem to be with Mr Pett's strategem to try what work the apprentices of the yard could do, nor are less satisfied with the issues thereof, in that we see not only that they are not so little serviceable in the yard as we have been apt to think, but that both they and their masters are capable of doing more or less than they do as they are more or less looked after. Pray let Mr Pett know what we have writ. So we remain.

July 72. Many most obvious instances are now and before me of this ill effect of our practice in hiring victual [ships], water ships, tenders, etc., at so much per ton per mensem for freight and the wear and tear, the King finding and paying men and victuals, *viz.* that men in time of war and under the discouragements they now serve, which are such as that at this day several instances have by discourse been given to the Board by the

---

[1] Wondered.

commanders of ships now manning out to the fleet, and lying some of them in Long Reach, others in the Hope and others at the Nore, of men's leaping overboard to avoid the King's service, and many drowned in so doing; as also at a time when merchantmen give 45*s.* per month while the King gives but 24*s.*; are so hard to be got and yet harder to be kept. We being forced (*vide* letter to Sir John Robinson[1] of the 30th inst., desiring him to help us to a file of musketeers to guard the pressed men on board each of the victuallers now going to the fleet) to use violent means of keeping them after we have got them, the masters of the vessels, whose interest it is to keep out of the way of wear and tear,[2] are under no provocation nor temptation either to hasten their being manned or keep their men when they have them. By which means victuals lie long by their shipside for want of hands to take it in. We are forced to offer extraordinary wages to men by the day to take in the provisions while the ship is in manning and yet cannot be served, for fear of their being carried (when on board) to sea. And as the last remedy are forced to employ riggers and labourers from the yard to do this work, thereby neglecting the business of the yard and in themselves neither qualified nor willing nor by their distance able to do half a day's work that men in merchants' service are used to do, where also they are well paid. By which means demurrage is contracted on the victuallers' vessels or lighters, freight runs on and some wages unusefully on our hired vessels, convoy perhaps either stays or is lost, the work of this Office perplexed, the fleet in want, the service thereby disappointed and many more inconveniences contracted not here to be reckoned up; the masters of the vessels being all this while gratified hereby their freight running on, and no wear and tear incurred or hazarded. As a remedy to which, unless better can be found, it seems at present most reasonable that, whatever almost the increase of the freight be, the masters be obliged to victual and man, to be subject to the musterings of our clerks of the cheque and muster-masters, with defalcations from their freight and other satisfaction for what time and service shall be lost from their want of their full complement of men.

---

[1] Lieutenant of the Tower.
[2] Sc. the cost of maintaining their vessel was increased if they ventured into open water. See Glossary: 'wear and tear'.

Col. Middleton to this day notwithstanding the many articles wherein he as Surveyor has for so many years known himself concerned, owns by his letter of the 26th of July 72 not to have, and therefore much more not to be conversant with, the Lord High Admiral's Instructions to Commanders, he now pressing for the copy of them which the Board of their own accord (out of their doubtfulness of his minding or knowing them, occasioned by his giving leave to Capt. Le Neve of the *Plymoath* upon the coming in of his ship to Chatham to come to London,[1] giving opportunity thereby to the whole ship's company to leave their ship and the work thereof) had said in their letter of the 25th they would send him.

The trial of Mr Bowyer's weights.

(An instance given me by Mr Tippet of the lightness of the weights found in the several yards in his present survey, 26 July 72. *Vide* a useful letter of the Board's wrote thereupon to Comr Tippets 26 ditto).[2]

Iron
- a 7lb. weight is 6¾oz. too light
- a 14lb. weight is 4oz. too light
- a ½cwt 1lb. 12oz. too light
- a ½cwt 1lb. 4oz. ⎫
- a ½cwt 0lb. 15oz. ⎬ too light
- a ½cwt 0lb. 8oz. ⎭
- a ½cwt 1lb. 2oz.
- a leaden cwt 1lb. too light

Belonging to the stores
10 lead ½cwts – exactly true
1 iron ½cwt wanting his lead cap 3lb. 3oz. too light
4 iron ½cwts exactly true
1 lead ½cwt 17oz. too light
1 iron ½cwt 4oz. too light
1 iron ½cwt 3oz. too light
1 iron ½cwt 2oz. too light

---

[1]The most recent Instructions to Commanders (28 Mar. 1672) required that a flagship should always be in that part of the fleet which lay about Sheernesss to protect ships in the Medway: PRO, ADM 2/1, f. 70*r*.

[2]*CSPD 1672*, p. 280; cf. also ibid., p. 298. Tippetts had just succeeded Middleton as Surveyor in June.

1 iron ½cwt 5 ⎫
1 iron ½cwt 15 oz. ⎬ too light
1 lead ½cwt 2oz. too light
1 iron ½cwt 1lb. 8oz. too light (the cap wanting)
1 cwt iron 2lb. 8oz. too light (the cap wanting)
7 iron cwts true
                                    Novembr 12. 1672.

This ill usage of masters, and their work taken out of their hands by commanders grows thick upon us, and may prove fatal, more ships (and those great ones) having been brought aground within this twelvemonth than can be remembered within twice twelve years before; and once this summer the whole fleet were mistaken, as coming (as they thought) up the Swin[1] and make the North Foreland before they knew where they were.

Capt. Beach this summer discharged Eglestone, his master, and under his hand to the Board charged him with an utter ignorance of knowing how to navigate a ship, while under a most solemn examination of him at Trinity House he is reported to be from thence a second time as a seaman of extraordinary abilities beyond the generality, and not only has an extraordinary report given him to myself by Capt. Bowen, under whom he had formerly served, but does at this day well discharge the office of master in the *Happy Returne. Vide* page [266].

14th November 1672. Sir Tho. Allin and Sir Jeremy Smith having lately for some weeks together been at Chatham to pay off the great ships come in to be laid up for this winter, the payment whereof for want of money to do it generously and to the satisfaction of the seamen was limited by many rules given us on purpose by the King and his Cabinet Council signed by Sir Joseph Williamson; they do publicly tell us both at the Board and before his Royal Highness, seconded by Sir Thos Osborne, that such is become the aversion among seamen, that those who cannot scape from it by running away (which they all labour to do, to the avowed forfeiture of their wages), do industriously deny themselves to be able seamen, and pretend themselves landmen (though known by the officers of the ships to be able, and so by them rated in the ships' books) to the end they may not be

---

[1]The East and West Swins were channels running NE from the Nore.

turned over, as all the able men by order are to be, into other ships. On which consideration, it is not only to be observed, that the ability of a poor seaman is hereby rendered matter of grievance to him, but that these gentlemen by their own confession (or rather indeed with some boasting of their good service therein) do declare that they have taken the poor seamen at their words, and made them ordinary, and yet turned them over into other ships.

Novembr 12th 1672. Vide page [265] about the ill usage of masters.

This day information is put into the Board by one Danll Andrews late master of the *Plymo.* under Capt. Le Neve, setting forth under his hand his captain's turning him out of his cabin and taking his charge out of his hand, with such abuses as that he was driven to apply himself to Capt. Narborough (commanding the *Prince* under his Royal Highness) for leave to be discharged;[1] and to show that it was not out of any dissatisfaction to the service, he immediately attended the Board by petition for another employment, and was so well esteemed of as a master, that Capt. Haddock himself being present at this his application desired that he might be appointed to him for his master now going out in the *Lyon*, and was so.

A more pregnant instance cannot be given of the loss the King sustains by the wants of money than the time which so many ships, and great ones too, lay in pay in the River of Thames and in the Downs (to lessen the scandal and clamour of it) in the year 1671, for no other reason but want of money to pay them off, some of them lying in that condition (I very well remember) a longer time in victuals, wages, wear and tear than the time they had been abroad doing his Majesty service from their going forth to sea.

12 March 7^1/$_2$. Worthy noting that this day Mr Harrison a merchant, in contracting with the Board for hemp and therein insisting immovably upon having his money advanced for his

[1]His petition is summarized in much the same terms in *CSPD 1672–3*, p. 157. He produced a certificate of competence from Trinity House dated 19 October: ibid., p. 627.

security into a third hand, he propounded Mr Lindsey the goldsmith, against whom the Board objected as being a banker and thereby at this time made unfit (by the late postponing of payments)[1] to have moneys of his Majesty's unnecessarily put into his hands.[2] We thereupon propounded Mr Thompson, a setter-up of a new bank – unconcerned with the King.[3] Whom Harrison, without reason shown, declining, the Board propounded Sir Tho. Osborne their Treasurer. Which he in like manner refusing, he propounds Col. Middleton, and insisting upon this manner of security, or no hemp to be expected from him, the Board was driven to yield to him herein, and accordingly the contract made to run so. *Vide* the contract itself.

Decembr 72. Capt. Berry, commander of the *Resolution*, came to the Board desiring an order to search the East India ships now going forth, for some of his men that were newly run away from him. Upon which, being asked upon what certainty he demanded it, he answered that he was sure of three, and had from thence and otherwise reason to believe, that many more of his men that are run away were entertained upon the East India ships. Upon which being again asked whether they were new men or some that had been any time with him, in regard of the King's saving thereby the wages due to them, he answered that two of them had eight months and that the third would at the end of this have belonged to him eleven months. Which led the Board to a sad contemplation of the general aversion the common seaman is come to the King's service.

---

[1] The Stop of the Exchequer: q.v. above, p. 258 & n. 1.
[2] John Lindsay did in fact go bankrupt but not until 1679: R. D. Richards, *Early Hist. Banking in Engl.* (1929), p. 25.
[3] This was possibly Robert Thompson whose loan to the government of £351 had been repaid in August 1670: *CTB 1669–72*, p. 655.

II THE BROOKE HOUSE PAPERS

(i) PEPYS'S DEFENCE OF THE CONDUCT OF THE NAVY

Letter from the Brooke House Commissioners to the Navy Board, 29 Sept. 1669[1]

My Lords and Gentlemen,
Upon consideration of the Instructions given you in charge, and some things that have occurred to our observation about your proceedings in the management of his Majesty's naval affairs entrusted to you during the late war, we have collected several heads, contained in the enclosed paper,[2] which we have thought fit to communicate to you, to the intent we may receive your answer thereupon; which, in respect of the near approach of the Parliament's sitting,[3] we desire you to return to us with all the speed that may be. And so we rest,
    Your Lordships' etc. humble servants,
    Halifax. William Brereton. George Thomson.
    Jo. Gregorie. Giles Dunster.

Pepys's General Defence of the Navy Board: his letter to the Brooke House Commissioners, 27 Nov. 1669[4]

My Lords and Gentlemen,
The trouble your Lordships will receive from this paper is

---

[1]PL 2554, p. 2 (copy); HLRO, Main Papers 26 Oct. 1669, 213 C, f. 4r (original); HMC, *8th Report*, App., pt i. 131 (copy).
[2]That is, their report, 29 Sept. 1669, in HLRO, loc. cit., ff. 2r–6v; summary in HMC, loc. cit., 128–9.
[3]The 8th session of the Cavalier Parliament was opened on 19 October.
[4]PL 2554, pp. 113–59 (original, in Hayter's hand, recovered by Pepys at cessation of the Commission: ibid., p. 111); ibid., pp. 11–97 (copy in Gibson's hand); PL 2874, pp. 509–81; Bodl. Lib., Rawl. MSS A 457.

grounded upon what (since my return into England)[1] I find to have in my absence passed between your Lordships and the Officers of the Navy touching certain Observations by you made upon some proceedings of theirs in reference to the late war and the management thereof. A copy of which Observations you were pleased to transmit to them by letter of the 29th of September last, and thereto received answer by like letter from the Lord Brouncker and Sir John Mennes dated the 11th of October,[2] wherein (submitting themselves to your further directions) they acquaint you that of eleven persons therein enumerated (who serving his Majesty as Principal Officers or Commissioners of the Navy within the said war, seem equally concerned in your satisfaction) three only continue in present relation to this Office, of which themselves being two were then only in town, the third (naming me) being absent – who, as Clerk of the Acts and (to use their own phrase) as a person constant at the Board, was best able to give an account of the actions of the Board in general.

Which matter having considered, together with your expectations of a speedy answer, whilst at the same time I find it as uneasy to procure from the whole number, as these judge it unfit for so small a part as are remaining to take upon them the delivering the sense of more than themselves in defence of matters acted so long since, in the hurry of a war, and under such difficulties as may well render the recovery of circumstances very uneasy; especially when to be done by those who, though present, might not yet be consenting to all that may now fall under question – I have made it my care to consider by what expedient your Lordships might (without delay) receive a competent view of the satisfaction to be expected from the Officers of the Navy, without prejudice to what answers more perfect you may hereafter see cause to demand from or be offered by the said Officers in reference to any part of their common or distinct duties concerned herein. And in order hereto reflecting upon myself and what the abovesaid report touching my particular capacity of giving an account of the general actions of the Board might lead your Lordships to look for from me, I have employed what liberty his Majesty's other services (with a sorrowful interruption

---

[1] On 20 October: below, p. 334.
[2] HMC, loc. cit., i. 131 (where the date is given as 12 October).

otherwise happening) by the sickness and death of my wife[1] have spared me since my return in putting together what I could in so little time recollect touching the duty, debates and acts of this Board in relation to the failures charged on them in your said Observations, not neglecting therein the faithfullest helps I could obtain either from memory, papers or books, those only of our contracts excepted, remaining in your Lordships' hands, the free perusal whereof had your Lordships thought fit to grant, might probably have administered matter for answer to such particulars as may otherwise happen not to occur.

Which recollections having summarily digested into answers suitable to your own method, and holding myself prepared to justify them by all fair evidences of truth, I here humbly lay them before your Lordships.

Observation 1st[2]

We do observe that some naval provisions contracted for (which appear to us to have been most necessary for the service and preservation of his Majesty's fleet) have not been delivered in by the contractors according to their contracts, and that such as were less useful (if not altogether unfit and unserviceable) have been received into his Majesty's stores, and yet no remedy appears to us to have been taken or sought for against the said contractors, but on the contrary great sums of money have been imprested to them and continued upon imprest, and bills made out to them on which the imprests have not been discounted.

Contract with Sir Wm Warren for Gottenburgh masts July 21. 1664 not delivered according to contract, in point of time and dimensions.[3] And contract with the said Sir Wm Warren and Capt. Taylor for New England masts 16 Augst 1664 not delivered as aforementioned.[4]

---

[1]She died on 10 November.
[2]Pepys gives his own summaries of the 18 Observations. (Here the order of his sentences is occasionally altered in the interest of clarity.) The Observations are to be found in HLRO, Main Papers 26 Oct. 1669, 213 C, f. 9r-v.
[3]See above, pp. 79–81.
[4]See above, p. 115.

Answer

1. As to breach of contracts in point of time: the Officers of the Navy will upon examination be found fully discharging their duties, not only in the timely providing good rules for the securing his Majesty against all prejudices in this particular, but in their endeavours of seeing the same duly executed, by rejection of the goods or otherwise, as often as (the matter of fact appearing to them) they have found the same of advantage to his Majesty. Which case can rarely be thought to have happened during the war, when besides the constant urgency of his Majesty's services, dearth of stores and continued rise of price rendering impracticable the rejection of goods, their own great failures in point of payment did for the most part leave them little remedy against the contractor for lapse of time.

2. For what concerns their receiving of goods less useful, unfit, unserviceable, or not answering contract in dimensions: the Lord High Admiral, well knowing the incapacity of the Officers of the Navy collectively considered are in of controlling the delivery of stores into the yards, while the gross of their duties calls indispensably for their attendance here, has by his Instructions placed the security of his Majesty in this particular upon especial hands, *viz.* the Surveyor of the Navy, together with the storekeepers, clerks of the cheque, masters attendant and shipwrights of the several yards; not only prohibiting the receipt of goods unfit, but requiring (as the guide for this Board in their signing bills to the merchant for what shall be received) that the said Officers do certify to them all manner of defects and unsuitableness to contract. To which as this Office, out of their endeavour of improving what is here provided, have long since by their own order added the clerk of the survey in conjunction with the rest in certifying the quality of goods received; so did his Majesty make a yet greater provision for himself by establishing a Commissioner Extraordinary in the out-yards of Harwich and Portsmouth[1] (as Comr Pett was before at Chatham) during the greatness of our late action, for directing and supervising all under-officers, as in other things, so in their due complying with the Instructions of his Highness and this Office in the particular now before us.

---

[1] John Taylor and Thomas Middleton respectively. They began work in November 1664 and were empowered to act independently of the Board if necessary.

Which being premised, the Officers of the Navy may (to my best recollection) challenge the whole world to allege one instance of prejudice sustained by his Majesty from their ordering either the receipt of or payment for the least parcel of goods unuseful, unfit or unserviceable, where any advice or caution from the Surveyor or any of the said Commissioners or under-officers hath appeared to them of their being so.

3. As to the former of those contracts which you are pleased to pitch upon in proof of your present Observation, I shall only beg leave to acquaint you that upon a like exception of non-performance started in the year 1665 by some persons whom this contract had disappointed in the market they hoped to have made upon the King (as will be further seen in the answer to the 16 Observation)[1] this matter was then by especial appointment of his Grace the Duke of Albemarle (acting as Admiral in the absence of his Royal Highness) solemnly inquired into, and Sir Wm Batten himself concurring (who for some reasons had been prevailed with to promote the complaint), received this resolution from a full Board now extant under all their hands, *viz.*:

Memorandum:
That in pursuance of his Grace the Duke of Albemarle's direction for our inquiry into Sir Wm Warren's proceedings in pursuance of his contract made with this Board for Swedes masts, we have accordingly proceeded in examining the letter of the said contract and Sir Wm Warren's proceedings on and performance of the same, and do find that he is not chargeable with any failure on his part in relation to the said contract.
   Brouncker. J. Mennes. Wm Batten. P. Pett. S. Pepys.[2]

4. For the other of the 16 of August (64) for New England masts: if (as I doubt not) miscarriage at sea may be admitted in plea for non-performance of a contract wherein danger of the seas is expressly excepted, and if attendance[3] for convoy may be the like for lapse of time, where the contractor is not (nor in this case ought on his Majesty's behalf to have been) left at liberty to proceed without it, the imperfect execution of this contract will not be found inexcusable to the merchants, and much less to the Officers of the Navy, in their reception of the goods at a

[1] Below, pp. 307–15.
[2] Dated 13 Jan. 1666: PRO, ADM 106/3520, f. 27*v*.
[3] Delay.

season which, though later than was wished, was yet very happy for the supply of the King's stores then in want thereof.

5. That much money hath been issued by the Officers of the Navy by way of imprest will neither be denied by them, nor (I believe) be much wondered at by any that shall consider them as persons lying evermore under such an incapacity of making good their undertakings to merchants in point of payment as left them destitute of any other means of obtaining credit from those they had failed upon their old contracts than by advancing them money upon credit of the new. An expedient which, moreover, will be found not to have wanted the further justification of lowering the rates, or at least preventing that rise thereof by which merchants would in an over-proportion have provided themselves an amends for the uncertainty of their payment. And yet, in prospect that this answer on behalf of the said Officers may possibly become as public as their charge which they meet with in every hand, and for the satisfaction therefore of such (as such there are) who do unwillingly allow of any argument (no, not necessity itself) that is not backed by the practice of those that preceded them in the time of usurpation, give me leave to assert that, respect being had to the difference between the condition of the present Officers and theirs, to whom it was more rare to fail their day of payment than to these to keep it, their use of imprests was less confined than this now in question, and their regularity not superior in seeing them cleared, as may appear from the declaration of their Treasurer's last account in the year 1660 in which above 250,000*l.* were at that time depending in the Exchequer in imprests uncleared,[1] and of them considerable sums relating not only to the Dutch war seven years before, but others in arrear for no less than ten years before that, and of each sort no small part resting unsatisfied at this day.

6. Which last nevertheless I mention not with intention of anticipating what better answer you may receive from the Comptroller of the Navy, who, standing singly chargeable with the care of seeing right done to his Majesty in the due defalcation of imprests and regular charging thereof on the Treasurer, it will not be needful to interest the name of the Board in this particular otherwise than by observing that as (for securing his Majesty against the insolvency of persons to whom they have granted imprests) they have generally taken care not to exceed the debt

---

[1] The Treasurer was Richard Hutchinson.

then actually owing them from his Majesty, so have they in particular behaved themselves from time to time in reference to Sir Wm Warren, by whom there at this day lie deposited in the hands of the Lord Brouncker (as his Lordship informs me) perfect bills to such a sum as secures the King (within 4220*l*.) against the utmost value of all the imprests he stands debtor to, besides pretences depending in the Office to many thousand pounds unadjusted, out of which his Majesty may have it also in his own hands, both to satisfy himself that sum, and discharge what may appear due upon the mutual account between himself and Sir Wm Warren relating to interest.

Observation 2d

That great store of shipping have been by them hired and paid for out of his Majesty's treasure to fetch goods for contractors, whereas goods bought into his Majesty's stores ought to have been delivered without charge to his Majesty in time of peace, and in case of war the King ought to have paid but a small part of the seamen's wages, and in some cases demurrage, and that for provisions contracted for only and no others, as by the said contracts appears.

10,000 tons of shipping and upwards have been paid for, for the fetching of masts and other goods.

Answer

1. Not to dispute the calculation of these 10,000 tons of shipping (wherein nevertheless I am apprehensive of some mis-reckoning), nor yet to take upon me the delivering what cannot avowedly be had from any other hand than that of the Comptroller in reference to the determining the charge at which these or any other provisions have been served into his Majesty's stores, I shall out of my particular desire of contributing all that occurs to me towards your Lordships' present satisfaction humbly observe that the article before us seems wholly raised from the not distinguishing between the masts served in upon the contract quoted by

your Lordships and others delivered upon a subsequent treaty with the said merchants by particular direction of his Majesty and Royal Highness.[1]

2. The latter of which being to be brought in the heat of the war, it was upon reasons then prevailing (and now, if called for, ready to be exposed) judged not only advantageous but necessary for his Majesty to have it done by ships and men in his own pay.

3. But of the former, not one stick (as far as I ever understood) was brought in any ship hired by this Board, or came to his Majesty at other charge, either by increase of freight or wages, than the simple price contracted for in time of peace.

Observation 3d

That the books of the Treasurer of the Navy have been by them signed though the true times of his paying bills therein contained have not been expressed, whereby the accounts are rendered untrue in fact, and we disabled from finding out the preference of one before another in payment.

This appears through the Treasurer's whole account and likewise several great sums have been charged as paid in the preceding year which have not been passed by their Board till the following.

Answer

As it was never enjoined, so neither has the practice of any age shown it to have been esteemed the work of the Officers of the Navy in passing the accounts of the Treasurer to take cognizance of the dates of his payments as any part (much less so essential a one as your Lordships seem to make it to the truth) of the said accounts.

Nor can that silence either in practice of the Lord High Admiral's Instructions be judged to arise from any overlooking of the inconvenience here imputed to the non-observation of this circumstance, since as the contrary would impose upon the

---

[1] This referred particularly to purchases made by Warren in Hamburg by commission and not covered by contract: see below, pp. 392–3.

Officers of the Navy the signing to the truth of what they are in no wise privy to, and therefore unable to control; so will it be found wholly unnecessary in a constitution like that upon which the Admiral's Instructions were founded, where (as it seems to have anciently been) the Treasurer of the Navy being satisfied his assignments seasonably and in specie, was, by his ability to pay all, not subject either to the guilt or censure of making preferences. But since (by what misfortune I shall not inquire) it has so fallen out that the affairs of the Navy have met in the late war with payments very ill suited either to the greatness or seasons of its expense, the Lord High Admiral taking into his care the considering how the imperfect supplies of monies we received might be best improved in the method of its payment and particularly in reference to this point of preference, he was pleased by especial Instructions in December 1665 (among other things) to direct that an account of the several payments of the Treasurer should be weekly transmitted to this Office.[1] Which being accordingly done by lodging the same with the Comptroller, you may from that time receive from Sir John Mennes for before and the Lord Brouncker for since Janry 1666[7] what satisfaction your Lordships shall think fit to demand in relation thereto.

Several cases may be assigned (as I conceive) wherein a payment made in a letter may even for regularity's sake be brought into the account of a year preceding, especially according to that method by which the Lord High Admiral's Instructions seem to have designed the marshalling the Treasurer's accounts more by the distinction of services and estimates relating thereto than the preciseness of time wherein any part of that service was either done or paid for. But the Lord High Admiral having been pleased to place the care of right disposing the Treasurer's payments in the passing his accounts not upon the Board in general but the Comptroller singly, as may be found in the 5th and 6th articles of his Instructions in these words:

5. To be first not only by priority of place but of duty that shall sign the Treasurer's accounts and cancel all bills and books digested into his Ledger Book, the better to enable him upon sight of all books and bills to control all wilful neglects and oversights in the Treasurer himself or his fellow Officers in all payments made proper to those accounts.

[1] See below, p. 369.

6. To state upon all bills and debentures to be passed by himself or his fellow Officers the titles or heads upon which those bills are proper according to the estimate of the service for which these provisions were supplied, as to govern the Treasurer in disposing them to their proper place or service so as to enable himself to keep his control or compter book of the Treasurer's account exact and even in the expense and issues of each store.[1]

I shall not by interposing in this particular prevent the fuller satisfaction your Lordships may expect from the proper Officer.

Observation 4th

That although imprests have been ordered to be abated upon several bills, yet the said Principal Officers and Commissioners have signed the Treasurer's books allowing the full bills (and that in some cases when the imprests upon the bills have been stayed and not recharged by the said Treasurer) whereby allowance is made to the said Treasurer both of the imprest and full bill, and his Majesty thereby in danger of losing the money imprested if the party that received it should prove insolvent, and though it should be afterwards repaid yet his Majesty doth in the meantime lose the use of the money.

There are sundry imprests stayed and not charged, and 150,000l. and upwards paid in imprests, a great part whereof ought to have been stayed.

Answer

Included in my answer to the close of the 1st Observation.

---

[1] *Oeconomy*, pp. 53–4.

Observation 5th

That they have signed the books of the said Treasurer though there were comprised therein sums for which no bills or books had been formerly by them signed, and so no voucher or warrant was extant for their signing the same.

As appears by all the Exchequer fees and divers books for yards being brought to account without any Commissioner's hand to the same.

Answer

The fact is owned as a procedure not only consonant to ancient practice but in itself (with submission) not chargeable with any injury implied therein to his Majesty by how much[1] the warranting a payment to the Treasurer, whether by signing a bill or book to be afterwards, upon cancelling, transferred into the ledger, or by signing to the ledger immediately, renders not his Majesty's security greater or less, provided the same be done with equal satisfaction first taken by the Officers of the Navy in the warrantableness of the payment.

Which as I doubt not but your Lordships will find to have been the case in reference to the books here mentioned, by their having passed all the previous examinations requisite for the rendering them allowable, so I presume the certainty of the Exchequer fees known to the Auditors and capable of no other variation than what attends the diversity of the sums received required no other voucher than what appeared to the Comptroller and the rest of the Officers at their allowing them on the ledger.

Observation 6th

That they have issued bills for very great sums of money and passed the same on the said Treasurer's ledgers, wherein no men-

---
[1] In that.

tion is made of the services or species and quantities of goods for which such bills were signed, nor of his Majesty's yards or storehouses into which such goods were delivered.

As in bills made out to Mr Lanyon and others.

Answer

Your Lordships having by your letter of the 2d inst.[1] thought fit to declare the instances specified in your first paper to be all you judged necessary to be given this Office in confirmation of the particular you are therein pleased to charge it with, my answer is by your Lordships necessarily confined to the mentioned case of Mr Lanyon, agent for his Majesty (during the late war) in attending the occasions of his Navy at Plymouth. Upon which I have humbly to say that your Lordships will not (I assure myself) upon examination find the bills of this merchant in the manner they issued from this Office (however their entries in the Treasurer's ledgers may represent them) to fail in expressing both the place and service where and on which the goods therein paid for were employed, with reference to the particulars thereof resting in this Office or the hands of the Surveyor, in order to the charging therewith the proper officers of the King's ships accountable for the same.

Observation 7th

That the care and oversight of all inferior officers of his Majesty's Navy being part of their charge, the said Principal Officers and Commissioners have neglected to examine the proceedings of the said inferior officers in management of the King's affairs committed to their trusts or to cause their miscarriages to be amended, whereby his Majesty hath been and further may be greatly damaged and his naval affairs much disordered; and particularly, the storekeepers having kept no order of time in their entries of provisions received, and many times have received in provisions of great

[1] HLRO, Main Papers 26 Oct. 1669, 213 C, ff. 85–8.

value, in some cases where no contract was made, in other cases where copies of contracts made have not been transmitted to them, and that done by warrant of the said Principal Officers and Commissioners, whereby such storekeepers have been disabled from certifying whether the provisions so received have answered the contracts for goodness, usefulness and time of delivery, and thereby the said Principal Officers and Commissioners were at liberty to give what prices they pleased and pass by defects as themselves should think fit, to the prejudice of his Majesty's affairs.

Answer

Would your Lordships' leisure have permitted your receiving from the Officers of the Navy either *viva voce* or otherwise the answers they should have been ready to have given your Lordships upon any instances lying before you (if such there be) wherein they may seem to have passed by the neglect or miscarriage of any inferior officer coming to their knowledge, I doubt not but your Lordships would have been so far satisfied of the pains and time spent by this Board in the detecting and examining the negligences and misdemeanours of all persons both officers and others, with their appeals thereon to the Lord High Admiral, and the manifold instances to be shown of their proceedings against the convicted, by imprisonments, defalcations and sometimes loss of wages, by suspension from and frequently the final forfeitures of their offices,[1] and lastly prosecutions at law where other ways of righting his Majesty lay not open to them, and all this under the burden of a war doubled by the difficulties extraordinary with which they were to undergo it – I doubt not (I say) but your Lordships would have been so far satisfied therein as sooner to have judged it matter of wonder that they could spare so much than censure that they spent no more of their time in the works of this sort.

It is true if, by the neglect complained of, your Lordships' intentions be their not visiting the out-yards and the officers therein with that frequency which might be looked for and which at other times they have done, it is confessed. But so as not to

---

[1] As in the case of John Browne, storekeeper at Harwich (see below, p. 385 & n. 1).

leave any tincture of neglect upon the Board, the fullness of whose employment during the war on the other indispensable occasions of his Majesty's service was so far foreseen by his Majesty and the Lord High Admiral as to acquit them of this duty by establishing a special Commissioner in each of the out-yards,[1] as Commissioner Pett had been before at Chatham, without other charge upon them than the good government of his officers and conduct of his affairs within their respective provinces.

For what concerns the storekeepers not observing any order of time in their entries of provisions received, give me leave to observe that the Officers of the Navy being (as is already said) incapable as a body to be present at the delivery of all stores, a particular officer is appointed by his Majesty and the Lord High Admiral by the title of clerk of the cheque for the keeping a book of control of all the storekeeper's receipts, whose firm[2] with the storekeeper is made the voucher to this Board of the truth of those receipts. And that this Board is not unmindful of obliging them to the keeping an account of the time as well as other circumstances relating to these receipts. I appeal to your Lordships' examinations whether you have found any bill accepted by this Board from the storekeepers for goods delivered into the King's stores wherein not only they but the clerk of the cheque have not taken care to express either the time of delivery or any other circumstance that might render them as satisfactory as any method of bills of like kind your Lordships have met with, either of late times or those more ancient.

That goods have been provided and their delivery into stores warranted by the Officers of the Navy without the formality of a contract solemnly made at the Board is owned as a proceeding not only agreeable to ancient practice and the present Instructions of the Lord High Admiral[3] providing rules for the better government of themselves and under-officers in relation thereto, but in many cases advantageous and very often indispensable, especially in this, where the Plague in the beginning of the war driving away the sellers and the Fire at the end of it multiplying the buyers, together with the want of credit through the whole, necessitated these gentlemen to hunt for that abroad which in the former war

---

[1] See above, p. 274 & n. 1.
[2] Confirmation.
[3] *Oeconomy*, p. 38.

from the currentness of their payments those before them were courted to take at home.

And yet since the practice of that time is by many so much made the standard of good management, I shall (for the satisfaction of others more than any real advantage I pretend to raise from it to the cause in hand) add, and am prepared to make it appear, that the contracts extant in the books of that time do not in any wise outgo in the circumspectness of their drafts those of this Office now lying before your Lordships, but are vouched with much less authority, as being rarely signed by more than two, but more frequently by a single hand or none at all – whereas these here instanced in of Sir Wm Warren's want not the attestation both of the advice and assent of each Principal Officer and Commissioner (to no less than seven) then serving at this Board. No, my Lords, you will easily be convinced that the use of contracts was generally in less practice, and instead thereof particular commissions and purveyances employed in another-gates proportion than under all the inducements and straits above-mentioned, it will be found to have been done by the Officers at this day charged therewith.

Nay, let it yet be added (in opposition to whatever can be but suspected touching the present Officers of the Navy) that the managers of the naval affairs in that time were so little exempted from the imputation of trading for naval provisions as from the current belief of the truth thereof (justified enough from their own books) to give occasion to his Royal Highness in his re-establishing the ancient Instructions of the Earl of Northumberland to add (among others) that new one of his own extant in the book now before your Lordships, beginning thus:

> It being supposed that of late times persons employed in the affairs of the Navy and many inferior officers of the Navy traded for such commodities as were used in the Navy, they are from the ill consequences of it to take care that neither themselves nor any inferior officers in the Navy trade in any such commodity, etc.[1]

If (as is alleged) any warrants have passed the Board for the receipt of goods contracted for without transmitting to the storekeepers a copy of the said contract, give me leave in this case to do my duty to my fellow Officers in discharging them

[1] Ibid., pp. 18–19.

and taking the blame thereof upon myself, whose particular part it was to have prevented that omission, unless where the said warrants shall have been sent from any of the members of this Board without my privity. But as in the many hundreds of contracts made by this Board neither my mind nor memory doth upon best recollection charge me with one instance of this kind, so if the known pressure of business, which for several years hath lain upon my hands, may (as it is easy to admit) have at any time occasioned me such an oversight, I shall nevertheless appeal to your own thoughts whether the inference you are pleased to make upon this subject may not be wholly withdrawn when you shall have considered the 4th article of the storekeeper's Instructions[1] lying before you, wherein the Lord High Admiral, out of a direct prospect of such a case, expressly commands him:

> To receive no provisions contracted for though warranted thereto without a copy of the contract attested by the clerk of the records.

Adding, in plain bar to the whole scope of your Lordships' inference:

> And upon view of the provisions, to compare it and the contract together, taking care that in all points it accord therewith, and wherein it differs from or comes short thereof, not to receive the provisions at all, but certify the defects to the Officers and receive their order what further to do therein.

But since upon the contrary presumption of their having it in their power 'to give what price they please and passing by defects as themselves shall think fit, to the prejudice of his Majesty', your Lordships have thought good not to limit your charge to crime actual, but extend it to what you find only possible (upon which terms not this Board only, but every hand else wherein trust is reposed, may (as such) be reputed criminal) your Lordships will not be offended if, since no instance is given wherein they have made the use which the inference supposes, I tender another in behalf of the Officers of the Navy, namely that the unblameableness of the said Officers, while possessed of an extraordinary, ought to be construed to their advantage in the exercise of the ordinary, trust reposed in them by his Majesty.

---

[1] Ibid., pp. 78–9.

Observation 8th

That they have not taken a yearly account of the receipts and issues of his Majesty's stores, by reason of which it is not to be known what of the said stores have been embezzled or employed to private uses, nor what was wanting to supply future occasions, and what particular species, qualities and quantities of provisions were most necessary to be provided.

No such annual account or survey of his Majesty's stores appears to us, though they have been sent for.

Answer

That storekeepers' accounts have not been balanced at any time, nor general surveys annually taken during the war, is confessed. But so as that the omission thereof (however upon examination it shall appear in reference to the [officers] concerned) will not be imputed to the failure of the Officers of the Navy jointly, who neither by practice nor the reasonable construction of the Lord High Admiral's rules in this matter have or can be thought chargeable with the non-execution thereof. Forasmuch as if the survey now in taking after five months' labour by the Surveyor, and that in a time of peace, be not yet completed, how impracticable would any such attempt be for the whole Board in a time of war when (as it lately was) besides the manifold increase of the King's stores, as well as of the occasions of employing them, the distinct duty of each Principal Officer was such (I may safely affirm it of my own) as during the whole war neither did not could without prejudice to his Majesty have dispensed with my attendance on it so many days, as the taking one such survey and balance would at that time have called for months.

Upon whom then the care of seeing the storekeepers' accounts annually balanced doth properly lodge appears in the 3rd article of the Comptroller's duty, who is therein directed:

To peruse and examine the storekeepers' books at the end of every quarter, and at the end of every year to take a general audit of their accounts of all provisions received and issued and expended upon all works and services proper for that year, distinguishing the warrants both for receipts and issues upon every particular head proper to each particular service, and presenting to his fellow Officers the balance of the general store and particular expense, etc.[1]

Which being so, and that nevertheless this great work of balancing storekeepers' accounts hath hitherto met with no performance, I shall not offer at anything which may more satisfactorily be expected from the proper officer touching the grounds of this failure otherwise than by laying before you such light towards the making a right judgement in this matter as being to be collected from the records and other helps of my office can neither be expected from any other hand, nor the present mention of them be without unfaithfulness omitted by mine, *viz.*:

1st – That the Officers of the Navy have evermore been sensible of the importance of this work and expressed the same not only by their frequent advice to the Comptroller on that behalf and concurrence with him in all things conducing to the attainment thereof, such as their letters and injunctions to the storekeepers, with the procuring from the Lord High Admiral an increase both of salaries and instruments where the same were found necessary, but early endeavour (at least some of them) to compass what has been effected since January 1666[7], namely the lightening the Comptroller of some other of the weightiest parts of his duty,[2] by which he might be the better enabled (with the additional help for that purpose also allowed him) to go through the remainder, whereof this of balancing storekeepers' accounts is a principal share.

2dly – That the balancing storekeepers' accounts is not the sole security provided for his Majesty by the present constitution of the Navy against the embezzlement of his stores, the Lord High Admiral having committed the safety thereof to other hands besides that of the storekeepers, namely the porter of the yard in the 1st, 2nd, 6th and 7th articles of his duty,[3] and the clerk of the cheque in the 8th of his[4] – and this not only in distinction from but distrust of the security pretended to reside in the store-

---

[1] *Oeconomy*, pp. 51–2.
[2] Brouncker and Penn were then appointed to assist him: see above, p. 176 & n. 1.
[3] *Oeconomy*, pp. 145–6, 148–9.
[4] Ibid., pp. 104–6.

keepers' balancings, as your Lordships will find in the 6th article of the first branch of the storekeeper's Instructions,[1] where that officer being strictly enjoined to a personal execution of his duty unless in case of sickness or other extreme necessity, when and during which only he is permitted to act by deputies of good report for demeanour and trust, and for whom he will be accountable. The ground of this so extraordinary caution is in the preface of the said article expressly declared to be:

> The greatness of that officer's trust, which at some times and in some cases renders it very difficult (if possible) to trace him therein.

And if the Earl of Northumberland found it reasonable to mention the tracing of a storekeeper with an 'if possible' under the inconsiderable action of the Navy thirty years past, how much less wonderful ought to seem the non-performance of that work since?

3dly – Which consideration leads me to what I have next to observe, *viz.*, that there is no memory remaining or record yet come to my view of any balance taken from any one storekeeper from the time of the first framing of these Instructions (whether under the late King or during the time of usurpation) to this very day. But so much the contrary, that when in the year 1656 (and no sooner that I can find) the Commissioners of the Navy then acting attempted the bringing storekeepers to a balance of their receipts and issues, and received from them a joint declaration of their incapacity to obey them therein, it does not appear that the said storekeepers fell under any censure for such their answer, or that anything was insisted on from them or committed to any other hands, by which the balance of one storekeeper's account was obtained during the whole time of that Republic. In which (besides other evidence) I humbly submit myself to the memory of one of the honourable members of your own number,[2] as well as to another now serving your Lordships and acting all that time at Deptford.[3] And yet,

4thly – The success of their war abundantly shows the want of this balance not so fatal as the ignorance in the state of their stores (here supposed necessarily attending it) must have

---

[1]Ibid., pp. 76–7.
[2]Thomson.
[3]Edmund Portman, secretary to the Commission.

unavoidably proved in a time of such action. Nor will this in the reason of it appear of so uneasy admission, when it shall be considered that those species thereof which, being of foreign growth and greatest expense, call for a constant and early provision (such as masts, fir timber, hemp, tar, rosin and canvas, etc.) are also in bulk so discernible as without any curiosity of search will by plain inspection timelily admonish the Surveyor and his instruments of their consumption and the necessity of a supply, whilst on the other hand those less discoverable (such as nails and ironwork of all sorts, chandlery, blockmakers' and turnery ware, etc.) are, by being of home preparation, almost as soon supplied as wanted. Insomuch that as the first war answers by its success for itself, so I may with assurance on behalf of the present Officers of the Navy invite any man to instance one miscarriage or delay happening in this from the untimely discovery of the want of one species of provisions.

5ly – Nevertheless that your Lordships may see by an evidence above all exception how much the matter now in debate of balancing storekeepers' accounts hath and is at this day attended to by this Office, give me leave to acquaint you that when from the close of the late war his Royal Highness found leisure and opportunity of informing himself in what from the experience thereof might be found requiring regulation in the future conduct of this Office, he did among other Instructions sent them thereupon in November 1668 not only enjoin for the time to come the balancing of storekeepers' accounts as a duty wholly indispensable,[1] but to obtain from his Majesty in Council in February following an establishment of several officers to be at the disposal of the Comptroller for the more effectual enabling him to go through therewith.[2] In pursuance of which, it is to be hoped that the next year will produce such fruits of this method as do not appear to have ever been pretended to, much less arrived at, in any time past.

For what remains to be said upon this Observation, touching the not taking annual surveys: though neither practice nor rule hath placed it, nor the nature of his Majesty's service will admit

---

[1] See above, p. 252 & n. 1.
[2] By the Council order of 12 Feb. 1669 special officers were to be appointed in each yard for this purpose and the Comptroller was provided with an extra clerk: PL 2242, pp. 143–4. Real improvement, however, came only with the establishment from 1671 of an extra Commissioner who was put in charge of the storekeepers: Ehrman, *Navy*, p. 182.

it to lie upon the Officers of the Navy jointly, yet will they be found so far to have concerned themselves in this particular with the Surveyor (whose single duty this is and has been ever esteemed and owned) as not to have wanted a survey in more than one year since their admission on this trust, till the war (as before) rendered it impracticable. Whilst on the contrary I find not one general survey made by their predecessors in ten years before, either in peace or war.

Observation 9th

That for ought appears to us, musters of the whole fleet have not been taken by the said Principal Officers and Commissioners or their clerks in the Narrow Seas once in three months, according to their Instructions in that behalf.

Answer

'Tis true that the Officers of the Navy have not either personally or by their clerks kept themselves to the taking any quarterly musters of the fleets – and yet may be presumed wholly free from any imputation of failure in this matter when you shall be pleased to add to that part of the Instruction here quoted by your Lordships that other by which this duty is wholly restrained to their doing it:

Where there is not a particular muster-master stated by the Lord High Admiral to execute the same.[1]

Which has at no time been the case in the late war, wherein (besides the extraordinary muster-masters and cheques established at Gravesend, Harwich, Plymouth and Kinsale) the fleet in the year 1665 was supplied with three, and that in 1666 with nine, whose performances not answering what was expected from them, this Board failed not in their representing it to the Lord High Admiral, who thereupon was pleased (according to the

[1] *Oeconomy*, p. 40.

degrees of their neglect) to punish some with loss of their wages and others with the addition of imprisonment.[1]

To which, notwithstanding, I might add that the Board have not omitted, sometimes by their clerks and at others by themselves, upon the going out or return of a fleet, to take extraordinary musters.[2] Nor from the sense they have had of the damages his Majesty has been liable to by the imperfect methods heretofore used in the keeping of muster books, to exercise much care in their endeavours of remedying it by the invention, publishing and enjoining the use of a method much more perfect for the obviating all the evils hereafter mentioned by your Lordships in relation to clothes and tickets than was ever yet arrived at by all that appears of the practice of our predecessors.[3] But making it not my business here to show what they have exceeded in, but what in truth they have not fallen short of the duties imposed on them, I shall forbear that trouble and proceed to the next Observation.

Observation 10th

That they have passed the accounts of boatswains and carpenters of his Majesty's ships before the respective pursers have been by them called to account what check they have kept upon the said boatswains and carpenters as by their Instructions the said pursers are obliged to do, and thereby his Majesty hath or might have been endangered through the embezzling of his Majesty's stores; nor have they compared and examined the accounts of the pursers and slop-sellers, whereby his Majesty hath been charged with extraordinary sums for clothes on the account of Runs.

---

[1] In the Diary at 16 Jan. 1667 Pepys has an account of the meeting at which these decisions were made. The Duke had wanted to give to the successful mustermasters (among them Balty St Michel, Pepys's brother-in-law) not only their own pay but part of that of their unsuccessful colleagues. But Pepys resisted the proposal, which might have been misconstrued because of Balty's relationship to him. Cf. *Diary*, viii. 83.

[2] Clerks were employed in 1664, 1665 and 1666 to take musters at the fleet's coming in – Brouncker taking charge on the last occasion.

[3] Pepys had designed a new muster book (see below, p. 402; cf. *Diary*, vii. 100), but irregularities still occurred, mainly through the carelessness of clerks in the Ticket Office.

Answer

For their passing the accounts of boatswains and carpenters without regard to the check therein kept by the pursers, it is humbly answered that as I am able (by several acts of the Board) to satisfy your Lordships in their endeavours of promoting this method of passing the said accounts by encouraging and assisting pursers in the gaining copies of the said officers' indents, as often as by the pursers' complaints on that behalf they have understood the same to be denied them, so will the Officers of the Navy be found not only not passing the accounts of boatswains and carpenters in the manner here suggested, but to have at no time intermeddled with the passing them either in that or any other; and this without any blame attending them for neglect, forasmuch as there appears neither practice nor Instruction of the Lord High Admiral to interest the whole Board in any degree relating to this matter otherwise than in their inspecting 'if they please' (for it is no farther enjoined) the yearly declaration thereof, which the Surveyor by the 5th article of his duty is indeed obliged to present to them[1] – though the little performance it hath met with be another of the matters in which his Royal Highness has been pleased in his regulations above-mentioned to exercise his care in the requiring its better performance for the time to come.

For their not comparing the books of the pursers with those of the slop-sellers: as with submission I cannot discern whence this should be esteemed so certain or even probable an expedient against the evil here suggested, since the slop-seller, being not any officer of the King's nor acting under any other obligation than that of his own profit, may easily be supposed inclining rather to the benefit of the purser; so should this nevertheless be concluded of use for the time to come, the non-observing it for what's past cannot (I presume) be charged on the Officers of the Navy as a crime, where neither practice nor precept appears to have called for it from them – but on the contrary, both the rules and practice of the Navy have provided his Majesty the same security in the case of clothes as in that much greater article of seamen's wages, namely the hands of his commanders, masters and boatswains.

[1] *Oeconomy*, pp. 64–5.

Observation 11th

That they have not taken care for the instruments employed under them for making forth of tickets to examine the tickets by their indentures or counterparts, whereby their clerks have had opportunity to deliver forth some of the said indentures or counterparts to persons who have made use of them to make false tickets by.

As appears by depositions upon oath before us.

Observation 12th

That they have not constantly used to examine tickets by the sea books and muster books by comparing the sea books with the muster books of the respective ships, whereby many false tickets have been passed, many of them to Runs, others to seamen as able who were but ordinary, grummets or boys, and in divers of them the time of service enlarged beyond its due bounds.

As appears likewise by depositions upon oath.

Observation 13th

That they have not caused a register to be constantly kept and transmitted to the Treasurer of the Navy of all tickets passed in the Office, to prevent the defrauding of his Majesty; nor doth it appear that they have taken care to get lists of tickets paid by the Treasurer to be transmitted to them, which hath not only contributed to the inconveniences in the next preceding head mentioned, but hath also occasioned the passing of double tickets to the same person for the same time of service and in the same ship, and consequently the making of double payments, and those allowed by the said Principal Officers and Commissioners on the sea books and Treasurer's ledgers respectively.

Answer

These three Observations terminating all of them in matters relating to the examining, signing and paying of tickets, your Lordships will allow me to give them this joint answer.

1st. That as to the facts here asserted by your Lordships and touching which you have by your said letter of the 2nd inst. been pleased to decline communicating the instances relative to the same, there seems no other room left for present answer thereto than that where the necessity of multiplying tickets have been increased, and consequently the manifold disorders attending them, it ought not to be doubted but errors will be found; since, when you shall have leisure of inquiring into the management of the former war, when the action was neither so great nor by the timeliness of their payments either the use of tickets or the grounds of disorder arising therefrom bore any proportion with those of this, you will soon be satisfied that even in those days tickets were passed with imperfect examinations. Nay, I have grounds of believing you will find all the errors upon tickets (either single or double) appearing in the making up the Treasurer's books at the end of that war to have been allowed to their Treasurer upon his account, and that to no inconsiderable sum.

2. But supposing the truth of the facts here asserted, and proceeding thereupon to the consideration of the inferences you are pleased to deduce from them, *viz.*:

> That the not examining of tickets by their counterparts hath given the clerks of the Officers of the Navy some opportunity extraordinary of doing what has proved prejudicial to the King. That the passing of many false tickets, and to Runs, with others untrue as to the quality of the person and the time he served, hath arisen from the want of a constant comparing of tickets with the sea books. That his Majesty must be defrauded where a register of tickets passed in the Office is not constantly transmitted to the Treasurer of the Navy. And lastly that their not taking care to get lists of tickets paid by the Treasurer to be transmitted to them hath contributed to the passing false tickets, tickets to Runs, tickets mis-rated and false cast as to the allowance of time, and moreover occasioned the passing of double tickets to the same person for the same time of service and in the same ship.

If your Lordships' meaning therein differ not from what the plain construction of the terms they here run in seems to discover, I beg I may without offence confess my present inability to discern the cogency of the said conclusions, but yet with a profession of my readiness when commanded not only to expose to you the grounds thereof (which to avoid prolixity I at present forbear) but to submit to what upon hearing them your Lordships shall be pleased to determine.

3. Forasmuch as, should both the facts and the consequences thereof here suggested be all of them admitted, it would not nevertheless (as I conceive) fall to the share of the Officers of the Navy in general to stand answerable therefore, by how much[1] (besides that the works here insisted on of examining tickets by their counterparts and transmitting reciprocally between them and the Treasurer lists of all tickets signed and paid are nowhere enjoined them) the care of seeing right done to his Majesty in the examining and passing of tickets in order to payment, and allowing them to the Treasurer when paid, hath by the Lord High Admiral's Instructions (both old and new) been made the special duty of the Comptroller, and both anciently and at this day owned as such by that Officer.

But that the Officers of the Navy may however appear not to have neglected the taking into their common care the good conduct of that affair, as of a matter wherein during the war both his Majesty and the subject were so nearly interested, I shall, of the several acts of this Board testifying their desires of serving his Majesty and assisting the Comptroller in this particular, trouble your Lordships with the present recital of that one only which follows, and wherein you will (I fear not) find abundantly expressed the endeavours of this Office to obviate as much as in them lay all the evils (whether those here mentioned by your Lordships or others) appertaining to this business of tickets.[2]

17th January 1666[7]. For the bringing into better method the present disorders of the Ticket Office, both for the safety of his Majesty and all persons concerned to apply themselves thither for the examination of tickets, it is hereby this day ordered:

---

[1] In that.
[2] There is a copy of this order in BL, Add. MSS 11602, ff. 317–18. It was designed to silence the clamour about tickets which had been raised in the House of Commons and elsewhere: *CSPD 1667–8*, pp. 457–8.

1st – That the several ships, great and small, which are or shall be during this war employed in his Majesty's service, being distributed into four equal parts by the letters of the alphabet with which each vessel's name begins, the four clerks hereunder mentioned shall daily attend to the dispatch of such tickets, and no other, as shall for the said division appertain to him, and which he shall accordingly receive either from the party concerned or from an officer by us hereunder appointed for the receiving of tickets from all persons in general, and distributing the same among the same four clerks according to their said divisions following:

   Mr Nathaniel Whitfield.. A,B,C,D,E.
   Mr Wm Barbour............. F,G,H,I,K.
   Mr James Carkesse......... L,M,N,O,P,R.
   Mr John Seddon.............. S,T,V,W,Y,Z.

2 – That the said four clerks do forthwith apply themselves to the reducing of the several books now lying in the office for each ship in his division to one perfect book, and that the same be from henceforwards constantly observed for all books which shall hereafter be brought into the office, and that none but the perfect book of any one ship be applied to for examination of tickets, but that therefore from time to time the clerks examiners do each for his own division safely lay by in a place apart the books of each ship so soon as the same are succeeded by one more perfect.

3 – That the said four clerks do day by day enter into a book provided for the purpose the person's name, the ship, and sum of every ticket he shall that day examine, with the number answerable to the number he is to affix upon each ticket; which daily abstract is to be by the same clerks by turns transcribed into the like book for the Treasurer, and to be carried to and again between the office of the Treasury and the Ticket Office daily by the messenger attending the Ticket Office for entries of the abstracts of each day, which is strictly to be observed for prevention of double passing of tickets for the same service and double payments in the Treasury Office, and for securing as well the King in case of tickets pretended to be lost, as the subject in case where they really are so.

4 – That the said four clerks shall according to their divisions, in the absence of the rest of his Majesty's Principal Officers and Commissioners, attend these under-named resident within

his Majesty's said office, for the timely signing of the tickets by each of them examined, *viz.*:

Mr Carkaiss......................	Sir John Mennes
Mr Whitfield.....................	Sir Wm Batten
Mr Barbour......................	Sir Wm Penn
Mr Seddon.......................	Samll Pepys Esqr.

And it is hereby understood that the signer of any ticket is to be indemnified in the doing thereof against any errors of the clerk examining by that Principal Officer or Commissioner to whom the said clerk particularly relates, and for security to all, that the casting of all tickets be before payment checked (as they used and ought to be) by some person on behalf of the Treasurer, with the letters of that person to be set to the re-castings.

5 – That no other clerk relating to this his Majesty's Office shall examine any tickets without the knowledge and satisfaction of that clerk to whose division the said ticket belongs, and that no commander, purser, or other person not relating to this Office be permitted to handle or inspect any book remaining in the Ticket Office upon any pretence whatsoever.

6 – That Mr Simon Waterson do from day to day attend at the Ticket Office, there readily to receive from each person tendering the same what tickets shall be brought him, and forthwith enter the name of the ship and person concerned in the said ticket, and then deliver the same by account to such of the examining clerks to whose division it belongs, and the said ticket being examined and signed, to remand it of the said clerk so as to give an account of the disposal of each ticket which shall be proved to have been delivered to him.

7 – That after the last of this instant January the said clerks do in no wise examine or receive for examination any written ticket, for avoiding the many counterfeits which are abroad and whereof some have been found, and moreover that for the timely recovery of that useful practice (of late wholly neglected) of comparing each ticket with its duplicate remaining in the office for prevention of counterfeits, the said clerks forthwith cause all the duplicates resting in the office of tickets already abroad to be burned, saving those lettered Ch[1] (the letters now ensuing) and that the said clerks each for his own division do see that no tickets so marked or with any of the succeeding letters of the alphabet be hereafter by them examined and tendered for signing

---

[1] ? Checked.

without the duplicate thereof at the same time presented therewith and cancelled by the clerk that examined it.

Lastly, forasmuch as we have declared that we will report to his Royal Highness the care and pains which shall appear to have been taken by the persons above-mentioned in the receiving, examining and issuing of the said tickets, in order to a proportionable consideration to be given them beyond their ordinary salaries:

We do hereby strictly forbid any of the said five persons[1] to demand or receive any reward or gratuity from any person for any service done in pursuance of these our orders, upon penalty of losing their places in case of any complaint and proof made of their having so done.

And it is hereby declared that every of the orders above-written shall become of force upon Monday the 21 inst. (saving the 7th, to which a longer time is assigned) and that therefore the said clerks are hereby required forthwith to apply themselves to the preparing of books and all things else previous thereunto.

Brouncker, J. Mennes, W. Batten, S. Pepys.

Observation 14

That through the want of their care to prevent it, the pursers have received money of the Victualler instead of victuals,[2] whereby men serving in some of the ships on or near the coasts of these kingdoms have been put to short allowance.

Answer

That the King's ships have some of them been at short allowance in the Channel is (I presume) as little to be questioned as its unfitness for his Majesty's service that they should have been so. But as the generality of the want of victuals pretended (and that

---

[1] The four examining clerks and Simon Waterson who registered the tickets on their being given in (above, para. 6).

[2] Pursers were authorized to receive money only for the purchase of dry provisions abroad.

in the Generals' own ships)[1] makes it less probable to have arisen from the cause here suggested, especially whilst there are so many others more considerable and undoubted (such as among the rest excess of supernumeraries and throwings overboard of provisions in preparation for fight) which not only may but must have contributed greatly to this want thereof, both by preventing their taking in so much and occasioning the spending it faster than of right they should have done; so should the contrary be admitted to have fallen out by any secret transactions between the Victualler and pursers, the miscarriage (I presume) will not nevertheless be held chargeable to the 'want of care in the Officers of the Navy' wholly unconcerned therein, but to the commanders of those ships wherein such disorders have been committed, forasmuch as to them alone the care both of seeing the provisions duly received on board and controlling the expense[2] of them there is entrusted by the Lord High Admiral. As appears in the 6 and 7 articles of the general,[3] with the 1, 2 and 3d of the additional Instructions of the Lord High Admiral to commanders.[4]

Observation 15

That they have bought goods for the service of the Navy at such prices that his Majesty hath been charged for them at much greater rates than they were truly worth.

Capt. Cock is paid for Flaunders hemp 50l. per ton and for Q[uinsborough] and Riga hemp 57l. Mr Deering the like price and others.

Answer

If by prices truly worth your Lordships' meaning be those at the same time current between private merchants for ready money, the Officers of the Navy have long ago loudly enough

[1] Those commanded by Rupert and Albemarle in 1666.
[2] Consumption.
[3] The General Instructions of 1662 (*Oeconomy*, pp. 25–7).
[4] See below, p. 412 n. 3.

declared the truth of that charge by their frequent, as well as mournful, representations thereof to his Majesty, his Royal Highness and the Lord Treasurer; and that not in general only, but with descendings even to the particular instances of the scandalous difference between the prices they have been forced to submit to on their terms of payment and what they have at the same time been by the same hand offered to be served at on those of ready money.

Thus it was that when after long condoling among themselves the unhappy state of his Majesty's affairs under their care, and many verbal complaints on that behalf made at their attendances on the Lord High Admiral, they found it necessary for their own justification as well as for the rendering the same the more impressive to betake themselves to representation thereof in writing. Thus (I say) it was that in a solemn address to his Royal Highness in May 1666 on this subject[1] *they discharged themselves as to the point now in question in the terms following:*

But (may it please your Royal Highness) his Majesty suffers not only under that loss [meaning the loss of time, of which they had been speaking][2] but the expense of his treasure also increased by the excessive rates we are forced to give for everything his service wants; the merchant resolving to save himself in the uncertainty of his payment by the greatness of his price, while the constant occasions we have for a long time had of exhausting our stores without capacity of giving them proportionable supplies necessitates us to look out for and embrace almost any bargains we can procure, though at rates ourselves know to be very excessive.

After which, going on to give his Royal Highness an instance of the matter they are complaining of, they prove therein so fortunate as to pitch upon the very particular your Lordships have thought fit to make the present example of their excess, *viz.*:

A hemp merchant (that from 60*l*. first demanded had fallen to 58*l*. and at last was prevailed with to accept 57*l*. per ton) being

---

[1]Longleat, Coventry MSS 97, ff. 19–20; drawn up by Pepys 'very betimes' on the morning of 12 May, according to the Diary. Copy in Coventry MSS 96, ff. 110–11; entered into Pepys's letter book: NMM, LBK/8, pp. 394–7 (printed *Further Corr.*, pp. 133–6).

[2]Pepys's parenthesis.

reproached by us that a private person had very lately bought of the same goods at 49l. 10s., he immediately replied that he would thankfully exchange the price he had then agreed with us for of 57 for 49 to be paid ready money, which is 16 per cent difference.

Thus it was that in another like address to his Highness in July 1666[1] the Officers of the Navy will be found, among other open expressions of their griefs in this matter, delivering themselves thus:

We crave leave of your Royal Highness now to add that, having with all humble and repeated importunities and by no less mediation than that of your Royal Highness endeavoured to represent to his Majesty and the Lord Treasurer our apprehensions of the consequences of this want, we see not any arguments behind from whence we may with reason hope for more success than from those already used, but contrarily do with much grief consider ourselves reliefless under all those difficulties your Royal Highness hath so often been disquieted with our complaints of, and of which the daily growth is such as without speedy remedy will soon verify the worst presage we have in any of our addresses made concerning the same.

It only remains for us to beg that we may be permitted sometimes to represent to your Royal Highness such instances of our misfortune as may best express the same and justify our former and present importunities to my Lord Treasurer for relief therein.

That (of many) which we shall pitch on for your Royal Highness's present trouble concerns hemp, that essential requisite of his Majesty's naval stores, concerning which your Royal Highness may please to be informed that what in the years 1661 and 62 through the uncertainty of payments and troubles in the country from whence it comes was sold at 55l. per ton did afterwards by the bettering of our credits in the year (63) fall to 42l., and so continued with little increase till by the greatness of our expense in prospect of a war and an untimely decay of our credit through the failure of our supplies of money it rose to 50 and 55, and in May last (for the last parcel we

---

[1]Coventry MSS 96, ff. 112–13, 14 July, 'a laborious letter' (*Diary*, vii. 205); entered into Pepys's letter book: NMM, LBK/8, pp. 398–400 (printed *Further Corr.*, pp. 137–40).

bought) 57*l.* per ton. Since that time (as great as our consumption is) we have not been tendered any otherwise than by a late proposition sent by an unknown hand to my Lord Brouncker to be communicated to the Board with offer of 1000 tons of the same hemp at the same price of 57*l.* per ton, but with these further conditions, etc.

Where, having given his Highness a particular thereof, they proceed and say:

> We need not animadvert to your Royal Highness upon the nature of these terms, they enough speaking their own unreasonableness. And yet, as unreasonable as they are, we durst not but yield so far to our necessities and the necessary care of preserving ourselves blameless as to make some return to the proposer, whereunto he hath sent his reply; the particulars whereof being long, we have chosen to present them to your Royal Highness by a duplicate of the whole, enclosed for your Royal Highness's own perusal, if you shall think fit, but more especially that they may be transmitted from your hand to my Lord Treasurer, whose particular direction we humbly pray to have in this matter, we neither daring to accept of the proposal without his Lordship's approbation, nor being able to perform our part therein without his assistance, nor on the contrary willing without his Lordship's command to reject it at a time of so much want and expense of that commodity, having no assurance that the merchants of the town do make their customary provision, and being ourselves wholly unable by ready money to make a provision (as heretofore) by our own commission.

And thus it was that in that yet more particular representation given his Highness in November 1666[1] of the then ruinous state of his Majesty's affairs they will be found disburdening themselves as to this particular in manner following:

> We are yet once more constrained to become troublesome to your Royal Highness upon that subject on which we have by your Royal Highness's favour been so often suffered to importune you, namely the want of money and the effects of that want under which his Majesty's service hath been so long

---

[1] Navy Board to Duke of York, 17 November; entered into Pepys's letter book: NMM, LBK/8, pp. 413–18 (printed *Further Corr.*, pp. 146–54). See *Diary*, vii. 373.

sinking; nevertheless do humbly hope and believe that neither the frequency of our former addresses nor plainness of this will lead your Royal Highness to judge us forwarder in our complaints than becomes us, forasmuch as standing accountable for all miscarriages within the power of our understanding or care to prevent, we find ourselves wholly unfurnished of any other way of acquitting ourselves under this difficulty than by a timely and continued declaration of it and its effects to your Royal Highness.

Here giving him an account by particulars of the disappointments they have continually lain under in the payments of the moneys promised and expected, they add:

What then must be the condition of his Majesty's stores and the credit of this Office, or its capacity either of building the new ships designed or refitting the old for the service of the next year, although your Royal Highness cannot but already collect in general, yet that you may see how far this lack of money hath diffused itself by its ill effects through every part of the naval service, and by that means judge better of the necessity and method of remedying it, and that ourselves may still be found mindful of our duty in a due representation thereof, we have assumed the liberty of laying before your Royal Highness the truth of our condition in most of those circumstances wherein your Royal Highness might expect our service should be of greatest use to his Majesty.

1 – And first, in the seasonable providing such supplies of stores as may answer the expense and wants of his Majesty's ships. Which we have been so unable to perform as in three months past not to have compassed the contracting for provisions to such a value as we have frequently heretofore done in fewer days, *viz.* 8000*l.*, and that but for five parcels of goods, a useful part whereof (being agreed for with condition of our advancing but 100*l.*) we have lost, from our inability to procure that sum. Nay, so far are we from complaining (as heretofore) of being only forced to give excessive rates that we cannot now at any rate prevail for any supplies without present money. Insomuch that with the 5000*l.* his Majesty was pleased lately to order us for the setting anchor-smiths to work against the next year we have not been able to invite any of them thereunto by what we could advance towards their making new,

unless at the same time they might be satisfied for what anchors we were already indebted to them for.

And as an instance of what answers are given us where we are forced to press for goods upon credit, we were lately asked 30s. per l. ready money for iron furnaces to be sent to Harwich, with a refusal of 50s. to be paid by bill.[1] And much more may your Royal Highness easily believe is the averseness in all persons to credit us in greater, if we be thus treated in matters of so small value; which yet even in small things is oftentimes of as injurious consequence to his Majesty as in greater – witness broom and reed, the want whereof (unless enabled by money to furnish ourselves therewith) will instantly prevent us in the cleaning any more of his Majesty's ships as it hath already set us backward in the dispatch of those last gone out.

Again, your Royal Highness may please to consider the further instance of the coming in of two Swedes some days since to Portsmouth loaden with deals (a commodity much wanted there), offering them us at 8l. *per centum* ready money, which we not being furnished with to give, they were invited to come about to London, where we must pay for them or the like 11 or 12l. *per centum*, and be moreover at the charge and hazard of sending them hence to Portsmouth.

After which the Officers of the Navy passing with like distinctness through the miseries his Majesty's service suffered in every other branch of the trust committed to them, they conclude this their address thus:

All which we do humbly leave with your Royal Highness as that which we could not with faithfulness either decline or delay the laying before you, having no other possible way open to us of contributing to the preservation of this great affair from a total and imminent miscarriage.

I could, my Lords, with little pains appear very voluminous on this subject, as well on that part of it which relates to the distress wherein his Majesty's service universally remained during the whole war, as what concerns the restless care exercised by the Officers of the Navy in their seasonable representations of the same. But the present matter calling for no more than what serves to illustrate the demeanour of the said Officers under the

---

[1] Treasury bill.

necessities they were driven to of buying provisions at excessive rates, I have chosen rather to confine myself to what is already offered than by further enlargement therein to adventure upon the giving your Lordships any unnecessary trouble.

To go on then with your Lordships' present exception, give me leave to add that as the Officers of the Navy do not only not disown but appear to have themselves been the readiest and loudest in their complaints of that hard usage by which they have been driven to the accepting at dearer, what with ready money they might have supplied themselves with at cheaper, rates, so I am not doubtful on behalf of the said Officers to invite the whole world to assign one instance where they have omitted to prefer the cheaper when but equal in goodness and the other terms of payment and delivery.

No, my Lords, I do (as far as the utmost of what I am privy to of their managements can inform me) apprehend them so little chargeable with a prevarication of this kind that when the prices they have given, aggravated in the severest manner by their wants and badness of payment, shall be maturely examined, I assure myself your Lordships will not begrudge them in this particular (no more than in those already mentioned) the benefit of that clause wherein for the enabling you better to distinguish of the evils you are commissionated to inquire into, the Parliament has in their great justice been pleased to point you to the '**inspecting and examining of former accounts**'.[1]

Which granted, it will soon appear how little the supposed husbandry, supported by a constant purse during the first Dutch war, hath outflung this Office under all its difficulties in this point of cheap buying, since (to pass over what might be observed to its advantage upon commodities of less value) it hath not yet occurred to me that in those of the greatest, and of greatest consumption as well as difficulty to procure, the present Officers have exceeded, but for the most part not come up to the prices given by their predecessors. In which to be a little particular and therein submitted to the contract books lying before your Lordships, allow me to observe that the highest rate legible in the contracts of this Office for Noyalls canvas is equalled by as large a one in theirs, *viz.* 18*l*. 10*s*. per bale. For cordage I find them

---

[1] In the preamble to the Act the Commissioners were authorised to 'inspect and examine all such further accounts as they shall think necessary': 19 & 20 Car. II c. 1. The quotation is written in black letter script.

paying 52*l*., for which no contract of this Office hath exceeded 45*l*. For tar they could afford 20*l*. for what his Majesty has not at the highest been charged with above 15*l*. 10*s*. Nor above 18*l*. for pitch, for which I find them giving 28*l*. 6*s*. 8*d*. And lastly (referring your Lordships to the next Observation for the difference between their pennyworths in the point of masts) give me leave to observe even for hemp itself the particular you are pleased to instance in (but with a mistake as to Capt. Cock, whose price never arose to 57*l*.) that although the present Officers have owned themselves giving no less to some others, I have nevertheless already made it out to your Lordships from their early complaints thereof to his Royal Highness that this arose not either from their not searching after, insisting upon, or not being able to have bought it even below the market price with ready money, *viz*. 49*l*., while it may as readily be shown that the price current among private merchants within the first war exceeded not 30*l*. to 36*l*., when (notwithstanding the credit of their treasury) the Commissioners then acting will be found giving 45*l*. and 46*l*.

Observation 16

That in buying of provisions they have preferred some persons before others, as also in prices and making out of bills, and have tied up themselves to take naval provisions of some, excluding others.

Sir Wm Warren and others preferred when more would have served but rejected.

Answer

Well knowing how little persuasive any general assertings of the integrity of this Office can prove under the opposition of a particular instance, I shall spare the use of what testimonies might in abundance be produced in their favour upon this subject, and apply myself directly to the informing your Lordships touching the demeanour of the said Officers in that instance, in the choice whereof, as your Lordships have no doubt proceeded with special regard to your own satisfaction, so do I think it the most fortunate to them, as having thereby opportunity of doing themselves right in a case wherein (as it often happens) they have found themselves under the severest and most public censure, when if well examined (as they conceive) deserving most the contrary.

The instance then is that of Sir Wm Warren, who being by the present Officers of the Navy at their entrance into this trust found (among others) trading therein as a Norway merchant, was (as the King's occasions called for it) summoned with the rest to treat with them, and as his prices exceeded or came under the offers of his neighbours, either contracted with or rejected.

And so it stood between them and him from the year 1660 till towards the end of 1663 when, his Majesty's stores calling for a considerable supply of Swedes and Norway masts, the Officers of the Navy in their deliberation how the same might with most advantage to his Majesty be obtained, considered with much affliction the strait under which they found the King's service then lying by an engrossment of the mast trade into so few hands as to render them unable in three years' time to contract for one mast with any other than the two persons here named, *viz.* Mr Wood and Capt. Taylor.

For remedy whereof they thought it greatly importing his Majesty's service to encourage tenders from any others, especially when the first essay they made therein carried with it such conviction of the benefit thereof, as is legible in the contract thereupon made with Sir Wm Warren in September 1663 for 450 masts, at prices not only 10, others 15, some 20 per cent lower than the lowest they had been able for three years before to buy of them above named, but lower than the lowest that (upon a search then purposely made) the like goods had been contracted for in ten years before by those they succeeded. For the truth of which I yet appeal to the books of both times.[1]

After which his Majesty's occasions calling for no further supply of that commodity until about June following, when intimation was given them of a probability of a breach with Holland, the Officers of the Navy then betook themselves to the consideration of a seasonable supply of those principal stores which, being also of foreign growth, required timelily to be secured. Among which masts being in the first rank, and a computation of the

---

[1] For the contract, see above, p. 9 and n. 1. By 'books' is meant contract books.

numbers thereof of each dimension requisite being first demanded from the Surveyor, they concluded upon contracting for the same with what speed they conveniently could, having in the meantime, *viz.* about the 4th of June, occasion of contracting with Mr Wood and Blackborough for two smaller parcels of masts, and therein of receiving full confirmation in the advantageousness of their late contract with Sir Wm Warren, to whose prices (though pressed with his example) the said Wood and Blackborough could not on this occasion be prevailed with to descend.

Whereupon, and being urged by the daily increase of circumstances portending a war, the Board resolved to proceed without delay to the securing as much as might be and on the best terms they could the quantities of masts calculated as before.

Which resolution proved the ground of the former of those two contracts instanced in by your Lordships,[1] and touching which I now come to show how little the Officers of the Navy will be found chargeable with the giving Sir Wm Warren either of those species of preference here suggested, *viz.* of *buying, price* or *making out of bills.*

And first, for that of *buying*: give me leave to observe that albeit his former undertaking, so much below what any had taken before him or would so lately accept of after him, might have easily directed them again to Sir Wm Warren, they did not nevertheless omit in the strictest manner to express their endeavours of enlarging the market, and therein testifying the little preference Sir Wm Warren either had or could deserve from them.

Which to prove, I shall (I presume) need no second medium after tendering your Lordships a copy of the invitation sent to Mr Wood and others the 28 of June 1664 in the words following, *viz.*:

Sir,
It being the intention of the Principal Officers and Commissioners to proceed upon Thursday morning next to the making a contract for a supply of Gottenburgh and Norway masts for his Majesty's service, you are hereby advertised thereof that if you shall think fit to make any tender of such goods to be brought directly from the ports they come from and delivered fresh into his Majesty's yards of Deptford, Woolwich,

---

[1]That of July 1664: see above, pp. 17–18.

Chatham and Portsmouth in such quantities as shall upon further considerations be thought fit, you may please to prepare in writing and offer to us at that time the rates you will expect for each sort of masts from 24 hands downwards. Wherein we desire you will set down the lowest price you will be contented to offer them at, that we may without loss of time be directed to accept or refuse the same as we shall find it to exceed or come beneath what shall be tendered by others. This I do signify to you from the whole Board, and rest,
    Your friend and servant,
    S. Pepys.

Distinct copies whereof were at the same time also sent to other merchants, namely Mr Dering and Mr Blackborough, as well as to Sir W. Warren, who with their partners were then the principal dealers of the town for that commodity.

As to the preference of *price*: the prices of this contract have, as is already observed, proved no other in its performance than those of September 1663, outdoing in their moderateness not only all examples backward but whatever was either offered upon the invitation now mentioned or have been contracted for with any other since. Wherein I humbly appeal to the contract books resting with your Lordships.

Lastly, for that of *making out his bills*: the preference your Lordships intend in that particular must (I suppose) lie either in their extraordinary dispatch, or over-rating.

If the former, I must humbly acknowledge my fears that when your Lordships shall more fully understand with what pace this Board has moved in the passing the bills of Sir Wm Warren, you'll find more reason to censure its delay than dispatch, there not occurring to me one person among the thousands with whom this Office have had to do whose bills have in any proportion lain so long unadjusted – too long, to be sure, on the King's behalf where his demands may not have deserved allowance, and too long, it's probable, on his where they have been found otherwise. At least he may be well thought to have esteemed it himself so, when (without touching at the merits of his cause, but complaining of delays) he twelve months since betook himself by petition to his Royal Highness barely for dispatch.

If the latter: though the proper work of my place has within the time of your Lordships' inquiry been such as to render me very little privy to the adjustment of any accounts or rating of bills, and so cannot knowingly undertake for anything in this particular, yet I well hope the Comptroller, who (with the assistance appointed him by his Royal Highness upon occasion of that petition) hath, as principal in the rating all bills, had the particular care of seeing right done his Majesty in these, will be able to justify both himself and the Board against any imputation of preference allowed Sir Wm Warren in this circumstance also.

Having thus given your Lordships an account of the proceedings of the Officers of the Navy in what concerns their contract of July, I shall go on to offer you the like satisfaction touching the other of the 16th of Aug 1664 for New England masts,[1] and in the same method show your Lordships that upon satisfaction first given them from the Surveyor of the want of masts of that country, with a particular of the numbers and dimensions thereof requisite to be provided, they proceeded to the contracting with Sir Wm Warren for the same, with no less caution and clearness from any guilt of preference than in the former.[2]

For as to that of employing him in neglect to others: I am no less prepared to lay before you the copy of the invitation sent on this occasion also to Mr Wood the 26 of July 1664 in the words following, *viz.*:

Mr Wood,

Being willing to receive any tenders of yours and others for 35 New England masts to be felled for the next season and brought the beginning of the next year, of which

$$\left.\begin{matrix}10\\11\\14\end{matrix}\right\} \text{ to be diameter } \left.\begin{matrix}35\\34\\33\end{matrix}\right\} \text{ inches}$$

We have appointed Thursday morning next to receive what offers you shall make us, which we desire you to bring in writing sealed up. Which notice we have likewise given to others. We are,
     Your affectionate friends,
   J. Mennes, W. Batten, W. Coventry, S. Pepys.

The copy of which was also the same day directed to Capt. Taylor and Sir Wm Warren, the only known dealers at that time to New England for that commodity.

---

[1] See above, p. 73.
[2] According to the Diary, Pepys was 'very hard' with Warren on 12 August about this contract – 'even to the making him angry'.

For the other two ways of preference, namely in his prices and making out his bills: referring the latter to what has been newly said in the like case of the contract of July, I am, as to the former, ready to show your Lordships that they were such as came beneath not only all that was now tendered upon this invitation, but what had been contracted for either by this Office since his Majesty's restoration or its predecessors in ten years before, and that to no less difference in some of them than 30 and 40 per cent – besides the addition of a covenant obliging him to such a performance in point of lengths as had never been before required, but since by his example continued to the great advantage of his Majesty.

And so, my Lords, have I summarily told you the story of these two contracts, concerning which were this to become public in any other method than that of an address to your Lordships (the respect to whom restrains me), I could easily think myself excusable in the letting fall something which might express resentment of the hard usage this Board hath met with in the censure so universally cast upon what (if in anything) they must be owned to have merited better. But, my Lords, having already had occasion of pointing your Lordships in the beginning of this discourse to the true rise thereof, and having in my present care the providing satisfaction for your Lordships and not the Officers of the Navy, I shall forbear any such excursion here, and go on to what yet remains to be spoken to upon this Observation, *viz.*:

Their tying up themselves to take naval provisions of some, excluding others.

Touching which there occurring nothing to me in the whole dealings of this Office that might offer ground for such a suggestion, saving the following clause in the latter of these contracts,[1] *viz.*:

It is also hereby agreed for the better encouraging and enabling the said contractor to perform this contract that they shall not contract with any other person for any supply of New England masts before the end of the ensuing winter, unless the said contractor shall first have refused the price given to such other person for the said supply.

[1] That of 16 Aug. 1664 for New England masts: listed *CSPD 1664–5*, p. 132.

I shall humbly offer your Lordships this satisfaction in defence of the said clause, *viz*.:

That the service being under a necessity of this supply, and the contractor insisting immovably upon their allowance of this condition (for avoiding that rise of price in the country which a competition in the market might subject him to), the Officers of the Navy were not at liberty to refuse him, in regard that Capt. Taylor (who was the only other of the three invited that answered us with a tender) did in his said answer demand the same covenant, yet with higher prices. Nor could the granting him the refusal of serving what further masts of that sort they should have occasion of contracting for that winter (which is all the said clause can amount to) have been then reasonably judged of any prejudice to his Majesty, in regard that the number of masts provided for in this contract was deliberately calculated by the Surveyor as a supply of that kind answerable to all the occasions of his Majesty's service then in view.

But, my Lords, that I may at once satisfy you not only in this, but (I hope) in whatever else can remain of doubtfulness in your Lordships touching the partiality of this Office to Sir Wm Warren, give me leave from what hath since arisen upon this very clause to draw an evidence so convincing both of the general endeavours of the Officers of the Navy to encourage a plurality of traders and the little inclination they had towards the suspected preference of Sir W. Warren, as (in the crowd of other testimonies pressing to come before you) to make it seem unnecessary and therefore less respectful to your Lordships to trouble you with any other.

Which is that when, upon the coming in of the fleet and some unexpected difficulties rendering the supply of great masts from Sweden uncertain, the Surveyor informed the Board in the requisiteness of its making a further provision of masts from New England, they upon satisfying themselves in the having given Sir Wm Warren (according to the intentions though not the letter of his contract) scope sufficient for buying up of his parcel, were so far from 'tying themselves up to Sir Wm Warren and excluding others', that neither the urging the letter of his contract nor the merit of his prices (wherein none yet pretended to the underbidding him) could prevail with them to the making use of him in this new occasion, but that before the end of that winter, namely in Janry 1664[5], they contracted for another ship's loading with Mr Child and Mr Shorter, though at Sir Wm Warren's own prices.

Which having said, and I hope not without satisfaction to your

Lordships in reference to the particular case of Sir Wm Warren, I shall not offer you any other trouble upon the general demeanour of this Office in relation to others than the proposing to your inquiry the common style of their written and verbal instructions to their purveyors, suitable to this that follows:

Mr Mayors,
It being intended that we speedily come to a considerable contract for deals of ordinary lengths, such as Dram, Longsound, Swinsound, etc., and for fir timber of all sorts, pray take your time to go (as soon as you can) to the persons undermentioned and who else you know likely to treat with us for the same, to see served what we can now and what quantities (as large as they will) next year, praying them to prepare in writing their proposals as distinct as they can, and their lowest prices at which they will serve, to prevent loss of time in bartering with each several person, and these to be brought in by Saturday next at furthest.
7 Decembr 1664.   Yours,
                                   S. Pepys.

Sir Wm Warren   Mr Walker
Mr Wood   Mr Dering
Mr Blackbury   Mr Smith
Capt. Chester   Mr Dyson and
         Mr White.

To which might be added their assigning, publishing and observing a fixed day weekly on which merchants might with certainty be received with their tenders of provisions,[1] conformable to what you may find observed in the two invitations above exemplified in the case of Sir Wm Warren. And the diversity of persons with whom they shall be found to have dealt for each species of naval provisions, though this diversity (God knows) very unequal to what they probably would have rendered it, had it been as easy to have found hands to trust them as they have carefully done their parts in inviting them.

But there lies the grief; and with that I shall betake myself to what seems the properest close for my discourse on this subject, namely that with which the Officers of the Navy, after enumerat-

---

[1] By an order of 12 June 1662 Thursday mornings were appointed for the purpose: PRO, ADM 106/3520, f. 6r.

ing in their letter to the Lord High Admiral in November 1666[1] several instances of the bad bargains they were then driven to make, do shut up their said report in that particular, *viz.*:

Nor doth this, may it please your Royal Highness, arise from the scarcity of many of the commodities we want, or our want of inquiry after variety of sellers, for our purveyors have been employed and do return us plenty enough of offerers, as particularly for large timber and plank – Mr Cole, Blackborough, Morecock, Barnes, Kingsbury, Lady Culpeper and others, but with a peremptory demand of ready money, or an utter refusal of treating with us upon any other terms. And if they who (as most of these are) have been acquainted with the sureness though lateness of the King's payment and are in some measure obliged by the great sums at this day remaining due to them, do decline further serving us, much more may it be expected from strangers, who stand neither under the obligation of the latter, nor have been tempted by any conveniency from the former.

Observation 17th

That they have not taken order for paying off some ships when they have come in to port, but let them lie at the King's charge for divers months together, whereby the King's treasure hath been wasted, and as a consequence thereof the King's ships have come to be paid by tickets, and the discontent of the mariners thereby occasioned.

As appears by their own list sent us.

Answer

I humbly offer to your Lordships' fresh consideration that list here mentioned, with the memorandum annexed thereto;[2] which

---

[1] The letter of 17 November cited above, p. 303 n. 1. The passage quoted in the lines that follow is in *Further Corr.*, pp. 148–9.
[2] Untraced.

having been sent your Lordships in my absence, I have since my return perused, and with submission conceive other reasons laid down of the ships' lying long in pay, and seamen's being sometimes discharged by ticket, than the want of order taken therein by the Officers of the Navy.

For, my Lords, if by 'their not taking order' your intentions be their not issuing orders originally for the bringing in or paying off of ships – that, my Lords, is an authority resting only in the hands of the Lord High Admiral.

But if it be a supposition of their not having issued their orders to their Treasurer, pursuant to the Lord High Admiral's to them, I hold myself provided to satisfy your Lordships that the Officers of the Navy have not acquiesced in the issuing only, but proceeded to the inculcating their said orders with arguments drawn from the most powerful considerations of the wasteful expense of his Majesty's treasure and the preservation of content and good discipline among the seamen. The latter of which they will also be found to have been so solicitous for, as not to have limited themselves to what the Lord High Admiral in the 10th article of his general Instructions[1] calls for from them, in which (upon a presumed continuance of the ancient efficacy of the Lord Treasurer's assignments) no other part is laid upon this Board towards the 'preventing the clamour of poor men for lack of their pay' than their presenting by estimate to the Lord High Admiral seasonably once a year the charge of the victuals and wages of all his Majesty's ships at home and abroad.

No, my Lords, it will be easy to show that in their solicitations on this subject they have neither stinted themselves to times nor methods, persons nor places, arguments nor style, by which they might have prevailed for the prevention or removal of those ruinous effects of the untimely and unsuitable supplies of money under which his Majesty's service hath ever suffered, as in all other regards so particularly in the two instanced by your Lordships in this Observation, namely the wasting of his treasure and discontent of his mariners.

---

[1] *Oeconomy*, pp. 29–30.

Observation 18th

That whereas there have been several prize ships and goods delivered to them by the Commissioners for Prizes, they have not charged themselves with the receipt of some of the said ships and goods, a list whereof is hereunto annexed.[1]

Answer

That the Officers of Prizes may as well err in the over-charging them of the Navy as that they of the Navy ought not to be thought inclining to the under-charging themselves may be reasonably collected from the contrary mistake of the former no less than the contrary practice of the latter, when in the year 1667 this Office did voluntarily charge itself with a considerable number of ships more than they of the Prize office (by a list of their own calculated to that purpose) had made them chargeable with. A difference also which (I have grounds to believe) your Lordships want not instances of to the advantage of the Officers of the Navy even in the lists from both Offices lying before you at this day.

But, my Lords, to give you a closer answer to this matter, let me have leave to say that the Officers of the Navy cannot be rendered chargeable by the Commissioners of Prizes either with the ships and goods mentioned in this list, or any other, by any account of theirs acknowledging their receipt thereof. What then the Commissioners of Prizes can pretend to charge them by must at the most be the receipts of those storekeepers and others to whom they would be believed to have made their deliveries. Which receipts having at no time hitherto been communicated to this Board, the Comptroller of the Navy could have no other guide in drawing up that account sent your Lordships than the reports he could collect from the several under-officers of the King's yards charging themselves with the same.

I cannot therefore think your Lordships will esteem it any

---

[1] In the debate before the Privy Council on this Observation Pepys pointed out that this was a revised list which omitted the ships about which the Commissioners had found that the Navy Board had not acted improperly: below, p. 432.

unreasonable prayer on behalf of the Officers of the Navy that the charge laid immediately on them in this Observation may be transferred upon those storekeepers and others to whom the Prize Office can pretend any deliveries; and that your judgement may be suspended even concerning them also, until that Office makes better proof of the difference suggested by your Lordships between the charge and discharge of the Officers of the Navy than (upon my private recollection, though little conversant in the state of that affair) I dare at present pronounce them to be by more than three-fourths of the value of the particulars mentioned in your Lordships' list. As may appear by the notes thereto here humbly subjoined.

Your Lordships' list of the ships and goods pretended to have been delivered to the Officers of the Navy by the Commissioners for Prizes, of which the said Officers are said not to have charged themselves with the receipt		My notes thereon
	l. s. d.	
De Ruiter, a man-of-war	860. 0. 0	More men-of-war of this name taken I never understood than two, both of which the list of the Officers of the Navy owns, distinguished (as they were to them) by the names of *Guilder de Ruiter* and *Sea Ruiter*. Whether some mistake may not have been occasioned by a third vessel which hath sometime gone by its Dutch name *De Ruiter* and sometime by its English version *The Horseman*, under which latter I find her long since owned by this Office to the Court of Admiralty and

		among others did lately lie sunk at Woolwich, I humbly submit to inquiry. But that there was any other man-of-war of this name than what their list owns will not, I am sure, appear.
Great Molen	30. 0. 0	The Officers of the Navy have at no time either victualled, manned, disposed of, nor have at this day any such vessel in their possession, and therefore an undoubted mistake in the bringing her to their charge.
George of Stroud	199. 0. 0	I dare affirm no such prize ever to have been delivered to the Officers of the Navy. A ketch indeed of that name this Office did hire among others during the war to attend the fleet, which being (as I am informed) taken by the enemy and afterwards re-taken, was delivered back to her owner Capt. Wood, master of the *Catherine* yacht.
Blew Boare	192.13. 0	Such a vessel was, it's true, once in the possession of the Navy, but returned to the Prize Office as unfit for the use she was designed, and by themselves afterwards (as they well know) sold to Sir W. Warren.
Prince of Denmarke	2360. 0. 0	This ship, a man-of-war, will be found in the list before your Lordships under the name of the *Young Prince*, by which the Office of the Navy received her from the Prize Office.

Dogger boat of Rochester	61. 0. 0	The Navy Officers' list doth own a dogger under the name of the *Golden Fortune* dogger which, having been delivered to their use at Chatham, so here she hath ever since been employed, and no other appearing charged on them by this name, cannot but be the same with the vessel here mentioned.
Endraught	80. 0. 0	The Officers of the Navy have at no time either victualled, manned, disposed of, nor have at this day any such vessel in their possession, and therefore an undoubted mistake in bringing her to their charge.
Wappin of Franiken	1050. 0. 0	The Officers of the Navy do in their list own to your Lordships this very vessel under the name of the *Franikin*.
White Rose	1305. 0. 0	The wreck of this vessel is at this day remaining at Harwich, which being there sunk in the harbour as a fence for the ways, lies not within the charge, though within the notice of the Navy, and so happens to have no place in their list.
St Lawrence	60. 0. 0	The Officers of the Navy have at no time victualled, manned, disposed of, nor have at this day any such vessel in their possession, and therefore an undoubted mistake to bring her to their charge.
Boat belonging to the *De Ruiter*	2. 0. 0	Your Lordships' silence touching the boats of any other prizes, though the list from this Office takes no more notice of

		theirs than this here mentioned, doth (with the consideration of the small value here put upon her) make me not doubt but this like the rest is included under the general terms of the furniture belonging to each prize.
143 large ash oars out of the *Hoveling*	17.17. 6	The Officers of the Navy do own in their list this precise number of oars to have been received at Chatham out of a ship coming in thither loaden with timber and plank, and well known to the Prize Office to be no other than the *Hoveling* here named.
One anchor of 14 cwt and a cable of 23 cwt out of the *King Solomon of Amsterdam*	40.14. 0	No wonder if the Officers of the Navy charge not themselves with this particular, though upon my inquiry I have lately found that the Prize Office did indeed issue such a cable and anchor to the *Eagle* frigate; for it being done at sea out of the check of any of their Officers, this Board could not receive any regular cognizance of it from other hands than that of the Prize Office, to which I appeal whether to this day any such notice hath been by them given thereof.
Also two hawsers	–	The same.
6400 deals out of the *Hope of Camphire*	96. 0. 0	This depends upon your Lordships' inquiry by what vouchers the Prize Office prove their delivery thereof.

Loading of the *Dove of Sardam*	2552.10. 8	The list of the Officers of the Navy owns 31 masts from 22 to 14 hands received at Chatham out of the *Dove* prize, besides deals and fir timber, which may be well esteemed a ship's lading, and arise to the full value of this appraisement.
Lading out of the *Hope of Henlopen*	446. 0. 0	They do also own 90 masts received out of this very ship at Newcastle, which in like manner may be very well valued at the full of this appraisement.
An anchor out of the *Burweek of Alkmer*	7. 0. 0	I offer it to your Lordships to inquire whether the anchor was not delivered at Hull, where the Officers of the Navy had none acting under them either to receive or give discharge for the same.
120 ton of wine out of the *White Lamb*	–	That wine hath been delivered at sea for supply of the fleet, this Office hath by common fame understood, but never so as to be privy to the doing it, much less either to stand chargeable for it, or to have been enabled from any advice from the Prize Office to give a regular charge at the coming in of the fleet to the person accountable for it.
Lading of the *Woodmer[chan]t*	–	What this lading of hers was, or where she was discharged of it, I know not; but this I know and do affirm that she came empty into the hands of this Office, and that the first possession they had of her was in the River

Lading of the *Golden Hand*	–	of Thames after her return with Sir John Harman's fleet in the year 1665 from Gottenburgh. What her lading also was or how disposed of I am not able to say, but can with the like certainty affirm not only that she came empty into the hands of the Officers of the Navy, but that the first notice they had of her was when (by order, as I suppose, from the fleet) she was sent into the River in the time of the Plague, and placed at Gravesend for the receipt of the Dutch prisoners.
$4\sfrac{3}{4}$ cwt of deals short accounted for out of the *Mouse of Amsterdam* 12 cwt 2 q. 17 deals short of those out of the *Wheele of Fortune* 3000 deals short of those of the *Mermaid of Amsterdam*	–	Submitted to your Lordships' inquiry as in the case of the other parcel above-mentioned.

Thus, my Lords, have I gone through with your Lordships' Observations and what on behalf of the Officers of the Navy hath occurred to me touching the truth of their demeanour in all matters contained therein. In which, though the satisfaction wherewith your Lordships have been pleased to receive what I have hitherto been on other occasions led to present you with, might make it seem unnecessary for me to doubt your belief of my faithfulness in this particular, yet because a great part of those before whom this may come are strangers to more of my demeanour in the Navy than what they have collected from those exercises of my duty to which the late inquisitions have sometimes publicly called me, and which from their common tendency to the doing right to this Office have been so unhappy as to raise in some an apprehension of my having taken upon me the general advocateship of the management of the Navy in prevention to the endeavours on foot of discovering what hath been amiss therein, give me leave for my justification to such to say that, as in my particular I depend not in any degree upon the issue to which the justification of the Board in general can be brought, by how much they who know least of the labour of my proper place during a war will easily discharge me from any responsibleness for what concerns the performances of others. So I do appeal, not only to all whose occasions have made them privy to the conduct of this Office how little such a suggestion suits with my known deportment among my fellow Officers, but to the justice also of his Royal Highness, whether the constancy and fervour with which I have ever laboured to discharge my duty of laying open to him what may have appeared amiss among them, with tenders of my humblest advice towards its remedy, hath not exceeded all that this paper or ought else of my endeavours in this kind can be thought to express of industry or concernment in their defence.

Which being so, I cannot doubt but my present undertaking will be found a duty doubly allowable. Once, from the obligation of my place, as having the custody of those records in the absence of my fellow Officers by which (if together) they might with the assistance of their own better memories have probably rendered your Lordships an answer yet more perfect. And then, from that justice by which, having not (as is already said) forborne the free discharge of my duty in what I have apprehended calling for amendment, I could not hold myself excusable in the not asserting (in the manner I have here done) what in their absence I conceived due to them in the matters here in question.

To shut up then your Lordships' present trouble, you will be pleased to allow me liberty of leaving with your Lordships this paper, as the result of what my faithfullest recollections could yet direct me to tender you in behalf of those gentlemen Lord Berkeley, Sir G. Carterett, Sir Wm Coventry, Sir John Mennes, Sir Wm Batten, Sir Wm Penne, Comr Pett, Mr Pepys, Lord Brouncker, Sir Tho. Hervey, Earl of Anglesey, whose present separation prevents my delivering it in any other name than that of my private essay towards their general answer; submitting to your Lordships the choice of your own method of gathering your satisfactions from the rest, either by their concurrence to some common, or their tender of distinct, answers. In which latter, as the nature of my employment and the method of its execution entitles me to a defence therein not applicable to the rest of the Board, so upon which of these two soever your Lordships shall think fit to pitch, such, my Lords, is my assurance both of your justice and my own unblameableness as to think myself safe even in the unbespeaking[1] all favour in whatever shall have reference to my particular.

My Lords and Gentlemen,
Your Lordships' most humble and most faithful servant,
Navy Office, S. Pepys.
27th November 1669.
Jurat 12 Janry 1669
Giles Dunster

Pepys's Particular Defence: his letter to the Brooke House Commissioners, 6 Jan. 1670[2]

My Lords and Gentlemen,
Your Lordships' silence to what I (now some weeks since) presented you with relating to the common defence of this Office, joined with what hath lately come to my notice touching your acceptance of separate answers on the same subject from some particular members thereof, leads me to the thinking it seasonable for me to put into your Lordships' hands something of what may hereafter come more amply to you in right to myself. The distinct

---

[1] Renouncing.
[2] PL 2554, pp. 98–106; copies in PL 2874, pp. 576–81; BL, Sloane MSS 2751, ff. 25v–27r.

duty of whose place as Clerk of the Acts being not to be denied to have shared in the increase of trouble occasioned by a war, equal (at least) to that of any of my fellows, especially those of them who, standing charged with little of the active, were at more leisure to attend only the consultive part of the Office, I cannot conceive any person conversant in the business thereof will scruple to allow the well executing my single share thereinfor a task sufficient to exercise the best industry of one man, without the additional charge of an accountableness for the reasons and actions of others.

To give your Lordships therefore a summary account of the method wherein I have in my particular place endeavoured to discharge my duty to his Majesty, both in the diligence of my attendance on it, the effects of my performance of it, and uprightness in both, give me leave to say:

1st – That for what respects my diligence: as no concernments relating to my private fortune, pleasure or health did at any time (even under the terror of the Plague itself) divide me one day and night from my attendance on the business of my place, so was I never absent at any public meeting of this Board but upon the especial commands of the Lord High Admiral, and that not thrice during the whole three years of the war. To which let me add that in my endeavours after a full performance of my duty I have neither made distinction of days between those of rest and others, nor of hours between them of day and night, being less acquainted during the whole war with the closing my day's work before midnight than after it.

And that your Lordships may not conceive this to arise from any vain assumption of what may be grounded more upon the inability of others to disprove than my own capacity to justify, such have ever been my apprehensions both of the duty and importance of my just attendance on his Majesty's service that among the many thousands under whose observation my employment must have placed me, I challenge any man to assign one day from my first admission to this service in July 1660 to the determination of the war August 1667 (being a complete apprenticeship) of which I am not at this day able upon oath to give an account of the particular manner of my employing the same.[1]

2ly – That although this resignation of my whole time and

---

[1] A reference to the Diary.

strength to the service of his Majesty might in other cases be admitted for the equallest method of rating my performances, and albeit that other, by which alone your Lordships seem inclined to measure the same, namely the exactness of their conformity to and compliance with the ancient Instructions of the Lord High Admiral, calculated for a time of peace and small action, will not (I conceive) either in the reason, practicableness or intention thereof be upon examination insisted upon as such during a war, yet to the end that when your Lordships shall find me reasonably urging the same in behalf of the Board in general, you may not apprehend me interested in the behalf of that argument from any use I have to make of it in reference to my particular, to whom the meanest article of a Navy Officer's duty ever seemed of too much moment to be left unexecuted without the communication of it and the reasons thereof to the Lord High Admiral, let it not be thought ostentation for me to own the result of my humble labours in his Majesty's service by pretending to the having strictly answered every part of those Instructions incumbent on myself; and that in such method as to be willing to submit the same (while under the most tumultuous difficulties of a war) to be compared with and censured by what can be found of most methodical in any of my predecessors during the most leisurely time of peace, though (to say more) your Lordships shall at the same time find the work of my place to have exceeded by little less than a tenfold proportion that of my predecessors in the busiest time of their war.[1] Wherein your Lordships are humbly referred to the written evidences of both, now extant.

And yet, that after having thus acquitted myself in my particular duty I may not be found unmindful of what your Lordships seem to expect from each member in the justification of the acts of the whole, I shall take upon me further to say that though the fullness of my proper employment may (I doubt not) be reasonably offered in defence of my necessary concurrence with others in matters foreign thereto, yet forasmuch as through the frequent absences of my fellow Officers during the late war (and that sometimes for weeks together) hundreds of letters and warrants have for the dispatch of his Majesty's service been necessarily issued under my single hand and advice, I shall alone undertake

[1]In September 1668 Pepys drew up a calculation comparing the volume of office business transacted during the two Dutch wars, based on the number of letters, orders and contracts dealt with: PL 2242, p. 100. The figures are given in Tanner, *Catalogue*, i. 31 n. 3, and according to Tanner represent a sixfold increase.

for every such act, without the support of any defence for the possible imperfections thereof, deducible from my want of their advice, who stood equally obliged to an attendance with me on the same.

Nay further, forasmuch as though in the quality of my employment it hath in an especial manner been esteemed my part to subscribe to the determinations of the Board, it may have so happened that my advice has nevertheless taken place in matters where one only of my fellow Officers may with myself have been present at the debates, I am contented also to stand personally accountable for every such act of this Office vouched but by one hand more than my own; leaving to your Lordships the considering how far you will expect the like from me in cases where I shall be found subscribing only to the resolutions of a greater number, and those either by the nature or leisure of their proper places more concerned for and better instructed to guide the Board then and justify it now in the reasonableness of the same.

3dly – That as I expect not that either my diligence or best performances should be held worthy owning otherwise than as they are accompanied with integrity to my master and fair dealing towards those whom his service hath led me to have to do with, so I do with good assurance desire the whole world to allege one instance to the prejudice of the same, having the comfort of being able to affirm that my conscience in its strictest retrospections charges me not with any wilful declension from my duty, either in the faithfulness of my deportment therein, or care of rendering it the least expenseful to his Majesty – the execution of my place (under the utmost pressures of the war and the necessary increase of charge attending it) being to be found of less cost to his Majesty by one half than any other branch of the work of this Office, or what (by the necessary latitude given me with the rest of my fellows on that behalf) I might without censure have rendered my own to have been, and thereby not only gratified myself with a greater leisure of attending my private concernments, but prevented that untimely ruin of my eyes by the constancy of their night services during the war, which renders the remainder of my life of much less content or use to me than can be supplied by any other satisfaction than what flows from the consideration of that duty to his Majesty to which I sacrificed them.

And as to my behaviour towards others in reference to those gratifications which both practice and the quality of my place might justify an expectation and acceptance of, when (by the direction of the Lord High Admiral or the Board) employed in matters of lawful favour to private men, especially while the trust and burden of my place falling short of none of my fellows, no other reason than the consideration of such advantages incident thereto has been ever assigned for that difference of encouragement current amongst us by which the wages of the Clerk of the Acts stands inferior not only to what attends the lowest of his fellow Officers but to the avowed profits of some of their servants,[1] I shall with the same openness and truth wherewith your Lordships have in every other matter (relating no less to myself than others) found me ready to assist your inquiries humbly say:

1st – That from the first hour of my serving his Majesty in this employment I did never to this day directly or indirectly demand or express any expectation of fee, gratuity or reward from any person for any service therein by me done or to be done them.[2]

2dly – That no gratuity, though voluntarily offered, hath ever met with my acceptance where I found not the affair to which it did relate accompanied with the doing right or advantage to his Majesty.[3]

3dly – That the sums wherein I stand at this day in disburse on occasions wholly relative to the execution of my said employment during the war, and which (amounting to above 400*l.*) my fellow Officers have in their respective places either not at all known, or been reimbursed the same from his Majesty, do far exceed whatever profits have accrued to me from my said employment within that whole time.

4 – Lastly, that I have in this place been in general so little solicitous in the study of my private fortune as to own with fullest and most humble thankfulness the favour and bounties of his Majesty to me under my low endeavours therein; though in exchange for near ten years' service, and those the most valuable of my life for such improvements, I find not my estate at this day bettered by one thousand pounds from all the profits, salary or

---

[1] E.g. John Fenn, cashier to the Navy Treasurer: cf. above, pp. 119–23.
[2] The question of his alleged corruptibility is discussed in *Diary*, vol. i, pp. cxxiii-cxxiv.
[3] Cf. *Diary*, iv. 415: 'As I would not by anything be bribed to be unjust in my dealings, so I was not so squeemish as not to take people's acknowledgement where I have the good fortune by my pains to do them good and just offices.' The many gifts he received from Warren, the timber merchant, and Gauden, the Navy Victualler, did not deter him from joining his colleagues in criticising them.

other advantages arising from my said employment beyond what it was known to be at my admission thereto.[1]

Into the truth of all which I do not only invite but pray your Lordships to exercise your strictest inquisitions; being ready to justify the same not only by oath but by a double retribution of every penny or pennyworth of advantage I shall be found to have received either in manner or value different from what I have here declared.

Which leaving with your Lordships as an appendix in my own right to what you have already received from me on behalf of the Board in general, and submitting both to your disposal, I remain,

My Lords and Gentlemen,
Your Lordships' most humble and most faithful servant,
S. Pepys.
Navy Office,
6 January 1669[70].

Pepys's Address to the King, 8 Jan. 1670[2]

Sir,

Your Majesty's having been pleased with one hand to receive what has been offered you in charge against the Officers of your Navy, I cannot without offence to your justice doubt your vouchsafing me the other, for what in most humble manner I come to tender your Majesty in their and my own behalf, being a duplicate of what hath lately gone from me in answer to the Observations of the Commissioners of Accounts.

In which, as I have aimed at the doing all (fair) right to my fellow Officers, so has it not been without regard also to the honour of your Majesty's service, which seems not a little interested in the removal of what at this day meets (as I apprehend) with too easy an admission, namely that the different issues of the former and later war with the Dutch are chiefly chargeable on the different degrees of method and good husbandry exercised then and now by the managers of this Office.

---

[1] According to the best evidence – that of the Diary – £7000 would be nearer the mark: *Diary*, x. 103–4.
[2] PL 2554, pp. 5–8; 2874, pp. 509–11.

Not but that those acting in the former have [not] left us many things worthy imitation, and which I have not only borne witness to in my particular practice, but may one day have opportunity of doing it by a more solemn representation of them, as such, both to your Majesty and the public.[1]

But because better success did attend them than it has pleased God to allow us, that therefore this success must (to the depreciating all that comes after them) be necessarily referred to some transcendency in their methods, while the whole style of the transactions of that time demonstrates a principle, as in other things so in those of the Navy, wholly incompatible with that of forms; as having neither directed themselves by the ancient Instructions of the Lord High Admiral (now urged to our prejudice) nor bound themselves up by any other of their own. Nay, when neither in the balancing storekeepers' accounts, frequency of their surveys, tenderness in granting or regularity in clearing imprests, use of tickets or infallibility in their examinations, uninterestedness of their contracts or lowness of their prices, or any other of those circumstances wherein your Majesty's present Officers are deemed most peccant, they will be found to outdo or in many of them even to come up to what hath been arrived at under your Majesty's government. This (I say) seems a concession so injurious to the honour thereof as in faithfulness thereto I durst not in my following[2] discourse permit to pass unreflected on.

Especially when I consider not only the issue of what's past, wherein (as it will ever be in actions like this, while managed but by men and subject to disappointments from plague, fire, etc., neither to be foreseen nor obviated) so many real failures must inevitably be looked for as shall not need to be aggravated by the suggestion of others, which indeed are not; but [are] the fatal effects of any miscalculations of the means designed for securing your Majesty's better success to come.

To which mistake I cannot see what can contribute more than an assignment of our present miscarriages to the want of what our predecessors under all their successes were no greater masters of than we; but so much the contrary, that whoever shall have opportunity of taking the same leisurely view of the management

---

[1] His plans to work on a history of the Navy varied. In 1664 it was to be a history of the Cromwellian war; in 1668, a wider history: *Diary*, v. 178; ix. 26. The project never advanced beyond the collection of materials.
[2] Here printed above, pp. 271–330.

of that time which my employment under your Majesty has led me to will easily concur that there appears not anything in the whole conduct of that age to which (under God) their success can be more duly attributed than a steady pursuit of all means conducing thereto, both in preference and exclusion to all impediments arising from considerations either of thrift or method.

Of which, and what else my best observations upon the managements and events of these two great actions, together with the collections which by your Majesty's command I have at my late being abroad made on the same subject relating to our neighbours,[1] may have furnished me with, improvable to your Majesty's future service, neither my common duty as a subject nor especial obligations as the eldest (though otherwise the least worthy) of your Majesty's servants enjoying at this day the honour of that name in this Office will suffer me to want, much less to let slip, a more fit occasion of exposing to that gracious censure[2] with which your Majesty hath ever been pleased to encourage the humble offers of,
Royal Sir,
　　Your Majesty's most loyal, most obedient and faithful subject and servant,
Navy Office,　　　　　S. Pepys.
Janry 8th 1669[70].

Pepys's Address to the Duke of York, 8 Jan. 1670[3]

May it please your Royal Highness,

I beg leave of presenting your Highness with this transcript of what lately went from me to the Commissioners of Accounts in the general behalf of this Office.

Concerning which, having not on other occasions spared the opening to your Royal Highness what in its management hath appeared needing your notice and correction,[4] your Highness will

---

[1] For his recent visit to the Netherlands and France, see below, p. 334 & n.2. His 'collections' have not been traced, but a note written after his return enviously referred to the 'prodigality' of Dutch naval expenditure: below pp. 400–1.
[2] Esteem.
[3] PL 2554, p. 9; 2874, p. 512.
[4] The inquiry made in 1668 into the efficiency of the Navy Board: see below, p. 342.

not (I assure myself) be displeased with my present endeavours in its defence in matters challenging the same.

Which, with what I have since added in particular right to myself, is in all humility submitted to your Royal Highness's censure and favour by,

Sir,

Your Royal Highness's most obedient and most faithful servant,

S. Pepys.

Navy Office,
Janry 8. 1669[70].

(ii) PEPYS'S BROOKE HOUSE JOURNAL

A Journal of what passed between the Commissioners of Accounts and myself before his Majesty in Council, touching their Reports and Observations upon Sir George Carterett and the Navy Office; as also the pretended diversion of moneys to other uses than the war's[1]

At my return from France October 20. 1669, I met with a parcel of Observations sent to this Office by the said Commissioners in my absence.[2] To which the Lord Brouncker and Sir John Mennes had by letter referred them to my return for an answer.[3]

I applied myself as soon and as far as my business of Alborough and with the sickness and death of my dear wife would admit me to the preparing an answer thereto, which I compassed by the 27th of November,[4] and carried it myself the 29th, where finding the Commissioners out of the way, I left it with their clerk and my old acquaintance Mr Simmons,[5] having communicated the foul copy thereof only to the Duke of Yorke, Lord Brouncker and Sir Wm Coventry, the last of whose advice I took through the whole.

Once by order from the Committee of the House of Lords and another time by command of the Duke I attended their

---

[1]Printed from the only surviving copy, PL 2874, pp. 385–504. For the manuscript, see above, Introduction, pp. xxxv–xxxvi.
[2]Pepys, accompanied by his wife, had gone to the Low Countries and France in August.
[3]HLRO, Main Papers 26 Oct. 1669, 213 C, f. 64r (letter, 12 October): summary in HMC, *8th Report*, App., pt i. 131.
[4]For the answer, see above, pp. 271–325. The business of Aldeburgh was a parliamentary bye-election in which Pepys had been defeated by a local candidate: B. D. Henning (ed.), *Hist. Parl. The Commons 1660–90*, i. 395; R. G. Howarth (ed.), *Letters and Second Diary of S. Pepys* (1933), pp. 37–8. Polling had taken place on 9 November. His wife had died on the 10th.
[5]Will Symons (often mentioned in the early months of the Diary), an underclerk to the Commonwealth Council of State, had lost his place at the Restoration: *Diary*, x. 406.

examination of Sir G. Carterett's business,[1] and as there was occasion informed the Lords in what was before them, but never unasked, though even that did not suffice to prevent the dissatisfaction of the Lord Brereton and Col. Thomson[2] with my appearing at all in this business. December, I received order from the Clerk of the Council to attend the King therein, to do the like office at the Council Board upon occasion of his taking into examination of Sir Geo. Carterett's matters. And was from day to day verbally directed to repeat my attendance, which I did to the great satisfaction of the Commissioners of Accounts as well as good success to Sir George, who several times so far owned his obligations to me therein, though assisted by Mr Ayliff and my old chamber-fellow Mr Sawyer, counsellors,[3] as to tell me that he had more reason to present me with fees than his counsel; although I ever made it my care not to interpose in any wise between the said Commissioners and him upon any less warrant or inducement than the King's particular command, which I so far took care of and am able so far to justify, as to be able to appeal to the Commissioners themselves, among whom when the Lord Brereton did once or twice take occasion to stop me in my discourse, I ever replied that what I was doing was in obedience to the King's command, and therein appealing to his Majesty, he did always answer for me to my Lord Brereton that he had called upon me to speak and thereupon commanded me to proceed.

One thing I must remember, that when they came to the article of Sir George Carterett's charge relating to his paying moneys to the Officers of the Navy contrary to the Duke's Instructions, they in the list of the said Officers placed me in the van;[4] but my Lord Brereton did in the beginning of his discourse thereupon declare that they did think it their duties to name me, though they had lately received full satisfaction from me in this whole matter. Whereupon I begged leave to inform his Majesty that though justice be at all times welcome and that what they had now said to his Majesty they had already (unknown to me) declared on

---

[1] A committee of the House of Lords appointed on 6 November to consider the report of the Brooke House Commission had begun by considering the charges against Carteret: *LJ*, xii. 261–2; HLRO, Main Papers 26 Oct. 1669, 213 C, n.f.

[2] Lord Brereton was chairman of the Commission, and Col. George Thomson its spokesman on naval business.

[3] Joseph Ayloffe, of Gray's Inn, and Robert Sawyer (kt 1677 and later Attorney-General), a Magdalene contemporary of Pepys.

[4] Pepys was charged with having sold flags to the Navy.

the like occasion to the House of Lords, yet that it had been a much more obliging part in him to have done me the same right in the House of Commons, with whom they suffered it to be received, as it does at this day remain, as a blemish or at least a ground of dissatisfaction against me, though I appealed now to them whether they had ever received any other satisfaction from me than what I gave them by letter in August last, long before the meeting of and therefore much more before their delivering their report to the House of Commons. To which the Lord Brereton replying that they had not then had time to consider my answer, but that however they had done me the right to lodge my said answer in the House of Commons, where he said it now lay; I answered that as I had given the said Commissioners no new satisfaction (wherein I appealed to themselves) so I did observe in like manner to the King, that at the instant that I brought my letter to them about this matter of flags, 'twas read to them in my presence by my old acquaintance Mr Simmons, now their clerk. To which he made no return, but the King and everybody else as well as the said Commissioners declaring their being satisfied in the business, I suffered it to go off, and so it ended.

Janry 3. 1669[70]. By letter from Sir G. Downing[1] this day, I was commanded from the Lords of the Treasury to meet with and assist Sir Robt Long and Sir Philip Warrick in the preparing an answer to the exceptions made by the Commissioners of Accounts to several sums claimed in Sir G. Carterett's account to the value of 514,000*l.* which (to use their own words) they most humbly conceive are for other uses than the war.[2]

Accordingly I met them at Sir Philip Warwick's, where with Sir G. Carterett we run over the particulars, and I taking the minutes of the particular points wherein they could help me, though very unsatisfactory to me, give me matter of much wonder to find a case of such importance to the King no earlier studied nor at this day better understood. They committed it to me to digest, with the addition of my own thoughts thereupon, so as to be able to manage the matter on behalf of his Majesty before the Commissioners of Accounts at the Council Board.

[1] Secretary to the Treasury Commissioners, whom Pepys had served as a clerk in the Exchequer under the Commonwealth.
[2] Above, pp. xxxii–xxxiii. This was the most serious charge they made: see below, pp. 366–7, 372–5.

Janry 4th. Sir Rt Long, Sir Philip Warwick and myself attended the Lords of the Treasury early in the morning. Where Sir John Duncomb only present, with whom having discoursed a little on this matter, he carried us up to the King, where present the Duke of York, the Lord Keeper,[1] [the] Duke of Ormond, both the Secretaries of State[2] and others, the manner of managing this matter was considered and the doing of it laid by the King upon me, to be assisted as there should be occasioned by the said two knights in points relating to the Treasury.

Then going into the Council Chamber, and all persons called in, there was found to appear on behalf of the Commissioners of Accounts the Lord Brereton only, who informed his Majesty that Col. Thomson was come as far as Brooke House with intention of accompanying him to the Council, but that there he found himself so ill as not to be able to go further, and that for the rest of them, they were wholly strangers to the matter in hand, by reason that that part of the work of their Commission which respects the Navy was committed to and examined by Col. Thomson only of the whole number.[3] Upon which score the rest thought it unnecessary for them to attend here. Upon which the King judging it unfit to enter upon this matter without Col. Thomson as being one heretofore conversant in matters of the Navy, the Board adjourned till the next morning if then Col. Thomson should be in condition to attend.

January 5. This morning Col. Thomson being present with others of their number besides my Lord Brereton, the King entered upon the debate, where after their sending him more at large that which was abstractedly set down in their report, it was in the first place observed that from what (on occasion of Sir G. Carteret's business) had been touched upon by me and others relating to the general charge of the war, they did in this paper expressly own this 514,000*l.* to have been paid out on uses of the Navy, though in their report they were so far silent therein as, by saying only that it was for other uses than the war, to have given occasion to the world's believing that it had been to uses

---
[1]Sir Orlando Bridgeman.
[2]Arlington and Sir John Trevor.
[3]His colleagues concentrated on Treasury matters. Thomson had served as a Commissioner of the Admiralty and Navy in the Commissions appointed in December 1652, May 1659 and February 1660: Aylmer, *State's Servants*, p. 14; Firth and Rait, *Acts and Ordinances*, ii. 1277, 1407.

of pleasure or other private respects of his Majesty's, which it will be very hard now by any means to undeceive them in. Of which the King largely expressed his resentment, and was thereupon answered by them, that they had it in their expectation to have opportunity of doing his Majesty right therein when they came to open this matter in Parliament; and being then minded by the Lord Keeper of what they some days since, upon occasion of Sir G. Carterett's business, voluntarily declared at the Board, that his Majesty had laid out above 300,000*l.* on the occasions of the Navy out of his private revenue more than what would satisfy this 514,000*l.*; they did again own the same, and in proof that they did purpose to do his Majesty right therein, they tendered to the King a copy of an account they delivered to the House of Commons[1] by the House's command and subsequent to their report, wherein they pretend to have shown them how much his Majesty had disbursed of his private revenue on the service of the war and Navy. But upon reading this it proved not satisfactory in regard to what it seemed to say of advantage to the King in one place, it seemed to take it away again in another. But upon the whole they did publicly own what is above said, *viz.* that the King had disbursed of his private revenue more by 300,000*l.* than what would clear this 514,000*l.*, and so the whole audience comprehended it. Then the King commanded me to open their report by particulars relating to this 514,000*l.*, which I did in a manner greatly satisfactory to the King and audience, though the contrary to the Commissioners of Accounts at least in two particulars. The one, that wherein I greatly surprised them as well as the King's officers too, which was my denying the 1st of Sepbr 1664 to be reputed for the commencement of the war, or that the Act did make either that day or any other day the bounds of the war's beginning,[2] but that whatever was done by his Majesty and whenever preparative to the war, all was to be reckoned within the war and the intent of the Parliament's grants of money for the maintenance of the same. Which having largely opened, my Lord Brereton replied that he wondered that one Com-

---

[1] BL, Add. MSS 30999, ff. 1*r*–3*r* (printed *CTB 1667–8*, pp. lviii-lix). According to these figures, the King had spent £439,174 from his customs revenue and £339,960 from his prize money.

[2] According to the preamble of the Act, 1 Sept. 1664 was the date from which calculations of the expenses of the war were to be made – that is to say the cost of the naval actions of 1664 prior to the declaration of war in the following February (mostly in N. Africa and N. America) was not to be included.

missioner of the Navy should undertake the construction of an Act contrary to the judgement of nine Commissioners appointed by that Act, to which I replied that I look upon this Act like all other statutes penned for the information and therefore to the understanding of every Commissioner, and that therefore as an Englishman and as one principally concerned therein I did challenge a right of delivering my sense of it, especially in a matter wherein as I conceived there lay so little mystery, and therefore till his Majesty's learned counsel had delivered their opinion therein I desired mine might be admitted in behalf of his Majesty.

The other was upon occasion of my saying that the inferring (as is pretended) from an estimate of the Navy Office which would not amount to 90,000*l*, that the ordinary charge of the Navy during the war did come up to 190,000*l*.,[1] was an unjustifiable inference. To which my Lord Breereton very eagerly replied that he did believe that gentleman would not say what he had now said in another place,[2] which being an insolence more reflective on the honour of his Majesty and that Board than myself, I silently suffered to pass, expecting that the King or some of the Lords would in their own honour have taken notice of it, as several of them afterwards told me, it had been but fit they should, though at this juncture and with these men, it was more prudent for the King indeed to take no notice of it. But the King did afterwards at dinner call me his advocate, and made much sport with my Lord Brereton's manners and dissatisfaction with my opposing him and his eight brethren in the construction of their own lesson.

Janry 6. Waiting at noon upon his Royal Highness and praying his getting me opportunity of waiting upon his Majesty and himself to offer something relating to what passed yesterday at the Council, he directed me to attend the King and him at dinner, after which they were pleased with my Lord Arlington to withdraw with me to a corner of the room, where I began first to desire I might receive his Majesty's censure[3] of my performance yesterday, which his Majesty was pleased to tell me it was to his perfect satisfaction, giving me several times thanks for my care therein. He also, upon my humble demand concerning it, told me that he did not apprehend that I had said anything unbefitting him

---

[1] It amounted to £80,000 in 1670: BL, Add. MSS 11602, f. 224*r*.
[2] That is, in Parliament, which was now in recess. Cf. Brereton's similar charge below, p. 358.
[3] Opinion.

in reference to the Commissioners of Accounts, and thereupon enlarged very earnestly upon the ill behaviour of my Lord Breerton in relation both to himself and me, in all which his Royal Highness and my Lord Arlington took occasions of signifying their concurrence with his Majesty to my advantage. I thereupon prayed leave that since what had been by me said found satisfaction with his Majesty as well as it seemed to do to all that were present at the debate, I humbly advised that his Majesty would be pleased to consider by what ways to improve the same, so as (if possible, which I expressed my doubt of and therein was seconded both by his Majesty and the rest) to rectify the opinions of the world occasioned by this reporting of these gentlemen that his Majesty had employed to his private uses of pleasure, etc., not only the 514,000*l.* here mentioned but near 300,000*l.* more in the moneys applied to the Ordnance and Guards. Here my Lord Arlington took occasion to put his Majesty in mind of what (as he said) he had the last night advised his Majesty, *viz.* that his Majesty would be pleased to cause the substance of this discourse to be put into writing, and that therefore as he did believe that Mr Pepys was the best informed of any man to do his Majesty this service, so (he added) that though Mr Pepys was by, yet he should not refrain to say that his style was excellent and the fittest to perform this work; though he would have it recommended to him to study the laying it down with all possible plainness, and with the least show of rhetoric if he could. Which motion the King embraced, and accordingly laid it upon me as a matter much importing him. Wherein I humbly submitted myself to his Majesty's disposal, and in order thereto offered it as my opinion that it would be necessary for me in matters relating to the Exchequer and construction of the Act to have the assistance of Sir Robt Long, Sir Philip Warwick and the King's Counsel. His Majesty referred me therein to be supplied by my Lord Arlington, and so with expressions of his gracious opinion of my services dismissed me.

I went home this day full of intentions to send a letter to my Lord Brereton testifying a due resentment of his yesterday's challenge in his Majesty's presence and while in debate of a matter strictly relating to his Majesty. But upon second thoughts suspended it, until I had seen further.

Jan. 7th. I attended this morning my Lord Arlington and received his letter to Sir Philip Warwick, making an advantageous mention of my discourse at the Council Board and bespeaking me in his Majesty's name both his own assistance, Sir R. Long's and the King's Counsel. This done I do visit Sir W. Coventry, whom I had not seen from before my sending him my general answer to Brooke House.[1] I dined with him and find that both him and Sir John Duncomb did labour to bespeak my expectation of receiving all severe usage from the House of Commons, which I without much trouble do embrace the thoughts of, as being much more willing to be at ease than hold[2] my employment with so much trouble as I have of long done and must still look for, while yoked with persons who every day make work for future censure, while I am upon the tenters in their preservation from the blame due to their failures past.

Monday Janry 10th. By order of Council dated [Jan. 7th][3] brought to the Board on Saturday this Office was directed to attend the Council to answer to the Observations relating to their management. Before the Council met [I met] the Duke of York walking in the Park, who upon seeing me told me that he had newly met Sir W. Coventry (who was walking in the Mall with Sir Philip Warwick), and that he had told them that he was concerned in this morning's work in the Council, to which I replied that I could wish he were concerned a little nearer us. Whereto the Duke publicly answered that that were too much in all conscience for the Commissioners of Accounts, Willm Coventry and me both upon them at once; and repeated the same aloud to Sir Wm Coventry when meeting him at his next turn, who answered that he reckoned himself safe enough in Mr Pepys alone. Thence to the Council Chamber, where, before the King and Board met, I by the Duke of York got the King to withdraw into his closet with the Duke and me, where I presented him with a copy not only of my general answer but of another bound up with it containing a particular answer relating to myself dated the 6th inst., which I forgot to mention in its proper place, and my sending it to [the] Commissioners of Accounts by Wm Griffen

---

[1]Coventry was a Commissioner of the Treasury, but no longer a Commissioner of the Navy.
[2]MS 'would' – a mishearing by the clerk who was writing at the dictation of a colleague: cf. above, Introduction, pp. xxxv–xxxvi & n. The vowel sounds of 'would' and 'hold' were similar in this period.
[3]Blank in MS.; date supplied from draft minutes of Council: BL, Stowe MSS 489, f. 250v.

the 7th. Before these two I affixed an epistle to his Majesty,[1] which at my presenting him the book I took liberty to read, and then gave it him, desiring that his Majesty would be pleased not to look upon me as one asserting the management of the Navy so as to desire to be understood as if there had been no failures in our management, for failures there had been, and not only myself had done my duty in representing the same to his Royal Highness, but his Royal Highness proceeded long since to the providing proper and timely remedies for the same.[2] But that forasmuch as the greatest part of them would be found imputable to the age and weakness of a servant by name Sir John Mennes, who besides the merit of having served his royal grandfather, father and himself, spending his whole youth and strength therein,[3] was moreover one that would be found a gentleman of strictest integrity, and that his weakness both of mind and body had been hastened upon by him his labours in his Majesty's service in unseasonable attendances upon pays of ships, etc., I prayed that his Majesty allow me liberty, when in my discourse I should be led to the confessing some frailties of his, to mention him with tenderness under the character I have here given him, and as one whom in that regard his Majesty had been pleased to indulge under a more imperfect execution of his duty than what ought and would have been expected from another. Wherein being seconded by his Royal Highness, his Majesty was pleased to own with great kindness his well liking of all I had done and said, and directing me to act accordingly, he went forth and so to the Council Chamber. Where all being settled, the Lord Brereton acquainted his Majesty of the attendances to which they had of some time been obliged upon his Majesty and the two Houses of Parliament having prevented them in making the uses of the answers they had received from this Board which otherwise they should have done, they were not in present readiness to make any regular entrance upon their Observations relating thereto, and therefore proposed that, forasmuch as it was possible, upon perusal of our several papers they might find reason of discharg-

---

[1] These documents are reproduced above, p. 271–332.
[2] In July 1668 Pepys had submitted a long report to the Duke about the Board's failures. It had led to the Duke's calling for reforms: see above, p. 252 & n. 1.
[3] Born in 1599, he had served in the Navy since his youth, holding several commands from 1626. (He had also held high military command in the Scottish War and the Civil War.) During the revolution he had been a Rear-Admiral under Rupert, and a royalist agent abroad; at the Restoration he was C-in-C of the Narrow Seas 1661–2.

ing either the whole Board of some particulars of the said Observations, or some particular members of us in reference to those single duties, which by the way my Lord Brouncker meeting me this morning in the Park, told me that he had upon conference just then with the Lord Brereton found his Lordship owning an inclination to think, from some new light he had received upon perusal of four several answers to what he before thought equally incumbent upon the whole, his Majesty would be pleased to allow them some time to peruse and consider our several answers, that so he might not necessarily trouble his Majesty in what they could without it receive satisfaction from us. Here his Royal Highness rose up, saying that the proposition was very reasonable, provided that when in those they should receive satisfaction [in], it might not be thought sufficient for them to say that they were satisfied, but that the grounds of such their satisfaction should be laid open to his Majesty and the Lords, that they also, since our crimes were public, might be as publicly informed in the grounds of our being discharged thereof. Which being said, his Majesty signified his full approval of it, and adjourned the Board till Monday next, directing us in the meantime to attend the Commissioners of Accounts in order to their satisfaction as often as it should be demanded of us.

Wednesday Janry 12. In pursuance of a warrant brought yesterday to the Board, we, *viz.* Lord Brouncker, Mennes, Middleton and myself attended Brooke House, where having chairs set us, and there being present Mr Dunster, chairman, Sir Wm Turner, Sir James Langham, Col. Osborne, Mr Gregory and towards the end my Lord Halifax came, they administered the usual oath to us. Which being done, they asked us each for himself whether the papers come from each of us were true; to which we separately swore that they were. They then demanded whether that which I had given in, as the general answer of the Board, was also true. My Lord Brouncker answered yes, as to all that concerned him. Sir John Mennes did the like, though, poor man, to that day he had not seen one word of it. Then they came to me with the same question, and received answer from me that I neither had wrote nor presented it to them as the general answer of the Board, I neither having had their advice therein, nor made them privy to it. At which being much surprised, they presently asked me what I meant by it. I replied that my meaning was plainly express[ed], which I then read to them, declaring it to be but my private essay towards their general answer. To which they seemed prepared to make us no present return, but that in regard they came not to them under oath they neither could nor had taken notice of these papers, and so had not considered in what name I had sent them this book. To which I might, but forbore to, answer not only that in their letter to the Board desiring the Duke's instructions at Oxford about payment of money,[1] they had grounded this their demand expressly upon Mr Pepys's late report, but that being this morning bid with the rest of us to withdraw into the back room, I found Sir Jonathan Trelawney busy with one of the accountants of this Office, where he told me he was beholden to me for the trouble he was now put to by denying to have received what prizes and prize goods he as one of the commissioners thereof at Plymouth had charged this Office with. Where looking on the tables, I found a copy of my notes on the 18th Article[2] made the measure of their inquiries, and upon discourse with Sir Jonathan, as well as lately with Mr Newport,[3] do understand that upon the arrival of my general answer they found themselves at a loss to prove that article, and therefore sent to the several Prize Officers concerned, giving them as I understand to the end of this month to justify what they in their report had so peremptorily charged us with so long since. They then began to talk loosely of the want of Sir Wm Warren's account,[4] asking when the same would be fully finished. Whereto my Lord Brounker answered he believed not these three months. They then seemed much to wonder at it, and one of them (Sir Wm Turner) moved that they might give that answer to the King which my Lord had now given them, and desired the chairman to ask in whose particular hands the dispatch of those accounts lay. To which Sir John Mennes answered that it lay in his, and that he had taken much pains therein and employed two [of] the ablest accountants in London about them; that he had also made several objections long ago to the account and lodged them at the Board, and that he could never get Sir W. Warren to satisfy him therein. And so was running on (God knows whither) when Sir Wm Turner desired that he might have a plain answer in whose charge the stating of Sir W. Warren's account lay. I then spoke, telling them that to give it them plainly and shortly, it lay,

[1] See below, p. 421.
[2] For the 'Article' (Observation), see above, p. 317.
[3] Andrew Newport, sub-commissioner of prizes, Portsmouth.
[4] See above, p. 148 & n. 1.

as Sir John Mennes had rightly told them, in his particular hand as Comptroller to state these as all other accounts. But that from a certain time upon petition of Sir W.W. to the Duke for better dispatch, his Highness had directed the Lord Brounker to join with him in the stating of this particular account;[1] so that it at this day lay under the care of Sir J. Mennes with the assistance of the Lord Brounker. Here Col. Thomson would have entered into a discourse upon what he hath frequently hinted at, that the 18th of our General Instructions[2] entitled the whole Board to seeing every particular member's duty performed. To which I returned that this would be found an objection very easily solved when it should be thought seasonable to enter into the debate thereof, which some of the Commissioners saying it was not a matter to be disputed now, Thomson run on to say that he wondered it should be thought Sir John Mennes's duty, when in the Hambrough business Sir J.M. hath made oath that he never knew anything of that undertaking, neither in the beginning nor progress of it. To which nobody else making answer, I also was silent, leaving it to the having an answer more seasonable given to it when that matter shall be brought on the stage, and expecting an opportunity of confronting the oath then with the oath he this day made before the Commissioners of Accounts relating to my general answer, showing the esteem that ought to be laid upon the words and performances of this weak gentleman. They then asked whether these papers contained all we had to answer to the said Observations, to which Br., J.M. and myself answered no, but desired the liberty claimed by each of us in our single papers of offering what we had further to say to them as the same should occur to us upon debate, only the Lord Brouncker did by memory add a particular or two of no great moment which he had before omitted. And so without anything considerable more we departed, without hearing further from them before Monday following, saving by a letter wherein they demand an account of all those particulars which have in any bills passed within the war been referred to as remaining in the Navy Office.

Monday Janry 17th. The King met again in the Council Chamber where all being settled, the Lord Brereton, Thomson, Langham and Turner present in their side, Lord Brouncker,

---
[1] See above, p. 176 & n. 1.
[2] *Oeconomy*, pp. 39–40.

Mennes and myself with Sir Jere. Smith, Middleton and Tippets standing by one of us, Breereton produce[d] a paper containing an instance on the 1st Observation, namely Sir W.W.'s Gottenburgh contract for masts July 1664;[1] which being read, I took upon me to speak to the King, beginning with the laying a foundation for his distinguishing between what we were accountable for as particular Officers and what as a joint Board, declaring our not appearing there in the name of a Board, as having neither power nor lying under any duty of doing so; taking notice of the little advance made of so long time by the said Commissioners [in] the examining our answers since they were delivered to them, saying that though it had the appearance of a delay, yet that as to myself I was under no haste, being most willing to begin my defence where they pleased, be it with his Majesty or the Lords or the Commons, having nothing in design to offer in satisfaction to the King but what I was bold to say should prove every whit as satisfactory anywhere else, and that therefore whatever should be aimed of picking up all that could be a disadvantage to this Office, without notice taken of ought that should appear to its advantage, yet I humbly submitted it to his Majesty to choose his own method, whether by examining us apart in reference to our particular duties, or summoning the whole Board to join in a general answer, or entering upon what I as a private man had presented his Majesty with as my conceptions touching what might be expected in defence of the whole.

To this his Majesty resolved to begin with my answer, as if it were the general answer of the Board, and as we come to any points relating to this or that particular Officer to call for satisfaction from that Officer.

I then desired leave to read the preface and close of the said answer, which being done, I turned to that part of my reply to the 1st Observation, which relates to Sir W.W.'s Gottenburg contract.

But before I proceed further I must remember that so soon as I had done with the first discourse touching a supposed delay in the proceedings of the Commissioners of Accounts, or rather my taking opportunity of declaring an indifference whether my examination should commence with the King or Lords or Commons, the Lord Breereton cried with much vehemence that he wondered that that person durst say that concerning him which

[1] See above, pp. 273–7.

he would not say in another place, or words to that purpose, saying that they were far from studying any delay on purpose of bringing matters to the House of Commons rather than to his Majesty.[1] Upon which the Duke of York rose up and said that [as] his Majesty would not admit any unfit language to be used to them, so he thought it was not in his intentions to bear with any words as those my Lord Breereton had spoke, which expressed want of reverence to him and the place he was now in. At which my Lord Breereton seemed much troubled, offering at some short imperfect excuse; the whole assembly appearing much scandalized at what he said, when the King told him that he did not see any just cause Mr Pepys had given him of being so much concerned, he having not charged him with any endeavour of delay, but only declared that he should not esteem such a delay anyways injurious to him who was ready to make his defence as willingly before the Lords or Commons as [before] himself.

Where I am to remember that when I said this I did add that it was true I did in duty esteem it my part to labour after the giving his Majesty satisfaction in the first place, whose servant I was, whose bread I had long eaten, and for whose particular satisfaction the Parliament page 14 of their Act declare all these their inquiries to be designed.[2]

Here we entered into the merits of the cause and I showing, first, the performing of this contract to have been solemnly already inquired into, and declared to have been performed on Sir W. Warren's part, by Sir W. Batten himself.

I appealed to the King and Duke, who both remembered their being particularly consulted with in the framing this contract.

To their objecting the great charge the King was at in convoy to fetch the masts home, the King himself answered that the convoy was not sent only for his goods, but to answer also the importunities of his merchants to bring home theirs. Which answer was not only useful but wholly new to me, and what Sir W.W. tells me is true, there coming under that convoy about forty merchantmen besides the King's goods.

[1] Parliament being then in recess.
[2] Sect. iii of the Act establishing the Commission required the Commissioners to give the King a 'full and true account of how the said moneys have been disbursed or disposed of'. The reference here is presumably to the printed sessional copy. (The page number is unlikely and is possibly the result of a mishearing by the clerk.)

To their urging the great numbers of small masts wherewith their stores were clogged, I showed them how soon after the delivery of each of the two great parcels of masts by Sir W. Warren[1] great demands of small masts under 14 hands were demanded in each yard; that at the end of this war there were remaining three times as many masts above 14 as under 14 hands, to the great prejudice of his Majesty by so many great masts at this day lying unemployed; that since the war we have been driven to buy great quantities of small masts.

Tomson most ignorantly urging that there was more use of great than small masts in a war, I appealed to Sir Jeremy Smith as a seaman, and run him down so as to make him laughed at.

They brought an affidavit of Comr Pett's, wherein he basely complains of the illness of this contract; its not being performed; that the stores lying clogged with small masts which lay rotting in creeks, and were cut into sheathing board, etc.[2] To which I replied that I appealed to Mr Tippets and all present whether ever sheathing board was cut out of rotten wood. I then took notice of the unhappiness the King's Officers serving in this war lay under, beyond any of his Majesty's subjects triable in any other court, where as Englishmen they have a right of confronting their accusers at the time of their giving evidence, whereas we are liable to evidences taken we know not when, and not shown us till the minute we are appointed to answer. Where the Lord Brereton stopping me, saying that this was but what Mr Ayliff had several times urged in opposition to the plain Act of Parliament limiting them to no such rule of proceeding, I told him that what I had said was not to find fault so much with their proceedings or the power given them in the Act, but to bemoan the infelicity we above all others lay under by it. I then read the memorandum of the Board declaring Sir W.W.'s performance of contract, signed by Pett himself; at which the King and the whole audience showed great surprise at his perfidiousness in this deposition, and more when I read to them a letter of the Board to Sir W.W. of the 4th January 1665[6], signed by him also, wherein they again owned the great[3] satisfaction he had given them in the performance of his contract.

Here Col. Thomson was driven to say that they could not but

---
[1] See above, p. 36.
[2] See above, pp. 67–8.
[3] MS. 'with a great advantage the late'.

make the use they did of this deposition, not being able to judge of the truth of it, to which the King yielded, as to their doing their parts, but did severely take notice of the villainy and hypocrisy of Pett. The King did also himself declare that, when he was below at Chatham, Pett made use of no other excuse for his delay in supplying the fleet then at the Nore but the want of small masts.

Nay, against this shall be urged again in Parliament, I may provide myself to show not only the letters that passed between him and me touching this contract in July (as I take it) 1665, but the demands which had been from time to time made from Chatham, and a letter as I remember that he wrote to the Board, whereto we answered that he must make the best shift he could, for more masts we could not supply him with. And for their being unfit and unserviceable, it was no man's duty of the Board so much as his to stop the receipt thereof or complain of the same to the Board; which I appeal to him whether he ever did or no. For what he says of masts lying in creeks it is possible that this is no more than that for want of his care to keep the under-officers to their duty the King's masts were suffered to go adrift, till they met with some creeks and there lay, from whence since his leaving the Navy[1] several masts have been recovered by care of the look-outs.

For what he saith in his deposition that he never dealt for Navy goods since the King's coming in, but for a parcel of timber of the Duke of Albermarl's;[2] I observed it as a proof how much worse the management of the Navy is to be thought under his Majesty's government than it was in the late times, when Mr Pett could do no more than this now, who was able to do so much more of the same kind (as I am able to show) in the time of usurpation.

They brought also an affidavit of Mr Wood's charging us with making a prejudicial contract – that masts might have been had at better terms in the said time [and] that we were forced afterwards to buy masts of him at dearer rates.

I showed that Mr Wood was invited with others when the contract was made,[3] that no terms so good were offered by him or anybody; that the masts he offered had been viewed and

---

[1]Pett was suspended from his commissionership at Chatham in September 1667 and dismissed in the following February: Tanner, *Catalogue*, i. 15 & n. 6.

[2]This was in May 1667 when, along with two timber merchants, he bought timber from Albemarle's estate at New Hall, Essex: *CSPD 1667*, p. 17.

[3]See above, p. 311.

dubbed[1] by Comr Pett and me and found sap-rotten and decayed in 1662, and the best picked out that there were at any time to be had; that the buying these proves the contrary to that which is aimed at, namely, that the stores were clogged with small masts, for these were not masts of those great dimensions which Sir W.W. is reproached for the non-delivery of; I appeal to their best information by Mr Pett, Wood, or otherways, whether any bigger masts were brought into England or could have been brought than those we had; I challenged any man to show where the service suffered any injury for the want of great masts during the war. I showed lastly that Mr Wood was a party in the complaint as having been greatly disappointed by our sending this merchant to market, we having in several years after the King came in not been able to serve ourselves with masts from any hands but his or Capt. Talor's, so that he hath evermore endeavoured to bring disgrace upon this contract.

They then urged that offers were made us by others to serve us with masts cheaper upon condition, to which word they were no sooner come but the King prevented them, saying upon condition that they might have them in Dutch names covertly and trade with the Dutch,[2] which condition, saith the King, I leave any man to judge how much more beneficial that would have been to me, which unexpected stroke from the King himself (being new, I confess, to me as well as them, but very seasonable) struck them dumb. This I perceive they had from Capt. Shorter, and as I remember, Pett said something of it in his deposition, as I am sure I did to him in my above-mentioned letter of July 1665.

[*Marginal note*] This was Mr Shorter whom Comr Pett had tampered with as Pett in his own deposition discovered, and as appears by a deposition of Shorter's of which I have got a copy, and proves unexspectively advantageous to us, offering to serve us upon no other terms than that of convoy or a dispensation from the Act of Navigation.

Then Thomson abruptly told me that we had got a new way of measuring masts at the butt-ends.[3] I asked him whether this

[1] Trimmed.
[2] Dutch dealers sold naval stores to English dealers right up to the outbreak of war, and possibly beyond.
[3] For Warren's account of this dispute, see BL, Add. MSS 9316, ff. 105–6. Thomson alleged that Warren had been overpaid for his masts by having them measured from the butt-ends rather than from the partners.

were any other way than what he used to measure a mast in his time. He replied shortly that he neither did nor had anything to do with measuring of masts. I told him that I meant not him but his under-officers, and did affirm that if any other way was now used of measuring masts than the old way of doing it at the partners (unless where as to the ascertaining the lengths of masts we had in our time regulated this matter beyond all that ancient practice could show us) it was not by our order or with our privity; but if to the King's disadvantage the fault ought to be charged upon the mast-measurer, which we should punish as soon as discovered, but I did verily believe there was no such thing. Thomson answered me that he was able to show a bill filled up with a considerable quantity of masts, wherein they were expressly said to be measured at the butt. I told him when we saw it it should have an answer.

Memorandum: that having since spoke with Sir W. W. about this business, he tells me that such a bill there is, filled up as he remembers by Mr Fist, then a new clerk not acquainted with the form of a mast bill, and that he is able to make it appear that the masts were measured in the manner they ought to be, and it was only a mistake of the clerk in wording the bill.

Besides, saith he, if by butt they mean the very butt-end, it is a folly to think any mast-merchant so ignorant, for that several feet from the very end towards the foot of the mast they taper it again.

Then Tomson started in the same abrupt manner a cavil about Sir W.W.'s not delivering to the King the right masts which were but as a present to him from those of New England.[1] The thing being wholly new as well as improper to the thing in hand, I told him that Sir W.W. ought to give satisfaction to those of New England, and that neither the King nor his officers were concerned in it, the King saying, very well, that he thought it a very worthy present and received what was given him without looking the given [sic] horse in the mouth.

[*Marginal note*] Since this, Sir W.W. being told thereof by the Board, he hath brought us a very full proof from Woolwich yard of his having done full right both to those of New England and the King in this business. *Vide* the certificate.

Upon discourse with Sir W.W. since, I am sensible that in my

---

[1]The phrase 'those of New England' here and later in the sentence and at p. 137 above means the people of New England, a phrase which occurs at p. 352.

opening the terms of this contract [I] thought it succeeded very well, yet whereas I insisted only upon the preface of it, wherein it is said 'that in order to the supplying his Majesty stores', and not 'that he did undertake to supply his Majesty's stores', I might, had my memory been ripe in the terms of the contract, have to very good purpose gone further and said that even in what he did undertake to bring, namely two ships' lading by Christmas 1664 and four more by July following (in pursuance of which I showed them that he did not only actually deliver five ships' lading, but – had they not miscarried at sea – would have delivered four more before the said December) he was not obliged to bring these further than 'with submission to the seas and restraint of princes', and as to their dimensions not at all otherways than the biggest he can procure. Which serves to admonish me when this shall come to be re-argued to be sure to read over afresh the contract itself.

Thus ended this day's work with an adjournment till Thursday next, with appearance of most perfect satisfaction to the King, the Board and all bystanders.

Wednesday Janry 19th. I received a letter from Brooke House demanding speedy satisfaction from me whether and what notice (if any) Sir W.W. did give the Board pursuant to his contract before the end of April 1665 of his ability or inability to bring further quantities of masts that year.

Thursday Janry 20. We attended his Majesty again at the Council Board, where the Commissioners of Accounts fell upon the second contract, *viz.* for New England masts,[1] insisting upon his having delivered much short both in time, number and dimensions the quantity he undertook. Whereto I showed that by the contract, danger of the seas was excepted, and accordingly a ship he lost, *viz.* the [*Neptune*],[2] that he stayed for convoy as might appear by the evidences, I said I was then ready to show of his applications to us from time to time for convoy, that of the thirty-six great masts he did deliver about twenty-five including the two which he had provided and shipped in part of his contract, though afterwards at the desire of the people of New England they were delivered to the King as a present from them, that he did deliver

---
[1]That of 16 Aug. 1664: HMC, *Lindsey* (*Supp.*), p. 147.
[2]Blank in MS.; name supplied from HMC, loc. cit. p. 148.

(afterwards at our particular desires by several letters I was then ready to show), smaller masts from New England grounded upon the notice we had of the incertainty or rather improbability of our being supplied with the great masts we desired from Gottenburgh. Upon which consideration, we by two letters which I was ready to show authorized him to bring masts from New England answering those dimensions which he would have had from Gottenburgh, and therein by the advice of the Surveyor were more pressing to have these than the whole number of the great ones, and that not without good reason, as may be collected from the number of great masts of New England now lying useless and perishing in stores, and the want of those of the lesser dimensions.

Here the King endeavoured to bring it to a short issue by asking what damage his service had received by having of too few great ones (as is by them supposed) and too many little ones. I answered by appealing to them as I did the other day, whether they can assign any one case where the King's service suffered any delay or prejudice from the want of great masts during the whole war. To which they (as then) made no reply, but suffered that point to be gained for our advantage. It comes in my mind now what I have no sooner thought of, but may perhaps be useful hereafter, to inquire in which sort of masts whether the greater or less the profit of the merchant may be thought most to lie, it seeming to me that it should lie in the greater, which should it prove true would become an unanswerable plea for the impartiality of our proceedings in reference to the merchant by suffering him (as is suggested) to clog the stores with small in lieu of great masts. And further I do not remember that I have yet made use of this answer to their general complaint of our clogging the stores with unnecessary masts, which by my own confession is true, though in a quite contrary sense to what they charge us with, who lay it upon our excess in small masts, whereas most obviously it ought (if at all) to be objected to our lavishness in buying of great masts; which answer is this, *viz.*, that whereas they have said that he [who] would build a brick wall would first calculate the length and other dimensions of it, and then govern himself thereby in the number of bricks he should provide for doing the same, it is to be replied that in a war no dimensions can be taken at least by us under-officers of the duration of that war, and that therefore we have no other rule to guide us in our proportions of stores than the consideration of the prejudice his Majesty's service would be liable to by any want, and not by what possible damage he might sustain from a surplusage of stores resting at the end of the war. Besides that, as I remember, our very Instructions leads us even in time of peace to the labouring after the being possessed of a year's stores of all sorts of sea service for [the] whole fleet;[1] and if so, how much more ought to be done under an uncertain war, especially when we reflect on the Lord High Admiral's farewell letter Janry 1664[5] cautioning us against the blame that would arise from any damage his Majesty should receive either from thrift in general or the want of this very species of goods in particular.[2]

Memorandum: that some want I found of it this day makes it necessary for me against our further debates on this matter in Parliament to have my quotations of letters, warrants and other papers regularly set down in a paper in my hand, with reference to the papers themselves in another, to attend me to prevent either my forgetting to make the benefit of them or being at too much trouble in the turning to them.

They then went to the giving an instance of our expending his Majesty's money upon stores unuseful and what should it be but the Swedes iron brought in Sir W.W.'s ships, which they say we had no need of and had no use for, and yet imprested present money to Sir W.W.'s warrants for it, that we sold it to loss to the King besides his charges in the loading[3] and issuing it, that it occasioned the making of bolts and other ironwork with Swedish iron which ought to have been made of Spanish, and insinuated that we imposed hardship on those we sold it to, who were driven to part with it at a lower price than they were forced to pay the King for it; and in proof hereof brought an affidavit of Russel's, which affidavit will be requisite for me to get a copy of.

Memorandum: I find a letter of Comr Pett's to myself dated Janry 6. (64 [65]) wherein he allows the usefulness of Swedes iron for anchors and other uses.

[1] This appears to be a mistake. The Instructions of 1662 simply required the Board to keep six months' stock of cordage in peacetime: *Oeconomy*, pp. 21–2.

[2] This 'farewell letter' (so subscribed) is mentioned twice again (below, pp. 388, 420), on each occasion by that description. Only here is it given a date – 'Janry 1664' (i.e. 1664/5), written quite clearly. A later date in 1665 would be more likely when the Duke was setting off to join the fleet. There is a letter from the Duke to the Navy Board written on 22 March 1664/5 'before I leave London' which in both substance and wording corresponds (though not completely) with the summaries given in these references. See the copy in PRO, ADM 2/1745, f. 118*r-v* (I owe this reference to Dr R. Saville).

[3] MS. 'landing'.

To all this I answered, first, though I doubted not but to be able to give his Majesty satisfaction herein upon the first hearing this instance, yet that I thought that it could not but be allowed for a piece of great hardship, that having wrote to the Commissioners of Accounts for what further instances more than those they had then given us in proof of their report, and receiving answer from them that they had given us all they thought necessary for us to have, they should now surprise [us] with one never till now mentioned, and thereby as much as in them lay drive us either to the making an imperfect answer to it, or suffer it (at least for the present) to remain good against us. Whereto my Lord Breereton made no other reply than that it was true they had given us that answer and that they at that time thought no other instances necessary, and that having since met with this of the iron, they could not but make use of it and offered us before the King, which I laid hold of, that we should if we desired it have any instances communicated to us which they had before them to make use of.

I then went on to answer the objection, and showed at large that it had been groundless rigour to deny the merchant the benefit of bringing iron and forcing him to ballast his ship with stones, where such a commodity would better improve[1] the room. That we were greatly in debt to our smiths, not only to the prejudicing them by the want of their money, but the disabling them thereby for want of materials to go on with his Majesty's work. That therefore being unable to pay them with silver (and finding the merchant willing to trust us therewith), we were willing to pay the smiths with iron as far as they desired it, both for their particular reliefs and for the removing their pretence of want of materials wherewith to go on with the King's work. That this to the best of my remembrance was never imposed on any of them, nor offered to them but as they desired it, in which it will hereafter be fit for me to be more positive. That to the best of my remembrance we never sold it for less, but a good part of it for more than it cost the King; so as not to doubt, but the difference will bear all the King's charge in this receipt and issuing; which let me hereafter also be better informed in. That no money was imprested to Sir W.W. for this particular commodity otherwise than as in general for the goods he had and was serving his Majesty with. That the bill for imprest allowed for the non-

[1]Make use of.

payment of the money due for this iron was pursuant to our agreement, and that pursuant to an order of Council. That this was not the only time of smiths being paid with iron, I having found the like to be done in the first Dutch war; to which Tomson replied that he did think indeed some such thing was done with a small parcel of Swedes iron taken in a prize. I answered that that difference is not the case at all; they being as much paid with prize iron, and having it as much in their power to use it in the King's service, though prize, as if bought. Let me inquire further into this. That if too much use hath been by the smiths made of this iron in the King's works, it was not from any new covenant or permission from us, or from any greater opportunity hereby given them of making use of this iron than they might have had, had not we supplied them therewith, and they found it to their advantage. The King's security against this abuse depending upon his officers in the yards in inspecting the King's works, and particularly the master shipwright, besides Comr Pett as superintendent over the whole, and who received his salary for no other service than the doing thereof in that single yard where this deponent[1] wrought. Col. Thomson did here call for Russel's deposition to be read, which being done, I answered that I questioned whether those gentlemen were not mistaken in the paper they designed to have read, this containing nothing to invalidate anything I had said, but seemed rather drawn to confirm the whole, myself owning, as I had already before it was read, the whole substance of the deposition. At which the whole Board seemed at a stand, owning it to be true, and the Commissioners left without reply. Something I remember the deposition insinuated touching his having heard of anchors being made for his Majesty all of English iron,[2] which I owned as a laudable attempt of this Board suitable to what his Majesty did so well approve of in our attempts after the English manufacture of sailcloths; it being our purpose herein upon some good invitation given us to make an experiment of anchors made of iron of his Majesty's own growth in the Forest of Deane, thereby to see if we could become masters of that commodity without being obliged to other princes for them.[3] Which answer seemed very satisfactory,

---

[1]Russell; of Chatham.
[2]Contracts usually specified the use of Spanish iron: Sir W. Beveridge et al., *Prices and wages in Engl.*, i. 658.
[3]Sir John Winter had put forward a proposal to use iron from the Forest of Dean for the Navy in 1665: see *Diary*, vi. 62 & n. 2.

and may, I believe, be rendered much more so by my recollecting the proceedings of the Board in this particular.

Something I remember Tomson or else Russel in his deposition I took notice of touching Swedes iron made use of in the making of a chain for his Majesty, I suppose that at Chatham.[1] It will not be amiss for me to recollect that matter also, though it be already in general answered.

Something hereabouts gave occasion to my asserting their having a survey of the stores as they were before the war and presently at the end of it, with an account of the issues and receipts between, and that these they have had delivered them the latest above a year ago, which the King took ready hold and charged the Commissioners of Accounts with their groundless repeating so often their want of light touching the state and expense[2] of the stores, and thereupon called for the letter our Board had lately wrote to the Lords of the Treasury and which now lay in the Clerk of the Council's[3] hand about the times of the delivery of those books of survey, receipts and issues, by the Comptroller and Surveyor. Which being read, they owned the truth of its contents, but urged that the first survey was six months before the beginning of the war, and that the books of receipts and issues being wholly inmethodical, it was impossible ever to collect the true state of the stores out of them. To the first I said that the survey was taken at the usual season of the year for taking the surveys, that no direction was ever given for making more than one in a year, much less at that time for the taking one the 1st of Sept. 1664, besides that surveys are chargeable at all times, difficult in time of peace and hardly possible nor in any ways necessary but rather obstructive to his Majesty's service to be taken in a time of war.

To the second, I said that the Comptroller being absent, nothing could be now properly given them touching the method of the books, whereof Tomson showing one, and I finding him with too much reason objecting against its want of method, I thought it best to say the least to it, and therefore studied how to put it off with fewest words and the best grace. Which I did (as I think) without leaving any blemish behind it. But since upon recollection I find a very good answer to it: which is, that though

---

[1] The chain which the Dutch ships broke through in the raid on the Medway.
[2] The amount used.
[3] Sir Edward Walker.

they asserted the contrary, we are not obliged to deliver them books to their satisfaction, but rather in the true form wherein they are kept, and that therefore the Act doth expressly provide (as I remember) that they shall have authority to new form any books or accounts as they shall see cause.[1] By which they may well be answered, that the true form that these books are kept in were sufficient for the uses the said books were intended, *viz.*, to enable the storekeepers and officers of the yards to make out true bills, both in behalf of the King and merchant for the goods delivered into stores, appealing to them whether by any of the bills they have seen they find reason to assert the contrary, and if they do, let them assign instances. But that if they have any further uses than what were intended to be made of them by them that kept them, it is by the Act made their proper work to put them into the form they would have them. Let me consult the Act well herein.

Some occasion or other, I remember, my Lord Breert. took to say that as much as Mr Pepys had lately thought fit to charge them with delay,[2] or at least he thought they did make delays, yet, etc., to which I replied by appealing to his Majesty and the Lords whether I did at any time charge them directly with delay, but that, as to what I thought concerning it, I did hope his Lordship did not think it unfit for me to challenge a liberty of thinking as I see cause.

They then proceeded to the last part about imprests, pressing very earnestly the great value of the imprests granted to Sir W.W., and that in a particular beyond what we were obliged to do by any contract appearing. I replied shortly that we are not bound up to give imprests only pursuant to contract. That imprests are granted justifiably upon these occasions: *viz.*, either where a service is to be done by a person not under contract but under a general trust of doing it, and dispensing the money necessarily advanced him in order thereto; or where some person undertakes a service or a supply of stores upon condition in the contract to have such a sum of money by way of advance, partly to secure him against the too common failures of our payment and partly to enable him the better to perform the contract, and neither of them without a beneficial influence to his Majesty in the price of the undertaking; or where the service being in a good measure

[1] 19 & 20 Car. II c. 1, sect. i.
[2] See above, p. 336.

performed or the contract for stores in a good part complied with, the party from several circumstances on his side or ours cannot conveniently have a perfect bill presently made out to him to enable him to receive his payment thereupon. That in every of these cases Sir W.W. hath had right to imprests, and hath not received any but in one or other of the said cases, and therein I appealed to them to give an instance of the contrary, alleging that to my best knowledge he never received imprests where he was not indisbursed twice as much for his Majesty as the imprests comes to.

That 'tis[1] true 34,000*l.* worths of imprests lies at this day out against him, but that above 29,000*l.* thereof is actually at this day discharged by bills perfectly adjusted between the King and him and now lying in the Lord Brounker's hand, as the King's security for so much; and that there lie also before us pretences of his unadjusted to above 20,000*l.* more, which, as it is too soon for us to assert their being all reasonable, so seems it no less too soon for the Commissioners of Accounts, till they had examined them, to condemn any part of them – at least so as out of above 20,000*l.* not to allow so much to be good as to secure his Majesty in four or five. Which seemed an answer wherein every man acquiesced, saving the Commissioners of Accounts, who took occasion thereupon to fly out upon the delay of his account, which I answer by saying in whose hand it lay, *viz.*, Sir J. Mennes's, with the special assistance of the Lord Brouncker by direction of the Lord High Admiral, and that upon the petition of Sir W. Warren to his Highness for dispatch. In which his Highness seconded me that Sir W. Warren had several times by petition and otherwise applied himself to him with his desires of his mediation with the Commissioners of the Navy for the dispatch of his accounts, which he very well observed, and so did the King too, to be no sign of a merchant's desire of defrauding the King, or looking upon himself as his debtor. And so as I remember the matter ended without anything sticking upon of blame therein.

In this discourse my Lord Brereton interposed one word relating to the loss which his Majesty may be supposed to sustain by the lying of so much money in Sir W. Warren's hands, and thereupon besides what I had asserted of his never having money imprested to him before he had disbursed to much greater value for his Majesty, I said that Sir W.W. was very willing and stood

---

[1]MS. 'his' (a mishearing).

prepared to come to a mutual account to his Majesty for interest, and seemed to be positive in it that Sir W.W. would be a gainer from his Majesty upon such an account.

It comes into my head to observe that if it shall happen to be objected hereafter touching what I have lately set down about their pretended incapacity of gathering a true state of his Majesty's stores from the survey books and other books delivered to them, and that to justify this their pretended incapacity they should allege that no books of receipts and issues had been delivered them for the time between the taking of the first survey till the 1st of Sept. 1664, it may well be answered that 'tis true, and that the said books of receipts and issues were limited in their commencement by their own order and the Act too to the 1st of Sept. 1664, and so no blame due to us or our officers that they commenced no earlier.

They then proceeded to the 2nd Article,[1] but before they could enter into it were stopped by his Royal Highness moving that one part of my answer to the first might be read to his Majesty, by which he might see how little the management of his officers in this great point of imprests hath been worse than that of the late times. To which the Commissioners of Accounts offered to give a prevention by saying (and it was pretty to hear Tomson himself urge it) that they would never govern themselves by the practice under the times of usurpation, but did limit themselves to the comparing the present management with these within the times of his Majesty's royal predecessors; however, his Royal Highness adhered to his motion and was seconded in it by the King himself that whatever they meant, the world had a general conception that the management of his officers came so much beneath those of the late times as to draw therefrom inferences of no small reproach to his government, and that therefore both for his own and others' satisfaction then present he directed me to read that part of my answer,[2] which having done, the King took up the substance of it, saying by way of irony, 'These were the methodical proceedings of those angelical times.' Whereupon Tomson took occasion to say that it was very true indeed that towards the latter end of those times their payments grew very bad, and so they were forced to pay great sums by imprest, and those by the disorder arising from want of money not so regularly

---

[1] That is, the 2nd Observation: above, p. 277.
[2] Above, p. 276.

and readily discharged as otherwise they would have been. To which I returned that this was the true description of the grounds of our imprests, and that it seemed very hard that what he thinks an excuse from the same effects in theirs should not be thought equally good for those in our times, though yet the value of imprests uncleared by us even in a time of war and greatest wants of money comes much short of what theirs appears to be even in times of peace and much other credit for payments. This being said, they again fall to [the] 2nd article; which being read, and something enlarged thereupon by the Lord Brereton, I read my answer, and then discoursed upon it by showing that the full number of masts contracted for by Sir W.W. in his contract of 6 July [1664] was delivered by December following, whereas he was obliged to no more than six ships' loading by the July after that. That it is true they answered not in dimensions to those aimed at in the contract, but that the merchant had undertaken nothing certain more than his utmost endeavours in reference to the dimensions; and thereupon I again appealed to the best information whether any greater masts than those brought by Sir W.W. was from that time brought into England by any other hand, or proof made to them that bigger could have been brought by him. That whereas they pretend his delivering only small masts, and that Mr Wood had offered us at cheaper rates a parcel of bigger, which we were afterwards by this ill[1] management of ours forced to buy at dearer rates of him, I showed that in this parcel of 977 Sir W.W. had delivered above 80 masts of above 14 hands, whereas in the parcel of above 420 masts tendered by Mr Wood (as the same among the papers in my office appears under the hand of Gelstrop, Sir W. Batten's own clerk) I do not find above 13 masts of above 14 hands.

I then went on to show that his Majesty, having advice that the King of Sweeden had made a proclamation prohibiting the expectation of felling of any more masts in Sweeden for seven years,[2] and to the end that the Dutch might be prevented in their market of masts from thence, where they were very busy to have bought up what they could, as the King of France also was at the same time, did take into his consideration (upon some advice also thereupon given his Royal Highness by letter from Sir W.W.,

---

[1] MS. 'in' (a mishearing).
[2] The information seems to have come from Warren in a letter to the Navy Board (4 Apr. 1665): *CSPD 1664–5*, p. 292.

which letter was communicated by his Highness to this Board, and the same now ready to be produced by me) how to engross into his own hands all the masts then to be had, and thereupon conferred several times with Sir W.W. both at Whitehall and Worcester House, and commanded him by all means of speed and privacy to apply himself to the buying up for his use whatever masts were to be procured at Gottenburg. In the truth of which appealing to the memory of his Majesty and Royal Highness they did both most readily avow the same, with these very considerations on which it was grounded, and which I then showed them proved so successful that the Dutch to the best of our information were never able to compass any supply of masts from thence during the whole war, but were driven to go to Russia for their supply, wherein (I replied, upon the word of Sir W.W.) they were driven to give 100*l.* for that mast which Sir W.W. affords the King at 36. Nay, that the King of France neither could furnish himself thence otherwise than with what the Crown of Sweeden sent him as a present during the war.

That his Royal Highness did at our attending him communicate these directions of his Majesty to us, upon which Sir W.W. proceeded to the providing them and we to the receiving them, without making any formal contract in a case where his Majesty upon so good reasons commanded so much privacy to be used. And this I urged in answer to what Thomson had pressed, *viz.*, that in their demanding from me all the contracts which had been made in the Navy during the war I had given them no account of this. To which (I say) I gave this answer – to the satisfaction of and owned as such by the King – that the privacy with which this was to be managed would not admit of the formality of a public contract.[1]

Then I proceeded to tell them that the freights of ships and the wages of men growing very high above the common rate in time of peace, Sir W.W. did inform us that though he had proceeded by the King's directions to provide the masts, yet that he under those difficulties durst not undertake to bring home the said masts, but left it to the Board to consider of the way of bringing them home, who laying before them that men might be pressed into his Majesty's service at 24*s. per mensem* whereas in merchants' service they now stood upon 40 or 45*s.*, and that men by being in his Majesty's pay, as they would be less liable to their

[1]For purchase by commission, see below, pp. 386–92.

being carried away by the pressmasters of his Majesty's other ships, so they would become subject to the laws martial and consequently be more under government. All which considerations made it seem much more eligible in reference to the effectual bringing home of the goods to send for them by ships and men in his Majesty's own pay than trust to the hazards attending their being to be fetched by the merchant in ships of his own, the Board upon debate hereof before the Lord High Admiral did conclude upon their hiring of ships themselves to fetch them with, and therein (whatever is said of 10,000 tons) were so sparing that the ships they sent were not able to bring them all, witness some hundreds of them lying at Gottenburg to this day.[1] Besides that it behoving the Office of the Navy to secure above all things else their being effectually brought home, this seemed the only way to do it by employing of ships in a manner subject to our own directions only and sending them with convoy. Whereas no private merchant would ever have stood to the demurrage in attendance for convoy,[2] but have made insurance upon their ship and goods and so adventured to bring them over in defiance to whatever danger they could be subject to in their coming, by which means the goods being made liable to loss, the King would surely[3] have paid in the effects of that loss, for which possibility he might have had saved in the price of the goods.

Here they began to insist upon the great charge of freight of these ships, arising as I think they said to about 30 or 40,000*l*., whereas that part thereof which the merchant hath paid towards it amounts not to above 4 or 5. To which I told them that it was not of any moment whether the part the merchant bore towards it amounted but to 4000 or 3000*l*. or any less sum. But whether we have not faithfully defalked from him so much as the freights of the like ships would by a rational medium have amounted to in time of peace; which and no more was what the merchant was to pay. And that this defalcation was thus reasonably made by us. I told them that the Board to my best remembrance governed themselves by no worse information than of some of the most

---

[1] On 29 Sept. 1669 Warren wrote to the Board about the 360 masts he had bought in 1666 but which were still at Göteborg. His factor there had tried but failed to dispose of them, and he now – in vain – asked the Board to arrange their transport: *CSPD 1668–9*, p. 502.
[2] Sc. would have been content with demurrage in cases where the delay was caused by waiting ('attendance') for convoy.
[3] MS. 'sorely' (? a mishearing).

notable Norway merchants upon the Exchange, and among others Mr Wood, to whom they had been beholden for the affidavit read the last day to the prejudice of this matter.[1] And that therefore what it came to more ought not to be imputed either to the merchant or us as a fault, because subject therein to his Majesty's greater occasions in the fleet, by which means not only the merchantmen hired to fetch these masts were in the beginning of the year 1666, when ready, employed to carry victuals to the fleet rather than do nothing for want of the Generals'[2] being able (notwithstanding our requests in writing on that behalf) to spare them convoy till they had fought the Dutch; so when after the fight[3] they arrived at Gottenburg and were there laden under the convoy of two or three 5th-rate ships, the news of the King of Denmark's intention to send twelve men-of-war to Gottenburg to destroy our ships there[4] were such as to give ground for expresses to be sent immediately from England to command them not to budge from thence till further force was come to them, which occasioned their stay there a long time till Capt. Robinson came thither with his fleet to bring them home,[5] as (if I mistake not) the other ships the last year 1665 under the single convoy of the *Convertine* were forced to do till Sir John Harman came with his fleet to bring them home,[6] all which charge though very considerable is not at all to be imputed either to us or the merchant, but to the contingent state of his Majesty's affairs, not to be avoided without having submitted the whole issue of the war to the dangers which without convoy these essential goods must have been submitted to if adventured to have been brought home without it.

About this matter Tomson found occasion of asserting two or three times, though not to much purpose here, that it is not in the power of the Officers of the Navy to constitute any man a purveyor or factor for them for goods to be brought from abroad. Which, though I passed by as impertinent here, yet conceiving him to have moved it with some vehemence as a matter of weight and which perhaps he may have occasion of offering more

[1] See above, p. 349.
[2] Rupert and Albemarle.
[3] The Four Days Fight, 1–4 June 1666.
[4] War had been declared on Denmark in September.
[5] He sailed with a squadron in November 1666 and returned in the following January: *CSPD 1666–7*, pp. 317, 419.
[6] They had returned in December 1665. Among them were 10 mast ships: ibid., *1665–6*, p. 97.

seasonably, it may not be amiss for me that in this case Sir W. Warren was not made a purveyor by us but by the King and Duke; that the Commissioners of the Navy in the former war did take upon them to employ whom they thought fit abroad, and in another-gates manner by sending abroad a brother of Hopkins, not only without a trust of buying the goods there, but with the providing and carrying forth a cargo from hence to be bartered in New England (as I take it) for masts there,[1] and lastly that by the 1st Article of our General Instructions this as well as all other matters conducing to the well being and well governing of his Majesty's Navy is entrusted to us.[2]

Memorandum: that in this day's discourse I drove them frequently to a confession of their being unready to argue this matter, having never had time yet to examine our answers. Upon which the King made great observation, taking notice of their readiness to give in charges against men before they were prepared rightly to understand the same.

I did also in the beginning of this day's discourse touching Sir W. Warren's non-performance of his New England contract when hindered therein by the dangers of the sea and want of convoy,[3] I surprised them with an observation that the Parliament had in their Act limited their inquiries to five sorts of faults by the names of negligences, abuses, frauds, exactions and defaults,[4] and thereupon desired that they would tell me which sort of fault of these five it is that they would in this be understood to charge upon us. Which sudden dilemma seemed to startle them as well as the whole company, and received no other reply from them than that to give me an answer to this were to deliver a judgement, whereas they meant these for nothing but observation. I replied, and was therein seconded by the King, that in common estimation these 'Observations' as they call them are interpreted for no less than judgements against us, and that if they are not so, we desire to know what they are to be reckoned, being delivered in the terms of observations of things which they deliver most positively. They answer the King that they did not mean them for judgements, but (however the world took them) as

---

[1] Edward Hopkins (a returned New Englander) was a member of the Admiralty Committee, 1652–5: Aylmer, *State's Servants*, p. 132. His brother was possibly Henry, a Limehouse shipwright: *CSPD 1653–4*, p. 462.
[2] *Oeconomy*, pp. 20–1.
[3] See above, p. 275.
[4] 19 & 20 Car. II c. 1, sect. i, where the offences are recited in a different order.

matters wherein they were at present dissatisfied, and did therefore expect satisfaction from us therein.[1] After which the King seemed to express great resentment of the method they proceeded in, so much to the scandal of his government and officers.

It is not amiss to remember as an instance of their hastiness in making these Observations against us, that the deposition of Shorter,[2] calculated as one of the greatest convictions of our ill management in the business of the Gottenburg contract with Sir W.W., bears date (as I take it) but of the 14 of this month, which is three months after their Observations delivered to the Parliament.

This day bears date my answer to their letter of yesterday, wherein I send them a copy of Sir W.W.'s letter of the 4 of April 1665 on the subject they demand satisfaction,[3] wherein I add my desire on behalf of the Board in pursuance of their offer this day before the King of what instances they have before them more than what they have already imported to us in proof of their Observations. This I did in order to good use to be made of it whether they grant my request or not.

Friday Janry 21 1669[70]. I was unexpectedly summoned with Sir P. Warwick and Sir Rt Long to attend the King in Council this morning, which I did, though by my endeavours of seeing Du Vall carried to his execution[4] I happened to come after the business was over. But understand it to be the King's having called the Commissioners of Accounts before him to receive from them what they would offer in order to their doing him and the government right in the mistake they had led the world into to his prejudice about his diverting so many hundreds of thousands of pounds to other uses than the war.[5] Wherein the King was forwarded by my Lord Keeper, Duke of York, Lord Bridgwater, Lord Ashly and Sir Thom. Clifford, most of which prosecuted the motions I had started touching the Act's giving no ground either to the limiting the beginning of the war to the 1st of Septembr 1664 or to the making any difference between ordinary

---

[1] This was the point which the Commissioners made to the Commons when the meaning of the word was debated in the House on submission of their report: see above, Introduction, p. xxx & n. 5.
[2] Untraced: see above, p. 350.
[3] See above, p. 352.
[4] The execution at Tyburn of Claude Duval, the handsome and gallant highwayman, attracted large crowds.
[5] See above, p. 336.

and extraordinary charge of the Navy; Sir Thomas Clifford also particularly urging that the Act doth require them as well to assign[1] those other uses as to say in general that money was diverted to other uses than the war. Upon all which my Lord Breerton answered that he should be ready to make his Majesty all reparation in anything wherein he had committed any mistake, but that he could not yet see that he had committed any. At which the King it seems grew very angry, and expressed in words of greater resentment than ever he did yet, charging all the evil he suffered thereby upon the hands of those five of them which signed this report. To which Lord Breerton replied that though it is true that Lord Halifax and Mr Pierrepoint did refuse to join with them in the signing of the report in general, yet that they[2] were both consenting to these words for which they[3] were at this time so much censured, but that if his Majesty commanded anything from them they should be ready to obey. The King replied that he would command nothing from them nor should they have it to say he did, and that if they did not think fit to do him right he would find his own way of doing it, therefore left them to do as they saw fit. After which it at last came to this issue, that they would farther consider this matter and set down the particular uses which they cannot allow to belong to the war, and attend the King with their resolutions therein this day seven-night.[4]

Monday Janry 24th.[5] The King and Council being met, and the Commissioners and we (*viz.*, my Lord Brouncker and myself) called in, their 3rd Observation was read,[6] with a paper annexed opening the proof thereof.[7] Upon which I read my written answer,[8] and then in discourse showed them [*firstly*] that the crime here charged upon us was our not doing what [was] never enjoined us, [*secondly*] what in no age was ever practised, [*thirdly*] what we could not have attempted to have done without unfaith-

[1] Specify.
[2] Halifax and Pierrepont.
[3] The other Commissioners.
[4] See below, p. 372.
[5] Marginal note: '*Vide* the following notes on the 6th Observation': below, pp. 381–4.
[6] This alleged 'that the books of the Treasurer of the Navy have been ... signed though the true times of his paying bills ... have not been expressed': above, p. 278.
[7] HLRO, Main Papers 26 Oct. 1669, 213 B 18, f. [105r]; summary in HMC, *8th Report*, App., pt i. 133.
[8] Above, pp. 278–80.

fulness, [*fourthly*] what in itself is impossible to be done, and lastly what as soon as we were enjoined it and enabled thereto has as far as it is possible been punctually executed.

To the first of which they wholly answered with silence.

To the second the like; saving that, I appealing in my discourse to Col. Tomson's observation as to the practice of the late times, he desired leave to be rightly understood by his Majesty how far he was to be looked upon as concerned in and acquainted with the practice of those times, which was that he never was employed in the time of Oliver but only at the latter end under the Parliament,[1] but could not say anything of the practice of that time, contrary to what Mr Pepys had said. But that it being a matter for want whereof his Majesty had sustained damage, they thought it their duties to lay it before him.

The third I proved by showing the Officers of the Navy not to be privy to the days of the Treasurer's payments as not being present, and therefore unable knowingly to sign to the same in his ledger, whereto they made no reply but that they looked upon it as their duty to represent it.

The fourth I showed by laying open to them the practice of the Navy in bringing as far as is possible all the wages upon the same ship under one head in the ledger, though the same be made up of several sums paid by tickets upon an hundred several days, and therefore that it is impossible truly to assign any one day for the payment of the gross sum as it lies in the ledger, the like I did in the case of perfect bills, where the parties had received part thereof by one or more sums advanced by bills of imprests, which being delivered up to the merchant in part of payment of the perfect bills, the whole perfect bill cannot be said paid at any one certain time.

Here being led also to take notice of the greatness of the action, and how much more easily all these things might have been done in a time of less action as heretofore, and therein the King also seconding me, Tomson replied that method might as easily be observed in a great action as in a little one, and instanced that a defect in architecture might be sooner observed in Paul's as Pancras,[2] at which position and instance the King and the Board seeming to make mirth of it, I thought it unnecessary for me to return any answer to it, though I had an instance in

---

[1] That is, under the Rump, between December 1652 and April 1653.
[2] A small church in Cheapside; burnt down in the Fire and never rebuilt.

my mind with my Lord Breerton as an understander of music[1] would have allowed me for good, *viz.*, that a theorbo is neither so soon put nor so easily or cheaply kept in tune as a violin or trump-marine, nor a harp as a Jew's trump.[2] For the last I appealed to themselves whether they did not so soon as demanded receive from us the weekly accounts of the Treasurer of the Navy of the payments by him day by day made from the first time of our being authorised thereto by the Duke's Instructions mentioned in my answer.[3] Which they owned to be true, but that they knew of no such Instructions when they made these Observations. To which I replied that there wanted nothing but their not [having] timely given us notice of their dissatisfactions to their having seen these Instructions long ago.

Here the King took upon him to observe their hastiness in giving judgement upon men before they were heard. Whereto they answered that they intended not these Observations to be received for judgements, for they were not to be thought so. The King answered they were esteemed no less in the case of Sir G. Carterett.[4] To which they yielded, saying that there was a great difference between those upon Sir G. Carterett and these – by how much those had been examined with Sir G. C.'s answers thereupon, which these had not, and that therefore they meant not that these should be esteemed any other than what at first view appeared to them before our answers thereto were made, and what they, upon examination thereof which they are now upon, may possibly find satisfaction in, and as they do shall own the same. I told them nevertheless that however they differed in their understanding them, the world thought them of the same nature with the other, by how much they were presented to the King and Parliament under the same positive title of 'Observations'. They answered they knew not by what other name to call them, but that their meaning was no other thereby than what they now say. And so this point went off.

For the latter part of their instance relating to our bringing things to wrong years in the Treasurer's account, I found little

---

[1] Pepys had once heard Brereton play the organ 'very handsomely' in Carteret's house: *Diary*, ix. 11.

[2] A theorbo was a large variety of lute; a trump-marine a large stringed instrument with sympathetic strings; and a Jew's 'trump' (or Jew's harp) a variety of whistle.

[3] See above, p. 279.

[4] The Commons had come within an ace of impeaching Carteret on the basis of their 'Observations': see above, Introduction, p. xxxi.

occasion for saying anything thereon more than what I had set down in my written answer which I run over in discourse, showing and appealing to their own Observations whether they had ever seen or heard of any Treasurer of the Navy's account, either in former or late times, wherein any such distinction of years was precisely kept to, asserting that there was none, at least since the Navy became so great as for many years it hath now been. That as I have observed, when three or four ships only were kept abroad and not one built in many years, and the Navy itself not a fourth so big, something of this kind might have been expected; but even at that time, when it was thus in some measure possible, the Admiral's Instructions directed us to a method of sorting the Treasurer's accounts quite different from what these gentlemen now expect, namely not according to years or time but the various occasions of service, as appears by the Comptroller's Instructions here quoted, where I am to observe that they in their paper justifying this article did quote the same article of the Comptroller's duty, but in discourse did insinuate that by the 18th article of our General Instructions it was made all our duties.[1] But that being now mentioned but by the by, I took no notice of it, as being a point fit for a more solemn handling when they shall make use of it in some occasion of more moment to the Board.

Upon this head – it was (as I remember) of the difference between the proportion of the work of the Navy anciently and now – that Tomson said what I have already taken notice of, that a great action may be managed with as much method as a little one. And here it was that I first took occasion to object against their late declaring that they did not govern themselves by anything of what was practised in the time of usurpation,[2] thinking it necessary to tell his Majesty that I thought we had reason in our defence to have reference to the management of that time, first in regard to the honour of his own service and government by letting the world see that, whatever was insinuated to the contrary, matters in the Navy have been at least as well [managed] or rather much better than in the time of usurpation. Secondly, that since the good managements wherever they can find them are made use of to the reproach of ours, it seemed but reasonable that ours, where there is ground for it, should confront with theirs, and that our lesser failures, where there are any, should

[1] *Oeconomy*, pp. 39–40.
[2] Cf. above, p. 360.

appear to the world compared with those of the same kind but in degree greater to be found under the management of our predecessors. Thirdly, that since it is allowed generally as one rule by which to judge the performances of one man that they be compared with the performances of another in the same affairs and under the same circumstances, there is no time to which ours can be so properly compared as that of the first Dutch war, when the action did beyond all other times approach to that of ours, though neither in the greatness of the work nor the difficulties attending it did even this[1] fully come up to our case.

To all which the King gave his full allowance and the whole company discovered[2] their doing the like, the King himself enlarging upon the liberty taken by people everywhere, in every coffee house, and therein appealed to the company then present whether they had not met with discourses to the prejudice of his and his officers' managements by quoting how much things were better done in the Navy in the late times, "those pure angelical times" (saith the King), to which I added, "those times concerning which people discourse in matters of the Navy as historians do of the primitive times in reference to the church".

They then proceeded to the 4th Article,[3] after reading of which I read the close of my answer to the 1st Observation,[4] and discoursing a little thereupon neither offered nor met with anything (as I remember now) saving that the King asking what real damage he either had or was in danger of sustaining by this use of imprests or the not regular defalking them, I answered as I believed none, for that the Comptroller, Sir J. Mennes, whose part it was to have defalked them, has been some time and is at this day looking after the recovering from the parties what they had received too much. To which the Lord Brouncker added that the whole sum thus in question accounted not to above 6 or 700*l*. (as I take it and am sure he said under a 1000*l*.) and that the parties concerned therein were so solvent as that he did not think the King would lose anything by it. The Commissioners objected nothing to any part of this, but said it was their duty to lay the whole before his Majesty as they found it, and that indeed they had not yet had time to examine these matters and our answers but that they were upon it, and that so soon as they had done

[1] MS 'even this did'.
[2] Expressed.
[3] That is, the 4th Observation: above, p. 280.
[4] Ending above, p. 277.

they should lay before his Majesty their opinions as they should then find cause to report concerning the whole. And so the King adjourned *sine die*.

Friday Janry 28th 1669[70]. By order of the [*blank*] for the Solicitor-General,[1] the King's learned Counsel, Sir Rt Long, Sir Phil. Warwick and myself to attend the King in Council this day at 3 of the clock, I accordingly attended with the rest where, the Commissioners of Accounts present and as great audience as the chamber could hold, the Commissioners of Accounts presented a paper[2] going over the heads of that part of their report relating to the sums excepted against Sir G. Carteret's account as being for other uses than the war, wherein I found not that they offered anything new to the King's advantage but their lessening the 65,000*l*. for interest by 15,000*l*. which they had since found to belong to moneys borrowed since 1st Sept. 1664, and declaring that they did in their private opinions think it reasonable that his Majesty should be allowed the charge of his preparations, though they do yet adhere to their thinking themselves bound up to the allowing of nothing before Sept. 1. 1664.[3] For what concerns their owning the whole to be for the use of the Navy, Guards and Ordnance, it was no more than what they had owned in their first report to the Parliament, though not so much attended to, but yet more plainly expressed in the paper they lately gave his Majesty in illustration thereof.[4] They close with great professions of fair meaning towards his Majesty, whatever ill use may have been made thereof by others' construction thereof. This paper of theirs being read, a silence for a while remained, myself though prepared and expected by the King and my papers in my hand ready for it, yet thought it unfit for me to begin the day until I had seen whether the King's Counsel would first offer anything or the King command me to speak. By and by the King spoke to Sir Hen. Finch to deliver his opinion in point of law, who thereupon began a very eloquent and elaborate harangue consisting chiefly of compliments to the Commissioners of Accounts both in the greatness of their trust beyond whatever was yet committed to any subjects and the expressions of their

[1]Sir Heneage Finch.
[2]Untraced.
[3]By this they meant that the expenses paid from the King's own revenue before 1 Sept. 1664 would be allowed, but not those paid from the public revenue.
[4]See above, Introduction, p. xxxi & nn. 1, 2.

duty and respect to his Majesty in this paper, he did handsomely make a show of proving the King's right to any allowance for his preparation, and that the Parliament (as he thought) had abundantly expressed their minds accordingly both in the preamble of the Act to the Royal Aid and this of the Act for Accounts,[1] and quoted one place more,[2] saying that when the Parliament comes to tell what would be collected out of the accounts, books and papers to be delivered in by several accountants and officers of the Navy, and after mentioning what moneys had been received and issued and stores employed after, and what ships his Majesty had upon, Sept. 1. 1664, they do then say what moneys have been paid or delivered and where the same was so paid or delivered, and how and at what time or times the same have been so disposed of, being words general and to be referred to moneys before, as the former[3] respected moneys after, the 1st of Sept. But lest he should be thought to take upon him the construction of the Act, of whose meaning he said he knew well whom the Parliament had made the judges, he did again and again industriously repeat that what he said herein was his private opinion, not in opposition but with all submission to what those Honourable Commissioners should declare concerning the same, whose believing themselves tied up to this first of Sept. he said he was confident was the reason of their excepting against these sums as relating to other uses than the war. And that therefore what he would propose was that under the infelicity of this obscureness in the Act these gentlemen might be desired to state the expenses of the war both ways, that is to say once as they have done, limiting themselves to the 1st of Sept., and then as the reason of the thing and the words of the Acts seemed to him (with submission) to warrant, and as the Commissioners themselves do now declare it in their private judgement to be reasonable, with the charges included of the King's preparations. He then fell to enlarge upon the care his Majesty had had, and therein undertook peremptorily to assert what the sum was that all the aids given the King for the war did amount to. And that the King had not only applied every farthing of the proceed thereof to the service of the Navy, Guards and Ordnance, but

---

[1]The operative phrases were (in the Act granting the Royal Aid) 'to equip and set out to sea', and (in the Act establishing the Commission) 'for the preparing and setting forth a fleet': 16 & 17 Car. II c. 1, sect. i; 19 & 20 Car. II, c. 1, sect. i.
[2]In the preamble of the Act establishing the Commission.
[3]That is, the passage from the preamble previously cited.

moreover all his customs and the whole proceed of his prizes[1] to a farthing, besides his submitting to account the moneys freely given him (though [not] enumerated among the rest of the sums in this Act) for the use of his Guards.[2] And this he said was as clear as the day, and would appear so to whoever would examine it. He by and by affirmed as positively that the King had spent 400,000*l*. out of his private revenue – above 400,000*l*. – for the use of the war more than all the moneys given by the Parliament amounted to.[3] And added that thus his Majesty had done his part in reference to his people – insinuating, and that pretty plainly, that failures may have been in his officers in the disposing of the said moneys, at least in that of applying the moneys without distinction to their proper uses as coming to them indeed promiscuously, and closed with the like elaborate eulogy to the said Commissioners as having fully discharged their duty and respect to his Majesty, and (which I forgot to mention)[4] did propound this expedient of their double stating the accounts as that which would be a middle way of doing his Majesty right without any retraction on the part of the said Commissioners.

After this was done my Lord Ashly[5] rose and offered something touching the charge his Majesty had been at for the use of the war out of his private revenue, and that he was at this day upon the accounts, and the difference in the state of his stores and ships above a million of money worse than he was at the beginning of the war. Then my Lord Chamberlain[6] moved that the company might be bid withdraw, which was accordingly done, only we and the King's Counsel directed to stay. Where, the room being voided, it was first moved by the Duke of York that some way should be considered of making so much of this their paper

---

[1] Revenue from customs and prizes was part of the hereditary income of the Crown, for which the King was not normally accountable to Parliament. Nevertheless he had agreed in the Act establishing the Commission to have it included in the scrutiny.

[2] These sums were given under the terms of an Act of 1661 (13 Car. II c. 4). They amounted to £400 in 1667–8 compared with £47,000 in 1661–2: C. D. Chandaman, *Eng. Public Revenue 1660–88*, pp. 348, 351–2. The army is not mentioned in the Act.

[3] A calculation made in September (?) 1667 put the King's contribution at £4,120,636, including loss of revenue and loss of and damage to ships: *CSPD 1667*, p. 471. Parliament's contribution amounted to above £5m.: see above, Introduction, p. xxiv.

[4] The expedient is in fact described a little earlier in the paragraph.

[5] Chancellor of the Exchequer.

[6] The Earl of Manchester.

public as did offer anything towards the King's satisfaction which he yet said was short of doing him right. Sir Tho. Clifford having first said that their paper was satisfactory as having owned all the money to have been laid out to the use of the war, and was therein seconded by my Lord Arlington, and in a great measure thirded by Sir John Duncomb, as to the satisfactoriness of the present paper. But were opposed therein by the Duke and my Lord Ashly and the rest of the Board, the King himself declaring that he thought they had made the matter worse, it being found upon reading their paper a second time that they had given him only a few good words, correcting only 15,000*l.* to his advantage in the sum of interest, but adhering to their excluding him from satisfaction for any of his disbursements for the war before Sept. 1664.

I confess I was extremely sick of this day's passages, and particularly the Solicitor's speech, blessing my fortune that I happened not to begin the day, my discourse being likely to have been of a sense so much contrary to the Solicitor's and what I now find to be to some of these Lords now named, and being I confess after so elaborate and elegant a discourse of the Solicitor's unwilling to expose myself to the contradicting him with another so much inferior in the style of it, besides that I did not think it convenient for me to take upon me the justifying the point of law on his Majesty's side further than he had done, though I think he left me abundant room for so doing, and particularly where the Parliament, after enumerating the other several sums, doth expressly require them to take the accounts of all moneys expended in the fitting etc. of his Majesty's Navy,[1] which if I mistake not is a proof not inferior at least to any that he made use of.

The Board run on then to take notice that the paper now delivered was not signed by them, and debate whether it was not necessary to have them sign it, where the Solicitor moved that it might be asked of them as a thing wherein his Majesty found satisfaction, it being otherwise an act they might make difficulty of doing if they should think it was only to give under their hand what would turn only to the King's displeasure. Herein he was seconded by my Lord Arlington and Sir Thom. Clifford but opposed by the King himself and the rest of the Board. My Lord of Oxford moved that they might be directly bid to sign it without

[1] See above, p. 306 & n. 1

giving any account more or less of the reason of it; at last it was moved and agreed to, and the Commissioners being called in, the King accordingly told them that looking over the paper again he found they had forgot to sign it, and therefore tendered it them to sign. Which Lord Breerton taking into his hand, said that they should be ready to do it, but that it could not be done that forasmuch as, though they were a quorum, *viz.*, himself, Tomson, Langham, Turner and Osborne, yet the latter had not signed as being both out of the way, the former on his mayoralty,[1] the latter beyond sea, and that therefore they would not, as he believed and themselves also said, think themselves concerned to sign this paper, but that it should be signed, and sealed also, if his Majesty pleased (which he left to them to do as they saw fit) and delivered back to his Majesty.[2]

What the Board had proposed touching the method of publishing this paper was shut out of doors by the subsequent disputes touching the satisfactoriness of it. But that which had been offered about it was printing it, directing some of the members of this Board to declare it in both Houses, or my Lord Keeper's bringing it into his speech at the opening of the session, which last was concluded on as the only proper way.[3]

Memorandum: that my Lord Ashly moving for something to be demanded further of the Commissioners of Accounts, Mr Solicitor shook his head and whispered to me that he did not think it expedient that these gentlemen should be teased with any ungrateful questions or being put upon any unnecessary trouble. I told him I was of the same mind, but that yet, as I would not have them put upon any unwelcome trouble, so I desired him to consider how far it would be advisable for the King to put them upon that work which he had propounded and which they seemed readily to have embraced, namely the stating the charge of the preparations, because I had reason to doubt we should not be

[1] Turner was Lord Mayor 1668–9.
[2] For the paper, see above, Introduction, p. xxxiii & n. 4.
[3] In his speech on 14 Feb. 1670, Lord Keeper Bridgeman said: 'His Majesty hath not only by his ministers, but in his own royal person, examined the accounts touching the expenses of the last war, and hath thought himself concerned to let you know that all the supplies you have given him for the war have been by him applied to the war, and no part of them to other uses. Nay, so far from it, that if the preparations towards the war shall be taken for the use of the war, as they must be, a great part of his own revenue, to many hundred thousands of pounds, hath been employed also.' Moreover, he added, the King, besides suffering loss of customs and excise revenue during the war, had now to provide for the repair and replacement of his ships: *LJ*, xii. 297–8.

able to justify the 800,000*l.* which the King had declared the charge of his preparations to have amounted to. He presently replied he was confident it would be made good within a very little. Wherein finding him so unexpectedly confident, I thought it to no purpose for me to say more to him; though saying the same by and by to me Lord Ashly he told me he thought the Solicitor was mad and that he wondered in the name of God by what or whose measures he had gone on in this his discourse, saying he was sure they were none of his; though I find by him while I was waiting the other night for him at the Attorney-General's[1] chamber, his Lordship was by mistake expecting me at the Solicitor's, where he did discourse with him the business, but disowns his giving him any ground for this his discourse.

The Commissioners of Accounts being withdrawn again, the Board only considered of a day for proceeding on their Observations, and pitching on Tuesday next, adjourned, myself being [and] (as I afterwards found) both the King and most of the bystanders that understood the King's business exceedingly dissatisfied with this night's work.

Tuesday February 1. 1669[70]. The King and Council being sat and the company called in, the Commissioners of Accounts (there being present there Lord Breerton, Tomson, Langham, Gregory and Turner) began their 5th Observation[2], proving by several particulars, chiefly as I remember consisting of ships' books and yard books, that [we] had signed the Treasurer['s] ledger for payments where no bills had been first passed, amounting to above 50,000*l.*, and grounding this their charge upon its being a breach of the 14th General Instruction[3], where in passing the Treasurer's accounts we are bid to cancel our own warrants.

To which, after reading my written answer,[4] I had occasion among other discourses principally to insist upon the following notes, *viz*:

That what they herein charge us with is no more than our not doing what was never enjoined us, what our predecessors in former and later times never observed more than we, and what in itself is but an indifferent matter of form only. The first I

[1] Sir Geoffrey Palmer's.
[2] Above, p. 281.
[3] *Oeconomy*, p. 35.
[4] Above, p. 281.

proved by showing that it is true the cancelling of our warrants is enjoined – and reasonably – for preventing the being of two warrants in being at once for the Treasurer's payment of the same sum, and that therefore not to cancel the loose warrants where there were any abroad would be a breach of this Instruction; but this doth in no wise either make it a crime not to cancel the loose warrant where there never was any, or to make our allowance of a payment by signing immediately to the ledger without any previous loose warrant for the same. For the second, touching practice, I appealed to themselves, who replied that for the ancient practice under the King's predecessors, it did not appear to them what it was, and that for later practice they seemed to urge it as a matter of pains to them to be driven to repeat what they have so often said, which is that they would not [make] nor had at any time made use of the practice under [the] usurpation in the justifying or condemning any present act. To which last I answered by repeating what I have heretofore said, that we are censured and reproached by the good acts of those days, and that therefore it is but justice that we should have the equal benefit of making use of the practice where it hath been less perfect than ours. But that since this was so grievous to them, I would ask but one condition, which being granted I would be contented never to use that manner of argument more, which is but that these Commissioners would report that, as bad as our managements have been, they have been better or at least as good as those under the late usurpation; for I declared that whatever pretences I may have of having out-done any of their performances in the late times,[1] yet I would be contented to stand by the issue of such a censure that I had done in this war as well as the like works were done in any other time.[2] Besides, the King did add, that no time was so proper for us to be compared with as those times of action, which came nearest in its burden to ours. To which I may hereafter add what now comes into my mind, that Col. Tomson, in the case of Sir G. Carterett's being allowed Exchequer fees, owned that he had looked back as far

---

[1] E.g. in the sheer volume of office work: see above, pp. 327–8.
[2] Pepys calculated that the Commonwealth government, in the first year of the First Dutch War, paid £171,785 more than the King paid in the first year of the second war for the same goods and services: PL 2589, pp. 117–18. There are other similar calculations by Pepys in Bodl. Lib., Rawl. MSS A 181, f. 36r and ibid., A 195a, f. 241r and (by Gibson) in BL, Add. MSS 11602, f. 93r. Cf. *Diary*, vii. 307; ix. 484.

as Queen Elizabeth's time and could find no precedent for it, though I find him mistaken, for in a ledger of her time which I have, there doth appear an ample precedent for this allowance.[1] And that he this day upon occasion of this very article afterwards [did] say that in those times[2] they did not keep the ships' books six months or a year unmade up after the pay as we have done, or trusted our clerks in making them up, but that they were made up by the Commissioners themselves and that as soon as ever the ship was paid, which (that is to say the latter)[3] though I told him it was untrue and therein appealed to Mr Portman then present, as I have since done to Mr Hayter, who tells me that they did in those days not only rely wholly upon the clerks' making up their books, but that they have committed the whole trust of managing a pay, as, if I mistake not, in particular that Mr Lewes has been sent down alone to a pay to act both as a paymaster, comptroller and clerk; yet I say this doth abundantly show that where the practice either of ancient or late times will wound us they do not spare to quote it. As they did also this day upon the next article in the case of parish duties, where Tomson did industriously,[4] and as it were by head and shoulders,[5] endeavour to bring reproach upon us for our making the King pay parish duties, saying that he did not believe that the Commissioners in the late times made the State do it; it seemed to him very unjust that the King should give us the benefit of a house and we make him pay the duties of it. To which I replied that they, for all the self-denyingness of those times, did make the State pay parish duties. That, it is true, church duties they might not [pay] as seldom going to any.[6] On which subject I might have added that the making their master pay for a house at all was more than ever we or our predecessors had in any time before done or probably should have now, had not his Majesty been heir to one of their purchasing for us.[7] As to the third[8] (that the matter in

[1]This was in 1566: PL 2874, p. 367.
[2]Under the Commonwealth.
[3]'The latter' must refer to the employment of clerks to make up the books.
[4]Persistently.
[5]With some violence.
[6]Preferring to attend conventicles. Thomson, for instance, was a Fifth-Monarchist.
[7]The Navy Board had occupied rented premises until 1649 when it moved to Tower Hill and shared a building with the Victualling Office. In 1654 a building in Seething Lane was bought for their use: T. F. Reddaway in *Bull. Inst. Hist. Research*, xxx (1957), pp. 175–88.
[8]The third of Pepys's points in addition to his written answer.

question is but matter of form) I explained it to the King, showing that the bills they would have first signed are not the vouchers of the ledger nor that anything new is vouched in the ledger by being put into the ledger, it being no more than the putting that up in one bound book for the conveniency of the Auditors[1] what before had to the great hazard of the Treasurer but yet unavoidably in regard of the private men to whom payments are due from the Navy – and who therefore till they can be paid do reasonably insist upon having the warrant for their payment lodged in their own hands, as especially they or their successors may at all times be able to make and prove their pretence to such a sum. That whereas the Treasurer at his own great hazard, and for the benefit of the service, doth adventure to make some payments such as to the yards, ships, seamen upon tickets, and Exchequer fees without any present voucher signed under three hands, and that the books for the first three have not been able under a war to be dispatched presently but, at the Treasurer's hazard, as I say, lie unperfected a great while after, the Treasurer and Comptroller – the last of which by his especial duty is made the sole comptroller over the whole Board in the making up the Treasurer's accounts – do at the day of the audit bring the said ships' and yard books, together with the Treasurer's demand for Exchequer fees (for which no receipt is ever given him), which having all the examinations made by the Comptroller previous to his and the Board's allowing the same, and upon which, were it not at the instant of signing the ledger the Board would proceed to the signing to the said distinct books and papers, they do forbear the signing the same as being a useless thing to sign what at the same moment they must unsign again by cancelling, they spare, I say, to sign those loose things and sign only to the ledger. And to show that this is only matter of form, the transferring of these private notes into a ledger, I observe to them that the Treasurer in the late times, Mr Hutchinson, thought fit to omit it wholly and passed his accounts by the loose papers by which (if these be any difference) the State then lost the benefit of one examination and security against counterfeit signings or false enterings or any practice incident to the corrupting of their bills, which the King hath by the ledger's being examined and made up by the Comptroller. My Lord Brounker indeed added that the ledger was somewhat more than barely putting in one book

[1] The Auditors of Receipt in the Exchequer.

what was before in loose papers, namely the sorting of the King's expense under several heads what before lay scattered, and by this means that his Majesty's expense, in the nature of either, as to services or sorts of stores might be better understood. Which though indeed it be true and doth give a nearer account of the intent of a ledger in general than what was before said, yet the contest not being about the definition of a ledger but how far the previous signing of loose bills or books is necessary, I did not see what present use was or could be made of it, the test being that which is to prove the signing of loose papers not to be the vouchers essential to the truth of fact in the accounts.

They then proceeded to the 6th Article,[1] which being read I opened the business of Lanyon's[2] quality at Plymouth suitable to one employed in the same quality at the same place and elsewhere in the first war; with the unavoidableness in behalf of his Majesty that the particulars justifying the bills should lodge in the office for the calling to account the persons answerable for the stores or other things contained therein, and I might have added for the preventing the present accountant his redemanding the same hereafter what he is now allowed, and what (should we part with the particulars by which he claims the same) he may with more security demand of us again, when we shall have forgot the same, or should we remember it, shall want the vouchers to prove it. This being said, and without offering on their side the instance then given of Mr Lanyon, they told us that they had many other instances in other cases where we have omitted to mention the particulars in the bill. I then took notice of our former desires in writing, and their promises before his Majesty, to communicate to us all new instances. Lord Breerton answered that we should have them when they had finished their examinations and before we should be called to answer to them elsewhere. Upon which the Duke moved that the pressing of instances might be suspended till that time. I replied that I should not desire it, but rather chose to submit what present answers I could give than leave his Majesty under the want of any satisfaction. Upon which they turning to Portman, their clerk, he tendered them a bundle of papers out of which they picked two, which being put into my hand, one proved a bill to Mr Smith our messenger, expressing the same to be for postage of letters,

---

[1] Above, pp. 281–2.
[2] MS. 'lawyers'.

parish duties, candles, etc., for the use of the office according to particulars lodged therein. Upon which I made the answer before mentioned, adding that it was not only agreeable to practice both old and new, and that I was ready to produce instances of their practices in the late times, but requisite for preventing the too great bulk of the ledger, and that whereas they objected that by this means the Lord Treasurer could not be thoroughly informed of the true expense of the Navy, the Auditors did upon all occasions of scruple have recourse for the particulars to our office where, for the reasons above mentioned, these particulars were ever thought more properly and usefully lodged than flung aside in corners as useless and cancelled papers in the Auditors' office. The other paper was a note of Mr Tucker's of some tar (as I take it) and rosin received from one Terrill for the service of the Navy without specifying to what yard it was delivered,[1] which paper they say is all that was sent from the Comptroller to them as the ground of their making a certificate to the Exchequer for the value of the said goods. I asked them for the original certificate, saying that we ought not to be judged nor can their Observations be proved from a scrip of paper of one of our officers, but from what passed from our hands, wherein I did believe we should be found to express all required of us by the Act of Parliament. They answered they had it not here. The King replied that then nothing could be proved. But upon the whole I fell to my old question, what prejudice they found the King to sustain in any of these particulars if they should so positively charge us herewith as in the rest with so many crimes against his Majesty, and was therein seconded by the King himself, who took notice largely of their so frequent acknowledging their unreadiness to make good any want of examination of their full[2] matters wherewith they charge us as so many crimes. They answered that it is true they could not yet instance anything of his Majesty's being damaged in this particular, having not yet gone through the examination of our answers and their own inquiries into this matter, but that they desired, as they had formerly done, that their Observation[s] upon us might not be interpreted for so many judgements against us, for they meant them not as such, but only as such errors which by what then appeared to them we seemed to

---

[1] For this dispute, see below, pp. 394–5. John Tooker was a Navy Board messenger and river agent.
[2] Sc. full examination of.

them chargeable with, until we could give them satisfaction therein, and that therefore they pretended to no more weight to be laid upon the said Observations to our prejudice than that the matters therein mentioned were true in fact. To which the King presently replied that the quite contrary appeared in the very first article of the performance of Warren's contract reflecting very severely upon Pett's villainy in his forswearing himself.[1] They answered that they only made use of Pett's evidence as a collateral proof of what they were before satisfied in the truth of from the letter of our contract. To which the King made some short reply that in all that they have already been satisfied, and that therefore they would spend no more time upon it.

Memorandum: that I have omitted one passage to the preceding Observation wherein to show them that we meant no more by signing the ledger than the transplanting into a book what we had formerly signed in loose papers, in opposition to what Tomson had urged about our signifying in the ledger our satisfaction in the moneys being paid, whereas in proof of the contrary nothing appears to verify the true payments of the fees allowed, I observed to them that the Officers of the Navy never did nor will in any[thing] think it safe for them to become accountable for the Treasurer's making true payments to the right persons upon the sight only of the names or marks of persons wholly unknown to us. Nay, where neither name nor mark appears, as by all practice it hath ever been in the case of tickets, that the Treasurer's possession of the bill, which he cannot be supposed to have but by the assent of the proprietor, and his being allowed the same upon his account, being a sufficient discharge to the King against the debt, and the Treasurer's being made accountable for the right payment thereof to the party, upon which score[2] I might have added it is that letters of administration are in case of executorship, and so letters of attorney in other cases, were never used to be tendered to us but to the Treasurers only for their satisfaction and justification. And that if it be anybody's work to inspect the Treasurer's making effectual proof of his payments, I suppose it to be the Auditors of Imprests, who do it in all other cases, I think, at least they do it in mine for Tangier;[3] as it seems requisite it should be done somewhere, that the King

[1] See above, p. 273.
[2] MS. 'sure' (a mishearing).
[3] Pepys had been Joint-Treasurer for Tangier since 1665.

and parties may not be made too much liable to the insolvency of a Treasurer in case of after-disputes touching the verity of the payment.

Upon this article I had fresh occasion of observing to his Majesty these gentlemen's proceeding to the charging us with crimes [was] only possible owning themselves not yet prepared to assign any instance of his Majesty's having undergone any actual damage from what, were it true, they here lay to our charge. And the same thing I had occasion to repeat touching the pretended irregularities of the storekeepers' entries in their books upon the occasion of the following Observation, *viz.*, the 7th, which they were next to proceed to.

Saturday February 5th. The King and Council met, and company called in, the Commissioners of Accounts, after reading the 7th Observation,[1] presented a paper containing instances,[2] as they would have it, to prove the truth of the first part thereof, namely our overlooking and not punishing the faults of under-officers. But it contained nothing but some instances of inmethodical and some double entries of goods received into his Majesty's stores, and particularly of Chatham and Harwich, and more especially of the latter. To which, after reading so far of my answer as respected this matter,[3] I took notice in the first place of their having failed in the asserting matter of fact, as I now also took leave to tell them they had in every article hitherto done but the 4th, wherein no blame can lie.[4] To the apparent violation of what themselves had the last meeting said to have been their only aim and what they pretended to have strictly done by and in their Observations, namely the right reporting matter of fact, wherein offering if they pleased to do the like in reference to the article foregoing, I observed them in this to have without exception condemned [us] in an universal neglect of looking to the behaviour of the under-officers, whereas I told the King I was ready to produce them a long list of instances to the contrary, if it were necessary to be done in a case where every leaf almost

---

[1] Above, pp. 282–3.
[2] Cf. HLRO, Main Papers 26 Oct. 1669, 213 C, f. 108r; HMC, *8th Report*, App. pt i. 133; where it is stated that (according to an incomplete count) there were 92 instances.
[3] Above, p. 284.
[4] This concerned the Board's alleged failure to check details of the Treasurer's ledgers: above, p. 280.

in our books gives a sufficient testimony thereof. Besides that I do challenge them to show me instance of any neglect of an officer discovered which we did fail of our neglecting our duties in the examining and punishing thereof; and did further show that even in the yard here mostly insisted upon, to wit that of Harwich, upon some discovery made to us of his irregular proceedings in his duty, we examined it, reported it to the Lord High Admiral, and had him turned out of his employment, and this above four years since in the beginning of the war.[1] For that of Chatham, the case of that yard was under Comr Pett, who particularly ought to answer for this failure there or show that he did complain to us of it, and that we did decline giving remedy thereto. But besides, these are not officers of our own choice, and consequently we [are] not accountable for them otherwise than for the correcting them so far as we are made to understand their defaults, which in all places where there are out-Commissioners it is certainly their part to see done, or the King loseth the whole benefit of the service expected from them. Moreover the injury to the King is neither probable nor can be great, which we are to fear from this error of the storekeepers, since from the known fallibility of mankind the clerk of the cheque is made a comptroller to him in his receipts and issues, and must not only concur with him in the mistake but must first lead the storekeeper to the same by being the person who first draws up the bill for the merchant; besides the concurrent testimonies of the clerk of the survey, master attendant and shipwright in their proper spheres, and the supposed control over all when the bills come to be examined by the Comptroller, who in case of any former bill made out for the same goods is supposed to make use of his former bill-book and the contracts, and thereby probably cannot oversee, but must rather discover the error – besides the further security his Majesty hath from the possible discoveries of the Treasurer when the bill comes to be paid, the Auditors when the Treasurer's account comes before them, and the solvency of the merchant to right the King when any such discovery shall be made. And to ratify this improbability which I suppose of the King's suffering anything hereby, I appeal[led] to them whether they had yet found the King [to suffer] in the whole time of this war, and in two years' examination thereof afterwards. To which

[1]This was the case of John Browne, storekeeper, dismissed in December 1665: *CSPD 1664–5*, p. 185; *1665–6*, p. 125; *Add. 1660–85*, p. 263.

they answered that they were not yet prepared to show any, but were upon the examinations thereof. Which is their constant answer, and to which I always reply by taking notice of their charging us only with possible evils rather than not at all, where they want actual ones, as they have hitherto still done. The Duke observed very well how unlikely this was to be designed by the storekeepers with intention of wrong to his Majesty because in the very same book they charge the same goods to the same [merchant] at the same place upon the same day twice: a cheat so discoverable as no man can be thought weak enough to venture his fortune upon the success of it. To which I add, when they may with much more security serve themselves with another [cheat] and every whit as advantageous: namely, by inserting different parcels at different times and of different men which were not received at all. Upon all which the King signified his full satisfaction and the hardship they offered us in making us accountable for the lapses of all inferior officers for whom we are no ways accountable otherwise than for the keeping them to the best of our powers to their duties and punishing them where they are found faulty; the omission of which they do not at all attempt to prove.

They then proceeded to the tender of a second paper containing instances of our providing and receiving goods otherwise than by contract, quoting that article of the General Instructions wherein we are forbid to buy any goods otherwise than by a contract first made.[1] To which I applied myself by making answer by discourse, without first reading my written answer thereto,[2] which since my recollection I find to have been attended with the inconvenience of having forgot the mention of some things to advantage; which inconvenience I must hereafter labour to prevent by reading always my written answer first. But I proceeded very happily to show his Majesty – both by two of the General Instructions, one of the Surveyor's and several of the storekeeper's,[3] (all quoted in my foul notes) – that as well by them as by constant practice of having a King's Merchant and other purveyors in his royal ancestors' time and the same much greater practice in the late times, as an express clause in our Commissioners' present patents, we have a full power of buying

---

[1] Art. 5 forebade any considerable quantity of provisions to be served in 'without contract made ... in a publick meeting': *Oeconomy*, p. 24.
[2] Above, pp. 284–5.
[3] *Oeconomy*, pp. 36–7, 38–9, 62, 90–1.

goods by commissions, purveyance and other ways than that of contract. To all which the King most fully agreeing, they offered nothing in opposition than that letter of the general Instructions, which I thereupon took up and showed it ought not to be interposed to the contradicting the whole tenor of the rest of his Instructions and practice in all times, and what neither he nor anything else can prevent the necessity of doing, namely of buying abroad and at times when no contractors can be had upon other terms than that of formal contract. They urged the chargeableness of some of these goods bought by commission, and particularly that of Sir W. Warren's, the King being put to charge [of] a convoy,[1] and appealing to any instance we could give of any goods provided in any of the King's predecessors' time when the Officers of the Navy made the King run the risk of bringing them home. I replied that the question was new but that as on the sudden I would not undertake to affirm anything of matter of fact so long ago without inquiry first made, so I asked whether he that had pretended to look so far backward (I mean Col. Tomson) as Queen Elizabeth's time in his other searches would assert that instances were not to be found, but supposing no instances, they would gain nothing by it since the commodities were very few in those days with which the King's expense,[2] such as it then was, might not be sufficiently supplied at home, as with his own iron, his own timber, his own plank, his own hemp (to which I might have quoted the Statute in Henry VIII's time, as I take it, about the town of Burfett)[3] and other goods, saving on art[icle]s which the common market without his sending for might with much ease supply sufficiently. But in the late times I was ready to show that they did find it necessary to undertake for the risk and charge of transportation, and that so much as for good[s] to be brought but from Yarmouth, from their creature Major Burton,[4] upon the quality of whose goods I may hereafter to good purpose have opportunity of insisting by comparing them with the quality of the worst bought by us. Besides, I told them, if

---

[1] See above, p. 363.
[2] The naval stores likely to be expended.
[3] Bridport, Dorset, an important centre for the manufacture of cables etc. from home-grown hemp. An Act of 21 Hen. VIII c. 12 protected its trade by forbidding the manufacture of rope in the immediate neighbourhood: F. Pulton, *Collection of... statutes* (ed. T. Manby, 1670), pp. 397–8; VCH, *Dorset*, ii. 345.
[4] William Burton, bailiff of Great Yarmouth and Navy agent there, c. 1655–8; a prominent republican MP in the Barebones Parliament; Admiralty and Navy Commissioner 1653–4: Aylmer, *State's Servants*, pp. 277, 419.

in that very instance which they have brought in opposition to our dealing with Warren, *viz.*, that of Shorter's offering us masts at the same time (though falsely) upon better terms, Shorter in his very deposition doth (as I take it) declare that his undertaking should be expressly by condition either of convoy or a dispensation with the Act of Navigation, that he might bring them in foreign ships.[1] I then prayed them to listen to the very first article of the Duke's Instructions, and tell me, and then applied myself to his Majesty, praying him also to tell me what he would have said to us, in case upon being convinced of the necessity of his Majesty's being supplied or his service ruined, and that being unable to procure them upon fair terms of contract it should have been told us – what need you stand upon contract? Have not you a full power given you of advising and consulting in and for all things conducing to the well being of his Majesty's Navy with authority and command to proceed therein by majority of voices?[2] And that therefore though other ways may be dearer, yet they are more certain and effectual, especially if it should have been added (which I have not yet thought fit to make use of, but leave it for some more eminent occasion) that the Admiral doth in his farewell letter[3] expressly charge you not to consider thrift or husbandry, but at our peril lays it upon us to see that the work be effectually done at any cost, suitable to what the Parliament itself limits its own inquiries to, *viz.*, that matters should have been done with no more care, fidelity and good husbandry than the nature of such services would admit; we should nevertheless say that notwithstanding all this we find ourselves bound up in one article (though it is true it was an article made with the rest in a time of peace, credit, plenty and little action, nor calculated for a war) to provide no goods otherwise than by contract, and therefore come what will of the service, we will abide by this article and make no other provision since we cannot compass it by contract. I asked what his Majesty would have said to us in such a case. He answered readily, and as happily as I could have wished, that he would have said we deserved to be hanged. I replied: "And that very justly." To which Tomson then took upon him to observe what the consequence of this answer would have been, namely the invalidating at once the

---

[1] See above, p. 350.
[2] Pepys here paraphrases the first article of the Admiral's Instructions of 1662: *Oeconomy*, pp. 20–1.
[3] See above, p. 354 & n. 2.

whole book of Instructions, leaving us by the power of the first to observe or dispense the observation of all the rest. To which I replied that as this was so, it ought to be allowed not only for a true but justifiable consequence, in regard that forasmuch as in the age when those Instructions were drawn[1] the Earl of Northumberland could have no competent idea either of the nature or bulk of the work of such a war, nor of the thousand contingencies attending the same, it is not reasonable to think that his Majesty's service should in its execution be bound up to the straitness of those scanty methods, but that the meaning of these Instructions should be no more than this, that where without prejudice by delay or otherwise to the service and where the same was also possible, those rules of the Admiral's should be observed, to prevent our falling into worse or at least uncertain methods of our own, which being unfixed would for ever keep the action of the Navy and the proceedings of this great Office in a state of disorders and uncertainties in its methods, liable to the humours, ignorances, or negligences, or perfunctory performances of the several particular hands which from time to time should be entrusted therewith, to the rendering also the tracing of their accounts and actions, especially when for any time past, very difficult; but that where the natures of the services would not permit of the nice attention to these rules, there the Principal Officers and Commissioners of the Navy, to whom the care of the execution of the whole is committed and was anciently without any such rules, should be judges of what is fit or unfit to be done therein, and proceed to do the same upon advice by majority of voices. To which explication of the nature of this constitution and book of Instruction[s] the King and Admiral did most readily concur, as being the only genuine and reasonable explication thereof. Wherein I might undoubtedly have not a little confirmed them had it been then what now comes into my mind to have said, that this exposition of the article and the consequence of it would but have put us into the same condition of doing his Majesty's service which those of the late times were of doing their masters', namely that of a freedom of doing what they judged most advantageous to their service without any limitation to rules of any sort,[2] and that I appealed to themselves

---

[1] In 1640, when Northumberland was Lord High Admiral.
[2] The Instructions issued under Charles I having lapsed.

and my written instances[1] whether our proceedings have not in all respects been such as may represent us as fit to have such a trust as they, Col. Tomson himself having disclaimed the valuing of the virtue of our management by being compared with theirs; and then again how unreasonable seems it that we should be expected not only to do as well but be condemned if we do not better than they in those times, and yet be denied equal trust, authority and capacity necessary for the enabling us to do the same.

I remember that upon the discourse of the business of our commissions Tomson did abruptly and from the purpose cry out with our having to do with foreign plank, saying with some insultingness that for his part he had served in the Navy and that he ever was and should still be for the good English plank. I replied that we also had served in the Navy as he and were as much in love with English planks as he, and that though we had formerly bought much foreign plank and were at this [time] under contract for some hundreds of loads more, yet to show our love to English plank I would undertake that upon the reasons which should be given his Majesty by the Officers of the Navy, and the satisfaction which I was confident his Majesty already had in the preferableness of his own plank, his Majesty should give him thanks to direct us where for a considerable advance of price we might be furnished with 2000 or but a 1000 or but 500 loads at this day of English plank to be had.[2] With which his mouth seeming to be stopped and the King expressing his full concurrence therein, they proceeded to the tender of a third paper, wherein they seemed to offer instances of warrants of the Board for receipt of goods contracted for without transmitting to them a copy of the contract. But when I come to hear them I found not one of them to be instances of that case, but instances of warrants for receipt of goods where there was no contract made, and so all at once I told them. They objected, first that several of these goods, and particularly and mostly in cases of Sir Wm Warren, were neither bought by contract nor by any commission that appeared. I answered that a commission is not necessarily to be given in writing: it sufficeth that we did direct the delivering in of the goods, they being no other but what his Majesty's service

[1] Pepys's 'paper of instances' relating to this Observation, now untraced.
[2] Supplies of English oak had been dwindling for some time: see R. G. Albion, *Forests and Sea Power* (Cambridge, Mass. 1926), esp. pp. 102–3.

stood in want of, and the prices the cheapest we could get, and the warrants for the receipt of them enough show that the goods were to be served in by direction from us, and with our satisfaction in the requisiteness thereof. They then urged our commission to Sir Wm Rider, Cutler, etc., as a contract for tar, hemp, etc. I answered that a contract, both in the general notion of it, and in the description thereof by the Admiral in the 5th General Instruction[1] so much by them insisted on, imploys as ascertaining what quantity, price and other circumstances which they shall not at all find in this our commission, wherein moreover express condition is made for the provision our said factors are to have for this their commission. Here they answered that a copy of this ought to have been sent to have enabled them to have described the quality of the goods. I answered that as the copies of nothing but contracts is enjoined to be sent down,[2] so neither is it necessary forasmuch as the storekeeper in his instructions is already in general told what he is to do in the receipt of and making out bills for any stores served in otherwise than by contract by certifying the quality, dimensions, etc. thereof as he finds them.

Memorandum: that as no instances of theirs gave occasion for it, so my forgetfulness to observe all along to read my written answer[3] prevented me, among other things, to show in the business of the storekeepers that we sign no bill for stores without the time specified for serving in thereof, and in the other business – of our gaining a liberty to ourselves of giving what prices and passing by defects as we think fit – that as we had never abused that liberty, so it was not a liberty by us sought after, but expressly and essentially committed and entrusted to us by the Lord High Admiral's own instruction,[4] as appears by my foul notes on this subject.

Some little disputes I remember there arose about the insurance of some goods of Sir W. Warren's, as iron, deal, pipestaves, etc., as also of the freight paid by the King and which we said was repaid him by Sir W.W. for pipestaves; but this chiefly falling within my Lord Brouncker's notice and his Lordship expressly taking upon him whatever should be found blameable

---

[1] *Oeconomy*, p. 24: the contract was to stipulate the 'quality, dimensions and price'.
[2] MS. 'done' (a mishearing).
[3] Above, pp. 283–6.
[4] *Oeconomy*, p. 37.

of the Board's proceedings in that matter,[1] and thereupon undertaking the debate thereof and satisfying his Majesty therein, I did not charge my memory with the passages thereof, as being a matter foreign to me, but passed[2] with good success, as by all circumstances appeared, of satisfaction to his Majesty and the Board.

Monday February 7th. The King and Council being sat and we called in, the Commissioners of Accounts, instead of proceeding to the 8th [Observation], produced a fourth instance to the 7th about that part of it which relates to the receipt of goods without contract,[3] or at least seeming grounded thereupon, though not very naturally. But upon an opinion that they could make something extraordinary of what they had the last day mentioned about our paying insurance for some iron, deal and pipestaves, which being put into Sir W. Warren's Hamburgh ships were lost and the insurance thereof with part of the rest paid for by the King, though the same were not bought by any direction or commission of ours, they resolved, rather than want the utmost benefit of what they could make on this occasion, to bring this matter in again under the name of a fresh instance. To which I was prepared to make answer, as my Lord Brouncker also did, who took upon him the justifying the proceedings of the Board in this matter, as having had the particular adjusting of the same, *viz.*, that though it be true that the goods were not bought by commission, yet they were useful to the King and we received them. To which particular they would have objected our having no use for pipestaves, but to that received present answer from me that the Victualler was at that time in utmost distress for pipestaves, which his Majesty confirmed by remembering himself that he and his Council were under great care how to supply him therewith, and to purpose had taken resolutions of helping him from Ireland, it being plain to them that the Victualler could not of himself provide them. I further showed that they were but a small quantity, and necessarily bought[4] as all private merchants are said to do, to whom I therein appealed, for the dry and

---

[1] Brouncker had responsibility for assisting the Comptroller in clearing Warren's account: see above, p. 176 n. 1.
[2] MS. 'lost' (a mishearing).
[3] Above, pp. 282–3.
[4] MS. 'brought'.

convenient storing of the hemp, and that what was bought[1] for the supply of the Victualler in straits to be repaid the King by the Victualler was but our duty to his Majesty's service in general; but we showed further that when Sir W. Warren came to pass his account he did frankly leave it to us either to repute the goods his and give him the benefit of that insurance which upon oath he had declared to us to have made in particular upon these goods, apart from what he had or was able to do for those goods which did come by commission from the King; or for us to take the goods, though lost, and take the assurance to the King, which insurance arising as my Lord Brounker showed to about 400*l*. and the goods lost not amounting to much above 200*l*., we took the goods to ourselves for the King and have the benefit of that insurance, by which his Lordship showed that the King had got almost 200*l*. clear by this parcel of goods. They urged it an improbability that a merchant should insure 400*l*. upon goods of but 200*l*. value. Lord Brouncker answered that the merchant had not then had from his factor a valuation of the goods and therefore made it his interest to insure enough, adding that the practice is familiar among merchants, according as they esteem the danger more or less and the insurance easy, to insure to a greater or less value than the goods are worth, and sometimes a bystander shall censure[2] that hath no goods there; but lastly it doth appear in fact by the merchant's oath, which we have no way of gainsaying, that he did really insure so much upon these goods. To which they did attempt to answer that by the commission he was obliged to insure all the King's, whereas he is found to insure only 200*l*. worth for the King besides this 400*l*. worth for himself, whereto I replied that it did appear to us at that time that he did insure as much as insurances could be procured for, and that he neither was obliged by his commission to insure all (wherein I appealed to the logical and grammatical construction of the words thereof) nor reasonably on his Majesty's behalf ought to have been, but left, as he was, to do no more in that point than as he should be by us from time to time directed; and this in regard that, the King intending to be at charge for convoy, it must seem very imprudent for us to condemn the King to pay insurance against that hazard which he had otherways at so great a charge as convoy resolved to secure himself against. To which Tomson

[1] Idem.
[2] Sc. it is agreed that a fellow merchant on the Exchange shall fix the sum.

impertinently answered that his Majesty had formerly said that his convoys went to secure the merchantmen as well as his own ships, but was presently replied to by the King that he hoped nobody would think him so far disposed towards the saving of other people's goods as not to think that by the same charge and convoy he meant to have the benefit thereof in preference[1] to his own.

This being over and they offering to proceed to the 8th Observation, I stopped them, desiring to be heard to two particulars that seemed the day before the last not capable then of being received by his Majesty with any other satisfaction than what depended upon his Majesty's choice of giving credit to my yes or Col. Tomson's no, being also nevertheless two particulars not otherwise worthy a single, much less a double troubling his Majesty than as these Commissioners had thought them worthy their instancing therein as matters of crime in his Officers. The business was that of our making his Majesty pay the parish duties of the house his office is kept in,[2] which Col. Tomson having thought fit to urge as unreasonable in us to put upon his Majesty for the house he voluntarily gives us to live in, I had answered that it was no more than the State had done to our predecessors in their time. To which Tomson making answer by denial of the same, I told the King I came now prepared to show him under the hand of Errington their messenger that paid them that the State out of their public treasure did evermore pay all these duties and other taxes and charges as long as they continued. To which I added that this were more unreasonable in them, if it must be unreasonable at all, by how much[3] they first made their masters buy an house for them, and then to pay all duties to that house, whereas we make ours only pay those duties, the house having cost his Majesty nothing, as being heir to it from the State. I might have added that what the King pays for, he or his officers have the benefit of it, whereas they made their masters the State pay among the rest of the duties a yearly allowance of 40s. to the parson, though they rarely, if ever, made the benefit of his doctrine by going to church.[4] But this last I forbore, having formerly hinted it.

The second thing was the paper of Terrill's signed only by Mr

[1] MS. 'reference' (a mishearing).
[2] Cf. above, p. 379 & n. 7.
[3] Sc. in that.
[4] See above, p. 379 n. 6.

Tucker without specifying the place or service for which the goods therein mentioned were provided,[1] which they bring as an instance of the 6th Article.[2] Upon which I showed them a copy of the order of the Exchequer issued to Terrill upon the certificate of this Office, both which they either have before them or might have had, wherein it doth appear expressly [that] the particular[s] of the goods were delivered. They answered frivolously that that paper was all they see. To which I replied that it was no fault of ours they saw no more, it being always in their power to have demanded what now upon the first demand is shown them,[3] and what upon the credit of the officers of the Exchequer I do believe they have already seen, besides that that loose paper of Tucker's had never[4] proved their Observation, since that charges us with signing bills without specifying place, service, etc. Whereas this paper of Tucker's neither is a bill nor signed by us, nor did we ever sign a bill at all for it, but a certificate to the Exchequer conformable to the method directed by Act of Parliament,[5] and that certificate expressly specifying every circumstance by this Observation pretended to have been wanting. To which they remaining wholly silent, the King called for the next Observation, which was accordingly read. But first let me remember that on some occasion or other upon discourse of bills and certificates, Tomson did by head and shoulders[6] quote a sum of 45*l*. which had been twice given by the Board to Sir W. Warren, *viz.*, once by bill and then by certificate to the Exchequer. To which I replied that this was a mistake of 45*l*. in an account with a merchant for above 40,000*l*. ("Yes", said my Lord Brouncker,[7] "above 100,000*l*.") And that mistake, saith my Lord Brouncker, long since discovered by ourselves and rectified, which Tomson would not own to be done before they had discovered it. But the King thought fit not worth his while to have that controverted, the error being no greater and already rectified, and therefore called for the next Observation.

[1] See above, p. 382.
[2] Above, pp. 281–2.
[3] That is, the order of the Exchequer referred to above.
[4] Sc. would never have.
[5] Sect. xi of the Act imposing the Eleven Months Tax (18 & 19 Car. II c. 13) whose proceeds were partly appropriated to the Navy. There is an office book containing abstracts of these weekly certificates signed by the Principal Officers between 31 Dec. 1667 and 31 Dec. 1668: PL 2583.
[6] Sc. in an interruption.
[7] MS. 'Breerton'.

The 8th Observation[1] being read, and by them opened by reading the articles of the Comptroller's and Surveyor's duty obliging them to balancing of storekeepers' accounts and taking of surveys[2] and the 18th of the General Instructions[3] as all, as they would have it, to the seeing it done, and declaring that no such balance had been by them seen, I began by craving leave in the first place to show the King and my Lords the nature of this work of balancing storekeepers' accounts, that it might be the better understood when we come to speak of its being performed or not performed; which being granted me, I shortly told them that it was no less than the taking an account of almost an infinite number of provisions great and small, foreign and domestic, under perpetual receipts and issues to almost as numberless number of services, and these in distant places, both on sea and on shore, while at the same time the charge thereof also lay in a great variety of hands full of employment during a war, who must be all taken from the other indispensable works of their places to attend the making up of this balance. And not only so, but the whole service must stand still, for without seeing the remainder of the stores, no balance can be made up, and how the remainder of stores shall be taken at a time when every quarter of an hour or less goods of one sort or other are issuing or receiving, or both, and that in sundry places of the same yard, so as it were impossible without a total standstill of the service to take a general survey at any one time, so can no balance remain true at any time an hour together. And therefore, this being the nature of the service, I proceeded to the reading my written answer as far as to the end of the 3rd article of the Comptroller's duty by me therein quoted.[4] Which having done, I took upon me to open the same by discourse according to the method which I had before set myself in the following paper, beginning with a profession of a willingness to make the worst of our case by adding to what the Commissioners had already said; the force of those two General Instructions, *viz.* thirteen and fourteen,[5] wherein not by a forced implication as they would have it out of the 18th, but in express terms the care of seeing storekeepers' accounts' balances seems to be laid upon the Board in general.

[1] Above, p. 287.
[2] *Oeconomy*, pp. 51–2, 60–1.
[3] Ibid., pp. 39–40 (MS. 'Instituting').
[4] Above, pp. 287–8.
[5] *Oeconomy*, pp. 33–6.

About storekeepers' balances. The end of the 13th General Article tells us we are to take the account of the storekeepers by meeting in the yards at convenient times in the year. When could that convenient time be, they being by the 13th bound at least twice – and our business in time of peace ever obliging us to meet thrice – in a week at the office, and therefore much more often in time of war? Myself[1] bound expressly to attend at every meeting, and not twenty-four hours absent from the office during the whole war, and but thrice absent from the meetings, and that by the Admiral's command, and letters coming continually early and late, and it may be said not one post or day free from letters or warrants issued from the Board. Myself able to give an account of every day's spendings. The Treasurer attends the Lord Treasurer, the Court, the Council, the Customers, the Excise Commissioners, the Exchequer, the bankers, the Parliament, and pays off ships or tickets, or other payments continually. The Surveyor, if he did it, had work enough to take up his time, in surveys of particular ships, boatswains' and carpenters' accounts, surveying of stores received, etc. The Comptroller in passing all accounts, examining bills, attending pays, etc. The Commissioners, one at Chatham, another attending the Admiral, a third either at sea or assisting in hastening out the fleets coming in,[2] the rest assisting at pays, at the Board or elsewhere, we (as sometimes myself) to be left alone with all the business of the Office and all the correspondencies thereof to the ships, to the yards, to the ports, to the Lord Treasurer, to the Council, to the Admiral and in his absence the Duke of Albermarle (as my Lord Craven[3] can witness), and lastly to all that daily had occasion of applying themselves to the Office. When then could this convenient time of the year be when none of us would be at leisure to take it, and much less those of the yard in condition without prejudice to the King's service (then always both summer and winter full of action) to give it?

The close of the 14th general article charging the Office jointly with the balancing yearly storekeepers' accounts.[4] But this is a work to which something must be done previous by a particular hand, as in the 5th article of the Surveyor's touching the balancing of boatswains' and carpenters' accounts, where the Surveyor is

---
[1]Pepys here repeats much of his defence of his own conduct at pp. 326–8 above.
[2]That is, Pett, Coventry and Penn respectively.
[3]Albemarle's close friend and associate.
[4]*Oeconomy*, p. 36.

to prepare and then lay them by way of declaration before the Board for their inspection, allowance, or questioning.[1] Just so the body of the Office is to balance the storekeepers', but, however, by receiving them from the hand of the Comptroller as [in] the 3rd article of his Instructions.[2] The like may be said of the Board's being entrusted with the balancing of the Treasurer's accounts (14th article general),[3] whereas the Comptroller by the 5th of his[4] is, by an express priority given him, obliged to prepare the said accounts for them.

The Comptroller, partly by his age and sickness, and partly by the multitude of other works above mentioned, has not been able to perform it. Wherein he is humbly submitted to his Majesty's indulgence, and therein hath the less reason to doubt his finding the same, when besides what is already said of his age spent and his weaknesses contracted in his Majesty's service, it shall appear that no part of the charge laid upon us or him, either in terms or by implication, touching this matter will be found to rest upon him, the charge amounting to this:

Viz., 1. That we have neglected this duty of balancing the storekeepers' accounts.

2. That by this means the King's stores have been liable to embezzlement.

3. That in this remissness we have failed in doing what others have done.

4. Lastly that his Majesty's service hath hereby been injured from our ignorance in what stores we were in want of.

To every one of which the four first of my five observations on this subject:

Upon the first of which, after reading the same out of my written answer,[5] I am ready to show the early endeavours of the Board after balancing of stores, and that by all probable expedients of compassing it, as:

1st. By beginning with but a little. *Vide* warrant the 31th of January 1662[3] to storekeepers to come to balance for canvas and cordage.[6]

---

[1]Ibid., pp. 64–5.
[2]Ibid., pp. 51–2.
[3]Ibid., pp. 35–6.
[4]Ibid., pp. 53–4.
[5]Above, pp. 287–8.
[6]That is, to give account of the amounts received and issued. Cf. the statement by the clerk of the ropeyard at Chatham: *CSPD Add. 1660–85*, p. 85.

2ly. By calling upon the officer appointed for the control thereof to do his duty. *Vide* warrant to the clerk of the cheque to keep counter books with the storekeeper in order to balancing his account.[1]

3ly. By attempting what could not be done everywhere, to do it in one place, where we looked upon the officer to be a man of most method amongst them, and a Commissioner present the best able to overlook him. *Vide* letters 30th March 1664. Comr Pett's letter to Mr Pepys.

> 31 March 1664. To the storekeepers at Chatham.
> 31 March 1664. To Comr Pett.
> 4 April 1664. Comr Pett to Mr Pepys.

After this the Board, upon some further advice from Comr Pett (which I have not yet looked out) for increase of pay to four of the storekeepers' instruments, warrants the clerk of the cheque[2] to see it done. This proving ineffectual, the Board resumes the consideration thereof with Comr Pett by their letter to him of the 2d Febry 1666[7]. In March following Mr Pett delivers the Board a paper of Holt's[3] dated the 5th, upon which they discourse with him before his Highness, where he undertakes for the seeing it done. The whole proceeding of which *vide* our letter to him 12 March 1666[7].

Since which having no success thereof, nothing was more done till the end of the war, of which more by and by.

Besides all which, some of us knowing the greatest part of this failure to arise from the Comptroller's inability to do his whole work, did endeavour earlily to ease him of part, that he might look after the remainder, and this in particular, but without success, till about Janry 1666[7] when Lord Brouncker and Sir W. Penn were made his assistants,[4] but yet this without effect as to the balancing storekeepers' accounts till the end of the war, of which we shall speak by and by. However, from hence it will appear that the Board, as much as in them lay, had it still in their wishes and endeavours to compass this matter.

---

[1] PRO, ADM 106/2507, no. 23; BL, Add. MSS 9315, f. 6*v*.; issued 25 Jan. 1664. He was to send copies quarterly or half-yearly to the Comptroller.
[2] At Chatham (Edward Gregory).
[3] Storekeeper at Chatham.
[4] See above, p. 176 n .1.

Having by discourse gone over the substance of this as well as my memory would enable me, and without anything forgot that I can recollect, I then went on to the second exception, touching the insecurity his Majesty's stores have been in under this want of a balance, and thereupon read my written answer on that head,[1] adding as it needed, but little enlarging upon by discourse.

I then advanced to the third, and having read what I had written thereon,[2] discoursed somewhat upon it, though without any fresh matter, and appealed particularly to Tomson not only for instance[s] under the late times but whether in those inquiries he hath formerly pretended to have made into the ancient practice of the Navy as far backward as Queen Elizabeth, whether he had ever even under the meanest action in any age heard of a balance of storekeepers' accounts taken.

I then went on the fourth, about the little prejudice this can be thought to have been of to his Majesty's service in the late war, where having read what I had written thereon,[3] the King was so fully satisfied with the reason as to prevent any enlarging of mine thereon, by taking it upon himself in his own vindication as well as ours (as he was pleased to call it) the giving a summary account of the success of our endeavours in the late war; which he was pleased to say was such as, but for the unhappy business of Chatham, we had no reason but to own to come up to the utmost of whatever was performed in the first Dutch war, or what the enemy could be said to have done in this; and so of his own accord run over the several instances of dispatch given by this Board in the fitting forth and the refitting forth of the fleets before and after fights, always sooner than the enemy could do, though the diversities of their Admiralties (as the King well observed) made it almost as easy to set out ten as two. To which I humbly took leave to offer the consideration of the difference between the charge which the late war is owned to have cost them and us. Which the King very readily took upon him also to speak to by saying that he had made it his work to inform himself in the expense of the Dutch in the late war, and finds it upon

---

[1] Above, pp. 288–9.
[2] Above, p. 289.
[3] Above, pp. 289–90.

very good information to have amounted to 11 millions sterling, whereas ours doth not come up to or at least not exceeds 6.[1]

But then, to show the esteem which both the Lord High Admiral and this Office hath ever had of the importance of this work of balancing storekeepers' accounts, besides the instances I have already given to the Board's care in the first of the four heads now mentioned, I read my fifth observation,[2] showing what the Lord High Admiral had done so soon as the end of the war gave him opportunity, and the hopes we may at present entertain of the good fruits thereof the next year beyond whatever past times have arrived at or pretended to.

[*Marginal note*] *Memorandum*: I here read the Duke's words in his letter of 9ber 25. 1668.[3]

Having done this in reference to balancing of storekeepers' accounts, I proceeded to that of taking surveys,[4] and thereupon read what I had wrote on that subject,[5] offering to prove the same by testimonies from the officers then and now best able to inform us, I mean Mr Acworth and Urthwaite. But it appeared unnecessary, the King and Lords expressing full satisfaction in this matter, and the Commissioners of Accounts offering nothing in reply but that these works being enjoined and not performed, they thought it was their duties to represent them in the manner they had done.

The King then called for the next Observation, *viz.*, the 9th.[6] Which being read and their paper containing only the general article of our duties obliging us to musters in the Narrow Seas every three months, and a declaration that they find the same not to have been done, there seemed to need no more answer than just the reading of what I had wrote,[7] wherein the King owned full satisfaction on our part, expressing his observation of the strangeness of their proceeding in charging us with a fault

---

[1]The actual expenditure was – and is – impossible to calculate exactly. Prof. Chandaman puts the figure in the case of England at not more than £5¼m., even including the naval actions of 1664 which preceded the declaration of war (*Eng. Public Revenue 1660–88*, p. 211). The Dutch probably spent the equivalent of c. £2m. (inf. from Prof. J. R. Bruijn, citing *inter alia*, J. C. de Jonge, *Geschiedenis van der Nederlandsche zeewezen*, Haarlem 1858, i. 703; J. M. F. Fritschy, *De patriotten en de financien van de Bataafse Republiek*, The Hague 1988, pp. 61–4.)
[2]Above, p. 290.
[3]See above, p. 252 & n. 1.
[4]MS. 'surveyors'.
[5]Above, pp. 290–1.
[6]Above, p. 291.
[7]Above, pp. 291–2.

for the breach of one part of an instruction wherein the very next words of the same instruction wholly acquits us, directing himself to Col. Tomson and saying that he would be once in his life ingenuous and own his being satisfied.

Memorandum: that I might have urged that our instructions to the muster-masters (and the performance of them too in a great measure) do exceed – much less come short of – what this instruction requires of us and the muster-masters, we obliging them to a monthly, whereas this expects but a three-monthly muster.

Memorandum: also, that it may not hereafter be unuseful for me to carry a specimen of the muster book by me prepared and by the Board established, and now for some years since in use, much exceeding anything formerly known.

The King then called for the 10th Observation,[1] which being read and a paper instancing two depositions of boatswains' and carpenters' accounts passed without any control made use of by the purser, there needed no other answer than what I had wrote thereon,[2] which was done and proved fully satisfactory, without the help of what further matter I might have added out of my foul notes, which, not foreseeing our advantage so far this day, I had not prepared myself to apply to.

[*Marginal note*] It may not be amiss hereafter to quote the Duke's last injunction in 9ber 68 about the Surveyor's bringing his declaration to the Board of boatswains' and carpenters' accounts.[3]

To the other part of this Observation, about comparing pursers' books with slop-sellers', after reading my written answer I gave them this short answer by discourse, that this expedient was first no other than to set a thief to catch a thief; secondly, to censure us (if it were good) for not doing what we were never enjoined with till now was never once thought of, and in which I did believe if it had been now but twice thought on, would never have been propounded; and thirdly, to find fault with the King's want of sufficient security against injury in this mean article of Runs, while the King hath no less[4] therein than what they themselves have nowhere complained of being insufficient in that article of a thousand times more moment to the King, namely that of seamen's wages, to which I might add that of

---

[1] Above, p. 292.
[2] Above, p. 293.
[3] This was required by the Admiral's Instructions of 1662: *Oeconomy*, pp. 294–5.
[4] Sc. no less security.

victuals and almost all other expenses of wear and tear, namely the hands of his commanders, masters and boatswains. To all which the Commissioners of Accounts remaining wholly silent, the King and Board broke up with most ample expressions at the Board, and much more afterwards, of the unanswerable satisfaction given them.

Saturday Febry 12. (69[70]). The King and Council sat, and we called in, the 11th Observation[1] was read and their papers of instances, upon which I propounded the reading of the 12th and 13th,[2] as relating all to the business of tickets, and for saving time capable of receiving a common answer. Which being agreed to, the other two were accordingly read, and then my written answer to the whole;[3] which being ended, my Lord Breerton took care to have it observed for future use that the instructions here read bore not date till Janry 1666[7].[4] I then began with this question: whether the fault they here blame us with be a fault of breaking some written instructions of the Admiral's or the practice of the Navy, showing and appealing therein to Tomson that in the late times they never offered at the establishing or observing any rules of comparing tickets [with] their counterparts till after the end of the first Dutch war, they having not so much as invented much less exercised the printing of tickets till then. Here my Lord Breerton interposed, saying that he had often answered this sort of question, fully as he thought, by saying that they did not hold themselves obliged to report miscarriages arising only from breach of a known rule or practice, but also everything wherein his Majesty may be found to suffer any evil, whether the same arises from breach of rule or not, and that as such they reported this; though he added that he thought there was a rule broke by the not doing what is here by them expected, and that is the 12th General Article,[5] containing directions for our proceeding in the passing the Victualler's account, wherein we are bid to compare our warrants with the sea books, and the sea books with the muster books, etc. His Lordship from thence inferring that if so much care is enjoined us in the business of victuals, much more

---

[1] Above, p. 294.
[2] Ibid.
[3] Above, pp. 295–9.
[4] That is, the Board's instructions about the payment of tickets: see above, p. 296 & n. 2.
[5] Of the Admiral's Instructions to the Board: *Oeconomy*, pp. 31–3.

ought it to be thought the Admiral's intentions that we should be strict in the examination of wages, I answered his Lordship, first, that it is true they were not tied only to take notice of breaches of rule, but that they had a double work upon their hand – one to blame the guilty for defaults past, against rules known, the other for the discovering any defects in our methods past in order to the rectifying the same for the time to come, and that therefore they might very justly offer anything of the latter sort as well as the former, but yet so as to distinguish between what is barely to be rectified for the time to come, and what through our non-observation of rule we are justly blameable for the suffering anything to have been done amiss in for the time past. I then showed him that no blame can be done to us in this particular from breach of rule, there being none, nor ground of condemning the methods of the Navy as imperfect in this matter, in regard that the examination of tickets by their counterparts is a matter wholly impracticable in a time of war, where ships being to be paid at the same time in sundry places, and the men thereon for the most part having tickets for service in former ships without opportunity either of sending or bringing them up for examination, it was impossible for them to be compared with their counterparts resting in the office, nor for the same reason (as is more largely expressed in my annexed notes[1] prepared for this day's work but little used) could those tickets be examined by the proper muster book, and this the State in the late times knew well enough, when they forbore either the enjoining or attempting the practising of it. But I showed them that our not doing it arose not from our not having the rule in esteem as far as it was practicable, forasmuch as Carkess himself, whose deposition and Seddon's they brought in proof of their Article,[2] does under his hand with another clerk Mr Whitfeild (which I read to them) certify that the examining of tickets by their counterparts was practised till the hurry of the war made it impracticable. I showed them also that it has been done together with the sending of lists to the Treasurer's office ever since the end of the war, and is at this day done. Tompson here objected that if it could not be done, why did we issue those instructions in Janry 66[7] now read?[3] If they could, why did we not make them sooner, before

---

[1] Below, pp. 411–16.
[2] Observation.
[3] For the instructions (about the issue of tickets) see above, pp. 296–9.

the gross quantity of tickets was issued? I answer that the said instructions being intended for a general regulation of that Office was necessarily calculated to comprehend all that ought to be taken in for the right settlement thereof, one thing having reference to another though not all equally practicable at the same time, but some more and some less. Secondly, that this being the act of the Board in general, they ought as a body to direct the whole to be done, leaving to the proper officer the sight of the same's being executed and answering to the Admiral for what was not done thereof. Which the Board, being incapable by their other joint and particular affairs, could not at all times take the care of seeing it done, or judging of the reason of the contrary. Thirdly, that should the Board have omitted to command what was fit to be done, it would alone have justified the not doing of it in those who were concerned to do it and see it done, and thereby left them under no necessity or provocation to do it, whereas by commanding it and annexing a promise of encouragement from the Lord High Admiral for their extraordinary care therein, it cannot but be thought a hopeful motive to the industry of the persons concerned to do their utmost in what otherwise they may be reasonably supposed to give themselves all ease in. Fourthly, that though the Board ought not to neglect any time in the rectifying what comes to their knowledge to be amiss in the managements of another office, and therefore had it come before them sooner would and ought to have established the same rules, yet in answer to Tomson's last queries, it may be observed that there was an apparent probability of this work becoming more easy and likely to be performed in regard not only of the King's resolutions then in taking of lessening his fleets,[1] but of the Comptroller's works being now divided into more hands, *viz*, the Lord Brouncker's and Sir Wm Pen's, and this particular part of it thereby better provided for either by Sir John Mennes, being at great leisure to look after it, or (which I did not mention) the Lord Brouncker's taking it upon him, which he must reasonably be thought to have done from his having taken upon him from that time the single directing the distribution of the rooms of the office, etc., I allotting one for his private use under lock and key, where he did from time to time visit the clerks, and at his own times sit and overlook their work.

[1] The decision made in the Privy Council in February 1667. The Dutch fleet invaded the Thames and Medway in the following June.

Here it may not be unuseful for me to examine, against the next time of this matter's coming into debate, what acts the Board will be found at any time to have passed in any matter relating to the Ticket Office before this of Janry 66[7]; though I doubt not but it will be thought enough justification to the Board that the practice of the Navy in this particular was so well known and so long used that it needed no written instructions of the Board to teach it now, but only the care of the officer concerned to see it practised or give account to the Admiral or them that it could not be. Only as to the care of and doing right to the subject it might be necessary for the Board to show some particular care at this time, and in that particular (though they may not be found to have done anything in reference to the King's part) I believe they will be found to have expressed their care in some acts, I mean as to the dispatch and seeing right to the subject without charge. It may be remembered also that from this time about Janry 66[7] my Lord Brounker did take upon him singly the answering of all petitions relating to tickets,[1] and that more petitions were then directed to him singly on that subject than to the whole Board.

To my Lord Breerton's objecting the 12th article,[2] I made little other present answer to it than by putting it off as an article wholly foreign to the business of tickets, and so let it pass as a matter which I was unwilling to stand by the event[3] of any pains I could then take to make the audience thoroughly understand the invalidity of this objection. But lest the same should be sprung again hereafter, it may be fit for me to remember what is now in my thoughts to say, *viz.*, first, that there being no analogy at all between the matter of this article and the matter in question, one relating to victuals, the other to wages, the one, *viz.* the former, a matter of ancient known practice, the other, I mean the printing of tickets with counterparts, never heard of either in ancient or later times till since the first Dutch war, there seems to be no more inference to the purpose intended to be drawn from this article than from any other article of the book, nor more appli-

---

[1] This followed from his being responsible for helping the Comptroller with the Treasurer's accounts: see above, p. 176 & n. 1.
[2] The Admiral's 12th Instruction to the Board was about the method of passing the Victualler's accounts: *Oeconomy*, pp. 31–3. Brereton was adducing it as an objection to the Board's case concerning tickets, and asking why payment of seamen's wages could not be checked by the Board in the same way as they checked payment for their victuals.
[3] Result.

cable to this point than to any other point not yet mentioned or discovered, wherein it may be thought his Majesty might have been better served than indeed he has. Secondly, that as they are not akin in the nature of them, so neither are they of any parallel consideration in their force and practicableness, the former relating to the paying of a Victualler's account at leisure, by general warrants and entire books, this the preservation of the nicety of a new form in the hurry of a war, in the management of an infinite number of loose single papers, each containing for every single man as many several circumstances to be attended to, if not more, than a warrant for six months' victuals for a whole ship's company. Thirdly, that wherein the cases are parallel, *viz.* in their passing the Treasurer's account for wages paid, I do not doubt but the Comptroller, whose particular work it is, will show that there has been as much care taken in the examinations thereof by comparing the establishment sea-books and muster books, as is in this article enjoined in the case of passing the Victualler's account, and is more properly directed in the 14th general and in the 3rd of the Treasurer's and 5th and 6th of the Comptroller's particular Instructions.[1] Fourthly and lastly, that the Commissioners of Accounts neither need to condemn us by a forced application of an article foreign to the matter, where the Admiral has provided a special Instruction to the present case, nor ought they, as I conceive, to condemn us by any other rule than that set us by the Admiral, which General Instruction 19[2] obliges us only to the mustering the ships etc. as is already said, returning those musters to the Treasurer, according to which he is from time to time to trace all tickets for men discharged before the pay, and at the pay the purser's sea books, 'for all men's names, entries, discharges and attendances that shall come to receive their pay, and thereby right the King in all arrearages that may happen either by the ignorance, neglect or wilfulness of the purser', whereas (which I am better to inquire into) this Office has not only evermore given directions for muster books to be sent to the Treasurer's Office, but signed no tickets themselves till the same had been examined by the muster books, and that examination attested by the clerk appointed thereto. For whose fidelity (though I did not as I have formerly observed open the last foregoing matter yet) I omitted not to tell his Majesty

[1] *Oeconomy*, pp. 35–6, 44–5, 53–4.
[2] Ibid., pp. 40–1.

that by the practice of the Navy expressly declared in our Instructions of Janry 66[7],[1] the particular master of the said clerk stands accountable, which condition I told him was read to stand in reference to any clerk of mine to the last penny of my estate, to which my Lord Breerton presently replied that he did believe that what I said was more than any other of our number would say.

Upon which my Lord Lauderdale rise up and asked what Carkes this was whose testimony had been this day read, whether the same that had been heretofore complained of and had been turned out of the Office, saying that that was a precious youth; wherein he was seconded by the King. I answered that it was the same. Upon which my Lord Brouncker, unasked, said that he was [his] clerk formerly and at this day, and that [as] for his re-entertaining him after being put out of the Office, it was at the request of several Members of Parliament who undertook for his good behaviour, and whose recommendation he thought to have been unfit for him to withstand.[2] Upon which his Lordship, tendering a written certificate and request on Carkases behalf signed by seven or eight Members of Parliament, replied for his justification in his retaking him; the same was read, with some jocular reflection thereon from the King and Duke. Upon which I added that however my Lord Brouncker was justifiable in the taking him back into his service, I did presume that the Board could not be thought to have omitted their parts in the getting of him once turned out, as they had by several other ways by reprehension etc., to their clerks, and publications of it in writing, endeavour[ed] to satisfy all the world in their desires of seeing justice done to everybody concerned in the receipt or payment of their tickets, and that as we had ourselves done all that was in our power in a time of so much action towards the correcting all that we found amiss in this matter, and although errors always was

---

[1] About the payment of tickets: see above, pp. 296–9.

[2] James Carkesse was dismissed for corruption in 1667 when serving under Brouncker in the Ticket Office, but was reinstated in the following year. He then became clerk to Sir Edward Seymour, who was Extra-Commissioner and later Treasurer of the Navy and the most powerful of his parliamentary friends. Carkesse was secretary to Seymour in 1673–6 in the first years of Seymour's service as Speaker. But he was an eccentric – to put it mildly – and by 1678 was committed to Bedlam, where he published *Lucida Intervalla* (1679), a collection of verses in which he represented himself as a rival of Pepys for the favour of the Duke of York. See *Diary*, x. 52–3; and the *Life* by Bernard Carcas (priv. ptd 1991).

and probably will be in matters of this nature, and that in the passing of Mr Hutchinson's account after the war errors in tickets paid to above 2000*l.* was discovered and borne by the State;[1] yet I for my part, and I did believe the rest would do so too, do not think that the loss arising from errors in this matter ought to be put upon the King, but that every Officer of the Navy ought to answer for his own and servants' behaviour therein, and that it was not only the desire but interest of those of us that pretends to have served his Majesty faithfully and diligently in this business to wish that the Commissioners of Accounts would exercise their severest care in the detecting and returning into the Exchequer[2] all persons accountable for any wrong done his Majesty therein.

Here I might have observed that whereas they reckon about 700*l.* error discovered in the third part of the books, which they say they have been yet able to examine, the former war was but half the length and in number of men not so great as ours, and yet the errors in tickets in theirs [amount] to above 2000*l.*

Here my Lord Breerton begun to enlarge upon the great number of errors now before them in tickets, finding no proper way of expressing it than by saying they alone would make a book as big or bigger than my answer now before them; and that though it was in some sense unfit to speak anything but good of the dead, yet that they could not but take notice that they had found great number of tickets to great value paid by Sir W. Batten to himself, and that Mr Fenn had done the like to much greater, insinuating that the like had been practised by others of the Board, but that they should be very ready to receive any satisfaction that should be offered them in reference to this matter. Wherein upon my Lord Brouncker's asking whether they had found anything of that kind in reference to himself, they answered they could not say that they had not yet discovered anything relating to his Lordship.

Upon which, finding that this discourse was like to end with some tincture at least of a possibility of blame upon the several members of this Office, which they would insinuate by an offer of a readiness in them to receive satisfaction from us, I thought it unfit for me in my particular to suffer it to rest so, and therefore took the boldness to tell them that whatever they would have

[1] Richard Hutchinson, Navy Treasurer 1650–60.
[2] The Court of the Exchequer.

the world think as to others, I did desire the whole world to show me to have been concerned directly or indirectly in any one ticket in reference either to any title to it or the payment or receipt of the moneys due upon it. At which my Lord Breerton with a look full of trouble and malignity answering, "How! Mr Pepys, do you defy the whole world in this matter?" I replied yea, that I defied both the whole world and my Lord Breerton in particular if he would be thought one of it. At which I could perceive the whole Board shaken with the surprise thereof, and my Lord Breerton himself struck dumb, so as no reply being at all made to it, nor further matter (as I remember) added on this subject, the King called after some pause for the next Observation.

Memorandum: that it would not be amiss for me against another time to have in readiness digested the substance of all my notes here annexed upon the 11th and 12th and 13th Articles,[1] as being very useful in case of coming to a strict answer to the particulars of the same, which now was prevented by a tumultuous falling into a discourse of the whole, so as no further use was made thereof than what is here by me above observed.

Memorandum: that from their much insisting, and that with great confidence, of the great number and value of the errors by them found in the casting and payment of tickets, it will be very advisable for me hereafter to take care to make it well understood that the business of the tickets was the part of a particular Officer,[2] not the whole Board's, and much less mine, and that I do most voluntarily desire and press them to proceed to the full execution of their duty and authority in returning all persons into the Exchequer upon whom any wilful injuries (or others, if they please) done to the King can be rightly placed.[3]

Memorandum: if they should again make any such mention of the length of my answer, that it may not be unfit for me to take notice that they have not hitherto been able to make any exception thereto but this of its being too long, which is to say more satisfactory than stood with their desire that it should prove to be.

---

[1] See below, pp. 411–16.
[2] Brouncker, acting for the Comptroller.
[3] The Act establishing the Commission required them to prosecute offenders in the Court of the Exchequer.

Notes on the 11th, 12th and 13th Observations of Brooke House[1]

Neither printed tickets, examination by counterparts nor lists of tickets sent the Treasurer till (54) after the first war, when peace made them practicable.

No injunction for examination of counterparts, and therefore though in other things they deny us the benefit of the practice of the late times, yet here they condemn us by it, and that for our not doing it in time of war, while they began it not till time of peace, and that[2] we pretend to have done as well as they.

An instance of the violence of seamen both in their times and ours.[3]

The evil supposed in the business of counterparts of little force [because]:

> 1st. Clerks might as well issue then the ticket as the counterpart, having tickets at their dispose at pays of ships either entirely paid by tickets or in part, besides tickets given to commanders, General, etc.
>
> 2dly. Neither ticket nor counterpart in itself sufficient to make ground sufficient for a false ticket, being to pass the examination of the Office by the sea books and muster books.
>
> 3dly. This examination being necessary and the combination of the clerks in doing the same, that unfaithfulness of theirs needed not the help of any counterpart or printed ticket, they having it in their power to have employed that unfaithfulness in the passing of written ones, which during the late war was wholly unavoidable.

That the Office did not neglect the use of examining tickets by their counterparts [because]:

> 1st. Their practice ever understood it to be done, being under the care of the Comptroller.
>
> 2dly. Mr Carcas and Mr Wittfeild do tell us that to their best knowledge it was done till the hurry of the war made it impracticable.

---

[1] Above, p. 294.
[2] Sc. peace-time practice.
[3] In protest against the failure of the Pay Office to redeem their tickets: cf. *Diary*, iv. 292 & n. 2.

3dly. That the Board in their willingness to recover this method did in Janry 1666[7] article 7th[1] by special instructions enjoin practice thereof.

Against written tickets:

1st. The practice of the Navy universally known.
2dly. The Admiral's Instructions constantly against it, *viz.* the 19th.[2]
3dly. Several written directions and publications to this Board against them.
4ly. The Office publishes a printed prohibition to commanders, and caution to seamen against written tickets.
5ly. The Office's regulation of the Ticket Office, by Janry 1666[7] article 7th.
6ly. The Admiral's present Instructions to Commanders,[3] article the 20th, strictly at this day as I understand observed.

The intention of my objecting against their inference from the not constant comparing tickets with the sea books is that the sea books are not to be had till the ships are paid off, while the tickets are indispensable to be issued and examined before the pay.

For not examining by the muster books, it is not owned by any clerk and, if proved, provision is made for the King's indemnity by the master of the clerk so faulty. Regulation Janry 1666[7] article 4th.[4]

Distinguish between faults blameable in clerks and mistakes incident and therefore excusable while committed in a hurry.

To the third inference,[5] I own that the sending a list of tickets passed to the Treasurer is of certain use in behalf of the subject, in case of a ticket lost, to prevent its being paid to wrong hand if not yet paid, and to the King in preventing the making out a double ticket, where it is allegedly paid. It is also useful to the King in cases of tickets where the hand both of the Principal Officers and the examinations of the clerks are wholly counterfeit, forasmuch as by this means no such ticket would appear in the list when compared. But where the ticket is truly examined and

---

[1] Above, pp. 298–9.
[2] *Oeconomy*, pp. 40–1.
[3] Issued in 1669: BL, Add. MSS 36782, f. 82v; Bodl. Lib., Rawl. MSS D 794, f. 11.
[4] Above, pp. 297–8.
[5] I.e. the Commission's 13th Observation: above, p. 294.

signed there this list is of no use to the King, besides that accidental one of informing him with more ease and certainty what tickets are paid or remain unpaid.

In which consideration only the practice hath been esteemed of sending such a list to the Treasurer, and understood by the Board to have been performed, at least as much as the hurry of the war would admit, having at several times called upon the persons concerned in the Ticket Office to keep it in practice, and particularly by their regulation in Janry 1666[7] article 3rd.[1] But as in the hurry aforesaid it seems very difficult that this should be performed, so had it been performed, it would have been in a great measure at least fruitless in a time of war, when men being to be paid their tickets at the same time in several places on shore and on float, and that upon one ship for service in another, the tickets upon which (for the necessary encouragement of seamen to continue in the service) such payments were made were incapable of being examined by the aforesaid lists lying in the Treasury Office or any other place whatsoever.

Which consideration is of unanswerable use to their objection of our not examining all tickets by their counterparts, as well as our not comparing them with their sea books and muster books, as being impossible to be performed, where, as it was almost every day's case during the war, ships coming in and going out again, which having been manned out of other ships or manned with men that had served or received tickets for their service in other ships could not be got to sea without paying these men, nay, and frequently ships newly fitted forth could not be manned but by inviting men on board with promise of paying them their wages due to them for other ships, there I say it was impossible for either counterparts to be looked into, or sea books and muster books compared, whilst nobody could either foresee what ships those men should belong to; and so neither what counterparts or books ought to be sent to the pay; or if that could be foreseen, could those books (though could the particular tickets [be] before known, the counterparts indeed might) be spared either from the Ticket Office, where there were constant occasions of making use of them, or from other ships, where at the same time they might be called for on the very same occasion; nor could the men be permitted to bring them up to the Office for examination, nor

---

[1] Above, p. 297.

the service allow time for their being sent up on that behalf and returned.

But so soon as the difficulty of the war was over, this list is said to have been duly sent. *Vide* Mr Carcas and Mr Whitfeild upon the 13th Observation.[1]

To the fourth inference, of our not having from the Treasurer a list of tickets passed:

1st. It is nowhere enjoined.

2dly. Never practised, even in the time when the method of printed tickets first began.

3dly. Wholly useless in any case where the ticket paid hath been examined by the Office, forasmuch as the sea book or muster book remaining with us, upon which this ticket was examined and is set off, informs us in whatever can be learned of caution from the Treasurer's list against the injuries there suggested.

And in cases where the Treasurer shall have presumed or have been necessitated to pay a ticket which hath not been examined by this Office, there the Treasurer must look to it to secure the King by taking care to communicate the same timely to the Ticket Office, that the said ticket may be set off on the books there, to prevent a future double ticket possible to be made, while the book stands open.

But in all cases of false tickets paid, tickets to Runs, tickets false in time of entry or discharge, over-rating of the men or the like, there this list is wholly ridiculous, forasmuch as the money being paid upon these tickets, this is but to endeavour to shut the door after the steed is stolen.

If it be said but by this means the injury being discovered, we are put into a timelier way recovering it from the seamen, it is answered:

1st. That the person will be very uneasy to be found.

2ly. Most probably insolvent when found.

3ly. That in right this discovery ought not to be the King's task, but the Treasurer's, ours, or our clerk's by whose default the said injury is contracted.

There is indeed a case, but that so rare as to be reckoned only

---

[1] The comments of Carkesse and Whitfield have not been traced.

possible where this list may have some use, namely where a ticket examined by the Office and paid by the Treasurer may have been forgot to have been set off on our sea book or muster book by the clerk examinant, in which case the Treasurer's list may give occasion to the supplying that defect by its being set off after payment. But this is so hard to be presumed as not to be worth mentioning or the having so troublesome an expedient provided for its remedy.

That the care of tickets hath always been, and been owned as it now is, a part of the duty of the Comptroller:[1]

1st. The 1st and 4th articles of the Comptroller's duty.[2]

2ly. The Lord High Admiral's instructive letter 9ber 1668,[3] the extract whereof on this behalf is annexed.[4]

3ly. The Board's letter to the Duke xbr 1st 1668; the beginning of the 1st article with all the 3rd. Which letter is signed by Sir J. Mennes with the rest of the Board. *Vide* also the Duke's letter thereupon of the 12th xb 1668.[5]

4ly. The Board's letter to the Duke 3d xbr 1668 about explaining his letter of the 25 of 9ber who he meant to be the comptroller charged therein with care of the Ticket Office, with the Duke's order of the 18th ditto, in which letter of the Board's they mention Sir J. Mennes's making difficulty of parting with any more of the known duty of his place without special warrant from the Duke.[6]

5ly. Brooke House, by letter of 4. 9ber 1668 to the Board demanding an account of tickets passed and unpaid during the war, Sir J. Mennes undertakes it for before, and the Lord Brouncker for after the time of the Lord Br's being made chargeable with that office and did return their answers to Brooke House immediately from themselves without any joint answer from the Board. The Board nevertheless hath

---

[1] The list that follows is of letters and papers concerning the division of responsibility between Mennes and Brouncker consequent on the appointment of Brouncker to help Mennes in the business of tickets.
[2] *Oeconomy*, pp. 49–50, 52–3.
[3] For the Duke's letter of instruction, see above, p. 252 n. 1.
[4] Untraced.
[5] PRO, ADM 106/17, ff. 257–9.
[6] The Board recommended that Brouncker, while assuming responsibility for tickets, should allow Mennes free access to his papers: BL, Add. MSS 36782, f. 79r-v.

itself in common[1] in this duty in all matters needing their help and assistance. *Vide* their regulation 17 Janry 1666[7].[2]

I condemn not examinations by counterparts as useless in reference to others without the Office, for so they are useful, and we in our very regulation above-mentioned and at other times do own them as such. But as to our own clerks, who are masters both of tickets and counterparts as well as the sea books and muster books, this doth not hinder them from the frauds which the comparing of tickets with their counterparts are said to subject his Majesty to, and without the combination of our clerks no other man can, though the counterpart be embezzled or made use of as in the Observation is suggested, impose anything upon the Office.

The King then calling for the 14th Observation[3] with their paper of instances,[4] and these being read, with my written answer thereto,[5] I enlarged thereupon by discourse, showing first, that though it be unusual and may by the weakening men's bodies be in some measure found inconvenient for seamen to be put to short allowance in the Channel, yet that the King cannot be said to have suffered anything thereby in the case mentioned and in other places; it is but what they desire.[6] Secondly, that the want of provisions was not more complained of anywhere than in the Generals' own ships,[7] where it is not to be thought but all care was used for seeing the same received on board in specie and well kept there. Thirdly, that the number of the supernumeraries in the fleet was such as to lead the Generals in 66 to demand one month's victuals extra in six to be sent them in consideration of supernumeraries. Hereafter let me be ready to evidence this by their or their secretary's letters. And *quere* whether something like this was not done the year before. Fourthly, that the ships happened in both years to fight presently after their taking in their victuals, so as to be forced to fling over much provisions to make room for wounded men, and clear their wings to come at

[1] Sc. accepts joint responsibility.
[2] Above, pp. 296–9.
[3] Above, pp. 299–300.
[4] Untraced.
[5] Above, p. 300.
[6] Because the seamen were compensated in cash (by 'pinch-gut money') when the ship was paid off.
[7] In 1666: cf. above, p. 300 & n. 1.

shot.[1] Against the next time let me be ready with the instances hereof. Fifthly, that the seeing provisions brought on board in specie is by the Admiral made the sole duty of the commander. Here I forgot to have by me the old Additional Instruction as well as the General[2] to prove it. And that this Board was nowhere obliged to take the care of it. Whereto my Lord Brereton objected to[3] the 11th General Instruction,[4] where the Board is authorized to give instructions to all inferior officers, among which pursers are there reckoned, and to keep a strict watch over them that they do their duties. To which I made little other answer than that this was impossible for us to see done, being tied to attendance here while ships lay in victualling at the several ports far distanced at the same time; besides that the King had appointed Commissioners and agents in all or most of the outports who might and ought to be accountable for all that the Board ought to see done in those places. This I mostly insisted on and was received as satisfactory by the King, though I did shortly hint at and might have more largely have insisted on each of the following particulars, *viz.*, first, that as far as we were able we did look after this by enjoining the Victualler and desiring the Commissioners of the outports to take care that victuals be all brought on board in specie. Secondly, that this has been done so as frequently to have victuals returned from the ship's side, commanders having frequently certified their ships being capable to receive no more. Thirdly, that in all times both old and new this work of seeing provisions brought on board in specie and stowing thereof has been reputed to belong to the commanders, masters, mates, midshipmen and quartermasters, and not this Board, wherein I appeal to Thompson. Fourthly, that the Admiral's warrants are grounded on the King's to him and ours to the Victualler on his to us, from which we dare not vary, though the warrants require more victuals than the ships can stow, which is also unavoidable in all long voyages, for supply whereof the pursers are assisted with credit for their wet provisions and bread. This I urged in reply, to which Tompson said

---

[1] The wings (q.v. Glossary) were supposed to be kept clear of all obstacles which might impede the work of carpenters and caulkers who had the duty of stopping up holes made by enemy shot.
[2] I.e. the Additional Instruction to Commanders as well as the General Instructions to the Navy Board.
[3] Sc. made an objection with reference to.
[4] *Oeconomy*, pp. 30–1.

that we ought to know how much provisions each ship will hold, thereby to prevent by applying ourselves to the Admiral the issuing warrants for more provisions than the ship will hold. The evil of which, says he, is that by this means the purser having credit for the remainder and the ship being lost, the King is charged with the loss of the whole provisions as if the whole had been on board. To which I further replied that care was always taken by this Board to command an account to be kept of all credits given the pursers, who in case of ships being lost are not allowed the whole of their supply without good satisfaction first given in what became of those credits. Upon which score several pursers are at this day sued in the Exchequer, and others denied to have their bond delivered up for want of this account of their credits. Fifthly, that credits were always and even in the first Dutch war given, and ought to be by reason that by the help of credits for one or two species of provisions, *viz.*, bread and beer, the ship's victualling is much lengthened to the great service of the King, beyond what it would be if all should be put on board; besides that the having these credits saves not only the multiplying and confusion of this Board's warrants to the Victualler for those broken proportions which are thus supplied by credits, but the wants of the ship to which they relate supplied by virtue thereof abroad, either at sea or in outports, without that loss of time which to the great damage to his Majesty's service must unavoidably accompany the ship's stay for a fresh warrant for every of the said supplies. Besides that bread and beer, the species for which credits are usually granted, are not only so bulky as the decrease thereof in their expense[1] is most easy to be discovered, but are such as may with most certainty be had everywhere, or wine and water in lieu of beer, whereas with the other species it is not so. Sixthly, that as often as any information has come to us of any purser's leaving provisions unnecessarily behind, or misemploying them when abroad, we have not omitted by ourselves or presentation thereof to the Lord High Admiral to punish the same.

After all which I appealed to them to inform his Majesty what service or design of his Majesty during the whole war has suffered any miscarriage by this want of provisions or the badness thereof, taking upon me the making some comparison between the management of victualling between this and the former war, wherein

---

[1] Consumption.

so many thousands of tuns and provisions were flung overboard, fleets come in for want, men mutiny, and the contractors but for the friendship which the interest of some of them found had probably been hanged for it, as it was threatened they should be. Thomson answered that Gawden was then one of them. I replied that Pride[1] was another, and that if Gawden did so well now, when alone, under the pressures of so great wants of money, what may it not be thought he would have done under so good payment had he been yoked with men like himself? In short I undertook to say that whoever shall hereafter come to tell the story of the management of this war, he will find more matter for wonder than censure in what relates to Sir Denis Gawden's part therein. In which the King and Duke very amply joined with me, and in their owning a full satisfaction in what relates to the Board in this Observation, and especially in that which I observed, *viz.*, that though it may be thought that some misbehaviour there may have been possibly in some pursers in their disposal of their provisions, yet that nothing at all appears why these Commissioners should in this their Observation so peremptorily charge the fault thereof upon the want of care in this Board.

Thursday February 17. 1669[70]. This day being appointed for another hearing at the Council, I was by my Lord Brounker first, then by Mr Slingsby, then by the King himself, and lastly by my Lord Lauderdalle, told that my Lord Breerton had given out that he would this day make good his challenge the last[2] touching my being concerned in the receiving money upon tickets, which therefore I expected, but in vain, nothing at all being mentioned of it at this meeting. But so soon as the King and Council were sat the 15th Observation was read, and after it my written answer.[3] Which being ended, I by discourse summed up the force of it suitable to the tenor of the following notes, saving what I have observed at the close of it touching the principal intention of the Admiral's Instructions being to be supported, that the work be done, and we at our peril to be made accountable for the not doing it, etc. Which finding what I had already said and discoursed sufficiently owned for satisfactory by the King, I

---

[1] Col. Thomas Pride, the regicide. He and Gauden, together with their fellow contractors, were reprimanded for their inefficiency by the Council of State in June 1652: M. Oppenheim, *Hist. Administration of R. Navy*, pp. 324–5.
[2] Sc. at the last meeting.
[3] Above, pp. 300–7.

spared to mention as unnecessary now and what may be more usefully reserved for hereafter, if it shall come unto any further debate.

Notes upon the 15th Observation

We complain ourselves first[1] of our excessive prices, and ourselves give the Admiral the very instances, and those, part of them, the very same now objected.

We tell the Admiral in the instance of the unknown proposer of hemp[2] how unreasonable the proposition is, saying that as we durst not agree to it without his approbation, we durst not reject it in the straits we were in without his leave and my Lord Treasurer's help if it should be accepted of.

That we were forced to offer 50*l.* upon credit, and be refused, when it was offered us at 30 ready money.

That we knew the market price and was offered by the merchant to sell [it] us under (*viz.* hemp) at the same time when we were forced to give him 57*l.*, he offering it at 49*l.* and the market price being 49*l.* 10*s.*

The Act directs Brooke House to the inspecting and examining former accounts for the better discovering of frauds, abuse, defaults, etc.,[3] of which this of giving more for goods than they are worth cannot be thought the least if true. If then the books of former accounts be examined, our prices will not be found to exceed, but, in goods of the greatest consideration, too short of the prices given in the late times.

But that which is to be said is that unless they can prove our giving more where they might have been served for less, the giving a great price, or indeed the giving of any price, cannot be esteemed a fault where we could not prevent it, forasmuch as the first thing intended in such an action is that the work be done, and we at our peril made accountable for the not doing it, first by the 1st General Instruction,[4] secondly by the Duke's farewell letter expressly declaring us inexcusable from any miscarriage from our too great husbandry and thrift,[5] thirdly by the Act

[1] Sc. we ourselves are the first to complain.
[2] See above, pp. 301–2.
[3] 19 & 20 Car. II c. 1, sect. i.
[4] *Oeconomy*, pp. 20–1.
[5] See above, p. 354 & n. 2.

itself where it is said 'and with such care, fidelity and good husbandry as the nature of such services would admit of.'[1]

And it was but necessary that this latitude should be given in an action calling for dispatch and pains in the managers who too probably might have been invited to the consulting their own ease, and suffering the work to want the despatch necessary, while furnished with so good a plea as their not being able to perform it, under the necessities and ill credit which[2] evermore were [?grievous],[3] at the same prices with which private men were served. And yet had our prices been so extraordinary, merchants by their failure in point of time would not probably have made work for the 1st Observation.[4]

All that Brooke House offered in opposition hereto was the observing the date of the earliest of these our complaints, and the showing instances of our height of prices before those complaints, and quoting the prices given by private merchants at that time for those goods. Whereto I answered first by observing that these instances are wholly new, and as in other case these Commissioners do not own any satisfaction in what is given to the instances there sent us, but labour still to surprise us with new ones not heard of before, though all to no purpose. For secondly, it is not the having complained in writing to justify us but the reason of that which is alleged by us in those complaints, namely the difficulties lying upon [us] for the want of money, and that those difficulties did so lie upon us before the date of these letters, I offered them to give them at any time proof of all sorts, and that our not quoting written addresses to the Duke of elder date than those in my answer arises (besides that it is possible I may have omitted to look further backward and thereby escaped what upon search might have occurred to me of elder date) partly from what is already taken notice of in my written answer of our contenting ourselves with the verbal laying our thoughts in this matter before the Admiral, and partly from the Admiral's being at sea, or else attending his Majesty during the Plague at Oxford,

---

[1] 19 & 20 Car. II c. 1, sect. i.
[2] MS. 'will' (a mishearing).
[3] The sense here seems to require the addition of some such word after 'were', which comes at the end of a line where accidental omissions most commonly occur.
[4] Above, p. 273; alleging that contractors had not spent all the money imprested to them.

so as we could not so properly present that to him ourselves in writing when we could wait upon him therewith, and open to him the particulars relating to the same. But that which I shut up all with, as what I insisted finally and principally upon in vindication of this Office, was that it was not our part to be accountable for the buying of goods at the prices now to be found in private merchants' books, in which all circumstances do not appear that should discover the difference between our bargain and theirs. [It] was this that I did assert in behalf of this Office and invited them by any instances to disprove it, that the Office did never omit to buy as cheap as they could, much less did ever give a greater price while under the same circumstances of price, time and delivery, quantity and dimension of the goods, etc., they would or were ever informed that they could have bought the same cheaper. Whereto Brooke House not offering anything in answer, the King owned his full satisfaction and called for the next Observation.

Which (*viz.* 16th)[1] being read with their paper of instances[2] as is usual, I proceeded to read my written answer,[3] and after it summed up in discourse suitable to the following notes, saving the last touching some words of Mr Wood's which I spared present mention of, reserving (if there shall be occasion) for future use. I do not remember they offered anything in objection to this my answer that was either extraordinary in itself or that did not receive a present full answer, saving two particulars touching Sir W. Warren's accounts which the Lord Brouncker took upon him to give present answer to by denial of what they alleged, and referring himself to the justifying that denial against the next meeting. The allegations of Brooke House were these: first, that we had made out two bills for the very same individual parcel of masts to Sir W. Warren. *Vide* the following state of these two objections and my Lord Brouncker's answers under his Lordship's own hand.[4] Which points I say referred for fuller satisfaction from the Lord Brouncker to the next meeting, and the King owning with their Lordships complete satisfaction touching this Observation, with words several times put in by the King

---

[1] Above, p. 307; alleging that 'some persons have been preferred before others' in the award of contracts.
[2] Untraced.
[3] Above, pp. 307–15.
[4] See below, pp. 424–5. The argument that follows is virtually the same as that used by Pepys in his 'Defence'.

and Duke of the serviceableness of Sir W. Warren and readiness on all occasions to furnish the King with ships or goods at[1] greater hazards and lower prices than others, his Majesty concluded the meeting.

The notes above mentioned on this Observation follow:

Sir W. Warren stranger to us and found dealing as a merchant with this Office when we came in.

No masts for two years bought of Wood and Taylor. Sir W.W.'s first contract Sept 63[2] the lowest ever made.

June 1664. Wood and Blackborrow sell us but above his prices.[3]

July 1664. Others invited as well as Sir W.W.[4]

Mr Wood owns in his affidavit the invitation and his refusal of it as not being to be performed, and yet owns his having some of 22 hands, but the true reason was his resolution declared to fetch no new till he had sold his old. *Vide* his tender in Augt 1663 wherein that is declared and his price therein higher than Sir W.W.'s.[5]

Shorter's own tender, so much insisted on, dearer than Sir W.W., uncertain in case of war, and to be brought by strangers' ships and men.[6]

Prices now demanded twice as great by Stockman and greater by Mr Wood, while Sir W.W. demands but the same. The invitation sent in the case of New England masts.[7]

The article of exclusion[8] neither injurious to the King nor avoidable in itself; propounded only at first by Sir W.W., nor kept by the Board.

Instructions to purveyors to look out for variety of merchants. Public days set for contracting.[9]

Variety of merchants serving the Navy with the principal provisions within the late war.

[1] MS. 'and' (a mishearing).
[2] For Norwegian masts: see above, p. 9 & n. 1.
[3] See above, p. 309.
[4] See above, p. 311.
[5] See above, p. 308.
[6] See above, p. 388.
[7] Above, p. 311.
[8] See above, p. 313.
[9] See above, p. 314.

Variety of merchants for the same goods at the same time, and yet not always the King's interest to buy of many, merchants selling better bargains in great parcels than in small.

A combination more to be suspected in Wood's high prices than W.W.'s low ones. How much more censure had been due had we bought Wood's old masts that were already upon the place at dearer prices instead of Warren's to be fetched now from abroad at lower prices. The Board's letter [to] the Eastland Company in general[1] shows their not inclining to particular merchants. I remember Wood's late words at the Board about being beaten out of his trade.

Monday Febr. 21. 1669[70]. The King and Council being met and we called in, the 17th Observation was called for; but before that was read my Lord Brouncker desired to be heard to the two particulars which were referred to this day for his Lordship to give his Majesty satisfaction in.[2] Which being granted, he showed, as to the first, that two bills were indeed made out for the same parcel of masts, one of them, namely the first, for the first cost only of the said goods, which was done in pursuance of a special demand to that very purpose sent to this Office from Brooke House demanding a certain list of bills by them mentioned to be filled up by the Board, whereof this was one. The other was a bill granted for the same goods wherein all the other charges of freight, etc., was added thereto, raising the bill to a much greater sum than the former. But to show the unreasonableness of this their exception and this Office's care to do the King right, my Lord Brouncker showed that at the time of signing the second, the first bill was cancelled, and in proof thereof produced the very cancelled bill, by which the impossibility also appeared of the Treasurer's being able as they suggested to charge the same twice upon his Majesty. To their second objection my Lord now showed, etc.:[3]

Objected by the Commissioners for Accounts that a bill of Sir Wm Warren's for 291*l.* 10*s.* was twice paid; being satisfied with

---

[1]Above, p. 314.
[2]These concerned Warren's account which Brouncker was dealing with in place of Mennes.
[3]The extracts from Brouncker's submission are also on an inserted leaf, and are written in two clerical hands, neither of which is that of the clerk who wrote the rest of the MS.

victuals (as appears under my hand upon the bill) and also allowed Sir G. Carteret upon his last ledger and not recharged.

But they are mistaken for that 291*l*. 10*s*. was part of the 1359*l*. 14*s*. charged in the front of the said ledger, as received from Sir W. Warren for victuals delivered him, *viz*., 750*l*. by the Board's order of the 11th of April 67 and 609*l*. 14*s*. by another order dated the 21th April 67.

With the former was satisfied one bill of imprests for the like sum.

With the latter three perfect bills were paid, *viz*.: one for 232. 11. 0. placed immediately before in the ledger; another for 291. 10. 0. which is the bill in question; the third for 85. 13. 0 the next but one after it.

<u>609. 14. 0.</u>

All made to Sir W. Warren and branded with the like note of being satisfied with victuals, and so entered in my books.

Objected also by the Commissioners that Sir W. Warren had two bills for the same provisons: *viz*., one dated the 9th of Nobr 67 for 924. 15. 5. The other dated the 29th of No. 68 for 3430. 14. 10.

But in these two they were mistaken, for the first bill was cancelled before the latter was made and was never delivered to him but remains in my custody, and so entered in my books. And was filled by the directions of the said Commissioners according to the rates of that time, for their satisfaction only; but afterwards when Sir W. Warren accounted for these goods one bill was passed for the whole charge, freight and demurrage.

Vide the annexed original.[1]

Which being said by my Lord Brouncker and improved as much as I held needful by my discourse thereon, to the satisfaction of his Majesty and the total silencing of those Commissioners, the 17th Observation[2] was read with a paper of instances[3] of the loss the King was at upon several ships particularly enumerated by their lying in harbour unpaid off. In reply to which I read my written answer,[4] and then proceeded to the discoursing largely

[1] Untraced.
[2] Above, p. 315.
[3] Untraced.
[4] Above, pp. 315–16.

thereon, grounded upon the following notes which for my memory I had prepared, though for shortness I spared the use of several (if not most) of the letters therein quoted, reserving their use to future occasions, and pressed the force of the whole by concluding with an observation of the unfortunate condition of the Officers of the Navy under the plain dilemma wherein by this charge from the Commissioners of Accounts they expressly stand, *viz.*, ships coming in to be paid off and we evermore under a want of money wherewith to do it; if we suffer them to lie in pay unemployed, we then fall under the censure of wasting his Majesty's treasure; if we discharge them into other ships, which cannot be done but by ticket, and this even at times when the King's service was at a stand for want of men in those other ships (which was the real case of most if not all discharges of ships by ticket, unless where it was done for saving the freight of ships hired) we are then arraigned for occasioning discontent to the seamen.

And with this I concluded, with the King's profession of his being fully satisfied in this matter.

The notes above mentioned relating to this observation were as follows:

The only point by the Admiral's Instructions wherein the Office is chargeable with the taking care for the payment of men's wages is by the 10th General Instruction, wherein they are obliged seasonably once a year to present the Admiral with an estimate [of] the charge of victuals and wages of ships in ordinary, or the ships in extraordinary, as the Admiral shall demand it.[1]

The former of which there was no occasion of doing it, the victuals and wages of the men in ordinary during the whole war not amounting to 2000*l.*, I believe not 1500*l.*[2] *Vide* my abstract of the ordinary charge of the Navy.[3]

In the latter, touching the ships in extraordinary, the account of estimates long since fully shows them we never failed in having presented some where there was no written order of the Admiral. But the Office was not content with this, but by all other means

---
[1] *Oeconomy*, pp. 29–30.
[2] Cf. above, p. 339.
[3] Untraced.

will be found to have been solicitous for the payment of ships off, and that not only by their constant letter[s] (pursuant to the Admiral) to their Treasurer, but to the Admiral himself, etc.

Collect:

20 7ber 65.	Board to D. Alb. about forwarding the payment of seamen.
28 Octo. 65.	S.P. to Peter Pett [about] want of money to relieve the seamen.
15. 9ber 65.	Board to D. York about want of money for ships out of service.
18 ,, ,,	Board to P.P. tell the plain state of their incapacity to undertake any payment.
6 Feb. 65[6].	Board to D.Y. The Board close with a desire of present money for tickets; a timely care of their gross demand for wages against Michaelmas.[1]

Board:

⎧ 10. 8ber 65.) ⎫	S.P. to W.P., and the Board to P.P. show care of cutting off growing charge.
⎨ 16 ,, ,, ⎬	
⎩ 30 ,, ,, ⎭	Board to P.P. show their care in payment of ships to hasten what would cut off most growing charge.
17. 9ber 66.	Board to D.Y. state the officers and seamen in ships and harbour unemployed yet in pay, for want of pay[2] most unruly.
6 xber 66.	Board to Sir G.C. show their discharging merchants' vessels to cut off charges – and press for money for men discharged in them.
11 ,, ,,	Board to Sir G. C. on the same.
18 ,, ,,	Board to Sir G. C. show their desire of cutting off charge but with tenderness to the men for money.
18 ,, ,,	S.P. to Col. Middleton. A pathetic close to express my sense of and grief for want of money.

Was the blame of the ships lying long unpaid at the King's coming in by the then Commissioners charged as a crime on

---

[1]Copy in BL, Add. MSS 9311, pp. 200–3.
[2]MS 'pay and yet'.

them as not having taken order for their payment, or were they blameable for those tickets by which the seamen were discharged for service before 1659?[1]

25th July 65. The Board to Sir G. Carteret, desire his absence at the Board might be constantly supplied by Mr Fenn's attendance.

Can the Board be thought to have been so unmindful of their own ease and quiet (if not for the King's service) as to have suffered themselves to remain under so much trouble and danger from the seamen's violence for want of their pay? For an instance, *vide* S.P.'s letter to Capt. Bassett, 2 xber 65, and of the 4th ditto to Sir John Robinson.

Notes upon the said Observation relating to the discharging ships by tickets

The Observation itself answers itself when want of money is considered and gives a good reason for the tickets, which were given only upon necessity to prevent growing charge and to put men upon the useful ships instead of unuseful.

Article 19th, General Instruction. The Admiral himself admits of men's being discharged by tickets before the pay.[2]

Article 4th of purser's doth the same.[3]

Article 4th of Treasurer's duty[4] supposes occasions relating both to his Majesty's service and the seamen's for men's being discharged, which to prevent the being done without money, and thereby the seamen discouraged, the Board is not forbid to discharge (for then the service might be retarded, as the Instruction intimates), but the Treasurer is ordered to solicit for money. The Board's opinion against tickets where it was not necessary, by being supplied with money to prevent them, was earlily discovered in their answer of the 31 October 65 to a letter of Penn and Pett's of the 25th Octobr 65 about their proposal of paying off the *Soveraigne* by ticket.[5]

---

[1] Cf. below, p. 429 & n. 5.
[2] *Oeconomy*, p. 41.
[3] Ibid., pp. 165–6.
[4] Ibid., pp. 45–6.
[5] Penn and Pett had objected that to pay the crew of one ship by cash would create jealousy in the crews of other ships who had served longer, and would bring men flocking into Chatham from plague-stricken areas: *CSPD 1665–6*, pp. 29–30.

Near 30,000 printed tickets appear to have been employed by the State between the end of 55[1] and the King's coming in, besides written ones.

By our general trust of providing for the well-being of the service, we are the judges of the occasion of discharging men, suitable to what is imployed[2] in the 4th article of the Treasurer's duty.

Memorandum: I find a letter from Comr Pett to the Board dated 1st 7br 1665 wherein it appears that he began the practice of discharging ships by ticket by removing 30 of the *Bendick*'s men to the *Guift* and the rest to the *Sta Maria*.[3]

The Board's judgement in the business of discharging by ticket (wherein I may be more amply referred to my discourse to the Parliament)[4] may be collected from their two reports on this subject of the 28 of Augt and 30th of Septembr 1667 to the King and Council.[5]

Great sums of money are yet due to seamen for service before the 14th March 1658[9] which might have in part been satisfied if the ships kept long uselessly in pay by the Commissioners of Parliament[6] had been discharged by ticket, and the money saved thereby in the growing charge thus cut off been made applicable thereunto.

Having thus concluded without any further reply upon this Observation, the King called for the next, when my Lord Breerton interposed, saying that having now gone through all those Observations in the management whereof as well as in their framing, and the next falling within the care of another member of their number, he desired before he took leave of his Majesty

---

[1] MS. '65'.

[2] Implied.

[3] PRO, SP 29/132, no. 5 (summary in *CSPD 1664–5*, p. 546). The original has '20' not '30'.

[4] The three-hour speech to the Commons delivered on 5 March 1668: *Diary*, ix. 102–4; reported in A. Grey, *Debates*, i. 71–4, and Milward, *Diary*, pp. 207–9.

[5] The Council had demanded that the seamen should be paid in money not tickets. On 30 September the Navy Board in consequence had reported that they would arrange to cash tickets twice weekly in the order in which the ships were discharged and that a notice to that effect would be posted at the Navy Treasury gate: PRO, PC 2/59, f. 281*r-v*; BL, Add. MSS 36782, ff. 64–5; ibid., 9303, f. 175*r*. Cf. *Diary*, viii. 397, 404, 454, 456.

[6] The Commissioners appointed by Parliament in 1660 to pay off the armed forces. The Act appointing them limited the arrears payable to those incurred after 14 March 1659: 12 Car. II c. 15, sects ii and iii.

in this matter he might be heard in something relating to what had passed between him and Mr Pepys, and wherein he understood it to have been suggested that he had affirmed something touching Mr Pepys more than he was able to prove, namely that Mr Pepys had received moneys upon tickets, which he said he was prepared to prove by a ticket which he then produced for 7*l*. odd money to one Capp of the *Lyon*, upon which ticket it was writ 'paid to Mr Pepys.' Having said which, and the ticket being offered to the King and Duke, the King put it into my hand for my perusal, which while I was doing, Col. Thompson voluntarily took occasion to observe to his Majesty (as near as I can in these very words) that they had discovered two or three more; they should not have troubled his Majesty with the mention of it, being so small a matter, had it not been that Mr Pepys had so positively taken upon him to assert his having never been concerned in the receiving money upon a ticket, which being so asserted, they thought themselves obliged to take notice of what they had found in disproof thereof. Which having been said, I betook myself to answer by observing, first, that in the many score thousands of pounds that had been paid in wages of seamen, and of that too great part in tickets, only one ticket could be found wherein any pretence could be of my being concerned therein. That nothing was offered to be objected either by my Lord Breerton or Col. Thompson against the truth of the ticket itself in any circumstance of it, but only a supposition that this one ticket, true as it is, was paid to me. Thirdly, that however these words 'paid to Mr Pepys' and by whom and whensoever they came to be writ, I did persist my defiance of any man to prove that this or any other ticket was ever paid to me.

Whereto my Lord Breerton answered that what he had said he was able to prove by the oath of Mr Stephen,[1] who had sworn the words to have been written with his hand, and that the money was paid to me. Upon which I replied that so much had been my constant resolution during the whole war to the having nothing to do with the payment or receipt of the money due upon any ticket or in any wise to be concerned for anything relating to a ticket more than the signing of them when brought to me by the clerks employed in the examination thereof, that it is not

---

[1] Anthony Stephens, clerk in the Navy Treasury. On 8 March Pepys wrote to him demanding an explanation in writing of his statement: *Further Corr.*, pp. 263–4. He there refers to the sum involved as £9 7*s*.

by any presumptuous guess but by a firm knowledge that I do take upon me to assert in defiance of the whole world my uninterestedness in anything of this matter, and therefore doubt not but the instance being now (and not before) given me, I shall be able even in this particular to show the little truth lying in this objection. Which having said, the King, with a smile and shake of his head, told the Commissioners that he thought it a vain thing to believe that one having so great trust and therein acting without any exception therein in matters of the greatest moment should descend to the so poor a thing as the doing anything that was unfit for him in a matter of 7*l*. 10*s*. And so this matter ended.

Memorandum: that so soon as my Lord Breerton mentioned this ticket, and before he produced it, I desired to know whether he did this in the name of the rest of the fellow Commissioners or only in his own, that I might know in reference to whom I[1] was to direct my answer.

To this he replied (but with a discovery of he being at some loss about it) that he did offer, as he did all the rest, in behalf of their whole number, as being done with their privity and consent, wherein turning himself towards the rest then present (which as I take it were Tomson, Gregory, Turner, Langham and Osbourne) by a seeming appeal to them whether they would deny it or not, they by their silence seemed to admit thereof, and thereupon I gave way to my Lord's going on to produce the ticket etc., as above, having first given his Majesty this account of the reason of my inquiring in this manner after what name this objection was delivered in; that were it delivered in the name of any particular member or members of their number under a quorum, I should have had the present satisfaction of knowing by what means to procure present reparation for the wrong offered me therein, whilst for what injuries may be supposed done by the whole, as a Board, his Majesty and the Parliament had thought fit to exempt them from any accountableness other than in Parliament. Which door being left open, I hope his Majesty would not be offended if in justification of myself and those others of his Majesty's servants and his government itself which may find just cause of reckoning themselves injured by these gentlemen, I take a time to make use of that provision made for our relief by an appeal to himself in Parliament.

Whereto his Majesty intimating by his countenance a silent

[1] MS. 'he'.

approval, my Lord Breerton bewrayed some disturbance at my motion, saying that their proceedings in the execution of the Act were such as they held most conducing to the rendering the same effectual, and such as they therefore thought justifiable in the power given them by the said Act, wherein if they erred they should very willingly be instructed by any explanation the Parliament should give them this their Act. And so this went off.

Then was the 18th and last Observation[1] called for and read, and my Lord Brereton and Thomson giving place, Mr Gregory advanced to their station, and in proof of the Observation tendered a list of particular ships and goods charged on and not owned by us. Which being read with my written answer,[2] I then by discourse opened the matter suitable to the substance of my said answer and read several parts of my reply to their list. In my doing whereof, Mr Gregory moved that my pains might be spared in reading those particulars which were not mentioned in the list now given in, and that I might answer to those and those only. Upon which I took leave to observe, first, the unfairness of their proceedings in being desirous to suppress anything that should discover their being satisfied. Forasmuch as their leaving out now what was in the former list sent us must I suppose naturally employ[3] their being satisfied in that particular by their taking no notice of this their satisfaction in their present list, and withstanding my making it appear to his Majesty by reading those particulars formerly urged against us which they now let alone, no bystander could have any ground to imagine but that they remain unanswered in the whole and every part of what they had before charged us with. Besides that, I observed that (if I was not mistaken therein) they did now not only suppress the old instances they are satisfied in, but bring upon us new ones by surprise, contrary not only to all fair proceedings, but to our repeated desires by letter of having the instances first sent to us, and my Lord Brereton's and Col. Tomson's repeated promises before his Majesty and this Board that we should have them. Which method of theirs I showed would moreover perpetuate the dispute without any end to be foreseen of it; while answers being given to satisfaction to this day's objection, that satisfaction shall never be owned but in lieu thereof a new race of objec-

---

[1] Above, p. 317; about prizes.
[2] Above, pp. 317–23.
[3] Imply.

tions shall be started, so as I plainly told his Majesty, my work must be to get a son and bring him up only to understand this controversy between Brooke House and us, and that his Majesty too should provide for successors to be instructed on his part in the state of this case, which otherwise would never likely be understood, either as to what thereof had already been adjusted or what remained further to be looked after in it. Besides, I observed a little more sharply to his Majesty, the method of these gentlemen in this particular suitable to their proceedings in the rest to be put to the justifying by affidavits of Wood and Shorter in January last, nay, and by evidences in the present case of later discovery than that (though all to so little purpose), what after a year and half's preparation and more they had the assurance so peremptorily to assert to the prejudice of this Office by these their Observations presented to the Parliament in October.[1] At this the King and the whole Board and all bystanders discovered by their murmur a disdainful resentment of these gentlemen's proceedings, and the King and Duke after their being up took notice of it in like manner publicly at supper as of a matter most enormous and oppressive.

I then in the second place proceeded to assert my written answer, which is that whatever was pretended by these Commissioners and now by Mr Gregory, not one particular in either of these lists are to my best knowledge chargeable on the Office of the Navy by anything that can rightly charge them, instancing particularly in the wine delivered and spent at sea, etc., but that at the most they cannot but pretend to prove the delivery of these things (supposing this also true, which I cannot admit) to some of the officers at the yards who, though they are by their places indeed made accountable to us, yet we were never nor can in any wise be esteemed accountable for them and their actions. To this Mr Gregory in a cynical, froward manner answers that for his part we (*viz.*, the Principal Officers of the Navy) are charged with all these things by the books of the Commissioners for Prizes, presently turning to one of their books and showing therein the 'Office of the Navy' are made debtor to such and such ships and goods. I replied that we were not accountable for the keeping of those books, much less for the wording of it, but

---

[1]Sc. the Commissioners are here, as elsewhere, attempting to justify their criticisms by affidavits sworn months after their Observations were completed and presented to Parliament. See above, pp. 348, 381.

that whatever was the meaning of the Commissioners of Prizes, who perhaps might call the under-officers of the Navy by the general name of the 'Office of the Navy', as esteeming them persons acting by and for us and accountable to us, I do affirm that the charge is wholly untrue in reference to us the Principal Officers and Commissioners of the Navy. To which Gregory snappishly answered that what he had reported was upon the entries in the books of the Commissioners of Prizes, and that he did not doubt but that they were able to justify the truth of their books, and this I drove him to repeat several times, and thereto adding that, to have justified this charge, he ought to have examined by what evidences the Prize Officers had placed these things to the account of the 'Office of the Navy', he frowardly returned: but what if he would have done so but could not get those evidences or any other papers or books from the sub-commissioners, but were answered that they had delivered all their books and papers to the Principal Commissioners for Prizes? I told him then he ought to have forborne so direct a charging us till those evidences did appear. Whereto he gave me his old answer, that he was confident those noble Lords would justify their books. Here my Lord Lauderdale[1] interposed, saying that had they known anything of this dispute, they would have seen right done to the Office of the Navy by calling their sub-commissioners to have explained the matter, adding that he was confident the goods were not delivered to the Office of the Navy but to the under-officers thereof in the yards, though the Office of the Navy in general was reputed debtor for it in their books, partly as those by whose desire the same were delivered for the Navy, and partly in general distinction to what was delivered for any other uses than the Navy. But that if his Majesty pleased, he and the rest of the Principal Commissioners for Prizes would take this matter into examination and give his Majesty satisfaction therein. Which the King approved of, declaring to Mr Gregory that he was sure some of these things could not, and that he did believe the rest were not, delivered to the Principal Officers of the Navy, but to the storekeepers and under-officers of the yards, and that therefore he ought to have fully informed himself therein before he had so directly charged us therewith.

And so this matter and the whole business of these Observations ended, with a profession of all satisfaction on his Majesty's

[1] A Commissioner for Prizes.

part in reference to every particular that I can remember either urged therein or offered upon the debate thereof by the Commissioners of Brooke House.

PRINCIPAL PERSONS

(often represented by initials)

George Monck, Duke of Albemarle, Captain-General of the Kingdom 1660–70	D.Alb.
Sir William Batten, Surveyor of the Navy 1660–7	W.B.
Lord Brereton, Brooke House Commissioner	Ld Bre.
Viscount Brouncker, Navy Commissioner 1664–79	Ld Br.
Sir George Carteret, Treasurer of the Navy 1660–7	G.C.
Sir William Coventry, Secretary to the Duke of York 1660–7; Navy Commissioner 1662–7	W.C.
John Cox, Navy Commissioner 1669–72	J.C.
Sir Denis Gauden, Navy Victualler 1660–77	D.G.
Sir Thomas Littleton, Joint-Treasurer of the Navy 1668–71	T.L.
Sir John Mennes, Comptroller of the Navy 1661–71	J.M.
Thomas Middleton, Surveyor of the Navy 1667–72	T.M.
Sir Thomas Osborne, Joint-Treasurer of the Navy 1668–71	T.O.
Sir William Penn, Navy Commissioner 1660–8	W.P.
Peter Pett, Navy Commissioner 1648–67	P.P.
Sir Jeremy Smith, Navy Commissioner 1669–75	J.S.
John Tippetts, Navy Commissioner 1668–72	J.T.
Sir William Warren, timber merchant	W.W.
James, Duke of York, Lord High Admiral 1660–73	D.Y.

GLOSSARY

admire, *v.* to wonder, be surprised at
another-gates, other-gates, *adj.* altogether different
apparel, *sb.* (of ship) outfit, moveable equipment
assign, *v.* to signalise, specify
attendance, *sb.* waiting

balk, *sb.* squared timber
band, *sb.* tie securing coil of rope; *see also* **great band**
bellropes, *sb.* ropes securing sails vertically
bewpers (blufers, bluffers), bunting (thin woollen cloth)
bewray, *v.* to show
bilboes, *sb.* iron shackles
bind, *v.* (in shipbuilding) to strengthen the body with knee-timbers, etc.
blufers (bluffers), *see* **bewpers**
boltrope, *sb.* rope sewn round edges of sails
boltsprit, *sb.* bowsprit
brand(ed), *v.* (of paper) labelled
break, *v.* to go bankrupt
bream (brim), *v.* to clean a ship's bottom by singeing with burning reeds, etc.
breechings, *sb.* heavy ropes securing gun-carriages
by how much, insofar as, in that

cabin lines, *sb.* ropes used to hold canvas walls of cabins
cablet, *sb.* cable under 10 ins in diameter
calcule, *sb.* calculation
call, *v.* to call on
can hook, sling used for hoisting
candle, sale by, auction in which the winning bid is the last before the candle goes out
caplaken, *sb.* gratuities
cast, *v.* 1. (of accounts) to make up. 2. (of canvas) to make

censure, *sb.* esteem, opinion, arbiter's verdict. *v.* to give expert opinion
centuries, *sb.* sentries
cheap, *sb.* bargain
chips, *sb.* small pieces of cut timber or plank
clench and splice *v.* to fix pieces of cable together securely
coach, *sb.* cabin under quarter-deck
collect, *v.* to recollect, deduce, calculate
colour, for, for the sake of appearances
combination, *sb.* collusion
compass, *v.* (of timber) curve
condescension, *sb.* concession (without implication of patronage)
considerable, *adj.* worthy of consideration
constr(ed), *v.* construed
conversation, *sb.* manner of life
course, in, (of payments) payments made in order of obligation
course, of, as of routine
curiosity, *sb.* carefulness, thoroughness

deals, *sb.* boards made of pine (red deal), or spruce (white deal)
defalk, *v.* defalcate, reduce by off-setting
demurrage, *sb.* detention of ship beyond the time agreed on; payment for demurrage
die-square, *adj.* square as a die
discover, *v.* reveal, express, confess
Dram timber, *sb.* timber from Drammen, Norway
dubbed, *adj.* trimmed with adze

earlily, *adv.* early
East-country, Eastland, *sb.* Baltic region
East Indies, *sb.* Indian sub-continent
employ, *v.* imply
event, *sb.* result

factor, agent (commercial)
firm, *sb.* confirmation. *v.* to confirm
flitch(ed), *v.* (of timber) split
foreigner, *sb.* usually one not native to or not enfranchised of a city
friend, close relative
frow, *adj.* (of plank) brittle

gouty, *adj.* (of canvas) rough
grave, *v.* to clean and seal a ship's bottom
great, by the, at an agreed price for the whole, by contract
great band, *sb.* superior variety of tar
gromet, grummet, *sb.* 1. ring of rope laid up three times. 2. youth ranking above ship's boy and below ordinary seaman
ground tows, *sb.* short-staple hemp used as ground tackle
growing charge, *sb.* compound interest

hamacco, *sb.* hammock
hand, *sb.* 1. signature. 2. unit of measurement (4 ins). *v.* (of sails): to furl or gather in
head and shoulders/knee, by, headlong, compulsively
Holland's duck, *sb.* smooth variety of canvas from The Netherlands or Germany
hounds, *sb.* shoulders on masthead
house, *sb.* 1. storehouse. 2. House of Commons
hundred, (of cordage); **hundredweight**, (of deals), *sb.* by convention reckoned as 120

impertinent, *adj.* irrelevant
imploy, *v.* imply
impress, *v.* 1. put pressure on. 2. recruit by force
imprest, *sb.* cash advance to government agent or supplier
indisburs(ed), *v.* out of pocket
industriously, *adv.* persistently, carefully, of set purpose
instrument, *sb.* clerk, agent
invite, *v.* induce

jealous, *adj.* fearful
jolliness (joleness), *sb.* insolent presumption
junk, *sb.* cordage of no other use than to make oakum

knees, *sb.* knee-shaped timbers

last *sb.* (of pitch): 12 barrels; (of tar): 13 barrels
late times, the, the Interregnum
lay, *v.* (of cable) to bind strands into cable; *see also* **twice-laid**
lignum vitae, *sb.* a tropical hardwood
line of numbers, *sb.* slide-rule marked out in logarithms
list, *sb.* strip added in sailmaking to strengthen sail and conceal seams

load, *sb.* (of timber) cartload one ton in weight
London dovetail, *sb.* variety of ironwork
Longsound timber, *sb.* timber from Langesund, Norway
loom, *sb.* inboard section of oar

marline-spike, *sb.* iron spike used in splicing
medium, sb. average rate, e.g. of cost (in victuals/pay) per man

Navy, *sb.* usually Navy Office/Board
necessary money, *sb.* money advanced to purser by Victualler for dry provisions (wood, candles, etc.)
nettings, *sb.* small ropes from top of the fo'c'stle to the poop
Normer deals, *sb.* variety of Norwegian deals
Noyalls (Noyles), *sb.* canvas from Noyal, Brittany

observable, *adj.* worthy of observation
officer, *sb.* official
open, *v.* to explain
ordinary, *adj.* (of ship) ships laid up in harbour, out of commission
overwork, *sb.* superstructure

painful, *adj.* painstaking
palm, *sb.* face of the fluke of an anchor
Park, the, *sb.* St James's Park
partners, *sb.* wooden frame in the deck at the point at which the mast passes through
pass hemp, *sb.* inferior variety of hemp
pay, *v.* to daub, smear
petty warrant, petty emptions, *sb.* supplies purchased locally
pipestaves, *sb.* wooden strips forming a cask
plate, *v.* to line with metal plates
poize, *v.* to weigh
Poldavis, *sb.* canvas from Poldavide, Brittany
poundage, *sb.* commission of so much per £ of money issued from Exchequer
practice, *sb.* trick
premio, *sb.* premium
present, *adj.* immediate
presently, *adv.* immediately
prise, *v.* to appraise
privative, *adj.* negative
prize, *sb.* price

propose, *v.* to question, examine
pursuit, *sb.* enquiry
purveyor, *sb.* purchasing agent paid by commission

quick, *adj.* sharp, penetrating

rag, *sb.* badly made object
recollect, *v.* retrieve information
reduce, *v.* arrange
reformado, *sb.* naval or military officer serving without commission
Rhine, Rine, *adj.* (from German *rein*, clean) variety of hemp of high quality
Ribadeux, *sb.* variety of knee timber
ruler, *sb.* slide-rule
runs, *sb.* runaway seamen, deserters

scantlings, *sb.* dimensions, units of measurement in shipbuilding
school(ed), *v.* scolded
seem, *v.* to pretend
shake, *sb.* (in wood) crack
sheath, *sb.* protective layer of wood on bottom of ship
shivers, *sb.* (in hemp) loose filaments
shot, *sb.* (of cable) two ends spliced together
shutter, *sb.* shuttle
shyness, *sb.* secretiveness
sized fish, fish of specified size
sledge, *sb.* sledge-hammer
slubbering, *adj.* hurried, careless
so-all, *adv.* nevertheless
Spanish table, *sb.* folding table
specie, species, *sb.* (of provisions) kind, sort
sprucia, *sb.* 1. spruce. 2. Prussia
standard, *sb.* upright timber
State, the, *sb.* the Commonwealth and Protectorate régimes, 1649–60
stealth, stealing
Straits, the, *sb.* the Mediterranean
stranger, *sb.* foreigner
success, *sb.* eventuality, outcome (good or bad)
Swinsound timber, *sb.* timber from Svinesund, Sweden

tally, *sb.* wooden stick used in Exchequer for accounting, notched and (for security) split in two matching parts
tell, *v.* to count
tenters, *sb.* tenterhooks
thimble, *sb.* metal ring used in splicing
Treasurer, the, *sb.* usually Treasurer of the Navy
Treasury, the, *sb.* usually Navy Treasury
treat, *v.* to negotiate
treenail, *sb.* cylindrical wooden pin
truck, *sb.* cap fixed on masthead
Turks, *sb.* usually Algerians
twice-laid *adj.* (of rope) new rope made wholly or partly of old; cf. **lay**

unbespeak, *v.* renounce
uneasy, *adj.* difficult
ungrateful, *adj.* unwelcome
unhackled, *adj.* (of hemp) uncombed

vail, *sb.* tip, gratuity
vane, *sb.* pennant worn at masthead showing direction of wind
vanity, *sb.* foolishness
verier, *adj.* comparative form of very
very, *adj.* 'really and truly entitled to the name' (*O.E.D*)
Victualler, the, *sb.* patent officer in charge of victualling of Navy
victualler, *sb.* merchant or ship engaged in victualling
Vitry (Vittry) canvas, *sb.* light and durable variety from Vitré, Brittany

wear and tear, *sb.* (of ship) a general term covering a variety of costs, including maintenance of ship at sea
Wibrough (Wiburg, Wiburger) tar, tar from Viborg, Sweden
wing, *sb.* those parts of the hold and orlop deck nearest to the sides
within square, *adj.* bent at an angle of less than 90°
withstanding, *adv.* moreover

INDEX

The arrangement of items within each entry is alphabetical. **Persons and places** are indexed under their modern form wherever possible, with any textual variants (except contractions which do not suggest discrete spellings) added in parentheses. **Peers** are indexed under their titles. **Titles and offices** are those held at the period which the volume covers, with a few later attainments noted in square brackets. Square brackets also include forenames of less well-known people; authorities for this information (for Navy personnel and civilian merchants) are given in the Appendix below. **Pepys** is denoted by P. The entries under his name are personal details. His professional functions are treated under the heading **Clerk of the Acts**. The section **Ships mentioned by name** gives, wherever possible, rate or type; if prize, provenance and date of acquisition; and reference to R. C. Anderson's *English Ships, 1649–1702*. Additional details/references are given for ships of the same or similar name, and in certain other cases. The **Introduction** is indexed only for matter not found in the text.

The indexer wishes to record his indebtedness to the editor for much advice and assistance, and in particular for providing identification of persons where necessary.

C. S. Knighton

Ackworth (Ackeworth, Acworth), [William], storekeeper, Woolwich: alleged embezzlement, 155; Batten's opinion, 58; incompetent accountant, 5 & n.5; information from, 50, 64 & n.7, 79, 97, 401; receives tar, 107; restored to place, 165 ~ alluded to, 75

Admiral, Lord High: Instructions, ('ancient') 327, (not applied temp. Commonwealth) 331; responsible for ordering pay, 316 *see also* Buckingham; Northumberland; York

Admirals (Flag Officers): avarice, 242–3 & n.; fail to oversee distribution of prizes, 208; negligence, 114

Admiralty, Court of: 318

Africa Company, Royal: ships lent to, 42

Albemarle (Albermarl(e)), George Monck, 1st Duke of, Lord General: command, 158 & n.4, 239, 300 & n.1, 364 & n.2, 416; letters to, 397, 427; orders from, (investigation of contract) 275, (payment of tickets) 159; timber bought from, 349 & n.2

Aldeburgh (Alborough, Albrough), Suff.: P defeated in bye-election, 334 & n.4 ~ alluded to, 134
Aldridge, [Henry], Navy Office clerk: 196
Algiers (Argier): expeditions against, (1661–2) 204 & n.1, (1664) 3 n.1, 42, (1668–9) 199–200 & n., 215
Allin, Cuthbert, soldier: 130
Allin (Allen), Sir Thomas [Kt 1665, Bt 1673], naval commander: concern for profits, 199–200, 242–3; criticized, 237; patrols Channel, 244 n.1; provisions for, 250; seamen's pay, 114, 265; voyages to Mediterranean, 141, 230, 236 n.1, 237 ~ alluded to, 204, 234, 235, 261
Amsterdam: 112 n.1
Anabaptists: admired by Penn, 20
anchors: bought, 16, 47, & n.2; break, 94; exchange sought, 131; iron for, (English) 356, (Spanish) 356 n.2, (Swedish) 354; lost, 200; prize, 322; stolen, 135
anchor-smiths: Navy Board's debts to, 304
Andrews, Daniel, master: 266
Andrews, [Thomas], merchant: 96
Anglesey, Arthur Annesley, 1st Earl of, Treasurer of the Navy 1667–8: account, 250–1 & nn.; payments, 207–8; removal, 202 & n.1; signature, 136 ~ alluded to, 325
Archangel (Archangell), Russia: tar from, 31
Arlington, (Sir) Henry Bennet, 1st Baron 1665 [Earl 1672], Secretary of State 1662–74: commends P, 340; negligence, 161; present at debate before Privy Council, 337; speaks there, 375(*bis*); to assist P in defending King over war finances, 340–1 ~ alluded to, 76–7, 78, 210, 251 n.3, 339
ash: 78
Ashley (Ashly), Anthony Ashley Cooper, 1st Baron [1st Earl of Shaftesbury 1672], Chancellor of the Exchequer 1661–72, Treasury Commissioner 1667–72, Treasurer of the Prize Commission: about prizes, 131; critical of Brooke House Commission, 374–5; speaks at debate before Privy Council, 376 ~ alluded to, 366, 377
Ayloffe (Ayliff), Joseph, of Gray's Inn, Carteret's counsel: 335, 348

Backwell (Backewell), Ald. Edward, banker: supplies pieces-of-eight, 3, 4 ~ alluded to, 98, 99
Baddicott, [William], ropemaker: 118
Badiley (Boddily, Bodily), Capt. [William], master attendant, Deptford: makes tarpaulins, 56; negligent, 72; perquisites, 50
balks *see* timber
ballast: excessive, 135, 220; Navy Board deceived over, 102 ~ alluded to, 355
bankers: dealt with by Navy Treasurer, 397 ~ alluded to, 258 nn.1,2, 267
see also Backwell; Lindsay; Meynell; Thompson
Banks, Sir John, merchant: 174 n.1
Barbary Coast: pirates, 27 n.2
Barbour, William: Navy Office clerk: 166, 297
Bargrave, Capt. Richard *or* Robert, royalist soldier: 222–3 & n.
Barker, Ald. [William], merchant: hemp from, 88
Barnes, [Alexander], timber merchant: 315
Barnes, Capt. Butler, naval officer: 139
barrels, casks, tuns: charges, 129–30; empty use, 134; thrown overboard, 419; water for ballast, 135
Barrow, [Philip], storekeeper, Chatham: 21 & n.1
Bassett, Capt. –, naval officer: 428
Batten, [Elizabeth], Lady, wife of Sir William: 197
Batten, Sir William, Surveyor of the Navy 1660–7:
contracts and supplies: advice, 353; consent, 11, 85; disputes, (cloth) 27–8, 29–30, 44, 48, 56–7, 82, (cordage) 40, (glass) 53, (ironwork) 37, 47, (timber) 5 & n.2, 6 & n.2, 9–13, 23, 36, 47, 51, 79–80, 91–2, 347; expertise, (cordage) 157; purchases,

(brickwork) 124, (ironwork) 37, (oil) 63, (timber) 15–16; shortages admitted, 15, 16
criticized: bad judgement, 126–7; contrariness, 56–8, 79; corrected/outsmarted by P, 13, 16–17, 40, 51–2, 88–9; favouritism, 10 & n.3, 16 & n.1, 54, 88–9, 95–6, 102; negligence, 15, 110, 117–18, 140, 141, 184, 186–7, 195, 397; poor book-keeping, 15, 17–18, 37–8, 131, 158, 184, 196–7, 212–13; sharp practice, 14–15, 19–20, 50–1, 88–9, 95–6
dockyards: critical of carpenters, 132; power in, 54; surveys, 15 & n.1, 17, 37; visits, (Chatham) 23, (Deptford) 117, (Portsmouth) 35
finance: hasty approval of estimate for building ship, 186–7; records delivered to Treasury, 357; suspected collusion with private shipbuilders, 131
information from: 16, 17, 19, 23, 37, 43, 67, 88, 353
pay and perquisites: bribed, 20; fencing for his house, 74 & n.4: private business, (in King's ships) 95–6, (using Office clerks) 196–7; salary and assessment, 101; ticket paid to himself, 409
relations with others: criticized by Ashley, 131; critical, (of C. Pett) 116, (of Warren) 80
sundry business: clerks, 19 & n.4, 67, 196, 298, 361; discovers cheat, 79; present at Board, 48, 85, 111; signature, 8, 53, 65, 66, 275, 299, 311
various: death, 182; lighthouses, 58 & n.6; MP, 50 & n.2, 102; share in privateer, 245 & n.5; surveyor for City ship, 118
~ alluded to, 21, 68, 325
Beach, Capt. [Richard], naval officer: 215, 265
Bergen, Norway: tar from, 31, 32, 39, 79
Berkeley (Barkely, Berkely) [of Stratton], John Berkeley, 1st Baron, Navy Commissioner 1660–4: clerks, 196; favours gentlemen captains, 221;

Ordnance Commissioner (1664–70), 120 & n.1; present at Board, 9, 82, 88–9 ~ alluded to, 325
Berry, Capt. [John], naval officer: 267
Berwick-upon-Tweed, Northumb.: 232 n.1
Beuningen (Beningham, Benningham), Coenraad van, Dutch ambassador: 229
bewpers *see* cloth
Bilbao (Bilbo), Spain: iron from, 38
Billop, Thomas, clerk to Matthew Wren: 252
Birch, Col. John, Trade Commissioner 1668–72: 216 & n.1
Birkhead (Birkehead), –, coppersmith: 61
Blackborne, Robert, Secretary to the East India Company: 205 & n.2
Blackborough (Blackborrow, Blackbury), [Peter], merchant: timber from, 309, 310, 314, 315, 423
Blackwall, Essex: 205
Blake, Gen. Robert, military and naval commander: praises English-made shot, 38 ~ alluded to, 20 n.4, 82 n.1, 228 n.1
Bland, [John], merchant: 3 & nn. 2,4
blocks, blockmakers: measurement, 26, 71 & n.1; winding tackle, 219 ~ alluded to, 16
blufers *see* cloth
boats, ships': 218
boatswains, bosuns (of ships): accounts, 194, 197, 198, 201, 214, 255, 292–3, 397, 402; appointment, 199; cordage for, 127; corruption, 44, 63–4 & n., 109, 113, 119, 127, 199, 201, 217–19; cut cables to make swabs, &c., 95, 124–5; demands, 129, 157, 199, 200, 201, 218; negligence, 156
boatswains (of yards): not to be masters of lighters, 155–6
Boddily *see* Badiley
Bodham, William, clerk of the ropeyard, Woolwich: 41, 71, 124, 127 n.1
Body (Boddy), [George], merchant: 189 & nn.2,3
Bohemia: oak from, 47 n.1
Boke, –, blockmaker, Chatham: 122
bolts *see* ironwork

boltsprits *see* masts
Bond, –, master: 141
Bourne, Rear-Adm. Nehemiah: 20 & n.4
Bow: 74
Bowen, Capt. [Peter], naval officer: 265
Bowyer, [Thomas], anchor-smith, Woolwich: 47
Bowyer, [William], merchant: 264
Boyce, [Richard], shipwright: 131, 182
brass: 38
bread rooms: 71–2 & n.
breaming: 134
Brereton (Breereton, Breerton), William Brereton, 3rd Baron, Brooke House Commissioner:
Privy Council debate: present, 337, 345, 377, 432; signature, 271; speaks, 355, 359, 361, 376, 381, 403 (*bis*), 409, (charges P with receiving ticket) 419, 429–32, (critical of P) 335–6, 338–9, 347, 348, 358, (dumbfounded) 410, (objects) 406, 417, (promises evidence) 432, (rude to King) 367, (supports P) 408
various: mocked by King, 339; musical talent, 369 & n.1; Parliamentary business, 339 & n.2, 342; P considers writing to, 340
bribery and corruption: 12–13, 19–20, 26, 37–8, 172 n.1
see also Ackworth; Batten; boatswains; captains; Carteret; Coleman; Gauden; Jennens; Lewis; Mayers; Mennes; Miller; sea officers
bricklayers, brickwork: 124, 133
Bridgeman, Sir Orlando, Lord Keeper 1666–72: present at debate before Privy Council, 337; speaks there, 338, 366; speaks to Parliament, xxv, 376 & n.3
Bridges, [Richard], linen draper, Cornhill: 83–4
Bridgewater (Bridgwater), John Egerton, 2nd Earl of, Brooke House Commissioner: 366
Bridport [*alias* Burport] (Burfett), Dors.: cordage from, 387 & n.3
Bristol: ships built at, 161 n.3

Brooke House, Holborn: building, xxviii & n.3
Brooke House Commission (Commissioners of Accounts):
general: established, xxiii-xxvi; membership, xxvi-xxviii; reports to House of Commons, xxix, xxx; termination, xxxiv
inquiries: accounts delivered to, 144 & n.2, 174; limited by establishing Act, 365 & n.4; list of bills demanded, 345, 424; Navy Board lacks records to answer, 197; P prompted to compile list of ships, 212; P warned to expect tough examination, 341; Warren's first contract, 148; will not look to Commonwealth precedent, 360, 370
Observations (general): meaning of word debated, 369; not judgements on Board, 382–3; sent to P, 334
Observations (particular): 1st (Warren's mast contract), 273–7, 346–61, 371; *2nd* (fetching masts), 277–8, 361–7; *3rd* (Treasurer's accounts not strictly kept), 278–80, 367–71; *4th* (imprests), 280, 371–7; *5th* (Treasurer's accounts signed without corresponding bills), 281, 377–81; *6th* (bills for large sums for unspecified purposes), 281–2, 367 n.5, 381–4; *7th* (storekeepers' records defective), 282–6, 384–95; *8th* (no annual surveys of stores), 287–91, 396–402; *9th* (no quarterly musters), 291–2, 402; *10th* (boatswains' and carpenters' accounts passed before pursers check them; storekeepers' and pursers' accounts not compared), 292–3, 402–3; *11th, 12th & 13th* (irregularities concerning tickets), 294–9, 403–16; *14th* (pursers given cash instead of provisions), 299–300, 416–19; *15th* (merchants overpaid for hemp), 300–7, 419–22; *16th* (favouritism for Warren), 307–15, 422–4; *17th* (ships unpaid and idle), 315–16, 424–9;

INDEX 447

18th (prize ships and goods not charged), 317–23, 344, 432–4
P's criticisms: charges not specific, 386; delay, 346–7, 358; divert Navy Board from other business, 254; evidence disputed, 277–8, 343–4, 356; evidence lacking, 286, 382, 385–6; evidence not examined, 371–2; evidence presented without notice, 348, 355, 381, 421, 432; frivolous, 395; Navy Board's answers not examined, 382; P himself criticized/exculpated, 335–6 & n.; strangers to Navy, 324, 337; unready to argue, 365
report: Lords' Committee to consider, 334–5 & nn.; publication proposed, 376; submitted to Board, 271 & n.2, 272 ~ alluded to, 337, 338
various: Buckingham's role, 148 n.1; clerk, 144; critical of King, 366–7; criticized by King, 357; discoveries reported, 177, 234–5, 236; oath, 343, 345; P wishes to report proceedings to King and Duke, 339
brooms, brushes, scrubbers: 119, 305
Brouncker (Brounker, Bruncker, Brunkard), William Brouncker, 2nd Viscount, Navy Commissioner 1664–79:
general: assists Comptroller, 176 n.1, 193 & n.1, 198, 288 n.2, 345, 359, 392 & n.1, 399, 406 & n.1, 410 & n.2, 415–16 & nn., 424 n.2; attends to petitions about tickets, 406; clerks, 166, 195–6, 408 & n.1; corruption/malpractice, 143 & n.1; hemp offered to, 303; muster taken by, 292 n.2; present at Board, 151, 158, 176, 179, 202, 246; records, inadequate, 212; register of attendance perhaps proposed by, 253 n.5; signature, 102, 136, 148, 150, 151, 152, 153, 154, 169, 172, 182, 188, 241, 272, 275, 299; visits Deptford, 117
information from: 138, 149–50, 174, 175, 197, 247, 248, 250, 277, 344, 419
Privy Council debate: discusses Brooke House business with P, 343; present, 345, 367; refers Commission to P, 334; reports to, 279, 422; speaks, 345, 371, 380–1, 393, 395, 409; submits rebuttal of Commission's charges, 424–6 & nn.
relations with P: discourses/visits, 149–52, 159, 166, 168, 234–5, 252; P critical, (absenteeism) 253, (forgetfulness) 203, 251; P praises, 195; P writes to, 148, 169–70; supports P, 147, 175, 194, 195, 199
relations with others: critical, (of Mennes) 148 n.1, 153, (of Penn) 147; reluctant to criticize gentlemen captains, 248; scientific interests, 252 n.3
~ alluded to, 152, 253, 325
Browne, John, storekeeper, Harwich: 283 n.1, 385 & n.1
Buat (Buatt), Henry Fleury de Culan, Heer van, Dutch opposition leader: 229 & n.4
Buckingham, George Villiers, 1st Duke of, Lord High Admiral 1619–28: 223
Buckingham, George Villiers, 2nd Duke of, politician: favours gentlemen captains, 221; hostile, (to Duke of York) 148 n.1., 225 n.2, (to Navy Board) 211
Buckridge, G., purser: 22
Burchet, –, merchant: 40
Burroughs (Burrows), [William], Navy Office clerk: 180 & n.2
Burton, William, bailiff of Great Yarmouth, Norf.: 387 & n.4
Byland, –, assistant shipwright, Woolwich: 173, 188–9, 247

cabins: captain turns out master, 266; coach, 132; excessive number and size, 219–20, 233; furnishings, 249
cables *see* cordage
Cadbury, [Humphrey], mast-maker, Deptford: 139
Cadiz (Cales), Spain: fleets at, 4, 201; goods from, 65 n.2; ship taken off, 200 n.2
calicoes *see* cloth
candles: price, 77–8 ~ alluded to, 382
canvas *see* cloth
Capp, [John], seaman: 430
captains, commanders:
bookwork/journals: accounts of

men in pay, 176–7, 248;
contempt for, 178; ticket records,
298, 412 ~ alluded to, 200
cupidity/negligence: concerning
cabins, 219–20, 249, 266; live
above means, 236; perquisites,
235; private trading, 200–1,
224 & n.1, 299–30, 236–7, 247,
249 ~ alluded to, 129, 156, 199,
218, 231–2, 238, 243
duties: dead men's effects, 140;
seamen's pay, 293; stores/
victualling, 199, 417
gentlemen v. tarpaulins: 183–4, 220,
221–30 & nn., 238–9, 248, 249
information from: 133, 260–1,
262–3; complaints, 95
malpractices/arrogance: collude in
pursers' frauds, 165, 178–9;
defraud chaplains, 113–14;
defraud pursers, 239–41;
defraud seamen, 204; hectoring,
259; impressment irregularities,
131, 204, 205–8; theft of tables,
alleged, 201; victualling abuses,
131, 132, 300, 402–3
pay: 42 n.2, 140, 244–5
relations with men: 'followings',
277 & n.1; maltreatment, 134–5,
208, 233, 236; master's work
taken over, 265; men's
preferences, 208, 215–16, 230–1
servants/musicians: as midshipmen,
134; barbers, 207; fiddlers, 207;
trumpeters, 134
social aspirations: 238
careening: 141
Caribbean: provisions for, 105 & n.1
Carkesse (Carcas, Carkaiss, Carkas,
Carkes, Carkess), James, Ticket
Office clerk: 297, 298; dismissal/
reinstatement, 408 & n.2;
information from, 130, 404, 411,
414 & n.1
Carl XI, King of Sweden:
proclamation by, 361
carpenters, joiners, sawyers: abuses,
43, 44, (corruption) 135,
(negligence) 131–2; accounts,
194, 198, 214, 255, 293, 397, 402;
appointment, 199; apprentices
worth more than masters,
261–2; charges, 90, 124; hours of
work, 45–6; wages, 260–1; work
in battle, 417 n.1 ~ alluded to,
14, 261

Carteret (Carterett), Sir George,
Treasurer of the Navy 1660–7:
business: accounts, 15, 62–4,
250–1 & nn., (scrutiny by
Brooke House Commission)
335 & n.1, 336–9, 369–70, 372–7;
bills allowed, 7–8, 424–5;
Exchequer fees, 378; letters/
orders to, 131, 161 n.2, 427, 428;
payments to merchants, 3, 98,
107, 121; present at Board, 48,
133; wartime duties, 397
criticized: collusion with corrupt
cashier, 123; negligent, 114, 195;
threat of impeachment, 369 & n.4
relations with others: letters from
P, 10, 101 n.2; reproves
purveyor, 13
resignation: 202 n.1
various: chamber organ, 369 n.1;
kinsman, 248 n.3; knowledge of
cloth, 82; private contract, 112 &
n.1 ~ alluded to, 80, 87, 296, 325
carving work: 26, 133
Castle, William, shipbuilder: builds
ships by contract, 117–18, 132 &
n.1.; estimate, 189; knees, (abuse
in) 102–5 & nn., (offered) 88–9,
92; masts certified, 54 ~ alluded
to, 130, 188
Castlemaine, Barbara Palmer,
Countess of, the King's
mistress: 14, 229
Castlemaine, Roger Palmer, 1st Earl
of: 230 n.1
Catherine, Queen: voyage to
England, 65 n.2
caulkers, caulking: charges, 90;
negligence, alleged, 108;
victuals for, 141: work in battle,
417 n.1
chandlery: 290
chaplains, ships': 113–14 & n.
Charles I, King: naval forces, 226 &
n.1
Charles II, King:
debate before Privy Council:
(i) *chairs proceedings*: 254, 337,
345, 367, 372, 384, 392, 395, 401,
402, 403, 410, 416, 419, 424, 429
(ii) *comments*: 336, 343, 347, 349,
360, 371, 378, 382, 383, 392, 394,
408, 434
(iii) *critical*: dissatisfied with
Commission's evidence/
methods, 338, 365–6, 375, 376,

377, 382–3, 401–2, 433;
interrupts, 350; objects,
(disrespectful language) 347,
(no apology) 367, (premature
judgement) 369, (repetitiveness)
357
(iv) *inquires/examines*: Dutch war
expenses, 400–1; evidence
offered by Navy Board, 366;
imprests, 371–2; shortage of
masts, 353; ticket produced by
Brereton, 429–30
(v) *private funds spent on war/
'other uses'*: 337–40 & nn.,
372–7; asks P to put facts on
record, 340; diversion of funds
repudiated, 366
relations with P: audience sought/
given, 335, 339, 341–2, 366, 372,
419; commands executed, 131,
162 n.2; dinner, 339–40; given P's
answer to Brooke House's
Observations, 336–8; makes P
spokesman for Board, 335, 337,
338, 347; P addresses/appeals to,
330–2, 346, 347, 358, 370, 384,
388, 394, 396, 431, 433; P's
report on naval administration,
191 n.2, 210, 251–2; P's service
to, 347; satisfied with P's
answers to Brooke House
Commission, 362, 386, 401, 403,
431, 434–5; seconds/supports P's
arguments, 339–40, 341–3, 347,
362, 365, 371, 383, 386, 388, 390,
395, 417, 419, 422, 422–3, 426
relations with others: Penn attends,
244; Warren, (appointment) 365,
(commendation) 422–3,
(contract) 347
reports/representations to: hemp
prices, 301, 302; tickets, 429; war
expenses, 372–3; Warren's
account, 344
sundry business: gratuity to spy,
161–2 & n.; instructions to Navy
Board, 362; Navy appointments,
(Commissioners) 210–11, 284,
417, (Comptrollership discussed
with Duke) 192, (contractor)
278, (purveyor) 365; restrictions
on pay of ships, 265; Stop of the
Exchequer, 257–8 & n.; visits
Chatham, 19, 349
various: amused, 368; at Oxford
during Plague, 421; laboratory
252 & n.3; mocks Petty's ship
design, 27; presents from New
Englanders, 137–8, 351, 352;
prevented from evaluating
captains, 209; reminiscences,
138, 222–3, 349, 362, 392; ship
admired by, 59 n.1; unreceptive
to anti-war views, 229; wit, 388,
408
Chatham, Kent, dockyard:
goods at/for/from: 63; balks, 51;
cordage, 155; hemp, 110 & n.3;
masts, 9, 55, 108, 115, 310;
plating, 71; timber, 321;
treenails, 15
officers: general: excuses for
absence, 257; letter to, 137;
particular: carpenters, 261–2;
clerk of the ropeyard, 398 n.6;
clerk of the survey, 214;
Commissioner, appointment,
191–2 & n.; nailer, 154–5;
shipwrights, 113, 155, (pressed)
160; storekeeper/stores, 173 n.2,
(abuses) 384, 385, (accounts)
112–13, (letter to) 399
shipbuilding and repairs: 132,
187–8 & n., 220, 257
ships at/from: 111, 129, 157, 204,
264, 320; unserviceable, 256
various: chain, 357 & n.1;
corruption, 26; customs dues,
35; pays, 247, 249, 265; P at, 112,
257; P's repute at, 18; Pett at,
112, 349 & n.1, (during war) 397;
Pett family domination, 19 n.1;
sale, 36–7; troubles, 21 & n.1, 112
~ alluded to, 133, 173, 184, 428 n.5
see also Barrow; Boke; Cox;
Gregory; Hempson;
Homewood; Moore
for Dutch raid *see* Medway
Chayford, – : 155
Chester, Capt. [Thomas], merchant:
314
Chicheley, Sir John, naval officer:
160–1 & n.
Chicheley (Chichly), [Thomas; Kt
1670], Ordnance Commissioner
1664–70: 120 & n.1
Child, [Josiah; Bt 1678], merchant:
313; proposed as Navy
Commissioner, 211
Chiverton (Cheverton), [Ald.] Sir
R[ichard], merchant: hemp
from, 87, 88

Chockely, – , servant to Batten: 74
Christiania *see* Oslo
Civil War: events, 222–3 & n., 226 & n.1, 228; fear of renewal, 225–6 & nn. ~ alluded to, 342 n.3
clapboard *see* timber
Clapham, [John], Navy Office clerk: 196
Clerk of the Acts [i.e. P's official functions]:
  business: bills queried, 102–3; business committed to, 75, 81–2, 87–8, 91, 164 n.1, 202, 247; business initiated by, 115, 167–70, 185–6, 211–12; deceived by Brouncker, 252–3; examines, (accounts) 137–8, (masts) 350–1; pay and expenses, 68, 101, (gratuities denied) 329 & n.3; predecessors' practice, 190–1, 327; proposes assistance for Comptroller, 175–6; protest about loss of hemp, 109–10; repute at Chatham, 18; seaman's testimonial, 265; signature withheld, 136, 153, 154; tradesmen beaten down, 124; visits ships, 257; wartime duties, 324, 326–30, 397
  clerks: 153–4, 253, 298; *see also* Gibson; Hayter; Hewer; Seddon
  debate before Privy Council: addresses Commissioners, 343–6; charges Commission with delay, 358; defends, (Board's conduct) 285–6, (imprests) 358–60, (length of his answers) 410; disputes/refutes Commission's evidence, 307, 316–23, 356, 367–8, 384–6, 390–1, 394–6, (criticizes lack of instances) 385–6, (exposes Commissioner's ignorance) 348; gives evidence, 352–3; notes for speeches, 354, 372, 384, 386, 391, 402; notes on Observations, 344; outwits Commissioners, 365; respects Solicitor-General's oratory, 375; silent when survey books criticized, 357; spokesman for Board, 272, 335, 336, 337, 338, 346; submission private not general, 343–4; ticket fraud charge, 410, 419, 429–32; war expenses compared with those of First Dutch War, 378 & n.2
  Parliament: evidence prepared for, 346–7, 349, 354; speech to, 429 & n.4
  record keeping: contracts, 12, 54–5, 112, 190, 351–2, 391; daily list of things undone, 140; fellow Officers' work done in their absence, 324; letter-book, 148 & n.2, 171, 192, 253; letters, (from) 36 n.2, 71 n.1, 104–5, 169, 427, 428, 430 n.1, (to) 54–5, 105, 399; memoranda/minutes/notes, 16, 17 & n.1, 35 & n.4, 57, 246, 336, (on Brooke House Commission's Observations) 344, 397–9, 410–16, 420–1, 423–4, 426–9; papers for debate before Privy Council, 354, 372, 402, (forgotten) 386, 391, 421; register of attendance at Board, 253 & n.5; shorthand, 119 n.2, 128; survey books criticized, 357–8 ~ alluded to, 6 & n.1, 40, 42, 79, 96–7, 97, 102, 110, 113, 114, 115, 131, 136–7, 151–2, 170, 172, 195, 212–14, 236, 237, 287–8
  relations with Duke of York: addresses, 332–3, 347; private audience, 191–3, 339; reports to, 126–7, 148 n.2, 187, 191–3, 342 & n.2; resists Duke's proposal, 292 n.1
  relations with King: addresses/appeals to, 330–2, 346, 347, 358, 371, 380, 384, 388, 389, 394, 419–20, 431, 443; attends, 335, 341–3; dines with, 339–40; service to, 347
Clerke, Capt. – , New Englander: 108
Clifford, Sir Thomas, Brooke House Commissioner: speaks in debate before Privy Council, 375 ~ alluded to, 367
cloth:
  general: manufacture/flax, 29, 31; measurement, 71, 72–3
  particular: bewpers/blufers, 24, 48, 52–3, 82–5; calico, 48, 49, 81–2, 83 & n.1, 84, 85; canvas, 56–7, 59, 60, 72–3, 219, 306, (charges) 13, 43–4, 51–2, 56, 398, (embezzled) 255, (varieties compared) 27–31; cotton, 172 n.1; kerseys, 172 n.1, 191, 249;

poldavy, 28; tarpaulin, 56; wool, 48 n.2
provenance: England, (Ipswich) 44–5, 57, 72, 219, (Norwich) 24, (Suffolk) 29, (West Country) 27–31; France, (Noyalls) 13, 28, 30, 51, 59, 72–3, (Vitry) 30–1; Netherlands, 27–31; Spain, 82
clothes *see* slops
Clothier, [John] merchant: bargain for cordage, 74
Clutterbuck (Cluterbuck), Richard, Navy agent, Leghorn: accounts, 143–5 ~ alluded to, 126–7 & n.
coach *see* cabins
coal: prices, 205, 209 ~ alluded to, 119
see also colliers
Cocke (Cock), Capt. [George], merchant: hemp from, 100, (prices criticized) 300, (P rejects charge) 307; planks from, (criticized) 46–7, (measured) 6; tar/pitch from, 33–5 ~ alluded to, 86
Cole, [Christopher], merchant: 315
Coleby, [Philip], merchant: 172 & n.1, 191
Coleman, James, master: corruption, 93 ~ alluded to, 108
Colepeper (Culpeper), [Judith Colepeper], Lady: timber from, 315
colliers (men): avoid press, 134
see also coal
Commonwealth (the State): nation's honour upheld by, 237; seamen employed by as captains, 223–4
Comptroller of the Navy: clerks, 290 n.2; duties, 192–4, 202–3, 276, 279–80, 281, 287–8, 290, 296, 344–5, 370, 380, 385, 396–401 & nn., 407, 415; journals to be delivered to, 200; needs to be able man, 217; salary and assessment, 101
see also Mennes: Slingsby (*bis*)
Connecticut (Kennedicutt), New England: tar from, 108
Constantinople (Constantianople): embassy to, 224, 229, 236
contracts, contractors: abuses, 44–5, 72, 132–3; arguments over, 6, 9–11, 18, 35–6, 48, 51–2, 53, 59–60, 74–5, 87–8, 91–2, 97–100, 189–91, 202, 266–7, 273–7, 307–15, 361–3, 383, 386–92, 422–3; goods delivered without, 51, 103, 282–6, 386–93; goods not answering, 5 & n.2, 24, 30, 54, 72, 85–6, 92, 117–18, 132–3, 283–6; goods over-priced, 300–7; goods superfluous, 35; loose terms, 145; negotiated by P, 9 n.1; private/commission, 112 & n.1, 114–15, 278 & n.1, 386–92; public days for tenders, 314 & n.1, 423; salvage, 135–6; shipbuilding and repair, 103, 117–18, 130–1, 132 & n.1; victualling, 250 & n.2; wartime complications, 277–8, (compared with First Dutch War) 327 n.1, 419 & n.1
~ alluded to, 33 n.1, 168
Cooke, Mark, master: 119
cooks: 257
copper, coppersmiths: 61, 78
cordage:
malpractices: cut for mean uses, 95, 124–5; embezzled, 5–6, 58, 109, 113, 118, 119; stolen, 125–6
manufacture: 31, 39–42; 108; hemp, 31, 39, 40, 71, 74–5, 95–6, 100, 112, 134, 290, (cheat in) 86–8, (contracts) 266–7, 391, (dry storage) 392–3, (lost in transit) 109–10, (offered against tax) 133–4, (prices) 300–7, 420, (prize) 131, (varieties compared) 119; in tar, 39, 78, 157–8; spinning, 41, 119 & n.1; strength, 39, 40–1; uncombed, 74
particular: bolt-ropes, 29, 127, 157; breechings, 116–17; cabin lines, 219; cables, 5–6, 39, 40, 42, 113, 118, 124–5, 127–8, 131, 200, 218, 321, 387 n.3; cablet, 218, 219; clench and splice, 113 & n.1; gromets, 219; ground tows, 127, 155; hawsers, 119, 218, 219, 236, 321; junk, 218; lashing line, 127, 218; mooring cables, 39, 94, 127–8; netting-rope, 127, 218; oakum, 127; port-ropes, 127; rope/ropeyards/ropemakers, 40, 127–8, 155, 157–8, 218–19, (abuses) 118; shrouds, 95; swabs, 95, 124; tackles, 116; tarred lines, 218; twine, 219; yarn, 41, 94, 95, 125
provenance: England/Dorset, 119 & n.3, 387 & n.3; Flanders,

100, 300; France, 94, 119; Latvia/ Riga, 39, 40, 74–5, 87–8, 119 n.3, 133, 300; Milan, 74–5; Netherlands, 40, 42; Prussia/ Königsberg, 40, 87–8, 133, 300; Russia, 39, 40, 112
various: defective, 94–5, 155; destroyed in fight, 260; extravagant demands, 94; prices, 306–7; storekeepers' accounts, 398 & n.6
Cotton, – , merchant master: 140
Council *see* Privy Council
Council of State: reprimands contractors, 419 n.1
Coventry, Sir William (Kt 1665), Navy Commissioner 1662–7, Secretary to the Duke of York 1660–7: discussions, (accounts) 17–18, 65–6, (anchors) 17, (contracts) 5, 10, 35, 84–5, (cordage) 42, 125, (dominion of seas/cause of war) 221 & n.1, 228–30, (gentlemen captains v. tarpaulins) 221–7; praised, 195; present at Board, 9, 48, 77, 80; reproves purveyor, 13; salary extraordinary, 76; signature, 8, 311; support sought by/given to P, 11 & n.2, 40, 82, 334, 341; wartime attendance on Duke, 397 & n.2 ~ alluded to, 36 n.2, 46, 58, 60, 87, 88, 119, 131 & n.1, 136, 325
Cowley (Cowly), [Thomas], clerk of the cheque, Deptford: P encounters, 26 ~ alluded to, 18 & n.3
Cox, Capt. John [Kt 1672], Navy Commissioner, Chatham 1669–72: appointment, 191–2 & n.; bribe to Batten, alleged, 20; flag-captain, 245 & n.1; information from, 220, 249 (*bis*); investigates defects in provisioning, 220; present at Board, 202; refuses to pay tickets, 247–8; signature, 247
coxswains: 204
Craven, William Craven, 1st Earl of, courtier and soldier: 397 & n.3
Creed (Creede), [John], Deputy-Treasurer to the Fleet 1660–3: 4
Culpeper *see* Colepeper
Curtiss, Theophilus, Navy Office clerk: 165–6

customs: dues, 35, 121, 374 & n.1, 376 n.3; officers (customers), 397
Cutler (Cuttler), William, merchant: dispute with, 185–6; hemp from, 100, 391; tar/pitch from, 33–4, 60, 97–100, (criticized) 106–7
~ alluded to, 86
~ son Thomas: 185 n.1
Cyclades, archipelago: 248 & n.1

Darcey (Darcy), Capt. [Thomas], naval officer: 157, 209
Davis, John, Navy Office clerk: 196
Davis, John, storekeeper, Deptford: corruption, alleged, 24 & n.2; information from, 56, 61; poor book-keeping, 61 ~ alluded to, 51 & n.1
Davison (Davidson), Sir William, merchant: 112 & n.1
deal, deals *see under* timber
Dean (Deane), Forest of, Glos.: iron from, 356 & n.3
Deane (Dean), Anthony [Kt 1675], assistant shipwright, Woolwich 1660–4, master shipwright, Harwich 1664–8, Portsmouth 1668–72: Batten's opinion, 57–8; difference with C. Pett, 116; discussion with P, 5–6; promotion, 58, 116; ship built by, 133 & n.3; supports Mayers, 92 ~ alluded to, 6 n.1, 122
demurrage: 7–8, 140, 148 n.1, 150 n.1; 174 n.1, 263, 277, 363 & n.2, 425
Denmark: war with, 364 & n.4
Deptford, Kent, dockyard:
goods at/for/from: blocks, 16; cloth/ flags, 31, 48, 52 & n.1, 56, 72–3; cordage, 42, 74–5; masts, 12; timber, 14, 15, 79–80, 91–2, 96, 183
officers: general: hours of work, 45 & n.1, 69 & n.1; order to, 137; stores in private houses, 255; *particular*: carpenters, 45, 69; clerk of the survey, 86, 255; master attendant, 86, 255; porter, 69; sailmaker, 255; shipwrights, 45 & n.1, 255; storekeeper/stores, 74–5, 145–6, 254–5
ships: building/launch, 118 & n.1; fleet from, 16; hulks, 184; lighters, 156 & n.1;

unserviceable, 256; wet dock misused, 255
various: construction work, 124; P visits, 24, 25, 26, 27, 42, 67, 68, 69, 70, 74, 85–6, 124; rigging house, 255; survey, 15; theft, 63–4; troubles, 69 & n.1
~ alluded to, 74, 216
see also Badiley; Cadbury; Cowley; Davis; Fletcher; Fownes; Harper; Hosier; Shish; Turner, T.; Uthwayt; Wells
Dering (Deering), [Edward], merchant: hemp, 300; masts, 13, 310; sheathing board, 57; tender for canvas, 51–2, 59
~ alluded to, 314
Desborough, [Maj.-Gen. John], republican leader: 237
Digby, Capt. the Hon. Francis, naval officer: 236–7 & n., 238
dockyards, private: King's ships repaired in, 130–1, 133
dockyards, royal:
malpractices: embezzlement, (cable) 5–6, (cordage) 155, (nails) 154–5, (timber) 69–70, (wages) 64–5 & nn.; negligence unpunished, 85–6, 126; private uses, 140; short measures, 264–5; stores in private houses, 255; thefts, 125–6, 154–5
officers (general): 128: extra, 291; Navy Board not accountable for, 434; pay increased, 399
officers (particular): boatswains, 155–6; clerks of the cheque, 62, 64–5, 141–2, 202, 263, (abuses) 385, (duties) 274, 284, 288, (records) 68, 231, 259, 399; clerks of the ropeyard, 62; clerks of the survey, 194, 196, 201, 217, 249, 274, 385; Commissioners, 64, (extraordinary/outports) 274–5 & n., 283, 290 n.2, 417, (ought not to command where previously serving) 191–2 & n., (wartime duties) 397; masters attendant, 50, 157 & n.1, 385, (duties) 274; porters, 288; shipwrights, 160, 385, (duties) 274, 356; storekeepers/stores, (accounts) 331, 391; (accounts defective) 5–6, 61, 146, 254–5 & n., (Brooke House Commission investigates) 282–91, 396–401, (deceits) 37, (duties), 274, 385–6, 391, (impropriety of also serving Prize Officers) 137, (overseen by Commissioner) 290 n.2, (prize goods not accounted for) 317, (salaries increased) 288, (stores clogged with unnecessary masts) 353–4, (surveys impossible in wartime) 289–90, 357, 360
various: alehouses adjacent, 70; goods transported between, 26; hours of work, 45–6 & nn., 69–70; letters to, 397; paying off, 196; payments to, 380; records, 377, 380–1; weights and measures, 23, 25, 26, 27–36, 41–2, 47, 48, 52–5, 70, 71 & n.1, 72–3, 85–6, 89, 91–2, 118, 119, 255, 264–5, 350–1; workmen, (diverted to victualling) 263, (knavery) 40, (pay) 186, 257
see also Chatham; Deptford; Harwich; Portsmouth; Woolwich
Doggett, [John], merchant: 133
dominion of the seas: 228 & n.4
Dorset: hemp from, 119
Dover, Kent: ships at, 133, 170, 171, 172
Downing, Sir George, Bt, Secretary to the Treasury Commissioners: letter to P, 336 & n.1
Downs, the: muster-master, 202; mutiny (1648), 222–3 & n., 226 & n.1; ships idle, 266
~ alluded to, 63, 94, 156, 172
Dowson, [Richard], master joiner, Woolwich: 43
Drake, Sir Francis: 223
Drammen (Dram), Norway: timber from, 14, 51, 90, 314
Dry, [James], master: 239
Dublin: harbour, 27 n.4; ship built at, 160 n.1
Duncombe (Duncomb, Duncum), Sir John, Ordnance Commissioner 1664–70, Treasury Commissioner 1667–72: P attends, 337; speaks at debate before Privy Council, 375
~ alluded to, 120 & n.1, 341
Dunkirk (Dunkirke), Siege of (1658): 228 & n.1
Dunster, Giles, Brooke House Commissioner: speaks at

454 INDEX

debate before Privy Council, 343, 344; signature, 271, 325
Du Teil (Dutel, DuTell), Capt. Jean-Baptiste, naval officer: 238–9 & n.
Duval (Du Vall), Claude, highwayman: execution, 366 & n.4
dyers, dyeing: 52, 82
Dyson, [John], merchant: 314

East India Company: merchants' knowledge of cloth, 82, ships, 42 & n.1, 200 & n.2, 267; Turkish embassy, 229–30 & n.; wages, 205
East India House, Leadenhall St: P at, 75
East Indies: 165, 200
Eastland Company: 86–8, 424
Eastwood, [Roger], purveyor, Portsmouth: 6, 111
Edgehill, [William], blockmaker: method of measurement, 26
~ alluded to, 16
Eglestone, – , master: 265
Elizabeth I, Queen: Spain her only enemy, 223
Ellery, – , carpenter: 124
Elliott, Capt. [Thomas], naval officer: 134, 243
Emsworth, Hants.: ship built at, 125 & n.2
English Channel (Narrow Seas): musters, 291–2, 401; patrol (1668), 244 n.1; short allowances, 299, 416
Epping Forest, Essex: timber from, 15
Erith (Eriffe), Kent: P at, 42
Ernle, Capt. John, naval officer: 260 & n.1
Ernle, Sir John, Commissioner, Storekeepers' Accounts 1671–6: 260 & n.1
Errington, [? Ralph], messenger of Brooke House Commissioners: 394
Evelyn (Euelin), John, diarist: 217
Exchequer, Court of: accounts submitted to, 64 & n.3, 150 n.1; Auditors, 64 & n.4, 150 n.1, 174 n.1, 281, 382, 385, (of Imprests) 383, (of Receipt) 380 & n.1; certificates to, 382, 395; fees, 281, 380, (allowed to Carteret) 378–9;

imprests uncleared, 276; order of, 395 & n.3; poundage on payments to Navy, 123 & n.5; P to require assistance in matters relating to, 340; Stop of, 258 & nn. 1,2, 267; suits in, 418
~ alluded to, 409, 410 & n.3
Excise Commissioners: attended by Navy Treasurer, 397

Falconer, John, clerk of the ropeyard, Woolwich: assists P, 32 n.1; death, 70, 71, 73–4 & nn.; information from, 69, 96
Falmouth, Charles Berkeley, 1st Earl of: 221 & n.1, 229 & n.1, 243
Fenn (Fen, Fenne), John, Cashier to the Navy Treasurer: business with P, 8; deputizes for Carteret at Board, 428; sharp practices, 119–23; ticket paid to himself, 409 ~ alluded to, 329 n.1
~ son Jack: ship built for, 122; underwrites father's dealings, 123
Ferrer, Capt. [Robert], soldier: criticized by Brereton, xxix
Finch, Sir Heneage, Solicitor-General: 372–3, 375, 376, 377
Fire, the Great: financial consequences, 284; housebuilding after, 173 n.2
~ alluded to, 331, 368 n.2
fireships *see* ships
Fishery, Royal: 183 & n.3
Fist, [Anthony], Navy Office clerk: 351
flags, flagmakers: abuses investigated by Brooke House Commission, 335–6 & n.; bill stopped, 63; contracts, 24, 48–9, 52–3, 81–5; faults, 56; measurement, 48; P instructed about, 24, 83
particular: ensigns, 48, 219; jacks, 24; pendants, 219; vanes, 219
Flanders: hemp from, 100, 300
flax *see* cloth: manufacture
Fletcher (Flecher), Richard, timber-measurer, Deptford: method of measurement, 70 & n.2; negligence, 85–6; succeeds Deane as assistant shipwright, Woolwich, 116 ~ alluded to, 6, 25
Foley (Folley), [Robert], ironmonger to the Navy: contract, 145
~ alluded to, 154–5

Ford, Ald. Sir Richard, merchant: examines account, 174 n.1; information from, 100–1; ships soldiers to Tangier, 75–6; son, 60
Formentera (Furmetera), Island of: 181 n.1
Fownes, [William], clerk to the storekeeper, Deptford: 61
France:
goods from: cloth, 13, 28, 30–1, 51, 59, 72, 306; cordage, 91, 119
naval affairs: forces allied to Commonwealth, 237 n.1; masts bought in Sweden, 362; P visits/observes naval management, 332 & n.1, 334 & n.2
Frederik III, King of Denmark: 364
freightage: 174 n.1, 263, 363, 426
frigates *see* ships
furnaces: 133

Gauden (Gawden), Ald. Sir Denis, Navy Victualler 1660–77: accounts, 193 n.1, (examined) 246–7, (not checked with pursers') 141–2, (passed) 14–15, 141–3; allowance of extraordinary provisions, 105; assists Penn, 147 & nn.2,3; contract, 250 & n.2; criticized, (backwardness) 230, (fraudulent collusion with pursers) 142–3, 299–300, 417–18, (functions questioned) 129–30, 142–3; (inefficiency in First Dutch War) 419 & n.1; information from, 128; P consults, 126–7; praised, 123 & n.3; requirements, (pipestaves) 392, (victuals put aboard in specie) 417; warrants to, 64, 141, 142, 417–18 ~ alluded to, 119, 137
~ son Benjamin: assists father, 250 n.2
Gelstrop [? Gilsthorpe, q.v.], – , Navy Office clerk: 361
Gibbons, [Thomas], Navy Office clerk: 196
Gibbs, Capt. [John], merchant: 183
Gibraltar: ships lost off, 108–9 & n.
Gibson, Richard, Navy Office clerk: discussions with P, (captains) 231–3, 237–9, (gentlemen captains v. tarpaulins) 227–9, (impressment) 215, (masters) 217, (pursers' frauds) 141 & n.2, 144, 181 n.1, (seamen) 258–60; handwriting, 252, (drafts P's correspondence) 169, (Navy White Book) xviii; information from, 157, 200–1, 204, 209–10, 245, 252–3; supports P's argument, 153–4
Gilsthorpe (Gilsthrop), – , Navy Office clerk: 196, ? 361 ('Gelstrop')
glass, glaziers: 25, 53 & n.1, 133; top lantern, 219
Godolphin, [Francis], master: 200
Gold (Gould), [John], merchant: 88
gold: 200 n.3
goldsmiths: Navy Board objects to bankers, 267; profit by paying in bills, 120–1
Gomme (Gum), Sir Bernard de, Chief Engineer to the Ordnance 1661–85: 77
Göteborg (Gottenburg, Gottenburgh), Sweden: masts from, 36, 54–5, 273, 309, 346, 353, 362, 366; masts lying at, 174, 363 & n.1; ships at/for/from, 129, 238, 323, 364 ~ alluded to, 33, 34
Graves, – , shipwright: 188
Gravesend, Kent: extraordinary muster-masters and cheques, 291; prison ship, 323 ~ alluded to, 205, 210 & n.2
see also Hosier
graving: 134
Greenwich, Kent: P at, 25, 26; shipbuilding at, 112; ship from, 183
Gregory, Edward, clerk of the cheque, Chatham: 21 & n.1, 399 & n.2
Gregory (Gregorie), John, Brooke House Commissioner: present at debate before Privy Council, 343, 377, 431; signature, 271; speaks, 432, 433–4
Grey (Gray), [Edward], merchant: 114–15
Griffith (Griffen), William, doorkeeper, Navy Office: 341
Grimsditch (Grimsdich), [John], naval officer: 237
grindstones: 71 & n.1
Grotius, Hugo, jurist: 228 & n.4

Guard, Royal: subvented from King's private revenue, 340, 372, 374 & n.2
Guinea (Guinney, Guinny, Guiny): ships at/for/from, 42–3, 48, 205, 239, 240
Gum *see* Gomme
gunners: appointment, 199
guns, ordnance: cleaning, 109; cordage for breechings, 127, (abuse) 117; manufacture, 38; naval guns frighten soldiers, 222; over-gunning, 132; removal delayed, 128; self-inflicted damage, 239 n.1
see also Ordnance Office
Gyles, Robert, sailmaker, Portsmouth: 43, 60

Haddock, Capt. [Richard], naval officer: 266
Haggon, Thomas, seaman: 232–3
Halfway Tree, point on Thames: 215 & n.2
Halifax, George Savile, 1st Viscount [Earl 1679, Marquess 1682], Brooke House Commissioner: dissents from report, 367; present at debate before Privy Council, 343; signature, 271
Halsall (Halsey), Maj. [James], Scoutmaster-General 1665–89: 140
Hamburg (Hamborough, Hambrough, Hambrow, Hamburgh): trade with/via, 33 & n.5, 34, 174, 278 n.1, 345, 392
Ham Creek (Ham River), nr Woolwich: reeds, 173; ships at, 173, 184
hammocks: 219
Hanbury, – , Navy Office clerk: 196
Harbin (Harbing, Harving), John, merchant: canvas from, accounts for, 94, (disputed) 13 & n.1, 72; contract, 51–2, 59–60, 73
~ daughter: bill of, 72
Hardwin, – , [? glazier]: 53
Harman, Capt. Sir John (Kt 1665; Rear-Adm. 1667), naval commander: information from, 134, 138, 209; rescues mast convoy, 364; West Indies expedition, 137, 245 ~ alluded to, 207
Harper, [Thomas], storekeeper, Deptford: clerk, 61; death, 145
~ alluded to, 103, 118
~ son: deputizes for father, 146
Harrington, [William], merchant: deals from, 50; hemp from, 87–8
Harris, [John], sailmaker to the Navy: instructs P, 29–31, 43–4
~ alluded to, 122
Harrison, – , merchant: 266–7
Hart, Capt. [John], naval officer: 220
Harvey, Sir Daniel, merchant: ambassador to Turkey, 224 & n.1, 229
see also Hervey
Harwich, Essex, dockyard:
goods at/for: furnaces, 305; oars, 85; timber, 90
officers: Commissioner, 274 & n.1, 284; extraordinary muster-masters and cheques, 291; storekeeper/stores, 137, (abuses) 384, 385
ships: repaired, 256; sunk for foundations, 95 & n.3, 320
various: floating stage, 106; letter dated at, 260; lighthouses, 58 & n.6
see also Browne; Deane; Taylor
Haslerig *see* Heselrige
Hawkins, Sir John: 223
Hayter (Hater, Haytor), [Thomas], P's Navy Office clerk:
business: pays, 8; pursers' accounts, 137; tickets, 130
information from: 143, 145, 152, 170, 206, 252, 254, 379
relations with P: at his elbow, 176; deputizes at Board, 252 n.4; supports argument, 153
various: handwriting, xviii n.5, 271 n.4; purveyor of petty emptions (1668), 145, 190
Hayward, Capt. [John], naval officer: 207, 209, 215
Hebdon (Hebden), [Sir John], merchant: contract for tar, 31 & n.1
Heemskerck (Hemskirke), Sir Laurens van (Kt 1669), Dutch traitor: 161–2 & n., 163
Heling, Capt. [Daniel], naval officer: 260
hemp *see* cordage: manufacture
Hempson, [William], clerk of the survey, Chatham: dismissed,

19–20 & n., 58; flatters P, 18–19; information from, 59
Herbert, Capt. [Charles], naval officer: 205
Hervey, Sir Thomas, Navy Commissioner 1666–8: clerks, 196 ~ alluded to, 325
see also Harvey
Heselrige (Haslerig), Sir Arthur, Bt, republican politician: 238
Hewer (Hewers), Will, P's Navy Office clerk: bribery accusation withdrawn, 172 n.1; handwriting, xviii n.5; information from, 159, 163, 190, 235–6; relations with P, (at his elbow) 169, 176, (supports argument) 154
~ alluded to, 45, 205
Hill, Thomas, merchant and P's friend: contract for tar, 60–1, 79, 97, 99
Hill, Capt. [William], naval officer: 93, 108
hinges *see* ironwork
Hispaniola, Island of: ships for, 164 & n.3
holds, store rooms: 135, 219–20
Holmes, Capt. Sir Robert (Kt 1666), naval commander: low birth no disqualification, 226 & n.3; men desert, 140; prevents passing purser's account, 239–41; raids Dutch coast, 162 n.1
~ father Henry: 226 n.3
Holt, [Nathaniel], storekeeper, Chatham: 399
Homewood, Edward, clerk of the survey, Chatham: 157, 199, 218–19
Hope, the, reach of the Thames: accident off, 111: goods to, 63; ships at/to, 141, 263 ~ alluded to, 133 n.2
Hopkins, Edward, Admiralty Commissioner 1652–5, and brother (? Henry), shipwright, Limehouse: 365 & n.1
Hornchurch (Hornechurch), Essex: timber from, 6 n.2, 58
Hosier, Francis, clerk of the cheque, Gravesend 1665, clerk of control, Deptford 1669–70: information from, 254–5 & n. ~ alluded to, 233–4
Houblon (Hublon), [Isaac, James jun., Peter], brothers, merchants and friends of P: 249
Howell, Richard, turner to the Navy: discusses Navy Treasury abuses, 119–23; his own malpractices, 59
hoys *see* ships
Hubbard (Hubbert), Capt. [John jun.], naval officer: 245, 246 n.1
hulks *see* ships
Hull, Yorks.: defence (1642), 228; seamen recruited, 227
~ alluded to, 322
Hutchinson (Hutchingson), Richard, Cashier to the Navy Treasurers: 180; Treasurer of the Navy (1650–60), errors in account, 409

Ibiza (Iueca, Iversy), Island of: 237 & n.1, 238
impressment: evasion/fear, 134, 139 n.3; exemption, 84 & n.2, 131, 134, 205–6, 231; men guarded, 263; Ordnance officials taken, 128 n.4; payment, (for discharge) 206 & n.1, (for exemption) 131; P reports to Duke, 203–10; pressmasters, 206, 363, (assaulted) 140; printed protections, 205–6; scruples over cause lack of men, 230; ship to ship, 128 & n.2, 234; superfluous, 129, 164, 204, 205, 209, 233–4; wages, 62–3, 160, 206–7, 362 ~ alluded to, 129, 215–16, 230, 257
Ingram, Richard, and father Robert, merchants: 4 & n.3
insurance, marine: 391–4
Ipswich, Suff.: canvas from, 44, 57, 72, 219 ~ alluded to, 130
Ireland: timber from, 392
Irish Sea: 27 n.4
ironwork, ironmongers, metalwork, smiths:
general: contracts, 145–6, 154–5, 391, 392; corruption, 135, 154–5; customs dues, 38 n.2; defects, 145; pay, 133; payment in kind, P defends, 355–6; prices, 36–8, 290; prize, 356; short measures, 264–5; varieties compared, 38, 354–7
particular: axes, 219; bilboes, 219; bolts, 37, 38, 133, 354; can-hooks, 219; Chatham chain,

357 & n.1; grapnels, 218; hatchets, 145; hinges, 145; nails/nailers, 15, 37, 70, 154–5, 290; plates/plating, 53 n.1, 71–2 & n.; port-hinges, 4; portnails, 255; sheet lead, 78; staples, 219; steel spades, 78; thimbles, 219; tin trucks, 219; wire, 78
provenance: England, (Dean) 356 & n.3, (Sherwood) 38; Netherlands, 38; Spain, 354, 356 n.2, (Bilbao) 38; Sweden, 38, 77, 133, 354–7
see also anchors; copper

Jamaica: capture of, 227, 228 n.1
James I, King: naval commands temp., 223
Jenkins, Daniel, master: 110
Jennens (Jenings, Jennings), Sir William, naval commander: corruption, 180 n.1, 236; petition for supernumeraries, 176–82
Johnson, [Capt. Benjamin], storekeeper, Portsmouth: 113
Johnson, [Henry], shipbuilder: 130, 132, 189
journals, ships': 167–8, 170, 183, 200 & n.3, 249

Kempthorne, Rear-Adm. John [Kt 1670]: 128 & n.5
Kent: royalist rising (1648), 222–3 & n.
Kingdon (Kingdom), Capt. [Richard], Commissioner, Prize Office 1665–7: 131
King's Bench prison: 240
Kingsbury, [Austin], merchant: 315
Kinsale, co. Cork: extraordinary muster-masters and cheques, 291; ship at, 160 n.1
knees *see* timber
Knight, Sir John, Navy agent, Bristol: 161 & n.3
Knip, [William], merchant: 87
Königsberg (Quinsborough), East Prussia: hemp from, 40, 87–8, 133, 300

Lake, Jo[hn], Navy Office clerk: 196
Lambert, Capt. David, naval officer: bills for pilotage, 63 ~ alluded to, 11–12

Langesund (Longsound), Norway: timber from, 314
Langham, Sir James, Brooke House Commissioner: present at debate before Privy Council, 343, 345, 376, 377, 431
Langston, Capt. [Anthony], naval officer: 234
Lanyon, [John], victualler, Plymouth: accounts, 282, 381
La Rochelle, France: expeditions to (1627–8), 227 & n.3
Lauderdale (Lauderdalle), John Maitland, 2nd Earl of, Secretary for Scottish Affairs 1661–80: information from, 419; speaks at debate before Privy Council, 408, 434 ~ alluded to, 173
launches (of ships): 90, 156
Lawson, Adm. Sir John: expedition against Algiers (1664), 3–4 & n.; embezzles chaplains' pay, 113–14; loyalty, 226; religious zeal, 114 ~ alluded to, 8, 144, 144 n.1, 207
Leadman, – , wood-carver: 26
leather: 219
Legg, Col. [William], Lieutenant-General and Treasurer of the Ordnance: 76–7, 77, 78
Leghorn (Livorne), Italy: victuals at, 126 & n.3, 143
Leith (Lieth), Midlothian: 185
Le Neve, Capt. [Richard], naval officer: 264, 266
Lever, Thomas, Purser-General: accounts, 65–6, 67
Lewen, – , sailmaker: information from, 29
Lewis (Lewes), Thomas, Victualling Office clerk: corruption, alleged, 66–7; information from, 66, 139; takes complete charge of pay, 379 ~ alluded to, 22
Lewsly, [Thomas], shipwright: 105
lieutenants: 205, 232, 237
lighters, lightermen: charges, 35
lighthouses: 58 & n.6
lignum vitae *see* timber
Lincoln's Inn Fields: 243
Lindsay (Lindsey), John, goldsmith-banker: 267 & n.2
Lisbon: action off, 82 & n.1; Queen's voyage from, 65 n.2
Littleton (Litleton), Sir Thomas, Bt, Joint-Treasurer of the Navy

1668–71: appointment, 158 & n.2; censured by Duke, 163; discredits Board, 202; dispute over contracts/signatures, 189–91; information from, 243; payments by, 208 & n.1; P questions over secret fund, 161–3; present at Board, 179, 180, 254; pursers' frauds pursued, 202; records, inadequate, 212 ~ alluded to, 152

Livorne *see* Leghorn

Lloyd, Capt. [John], naval officer: 207

London: rating assessment, 100–1; rebuilding, 173 n.2; St Pancras Church, Cheapside, 368 & n.2; seamen riot (temp. Charles I), 227 n.3; ship built by City, 118 & n.1; strategic importance in civil war, 225–6; water bailliage, 35 & n.3

Long, Sir Robert, Auditor of Receipt at the Exchequer: P assists, 336–7, 340, 341 ~ alluded to, 366, 372

Long Reach, in the Thames: 263

Longsound *see* Langesund

Lowe, [Capt. Henry], merchant: 85

Lucy, Thomas, merchant: rope from, 62

Ludman, Capt. Bernard, naval officer: 133 & n.2

Lyell, [Patrick], merchant: 185

Lyme Regis (Lyme), Dors.: defence (1644), 228

Maddox, Richard, Navy Office clerk: 165–6, 195–6, 198

Malaga, Spain: goods from, 65 n.2

Mall, the: 341

malpractices: collusion, 141 & n.2, 142–5; dead pays and similar frauds, 64 & n.7, 165, 174, 202–3, 234–6, 295–9, 414–15, (imaginary chaplains) 113–14; embezzlement, 37–8, 63–4 & n., 65, 69–70, 108–9, 113, 116–117, 118, 119, 134, 154–5, 239–42, 255, 292–3, 398, 402; forged tickets, 412, 414; fraud, 420; impressment irregularities, 131, 205–6; loitering by purveyors, 132; mistress on board, 248; profiteering, 59–60, 75–6, 79, 80–1, 86–8, 95–6, 97–100, 101–2, 114, 120–3; short measures, (flags) 56, (iron) 145–6, (masts) 53–5; stolen goods sold back, 135; stores in private houses, 255; vandalism, 133

Manchester, Edward Mountagu, 2nd Earl of, Lord Chamberlain: 374

Marescoe (Morisco), Charles, merchant: tar from, 60 & n.2, 98–100, 107

Margate (Margett), Kent: ship of (*named*), 110

marlin spikes: 218

Mason, [John], merchant: 190

masters: captains dependent on, 221–2; dislike gentlemen captains, 248, 249; in hired ships, 129; in merchantmen, exempted from press, 134; irresponsible, 135; journals, 183, 200; maltreated, 134–5, 265, 266; pay conducted by, 293; press men, 215; purchase cordage, 39; slow to man vessels, 263 & n.2; slow to receive victuals, 139; threatened by mutineers, 139–40; tickets defective, 217; unpopular, 243 ~ alluded to, 80 & n.2, 108, 119, 134, 141, 183 & n.2, 216, 232, 403

masts and spars:
general: abuses, 35–6, 67–8, 95–6, 423–4; alleged shortage of large masts during war, 353–4; bad supplied with good, 10, 114–15; carriage, dispute over, 166–8, 277–8; contracts, 9–13 & nn., 15–16, 18, 22–3, 35–6, 53–5, 67–8, 101, 114–15, 148–54 & nn., 273–8, (Brooke House/Privy Council debate) 344–66, 388; damaged/lost, 108, 109, 260–1; defective, 10, 138–9; lying idle, 174, 348, 349, 353, 363 & n.1; measurement, 23, 36 & n.2, 53–5, 71, 73, 101, 107, 138–9 & n., 273–7, 310, 311–12, 351, 353, 361; superfluous, 10, 15–16, 57, 353–4; trade in few hands, 308; unlading, 90; valuation/prices, 79–81, 101, 106, 107, 114–15, 290, 307–15, 422–5; wastage, 95, 106, 108

particular: boltsprits, 10, 22–3, 54, 55, 101, 107; foremasts, 101, 107, 260–1; foretopmasts, 260–1;

foretopsail yards, 108;
mainmasts, 101, 107, 260–1;
maintopmasts, 260–1;
mizenmasts, 107, 260
provenance: New England, 22–3, 36 n.2, 50, 54, 55, 71, 73, 115, 138, 148, 174, 273, 275, 311–13, 351–3 & n., 365 (*bis*), 423; Norway, 9 & n.1, 12, 308, 309; Scotland, 173 & n.2; Sweden/Göteborg, 36, 54, 55, 174, 273, 275, 308, 309, 314, 346, 362, 363 & n.1
mates: duties, 417 ~ alluded to, 134
Mathews, – , bricklayer: 124
Maxwell, – , merchant: 62
May, [Thomas], boatswain: widow of, 248–9
Mayers (Mayors, Meres), Robert, purveyor of timber to the Navy, Woolwich: corrupt, 12–13; letter to, 314; negligent, 79; spiteful, 92 ~ alluded to, 89 & n.1, 189 & n.3
Maynell *see* Meynell
Medcalf, John, soldier: 130
Mediterranean, the: actions in temp. Commonwealth, 237 & n.1; fleets in, (Allin 1668–9) 141, 199–200, 236 & n.1, (Allin 1669–70) 230, 242 & n.1, 243, (Jennens) 181, (Lawson) 144 n.1; provisions for, 105 & n.1; 219; ships for/from, 42 & n.1, 157, 205, 219, 233, 236
Medway, River: Dutch raid (1667), 134 n.1, 176–82, 184 & n.1, 225 n.4, 236, 247 n.1, 357 n.1, 400; protection ordered, 264 n.1; wrecks in, 135–6 & n., 236, 247 & n.1
Mennes (Minnes), Sir John, naval commander, Comptroller of the Navy 1661–71:
business: accounts, (passed) 21–2, 154, 250, (responsible for Warren's) 344–5; argues over contracts, 6, 11–12; assistance by City merchant, 174; assistance/duties lightened, (proposed by P) 175–6, (provided by Brouncker and Penn) 176 & n.1, 192–4 & n., 211–12 & n., 288 & n.2, 311, 344–5, 359, 399, 406 & n.1, 410 & n.2. 415 & nn.1,6, (provided by clerks) 67, 290, (transferred to Commissionership at large) 148 & n.1; attends pays, 397; buys oil, 63; clerks, 66, 67, 143, 149, 152, 167, 169, 195, 196, 198, 290 n.2, 298 (employed on private business) 197; examines bills, 397; examines journal, 167, 168, 170–1; information from, 148–50, 171, 206, 248, 249, 272; knowledge of cloth, 48, 81–2; orders cloth, 49; pays wages of East Indiaman, 205; present at Board, 9, 53, 152, 158, 176, 179, 202, 246; recovers excessive imprests, 371; responsible for tickets, 410 & n.2, 411, 415 & nn.1,6, (refuses to pay) 247–8; salary and assessment, 101; signature, 21–2 & n., 136, 148, 151, 153–4, 166, 169, 172, 186, 188, 198, 241, 275, 299, 311, 415; storekeepers report to, 317
criticized: contrary, 65–6, 67; corrupt, 143–5; forgetful, 202–3, 251; incoherent, 174; negligent, 151, 168–71, 185–6, 192–4, 195, 217, 343, (admitted) 168; P corrects, 115; P's hostility to, 11; poor book-keeping, 63, 66, 148–50 & n., 174–5, 185–6, (denied) 152–3; records, inadequate, 212; weakness/inability to do work, 198, 342, 343, 345, 398–9, (P tells Duke of) 192–4
critical of others: Batten, 14–15; Deane, 57–8; Penn, 82: C. Pett, 116; Comr Pett, 20–1
debate before Privy Council: absent, 357; answer to Brooke House Commission, 279, 407; present, 343, 346; records delivered to Treasury, 357; refers Commission to P, 334; reports on Warren's account, 346; speaks, 344, 345
various: long service/naval and military commands, 28 & n.1, 81–2 & n., 220 & n.1, 342 & n.3; poor health, 102, 175, 342, 398 ~ alluded to, 8, 15, 21, 29, 30, 47, 48, 65, 76, 80, 85, 89, 92, 97, 111, 276, 325, 382
merchants *see* Andrews; Barker; Barnes; Blackborough; Bland;

INDEX 461

Body; Bowyer; Bridges; Burchet; Chester; Child; Chiverton; Clothier; Cocke; Cole; Coleby; Colepeper; Cutler; Davison; Dering; Doggett; Dyson; Ford; Gibbs; Gold; Grey; Harbin; Harrington; Harrison; Harvey; Hebdon; Hill, T.; Houblon; Ingram; Kingsbury; Knip; Lowe; Lucy; Lyell; Mason; Maxwell; Morecock; Nelson; Norwood; Pemble; Play; Potter; Reymes; Rider; Risby; Shaw; Shorter; Smith, A.; Smith, E.; Stacey; Stanley; Stockman; Terrill; Upton; Walker; Warren; Webber; Weston; White; Williamson; Wood, W. (*bis*); Yorke; Young

Meres *see* Mayers

messengers: 64, 172

Meynell (Maynell), Ald. [Francis], banker: customs assigned to, 121; high rate of interest, 122 ~ alluded to, 98–9

Middleton (Midleton), Col. Thomas, Navy Commissioner, Portsmouth 1664–7, Surveyor of the Navy 1667–72:
business: accounts, 137, 174–5, 194–9; clerks, 166, 194, 195, 196, 198–9, 212; compared favourably with Batten, 184–5; criticizes, (Batten's negligence) 184, 197, (boatswains) 201–2, 218, (waste) 114; discharges shipwrights, 160; dispute over contract, 190–1; estimate for making hulk, 188; information from, 94–5, 109, 110, 116–117, 119, 124–5, 125–6, 129 & n.1, 131, 132, 134, 135, 139, 155–6 & n., 156–7, 173, 182, 184, 186–7, 188, 201 n.1, 214–15 & n., 216, 219–20, 246, 247, 248, 254, 255–6, 258, 261, 261–2, 264; investigates defects in provisioning, 200; knowledge of cordage, 157–8, letters to, 158, 427; present at Board, 152, 168, 176, 179, 199, 202; proposes captains have care of stores, 199; signature, 136, 148, 150, 151, 152, 153, 169, 172, 188, 194, 247; succeeded by Tippetts, 264 n.2;

survey by, 287; tender, 106; visits Chatham, 155, 214
criticized: ignorance, 264; indulgence of boatswain, 157; negligence, 141, 194–6; poor book-keeping, 165, 172; records, inadequate, 212
relations with P: P confronts at Board, 199; P discourses with, 199; withdrawal of Hewer bribery charge, 172 & n.1
various: approves seamen as captains, 184; present at debate before Privy Council, 343, 346; security for imprest, 267 ~ alluded to, 146, 152, 274 & n.1, 282

midshipmen: servants and musicians intruded as, 134, 207 ~ alluded to, 204, 233

Milan: hemp from, 74–5

Miller, Henry, boatswain: corruption, 93, 108

Milward, John, MP: xxix

Mings *see* Myngs

Minnes *see* Mennes

Minors, – , purser: 144

Mitchell (Michel(l)), [John], flagmaker: advises P, 24, 82–3; patterns, 84; prices, 48–9; unfairly criticized, 52–3, 84–5 ~ alluded to, 86

Molina, Antonio Francesca Mesia de Tobar y Paz, Conde de, Spanish ambassador 1665–9: 220 & n.2

Monmouth and Buccleuch, James Scott, 1st Duke of, and Duchess Anne: 229

Moore, [John], boatswain, Chatham: 236

Moray (Murray), Sir Robert, Keeper of the King's Laboratory: 252 & n.3

Morecock, [John *or* Robert], merchant: 315

Morisco *see* Marescoe

Moxon, Joseph, printer: 68 & n.2

musters: Board's conduct defended, 291–2, 401–2; muster books, 174, 178, 202–3, 259, 292, 294, 403, 404, 407, 411, 412, 413, 414, 415, 416, (P's design) 292 n.3, 402; muster-masters, 202, 263, 291–2, (Board's instructions to) 402 ~ alluded to, 42, 233, 263, 407

mutinies: in captain's absence, 139–40, mutinous manner of pressed men, 160; revolted fleet (1648), 223 & n.1, 226 & n.1 ~ alluded to, 227 & n.3, 419
Myngs (Mings), [Sir Christopher (Kt 1665)], naval commander: 207, 226

Narbrough (Narborough), Capt. John [Kt 1673], naval officer: 159–60, 266
Navigation, Act of: 350, 388
navigation, negligent: 108–9, 110, 265
Navy Board:
business/accountability:
(i) *general responsibilities*: accountability of individual officers, 345, 346; accountability to Duke, 405–6; accountability to Parliament, 431; attends Duke, 76, 126–7, 133, 158, 176, 179, 183, 199, 216, 219–20, 251, 255–6, 362, 363, 399, 421; attends Treasury, 216; decisions, 210, 242, 247, 256 n.1; impressment, 129; meetings, (adjourned) 253, (disorderly) 140, (diverted) 254, (open then cleared) 170; musters, 291–2; pays, 426; storekeeper's accounts, 397–8, 401; surveys, 287
(ii) *responsibilities disclaimed*: appointment of purveyor, 364–5; authentication of bills, 377–81; certain prize goods and ships, 317–23; collective inspection of accounts, 293; collective concern for tickets, 410; misconduct of dockyard officers, 433–4; provisions boarded in kind, 417; supervision of pursers, 417; witness to Treasurer's pays, 368
clerks and officials:
(i) accountants, 344, 373
(ii) *clerks*: advancement, 76, (by favour) 195–6, 198; dismissal, 408 & n.2; education, 196; extra, 174, 290 n.2; mistakes, 411, 412, (by new men) 351; musters by, 291, 292 & n.2; private work for masters, 196–8; seconded to Treasury, 165–6, 195–6, 198–9; ticket duties, 297–9, 411, 412,
414, 415, 416; trusted to make up books, 379; wages (clerks' own), 195, 196, 199 ~ alluded to, 62, 63, 67, 68, 176, 195–9, 250, 253, 405, 430
compared with predecessors:
(i) *Commonwealth*: 276, 284–5, 289, 292, 295, 306–7, 312, 349, 360–1, 365, 368, 377–80, 382, 387 (*bis*), 389–90, 394, 400 (*bis*), 404, 409, 411, 419 & n.1, 429, (P's memoranda/researches) 191 & n.2, 327 n.1, 331 & n.1
(ii) *other predecessors*: 360, 378–9, 387, 400
criticism by P:
(i) *Board's failings*: negligence, 194–9, 251, (inquiries into losses) 110, 111, (inquiries into masts defective) 139, (of own rules) 202–3, (of P) 140, 252–3
(ii) *other*: Board's advice ignored, 41, 159; private entertainment charged to Board, 19
debate before Privy Council: answers not examined by Brooke House Commission, 365; charges against Board, (and P's General Defence) 271–325, (P's Particular Defence) 325–30; individual Officers to report to Commission, 345; records delivered to Treasury, 357; ticket irregularities admitted, 409
finance: bills delayed, 61; cash, (advantage of) 94, (lack of) 131, 133, 279, 301–6, 426, 427–8, (provisions in lieu of) 355–6; credits/imprests/loans, 3–4 & nn., 6–9, 66, 143–4, 158, 168, 182, 189–91, 197, 202, 219, 242, 266–7, 273, 276–7, 280, 301–6, 331, 354, 355–6, 368, 371, 417–18, 420, 421 & n.4, 425, (challenged and allowed) 182, (criticized) 112, (interest rates) 3 & n.3, (lack of credit) 131, 284, (P defends) 358–60; salaries and assessments of Principal Officers, 100–1 & n.; taxation funding Navy, 395 n.5; travelling expenses, 68, 244–5; warrants for payments, 377–81
inquiries/reports: administration/ constitution of Navy Office,

191 & n. 2, 210, 251–2 & n., 332 & n.4, 342 & n.2; collision, 216; prices/victualling, 179–80, 300–6, 314–15, 421–2, (annual account of victuals and wages) 426; pursers' credits, 418; shipbuilding, 186–7, 220; state of ships, 137; storekeeper's negligence, 385; tickets, 429 & n.5; wrecks, 188, 247, 255–6
instructions from: tickets (1667), 296–9, 404, 408, 412, 413, 416
instructions/orders to:
(i) *Admiral's General Instructions (1662)*: 189, 194, 214, 274, 279–80, 284, 285, 286, 287–8, 288, 289, 291, 292, 293, 296, 300, 316, 335, 345, 354 & n.1, 365, 369, 370, 377, 386 & n.1, 388 & n.2, 389, 391 & n.1, 396, 397, 398, 403 & n.5, 406 & n.2, 407, 412, 415, 417 & n.2, 419, 420, 426, 428, (not to be interpreted literally) 388–9
(ii) *Admiral's additional instructions*: (1665), 279; (1668), 214 & n.2, 252 & n.1, 290, 415
(iii) *other orders*: purchase by commission, 278 & n.1; wrecks, 188
letters from: quoted, 240–1, 262, 309–10, 311, 314; read at debate before Privy Council, 348; wartime profusion, 397 ~ alluded to, 75, 148, 152, 214, 215–16, 246, 247, 250, 264, 357, 399, 415, 423, 424, 427–8
letters/petitions/reports to: quoted, 239–40, 261, 261–2, 271 ~ alluded to, 54 n.2, 139 & n.4, 140 & n.1, 148 & n.3, 215–16, 219, 232–3, 248–9, 262–3, 263–4, 266, 267, 349, 354 & n.2, 361 & n.2, 406, 415, 429
record keeping: quoted, 275 ~ alluded to, 8, 16, 45, 51, 62, 63, 66, 75, 94, 131, 152–3, 154 & n.1, 158, 165–6, 180, 189, 194–9, 201, 212–14, 217, 251, 279–80, 282–6, 287–91, 297–9, 306, 310, 377–81, 384–5, 395 & n.5, 402–16, 424–8
signatures: 53, 65, 136, 137, 145, 147, 150–1, 152–3, 154, 166, 169, 172 (*bis*), 190–1, 279, 285, 378–84, 395, 424,

(counterfeited) 412, (not warranties) 281
various: criticism of Penn, 146 & n.1; opponents of Board, 211
see also Anglesey; Batten; Brouncker; Carteret; Clerk of the Acts; Comptroller; Coventry; Ernle; Hervey; Littleton; Osborne; Penn; Slingsby (*bis*); Smith, J.; Surveyor; Taylor; Tippetts; Treasurer
Navy Office [i.e. the Board's premises, Seething Lane]: 379 & n.7, 382, 394, 405
Navy Treasury, Broad Street: abuses, 119–23; accounts, 62–3, 119–20, 123 & nn.1, 5; 144 & n.2, 193 n.1, 278–82, 368–72, 377–81; premises, 8, 163, 190, 297, 404, 407, 413, 429 n.5; relations with Navy Board, (Board's advice ignored) 160, 163, (Board's clerks poached) 165–6, 195–9; responsibility for widows and orphans, 250–1 & n. ~ alluded to, 9, 297
see also Anglesey; Carteret; Fenn; Hutchinson; Littleton; Osborne; Treasurer; Waith
Nelson (Nellson), – , merchant: cloth from, 82–3 & n., 84
Newburne, Thomas, broker: shares Batten's gratuity, 19–20
Newcastle-upon-Tyne, Northumb.: coals from, 209; masts at, 322; seamen recruited, 227 ~ alluded to, 158
New England: masts from, 22–3, 36 n.2, 50, 54, 55, 71, 73, 115, 138 & n.1, 148, 174, 273, 275, 311–13, 351–3 & n., 365, 424; presents from, 137–8, 351 & n.2; tar from, 108; voyage from, 93
New Hall, Essex: Albemarle's estate, 349 n.2
Newport, Andrew, sub-commissioner of prizes, Portsmouth: 344
Nicolls (Nicholls), Maj. [Henry]: 135–6 & n.
Nore, the: accident at, 111; provisions to, 130; ships at, 263, 349 ~ alluded to, 265 n.1
Norfolke, – , bricklayer: 124
North Country: impressment in, 206
North Foreland: 265

Northumberland, Algernon Percy, 10th Earl of, Lord High Admiral 1638–42: Instructions, 285, 289, 389 & nn.1,2
Norway: masts from, 9 & n.1, 12, 308, 309; merchants trading with, 364; tar from, 31–2, 39, 79; timber from, 14, 51, 75, 90, 314
Norwich, Norf.: bewpers from, 24
~ alluded to, 84
Norwood, Col. Henry, Deputy-Governor of Tangier 1665–8: 75
Norwood, John, lighterman and merchant: 137 & n.1

oak see timber
oars: defective, 85–6; prize, 321
~ alluded to, 15, 218
O'Brien, (Obrian, Obryan), Capt. Charles, naval officer: 131, 137, 244 & n.1, 229–30 & n., 236–7, 248, 249
oil: 63, 202
Ordnance Office: Commissioners appointed (1664), 120 & n.1; cordage supplied to, 117; corruption, 76–9; finances, 372, (better ordered than Navy) 120, (King subvents from private revenue) 340, 373; letters from/to Navy Office, 128 & n.4
see also Gomme; Legg
Ormond, James Butler, 1st Duke of, Lord-Lieutenant of Ireland 1661–9: present at debate before Privy Council, 337
Osborne (Osbourne), Col. [Henry; Kt 1673], Brooke House Commissioner: present at debate before Privy Council, 343, 431 ~ alluded to, 376
Osborne, Sir Thomas, Bt, [1st Earl of Danby 1674; 1st Duke of Leeds 1694], Joint-Treasurer of the Navy 1668–71: appointment, 158 & n.2, 208 & n.1; censured by Duke, 163; discredits Board, 202; dispute over contracts/signatures, 189–91; information from, 158, 180, 265; payments by, 208; present at Board, 179; pursues pursers' frauds, 202; records, inadequate, 212; refuses to secure loan, 267
~ alluded to, 152, 162, 254
Oslo (Christiania): deals from, 75

Oxford: Court at during Plague, 229, 344, 421
Oxford, Aubrey de Vere, 20th Earl of: speaks at debate before Privy Council, 375–6

Page, Damaris, brothel-keeper: 216–17 & n.
Palmer, Sir Geoffrey, Attorney-General 1660–70: chamber, 377
~ alluded to, 211
Palmer see also Castlemaine
parish dues: 379, 382, 394
Parliament:
Commissions: accounts *see* Brooke House; paying off armed forces (1660–1), 429 & n.6
finance: Crown's subordination in, 228; grants for war, 338–9, 372–6 & nn.
House of Commons: Committee on Miscarriages, 159 & n.1, 164 n.1, 296 n.2; P's speech on tickets, 429 & n.4
statutes: 21 Hen. VIII c. 12 (Bridport manufactures) 387 n.3; 12 Car. II c. 4 (tonnage and poundage), 38 n.2; 12 Car. II c. 15 (paying off armed forces), 429 n.6; 12 Car. II c. 27 (arrears of pay), 204 & n.2; 13 Car. II c.4 (free gift), 374 & n.2; 13 Car. II c. 9 (Navy discipline), 208 & n.2; 16 & 17 Car. II c. 1 (Royal Aid), 100 & n.1, 221 & n.2, 373 & n.1; 18 & 19 Car. II c. 1 (Poll Tax), 133 & n.4; 18 & 19 Car. II c. 13 (Eleven Months' Tax), 133 & n.5, 395 & n.5; 19 & 20 Car. II c. 1 (establishing Brooke House Commission), 306 & n.1, 338 & n.2, 339, 347 & n.2, 348, 365 & n.4, 366–7, 373 & nn.1,2, 374 n.1, 375, 382, 388, 410 n.3, 420–1 & nn., 432, (P resolves to study) 358; Navigation Act [i.e. 1651 c. 22 as reiterated and extended in several Acts of Charles II], 350, 388
various: Batten as MP, 50 & n.2, 102; impeachment threatened, (Carteret) 369 & n.4, (Penn) 244 & n.2; MPs recommend Carkesse, 408; Navy Board accountable to, 431; Navy Treasurer attends, 397; P

INDEX 465

defeated in bye-election, 334 &
  n.4; sessions, 102 & n.2, 244 n.2;
  271 & n.3
see also taxation
passengers: aboard King's ships, 164,
  181, 229–30 & n.; mistress
  disguised as man, 248
Pearse (Pierce), [Andrew], purveyor:
  information from, 66–7
Pemble, [John], merchant: 167, 168,
  169
Penn (Pen, Penne), Sir William,
  Navy Commissioner 1660–8:
  business: appointment, 212 & n.1;
  argues/complains, (canvas) 28,
  82, (cordage) 125; assists
  Comptroller, 146–7 & n., 176 n.1,
  193 n.1, 212 n.1, 288 n.2, 399,
  405, (fails in so doing) 146 n.1;
  assists P, 173 n.2; assists
  Victualler, 250 n.2; attends King
  and Duke, 244; clerks, 147, 298;
  criticizes captain, 134–5;
  criticizes carpenters, 132;
  defends contract, 11;
  economies, claimed, 146;
  examines accounts, 137–8;
  information from, 17, 57, 60, 108,
  170, 177, 428 & n.5; letters to,
  247, 427; orders flags, 84; present
  at Board, 9, 85, 111, 158, 168,
  (silent) 150, 151, (supports
  Duke) 158; salary, extra
  expected, 147; signature/refuses
  to sign, 136–7, 144–5, 148, 151,
  153, 154, 169, 172; successor,
  210–11; wartime duties, 397 &
  n.2
  criticized: avarice, 73–4, 147, 244–5;
  bad judgement, 126; clerks do
  his work, 147; corruption in
  accounts, 143–5; cowardice in
  battle, 20 & n.4; fraudulent pay
  claim, 244–5; impeachment,
  threatened, 244 n.2;
  incompetent, 138, 146–8;
  negligent, 146 n.1, 195, 246–7;
  records, inadequate, 212
  naval career: flag captain, 245 &
  n.2; prize-goods scandal, 244 &
  n.2 ~ alluded to, 20 & n.4,
  237 & n.1
  various: family, 73–4; health, 6, 244;
  private dealing, 245; privateer
  share, 245 n.5; religion, 20;
  servants fearful of, 172

  ~ alluded to, 152, 325
Pepys, Elizabeth: death, 250 & n.1,
  273 & n.1, 334 & n.4
Pepys, Samuel:
  business: Navy Board *see* Clerk of
  the Acts; Tangier, 7, 8, 383 &
  n.3
  personal: absent from work after
  Elizabeth's death, 250, 252 &
  n.4, 272–3; eyesight weakening,
  148 n.2, 211 n.1, 328; finances,
  9, 329–30 & n.; pride in oratory,
  429; privateer share, 245 n.5;
  slide-rule, 70 & n.2; visits France
  and Netherlands, 332 & n.1;
  watches execution, 366–7
  writings: Diary, 311 n.2, 330 n.1,
  (would enable him to account for
  daily employment during war)
  326 & n.1; projected history of
  Navy, 331 & n.1
perquisites/gratuities: cordage, 113,
  124–5; dinners, 26; fencing, 74 &
  n.4; financial, 14–15, 18, 19, 73,
  76, 234–5, (in cap) 35 & n.1;
  firewood, 19 & n.3; gold watch,
  73; plate, 9, 19, 50 & n.3; prize
  goods, (purser denied by
  captain) 237, (seamen) 208 &
  n.2; provisions (officers), 114;
  wine, 19
Perriman (Perryman), Capt. [John],
  river agent to the Navy Board:
  information from, 134, 200
Peterborough, Henry Mordaunt, 2nd
  Earl of, Governor of Tangier
  1661–2: 8
Pett, family: domination at
  Woolwich, 19 n.1
Pett, Christopher, master shipwright,
  Woolwich: employment
  discussed, 80; estimates from, 91,
  186–8; extra pay claim, 116;
  information from, 6 n.2, 25,
  49–50, 55, 68, 91, 130; inquiries
  by, 108; ships built by, 4–5 & n.,
  26, 46–7
Pett, Peter, Navy Commissioner,
  Chatham 1648–60, 1660–7:
  business: criticizes Warren's
  contract, 348; duties,
  (superintendent of whole yard)
  356, (wartime) 397; examines
  knees, 92; examines masts,
  349–50; information from/
  sought from, 23 & n.1, 26 n.1,

27, 36, 40, 41, 71 & nn.1,3, 72, 85, 110 (*bis*), 115–16, 132, 350, 354, 399, 427, 428 & n.5, 429 & n.3; orders victuals, 141; signature, 23, 275; visits Deptford, 117
criticized: delay in supplying fleet, 349; ignorant of dimensions of rates, 115–16; imprests, 112; responsible for abuses in Chatham yard, 385; villainy/hypocrisy, 18–19 & n., 20–1, 103–4, 112, 348–9, 383
dismissal: 349 & n.1
~ alluded to, 274, 284, 325
Pett, Capt. Phineas (I), master shipwright, Chatham: information from, 106; opinion of P, 18; pits carpenters against their apprentices, 261–2; seeks mast timber in Scotland, 173 & n.2 ~ alluded to, 26, 240
Pett, Phineas (II), of Limehouse: stores bought by, 50–1
Petty, Sir William, scholar: double-keel vessel, 27 & nn. 1–4
petty emptions: Hayter made purveyor, 145 ~ alluded to, 190
Pew *see* Pugh
Philip IV, King of Spain: 238
Pierce *see* Pearse
Pierrepont (Pierrepoint), William, Brooke House Commissioner: 367
pilots: shortage, 129 & n.2, 134
~ alluded to, 63, 217
see also Trinity House
pirates: 27 n.2, 226
pitch: 31–5, 78, 108, 112, 134, 202, 307
see also tar
Pitt (Pett), John, secretary and deputy-treasurer of Mediterranean fleet 1662–3: 144 & n.1
Plague, Great: Court removes to Oxford, 421; financial consequences, 284; seamen's distress, 234 ~ alluded to, 139 n.1, 323, 326, 331, 428 n.5
plank *see* timber
plating, platerers: 53 & n.1, 71–2 & n.
Play (Plea), Capt. – , merchant: canvas from, 31
plumbers' work: 133
Plymouth, Devon: defence (1644–5), 228; seamen riot (temp. Charles I), 227 n.3; ships at/to, 76, 170, 172
see also Lanyon; Trelawny
Plymouth, Mass.: tar from, 108
Pointer, [Thomas], Navy Office clerk: 143–4, 149, 150, 154, 167, 168, 169, 185, 197
Poole, Capt. William [Kt 1672], naval officer: information from, 231, 258 ~ alluded to, 204, 231–2, 245
port-hinges *see* ironwork
Port Mahon, Minorca: 260
Portman, Edmund, clerk to the Brooke House Commission: information from, 379 ~ alluded to, 289 & n.3, 381
Portsmouth, Hants., dockyard:
goods at/for/from: general: 16–17, 130; *particular*: blocks, 26; cloth, 31, 60, 73; cordage/hemp, 74, 94, 110, 140; masts, 12, 16, 22 & n.3, 35, 53–4, 95–6, 106, 166–72, 310; oars, 15; oil, 63; screws, 79; tar, 79, 254; timber, 168, 305
officers: general: mutually uncritical, 113; *particular*: clerk of the survey, 94; Commissioners, 191–2 & n., 274 & n.1, 284; master attendant, 94; Ordnance officer, 117; storekeeper, 43–4, 60 & n.1, 106
ships: at, 17, 111, 116–17, 135, 199; built/launched, 122, 125 & n.2, 156; run aground, 110–11
various: economies proposed, 139; harbour's usefulness, 135 & n.5; pay at, 8; seamen riot (temp. Charles I), 227 & n.3
~ alluded to, 136, 141, 162, 204, 245
see also Deane; Eastwood; Gyles; Johnson, B.; Ridge; Tinker; Tippetts
postage: 381
Potter, – , merchant: canvas from, 44–5, 57
Povey (Povy), [Thomas], Treasurer of Tangier Committee 1663–5: dealings with P, 8
press, pressing *see* impressment
Pride, Col. Thomas, regicide: victualling contractor in First Dutch War, 419 & n.1
Pritchard (Prichard), [William], ropemaker: 106

INDEX 467

Privy Council:
debate on report of Brooke House Commission: preliminaries, 334–7; proceedings, 337–435; P summoned/attends, 334, 366, 403, 419, 424; P's explanations accepted by Council 401, 403
letters/reports to: tickets, 164–5, 429 & n.5; wartime, 397; wreck, 188
orders from: assistance for Comptroller, 193 n.1; East India Company to pay for Turkish embassy, 229–30; end to tickets, 164 & n.1; 429 n.5; extra dockyard officers, 290 & n.2; Navy Board to defend management of war, 341 & n.3; payment for secret service, 162; payment of smiths, 356; prohibition of trading by King's ships, 200 n.3; restrictions on pay, 265; Stop of the Exchequer, 258 & nn.1,2; welfare of widows and orphans, 250–1 & nn.
various: Committee for the Navy, 186; concern for supply of pipestaves, 392; decision on disputed contract, 167
Prize Commissioners (Prize Office): goods sold, 131; Prize Court, 185 n.1; ship returned to, 319; storekeeper to, 137 ~ alluded to, 131, 317–22
prize goods/ships:
general: investigation by Brooke House Commission/debate before Privy Council, 317–23, 344, 432–4; perquisites of seamen/officers, 208 & n.2, 237; required by Board, 137, 185; revenue of Crown, 221, 374 & n.1; scandal concerning, 244 & n.2; sold, 131 & n.1
particular: iron, 356; masts, 158; ships, (allowed to Algerians) 200 & n.1, (manning) 210, (serve as auxiliaries) 109, 220, (sunk for foundations) 95 & n.3, 183 n.2
proclamation (Stop of the Exchequer): 258 & n.1
Prussia (Sprucia): timber from, 50, 189
Pugh (Pew), [James], Navy Office clerk: 63, 196, 197

Pulo Run (Polyroon), East Indies: 229 & n.3
Pumpfield (Pumfield), [Edward], ropemaker, Deptford: 74
pursers: accounts/records, (examination) 137, 147, 211, 247, 250, (malpractices) 21, 64 & n.7, 65–6, 66–7, 93, 137–8, 141 & nn.2,3, 142–3, 144, 165, 176–82, 202, 239–42, 257, 292–3, 402–3, 407, 418; credits to, 417–18; faults overlooked, 129; information from, 177; instructions to, 428; maltreatment by captains, 239–40; Navy Board not accountable for, 419; oath, 65 & n.3; provided with cash instead of victuals, 299–300, 416–19; supervision by Board impossible, 417; ticket records not to be meddled with by, 298
purveyors: accounts, 64; appointment not in hands of Navy Board, 365; corrupt, 132; Navy Board empowered to buy goods by purveyance, 386–7; practices, 189; variety of merchants to be sought by, 423 ~ alluded to, 106, 315
see also Mayers

quartermasters: duties, 418 ~ alluded to, 204
Quinsborough *see* Königsberg

Rainsborough, [Col. Thomas], Parliamentary naval commander: 226 n.1
Rawlinson, [Daniel], innkeeper: P visits, 66
Ré, Ile de (Isle of Rhe): expeditions to (1627–8), 227 & n.3
reed: 173, 305
reformadoes *see* sea officers
Reymes (Reames), Col. [Bullen], merchant and MP: attends Board, 30, 59–60; canvas from, 73; information from, 77; negotiates with P, 28, 29
Ribadeux, [? France]: timber from, 92
Rider, Sir William, merchant: contract for cordage, 74–5; goods from, 391; knowledge of cloth, 82; masts from, 16; ships soldiers to Tangier, 75–6;

surveyor for City ship, 118; tar and pitch from, 33–5, 60, 97–100 ~ alluded to, 86, 107
Ridge, [Richard], agent of the Navy Treasurers, Portsmouth: 243
Riga, Latvia: hemp from, 39, 40 (*bis*), 74–5 & n., 87–8, 119 n.3, 133, 300
rigging *see* cordage; sails
Risby, Capt. [Henry], merchant: 107
River *see* Thames
Roach, William: 240, 241
Roberts, [George], master: 254
Robinson, Ald. Sir John, Bt, Lieutenant of the Tower 1660–79: entertained by Penn, 172; letters to, 263, 428 ~ alluded to, 238
Robinson, né Roberts, Capt. [Robert], naval officer: 238, 364
Rolling Grounds, off Aldeburgh, Suff.: 94 & n.1
rope *see* cordage
rosin: lack of, 134 ~ alluded to, 290, 382
Royal Exchange (the Change): Norway merchants at, 363–4; P visits/negotiates at, 7, 11–12, 22, 36, 39, 43, 48, 59, 60, 88, 100, 149; rumours/news at, 201, 230, 248 ~ alluded to, 190
runaways *see* seamen
Rundall, [Edward], carpenter, Deptford: over-charges, 124
Rupert, Prince, the King's cousin; joint C.-in-C. ('General') 1666: naval career, (Civil War) 82 n.1, 237 n.1, 342 n.3, (Second Dutch War) 244 & n.3, 300 & n.1, 364 & n.2, 416 & n.7
Russell, – , purveyor: 103
Russell (Russel), – , official, Chatham: 354, 356 & n.1
Russell, Peter, master of the ropeyard, Woolwich: 75 & n.1, 94
Russia: hemp from, 39, 40, 112; masts bought from by Dutch, 362; tar from, 31–2
Ruyter, [Michiel Adriaanszoon] de, Dutch naval commander: 261

sailmakers: 43–4, 60
sails:
 general: abuses/corruption, 27–31, 43–4, 255; damage/loss, 129, 156, 200, (in fight) 260; manufacture/preservation, 27–31, (pickling) 156–7, (selvedge) 28–9, 30; trim, 56
 particular: mizen, 219; mizen topsail, 218; spritsail, 218; topsails, 157
St James's Palace: Duke's chamber, 211 & n.1; P at, 236
St James's Park: P's encounters in, 341, 343
St Michel, Balthasar, P's brother-in-law: muster-master, 292 n.1
sales (surplus stores): canvas, 56; cordage, 6; iron, 36–7; plate, 50–1 ~ alluded to, 58
Salkeld (Salkield), Lieut. Ralph, naval officer: 232 & n.1
salt: 156
Sandwich, Edward Mountagu, 1st Earl of, politician and naval commander; P's patron: Mediterranean voyage (1661–2), 65 & n.2, 204; prize-goods scandal, 244 n.2
Sansum, [Rear-Adm. Robert]: 227
Santa Cruz, Tenerife: 228 n.1
Saunders, – , naval officer: 227
Sawyer, Robert [Kt 1677]: Carteret's counsel, 335 & n.3
Scarborough, Yorks.: seamen recruited, 227
Scave, Nathaniel, master: 131
Scotland: Court and Council, 173; Second Bishops' War (1640), 342 n.3; timber from, 173 & n.2, 185
Scott, – , former Navy Office clerk: 59
Scott, Capt. [Thomas], naval officer: 232–3
Scott *see also* Monmouth
screws *see* timber
Seale, Capt. [Thomas], naval officer: 249
seamen (King's ships):
 general: aspirations to command, 224; aversion to King's service/discontent/disorder, 134, 207–10, 215, 231–4, 243, 249, 258–60, 265–6, 267, 315, 426, 428, (thieving) 37, (violent) 411 & n.3, 428; 'followings', 209, 216, 227 & n.1, 231; hope of plunder, 208 & n.2, 259 & n.2; irreligious, 260; maltreatment, 207, 231, 232, 233, 236; moved from ship to

ship, 164, 208, 209, 259–60, 266, 426; mutinies, 139–40, (temp. Charles I) 222–3 & n., 225–6 & n., 227 & n.3; runaways/ deserters, 140, 164 & n.2, 165, 174, 177 & n.1, 180, 202, 206, 215, 230, 236, 262–3, 265–6, 267, 292, 294, 295, 402, 414, (legitimate absentees treated as deserters) 233, (seamen pretend to be landsmen) 265; shore leave, 207, 233; shortage 230, 426; sick and wounded, 165, 179, 181, 416, (recovered) 164; survivors, 108, 164

pay: abuses, 64 n.7, 176–82, 208; annual estimate reported to Duke, 426; arrears/owed, 140, 158–61, 204 & n.2, 207–8, 231, 233, 259 & n.1; compared with merchant service, 42–3, 205, 209, 231–3, 258–9, 263, 362–3; covenants for, 204; deductions/ forfeits, (chaplains' groats) 114 & n.1, (desertion) 233, (failure to re-engage) 230, 243; in hired ships, 262, 277–8; lack of cash for pay, 135, 208, 265, 266, 427–8; numbers in pay, 129, 258–9 & n.; 'pinch-gut', 416 n.6; raised, (false promise) 134, (temp. Commonwealth) 203 & n.4; records/pay books, 177–8 & n., 196, 265, 368, (errors in) 174; short allowance, 181 & n.2, 299–300, 416; soldiers paid and seamen not, 128, 203; wasted because ships idle, 216 ~ alluded to, 209–10, 258, 293, 380, 403–16, 428–9

rates etc.: able, 134, 265; ordinary/ boys/grommets, (paid as able) 294; supernumeraries, 164, 176–82, 209, 234, 300, 416; volunteers, 209, 215, 231, 233, 259

see also impressment; tickets

seamen (merchant ships): desert to King's service, 42–3; mutiny then fight Spaniard, 243; pay, (better than King's service) 362, (half) 210 n.2, (raised because of impressment) 203 & n.3, 205, 209, 216

Seamour *see* Seymour

sea officers: collude with fraudulent pursers, 165; corrupt, 92–3; extravagant accommodation, 219–20; deceased, care for effects of, 140; gentlemen v. tarpaulins, 222–3, 231–2, 233, 237; junior, 222, 232, 238; negligent, 108–9 & n., 110; pay, 42 & n.2, 140, 207; pension, 160–1 & n.; reformadoes, 164, 232

see also captains; lieutenants; midshipmen

secret service: payments for, 161–3; royalist, 342 n.3

Seddon, John, Navy Office clerk: deposition by, 404 ~ alluded to, 196, 297

Seething Lane: 379 n.7

Selden, John, jurist: 228 n.4

Seymour (Seamour), Capt. Hugh, naval officer: 232 & n.2
~ father Sir Edward, Bt, and brother Sir Edward, Bt, 232 n.2

Shales, [Capt. John], victualling agent, Portsmouth: 180

Shaw, Sir John, merchant: 136

sheathing board *see* timber

Sheeres, John, Navy Office clerk: 196

Sheerness, Kent: foundations, 183 n.2; ships at, 264 n.1

Sheldon, William, clerk of the cheque, Woolwich: malpractices, 64 & n.7

Sherwood Forest, Notts.: iron from, 38

shipbuilding and repair: contract, 103 & n.1, 115–16, 117–18, 125, 132 & n.1, 140; costs and estimates, 43 & n.1, 73, 90–1, 112, 125 & n.2, 132, 186–9, 257, 304; defective, 131, 132–3, 219–20, 257; delayed, 186–7; economy in building, 156; exceeding dimensions, 187; experimental, 27 & nn.1–4; spasmodic in earlier times, 370 ~ alluded to, 4–5 & n., 37 & n.2, 47 & n.1, 50 & n.1, 161 & n.3

ships (the King's):
general: draughts/capacities, 220, 416–18; economies at sea, 114; fitting/setting out, 3 & n.1, 12, 16 & n.2, 42 & n.1, 48, 65 & n.2, 131–2, 207, 244 & n.1, 245, 373 & n.1, 400, 413, 417–18; lists, (given) 213–14, 256, 318–23, (referred to) 212–13, 317–18, 373;

loss/damage/accidents, 418, (collisions) 132, 216, (explosion) 111, (Medway raid) 135–6 & n., 236, 247 & n.1, (run aground) 110–11, (storm) 58 & n.1; loss kept secret, 108–9; lying idle/kept useless in pay, 61, 183, 232, 315–16, 425–6, 427, 428, 429, (not manned) 257; payments to, 380; thefts from, 37; trading, 200; unserviceable, 255–7, 319
paying off: 196, 208, 230, 232, 247, 249, 259 & n.1, 265, 342, 379, 397, 407, 411–12, 425–9, (efficiency of temp. Elizabeth I) 379
records: books, 377, 379, 380, 416; letters to, 397
repair: by contract/in private docks, 130–1, 140; costs, 376 n.3; defective, 182; during action, 417 & n.1; neglected, 135
types [where so specified]: 1st-rate, 257; 2nd-rate, 91, 156, 257; 3rd-rate, 91, 135; 4th-rate, 91, 115–16; 5th-rate, 115–16, 156, 364; ammunition, 128; fire, 128, 246 & n.1, 256 & n.1; flag, 264 n.1; flyboats, 239, 256; frigates, 129; galliots, 109; hoys, 85, 141, 183 & n.2; hulks, 184 & n.1, 188; ketch, 91; lighters, 156–6 & n.; prison, 323; scout, 125 n.2; ships' boats, 218, 261; sloops, 125; victuallers, 128 & n.3, 128–9, 130, 142 & n.1; water, 128–9; yacht, 63 & n.2

ships (merchant): compared with King's ships, (better husbanded) 109, (less so) 231; hired by King, 6 & n.3, 33, 42 & n.1, 101, 110, 111, 116–17, 129, 140, 156 n.1, 173, 183–4, 219, 220, 319, 363–4, 426, (discharged) 427, (excessive charge of refuted by P) 277–8, (inconveniences) 262–3; lying long in freight, 128, 140; men put in from King's ships, 164; men take over, 243; molested by press, 216, 233
types [where so specified]: colliers, 129, 205, 209; East Indiamen, 42 & n.1, 200 & n.2, 267, (Dutch) 244 n.2; ketches, 129; lighters, 35, 81, 102, 155–6 & n., 263; smacks, 129; tenders, 262; transports, 75, 95–6, 140, 173; victuallers, 262–3; water, 262
~ alluded to, 27 n.2, 347, 423

ships mentioned by name in text or footnotes:
Adam and Eve hoy [Dutch prize 1665; Anderson, no. 359], 183, 214, 256; *Adventure* [4th-rate; Anderson, no. 28], 213, 258; *Advice* [4th-rate; Anderson, no. 93], 204, 213; *Anne (Ann)* [3rd-rate; Anderson, no. 210], 144, 213; *Anne*, the Duke's yacht [Anderson, no. 295], 63 & n.2, 214; *Antelope (Anthelope)* [4th-rate; Anderson, no. 180], 213; *Arthur of Bradley* [merchantman], 173; *Assistance* [4th-rate; Anderson, no. 92], 213; *Assurance* [4th-rate; Anderson, no. 29], 22, 58 & n.1, 213; *Augustine (Augustin)* [5th-rate; Dutch prize 1653; Anderson, no. 193], 12, 16, 75, 79, 95
Bear (Beare) [4th-rate; Dutch prize 1652; Anderson, no. 124], 5–6, 124; *Bendick* [unidentified], 429; *Bezan (Besan)* yacht [Anderson, no. 297], 214; *Black Dog (Black Dogg)* galliot [Dutch prize 1665; Anderson, no. 363], 214, 256; *Blue Boar (Blew Boare)* [flyboat; Dutch prize 1665; Tanner, *Catalogue*, i. 286], 319; *Bonaventure (Bonadventure)* [4th-rate; Anderson, no. 94], 144, 213; *Breda* [4th-rate; Anderson, no. 219], 22, 248; *Bristol (Bristoll)* [4th-rate; Anderson, no. 178], 213; *Burweek of Alkmer* [unidentified], 322
Cambridge [3rd-rate; Anderson, no. 370], 213; *Catherine (Katharine, Katherine)* yacht [Anderson, no. 296], 112, 214, 319; *Centurion* [4th-rate; Anderson, no. 96], 213; *Charles (Charles the 2d)* [1st-rate; Anderson, no. 443], 213, 245 & n.1; *Charles* yacht [Anderson, no. 298], 68 & n.1; *Chatham* smack, 214; *Chestnut* [ketch; Anderson, no. 258], 165;

Constant Warwick (*Warwick Constant*) [4th-rate; Anderson, no. 74], 213; *Convertine* [4th-rate; Portuguese prize 1650; Anderson, no. 91], 133, 364; *Crown* (*Crowne*) [4th-rate; Anderson, no. 218], 213
Dartmouth [5th-rate; Anderson, no. 234], 213; *Defiance* [3rd-rate; Anderson, no. 372], 117 & n.2, 132; *Deptford* ketch [6th-rate; Anderson, no. 357], 213; *Diamond* [4th-rate; Anderson, no. 107], 213; *Dove of Sardam* [prize; unidentified], 322; *Dover* [4th-rate; Anderson, no. 217], 213, 260; *Dragon* (*Draggon*) [4th-rate; Anderson, no. 26], 213; *Drake* [6th-rate; Anderson, no. 156], 213; *Dreadnought* [3rd-rate; Anderson, no. 211], 213; *Dunkirk* (*Dunkirke*) [3rd-rate; Anderson, no. 106], 213
Eagle [5th-rate; Anderson, no. 221 (as *Selby*)], 213, 321; *Eagle* [merchantman hired by King], 111, 117, 119; *Edgar* [3rd-rate; Anderson, no. 444], 161 n.3, 213; *Elias* [4th-rate; Dutch prize 1653; Anderson, no. 186], 92–3, 108; *Emsworth* sloop [6th-rate; Anderson, no. 441], 125 & n.2; *Experiment II*, 27 & nn.1–4
Fairfax [3rd-rate; Anderson, no. 172], 213, 237; *Falcon* (*Faulcon*) [4th-rate; Anderson, no. 377], 213; *Fanfan* [6th-rate; Anderson, no. 382], 213; *Flying Greyhound* [6th-rate; privateer; Dutch prize 1665; Anderson, no. 332], 245 & n.5; *Foresight* [4th-rate; Anderson, no. 97], 209, 213, 215; *Forester* (*Forrester*) [5th-rate; Anderson, no. 266], 213; *Fountain* (*Fountaine*) [5th-rate; Algerine prize 1664; Anderson, no. 304], 213; *Francis* [6th-rate; Anderson, no. 380], 213; *Francis* [fireship; Anderson, no. 400], 246 n.1; *Franekin* (*Franikin*) [flyboat; Dutch prize 1665; Anderson, no. 341], 320; *French Ruby* (*Ruby*) [3rd-rate; French prize 1666; rebuilt as 2nd-rate 1672; Anderson, no. 369], 213; *French Victory* (*Victory Prise, Victory Prize*) [5th-rate; French prize 1665; Anderson, no. 328], 213, 220 & n.4, 233; *Friezland* (*Freizland*) flyboat [Dutch prize 1665; Anderson, no. 342], 214, 256
Garland (*Guarland*) [5th-rate; Anderson, no. 223], 213, 216; *George* [E. Indiaman], 205; *George of Strood* (*George of Stroud*) [ketch; hired by King], 319; *Gloucester* [3rd-rate; Anderson, no. 209], 213; *Golden Fortune* [dogger; Dutch prize 1665; Tanner, *Catalogue*, i. 280], 320; *Golden Hand* [fireship; Dutch prize 1665; Anderson, no. 335], 323; *Golden Sun* (*Sunn*) [merchantman], 166–7, 175; *Great Alexander* [French prize 1651], 237 & n.1; *Great Duke of York* (*Great Duke of Yorke*) [merchantman], 148, 154; *Great Gift* (*Guift*) [5th-rate; French prize 1652; Anderson, no. 134], 429; *Greenwich* [4th-rate; Anderson, no. 374], 213; *Guernsey* [5th-rate; Anderson, no. 225], 213; *Guilder de Ruyter* (*Guilder de Ruiter*) [4th-rate; Dutch prize 1665; Anderson, no. 316], 318
Hampshire [4th-rate; Anderson, no. 181], 213; *Happy Edward* [merchantman hired by King], 117; *Happy Return* (*Happy Returne*) [4th-rate; Anderson, no. 214], 213, 265; *Harp* (*Harpe*) [6th-rate; Anderson, no. 259], 160 & n.1, 213, 256; *Harwich* hoy [Anderson, no. 290], 141, 214, 256; Harwich muster boat [cf. *Musterboat* smack, below], 256; *Henrietta* [3rd-rate; Anderson, no. 206], 213, 261; *Henrietta* yacht (*Heneretta Yacht*) [Anderson, no. 301], 26, 47, 214; *Henry* (*Harry*) [2nd-rate; Anderson, no. 245], 28 & n.1, 213, 220 & n.1; *Hope* galliot, 214, 256; *Hope of Camphire* [Quimper], *Hope of Henlopen* [Dutch prizes; cf. *Hope*, 4th-rate taken 1665; *Hope* hoy taken 1666 (Anderson, nos 320, 420)], 321,

322; *Horseman* (*De Ruiter, The Horseman*) [flyboat; Dutch prize 1665; Anderson, no. 345], 318; *Hoveling* [unidentified], 321
James [2nd-rate; built 1634; Anderson, no. 3], 213; *James* hoy [Anderson, no. 360], 254 & n.2, 256 [as galliot]; *James* (*Jemmy*) yacht [Anderson, no. 299], 68 & n.1, 214; *James* of Southampton [merchantman hired by King], 140; *Jersey* [4th-rate; Anderson, no. 215], 213, 215, 239; *Joseph* [fireship; Anderson, no. 404], 245
Kent [4th-rate; Anderson, no. 121], 213; *King Solomon of Amsterdam* [Dutch merchantman; sunk 1664; *Diary*, vi. 19 & n.3], 321; *Kitchen* (*Kitchin, Roe Kitchin*) yacht [Anderson, no. 454], 47, 214
Leopard [4th-rate; Anderson, no. 286], 213, 224 & n.1, 229–30 & n., 236, 247–8, 249; *Leopard* [E. Indiaman], 42 & n.1; *Lighter* hoy, 214; *Lion* (*Lyon*) [3rd-rate; Anderson, no. 15], 213, 218–19, 261, 266, 430; *Little Victory* (*Victory, Victory Litle*) [5th-rate; built 1665; Anderson, no. 330], 174, 213; *London* [2nd-rate; built 1656; Anderson, no. 244], 111; *Loyal London* (*Loyall London*) [2nd-rate; built 1666; rebuilt 1670 as *London*, 1st-rate; Anderson, nos 367, 449], 118 & n.1, 236, 257; *Loyal Merchant* (*Loyall Merchant*) [merchantman hired by King], 101, 107; *Loyalty* [E. Indiaman], 75
Madras [E. Indiaman hired by King], 116; *Maria Sancta* (*Sta Maria*) [4th-rate; Dutch prize 1665; Anderson, no. 318], 429; *Marigold* (*Marygold*) hoy [Anderson, no. 203], 214; *Mary* [3rd-rate; Anderson, no. 89], 94, 95, 213, 260; *Mary* yacht [Anderson, no. 292], 214; *Maryner* [unidentified], 157; *Mary Rose* [4th-rate; Anderson, no. 216], 213; *Merlin* yacht [Anderson, no. 383], 161 n.3,

214; *Mermaid* [5th-rate; Anderson, no. 112], 213; *Mermaid of Amsterdam* [Dutch prize], 323; *Michael* (*Michaell*) [unidentified], 173; *Milford* [5th-rate; Anderson, no. 224], 182, 213; *Monck* [3rd-rate; Anderson, no. 285], 213; *Monmouth* [3rd-rate; Anderson, no. 429], 141 & n.1; 213; *Monmouth* yacht [Anderson, no. 384], 214; *Montagu* (*Mountague*) [3rd-rate; Anderson, no. 208], 213, 236 n.1; *Morning Star* [E. Indiaman], 200 & n.2; *Mouse of Amsterdam* [Dutch prize], 323; *Musterboat* (*Musterboate*) smack [cf. *Harwich* muster boat, above], 214
Neptune [merchantman], 352 & n.2; *Newcastle* [4th-rate; Anderson, no. 174], 204, 213; *New York* (*New Yorke*) [unidentified], 95; *Nightingale* [5th-rate; Anderson, no. 113], 213; *Nonsuch* (*Nonesuch*) [4th-rate; built 1646 wrecked 1664; Anderson, no. 27], 108–9 & n., 213 [where the next is presumably meant]; *Nonsuch* [5th-rate; built 1668; Anderson, no. 445], 156, ? 213; *Norwich* [5th-rate; Anderson, no. 233], 213
Orange [5th-rate; Dutch prize 1665; Anderson, no. 329], 213; *Oxford* [5th-rate; Anderson, no. 248], 213
Pearl (*Pearle*) [5th-rate; Anderson, no. 115], 213; *Phoenix* [4th-rate; Anderson, no. 25], 108–9 & n.; *Plymouth* (*Plymoath*) [3rd-rate; Anderson, no. 171], 213, 264, 266 *Portland* [4th-rate; Anderson, no. 176], 108, 213, 220 & nn.2,4; *Portsmouth* [4th-rate; Anderson, no. 95], 213; *Portsmouth* ketch [6th-rate; Anderson, no. 358], 213; *Portsmouth* sloop [6th-rate; Anderson, no. 442], 125 & n.1, 213; *Prince* [1st-rate; Anderson, no. 448], 186–8 & n., 257, 261, 266; *Princess* [4th-rate; Anderson, no. 289], 213;

INDEX

Prosperous [fireship; Anderson, no. 410], 245 & n.4, 246 & n.1
Rainbow (*Rainebow*) [2nd-rate; Anderson, no. 6], 213; *Reserve* [4th-rate; Anderson, no. 98], 213; *Resolution* [3rd-rate; Anderson, no. 205], 133 & n.3, 213, 267; *Return* (*Returne*) [E. Indiaman], 205; *Revenge* [3rd-rate; Anderson, no. 207], 213, 217, 233; *Richmond* [5th-rate; Anderson, no. 247], 213; *Roebuck* [6th-rate; Anderson, no. 381], 213; *Roe* ketch [6th-rate; Anderson, no. 242], 213; *Royal Charles* (*Charles, Royall Charles*) [1st-rate; built 1655 taken by Dutch 1667; Anderson, no. 231], 110–11, 125 n.1, 245 & n.2; *Royal Charles* (*Royall Charles*) [merchantman], 139; *Royal James* (*Royall James*) [1st-rate; Anderson, no. 276], 184 & n.1, 188, 236, 247; *Royal Katherine* (*Royall Katharine, Royall Katherine*) [2nd-rate; Anderson, no. 302], 4–5 & n., 43 & n.1, 73 & n.3, 90, 91 & n.2, 186 & n.1, 213, 257; *Royal Oak* (*Royall Oake*) [2nd-rate; Anderson, no. 303], 184, 236; *Royal Sovereign* (*Soveraigne*) [1st-rate; Anderson, no. 1], 141 & n.1, 213, 428; *Ruby* [4th-rate; built 1651; Anderson, no. 108], 177, 180 n.1, 213 [see also *French Ruby*]; *Rupert* [3rd-rate; Anderson, no. 373], 58–9 & n., 213

St Andrew [1st-rate; Anderson, no. 450], 186–8 & n.; *St David* [4th-rate; Anderson, no. 430], 213, 258; *St George* [2nd-rate; Anderson, no. 8], 213; *St Michael* [Petty's 4th prototype; 1684], 27 n.4; *Sampson* [unidentified], 100, 106; *Sapphire* (*Saphire*) [4th-rate; Anderson, no. 110], 135, 181, 204, 213; *Sea Rider* (*Sea Ruiter*) [flyboat; Dutch prize 1665; Anderson, no. 351], 318; *Seaventure* [transport], 214; *Society* [merchantman hired by King; Anderson, no. 1191], 128; *Sophia* [5th-rate; Dutch prize 1652; Anderson, no. 137], 42, 131; *Speedwell* [5th-rate; Anderson, no. 246], 213; *Spy* (*Spie*) sloop [6th-rate; Anderson, no. 426], 213; *Stathouse van Harlem* [4th-rate; Dutch prize 1667; Anderson, no. 431], 213; *Success* [5th-rate; Anderson, no. 277], 213, 260; *Swallow* [built 1634 sold 1653; Anderson, no. 19], 82 n.1; *Swallow* [4th-rate; built 1653; Anderson, no. 179], 133, 213; *Sweepstakes* (*Sweeptakes*) [4th-rate; Anderson, no. 378], 213

Thomas and Margaret ketch of Margate, 110; *Tiger* (*Tyger*) [4th-rate; Anderson, no. 24], 213, 258; *Tower* smack [Anderson, no. 446], 214; *Triumph* (*Tryumph*) [2nd-rate; Anderson, no. 5], 213; *Truelove* (*Trulove*) [6th-rate; royalist prize 1647; Anderson, no. 53], 214, 256

Unicorn (*Unicorne*) [2nd-rate; Anderson, no. 10], 213

Victory [2nd-rate; built 1620; Anderson, no. 13], 213 [see also *French Victory; Little Victory*]

Warspite (*Warrspight*) [3rd-rate; Anderson, no. 371], 132, 213; *Welcome* (*Wellcome*) [4th-rate; Dutch prize 1652; Anderson, no. 128], 42; *Wheel of Fortune* (*Wheele of Fortune*) [perhaps *Fortune* fireship (Dutch prize 1666; Anderson, no. 399) or *Fortune* flyboat (Dutch prize 1666; Anderson, no. 418)], 323; *White Lamb* [Dutch prize], 322; *White Rose* [flyboat; Dutch prize 1666; Anderson, no. 419], 320; *William and Mary* [merchantman hired by King], 6 & n.3; *Woodmerchant* [Dutch prize], 322; *Wyvenhoe* (*Vivenhoe, Wevenho*) ketch/pink [Anderson, no. 425; converted to pink 1668/9 (Tanner, *Catalogue*, i. 292)] 214, 261

Yarmouth [4th-rate; Anderson, no. 175], 109, 213, 232; *York* (*Yorke*) [3rd-rate; Anderson, no. 212], 213; *Young Prince* [4th-

rate; Dutch prize 1665; Anderson, no. 326], 319
Zealand (*Zeland*) [4th-rate; Dutch prize 1665; Anderson, no. 322], 172
shipwrights (King's service): hours of work, 45–6 & nn.; survey repairs in private docks, 130–1
~ alluded to, 117–18
shipwrights (private): consulted, 118; demands, 130
Shish, [Jonas], assistant shipwright, Deptford: certification questioned, 182; complaint about shipwrights, 45–6; estimates/valuations, (bricklaying) 124, (shipbuilding) 91, (timber) 14, 80, 139, 174, (wreck) 188–9, 247; incompetent in measuring, 70 & n.3, 138–9; information from, 26, 103, 104, 132, 256; letters to, 102; private work for Batten, 74; private yard, 45 n.1; report on private yard repairs, 130; ship built by, 4–5 & n.; timber work, 117–18
Shorter, Capt. [John], merchant: deposition by, 350, 366, 433; masts from, 388, 423
~ alluded to, 79, 313
shot, shot-makers: 38
shrouds *see* cordage
silver: lack of for payment, 355
~ alluded to, 200 n.3, 249
Silvester (Silverster), [Edward], smith: 135
Sindry, Daniel, purser: 239–41
Slater (Sliter), [John], Navy Office messenger: letter to P about cordage, 39
slaves: redeemed, 181 ~ alluded to, 165, 200 n.1
Slingsby, Sir Guilford, Comptroller of the Navy 1611–18, 1628–32: 14
Slingsby, Sir Robert, Comptroller of the Navy 1660–1: against perquisites, 50; information from, 419; praised, 195
sloops *see* ships
slops, slop-sellers: accounts, 402; frauds, 92–3, 174, 202, 292–3; soldiers better equipped than seamen, 203
Smith, Arthur, merchant: oil from, 63

Smith, [Edward], merchant: 314
Smith, Capt. Sir Jeremy (Kt 1665), Navy Commissioner 1669–75: appointment, 211; clerk, 250; information from, 94, 233, 248–9; pays ships, 265; P appeals to his naval experience, 348; present at Board, 242, 246; present at debate before Privy Council, 346; signature, 241; victualling contract, 250
~ alluded to, 204, 227, 234
Smith, John, seaman: 204
Smith, [Robert], Navy Office messenger: 381
Smith *see also* Smyth
smiths: payment in kind defended by P, 355
see also iron
Smyrna (Smirna): 247
Smyth, Richard, boatswain, Woolwich: 58 & n.3
soldiers: frightened by naval guns, 222; gentility among, 227; numbers greater temp. Commonwealth, 203; paid and seamen not, 128, 203; sent to Tangier, 75; supernumeraries, 164
Sole Bay, Battle of: 260–1 & n.
Southampton, Hants.: ship of (*named*), 140
Southampton, Thomas Wriothesley, 4th Earl of, Lord Treasurer 1660–7: letters/requests to, 301, 397, 420 ~ alluded to, 382, 397
Spain: goods from/of, (cloth) 82, (iron) 38, 354, 356 n. 2, (timber used in their shipbuilding) 104; relations with Britain, (alliance with Commonwealth) 238, (ambassador from) 220 & n.2, (war temp. Commonwealth) 227–8 & n., (war temp. Elizabeth I) 223; ship engaged by merchantman, 243
Spithead: 230, 243
Spragge, (Spragg), Sir Edward, naval commander: 205, 216–17, 233, 234, 235–6, 242 & n. 2, 242–3
Sprucia *see* Prussia
Stacey (Stacie, Stacy), [John], merchant: contract for tar, 61, 202; informs P about tar, 31, 99–100, 106

Stanes, Thomas, glazier: 53 & n. 1, 71–2
Stanley (Stanly), [William], merchant: 59
Stapely (Staply), [Joseph], ropemaker, Wapping: instructs P, 31, 39–40, 88
Starling, Samuel, ? notary public: 240
Stephens (Stephen), Anthony, Navy Treasury clerk: 430 & n.1
Steventon (Stephenton), [? John], purser: 22
steward: 215
Stockholm (Stock(e)holme): tar from, 31–5, 60, 69, 98, 107, (*canard* of burnt tarhouse) 97–100
Stockman, [Isaac], merchant: 423
Stockwith, Lincs.: 183
stores, storekeepers *see* dockyards, royal
Strachan, Capt. John, Navy agent, Leith: 185
Suffolk: cloth from, 29
surgeons: 63
Surveyor of the Navy: duties, 214–15, 274, 290, 293, 386, 396, 397, 397–8, 402
see also Batten; Middleton; Tippetts
surveyors: contract building and repairs, 132–3, 140
surveys: 12, 15 & n. 1, 17, 37, 331; books, 360; investigation by Brooke House Commission/ debate before Privy Council, 287–91, 396–401, (P acknowledges lack of method) 357–8; wartime impossibility, 287, 289–90, 357, 360
Svinesund (Swinsound), Sweden: timber from, 314
Swale, the, channel: 128 & n.6
Sweden: iron from, 38, 77, 133, 354–7; masts from, 36, 54–5, 174, 273, 308, 309, 313, 346, 363, (embargo on felling trees for) 361–2; tar from, 31–5, 60, 69, 97–100, 107; timber from, 129, 305, 314
Swins, channels: 265 & n.1
Swinsound *see* Svinesund
Symons (Simmons), William, clerk to the Brooke House Commission: 334 & n. 5, 336

tallow: 78

Tangier (Tanger): Commissioners for, 4, 7, 75, 76; finances, 383; P's service, 8, 383 n.3; ships hired for, 6 & n.3, 75; supplies for, 76–8; women for, 22 & n.2
~ alluded to, 201
tar: bad, 107; bad supplied with good, 79; barrels, (stolen) 69, (use of empties) 134; contracts, 60, 61, 69, 97–8, 107, 112, 202, 391; prices/purchase, 31–5, 60–1, 78, 79, 97–100, 254, 290, 307, 382; prize, 131; uses, (application to cordage) 119, 157–8, (tarpaulins etc.) 56; varieties compared, 31, 39, 108
provenance: New England, 108; Norway/Bergen, 31–2, 39, 79; Russia/Archangel, 31–2, 39; Sweden/Stockholm, 31–5, 39, 60–1, 69, 97–100, 107
tarpaulin *see* cloth
tarpaulins *see* captains
taxation: 100–1 & n., 133 & nn.4,5, 379, 394
see also Parliament
Taylor (Talor), Capt. John, shipbuilder, Navy Commissioner, Harwich 1665–8: bills for hire of ships, 6–9; foreman, 36; gratuity to P, 8–9; information from, 132, 133; letter to, 311; masts from, 36, 53–5, 115, 273, 350, 423, (monopoly of trade) 308, (tender) 313; ship built by, 118 & n. 1; storekeeper to yard/Prize Officers, 137
Teate, Capt. [Richard], naval officer: 74, 95
Teddeman (Tiddeman), [Sir Thomas], naval commander: 226
tenders: fixed days for, 314; invited, 311–12, 314, 349–50; unreasonable, 420, 423
Terrill, [William], merchant: 382, 394
Teviot (Tiviott), Andrew Rutherford, 1st Earl of, Governor of Tangier 1663–4: 75, 77
Thames, River ('the River'): blockade feared, 134; Dutch raid (1667), 134 n.1, 176–82; fleet preparing in, 244–5; gossip in, 215; harbours allegedly inferior, 135; masts, (lacking in) 12–13,

(lying idle, etc.) 36, 67, 115; moorings, 39; prison ship, 323; ships idle in, 128 (*bis*), 134 (*bis*), 140, 266; ship to be hired in, 16; shipwrights' advice sought, 188; strategic importance in a civil war, 225; timber kept from being carried away, 92; wear and tear not chargeable in, 263 & n.2; wreck clearance not responsibility of particular Principal Officer, 140

Thompson, ? Robert, banker: 267 & n.3

Thomson (Thompson, Tompson, Tomson), Col. George, Brooke House Commissioner: alone familiar with Navy, 335 n.2, 337 & n.3; criticized, (evidence delayed) 432, (ignorant) 348, (impertinent) 364, 393, (trivial complaint) 395; dissatisfied at P's appearing in debate before Privy Council, 335; P appeals to, 289 & n.2, 403, 417; present at debate, 337, 376, 377, 431; signature, 271; speaks in debate, 345, 348–9, 356 (*bis*), 365, 383, 388–9, 390, 417–18, 419, (accuses King of contradiction) 393–4, (Commonwealth precedents) 360–1, 368, (Elizabethan precedents) 378–9, 387, 400, (masts) 348, 351 & n.1, (parish dues) 379, 394, (survey books) 357, (tickets) 404–5, 430, (uses architectural metaphor) 368, 370

Ticket Office: clerks' errors, 130, 292 n.3; Navy Office clerks sent to, 196 ~ alluded to, 406, 408 n.2, 411, 413, 414, 415

tickets:
abuses: 292, 403–16, (captains' frauds) 235–6, (clerks' profits) 196, (entrusted to others) 234, 235–6, (false/irregular) 130, 164–5, 234, 294–9, (payment refused) 164–5, 208, 247–8
criticized/defended: clamour in Parliament/Committee on Miscarriages, 159 & n.1, 164 n.1, 296 n.2; condemned by Council, 164 n.1, 429 n.5; P defends in speech to House of Commons, xxi, 429 n.4
investigation by Brooke House

Commission/debate before Privy Council: Observations/answers, 294–9, 315–16; proceedings, 403–10, 424–6, 430–2; P admits possibility of blame, 409; P challenged by Commission, 419, 429–32; P's notes, 411–16, 426–9
payment: arrears, 158–9, 207–8; instructions by Navy Board, 296–9, 403 & n.4, 404–5, 408, 412, 413, 415–16; notice of encashment, 159, 429 n.5
various: Comptroller's responsibility, 176 n.1, 410; examination of counterparts impracticable in wartime, 403–4; precedents of First Dutch War, 331, 411, 429; printed forms, 411, 414, 429
~ alluded to, 368, 383, 397

Tiddeman *see* Teddeman

timber:
abuses:embezzled, 69–70; short measures, 36 n.2, 70, 77–9, 92, 117–18, 132–3
contracts/purchase: 5 & nn.2,3, 6, 15, 89–90, 168, 349 & n.2
defects: bad, 5 & nn.2,3, 6 & n.2, 91–2, 117, 132, 173, n.2; bent, 104 & n.1; cross-grained, 104; rotten, 36, 67, 132, 348, 349–50; rough, 89; unseasoned, 257; worm-eaten, 10
measurement/shape: 6, 70 & nn.1–3, 89, 104
particular cuts/uses: balks, 15, 51, 78; beams, 132; boards, 43; brush faggots, 261; chips, 69 (*bis*), 261; clapboard, 185; deals, 5 & nn.2,3, 7, 22 & n.4, 35, 43, 50, 70, 77–8, 79–81, 90, 96, 131, 189, 305, 314, 323; firewood, 90 & n.1, 106; handspikes, 219; housebuilding, 173 & n.2; knees, 6, 49–50, 88–9, 91–2, 102–5, 131; pipestaves, 391, 392; plank, 6, 47 & n.1, 257, 261, 315, 321; scantlings, 117, 132–3, 187; screws, 79; sheathing board, 14, 51, 57, 348; spars, 78, 131, (boathook) 219; treenails, 15
particular woods: ash, 321; deal, 72, 201 n.1, 391; fir, 290, 314, 322; lignum vitae, 15 (*bis*), 59; oak,

INDEX

390 n.2; pine, 22 & n.4; spruce, 22 & n.4
provenance: Baltic (East-Country), 6, 47 & n.1; Bohemia, 47 n.1; England, 390 & n.2, (Essex) 15, 58, (Lincs.) 183; Ireland, 392; 'Normer', 77 & n.1; Norway, (Drammen) 14, 51, 90, 314, (Langesund) 314, (Oslo) 75; prize, 131, 321, 322; Prussia, 50, 189; 'Ribadeux', 92; Scotland, 173 & n.2; Sweden, 305, (Svinesund) 314
see also masts and spars
Tinker (Tincker), Capt. [John], master attendant, Portsmouth: 6, 111, 135
Tippetts (Tippet, Tippets), John [Kt 1672], master shipwright, Portsmouth 1660–8, Navy Commissioner, Portsmouth 1668–72; Surveyor of the Navy 1672–86, 1688–92:
business: appointed Commissioner, 191–2 & n.; appointed Surveyor, 264 n.2; clerk, 196; duped, 59; information from, 16, 50, 54 & n.2, 105, 156, 184, 186–7, 188, 230–1, 264; investigates defects in provisioning, 220; P criticizes, (mast measurement) 54, (over-lenient) 113; plank used by, 47; present at Board, 152, 168, 176, 179; signature, 150, 151, 153, 154, 172, 188
debate before Privy Council: P appeals to, 348; present, 346 ~ alluded to, 136, 152
Tooker (Tucker), John, Navy Office messenger and river agent: 382 & n.1, 394–5
Tower of London: official, 77
see also Ordnance Office; Robinson, Sir J.
Tower Hill: 379 n.7
Treasurer, Lord *see* Southampton, Earl of
Treasurer of the Navy: accounts/duties, 276, 278–82, 316, 367–70, 385, 398, 424, 427, (tickets) 294–9, 403–16; comparison with Commonwealth, 370; poundage, 123 & n.5; resignation/removal, 202 & n.1
see also Anglesey; Carteret;

Littleton; Navy Treasury; Osborne, Sir T.
Treasury: bills/orders, 258 n.1, 305; Brooke House Commission mainly concerned with, 337 n.3; P assisted in matters relating to, 337
Treasury, Commissioners (of 1667): letter to, 357; Navy Board attends, 216; P attends, 336, 337; payments, 158, 161–2 & n.
Treasury, Commonwealth: 307
Treasury, Irish: 160 n.1
treenails *see* timber
Trelawny (Trelawney), Sir Jonathan, Comptroller to the Duke of York 1668–74, Commissioner of Prizes, Plymouth: 344
Trent, River: 183 n.1
Trevor, Sir John, Secretary of State 1668–72: present at debate before Privy Council, 337
Trinity House: criticized, 129, 217; masters certified by, 265, 266 n.1; P at Election dinner, 217 & n.2
see also lighthouses; pilots
Tucker *see* Tooker
tuns *see* barrels
Turkey: ambassador to (*named*), 224 & n.1
Turner, Thomas, purveyor of petty provisions 1660–8 then storekeeper, Deptford: 66, 73 & n.1, 97
Turner, Ald. Sir William, Lord Mayor 1668–9, Brooke House Commissioner: present at debate before Privy Council, 343, 345, 377, 431; speaks there, 344; ~ mayoralty, 376
turnery ware: 290
Tyburn: execution at, 366 & n.4

United Provinces of the Netherlands:
goods from: canvas, 27–8, 29, 30, 31; cordage, 40, 42; iron, 38
navy: Admiralty organisation, 400; P visits/observes naval management, 332, 334, n.2; prisoners, 323; recruitment, 259; seamanship, 224; show of force in English Channel, 16 n.2, 244 n.1; war expenses, 400–1 & n.
trade: covert wartime, 350 & n.2; Dutch East India Company,

209–10 & n., (cargo seized) 244 n.2; freedom of seas claimed, 228 n.4; prevented from obtaining Swedish masts, 362
various: Charles I's navy in, 226 n.1; coast raided (1666), 162 n.1; Englishmen serve in, 165
see also War[s], Dutch
Upton, [Hugh], merchant: 87, 133
Uthwayt (Urthwaite, Uthwayte), John, clerk of the survey, Deptford: information from, 52, 104, 127 n.1, 402; malpractice suspected by P, 102; private work for Batten, 74

Vane, Sir Henry, republican politician: protects Penn, 20
Viborg (Wibrough, Wiburg), Sweden: tar from, 98 (*bis*), 107
Victualler of the Navy: accounts, 193 n.1, 403, 406 n.2, 407
see also Gauden
Victualling Office, East Smithfield: 380 n.4
victualling, victuallers: abuses/defects, 64 & n.7, 75–6, 123 & n.3, 128, 129–30, 133, 138, 141–3, 178–9, 181 & nn.1,2, 215, 263; accounts/charges, 126, 176 n.1, 178, 183, 185, 211–12, 250, 402–3, 403, 406, (annual estimate to Duke) 426; investigation by Brooke House Commission/debate before Privy Council, 299–300, 416–19; Navy Board's ignorance, 129; payment in kind, 424–5; variety of employed in wartime, 418
victuals: carried to fleet, 364; extra for supernumeraries, 416; forfeiture, 233; freshness, 181; jettisoned, 141, 300, 416, 418–19; savings, 232; wastage, 216, 246, 266
particular: beef, 105; beer, 105, 128, 135, 220, 418; biscuit, 71 n.4; brandy, 105; bread, 7, 418; butter, 7, 105; cheese, 105; cider, 105; fish, 105; flour, 105; fruit, 105; oatmeal, 105; oil, 105; pease, 105; pork, 105; rice, 105; suet, 105; water, 418; wine, 19, 105, 322, 418
Vyner (Viner), [Ald. Sir Robert (Kt 1665, Bt 1666)], goldsmith-banker: advice from, 3 & n.4.

Wager, Capt. [Charles], naval officer: 207, 227, 232
Waith (Wayth), Robert, cashier to the Navy Treasurer: accompanies P, 67; contract for canvas, 44–5; criticized by Board, 161; grudge with Shish, 46; information from, 69, 69–70, 74, 104; knowledge, (of cloth) 29, (of ironwork) 36–8; payment to, 63; present at passing accounts, 15 & n.2, 176, 250–1; undercuts competitor, 57
Walker, –, merchant: 314
Walker, Sir Edward, Garter King of Arms: 227
Walthamstow, Essex: Batten's house, 74 & n.4
War, First Dutch: charge/expenses, 378 & n.2, 409, (iron) 38 & n.1, (uncleared at Restoration) 276; comparisons with second war, 330–1, 371, 378 & n.2; credits to pursers, 418; impressment rare, 203; prize, 95 n.3; purveyance, 365; smiths paid in kind, 356; soldiers, 222; tickets, 406
~ alluded to, 20 & n.4, 284–5, 289–90
War, Second Dutch:
approach: 16 & n.2, 59, 87, 97, 108, 134, 308, (causes discussed) 228–9, (date of commencement debated) 338 & n.2, 360, 366, 372 & n.3, 373
events: Four Days' Fight, 239 & n.1, 364 & n.3; Holmes's Bonfire, 162 n.1; Medway Raid, 134 n.1, 176–82, 184 & n.1, 225 & n.4, 236, 247 n.1, 357 n.1, 400; other actions, 239, 416; termination, 112
finance: alleged diversion of funds, 336 & n.2, 366–7, 372–5; charge/expenses, 221 & n.2, 279, 284–5, 339 & n.1, 378 & n.2, 426, (compared with Dutch) 400–1 & n.
management: comparisons with first war, 330–1, 371, 400; impressment, 204, 205–6; Navy Commissioners' duties, 397
reflections/repercussions: effect on

INDEX

pay, 259; P's memoranda, 128 × 143; rise in prices, 274, 301–7, 309; seamen's distress, 234
War, Third Dutch: 260 n.1
Ward, Lieut. James, naval officer: 243
Warren (Waren), Sir William, merchant:
  accounts/charges: alleged double payment, 395, 424–5; freight charges disputed, 166–71; imprests to defended by P, 358–60; long-delayed settlement, 148–54 & nn., 174–6, 192–4, 307–14, 344–5, 392 n.1, 422–3; passed, 393; prices, 14, 36, 307–9, (low/reasonable) 9–10, 11, 57, 106, 115, 423–4, (overcharges) 174 n.1
  contracts with/goods from: Board's favouritism alleged/refuted, 307–15; commission purchases in Hamburg, 174 n.1, 278 n.1, 392–3; particular commodities, (deals) 5 & nn.2,3, 79–81, (iron) 133, (knees) 6 & n.2, 49–50, 89, 91–2, (masts) 9–12, 13, 15–16, 18, 35–6, 80, 90, 106, 138–9, 344–66, 423–4
  criticized: by Batten, 9–11, 51; by P, 311 n.2; by Wood, 22, 36
  various: commended by King and Duke, 422–3; information from, 12–13, 15–16, 36, 73, 148 n.3, 148–9, 192, 361 n.2, 366; letters to, 148, 310, 311; marine insurance, 392–3; partnership with Taylor, 7; pilots recommended, 129; present at Board, 149; security for imprests, 358–60; ship sold to, 319
  ~ alluded to, 86, 285, 383, 387, 388, 390
Warwick (Warrick), Sir Philip, Treasury official: attends Lords Commissioners, 336, 337; business with P, 341, 366
  ~ alluded to, 372
water bailliage: 35 & n.3
watermen: unfit or unwilling, 139
Waterson, Simon, Navy Office clerk: 196, 298, 299 & n.1
Wayth *see* Waith
wear and tear: 263 & n.2, 266, 403
Webber, –, merchant, Greenwich: 104

Wells, John, storekeeper, Deptford: 127 & n.1
West Country: cloth from, 27–31; impressment in, 206
West Indies: fleets for, 134 (*bis*), 137–8, 245 & n.3
Weston, –, merchant: information from about iron, 38
Wetwang, Capt. [John], naval officer: 227
Whistler, [Henry], flagmaker: contract with, 24 & n.2, 52–3; goods from, 56 & n.1; tender, 49
  ~ alluded to, 81, 82, 83 & n.2
White, –, merchant: 314
White, John, master: 173
Whitehall, Palace of: Duke's Closet, 191; Robes Chamber, 179
  ~ alluded to, 27, 131, 158, 243, 251, 252, 362
Whitfield (Whitfeild, Wittfeild), Nathaniel, Ticket Office clerk: information from, 404, 411, 414 & n.1 ~ alluded to, 130, 297, 298
Wibrough, Wiburg *see* Viborg
widows and orphans: 250–1 & n.
Williamson, –, merchant, Thames Street: 82
Williamson, Sir Joseph, Under-Secretary to Arlington and Keeper of State Papers 1660–74, [Secretary of State 1674–8]: signature, 265
Wilson (Willson), T[om], Navy Office clerk; storekeeper, Chatham 1667–76: information from, 154–5, 236; victualling business, 67
Winchester, Hants.: gaol delivery, 125
Winter, Sir John, Secretary to Queen Henrietta Maria: iron interests, 356 n.3
Winter, [Thomas], merchant: contract for timber, 6 & n.2
Wood, Capt. [Robert], naval officer: 319
Wood, William (I), merchant: charges, 73, 107, 423, (freight) 364, (high) 424; checks Warren's masts, 73; contract for masts, 16, 35–6, 309–10; criticizes Warren's contract, 349–50; deals from valued, 50; deposition by, 433; favoured by Batten, 10 & n.3, 16 & n.1, 23; insists on seaman

480 INDEX

to command his ship, 183–4; letters to, 309–10, 311; masts from, 53–5, 67–8, 73, 95–6, 101, 107; monopoly of mast trade, 308; partnership with Howell and others, 122; P argues with, 11–12 & nn., 22–3; ropeyard practices, 40; sale of old cordage to, 6; tenders, 10–11 & nn., 67, 80–1, 349–50, 361; trickery, 114–15 ~ alluded to, 89–90, 102, 422
Wood, William (II), [son of the above]: deals in masts, 54, 81
wool *see* cloth
Woolwich, Kent, dockyard:
  abuses: 64–5, (negligence) 108, (theft) 63–4
  goods at/from: canvas, 52 n.1; cordage, 74; flags, 56; hemp, 140; masts, 35–6, 55, 309; timber, 15, 80, 91–2; treenails, 15
  officers: assistant shipwright, 116; clerk of the cheque, 90; glazier's shop, 25; letter to, 140; Pett family's domination, 19 n.1
  P visits: 56, 68, 74
  ships: building/launch, 5 & n.1, 37 & n.2, 43 & n.1, 47, 73, 186–8 & n.; hulk, 184, 247; sunk for blockade, 318–19
  ~ alluded to, 95, 351
  see also Ackworth; Bodham; Bowyer; Byland; Deane; Dowson; Falconer; Fletcher; Mayers; Pett, C.; Russell; Sheldon; Smyth
Worcester House, Strand, [Lord Chancellor Clarendon's residence]: 362
workmen: wages, 139 & n.1
Wren, Sir Christopher, architect: 136 n.3
Wren, John, messenger: 136 & n.3
Wren (Wrenn), Matthew, Secretary to the Duke of York 1667–72: clerk, 136 & n.3; discusses finance with P, 159; favours gentlemen/noble commanders on land/at sea, 223–4; information from, 216–17, 230, 236–7, 252; letters/orders to, 136, 193, 210; present at Board, 179, 185; sympathetic to Mennes, 193–4 ~ alluded to, 148 n.1, 192, 211, 245

yachts *see* ships
Yarmouth, Great, Norf.: goods from/via, 40, 387; schoolmaster, 238; seamen recruited, 227
York (Yorke), James, Duke of, the King's brother and heir-presumptive, Lord High Admiral 1660–73, [King James II 1685–8]:
  appointments/personnel: agrees to removal of Mennes, 148 n.1, (to his being assisted) 311, 345, 359; approves seamen as commanders, 183–4; chooses Smith as Commissioner, 211; commends Warren, 423, (appoints him purveyor) 365, (receives his advice) 361–2; dismisses master, 131; fixes carpenters' hours of work, 45 & n.1; increases Navy Office staff, 284; increases storekeepers' salaries, 288; orders to Capt. O'Brien, 224 n.1; prevented from evaluating captains, 209; promises advancement to Navy Office clerks, 76; punishes negligent muster-masters, 291–2 & n.; punishes pursers, 418; rebukes Jennens, 179
  business: authority as Lord High Admiral, 158, 162; business submitted to for decision, 178, 181, 242; care for balancing storekeepers' accounts, 401; consulted over contracts, 53, 347; Navy Board attends/reports to, 76, 126–7, 133, 158–9, 161, 176, 179–80, 183, 199, 216, 219–20, 251, 255–6, 301–5, 362, 385, 399, 420, 421, (Mennes only) 85, (Penn only) 244; Navy Board responsible to, 405; recommends register of attendance at Board, 253 n.5; reforms urged, 342 & n.2; saves ships from sale, 256–7; warrants, 418
  debate before Privy Council: criticizes Brooke House Commissioners, 433; dissatisfied with their report, 375; examines ticket produced by Brouncker, 430; letter read, 401; proposes publication, (of Commission's satisfaction by Board) 343, (of

vindication of King's conduct) 374–5; speaks, 347, 366, 381, 386; supports Board over impresm, 360
instructions/orders from:
(i) General Instructions to Navy Board (1662): 189, 194, 214, 274, 279–80, 284, 285, 286, 287–8, 288, 289, 291, 292, 293, 296, 300, 316, 335, 345, 354 & n.1, 365, 369, 370, 377, 386 & n.1, 388 & n.2, 389, 391 & n.1, 396, 397, 398, 403 & n.5, 406 & n.2, 407, 412, 415, 417 & n.2, 419, 420, 426, 428, (not to be literally interpreted) 389
(ii) additional instructions to Board: (1665), 279; (1668), 146–7, 214 & n.2, 252 & n.1, 253 n.5, 290, 401, 402, 415
(iii) instructions to commanders: (1669), 176 & n.2, 178–9, 300, 412 & n.3, 417 & n.2; (1672), 264 & n.1
(iv) occasional orders: captains' pay, 244 & n.1; collisions/leaks, 131–2; commission purchases, 174 n.1, 278 & n.1; finance, 77, 133, 158–61, 161 & n.2, 162 & n.1, 163, 175, 344; fleets to sea, 16 n.2, 48; hire of ship for ambassador, 220; hulks, 185, 188; laying up ship, 160; report on administration, 191 & n.2: sale of small vessels, 256–7; stop to press warrants, 210
letters/information from: 181–2, 209, 210, 251–2, 258, 362, ('farewell' letter) 354 & n.2, 388, 420
letters/petitions/reports to: 134–5, 136, 137, 146, 176, 179–80, 181, 184, 187, 191–2, 230, 249, 265, 283, 299, 301–7, 315, 347, 415, 426–7
relations with P: address from P, 332–3; attended by P, 339, 341–2; comments recalled by P, 138, 209, 220; orders P to attend examination of Carteret's business, 334; P advises/reports to, (defence of Navy Board) 334, 341–2, (impressment) 203–10, (naval administration) 191 & n.2, 210, 251–2 & n., 342 & n.2, (personnel) 192–3, 230, (Stop of the Exchequer) 258; P meets in Park, 341; P's service to, 324, 328–9; seconds/supports P, 211, 230, 340, 342, 359, 389, 419; special command for absence, 326, 397
sea command: 125 n.1, 158, 238–9 & n., 244, 245, 266, 354 n.2, (attended by Coventry) 397 & n.2
various: at Oxford during Plague, 421; friends, 232 n.2, 239 n.1; mocks Petty's ship, 27; opponents, 225 n.2; recollections, 362; reflections on naval architecture, 220; ship admired by, 59 n.1; wit, 408; yacht *Anne*, 63 & n.2, 214
~ alluded to, 275
Yorke, Edmond, merchant: 33
Young, –, merchant [? the following]: 172
Young, [John], flagmaker: bill, 63; contract, 48–9, 52–3, 81–5; fear of impressment, 84; goods from, 56 & n.1 ~ alluded to, 24, ? 172

APPENDIX TO INDEX

Authority is here cited where possible for the forenames supplied (in square brackets) in the Index for these categories of persons: Navy Office officials, dockyard officials, sea officers, merchants.
In addition to abbreviations listed above, pp. xv–xvi, the following are here used:

    Collinge   J. M. Collinge, *Navy Board Officials 1660–1832* (1978)
    DNB   *Dictionary of National Biography* (1st edn)
    Heal   A. Heal, *The London Goldsmiths 1200–1800* (1935)

Ackworth, William: *CSPD 1658–9*, p. 431
Aldridge, Henry: *Collinge*, p. 81
Andrews, Thomas: *Diary*, x. 8
Baddicott, William: *CSPD Add. 1660–85*, p. 431
Badiley, William: *Diary*, x. 17
Barker, William: *Diary*, vii. 420
Barnes, Alexander: *CSPD 1666–7*, p. 390
Barrow, Philip: *Diary*, x. 20
Beach, Richard: *CSPD 1665–6*, p. 108
Berry, John: *CSPD 1665–6*, p. 131
Blackborough, Peter: *CSPD Add. 1660–85*, p. 420
Bland, John: *Diary*, iii. 158
Body, George: *CSPD 1668–9*, p. 126
Bowen, Peter: Tanner, *Catalogue*, i. 328
Bowyer, Thomas: Bodl. Lib., Rawl. MSS A 180, p. 375
Bowyer, William: *CSPD 1665–6*, p. 134
Boyce, Richard: *CSPD 1665–6*, p. 554
Bridges, Richard: *Diary*, v. 292
Burroughs, William: *Collinge*, p. 89
Cadbury, Humphrey: Bodl. Lib., Rawl. MSS A 180, p. 375
Capp, John: *Further Corr.*, p. 263
Chester, Thomas: *CSPD 1664–5*, p. 131
Chicheley, Thomas: *Diary*, x. 60–1
Child, Josiah: *Diary*, vi. 255
Chiverton, Richard: *Diary*, x. 62
Clapham, John: *CSPD 1667*, p. 185
Clothier, John: *CSPD Add. 1660–85*, p. 420
Cocke, George: *Diary*, x. 69
Cole, Christopher: *CSPD Add. 1660–85*, p. 427
Coleby, Philip: *CSPD 1666–7*, p. 390
Colepeper, Judith: *DNB* (Colepeper, John)
Cowley, Thomas: *CSPD 1666–7*, p. 509
Creed, John: *Diary*, i. 86
Darcy, Thomas: Tanner, *Catalogue*, i. 342
Dering, Edward: *Diary*, iv. 415
Doggett, John: *CSPD 1665–6*, p. 130
Dowson, Richard: Bodl. Lib., Rawl. MSS A 180, p. 375
Dry, James: *CSPD Add. 1660–85*, p. 126
Dyson, John: *CSPD 1664–5*, p. 131
Eastwood, Roger: Bodl. Lib., Rawl. MSS A 180, p. 375
Edgehill, William: Bodl. Lib., Rawl. MSS A 180, p. 375
Elliott, Thomas: *CSPD 1665–6*, p. 259
Errington, ? Ralph: *CSPD 1666–7*, p. 314
Ferrer, Robert: *Diary*, x. 130
Fist, Anthony: *Collinge*, p. 101
Foley, Robert: *Diary*, x. 142
Fownes, William: Bodl. Lib., Rawl. MSS A 180, p. 375; A 212, p. 425
Gibbons, Thomas: *Collinge*, p. 103
Gibbs, John: *CSPD 1664–5*, p. 134

Godolphin, Francis: *CSPD 1668–9*, p. 234
Grey, Edward: *CSPD Add. 1660–85*, p. 429
Grimsditch, John: Tanner, *Catalogue*, i. 357
Haddock, Richard: Tanner, *Catalogue*, i. 358
Halsall, James: *Diary*, vii. 145
Harper, Thomas: *Diary*, x. 169
Harrington, William: *Diary*, x. 169
Harris, John: *CSPD 1664–5*, p. 134
Hart, John: Tanner, *Catalogue*, i. 362
Hayter, Thomas: Collinge, p. 109
Hayward, John: Tanner, *Catalogue*, i. 363
Hebdon, John: *Diary*, iv. 175
Heling, Daniel: Tanner, *Catalogue*, i. 364
Herbert, Charles: Tanner, *Catalogue*, i. 364
Hill, William: Tanner, *Catalogue*, i. 365
Holt, Nathaniel: PRO, ADM 20/9, p. 2
Houblon (brothers): *Diary*, x. 193
Hubbard, John: Tanner, *Catalogue*, i. 369
Johnson, Benjamin: Bodl. Lib., Rawl. MSS A 212, p. 447
Johnson, Henry: *Diary*, vi. 236
Kingdon, Richard: *Diary*, vi. 319
Kingsbury, Austin: *CSPD 1668–9*, p. 635
Knip, William: *CSPD 1664–5*, p. 132
Langston, Anthony: Tanner, *Catalogue*, i. 375
Lanyon, John: *Diary*, x. 229
Legg, William: *Diary*, x. 230
Le Neve, Richard: Tanner, *Catalogue*, i. 378
Lewsly, Thomas: PRO, ADM 106/3520, f. 18r
Lloyd, John: Tanner, *Catalogue*, i. 378
Lowe, Henry: *CSPD 1664–5*, p. 135
Lyell, Patrick: *CSPD 1665–6*, p. 548
Mason, John: *CSPD 1667–8*, p. 122
May, Thomas: *CSPD 1665–6*, p. 9
Meynell, Francis: Heal, p. 205
Mitchell, John: *CSPD Add. 1660–85*, p. 425
Moore, John: *CSPD 1668–9*, p. 2
Morecock, John or Robert: *CSPD 1664–5*, p. 131
Myngs, Christopher: *DNB*. Tanner, *Catalogue*, i. 387

Nicolls, Henry: *CSPD 1667–8*, p. 401
Osborne, Henry: *CSPD 1667–8*, p. 11
Pearse, Andrew: *CSPD 1656–7*, p. 517
Perriman, John: *CSPD Add. 1660–85*, p. 185
Pointer, Thomas: Collinge, p. 132
Poole, William: Tanner, *Catalogue*, i. 394
Povey, Thomas: *DNB*
Pritchard, William: Tanner, *Catalogue*, i. 396
Pugh, James: Collinge, p. 132
Pumpfield, Edward: *CSPD Add. 1660–85*, p. 110
Rainsborough, Thomas: *DNB* (Rainborow)
Rawlinson, Daniel: *CSPD 1663–4*, p. 638
Reymes, Bullen: *CSPD Add. 1660–85*, p. 171
Rider, William: *Further Corr.*, p. 19
Ridge, Richard: *CSPD 1668–9*, p. 649
Risby, Henry: *CSPD Add. 1660–85*, p. 242
Roberts, George: *CSPD 1668–9*, p. 497
Robinson, Robert: Tanner, *Catalogue*, i. 399
Rundall, Edward: *CSPD 1663–4*, p. 171
Sansum, Robert: Tanner, *Catalogue*, i. 402
Scott, Thomas: Tanner, *Catalogue*, i. 403
Seale, Thomas: Tanner, *Catalogue*, i. 403
Shales, John: *Further Corr.*, pp. 68, 69
Shish, Jonas: *Diary*, x. 397
Shorter, John: *CSPD Add. 1660–85*, p. 428
Silvester, Edward: *CSPD 1664–5*, p. 131
Slater, John: Bodl. Lib., Rawl. MSS A 212, p. 425
Smith, Edward: *CSPD 1664–5*, p. 136
Smith, Robert: Collinge, p. 139
Stacey, John: *CSPD 1664–5*, p. 132
Stanley, William: *Further Corr.*, p. 288
Stapely, Joseph: *CSPD 1665–6*, p. 132
Stockman, Isaac: *CSPD Add. 1660–85*, p. 424
Teate, Richard: Tanner, *Catalogue*, i. 412

Teddeman, Thomas: Tanner, *Catalogue*, i. 413
Tinker, John: *CSPD Add. 1660–85*, p. 232
Upton, Hugh: *CSPD Add. 1660–85*, p. 331
Vyner, Robert: *DNB*. Heal, p. 261
Wager, Charles: Tanner, *Catalogue*, i. 418

Wetwang, John: Tanner, *Catalogue*, i. 421
Whistler, Henry: *CSPD 1664–5*, p. 135
Wilson, Tom: *Diary*, x. 488
Winter, Thomas: *CSPD Add. 1660–85*, p. 89
Wood, Robert: Tanner, *Catalogue*, i. 426
Young, John: *Diary*, x. 493

Navy Records Society
(Founded 1893)

The Navy Records Society was established for the purpose of printing unpublished manuscripts and rare works of naval interest. Membership of the Society is open to all who are interested in naval history, and any person wishing to become a member should apply to the Hon. Secretary, c/o Barclays de Zoete Wedd Ltd, First Floor, St Mary's Court, Lower Thames Street, London EC3R 6JN, United Kingdom. The annual subscription is £30, which entitles the member to receive one free copy of each work issued by the Society in that year, and to buy earlier issues at reduced prices.

A list of works in print, available to members only, is shown below; very few copies are left of those marked with an asterisk. Prices for works in print are available on application to Mrs. Annette Gould, 5, Goodwood Close, Midhurst, West Sussex GU29 9JG, United Kingdom, to whom all enquiries concerning works in print should be sent. Those marked 'TS' and 'SP' are published for the Society by Temple Smith and Scolar Press, and are available to non-members from the Ashgate Publishing Group, Gower House, Croft Road, Aldershot, Hampshire GU11 3HR. Those marked 'A & U' are published by George Allen & Unwin, and are available to non-members only through bookshops.

Vols. 1 and 2. *State Papers relating to the Defeat of the Spanish Armada, Anno 1588*, Vols I & II, ed. Professor J. K. Laughton. TS.

Vol. 11. *Papers relating to the Spanish War, 1585–87*, ed. Julian S. Corbett. TS.

Vol. 16. *Logs of the Great Sea Fights, 1794–1805*, Vol. I, ed. Vice-Admiral Sir T. Sturges Jackson.

Vol. 18. *Logs of the Great Sea Fights, 1794–1805*, Vol. II, ed. Vice-Admiral Sir T. Sturges Jackson.

Vol. 20. *The Naval Miscellany*, Vol. I, ed. Professor J. K. Laughton.

Vol. 31. *The Recollections of Commander James Anthony Gardner, 1775–1814*, ed. Admiral Sir R. Vesey Hamilton and Professor J. K. Laughton.

Vol. 32. *Letters and Papers of Charles, Lord Barham, 1758–1813*, Vol. I. ed. Sir J. K. Laughton.

Vol. 38. *Letters and Papers of Charles, Lord Barham, 1758–1813*, Vol. II, ed. Sir J. K. Laughton.

Vol. 39. *Letters and Papers of Charles, Lord Barham, 1758–1813*, Vol. III, ed. Sir J. K. Laughton.

Vol. 40. *The Naval Miscellany*, Vol. II, ed. Sir J. K. Laughton.

Vol. 41. *Papers relating to the First Dutch War, 1652–54*, Vol. V, ed. C. T. Atkinson.

Vol. 42. *Papers relating to the Loss of Minorca in 1756*, ed. Captain H. W. Richmond.

Vol. 43. *The Naval Tracts of Sir William Monson*, Vol. III, ed. M. Oppenheim.

Vol. 45. *The Naval Tracts of Sir William Monson*, Vol. IV, ed. M. Oppenheim.

*Vol. 46. *The Private Papers of George, Second Earl Spencer*, Vol. I, ed. Julian S. Corbett.

Vol. 47. *The Naval Tracts of Sir William Monson*, Vol. V, ed. M. Oppenheim.

Vol. 49. *Documents relating to Law and Custom of the Sea*, Vol. I, ed. R. G. Marsden.

Vol. 50. *Documents relating to Law and Custom of the Sea*, Vol. II, ed. R. G. Marsden.

Vol. 52. *The Life of Admiral Sir John Leake*, Vol. I, ed. G. A. R. Callender.

Vol. 53. *The Life of Admiral Sir John Leake*, Vol. II, ed. G. A. R. Callender.

Vol. 54. *The Life and Works of Sir Henry Mainwaring*, Vol. I, ed. G. E. Manwaring.

Vol. 60. *Samuel Pepys's Naval Minutes*, ed. Dr. J. R. Tanner.

Vol. 65. *Boteler's Dialogues*, ed. W. G. Perrin.

Vol. 66. *Papers relating to the First Dutch War, 1652–54*, Vol. VI, ed. C. T. Atkinson.

Vol. 67. *The Byng Papers*, Vol. I, ed. W. C. B. Tunstall.

Vol. 68. *The Byng Papers*, Vol. II, ed. W. C. B. Tunstall.

Corrigenda to *Papers relating to the First Dutch War, 1652–54*, ed. Captain A. C. Dewar.

Vol. 70. *The Byng Papers*, Vol. III, ed. W. C. B. Tunstall.

*Vol. 71. *The Private Papers of John, Earl of Sandwich*, Vol. II, ed. G. R. Barnes and Lt Cdr J. H. Owen.

Vol. 73. *The Tangier Papers of Samuel Pepys*, ed. Edwin Chappell.

Vol. 74. *The Tomlinson Papers*, ed. J. G. Bullocke.

Vol. 77. *Letters and Papers of Admiral The Hon. Samuel Barrington*, Vol. I, ed. D. Bonner-Smith.

Vol. 79. *The Journals of Sir Thomas Allin, 1660–1678*, Vol. I, ed. R. C. Anderson.

Vol. 80. *The Journals of Sir Thomas Allin, 1660–1678*, Vol. II, ed. R. C. Anderson.

Vol. 89. *The Sergison Papers, 1688–1702*, ed. Cdr R. D. Merriman.

Vol. 104. *The Navy and South America, 1807–1823*, ed. Professor G. S. Graham and Professor R. A. Humphreys.

Vol. 107. *The Health of Seamen*, ed. Professor C. C. Lloyd.

Vol. 108. *The Jellicoe Papers*, Vol. I, ed. A. Temple Patterson.

*Vol. 109. *Documents relating to Anson's Voyage round the World, 1740–1744*, ed. Dr. Glyndwr Williams.

Vol. 111. *The Jellicoe Papers*, Vol. II, ed. A. Temple Patterson.

Vol. 112. *The Rupert and Monck Letterbook, 1666*, ed. Rev. J. R. Powell and E. K. Timings.

Vol. 113. *Documents relating to the Royal Naval Air Service*, Vol. I, ed. Captain S. W. Roskill.

Vol. 114. *The Siege and Capture of Havana, 1762*, ed. Professor David Syrett.

*Vol. 115. *Policy and Operations in the Mediterranean, 1912–14*, ed. E. W. R. Lumby.

Vol. 116. *The Jacobean Commissions of Enquiry, 1608 & 1618*, ed. Dr. A. P. McGowan.

Vol. 117. *The Keyes Papers*, Vol. I, ed. Dr. Paul G. Halpern.

Vol. 119. *The Manning of the Royal Navy: Selected Public Pamphlets 1693–1873*, ed. Professor J. S. Bromley.

Vol. 120. *Naval Administration, 1715–1750*, ed. Professor D. A. Baugh.

Vol. 121. *The Keyes Papers*, Vol. II, ed. Dr. Paul G. Halpern.

Vol. 122. *The Keyes Papers*, Vol. III, ed. Dr. Paul G. Halpern.

Vol. 123. *The Navy of the Lancastrian Kings; Accounts and Inventories of William Soper, Keeper of the King's Ships 1422–1427*, ed. Dr. Susan Rose.

Vol. 124. *The Pollen Papers: The Privately Circulated Printed

Works of Arthur Hungerford Pollen, 1901–1916, ed. Dr. Jon. T. Sumida. A & U.

Vol. 125. *The Naval Miscellany*, Vol. V, ed. N. A. M. Rodger. A & U.

Vol. 126. *The Royal Navy in the Mediterranean, 1915–1918*, ed. Professor Paul G. Halpern. TS.

Vol. 127. *The Expedition of Sir John Norris and Sir Francis Drake to Spain and Portugal, 1589*, ed. Professor R. B. Wernham. TS.

Vol. 128. *The Beatty Papers*, Vol. I, 1902–1918, ed. Professor B. McL. Ranft. SP.

Vol. 129. *The Hawke Papers: A Selection: 1743–1771*, ed. Dr. Ruddock F. Mackay. SP.

Vol. 130. *Anglo-American Naval Relations 1917–1919*, ed. Michael Simpson. SP.

Vol. 131. *British Naval Documents 1204–1960*, ed. John B. Hattendorf, R. J. B. Knight, A. W. H. Pearsall, N. A. M. Rodger and Geoffrey Till. SP.

Vol. 132. *The Beatty Papers*, Vol. II, 1916–1927, ed. Professor B. McL. Ranft. SP.

Occasional Publications:

Vol. 1, *The Commissioned Sea Officers of the Royal Navy, 1660–1815*, ed. Professor David Syrett and Professor R. L. DiNardo. SP.